Sociology

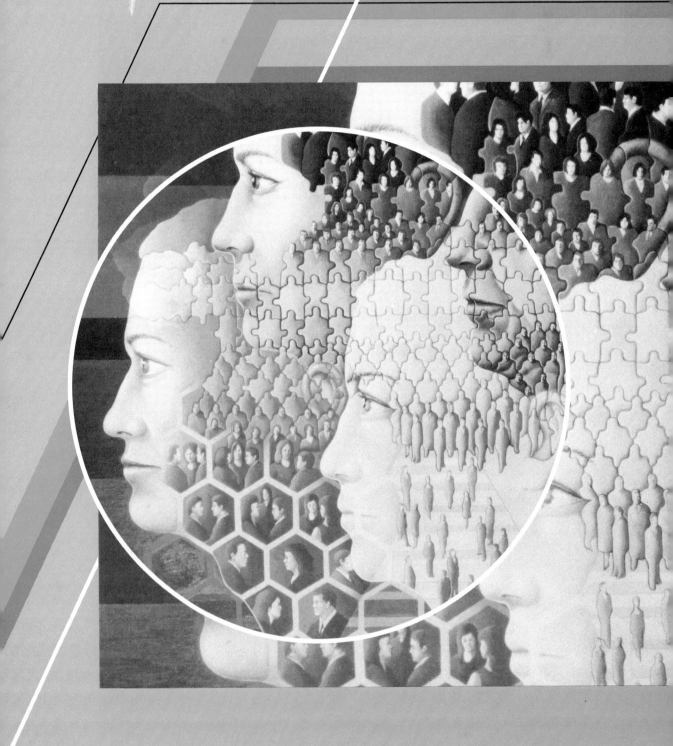

Sociology

Dean J. Champion
Suzanne B. Kurth
Donald W. Hastings
Diane K. Harris
University of Tennessee

with James A. Cramer

Holt, Rinehart and Winston
New York   Chicago   San Francisco
Philadelphia   Montreal   Toronto   London
Sydney   Tokyo   Mexico City   Rio de Janeiro
Madrid

Publisher   John L. Michel
Acquiring Editor   Marie A. Schappert
Developmental Editor   Rosalind Sackoff
Special Projects Editor   Jeanette Ninas Johnson
Art Director   Lou Scardino
Design   Caliber Design Planning, Inc.
Production Manager   Annette Mayeski
Portfolio Editor and Copy Editor   William Faricy

Photo credits are on page 519.

Library of Congress Cataloging in Publication Data
Champion, Dean J.
   Sociology.
   Bibliography: p.
   Includes index.
   1. Sociology. I. Title.
HM51.C425   1984   301   83-22682

ISBN 0-03-058979-7

Copyright © 1984 by CBS College Publishing
Address correspondence to:
383 Madison Avenue
New York, N.Y. 10017
4 5 6 7   032   9 8 7 6 5 4 3 2 1

CBS COLLEGE PUBLISHING
Holt, Rinehart and Winston
The Dryden Press
Saunders College Publishing

Preface

Collectively, the authors of this book have *over 70 years* of experience in teaching introductory sociology. During this time many trends have emerged in the introductory sociology course, but none so strong as the current need to make the discipline of sociology relevant to today's pragmatic students. We encounter among our students many who wish to learn about their world but who do not intend to pursue a career in sociology. While we must meet the needs of these students, we are also committed to the discipline and have a central goal we wish to accomplish when teaching the basic course. This goal is to provide a look at the world from a *sociological perspective*, the approach to events that makes sociology unique. With this dual purpose in mind—to meet both the needs of our students and the requirements of our discipline—we have created *Sociology*. The book is meant to be a basic introduction to the subject that presents students with a sound yet easily understandable treatment of how sociologists investigate social life and what they have learned about it.

Organization of the Text

The first chapter of the book introduces each of the major theoretical perspectives used by sociologists—structural functionalism, symbolic interactionism, and conflict theory. These theoretical approaches are integrated, when appropriate, throughout the text. This chapter also presents the basic tools of research, which are then applied when discussing research studies in later chapters to illustrate sociology's usefulness in everyday life.

In order for this text to be easily integrated into current course structures, *Sociology* follows a traditional format of micro to macro topics. The beginning sections—Parts I and II—contain the core concepts of the course. We recommend that these chapters be assigned in the order in which they appear. The subsequent chapters may then be rearranged to accommodate individual preferences or time constraints. The inclusion of a *running glossary* helps students learn new terminology as it is presented in each chapter. The glossary also provides an excellent reference for studying the basic concepts.

Unique Content Coverage

Although *Sociology* shares many common topics with other textbooks in the field, it is distinctive in regard to its coverage of many areas. Part III, for example, opens with a unique chapter on the postindustrial society. It examines the major institutions with a historical perspective, covering the development of today's society and the impact of modern technology.

Other subjects given special treatment in this text include the following:

- Full chapter coverage of aging.
- A separate chapter on gender.
- A complete chapter on social organizations, including bureaucracy.
- An extended section on the influence of mass media in the chapter on collective behavior.
- A chapter with combined coverage of political and legal institutions.
- An appendix on careers in sociology.

In addition to this exceptional coverage, *Sociology* includes numerous *cross-cultural* and *contemporary* examples throughout the text.

Special Features

Three high-interest areas in *Sociology* have been given additional coverage in a *photo essay* format. Chapter 2 includes a cross-cultural photo essay "The Eskimos: Living in Two Worlds." Emphasis on the "graying of America" was the basis of the photo essay in Chapter 9 on "Aging: Looking Back and Moving Ahead." This presentation illustrates the different roles that the older generation plays in our society. Finally, in Chapter 19 the photo essay on "Change: Visions of Society" asks the question "What now?"

Other highlighted material appears throughout the text in boxes under the following headings:

- **Controversial Issues**—covers the range of opinions about specific current topics.
- **People**—concerns new and interesting ideas about our society at a micro level.
- **Facts**—discusses basic research data which amplifies sociological issues.

In addition, each chapter contains a number of features designed to supplement the subject matter and engage the student's interest:

- Opening vignettes which introduce the material and provide actual examples of sociology at work.
- Outlines, thought questions, and summaries which guide students and help reinforce learning.
- Annotated suggested readings enabling students to pursue topics of interest.
- A running glossary which defines terms within the chapter.

Complete Teaching and Learning Package

Accompanying the book is a comprehensive set of supplementary materials to aid the instructor and student.

The *Instructor's Manual* provides sample syllabi, lecture notes, teaching tips, key terms, chapter-by-chapter summaries, and a list of films to facilitate the transition to a new text.

The *Test Bank* contains more than 50 multiple-choice questions per chapter, or over 1,000 items, to provide material for preparation of exams.

The *Computerized Test Bank* combines the items from the printed test bank with a test generator program for easy test preparation from a microcomputer. These disks are available for the Apple IIe, IBM P/C, and TRS 80 systems.

The *Study Guide* uses learning objectives, study tips and techniques, exercises, chapter outlines, key terms, and objective test items to enhance students' mastery of the text material.

Finally, the most innovative element in the package is a revised and expanded *CLEAR II* which includes enhanced programs from the original *CLEAR* with new material to complement lectures. This CAI (Computer Assisted Instruction) package helps students learn concepts, skills, and facts related to *Sociology*.

Although a good textbook is the essential ingredient for any introductory course in sociology, we feel that this package makes the teaching/learning program complete. We would be delighted to receive your reactions to our text and the ancillaries. Please write to us in care of the Sociology Editor, Holt, Rinehart and Winston, 383 Madison Avenue, New York, N.Y. 10017.

Acknowledgments

Sociology draws on our many experiences with our students and on numerous interactions with our colleagues in sociology and other disciplines. We owe a debt of gratitude to these associates who helped provide the ideas and examples which appear here.

We would also like to extend our appreciation to the many individuals at Holt, Rinehart and Winston/CBS College Publishing who helped orchestrate this massive project. Among them are Roz Sackoff, Senior Developmental Editor; Marie Schappert, Acquisitions Editor; John Michel, Publisher; Barbara Heinssen, Editorial Assistant; Jeanette Ninas Johnson, Special Projects Editor; Lou Scardino, Designer; and Annette Mayeski, Production Manager.

The chapters herein reflect our shared views of the sociological perspective, a goal which various reviewers have helped us to clarify. We appreciate their contributions to the preparation of *Sociology* and hope that many students will benefit from their efforts. Our special thanks to the following:
Karen Altergott, University of Missouri–Columbia; Stephanie Catalan, Massassoit Community College; Jack Dison, Arkansas State University; David Dobos,

Santa Ana College; Maurice Ethridge, Tennessee Technological College; Gilbert Fleer, Western Texas College; Joseph Healy, Christopher Newport College; Sidney Jackson, Lakewood Community College, Minnesota; Hugh Lena, Providence College; Larry Perkins, Oklahoma State University; Roland Pippin, Northwestern State University (Louisiana); Chad Richardson, Pan American University; Joslin Salmon, Triton College; Arnold Silverman, Nassau Community College; Kenneth Smith, University of Miami; Llewellyn Swan, Texas Southern College; Glenn Vernon, University of Utah; Eric Wagner, Ohio University; Thomas Yacovone, Los Angeles Valley College.

Contents in Brief

Contents

PORTFOLIO I: The Eskimos: Living in Two Worlds

3   Groups and Society   51

4   Socialization   73

7 Ethnicity and Race 150

PART THREE   Social Institutions and Organizations   **229**

10   Organizations   231

11   The Structure of Postindustrial Society: The Economic Order, Technology, and Work   254

12 The Family 277

13 Educational Structures 307

14   Religion   333

15   Political and Legal Institutions   355

PART FOUR   Social Dynamics   383

16   Population Parameters and Processes   385

17   Urbanization and Urban Life   416

18   Mass Behavior   447

Feature Contents

Controversial Issues

The Facts

People

1

Learning about Sociology

Why do people act as they do? Sociologists address this question in numerous ways. Some focus on the structure of society, others on social interaction. All are interested to some extent in how and what people learn (values, norms, skills) and how that learning affects social actions. As a member of society you too are interested in people's actions because they affect you all the time. Everyday you make guesses about how people will behave in specific situations.

If you were walking through a nightclub area of a large city after dark and lost your wallet with $350 in it, would you expect to get it back with your money still in it? Probably not. Someone could pick it up without anyone noticing or caring what was happening. The person who picked it up wouldn't know you and might not care whether you lost the money.

Yet in Chicago a young man who dropped his wallet with $350 in it got it back with the money in it. Two sisters from a small town in Tennessee were in Chicago to study at a Bible institute. They believed that turning the wallet in to the police was their Christian duty. Thus, although they were in a setting in which people often emphasize looking out for themselves, their actions were shaped by other social values.

Social scientists have developed terms to describe actions such as the sisters took (pro-social behavior, altruism, samaritanism). When people go out of their way to help others, their behavior is seen as extraordinary in today's society, for the news media often report how individuals and organizations directly or indirectly harm people through action or inaction. Organizations discharge toxic waste; people rob, murder, and rape other people; parents abuse their children and each other. Yet you should remember that these things are news because they do not happen all the time and because there is strong disapproval of these activities.

What is sociology?

Sociology *is the scientific study of patterns of human interaction. Although sociologists can learn about such patterns by studying behavior identified as wrong, many sociologists focus on ordinary behavior that is in accord with the prevailing rules of various social units. Some sociologists simply study the* structures *created to organize social life. Sociologists interested in social change look at violations of social understandings and conflicts between social units to understand the* dynamics *of social change.*

Sociology the scientific study of patterns of human interaction.

The Sociological Perspective

The Everybody-Knows-That Syndrome

How many times have you heard sayings like "you can't teach an old dog new tricks" or "birds of a feather flock together"? Such commonsense expressions suggest oversimplified and sometimes false truths about the behavior of humans and other animals. Although people point to occasions that seem to verify these expressions, on other occasions opposite expressions—like "it's never too late to learn" and "opposites attract"—seem to be correct. But if commonsense expressions seem true on occasion, how do we know when?

One of the tasks of scientific research is to sort out which commonsense beliefs are generally true. Take "you're never too old to learn": research suggests that under most circumstances our primary capacity to learn changes very little with age. And research also indicates that people do tend to prefer others who are similar to themselves (birds of a feather), but in some cases the attraction of opposites is functional.

Read the following statements about social classes, and on the basis of your present knowledge and perceptions, indicate which are true and which are false.

True or False:

_____ 1. Mental illness is more prevalent among upper-class people than among lower-class people.

_____ 2. Participation in organized religious activity is more common for middle-class people than lower-class people.

_____ 3. Lower-class children receive more encouragement from their families to continue their education than do upper-class children.

_____ 4. People from the lower classes often pay more for the things they buy than do people from higher social classes.

_____ 5. Lower-class people in the military have lower casualty rates than those from the middle and upper classes.*

Because sociology deals with the everyday social life we are familiar with, most persons possess commonsense views about its subject matter. But the true–false exercise you just did illustrates that we often cannot depend on common sense.

Your beliefs about social behavior are in part based on your past experiences and what you have been taught. But these beliefs are not formed according to the same criteria that sociologists use in investigating social behavior. Sociologists systematically collect data to test generalizations and beliefs, for they seek to understand and predict what factors influence social behavior and in what ways. Sociologists continually strive to obtain more complete and accurate information about social life and better explanations of why they find what they do.

The study of social life leaves the sociologist open to criticism. As sociologist Robert K. Merton (1959) notes, if the sociologist's investigation confirms what is widely assumed, then he or she might be accused of belaboring the obvious and telling what everybody already knows. On the other hand, if

*The even numbers are true and the odd numbers are false.

the sociologist's research reveals that widely held beliefs are untrue, he or she may be called a heretic. Then if the sociologist examines ideas considered socially implausible and finds they really are untrue, he or she is considered a fool for wasting time and money on research not worth doing in the first place. Finally, if the sociologist should turn up some implausible truths, then he or she must be ready to be regarded as a charlatan for claiming as knowledge what seems "definitely false." One United States senator has even regularly awarded "golden fleece" awards to federally sponsored research that he believes was not worth doing. Despite such criticisms, sociologists continue to seek to unravel the truth about social life.

Sociology and Other Social Sciences

Sociology is the scientific study of patterns of human interaction. Thus sociology involves the study of all facets of social life. Sociologists do not study behaviors that are not social, such as behaviors that are based on our human biology or on individual psychology. And although sociologists are interested in historical events and processes, they focus on social patterns. Similarly, sociologists may be interested in economic and political influences on human interaction, but they do not try to explain those influences. The other social sciences (psychology, history, economics, political science) contribute information useful to sociological analyses, but do not have the same goal of understanding patterns of human interaction as a product of numerous social influences.

Social Activism

People sometimes confuse sociology with socialism, a political belief system, or with social work, a human services profession. Sociology is neither. Sociologists personally endorse many different political belief systems and do not typically see themselves as human services practitioners. Indeed, the formation of social work as a separate professional field clarified to some extent the domain of sociology.

Many of the founders of sociology were not, however, dispassionate observers of society. Some were interested in reforming society or remedying social ills. Others were more radical and hoped for a more utopian future. Various early twentieth century American sociologists actively engaged in social reform activities, but others were ideologically opposed to social reform.

Sociologists still vary in their orientations to what today is called social activism. For some sociologists the study of social life leads them to want to change what they see. Most, however, believe that they should separate their academic activities and their social activism. And some believe that professional sociologists should simultaneously be social activists.

By examining the lives and works of the founders of sociology we can get a sense of the various stances sociologists take toward the social world.

What do you believe it means to "think sociologically"?

CONTROVERSIAL ISSUES · Sociological Interpretation

Sociology instructors often admonish students to think sociologically, to the consternation of the students who do not know what it means to "think sociologically." Early founders of sociology such as Max Weber argued that the study of social life required a special "subjective" approach. The researcher must take the perspective of the people being studied or the researcher will be unable to understand why they do what they do. Human beings think about what they are doing, unlike atoms or rocks. As a consequence, a researcher must take into account the research objects' (people's) thoughts and attitudes when analyzing their actions.

Various modern sociologists have described sociology as requiring a special critical stance (Bates 1967:13–14) or an imaginative stance as an art form (Nisbet 1963), as well as a mode for interpreting social life (Berger 1963; Berger and Kellner 1981). Underlying these various arguments is a common thread. Sociologists must be sensitive to people's perspectives and yet retain some detachment from their subjects so that they can report to others about what they have learned. For example, a sociologist who studies life in a religious cult must understand how the members of the cult view the social world and their own actions. Yet if the researcher adopts the cult perspective as his or her own, then the researcher can no longer analyze cult life as a sociologist but instead has become a cult convert.

Some sociologists believe that the study of humans is not inherently different from the study of other phenomena. But they too recognize that humans think and have values. These sociologists argue that researchers should be as "objective" as possible when studying social life—they should let neither their own values nor those of the people they are studying influence their reports.

The Sociological Tradition

Auguste Comte

The founder of sociology is generally recognized to be Auguste Comte (1798–1857), a philosopher who was strongly influenced by the events following the French Revolution. At age 16 Comte left his home in Montpellier for Paris, where he enrolled in the Ecole Polytechnique. He was expelled from the school for organizing a demonstration. In 1818 he met Saint-Simon, a famous French socialist, with whom he collaborated on a series of essays. When major differences developed between them, they ended their relationship with much bitterness.

Comte eventually reached the conclusion that he should develop his own ideas; he decided that he would not read any scientific writings, reviews, or even newspapers, to keep his mind from being contaminated by the thoughts of others. He called this practice "cerebral hygiene." During this period, he

The founders of the discipline continue to influence sociologists. The American Sociological Association is the major organization for modern-day sociologists. Alice

completed his first great work, *Positive Philosophy* (six volumes) in 1842. Twelve years later he produced his second major work, *Positive Polity*. He strongly believed in the importance of his ideas and he refused all royalties from these books because he felt they should be given to the world.

In his *Positive Philosophy*, Comte used the term "sociology" for the first time. Originally he wanted to call the new discipline "social physics," but a Belgian scientist Adolphe Quételet had already adopted that term. So Comte developed the term "sociology" from the Latin root *socio-* meaning society and the Greek ending *-logy* meaning a high-level study. Thus, the new discipline, sociology, involved the study of society on a highly abstract level.

Comte divided the subject matter of sociology into two major areas: social statics and social dynamics. The study of social statics involved the examination of how the institutions of society interrelated; social dynamics focused on how whole societies changed over time. Although different terms are used today, sociologists continue to examine both of these areas.

Comte also argued that knowledge passes through three stages: the theological or religious stage, the metaphysical or abstract reasoning stage, and the positive or scientific stage. Comte's aim in his positive philosophy was to advance the study of society to the third and last stage and to apply the methods of science to the study of society. By studying and reorganizing society along scientific lines, Comte hoped, as did many early sociologists, to improve society.

Herbert Spencer

Carrying on in Comte's tradition, the English philosopher Herbert Spencer (1820–1903) is sometimes referred to as the second founder of sociology.

Rossi has served recently as president of this association. From left: Karl Marx, Max Weber, Herbert Spencer, Auguste Comte, Emile Durkheim, Alice Rossi.

Although his father was a schoolmaster, Spencer received very little formal education. As a child he was taught at home because of his poor health. He acquired much of his advanced education through reading.

At age 17 Spencer went to London where he worked as a railway engineer for four years. After leaving the railroad Spencer became interested in journalism and eventually became an editor for the *Economist,* one of England's most influential publications. During this period he began writing his first book, *Social Statics* (1855), a systematic presentation of sociological analysis, which is often called the first sociology textbook.

The central theme of Spencer's work involves the application of Darwin's theory of evolution to social life. Spencer argued that like animal forms, human societies evolved from simple forms (primitive societies) to more complex forms (industrial societies). Through natural selection, those societies that adapt to their environment and compete successfully will persist. Spencer argued that social life is governable by the laws of conflict and competition and, as in the animal world, natural selection leads to "survival of the fittest." Incidentally, it was Spencer, not Darwin, who coined this phrase. Spencer believed that the doctrine of survival of the fittest would eventually lead to social progress, which in his view constituted social justice.

Some of Spencer's ideas are definitely not accepted today, but his extensive writings have had considerable influence, particularly on scholars interested in the evolution of society.

Emile Durkheim

The French scholar Emile Durkheim (1858–1917) was strongly influenced by Comte. In fact, many considered him the heir to Comte. Coming from a family of rabbinical scholars, he broke with family tradition when he became a university professor. However, religion remained one of his lifelong interests.

Durkheim received a doctorate degree from the University of Paris in 1893 and later returned there to teach social science. Four years before his death, he became France's first professor of sociology.

Durkheim's major focus was on the social forces that hold society together. He believed that social solidarity was based on the shared values and beliefs of the members of a society. He identified two types of societal solidarity. The first type is "mechanical solidarity." In primitive societies, in which people perform similar tasks, sameness provides a basis for mechanical solidarity. The second type is "organic solidarity," which is based on differences. In industrial societies people perform various tasks, most of them necessary for the continuation of the society. These activities are interdependent like the organs in a living being.

One of Durkheim's most notable achievements was his monograph on *Suicide* (1897), in which he looked beyond individual motives to social factors as explanations of suicide. This monograph combined empirical evidence (data on suicide) with a theoretical explanation and is considered the first piece of true sociological research.

Besides *Suicide,* Durkheim's well-known works include *The Division of Labor in Society* (1893) and *The Elementary Forms of Religious Life* (1917). Durkheim's work is frequently cited today.

Karl Marx

Unlike Durkheim, who stressed social solidarity in society, Karl Marx (1818–1883) focused on social conflict. Marx, a German socialist and philosopher, was the son of a Jewish lawyer who converted his entire family to Christianity. Marx attended the universities of Bonn and Berlin where he studied law, then history and philosophy. After an unsuccessful stint as a writer for a radical publication, Marx moved to Paris, where he met his lifelong friend and collaborator, Friedrich Engels. The pair wrote *The Communist Manifesto* (1848), a propaganda pamphlet dealing with class struggle, which is still read today.

To Marx, social change was brought about through the process of conflict between two opposing classes. This was the first modern theory of social change that emphasized a single, determining factor. He characterized history as a class struggle between the oppressed and the oppressors. Marx was an *economic determinist* in that he believed that the structure of the economy determined all other aspects of society. He argued that material conditions were at the core of class conflict; that those who owned and controlled the means of production were the oppressors and those who owned nothing but their own labor were the oppressed. Marx believed that the conflicting interests of these two groups or classes would inevitably lead the oppressed to overthrow their oppressors. Although Marx was pessimistic about the immediate future of capitalist industrial societies, he had a utopian view of society after the workers' revolution. Marx prophesized there would be collective ownership of the means of production, and then there could be a classless society.

Marx's three-volume *Das Kapital* was his major work. The first volume was published in 1867, and the last two volumes, edited by Engels, appeared after his death.

Some of Marx's ideas have been adopted as a political philosophy by various groups. Sociologists are most interested in Marx's contribution to the conflict theoretical approach.

Max Weber

Some have argued that much of the work of Max Weber (1864–1920) can be interpreted as a debate with Marx's ghost. Weber repeatedly refuted Marx's contention that there is a single determinant of social change, such as economic conditions.

Weber was born to a wealthy German family and spent his youth in Berlin. He attended three universities in Germany and received his law degree in 1885. He taught economics at the University of Heidelberg until his academic career was cut short by mental illness. He worked on his research and writing at home without a university appointment for nearly two decades.

His first work, *The Protestant Ethic and the Spirit of Capitalism* (1906), examined how belief systems might affect people's actions and in turn the economic system. He hypothesized that the Protestant ethic (admonishments to achieve salvation through hard work) influenced the development of capitalism. In the present book, Chapter 14, Religious Structures, further discusses Weber's work on religion.

Not only did Weber develop his own view of social change, but also he argued with those who simply wanted to adopt the methods of other disciplines for the study of human social life. Weber introduced the *Verstehen* method into sociology (Shils and Finch 1949). He believed that sociologists must not only employ objective methods but also must ascertain the subjective meanings that people attach to their own behavior and that of others. Through the process of *Verstehen*, sympathetic understanding, these meanings can be an object of study for sociologists.

Today sociologists still rely on Weber's descriptive analysis of bureaucracy (Gerth and Mills 1958), the organizational structure that is so prevalent in modern societies. (See Chapter 10, Social Organization, for further discussion of Weber's ideas on bureaucracy.)

Who were the founders of sociology? What were their major ideas?

As you can see, the founders of the discipline of sociology often emphasized different structures or social processes whether looking at similar or different social phenomena. They each made somewhat different assumptions about the nature of social life and thus developed somewhat different hypotheses. Their works laid the foundation for continuing variety within sociology. Over the years sociologists have developed various theoretical perspectives or approaches that they use when analyzing social life.

Theoretical Perspectives

Functionalism

A theoretical approach used by sociologists since the discipline was founded is called **functionalism.** Spencer and Durkheim used this approach, which focuses on society and on the interrelations of its parts (institutions). Underlying this approach is the assumption that societies form harmonious systems that tend to remain in balance. If one part of society changes, equilibrium or balance is only temporarily disrupted until other parts of the society change to create a new equilibrium. According to Alex Inkeles (1964:35), the key question for those who employ the functionalist approach is, "How is social life maintained and carried forward in time despite the complete turnover in the membership of society with every new generation?"

Those who use the functionalist approach examine societies to identify the structures that perform tasks necessary for the survival of organized social life. Every society has basic social needs, functions that must be performed if the society is to be maintained.

Each structure (institution) in society (familial, economic, political, religious) fulfills certain tasks or functions for the society. These structures persist because they are both useful and necessary, that is, functional. For example, the family, one of the major institutions in every society, fulfills the function of caring, protecting, and nurturing the young, and also helps to regulate sexual behavior. When the functions that a given structure (such as the family) fulfills are intended and recognized, they are referred to as **manifest** functions. But structures (institutions) also have functions that are neither intended nor recognized; these are called **latent** functions.

The religious institution or structure of the North American Zuni Indians had both manifest and latent functions. The manifest function of the rain dances was to bring about rain, although there is no evidence that these dances altered the weather. An unintended and unrecognized, or latent, function of these dances was that they promoted social solidarity by bringing all the group members together for a ceremonial occasion. Whether or not the manifest function of the rain dances was realized, the rain dances performed the latent function of contributing to the maintenance of society.

Not all that occurs in a society is desirable for its continued stability. Social patterns that contribute to the maintenance of a society are regarded as *functional;* those patterns that have negative consequences for a society are considered **dysfunctional.** Religion, for example, performs many positive

Functionalism involves examination of societies to see what structures perform tasks or functions necessary for the survival of organized social life.

Manifest functions that are intended and recognized by the members of the social unit.

Latent functions that are neither intended nor recognized by members of the social unit.

Dysfunctional social patterns that have negative consequences for the social unit.

functions for society. These functions include reinforcing basic values, serving as a means of social control, and creating a community of believers. On the other hand, religion can be dysfunctional in that it can divide society, promote conflict, and justify persecution of those who hold divergent beliefs.

The functional approach is useful because it permits sociologists to examine how the same functions are performed in different ways in various societies or in one society over time. The distinction between manifest and latent functions encourages sociologists to examine the unnoticed consequences of social arrangements.

Yet some sociologists are critical of the functional approach. They argue that some patterns in society persist although they serve no particular function. Another criticism is that a pattern may be functional for some groups in society but may be dysfunctional to other groups or to the society as a whole.

Conflict

Other sociologists believe that tension and conflict are inevitable in society. Marx and Georg Simmel (1955) perceived conflict rather than harmony as the appropriate focus for the study of social life.

Sociologists who take a **conflict perspective** believe conflict is an *inevitable* outgrowth of social life. Those who adopt some of Marx's theoretical ideas, who take a neo-Marxist perspective, emphasize struggles between those who control and those who are controlled by the others. They take this view whether looking at how poor people are treated by our criminal justice system or how women are treated by men.

> **Conflict perspective** assumes that conflict is an inevitable outgrowth of social life.

Those who follow the tradition of Simmel agree that conflict is inevitable, but they do not tie it to a class struggle. Conflict is always going to occur, because people have different values and thus desire to pursue different courses of action. Conflict can lead to revolution, but it can also culminate in compromises.

Symbolic Interaction

All sociological theories focus on somewhat different aspects of social life. **Symbolic interactionism** focuses on two basic questions: How does society shape individuals? and, How do individuals shape society?

> **Symbolic interactionism** proposes that humans are the only animals to have complex forms of social organization because they can communicate with symbols.

Symbolic interactionists point out that humans are the only animals to develop the elaborate forms of social organization we call societies. George Herbert Mead (1934), the social philosopher whose ideas shaped what is today called symbolic interactionism, argued that because human animals can use language and think, they are capable of things other animals cannot do. Language permits us to learn about things we never directly experience and to plan for things we have yet to experience. Current debates about whether other animals such as dolphins have shared symbols with which they can communicate do not undermine Mead's point. Humans appear to be the only animals who can engage in the complex symbol manipulation that underpins human social life.

Individuals are born into ongoing social units. They become social beings as they learn to assign the same meanings to symbols as people already in the social unit assign to them. Typically, infants are taught symbols by their parents. Charles Horton Cooley (1922) believed the family and other primary groups served as the "nursery of human nature."

One of the important things people can do with symbols is to think about what they have done, what they are doing, and what they would like to do in the future. The behavior of nonhuman animals is explained chiefly in terms of instincts. A dog or cat responds to threatening situations in instinctive ways (body posture, vocalizations—growls or hisses). Other aspects of animals' behavior can be explained in terms of past learning or reinforcement. We can use rewards and punishments to teach pets not to jump or climb on furniture.

Humans, like other animals, acquire or discard patterns of behavior depending on reinforcement. Yet unlike other animals, people can think about what they are going to do. A stimulus does not produce an automatic response. A person may think of a new response to a stimulus. Herbert Blumer (1937), the sociologist who coined the term symbolic interaction in the 1930s, argues that human beings can create or construct responses. In fact, the social worlds in which we live are continually changing, for we are continually negotiating with one another over the meanings of symbols and actions. Thus individuals shape the societies in which they live.

Exchange

Why do people act as they do? According to exchange theorists, people are aware that some actions provide them with greater benefits than other actions. The first sociologist credited with examining human interactions from an **exchange perspective** was the German scholar Simmel. He suggested that the feeling of gratitude a person experiences when someone else gives a gift provides an important form of social glue, for the person feels obligated to the giver (Simmel 1950). Other sociologists touched on the idea of exchange during the first half of the twentieth century, such as the American sociologist Willard Waller, who looked at the "rating and dating complex" of college students. Anthropologists looked at exchanges in kinship networks and at the role of gifts in social life.

Exchange perspective people's actions are shaped by their perceptions of what behavior will produce the most desirable outcomes for them.

In the second half of the twentieth century, sociologists, psychologists, and anthropologists began to develop modern social exchange theory. Harvard sociologist George C. Homans (1961, 1974) argues that social exchange is an elementary form of social behavior. If we can understand what happens between two individuals, then we can better understand what happens in very large and complex social units.

Basically Homans argues that we can look at social interaction as social exchange. If another person engages in an activity that produces something of value to me, that person has given me a **reward.** Unfortunately, when I

Reward activity of another person that I value.

interact with that person, I am of necessity foregoing doing something else. My foregone opportunities involve some potential rewards; the opportunities or rewards that I forego are my **costs.** Exchange theorists believe that people weight the relative benefits of interacting with various others by subtracting potential costs from potential rewards. I will presumably choose to interact with others when my outcome or profit level (rewards minus costs) is most attractive.

Costs the opportunities or rewards that I had to give up.

People do not always have "free choice" about whom they will have as exchange partners. Some people such as kin may expect us to provide them with rewards. Participation in the social networks described in Chapter 3, Groups and Society, may establish exchange patterns for participants.

Compare and contrast the four theoretical approaches.

These theoretical perspectives provide sociologists with ways of looking at social life. A theory proposes relationships between things. Sociologists are interested in establishing whether or not theories are valid, whether the relationships that they propose do in fact exist in the "real" world. Researchers develop specific statements of proposed relationships—called hypotheses— and empirically test them. **Hypotheses** propose relationships between two or more things.

Hypothesis proposed relationship between two or more things or ideas.

> *Example:* Students who read the textbook assigned for a course do better on tests based on the textbook than those students who do not read the textbook.

This hypothesis proposes a relationship between two things (variables); studying and test performance.

Researchers cannot simply argue that they believe a hypothesis is valid; they must demonstrate to other people's satisfaction that there is reason to believe a hypothesis is valid. People rely on the scientific approach to establish the validity of hypotheses.

The Scientific Approach

We continually hear reports of what people think about political candidates, toothpaste, the economy and just about any other topic imaginable. Some of these reports are scientific, some are not. Some reports are intended to inform us, others to persuade us. Most of us are somewhat skeptical about at least some of these reports. Why?

Some reports about products are presented by the makers of the products. Consumer groups have made us aware that advertisers sometimes exaggerate and sometimes mislead us about products. Governmental regulations have been introduced to prevent advertisers from claiming a product is "low calorie" unless it is. Various companies have had to spend money running "corrective advertising" because they had made advertising claims that could not be substantiated. The company that makes Listerine mouthwash, for example, had to run ads indicating that using Listerine does not prevent colds and sore throats (Horowitz 1979).

On local television news programs, reporters sometimes interview people on the street or in shopping centers to assess public opinion. Newspapers and television programs also report the findings of polling organizations that systematically survey samples of the population about their opinions. The scattered on-the-street interviews do not qualify as scientific surveys, but polls conducted by organizations formed by George Gallup, Louis Harris, and Daniel Yankelovich do meet the criteria of scientific surveys.

The polls that qualify as scientific provide people with information about what specific questions were asked of what people during a given time period. Simply reporting this information is not enough, although having such information permits the person reading the report to make an informed decision about whether or not to pay any attention to it. If a political candidate reports that a survey shows most people support him or her, you might consider the results more believable if the general public were surveyed than if the candidate's financial supporters were surveyed.

The **scientific approach** involves careful observation and measurement of the phenomena being studied. The researcher's hypotheses establish the nature of what is to be studied.

Scientific approach involves careful observation and measurement of phenomena under investigation.

After a researcher has collected information, the researcher can *describe* an event or situation. However, accurate description is only the initial goal. Scientists analyze their data, often employing statistical tests, in order to *understand* how different phenomena are related to each other. If the relationship in a hypothesis is supported by the data, the researcher has achieved another goal, *explanation.* The theories from which hypotheses are derived provide explanations. Ultimately, the goal of science is to *predict* what will occur. Most sociologists find it difficult to predict, for human actions are the product of many diverse influences.

Interplay of Theory and Research

We have introduced information about theories and about scientific research. Now we consider how they interrelate. Theories are systematic presentations of ideas about how phenomena interrelate. Some theories are more appealing to us than others because they coincide better with the views we held before we read the theory. Yet personal taste is not an adequate criterion for judging the worth or value of a theory.

Other criteria used to evaluate theories are how adequately they appear to account for what is already known about the world. When people had

CONTROVERSIAL ISSUES · Predicting the Future

Many people would like to know what the future will bring simply because they are curious. As an individual you might like to know what job opportunities will be like in the future so you can decide what you should study in college. Or you might like to know what a particular person will be like in the future, so you can decide whether or not to marry him or her. Most of us do not turn to soothsayers or fortune tellers to learn about the future. We try to rely on the opinions and guesses of people who are experts.

There are many kinds of experts predicting the future. Newsletters are published by stock market analysts who try to predict sound investments. Companies thinking about introducing new products conduct market research to learn if people will be interested in the product, how much they are willing to pay for it, and what kind of advertising will work best. The government employs economists to forecast the government's future income, and whether the economy will expand or decline. Demographers predict how fast the population will grow in the future. Pollsters (Yankelovich 1981) and others (Toffler 1970) attempt to identify directions in which people are moving.

Forecasting the future is always risky, for many different things may influence what occurs. In 1949 George Orwell's pessimistic political novel *1984* was published. Presumably his novel was intended to shock people into thinking about how political belief systems and technological changes could work together to shape a totalitarian society in which "Big Brother" controls our behavior through electronic surveillance and sophisticated propaganda techniques. If you read *1984* today you might laugh about ways in which society is not like he predicted or be appalled by the ways in which it is.

Generally, sociologists experience ambivalence about predicting the future. In part they are reluctant to predict because their theoretical models and research methods are not as well developed as they would like them to be. But also they are apprehensive about the uses that might be made of knowledge about how human behavior is shaped. If you can predict what will lead people to behave in certain ways, then possibly you can *manipulate* people to behave so as to suit your own purposes.

limited knowledge about our planet, they theorized that the Earth was flat. We laugh at that idea today because we have information that clearly contradicts that theory.

Sometimes more than one theory can be used to explain or account for the same observable facts. When confronted with such dilemmas, scientists have tended to prefer the theory that most simply accounts for what is known. The most parsimonious theories are usually preferred.

At times it is frustrating to read about theory evaluation because you wonder why researchers do not simply prove which theories are true and which are false. However, we cannot prove which theories are true, but only which theories are not true. Scientists compare information they obtain from their investigations with what is hypothesized. If over a series of tests, studies indicate that a hypothesis is not true, they can discard the hypothesis. If over a series of tests, studies provide support for a theory, we can say that the theory has not been disproved, but we cannot say we have proved that it is true.

Just as various theories about the physical world have been discarded because evidence gathered over the years did not support them, theories about the social world have been discarded also. At one time Cesare Lombroso (1911), a founder of the field of criminology, argued that people were deviants or criminals because they inherited particular physiological characteristics. He argued specifically that criminals could be identified by their head shapes.

As Charles Darwin's ideas about evolution became accepted, some social scientists applied notions about the survival of the fittest to their analyses of social life. Theorists who adopted such ideas believed that social welfare programs were misguided, for they disrupted the natural order. The fittest were those who experienced success. Advocates of laissez faire, which means doing nothing to change social inequities, were classified as "social Darwinists" (Herbert Spencer, William Graham Sumner).

Lombroso's ideas and those of the social Darwinists have been rejected because scientific research findings did not support them. Sociologists employ a diverse set of research strategies in their attempts to confirm or disconfirm theories. Each of these research strategies or methods has strengths and weaknesses.

Research Methods

⊕ Sample Survey

If you want to know how many college students plan to marry before age 25, or whether they plan to have children, or how important physical attraction is as a criterion of mate selection, why not ask them? Other research procedures may provide us with more specific information about people's behavior, but the sample survey gives us information about trends among college students or other populations we are interested in. The **sample survey,** as its name suggests, has two parts: the sample and the survey.

Once a researcher decides what people's actions or beliefs are of interest—college students, cult members, divorced people, or ex-convicts, for instance—the researcher is typically confronted with a relatively large population. It is expensive and time-consuming to collect data from every member of a population. Every ten years the United States Government conducts a census of the population. While much valuable information is obtained, it is cumbersome to deal with so many cases. Researchers using the census often do not use all people when analyzing characteristics of the population, but rather use a "1 in a 1,000 sample" of the population.

Sample survey a research method which involves collecting information from a sample of the population.

Sociologists, typically, do not collect data from all members of a population, but rather select some members of a population for study—a sample. To be able to make generalizations about the population from their findings about a sample, researchers must use a sample that is representative of the population. There are a number of ways to select a representative sample. Researchers do not want a biased sample, one that does not reflect the characteristics of the population. If a survey were given only to the students in your introductory sociology class, could you generalize about all college students from the results? The answer is no.

One type of sample that is representative of the population because each element of the population has an equal chance of being included in the sample is called a random sample. Various states sponsor lotteries in which people pay money for a lottery number. The winning lottery numbers are randomly selected. Each digit of the winning number is pulled from a container of numbers. If winning lottery numbers were not randomly selected, people would be angry, for their chances of winning would be altered.

Researchers often do not want a completely random sample. For example, a pollster may be interested in which candidate is most likely to be elected President of the United States. A random sample of 1,500 might not include people from all parts of the country. Since we know that people in different regions of the country have voted differently in the past, we might advise the pollster to divide the country up into regions (strata) and sample people within each region, to develop a *stratified sample.*

A researcher conducting a sample survey may directly ask questions or may mail questionnaires to people.

After the researcher selects or "draws" a sample, the researcher is ready to administer the study. Questions may be mailed to people, asked over the telephone, or presented in a face-to-face interview. The questions may be carefully worded so they can be easily understood and are not ambiguous. Also care must be taken so that questions do not sway or influence responses. The following questions are worded in such a way that they force the subject to respond negatively.

Do you think the President has the right to enslave the American People?
Do you agree that college students must be pampered or they will become frustrated and upset?

Such questions are loaded or biased.

After the researcher receives the respondents' answers, the researcher typically uses statistical techniques to analyze them. Hypotheses may be accepted or rejected depending on the results of statistical analysis.

The survey is an invaluable method for systematically and efficiently obtaining information about large numbers of people, for the researcher uses statistical techniques to generalize about the target population based on the samples' responses. However, the survey has some disadvantages. People are not always truthful in their answers, especially when the questions concern things which they do not want other people to know. At times people may truthfully report their attitudes, but they do not behave as we might expect, given their attitudes. For example, people may disapprove of sexual relations outside of marriage but participate in them.

Content Analysis

A questionnaire administered as part of a sample survey may include questions which do not have a limited number of response choices. They are called open-ended questions.

Fixed Response Choice Question

Select the statement which *best* indicates why you enrolled in an introductory sociology class.

a. personal interest
b. friend's recommendation
c. requirement for my program
d. fit my schedule

Open-ended Question

Why did you enroll in an introductory sociology class?

Before a researcher administers a questionnaire with fixed response choices, he or she may look at questions on other survey questionnaires and/or conduct a pre-test to develop what the researcher believes is a good set of answer choices. When a researcher uses an open-ended question, response categories are established after the questionnaire has been given. The researcher reads respondents' answers to see what themes or categories appear in the answers. In other words, the researcher analyzes the content and develops categories.

Sociologists also may examine official reports (records of divorce settlements or suicides, for example), diaries, magazines, television programs—in fact any record (printed, audio-taped, video-taped, or painted) of people's individual or collective experiences. Through use of **content analysis** procedures, sociologists can learn many things which people might not be willing or able to tell a survey researcher.

Advocates of content analysis argue that researchers should not in advance of collecting data limit what responses people can give or what categories will be used. They want the data to "speak for themselves." Critics believe that content analysis gives the researcher too much latitude, too much opportunity to impose his or her perspective on what people said or did.

While sociologists may learn about people's beliefs and behaviors through having them respond to survey questions or examining documents and records, another basic way to obtain information is through observation of people's activities. Early sociologists, such as Simmel, wrote essays about social life based on their familiarity with the social worlds in which they lived. In the first decades of the twentieth century, sociologists at the University of Chicago treated the city as their laboratory. Since then sociologists have elaborated observational procedures, distinguishing two types: participant observation and unobtrusive observation.

Participant Observation

Early American sociologists went out into the urban communities surrounding their universities to learn about gang life (Thrasher 1927), prostitution (Thomas 1923), and many other aspects of social life. During those early decades anthropologists were going out into the field to learn about vanishing North American Indian customs and about "primitive" societies around the world (Mead 1928). Because sociologists were participating in social activities in their own society while they were observing them, their research strategy was called **participant observation.** Anthropologists left what was known (their society) and entered the field (another society); consequently their research was called fieldwork.

During the 1930s and 1940s sociologists became concerned about establishing their discipline as a science and many of them turned to survey data and statistical analyses. Yet, some sociologists such as Herbert Blumer (1931) continued to promote and engage in observational research. In the 1940s William Foote Whyte reported in *Street Corner Society* (1943) on a participant observation study of unemployed men who hung around an urban neighborhood he was studying. During the 1950s, few studies achieved the status that Whyte's study did, although many students and professionals alike were intrigued by Howard S. Becker's article on "Becoming a Marihuana User" (1953), which outlined the steps people went through in defining marihuana use as

Content analysis a research procedure which involves development of categories based on study of content.

Participant observation a research procedure which requires that the researcher engage in the activities of the people being studied.

pleasurable. The 1960s apparently provided a more hospitable environment for participant observation reports, for there were studies of medical school socialization (Becker et al. 1961), bars (Cavan 1966), black street corner men (Liebow 1967), homosexuals (Humphreys 1970), TB sanitaria patients (Roth 1963), and dying (Glaser and Strauss 1965), to name a few topics.

As you look at the topics, questions about how researchers participate should come to mind. Obviously, researchers do not die or contract tuberculosis in order to conduct their research. But a participant observer is to varying degrees involved in the activities of those being studied. At a minimum a participant observer sits in the corner and observes what is happening. Sitting in the corner is a form of participation, for those persons being observed, whether subtly or obviously, alter their activities when someone new is with them. Typically, the participant observer does not sit alone in a chair but talks with people and participates to varying degrees in group activities.

No matter how active or passive the participant observer is, participant observation takes time because the researcher must wait for events to occur. On the grounds of efficiency alone, some people reject observation in favor of simply asking people about their activities. Yet advocates of participant observation argue that it is the best way to understand social behavior, because the researcher learns how people think about things and why they act as they do. And sociologists need to observe directly how people behave in ordinary settings in which they are comfortable.

Other critics of the participant observation method wonder if it is possible to participate in a group and then "objectively" report on its activities. Anthropologists tell tales of researchers leaving to study exotic societies and never returning because they "go native." Defenders of participant observation argue that human beings conduct all research, and thus values may affect any researcher's findings.

Unobtrusive Observation

At times sociologists observe social life without participating in the activities they are studying. Such observation is called *unobtrusive* because the researcher in no way affects or intrudes on what is being studied. In an airport or other public waiting setting, a sociologist may record what people do while they are waiting. A researcher may observe children's play behavior from a concealed observation post.

Unobtrusive observation sometimes is called "naturalistic" (Denzin 1977). People are observed in settings they normally are in and doing what they typically do. Implicitly, this research is being contrasted with research which involves people being in settings contrived by researchers and/or engaging in atypical activities. If a researcher puts a child in a special room alone with "experimental" toys and observes what the child does through a special window, the research activity may be unobtrusive but the research setting is not natural—children do not normally play by themselves in special observational rooms.

Unobtrusive observation a research procedure that requires that the people being studied remain unaware that they are being observed.

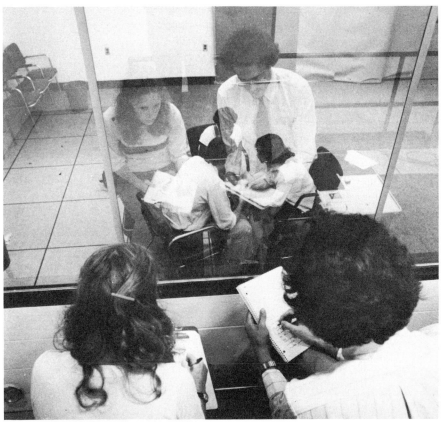

Researchers may systematically record information about group behavior without disrupting the group's activities.

Not all unobtrusive research involves direct observation of people's activities. Other unobtrusive research may involve analyzing materials left by people or generated about people. You can learn about people's lifestyles by seeing what they discard, what is in their "garbage." Or, you can examine records kept on them (such as academic, driving, military, credit, or medical).

As you think about various ways to unobtrusively study human behavior, you should begin to think about whether the individual has the right to know you are studying him or her and what, if any, right to privacy a person has.

Sometimes sociologists use more than one research method to examine social phenomena, for they recognize the various strengths and weaknesses of each method. By employing more than one method, they believe they can collect data which better test their hypotheses.

Yet, whether using only one research method or more, sociologists are still confronted by questions about the role of values in social research. From the time when sociology was first emerging until today, questions about the role of values in social research have been debated. All human beings have values. Can or should researchers put aside their personal values and be totally objective when conducting research? Today most sociologists recognize that it is impossible to be completely objective (Gouldner 1962). However, some sociologists argue that if sociologists want to be scientists and to be *seen* as scientists, they should be as objective as possible. Others argue that all sociologists can do is to state their values at the beginning of their reports so that readers can be aware of any biases that may appear in their research.

Do you believe social scientists can be objective?

THE FACTS · The Scientific Method

With all of the different studies we are confronted with every day, we must have some rules for deciding which studies to believe and which not to believe. We assume that research findings are valid, that they accurately reflect reality, if people follow specific steps in conducting their research.

By reading about and observing social life we begin to have questions about why people act as they do. The first step of any research project involves *formulation of the research problem* or question. You must define a problem which is capable of being empirically addressed. For example, you cannot establish the validity of various religious beliefs because they cannot be empirically tested; however, you can study people's religious beliefs and how they relate to their behavior. You must also remember to limit your statement of the research problem so that your task as a researcher is manageable. It might be interesting to learn how people's beliefs about sexual behavior change over their lifetimes, but it could take you all of your life to address this question.

Sociological theories suggest questions that can be empirically researched. For a research project questions are usually stated in the form of hypotheses. If we are interested in the relationship between religious beliefs and behavior, we might develop an hypothesis such as the following: college students who are very religious are less likely to engage in premarital sexual intercourse than students who are not very religious.

Once you have established your research question, the next step is to *review the relevant literature.* You want to learn how others addressed the question, what information they obtained, and what conclusions they drew from their studies. One study reported that teenage females were less likely to engage in premarital sexual intercourse if they attended church frequently (Kanter and Zelnick 1972). Another study found a similar relationship between sexual behavior and religious involvement for college students in the 1960s (Carns 1969). These studies suggest the hypothesized relationship existed for other groups in the past. We need to find out if college students in the 1980s are influenced by religious beliefs as students were in the past.

The third step in the research process involves establishing the *research design.* We must decide whom we are going to study—presumably college students on our campus. Then we must decide how we are going to collect information from them. For the sake of simplicity we will give them a questionnaire using questions asked in previous studies.

Now we are ready to engage in *data collection.* We will distribute the questionnaire to preselected college students on our campus. (Other types of projects might involve observing people's behavior; however, our topic does not lend itself to this research strategy.)

The fifth step consists of *data analysis.* We will categorize people by how religious they are and then compare the groups on whether they have or have not engaged in premarital sexual intercourse. If those who are most religious have by and large not engaged in sexual intercourse and those who are less religious have almost all engaged in sexual intercourse, our research hypothesis has been supported. Typically professional sociologists employ statistical procedures when analyzing their research findings, so they can more precisely communicate information to other professionals.

After analyzing the data, the researcher is ready for the final step, the *drawing of conclusions.* In a research report the investigator indicates whether or not the data (empirical findings) provide support for the research hypothesis. The investigator may note any qualifications or limitations of the study design when drawing conclusions. For example, if only students at a religious college were studied, the findings might not be reflective of college students in general. Such information will help subsequent researchers when they develop their research designs.

The accumulation of information from various studies provides the scientific underpinnings of sociology.

CONTROVERSIAL ISSUES • Research on Human Subjects: Ethical Issues

If you were ill and went to a doctor seeking treatment, would you expect the doctor to provide you with the proper treatment indicated by the diagnosis of your ailment? At one time poor people in the South were unknowing subjects in an experiment: one set of people diagnosed as having syphilis received proper treatment; another set did not.

If you agreed to participate in a study of human behavior conducted at a university, would you expect that the researchers would lead you to engage in behavior counter to your values or behavior that was psychologically or physically harmful to you? Psychologist Stanley Milgram (1965) had research subjects participate in a study in a "scientific laboratory." A confederate of the experimenter was placed in another room and presumably wired to receive shocks. The research subject was asked to administer a shock to the person in the other room each time the person made a mistake in reciting words. Each time a mistake was made a higher level of shock was supposed to be administered. The mechanism in front of the research subject noted different levels of shock intensity with "danger" at one extreme. Milgram's goal was to see if research subjects would *conform* to the demands of the experimenter to keep administering presumably stronger and stronger shocks. Milgram learned that many people would conform. What did the research subjects learn? Did they learn that they were capable of doing harm to other people? Was it psychologically damaging to the research subjects to learn such a thing about themselves?

Furor over various medical and psychological studies led various professional organizations to adopt codes of ethics for research. The federal government has established rules for using human subjects. Universities have committees that review research proposals which will involve human subjects.

Today people cannot be made to participate in research that will do them harm. Researchers must let potential subjects know what possible benefit or harm may result from participation in a study. Potential subjects must be informed. After they have been informed about possible consequences of participation, researchers can ask for their **informed consent.**

Informed consent exists when a research subject knows what the research project involves and agrees to participate in it.

Much sociological research involves no risk to the subject. If a person agrees to fill out a questionnaire, that agreement is taken as a sign of informed consent. However, sociologists typically inform possible participants in their research that their identities will be kept confidential, so that no one but the researcher will know who said or did what.

Which do you believe is more important—the scientist's need to know or individuals' rights of privacy?

Summary

Sociologists engage in the scientific study of patterns of human interaction. These patterns can be learned by observing ordinary behavior as well as behavior identified as wrong. Structures represent persisting patterns of human action. Sooner or later patterns change, so sociologists look also at the dynamics of social interaction.

Sociologists study what most people take for granted, social life. At times people suffer from the "everybody-knows-that" syndrome when informed of sociological research findings. People tend to selectively remember when commonsense expressions were empirically supported and to forget occasions when they did not hold true.

When sociologists study human interaction they may consider economic, political, historical, and psychological factors. However, unlike the social science disciplines that focus on one basic set of factors, sociologists try to understand patterns of human behavior as the product of multiple social influences.

The discipline of sociology traces its origins to Auguste Comte, who established the name sociology in the middle of the nineteenth century. Another early founder who carried on in Comte's tradition was Herbert Spencer. Two other founders, Emile Durkheim and Karl Marx, took somewhat opposing views of social life. Durkheim emphasized the importance of social solidarity, while Marx focused on the key role of conflict in shaping society. Another early contributor, Max Weber, questioned Marx's emphasis on economic factors. Weber believed that ideas or beliefs could be as important as economic factors in stimulating social change.

Modern-day sociologists draw on the ideas of the founders but, rather than using the perspectives of particular founders, they tend to adopt one of a variety of theoretical perspectives: functionalism, conflict, symbolic interactionism, or exchange. The functionalist perspective emphasizes stability within society. In contrast the conflict perspective emphasizes how societies change. Both the symbolic interactionist and exchange perspectives are used to focus on why people behave as they do in specific situations. Depending on what questions a researcher wants to answer, one theoretical perspective may be more useful than another.

Theories propose relationships among many different things. Sociologists cannot ascertain the validity of all aspects of a theory with one study. What they do is investigate hypotheses, proposed relationships between two or more things. If numerous hypotheses derived from a theory are supported by research findings, the general theory has been supported.

Hypotheses are accepted or rejected on the basis of scientific findings. Findings from studies that utilize the scientific approach are accepted because they are based on careful observation and measurement.

After a researcher has collected information, it is analyzed and reported to the public. Research reports may simply be descriptive. Sociologists typically hope to be able also to understand and explain the patterns of behavior they describe. Some sociologists strive to predict what people will do in the future.

Research hypotheses are often drawn from existing theories. Empirical studies may produce findings which cause researchers to modify or reject hypotheses. If hypotheses derived from a theory are not supported by research findings, eventually the theory may be rejected. Thus there is interplay between theory and research.

Sociologists draw on four research methods or strategies in their investigations of social life: sample surveys, content analysis, participant observation, and unobtrusive observation. Which research method is employed depends on the type of information the researcher needs as well as the opportunities the researcher has to collect information.

Whatever type of research project in which a sociologist engages, the study to some extent reflects the interests and values of the investigator. Rather than arguing that they can be value-free, most sociologists have the goal of being as objective as possible.

Suggested Readings

Earl R. Babbie. *The Practice of Social Research,* 2d ed. Belmont, Calif.: Wadsworth, 1979. Provides an overview of the methods and techniques sociologists use for conducting social research.

Peter I. Berger. *Invitation to Sociology.* Garden City, NY: Doubleday, 1963. A clear, concise introduction to the subject matter and purpose of sociology.

C. Wright Mills. *The Sociological Imagination.* New York: Oxford University Press, 1959. A classic discussion of some of the uses of sociology and the insights it can provide.

Everett K. Wilson and Hanan Selvin. *Why Study Sociology? A Note to Undergraduates.* Belmont, Calif.: Wadsworth, 1980. A brief statement of the uses of and rewards gained from studying sociology.

PART ONE

The Individual and Society

The following four chapters focus on culture—how it shapes and influences human behavior and in turn how human beings create and maintain culture. Chapter 2 describes culture, which is the social heritage of a society that is transmitted in each generation. From the time we are born until we die, culture regulates our lives. Our lives are spent in the company of others and in the context of groups.

In Chapter 3 we turn to a discussion of groups and how they influence the behavior of their members. The process through which we learn our culture and internalize and follow the rules of our society is socialization, discussed in Chapter 4. Because socialization alone cannot insure sufficient conformity, additional means of social control are needed. In Chapter 5 we look at social control—that is, a set of means that makes most individuals act as they are expected to act and, at the same time, we examine deviance, which is behavior that violates cultural expectations.

2

Culture

Unlike all other creatures, human beings are unique in that they are able to transmit ideals, knowledge, beliefs, values, and patterns of behavior from one generation to the next. This social heritage is called "culture." It is what makes our species human and sets us apart from other primates. As one anthropologist has put it: "Without the presence of culture, conserving past gains and shaping each succeeding generation to its patterns, homo sapiens would be nothing more than a terrestrial anthropoid ape, slightly divergent in structure and slightly superior in intelligence" (Linton 1936:79).

The Nature of Culture

Culture is such a pervasive part of human life that almost no human thought and behavior is free from its influence. And yet, we are seldom aware of this influence because culture is such a part of us that we take it for granted and are only vaguely conscious of it. The cultural patterns of our society often become so instilled that we follow them automatically and habitually. Kluckhohn states:

> Even those of us who pride ourselves on our individualism follow most of the time a pattern not of our own making. We brush our teeth on arising. We put on pants—not a loincloth or a grass skirt. We eat three meals a day—not four or five or two. We sleep in a bed—not a hammock or on a sheep pelt (Kluckhohn 1949:18).

Culture, then, may be thought of as a design for living or a road map that guides the behavior of members of a society, permitting them to live together in an organized, orderly manner.

Another important aspect of culture is that it helps us to predict the behavior of others and also permits others to know what to expect of us. A college professor can predict with reasonable certainty that students will come to class at a certain time and will sit in the seats in the classroom, not stand on them, or use them as weapons to hit each other over the head. If there are sufficient seats, no one will sit on the floor. Chances are that no student will come to class wearing a bikini or nothing at all. By the same token, the students can predict certain behavior about the professor, such as taking attendance and giving tests and grades. Students can also predict that no professor will come to class and do a tap dance or sleep instead of giving a lecture.

You may have noticed that in the preceding discussion, the term "culture" was used in a way different from what you are probably used to. In sociology "culture" has nothing to do with refinement or appreciating the finer things in life. Persons who prefer pornography to an artistic masterpiece, use vile language, or pick their noses are still considered to have culture in the sociological sense. To the sociologist all human beings are cultured in the sense that they are participants in the culture of their societies. One of the first definitions of culture and still the most widely quoted one was formulated in 1871 by Sir Edward Tylor, an English anthropologist: "Culture is that complex whole which includes knowledge, belief, art, morals, law, custom, and any other capabilities and habits acquired by man as a member of society" (Tylor 1871:1). In other words, it refers to the totality of what is learned by persons as members of society. For our purposes we define **culture** as the social heritage of a society that is transmitted to each generation. It is learned behavior that is shared with others.

A term often used synonymously with culture is "society." Although no culture can exist apart from a society of people and no society can function without cultural guidelines, for analytical purposes it is necessary to separate the two. A **society** is a group of people who live and work together and think of themselves as having social unity. A culture refers to the distinctive ways of life of such a group of people—the habits and values shared by members of a society. Society, then, refers to an organization of people whereas culture refers to a system of behavior and values.

> **Culture** the social heritage of a society that is transmitted to each generation; learned behavior that is shared with others.

> **Society** a group of people who live and work together and think of themselves as having social unity.

Components of Culture

Culture is such an inclusive, all-encompassing concept that to understand it more fully, we need to break it down into some of its principal parts: material culture, norms, values, and language.

Material Culture

The first major component of culture consists of physical objects or artifacts—things that human beings create by altering the natural environment. These include skyscrapers, jet airplanes, stone axes, clothing, teepees, and baseball bats. The book you are now reading is an artifact of **material culture,** as is the press that printed it.

The meanings and uses of an artifact may vary from culture to culture. In our society, for example, a ring means that a person is married when it is worn on the third finger of the left hand, but in some places, rings are worn, for the sake of beauty, through the nose.

> **Material culture** physical objects or artifacts that human beings create by altering the natural environment.

Norms

In a typical nudist camp there are rules of behavior that members follow in relation to one another that function for the maintenance of the group (Weinberg 1965:311–319). These include:

1. There should be no staring: This rule helps to prevent any signs of "over-involvement."

2. There should be no sex talk: Talking about sex or telling dirty jokes is considered unacceptable behavior.
3. Body contact is taboo: Nudists are careful to avoid body contact because of the way it might be interpreted.
4. Alcoholic beverages are not permitted: The purpose of this rule is to control any breakdown in inhibitions that could result in erotic overtures.
5. There are rules regarding photography: Taking pictures is a sensitive matter unless the individual is an official photographer.

This list of shared standards or rules for behavior is an example of **norms** that apply to a specific group within the society—members of a nudist camp. Some norms, which are the most significant, apply to the entire society. Our society has a powerful norm against a person having several spouses at the same time or taking the life of another human being. Norms define what we are expected to do and what we should or should not do in certain situations. They are the rules and regulations that govern the game of life.

Norms shared standards or rules for behavior.

One way sociologists classify norms is on the basis of the degree of disapproval that results when they are violated. Nonconformity to some norms may result in only mild disapproval of the violator, whereas infractions of other norms result in strong disapproval. Norms may be arranged along a continuum, although in many cases there may be considerable overlapping and the dividing line between them is not always sharp. By using this classification, the following norms are usually differentiated: folkways, mores, and laws (Davis 1948).

Folkways.　Customary patterns of everyday life that specify what is socially correct and proper are called **folkways.** Shaking hands, having cereal

Folkways norms that specify what is socially correct and proper in everyday life.

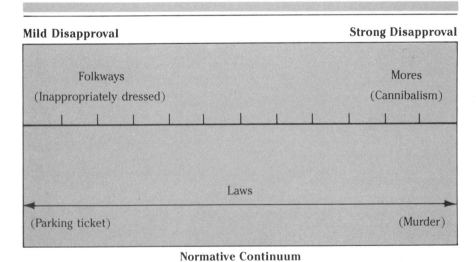

Normative Continuum

Figure 2.1

Suspicion and stark fear are the sources of the apparently harmless and polite gesture of shaking hands... In the distant past meeting with a stranger aroused immediate suspicion. Neither man knew the other's intention... Grasping their weapon all the more firmly, they could proceed on their way, perhaps giving each other the widest possible berth. Or, they could... become friends.

To do this they first had to make sure that there was no possibility of attack. So they laid down their weapons or kept their hands well away from them, displaying their empty palms. But to be doubly sure, and to prevent the other man from suddenly grabbing his sword, they clasped hands firmly.

The hearty handshake, therefore, did not in the beginning show friendship but distrust. Nor did the customary use of the right hand originate by chance. It was a precaution to immobilize the other man's weapon hand.

SOURCE: Adapted from R. Brasch, *How Did It Begin?* (New York: David McKay Company, Inc., 1966), pp. 71–72.

for breakfast, throwing rice at a bride and groom, bathing frequently, keeping one's lawn cut, and not drinking whiskey in church are examples of folkways in our society. Because folkways are not considered too important, when violated they carry only minor penalties such as a raised eye-brow or a critical remark. Folkways are not deliberately planned and often their origin is unknown. Once a pattern is started, however, it tends to persist even though the reason for it has long since disappeared. (See the box on handshaking.)

Mores. In contrast to folkways, mores are seen as extremely important and are considered vital for the group's welfare and survival. While the folkways specify socially correct and proper behavior, **mores** define what is morally right and morally wrong. As a consequence, their violation results in strong disapproval and even severe punishment. If someone chews food with his or her mouth open or wears a purple polka dot shirt with green pants, eye-brows may be raised, and the person may be the butt of jokes and ridicule. But no one would consider that person immoral or depraved. But if a person commits treason or murder or practices cannibalism, we react with disgust, horror, or shock; our deepest sentiments are offended. Persons who violate the mores may be ostracized, imprisoned, or killed. Conformance to mores is taken for granted and acceptance of them is usually without question by most people in a society.

Although folkways and mores are relatively durable, some do change, although the change is slow and gradual. Cigarette advertisements in the early 1980s had the theme "You've come a long way, baby," emphasizing how in the past the mores prohibited women from smoking in public. Not too many

Mores norms that define what is morally right and wrong.

PEOPLE · Dating Etiquette Sixty Years Ago

"On his first visit the man is not expected to remain longer than a half-hour," counsels an etiquette book written in the early 1920s. Upon leaving the woman's house the young man should not request permission to call again. If the woman desires to continue the friendship, she will send him a dinner or tea invitation.

The book goes on to advise that if the hour is late and other people in the house have retired, it is incorrect for the young woman to invite her escort for the evening into the house. Also it is not good manners for a young woman to thank her escort upon taking leave of him at her home. However, he may thank her for the pleasure of her company.

Other pointers on how well-bred young men and women should act are that when eating in a restaurant, it is not considered good form for the young woman to give her order directly to the waiter. She must give her order to her escort who then in turn tells the waiter. Also "no well-bred person kisses in public." Kissing is a form of greeting not practiced by people of polite society. Friends and relatives who kiss every time they meet are displaying poor taste and creating a bad impression.

SOURCE: Lillian Eichler, *Etiquette Problems in Pictures* (New York: Nelson Doubleday, Inc., 1922), p. 55.

years ago women didn't wear pants except on certain occasions, and men were expected to keep their hair short and well-trimmed. Both folkways and mores regarding the relations between the sexes have undergone considerable change in recent years. The boxed insert on this page tells of some changes that have taken place in dating etiquette in the past sixty years.

Laws. Laws differ from folkways and mores in several important respects. First of all, **laws** are enforced formally by a special political organization composed of persons authorized to use force if necessary. Also, laws are the result of conscious thought and deliberate planning. Finally, laws are more adaptable to changing conditions than are folkways and mores. The degree of disapproval and punishment of the violator of a law varies according to which law is broken. A person who exceeds the 55-mile speed limit by five miles an hour or so may get an informal rebuke or a ticket for speeding or both. Certainly his or her friends are not disgusted or repulsed by the incident. But suppose that same person ran over a child and never even stopped to look back. This act would elicit not only strong disapproval but strong punishment as well.

Many mores are incorporated into law and serve to reinforce it. In fact, laws are most effective when they are rooted in the mores. At times, however, the mores and folkways may conflict with the laws. National prohibition is an example of a law that was in conflict with the nation's mores. Enforcement

Laws norms that are enforced formally by a special political organization.

was so ineffective that the law was repealed 15 years after it had been enacted. On the other hand, some laws are passed in an effort to change the folkways and mores. The civil rights legislation of the 1960s challenged the traditional norms regarding racial patterns and required the instituting of new norms.

Values

Another important component of culture is values. Unlike norms, which constitute standards for behavior, **values** represent the standards we use to evaluate the desirability of things. They define what is right, good, and moral. The values of a society shape its normative system and guide the behavior of its people. By analyzing the norms of a society, one can determine the basic values of that society.

Values the standards we use to evaluate the desirability of things.

Each society has certain values that tend to set it apart and help distinguish it from other societies. In an attempt to analyze the dominant values of American society, Robin Williams (1970) identified fifteen major value orientations. Some of these are:

1. *Achievement and success.* We emphasize personal achievement, especially occupational success. We admire rags-to-riches stories and value the self-made man.
2. *Activity and work.* Closely related to achievement and success is the high evaluation that Americans place on work. Work is not only regarded as a means to success but as an end in itself. Many Americans are not happy and feel guilty unless they are doing something. Foreign observers are often amazed at our constant activity and dedication to work.
3. *Moral orientation.* Americans see the world in terms of right and wrong and good and bad. They tend to judge their conduct and that of others against certain ethical principles.
4. *Humanitarianism.* We are noted for our material generosity. Americans believe in helping others individually as well as collectively through organized charities and philanthropies.
5. *Efficiency and practicality.* Efficiency has become a standard by which we judge activity. Our emphasis on efficiency is associated with the importance we place on practicality and technology.

Other value orientations that Williams has singled out for analysis include progress, freedom, conformity, and democracy. Such a list is certainly not conclusive, but at best only suggestive. In addition, some of these values are highly controversial and have been challenged in recent years. Such an analysis does, however, provide us with valuable cultural insights.

Language

Why do we call a metal or wooden object with four legs that we use to write on a "desk"? There is nothing in the property of this object that is associated with the sound "desk." The connection between the word "desk" and the piece of furniture that it stands for is purely arbitrary. We might just as well have called it a jidget or a klugaboo. The word "desk" then is simply a symbol—a thing that stands for something else. The thing or event that the symbol refers to (in this case a four-legged object) is called a referent. "Human beings simply decide in the process of human interaction that some particular symbol will be used to refer to something else. Tying the symbol and referent together, then, is a human behavior pattern. The connection between the symbol and referent is a human product" (Vernon 1972:65). Thus there is no inherent relationship between the symbol and the referent. For communication to take place, it makes no difference what we call something as long as there is a mutual agreement as to what we are referring to. **Language** may be defined, then, as a system of symbols that have specific and arbitrary meanings in a given society. It is this symbolic communication or language that sets human beings apart from other species. With language we can go beyond transmitting simple feelings and emotions in the "here and now." It allows us to talk and think about the past and the future. Language enables us to learn from others' experiences and to accumulate knowledge from one generation to the next. In other words, language gives us the ability to transmit our learning to others. As a result, each new generation does not have to discover fire or invent the wheel but can build upon what has been passed on by the previous generations. This is probably human beings' greatest advantage.

Language a system of symbols that have specific and arbitrary meanings in a given society.

Human and Animal Communication.   How does our capacity for language compare with that of lower animals? The ability of primates to learn language has been demonstrated in various experiments, mainly with chimpanzees. It has long been believed that chimpanzees were smart enough to learn language, and much of the early work focused on attempts to teach them to talk. The record set in the 1950s for the number of words spoken by a chimpanzee was four (Fleming 1974).* In 1966 two psychologists, Beatrice and Allen Gardner, decided that instead of speech, they would try to teach a young female chimpanzee named Washoe the American sign language used by deaf people. In less than a year of training Washoe had learned 8 to 10 signs and produced her first combination of signs. As time went on, the number of combinations she knew increased—some she learned and others she invented herself. She made up "gimme tickle" to request tickling and "open food drink" to ask for the refrigerator to be opened. After four years of training Washoe had acquired a vocabulary of 160 signs.

Another researcher, David Premack, has taught a chimpanzee named Sarah to communicate by using small pieces of variously shaped and colored plastics. Each piece stands for a word. Sarah has been taught to place these symbols in a vertical line on a board to form sentences. Like Washoe, Sarah was able to transfer her knowledge outside the context of her training and invent new sentences. Both know about the same number of symbols, but

*Much of this material is adapted from Joyce D. Fleming, "The State of the Apes," *Psychology Today*, January 1974, pp. 31–50.

The chimpanzee Washoe learning the American sign language for "brush."

Sarah has been taught many more language functions than Washoe. For instance, she is able to use such parts of the language as class concepts, negation, pluralization, quantifiers, and the conditional.

At the Yerkes Primate Research Center, Duane Rumbaugh and his colleagues have taught a chimpanzee, Lana, to operate a typewriter-like instrument that is attached to a set of projectors and a computer. The computer records and analyzes what she types and then rewards her for a correct performance. In this way, Lana asks for food, drink, entertainment, and even human companionship. In one year of training, Lana's progress far outdistanced her teachers' expectations. She began inventing new sentences and even asking questions. For instance, when Lana saw an orange for the first time, and her keyboard had no symbol for the fruit, she improvised by asking for "an apple that is orange color." On another occasion, Lana was shown a box filled with candies. "Box" was a word that had been added to her keyboard only that morning. After punching the words she already knew, "bowl" and "can," Lana asked for "name of this." The reply came back, and she then punched out: "Give Lana this box."

From the work that has been done so far, it appears that with training chimpanzees can learn language. But there are several important limitations that set them apart from the way humans use it. First, none of the chimpanzees were able to advance in their communicative capacity beyond the level of a young child. Another difference is that language does not have to be taught to a child as long as the child is not kept in isolation. There appears to be a biological disposition for humans to use language that animals do not have.

Finally, chimpanzees do not learn language from other chimpanzees. Psychologists teach them. As a result, they cannot talk to each other and transmit their knowledge the way humans do.

Language and Perception. Persons' perceptions of the world are shaped by their language. Language functions not only as a means for reporting experiences but also as a way of defining experience. It serves as a guide to social reality, with each language representing a particular social reality. These are the central ideas put forth by Edward Sapir and his student, Benjamin Whorf, that are commonly known as the Sapir-Whorf hypothesis. In 1929 Sapir wrote:

> Human beings do not live in the objective world alone . . . but are very much at the mercy of the particular language which has become the medium of expression for their society. It is quite an illusion to imagine that one adjusts to reality essentially without the use of language and that language is merely an incidental means of solving specific problems of communication or reflection . . . the "real world" is to a larger extent unconsciously built up on the language habits of the group. No two languages are ever sufficiently similar to be considered as representing the same social reality. The worlds in which different societies live are distinct worlds, not merely the same world with different labels attached (Sapir 1929:207–214).

Human beings, then, shape the world by means of the patterns in the language of their society. The language we use guides our perceptions and tells us what is important and what to ignore. It does this partly by either making minute symbolic distinctions of items that are important or lumping together many dissimilar things that are unimportant. The Eskimos make fine distinctions between the various kinds of snow. But snow is relatively unimportant to us, so we have only one word for it. The natives of the Sahara have 200 words for dates, their main source of sustenance. At one time the Arabs had about 6,000 words in some way or another connected with camel. There were words for camels according to their color, function, body structure, lineage, and other various attributes. There were over fifty words alone to refer to camels in various stages of pregnancy. It may sound strange having so many words to describe one thing. But think for a moment of all the words we have to distinguish automobiles. Because of the importance of automobiles in our culture, we describe them according to body types—sedans, coupes, convertibles, compacts, fastbacks—as well as by make, year, and model. Another example of how language influences our perception of the world is expressed by Walter Lippman's famous aphorism: First we look, then we name, and only then do we see. The drawings in Figure 2.2 that illustrate this point are called "Droodles," a pastime that has been popular since the 1950s. Look at each of the drawings, and at first glance it will be difficult to figure out what they are. But after you name them, you can "see" them. (The "names" are given under each illustration.)

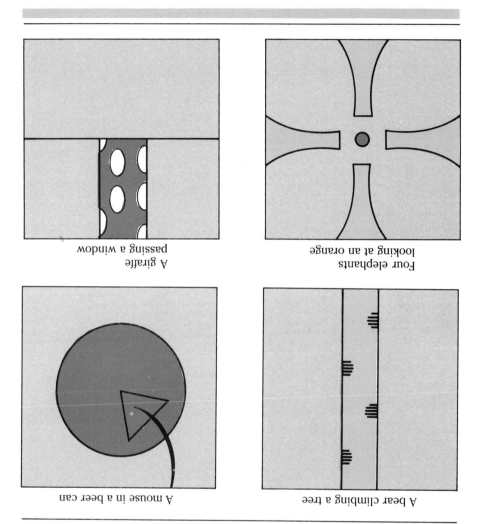

Figure 2.2 "Droodles" illustrate how language influences our perception.

Nonverbal Communication. Words are not the only symbols that human beings use for communication. They communicate by what has been referred to as the "silent language." This language includes gestures, facial expressions, body postures, and the treatment of space.

As an American family was boarding a plane in Ankara, they waved good-bye to their Turkish friends who came to the airport to see them off. But instead of waving back, the Turks started running toward the plane. The Americans were puzzled until they learned that in Turkey the gesture we use for "good-bye" means "come here." In Kenya our gesture for waving good-bye has a vulgar connotation.

CONTROVERSIAL ISSUES · And We Speak the Same Language

At the end of the day, a typical English office worker takes the *lift* and walks out of the building along the *pavement* to the *car park*. Once in his car driving along the *motorway*, he decides to stop for *petrol*. He pulls in at a *garage* when he *queues* up behind several *articulated lorries*. In addition to petrol, he notices that the car needs some oil so he lifts the *bonnet* and then opens the *boot* to have the air in his spare *tyre* checked. Being a bit short of cash, he pays by *cheque*.

Our office worker arrives home and turns on the *telly* while his wife prepares dinner. Feeling *peckish,* he eats some cheese and *biscuits*. For dinner his wife serves his favorite, *mixed grill.*

After dinner he and his wife *knock up* a *neighbour* they haven't seen in a *fortnight* because she has been away on *holiday*. They ask her to join them at the *pub* for a drink. Once there, they *put their feet up* and have several half pints of *bitter* along with some *crisps*. An American sitting at the next table leans over and begins to converse with them. He casually remarks: "Isn't it nice that we all speak the same language?"

British	American	British	American
lift	elevator	peckish	hungry
pavement	sidewalk	biscuits	crackers
car park	parking lot	mixed grill	several types of
motorway	interstate,		broiled meats
	freeway	knock up	drop by
petrol	gasoline	neighbour	neighbor
garage	service station	fortnight	two weeks
queues	lines up	holiday	vacation
articulated lorries	trailer trucks	pub	bar
bonnet	hood	put up their feet	relax
boot	trunk	bitter	dark beer
tyre	tire	crisps	potato chips
cheque	check		
telly	TV		

Communication can only take place if the person who makes a gesture and the one who sees it attaches the same meaning to it. Otherwise the wrong meaning or no meaning might be attached to the gestural symbol. Not only can the same gesture mean something entirely different in another society, but different gestures can have the same meaning. What could be more natural than greeting someone by shaking his or her hand? Yet, some people greet by joining their right hands and separating them so that a loud snapping noise is made. Polynesians stroke their own faces with the other person's hands. In

Eskimos live in one of the harshest and most forbidding of the world's climates. Summers are short, cool, and mosquito-plagued. Winters are long, dark, and cold. Food is scarce and hard to obtain. Despite this environment many Eskimos are gregarious, good-natured, fun-loving, and content. Traditional Eskimo society was one of equals. They acknowledged neither chiefs nor superiors; their language even lacks a term for such a person. What there was of social authority was shared by the community as a whole. Social control depended on the rule of public opinion. The approval and esteem of the group were a person's highest reward.

Eskimo technology was primitive, but they developed several basic tools—harpoons, kayaks, slit-type bone goggles, igloos—that are remarkably efficient for survival in their environment. They also learned to make fullest possible use of available raw materials for food, clothes, and tools. The arrival of modern, foreign culture destroyed much of the Eskimos' way of life. This foreign culture, much of it from the United States, brought concepts alien to Eskimo culture—individual self-fulfillment, master-servant relationships, measuring personal worth by material wealth, submitting to the will of another. Foreigners also brought diseases unknown to Eskimos—tuberculosis, smallpox, alcoholism.

Today many Eskimos live in permanent communities, in houses like those of other Americans. As they adopt this new culture, they tend to lose touch with the cycle of the seasons. Their children no longer learn the lore of hunting and sometimes do not learn their grandparents' language. Of course this process has another side: Eskimos also benefit from modern technology—such as rifles, radios, and TV. And the people who once brought the Eskimos new diseases now bring them modern medicine.

In some smaller communities, however, the hunting-trapping life persists
according to the old ways: taking from each season what each season
brings; sharing your food with all members of the group; rising to
superhuman efforts when the hunt requires it; and doing as you like and
letting others do as they like. The crucial problem that modern Eskimos
face is an extreme form of a problem facing all Americans: how to hold
on to the best of traditional ways while taking advantage of the benefits
held out by a new technology.

some Eskimo tribes persons greet a stranger by licking one's own hands, rubbing them first over one's face and then over the face of the person being greeted (Hiller 1933).

One of the most important types of nonverbal communication is facial expressions. We are constantly aware of how emotions are mirrored in facial expressions, and as a result we monitor the reaction of others by watching their faces. The term "poker face" is a good example of the importance of facial expressions in communication. Card players often exercise careful control over their faces so as not to give any clues to the cards they are holding.

In ordinary conversation the listener unconsciously guides the conversation not only by his or her facial expressions but also by gestures and posture. As Edward T. Hall and Mildred Hall note:

> If you observe a person conversing, you'll notice that he indicates he's listening by nodding his head. He also makes little "Hmm" noises. If he agrees with what's being said, he may give a vigorous nod. To show pleasure or affirmation, he smiles; if he has some reservations he looks skeptical by raising an eyebrow or pulling down the corners of his mouth. If a participant wants to terminate the conversation, he may start shifting his body position, stretching his legs, crossing or uncrossing them, bobbing his foot, diverting his gaze from the speaker. The more he fidgets, the more the speaker becomes aware that he has lost his audience. As a last measure, the listener may look at his watch to indicate the imminent end of the conversation (Hall and Hall 1971:139).

Another means of communication is by the manipulation of space between oneself and others. Hall (1959) reports that in our society a comfortable conversational distance is anywhere from $2\frac{1}{2}$ to 4 feet and at a social gathering it may range up to 7 feet. In other countries, such as those in Latin America and the Middle East, the preferred conversational distance is much closer. Many foreigners do not feel that they can talk comfortably unless they are very close. To an American, this closeness suggests unfamiliar intimacy, may arouse hostile feelings, and makes one feel uncomfortable and uneasy. When a person gets too close during a conversation, we often automatically and unintentionally back away. Hall has observed an American backing up the entire length of a long corridor while talking to a foreigner. Many foreigners interpret our backing away as being cool and unfriendly, whereas we think of them as being pushy and aggressive for talking at such close range. Lawrence Stressin (1971) notes:

> Anyone who has ever attended a party or reception in Latin America must surely have observed the self-consciousness of the uninitiated and stateside visitor, who keeps backing away from his native host to whom it is natural to carry on a conversation separated by inches. Last year at a businessmen's club in Brazil, where many receptions are held for newly arrived U.S. executives, the railings on the terrace had to be reinforced because so many American businessmen fell into the garden as they backed away (p. 3).

THE FACTS · Typical Nonverbal Communication
Found in Most Classrooms

Eye contact. Sometimes a student avoids eye contact when the teacher asks him a question. He may act very busy taking notes, rearranging his books and papers, dropping a pencil. Nonverbally he is saying to the teacher, "I don't want to be called on." Eye contact signs that the communication channel is open.

Arm extending. Have you ever seen a professor lecture all period without moving his hands at all? Galloway has shown that teachers who extend their arms toward the class have students who test better than teachers who keep their hands in their pockets.

Nodding. Teachers who nod affirmatively to their students encourage them to respond more and to respond better. Depending upon individual teacher, grade level, and class size, the optimum number of nods is usually one every 30 seconds. However, if the teacher consciously adopts the 30-second pattern the kids pick it up, and it becomes ineffective.

Hand raising. In volunteering classroom information a clever student knows how to make his raised arm look tired, as if he's been waiting interminably to be called on. He also knows how to raise his hand tentatively, as if he does *not* want to be called on. It seems that the hand-raising technique is not innate; students learn all these subtleties by around the fourth grade.

SOURCE: "Body Language," *Saturday Review,* May 1973, p. 78.

Cultural Variability

The range of variations between cultures is almost endless and yet at the same time cultures resemble one another in many important ways. All known cultures recognize certain categories that are often referred to as "cultural universals" (Murdock 1945). These include bodily adornment, courtship, dancing, education, family, food taboos, funeral rites, gestures, hospitality, religion, and sexual restrictions. While these categories are found in all cultures, specific content of each of them varies from one culture to another. For instance, all people adorn themselves, but they do it in various ways. Some put wild boar tusks through their noses, use quartz lip jewels, artificially elongate their lips and necks, tattoo their buttocks, scar their faces, or put holes in their ears. Some people believe in many gods (polytheism), others in no gods but in spirits and souls (animism), and still others in one god (monotheism); but all people have some type of religion. Some form of family life is found in all societies. Some men have two or more wives at the same time (polygyny), some women have two or more husbands at the same time (polyandry), and

Decorative ornaments from one culture are sometimes adopted by other groups.

some persons have several mates but at different times (serial monogamy). It is these variations within the cultural universal categories that give rise to two important concepts: ethnocentrism and cultural relativity.

Ethnocentrism

When the ancient Greek historian, Herodotus, wrote about differences in customs between Greeks and Egyptians, he noted with amazement that "these barbarians retired into the house to perform their excretory functions instead of taking to the street in civilized Greek fashion" (Linton 1945:27). From earliest times people have judged other cultures in terms of their own ideas, norms, and values. One's own culture is taken as a standard against which all other cultures are judged. Everything that differs from the way of life of one's own society often seems barbaric, uncivilized, or ridiculous. This tendency to regard one's own culture as superior to all other cultures is called **ethnocentrism.** It is a universal phenomenon.

To us, our way of selecting a mate, kissing, and dressing is the only proper way. But people in societies in which they choose their children's mates when they are 3 or 4 years old, kiss by rubbing noses, and wear only leaves consider our ways strange and inferior to theirs. Some societies would consider some of our food disgusting and unpalatable. We, in turn, feel the same way about their foods. As Dorothy Lee points out:

Ethnocentrism the tendency to regard one's own culture as superior to all other cultures.

We do not regard dragon flies as human food; the Ifugao do. They eat three species of dragonfly, as well as locusts which are boiled, then dried, then powdered and stored for food. They eat crickets and flying ants which they fry in lard. They eat red ants and water bugs and a variety of beetles. I doubt that I would recognize these insects as food, however hungry I might be. On the other hand, I regard milk as food, a fluid which some cultural groups regard with disgust akin to a mucous discharge (1959:157).

Ethnocentrism is a two-way street. Groups that we think of as backward and barbaric and that we feel superior to, have similar feelings of superiority to us.

Cultural Relativity

Rejecting the ethnocentric way of judging all other cultures in relation to one's own, William Graham Sumner in *Folkways* (1906) was the first to formulate the concept of **cultural relativity.** He argued that there are no universal moral standards of right and wrong and good and bad for evaluating cultural phenomena. Standards are relative to the culture in which they appear. Customs can only be judged by how well or how poorly they fit with other aspects of the culture. For instance, polygyny or having several wives is functional in a society where women are needed to work in the fields. Abandoning sick or disabled elderly persons who can no longer travel is the practical thing to do for a nomadic people.

> **Cultural relativity** the concept that all behavior patterns and customs can only be understood and evaluated in terms of the cultural setting in which they occur.

In the course of doing field work among the Havasupai Indians of Arizona, Elman Service (1973) interviewed Paya, an old man, about the tribe's customs. Each time Service asked him why the Indians acted in their peculiar ways, Paya would answer, "That's the way we do." "I was looking for a key to Havasupai culture, afraid of not finding it, and right there I patiently overlooked the truth: There is no key to understanding another culture except on its own terms" (Service 1973:10). Thus, if we are to understand the behavior of other groups, we must study them in terms of their values and ideas and not our own. It is helpful to ask such questions as: What functions does a custom perform? What needs does it fulfill? What meaning does the custom have for its users? Consider the practice among the polar Eskimos, for example, of offering one's wife to another man for the night as a form of hospitality. The following dialogue takes place between a white man, an Eskimo, Ernenek, and his wife, Asiak, about how Ernenek killed a man for refusing his hospitality.

"You said the fellow you killed provoked you?"
  "So it was."
  "He insulted Asiak?"
  "Terribly."
  "Presumably he was killed as you tried to defend her from his advances?"
Ernenek and Asiak looked at each other and burst out laughing.
  "It wasn't so at all," Asiak said at last.
  "Here's how it was," said Ernenek. "He kept snubbing all our offers although he was our guest. He scorned even the oldest meat we had."

PEOPLE · **Hungry Asian Refugees Snaring Dogs,
Squirrels in Park in California**

SAN FRANCISCO (AP)—Hungry Southeast Asian refugees are setting snares in Golden Gate Park for stray dogs, squirrels, pigeons, and ducks. The poachers in the large park in the middle of the city are believed to be from the primitive mountainous regions of Southeast Asia, said Jim Meyer, director of the Intergovernmental Committee for European Migration.

"It's not really strange in their culture," said Meyer. "All these people have really been transported very quickly into an entirely different culture. It's like coming from the tenth century," said Meyer.

The refugees undoubtedly are after food but whether they are driven to it out of poverty isn't clear. One woman, caught in a group of eleven Cambodians and Laotians foraging in the 1,200-acre park, was carrying four $100 bills with her.

Recently, one official saw a group of what he said were Southeast Asians hunting in the park. He gave chase and the frightened poachers fled, dropping their catch of 10 dead squirrels and eight pigeons.

Lt. Richard Shippy, who heads the park and beach patrol, made a grisly find recently of five dead dogs in a shallow grave with a plastic tarp over them. They were all skinned and had their heads cut off. The lieutenant went to call the SPCA, but when he came back the dogs were gone.

Samboun Sayasane, head of a statewide Laotian association, said the refugees probably did not know there was anything wrong with their actions. "Hunting and fishing is a way of life in Laos," he said. "Maybe they didn't realize these things belong to the city, the park, and to everybody. They just think it's nature that creates these things and they are free for everybody to have."

SOURCE: *The Albuquerque Tribune*, August 18, 1980, p. A–8.

"You see, Ernenek, many of us white men are not fond of old meat."
"But the worms were fresh!" said Asiak.
"It happens, Asiak, that we are used to foods of a quite different kind."
"We noticed," Ernenek went on, "and that's why, hoping to offer him at last a thing he might relish, somebody proposed him Asiak to laugh [have sexual intercourse] with."
"Let a woman explain," Asiak broke in. "A woman washed her hair to make it smooth, rubbed tallow into it, greased her face with blubber, and scraped herself clean with a knife, to be polite."
"Yes," cried Ernenek, rising. "She had purposely groomed herself! And what did the white man do? He turned his back to her! That was too much! Should a man let his wife be so insulted? So somebody grabbed the scoundrel by his miserable little shoulders and beat him a few times against the wall—not in order to kill him, just wanting to crack his head a little. It was unfortunate it cracked a lot!"

"Ernenek has done the same to other men," Asiak put in helpfully, "but it was always the wall that went to pieces first."

The white man winced. "Our judges would show no understanding for such an explanation. Offering your wife to other men!"

"Why not? The men like it and Asiak says it's good for her. It makes her eyes sparkle and her cheeks glow."

"Don't you people borrow other men's wifes?" Asiak inquired.

"Never mind that! It isn't fitting, that's all!"

"Refusing isn't fitting for a man," Ernenek said indignantly. "Anybody would much rather lend out his wife than something else. Lend out your sled and you'll get it back cracked, lend out your saw and some teeth will be missing, lend out your dogs and they'll come home crawling tired—but no matter how often you lend out your wife she'll always stay like new" (Ruesch 1951:87–88).

The above account illustrates that cultural patterns can only be understood and evaluated in view of the cultural setting in which they occur. Each culture must be seen on its own terms, because what is moral in one society would be considered highly immoral in another.

Subcultures

All complex, industrialized societies like our own contain numerous groups of people that possess distinctive traditions and lifestyles that set them apart from the larger society. Yet, at the same time, they participate in the larger society and share most of its culture. These groups are called **subcultures.** They may differ from the larger society in a variety of ways, including language or special vocabularies, modes of dress, values, religion, and foods.

Subcultures groups of people who possess distinctive traditions and lifestyles that set them apart from the larger society.

Subcultures may be based on religious differences or racial or ethnic differences as in the case of black Americans. Occupations such as the military or medical professions often give rise to subcultures. For instance, the military subculture is fostered by specialized training, long-term careers, and the segregation of military families from the rest of the community. The development of the medical subculture is aided by long years of training, technical jargon, and physicians' common set of goals and attitudes toward their profession.

Subcultures are also associated with social classes. When used in this sense, they are popularly referred to as highbrow, middlebrow, and lowbrow. The idea behind this is that our society is made up of a number of taste subcultures each with its own art, music, literature, television preferences, and the like. As Herbert J. Gans (1974) notes:

Among the three criteria that sociologists use most often to define and describe class position—income, occupation, and education—the most important factor is education . . . First, every item of cultural content carries with it a built-in educational requirement, low for the comic strip, high for the poetry of T. S. Eliot. Second, aesthetic standards and taste are taught in our society both by the home and the school. Thus a person's educational achievement and the kind of

In the United States, attending the opera is considered "high culture."

school he or she attended will probably predict better than any other single index that person's cultural choices. Since both of these are closely related to an individual's (and his or her parents') socioeconomic level, the range of taste cultures and publics follows the range and hierarchy of classes in American society, although the correlation is hardly perfect (pp. 70–71).

Gans differentiates taste subcultures into high culture and popular culture. He then subdivides popular culture into upper-middle culture, lower-middle culture, low culture, and quasi-folk low culture (Gans 1974).*

High Culture

This taste culture is created and dominated by "serious" writers and artists, and most of its users or public accept their perspectives and standards. Both the creators and users are generally highly educated persons of upper- and upper-middle-class status who work in professional or academic occupations. High culture not only tends to change more quickly than the other

*The material that follows is based on the work of Herbert J. Gans, *Popular Culture and High Culture* (New York: Basic Books, 1974).

taste cultures but at the same time it offers the greatest conglomeration of content. It contains both classic and contemporary elements, ranging in our society from medieval songs to complex modern music and from primitive art to abstract expressionism.

The fiction of high culture stresses character development over plot and the exploration of basic psychological, philosophical, or social issues. High culture prides itself on being exclusive and, as a result, its products are not meant for mass media distribution. Its art is distributed through galleries, its theater is concentrated largely in Europe and Off-Broadway, and its movies are often foreign. The small amount of high culture television that exists is shown on public television stations.

Popular Culture

Upper-Middle Culture.   This taste culture serves the majority of the upper-middle class. It includes professionals, executives, and managers who have attended the "better" colleges and universities. The music of this culture includes operatic and symphonic works of nineteenth-century composers. Its younger members are probably the major consumers of melodic rock and folk music.

In contrast to high culture, upper-middle fiction stresses plot over mood and character development and deals more with individual achievement and upward mobility. The upper-middle public reads the *New Yorker, Playboy, Ms.,* and *Vogue; Time* and *Newsweek* are primarily written for this public. Since this culture group purchases most of the hardcover "trade" books, they help to determine the best sellers. They also provide the largest audience for public television, network documentaries, and dramatic television specials.

Lower-Middle Culture.   This is the taste culture of the majority of Americans. It includes middle-class and lower-middle-class people in the lower status professions. Although some of the older members of this public have only a high school education, many of the younger ones have attended or graduated from universities or colleges.

This public prefers romantic and representational art to abstraction and harsh realism. The art of Norman Rockwell continues to be a favorite. The low-middle public makes possible the high circulations of such magazines as the *Reader's Digest* as well as a wide variety of women's homemaking and hobby magazines. Popular novelists such as Jacqueline Susann and Harold Robbins sell millions of copies of paperback books to this market. The low-middle public supplies the viewers for whom television makes the popular dramas, variety shows, and situation comedies.

Low Culture.   This culture is largely composed of skilled and semi-skilled factory and service workers and semiskilled white-collar workers. Most have either dropped out of high school or have obtained nonacademic high school educations. Low culture was dominant in the United States until it was replaced in the 1950s by the lower-middle culture. Though not as pronounced as in the past, some sexual segregation continues to exist among the low-culture public and is reflected in its art, literature, and movie preferences. For example, the women tend to like religious art and bright representational pictures, and the men often choose pinup pictures of overtly erotic women to hang in factories and garage workshops. Adventure magazines are written for the male public, and fan and confession magazines are written for the female public.

With an emphasis on morality, low-culture fiction is divided into good and evil and heroes and villains.

> The male action drama typically describes an individual hero's fight against crime and related violations of the moral order, or his attempt to save society from a natural disaster . . . He is depicted as an explicitly classless person who expresses important working-class behavioral norms; he is sure of his masculinity, is shy with "good" women and sexually aggressive with "bad" ones. He works either alone or with "buddies" of the same sex, depends partly on luck and fate for success, and is distrustful of government and all institutionalized authority. Clark Gable, Gary Cooper, and John Wayne were typical prototypes of this hero, and the fact that none of the younger stars of today's action films have achieved their level of popularity is indicative of low culture's loss of dominance. Conversely, the confession magazines feature the working-class girl's conflict between being sexually responsive in order to be popular with men, and remaining virginal until marriage (Gans 1974:90–91).

Quasi-Folk Low Culture.   This is the culture of those whose education stopped at grade school and who work in unskilled blue-collar and service jobs. Many of these people are rural or of rural background and non-white. Although information is scarce about this taste culture, it seems to be a simplified form of low culture with its content focusing on melodrama, action comedies, and morality plays. Its public reads mostly tabloids and comic books and prefers old Westerns and adventure type movies.

Summary

Culture is the social heritage of a society that is transmitted to each generation. Culture and society are interdependent and neither can exist without the other.

Norms are a major component of culture. Norms are standards or rules for behavior specifying what we should and should not do in certain situations. Norms may be divided into three types on the basis of the kind of disapproval that results when they are violated: folkways, mores, and laws.

Values are standards that we use to evaluate the desirability of things. Robin Williams has identified certain basic value orientations in American society. These include achievement and success, activity and work, moral orientation, humanitarianism, and efficiency and practicality.

Language is basic to culture, enabling humans to transmit their learning to others. Language shapes our perception and serves as a guide to social reality. It includes not only words but gestures, facial expressions, body postures, and the treatment of space.

All societies assume that their own culture is superior to all others. This phenomenon is called ethnocentrism. Closely related to ethnocentrism is cultural relativity, a principle that implies that all behavior patterns can be understood only in the cultural setting in which they occur.

Modern societies tend to be made up of numerous groups of people or subcultures that possess distinctive traditions and lifestyles that set them apart from the larger society. Subcultures based on aesthetic standards and tastes are referred to as high culture and popular culture.

Suggested Readings

Ruth Benedict. *Patterns of Culture.* Boston: Houghton Mifflin, 1961. A classic discussion of three societies that illustrates how culture affects social behavior and personality.

Marvin Harris. *Cannibals and Kings: The Origins of Culture.* New York: Random House, 1977. Discusses how cultures have evolved along similar paths and that their evolution may be predicted from a knowledge of their processes of production, reproduction, intensification, and depletion.

Ralph Linton. *The Cultural Background of Personality.* New York: Appleton-Century-Crofts, 1945. A series of five highly readable essays on the interrelationships between the individual, culture, and society.

Margaret Mead. *Sex and Temperament in Three Primitive Societies.* New York: Morrow, 1935. Using cross-cultural comparisons, Mead shows how gender traits of masculinity and femininity are culturally conditioned.

Philip Slater. *The Pursuit of Loneliness,* rev. ed. Boston: Beacon Press, 1976. As astute analysis of the pathologies of American society that are splitting our culture apart.

Robin Williams. *American Society.* New York: Knopf, 1970. An excellent text that offers, in Chapter 11, a penetrating analysis of the dominant values of American society.

3

Groups and Society

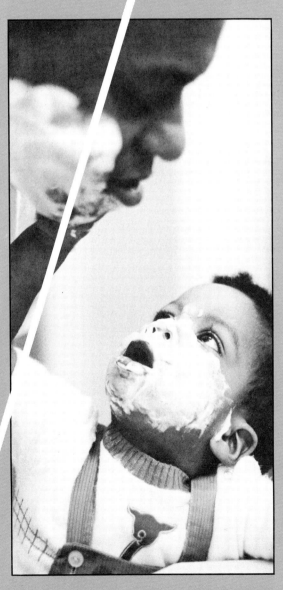

Pat Conroy's The Lords of Discipline, *although a caricature of military school life, neatly depicts many of the processes involved in the formation, maintenance, and dissolution of groups. Plebes, such as Will MacLean, Dante Pignetti, Mark Santoro, Tradd St. Croix, Bobby Bentley, Pearce, and Poteete, each from different circumstances, were instilled with a desire or expected by their families to attend Carolina Military Institute. Not only were they expected to attend, but to survive and eventually graduate as wearers of the Ring. The Ring was a symbol not only of survival, but manhood.*

The emotions of the incoming plebes—knobs—are plumbed and the mechanisms detailed as the rites of status denigration, dehumanization, and severing of social ties with the outside world proceed. Once plebes passed through the Gates of Legrand, they passed into the care of the upperclassmen and the Bear. Plebes began a period of testing to ascertain their moral character, physical stamina, and commitment to the Institute. Plebes with social stigmas or physical disabilities were given special attention by upperclassmen, hazed viciously, broken, and left the school, never to be mentioned again. Plebes who possessed traits particularly onerous to the image of the Institute, its traditions, and seen as a blemish on the pride of wearing the Ring fell victims to the secret organization, the Ten, an elite of true believers in the Institute's code and way of life.

Survivors of the freshmen year bonded together, transformed by the common experiences of harassment and punishment, and became the gatekeepers in the fall of their sophomore year. Despite the efforts of individuals to maintain a sense of individuality, distance, and aloofness, thereby avoiding a total brainwashing to the code, survivors ineluctable were marked by the taming and took pride in wearing the ring.

Although the desire to belong is exaggerated in *The Lords of Discipline,* people do want to form **groups** because, for most persons, loneliness and social separation are conditions to be avoided if at all possible. In some cases, they trigger feelings of anxiety, abandonment, or in more extreme situations, suicide. This desire to be with others gives rise to the belief that sociability is part of the human condition. One explanation is that the absence of in-born survival skills (instincts) in newborn infants requires a prolonged period of dependence on adults for satisfaction of basic needs and learning social skills. This period of dependency presumably predisposes individuals to turn to other persons and groups during their lives in order to satisfy needs of social intimacy. A second explanation views sociability as merely an outgrowth of expediency, since handling some kinds of problems is often more easily accomplished in groups than alone (Durkheim 1951).

Group "a specific number of individuals, where each recognizes members from nonmembers, each has a sense of what others do and think as well as what the purpose of the association is" (Golembeiski, 1962: 34–47).

How Groups Are Defined

In everyday conversation, people are not always clear about what they mean when they speak of a group. Three meanings are often implied by the term "group." First, some persons use it to refer to a set of individuals with some similar characteristic, such as age or occupation. This meaning emphasizes the *sharing of like traits* and is better called a **social category.** Second, individuals sometimes speak of a group as any number of individuals who meet occasionally or regularly and have a sense of who is present or absent, such as parents at a PTA meeting. This meaning stresses two conditions of group life: common presence and a minimum awareness of others. Third, still others use group to mean "a specific number of individuals, where each recognizes members from non-members, each has a sense of what others do and think as well as what the purpose of the association is" (Golembeiski 1962: 34–47). This meaning emphasizes three elements: common association, awareness of others, and socially shared goals. This third meaning is the essence of a social group.

Social category people who share a particular trait.

For sociologists, then, what makes a group is not just the similarity of traits among individuals or the physical proximity of individuals, but rather the fact that people interact. At the very least there must be at least two persons who interact, share a sense of bondedness—"we" versus "they," and have an idea what each will do and how the other will react. Interaction is the touchstone of group life. We are interested in understanding how individuals influence the quality of interaction and in turn how individuals are affected by the way that interaction occurs.

Some sociologists argue that social groups have common organizational features. Guidelines are established governing how one becomes a member or terminates membership. People agree to cooperate with one another in order to accomplish certain activities and reach common goals. People agree who will lead them as well as what each person is responsible for doing. They develop ways for getting everybody to understand what is commonly believed and expected of them as well as mechanisms for insuring conformity (Goffman 1961a).

What are the three definitions of groups used by people?

Some Dimensions of Groups

Six dimensions are often considered when discussing group life: size, degree of structure, nature of goals, identifiability of members, cohesiveness, and leadership styles.

Size

Social relationships range in numbers from two persons up to entire populations. Sociologists use size to distinguish among types of groups. A small social unit might be a **dyad** (two persons), a **triad** (three persons), or a collectivity of 20 to 30 individuals. Intermediate and large-scale relationships include various social units such as organizations, communities, and societies. Size affects the quality of interaction. Dyads are particularly fragile, for the removal of either party destroys the relationship. The addition of a third party in a triad reduces the fragility of the relationship, but sets the stage for the forming of a coalition, that is, two persons teaming up against the third. Conversation creates a bond between the talkers and may highlight common interests or foster sharing of secrets, but such conversation always leaves the third party, if only temporarily, in silent limbo (Caplow 1968). For instance, in some dormitory living arrangements with three persons, two of the individuals may talk a lot together, forming a close social bond, leaving the third person alone.

Dyad a two-person group.

Triad a three-person group.

How does size affect interaction?

As size of a group increases, the opportunities for each individual to interact with every other individual decrease markedly. Similarly, as group size increases, the goings and comings of individuals from the group become less noticeable. With the expansion of a group, individuals' treatment of one another becomes increasingly formal, behaviors become routinized, roles become elaborated in number and complexity, and tasks become more specific. Just imagine the growth of rules and regulations that arise as three or four high school friends interested in playing chess expand their membership, seek official recognition as a school organization, and eventually prepare to host a regional tournament. Size not only alters the quality of social exchange in small groups, it sets boundaries for the complexity of their organization.

Size also influences the readiness with which individuals disclose personal information, offer opinions, contribute new ideas, and generally feel free to participate. Dyads permit the highest levels of self-disclosure and participation. The addition of each new individual lowers the level of self-disclosure and inhibits the freedom of information exchange. People express uneasiness when revealing personal facts or private feelings without establishing a sense of rapport and belonging. Revealing such matters opens one to the possibility of being labeled "different"—or pushy, big mouthed, overly assertive, aggressive—and thus becoming a target for various forms of sanctions ranging from gestures of disdain to outright verbal and physical abuse.

Structure

By **structure** we mean the patterning of actual behavior. When people do the same things repeatedly in the same circumstances, we refer to the

Structure a pattern of behavior.

One type of group is represented here with the mayor of Englewood, New Jersey, and the planning board in discussion.

situation as having structure (Giddens 1982). In fact, people learn to expect that the same activities will occur in a particular kind of setting. If the activities are not performed, disorientation and feelings of being uncomfortable usually result. For example, before class, students take their seats, open their notebooks, and take out a pen or pencil, and wait for the instructor to begin talking. Should the instructor follow a format other than lecturing, students become uneasy, and remain so, until they get used to the new format.

Groups vary in their degree of structure from high to low. The military with its elaborate chain of command, detailed gradations in responsibilities, and codes of conduct is one of society's most highly structured social organizations. In a highly structured group such as a voluntary association with a constitution, officers, and agenda, every individual knows what norms the group values, what rituals are to be performed, who occupies positions of authority and responsibility, and what activities will occur at each meeting. In groups with minimal structure, questions such as "What is to be accomplished and how?" and "Who will take responsibility?" and "What issues need to be discussed?" are just some of the matters that individuals must resolve repeatedly whenever they get together. Friends, for instance, when deciding how to spend their leisure time, often repeat the familiar questions: "What do you want to do?" "I don't know, what do you want to do?" and so forth.

Give an example of a situation which is unstructured.

Nature of Goals

Just as groups differ in size and structure, they also vary in the nature of their goals. Some social relationships are geared toward the achievement of quite specific ends. Task groups often are set up among corporation personnel with the sole aim of identifying problems in management, marketing, or production and then preparing alternative strategies for solving these problems. Other groups—such as therapy groups, sensitivity groups, or training groups—have as their end product the recognition and the alleviation of emotional problems. Single parents, unwed mothers and fathers, divorcees, widowers, retirees, addicts, and alcoholics are just some of the varieties of people that form groups to learn how to identify the roots of their anxieties and to provide mutual social support in coping with and overcoming them. Still other groups persist simply for the pleasure of fellowship, such as boccie players in the park or regulars at the neighborhood tavern. In friendship groups, personal ties are maintained without any ulterior motives other than sharing common interests.

Identifiability of Members

Sociologists often catalogue social relationships using the yardstick of whether or not a person recognizes other individuals. In some cases, persons expect to treat others as "nonpersons." A waiter who seeks to become a "person" by being overly talkative, intruding in conversations, and frequently asking whether anything is needed, is offensive, and is often sanctioned with a poor tip. In other cases, persons find themselves in relationships, such as formal dinners or cocktail parties, where they make acquaintances, exchange pleasantries, and after the evening is over forget everyone they met. In such encounters one does not delve into personal feelings or goals of another person. One is expected to maintain a sense of decorum and formality by keeping the conversation flowing and avoiding serious topics, and at all costs avoiding a sense of intimacy. Such impersonal relationships are transient and not important in providing a participant with a sense of social belonging, defining oneself and one's associates. In still other instances, persons interact with people they know intimately: such people are crucial in marking their social identity, their community of friends, and their sphere of daily activity. (See the discussion of socialization in Chapter 4.)

In what kinds of social relationships is an individual treated as a "nonperson"?

Cohesiveness

The intensity of conformity, degree of social participation, feelings of satisfaction, and level of productivity in a group indicate a group's **cohesiveness.**

Cohesiveness the degree to which members of a group cooperate.

Group cohesiveness is usually measured in one of four ways. First, researchers ask individuals to list a specified number of friends. The more friends who are held in common by members of a group, the higher the cohesiveness of the group. The same principle is extended to examine the degree of social participation in social networks of various kinds, such as ethnic, religious, or voluntary collectivities. Sociologists assume friends interact with each other, thus jointly participate in the same groups. Second, individuals are asked to rate their feelings toward the group as an entity. The greater the esteem directed toward the group, the greater the group cohesiveness. Third, individuals are asked to evaluate their sense of belonging to the group. The more individuals feel rooted in the group, the greater the cohesiveness. Fourth, individuals rank whether they want to remain in the group. The greater the commitment to the group, the greater the cohesiveness. Each of these measures emphasizes the individual's perception of social and emotional ties to other group members or to the group as a unit.

Research on how cohesiveness affects varous kinds of behaviors is abundant. For instance, researchers have found that the greater the social cohesiveness of a group in a work setting, the lower the rate of absenteeism and the higher the level of social participation. Also, a cohesive group has less worker turnover and slowdowns. To reduce management-worker conflict in a Swedish Volvo factory, owners involved workers in the decision-making process, gave them shares in the company, and generated a sense of commitment to product and production. Similarly, individuals who express a sense of attraction toward others and to the group attend more meetings, are less likely to be deadwood, and are more likely to work toward promoting the group's goals. Members of a voluntary organization often recognize quickly that some members should not be given committee assignments since their sense of involvement in the group is less intense than that of other members.

Cohesiveness also is linked to ethnocentrism. As one's commitment to a group's goals, norms, and lifestyle is heightened, the distinction between in-group and out-group is sharpened. As the group's standards become the yardstick for judging the beliefs and actions of others, we find prejudices developing, and sometimes even discrimination (see Chapter 7).

A sociology instructor divided his class into two groups. Each group had to develop a language and a set of gestures that were unique. By the middle of the term, all the students in each group had to be able to engage in meaningful conversation using the made-up language. The students were to keep diaries. As the term progressed, an examination of the diaries made clear that in each group the students formed friendships which extended beyond the class, talked in their own language, became extremely ethnocentric, and began to see the other group's members as outsiders and inferiors, to be avoided. To compensate for this divisiveness, the instructor forced the two groups to interact, each using its own peculiar language. Only after one group had learned the other group's language, did the feeling of distinctiveness abate and the class once again see itself as an entity.

Although sociologists have conducted a great deal of research on ways to enhance group cohesiveness, they have not examined in as great detail conditions leading to the dissolution of groups. Many of the conditions that might bring about the breaking up of a group would be difficult to introduce experimentally. Also some would be unethical because of their harmful effects.

Identify some of the social conditions which threaten the cohesiveness of small groups? of large organizations?

Leadership Styles

Earlier sociologists and social psychologists assumed people should agree and cooperate with one another rather than disagree and engage in conflict. They also assumed that situations which were restrictive, inhibited individuals from expressing themselves freely and prevented them from fulfilling their native capacities were to be avoided. Thus, to understand the dynamics of groups and to define a good leader, some social scientists focused on which leadership traits marked a "good" leader as well as which traits affected behaviors and feelings of group members. More specifically, sociologists investigated which traits affected individuals' willingness to cooperate, to give support and approval to others, to express personal opinions and offer information and ideas, and to be satisfied with being in the group and working toward its goals. Extensive research found no clearly defined set of traits distinguishing leaders and nonleaders. However, sociologists found that groups in which the leaders and followers had similar personality styles—such as autocratic, democratic, or laissez faire—generally got along better than groups in which the personality styles of the leaders and followers differed. Further, both autocratic and democratic groups could get tasks performed efficiently. But democratic groups were marked by a sense of cooperation, friendliness, and supportiveness, whereas autocratic groups were less cooperative, more dependent on leaders for directions and guidance, and quite critical of lower esteemed members.

Research then shifted away from a search for personality traits making a good leader to investigating what kind of leader is required for accomplishing different types of tasks. Researchers found that the dynamics of interaction changed depending on the mix between leadership style—task oriented or social supportive—and the traits of members. Some members work best when tasks are clearly defined, others work best when leeway is provided in assigning who does what and when it must be finished. The leader's sensitivity to group members and the leader's style, assertive or passive, influences the opinions and ideas exchanged among members. Where leaders follow a dictatorial or tyrannical role, information flow between individuals is curtailed in volume, and problems were solved less rapidly than in groups with a more open and democratic style. Similarly, the kinds of opinions and information volunteered differed depending on the leader's approach to members. Under strong, assertive leaders, "groupthink" may occur. In groupthink situations, the information and opinions offered usually enhance the leader's position rather than criticizing it, and the range of opinions is reduced. In some cases people censor their own ideas rather than let the group weigh and sift information before reaching a consensual decision (Janis 1972). In more open groups, comments are more critical, opinions vary widely, and individuals reach common judgments after lengthy discussion.

The Individual's Ties to Groups

Central to any discussion of social groups is the distinction between primary and secondary groups.

Primary Groups

Primary groups may arise when individuals find themselves in close physical proximity, the number of individuals is small, and social bonds persist over time. More important than these spatial and temporal qualities are the qualities of interaction that bind the participants to one another. Face-to-face contact facilitates exchange of ideas, opinions, and gestures. This kind of communication breeds good feelings and strong ties between individuals. Small numbers heighten the potential for intense sensory contact. Frequency of contact and intensity of dialogue deepen one's feelings of intimacy with others. Some sociologists question whether primary group ties develop only in face-

Primary group   a group in which relationships are spontaneous, personal, and intimate.

Working together for community improvement is a form of primary group.

to-face settings or among small numbers of people (Faris 1932). They argue that intimacy can also arise when individuals are widely distant, such as among pen pals, radio ham operators, or computer users pursuing the same sets of problems. Whether one includes or excludes all three features—face-to-face interaction, small size, and a sense of intimacy—as essential to primary groups is not as important as recognizing that primary groups provide the individual with a sense of profound social anchorage. When defining the notion of the primary group, Cooley (1909) illustrated its qualities by talking about the children's play group, friendship bonds, and the neighborhood.

Primary groups, particularly in ethnic neighborhoods where choice of those with whom one interacts is often constrained by propinquity, serve to bind individuals together with a sense of community. (See discussion of communality in Chapter 7.)

In primary groups to which individuals elect to belong because of a particular ideology, the group may form a basis for political activity either to defend or oppose the status quo. Where primary groups channelize goals and their activities serve the ends of the community, institution, or state, they act as an integrative force; where they act as barriers, they facilitate conflict rather than consensus (Hastings et al. 1982).

Secondary Groups

Although not discussed specifically by Cooley, the **secondary group** stands at the opposite end of the social spectrum. It is the mirror contrast of the primary group. Individuals are widely separated, the group size is large, and social bonds persist only as long as contacts are maintained. The nature of the social exchange obviates feelings of belonging, is detrimental to any exchange of intimate ideas, opinions, or gestures that reveal the private self. Individuals interact as automatons, and the relationship fosters feelings of rootlessness and alienation (Davis 1948). The secretarial pool in a large insurance agency with hundreds of individuals processing forms and entering information on word processors is one example of a routinized and specialized secondary association.

Secondary group a group in which relationships are impersonal and widely separate.

Group Membership

Being included in a group gives the individual a sense of belonging—a sense of social location. Membership delimits social boundaries between various social relationships. It distinguishes "we" from "they." Membership serves as a statement of group identity denoting "who we are" for all people in the collectivity. For the individual, it serves as a statement of self-identity since it marks "who I am." (For a discussion of the ascriptive nature of ethnic group membership see Chapter 7.) In some cases, simply being assigned to a group is the basis for forming a self-identity and a group identity.

In Japan a person's identity is simply an extension of membership in a kinship network. A son or daughter becomes a representative of the kin group. His or her actions bring honor or shame, joy or sorrow to all kin members. In the United States individuals develop membership ties with a variety of groups ranging from family and friends to associates at work, but Americans are not expected to submerge their total identities to that of the group. Nonetheless, being accepted as a group member is important. Membership also confers social recognition. It entitles the individual to the rights and privileges of the group. In ancient Rome the father viewed the newborn infant and decided whether to let it be fed or not. Refusal meant death. Feeding the child conferred the legal status of family member and citizen.

Membership in a group also demands that the individual learns the rules and regulations of the group, its rituals and rhythm of activities. Once the individuals adjust to this normative order, they often experience a sense of freedom. They no longer have to struggle continually to sensitize themselves to the demands of others or work at making sense out of happenings that bombard them. The individual can relax and feel comfortable, for group life is regular and orderly. Anybody who has traveled abroad and had to speak a foreign language no doubt has felt the fatigue that comes from trying to keep up with the flow of conversation and making sense out of the bewildering barrage of strange events.

Conversely, being isolated from a group or, more generally, being without social ties often leads individuals to express feelings of alienation, loneliness, social loss, rejection, anger, frustration, and depression. The absence of social bonds often is invoked as an explanation for aberrant social behaviors or in more severe cases, self-destructive acts. Further, social isolation or exile are effective strategies for ensuring conformity, since individuals often fear loss of social support of others.

Reference Groups

Not only do groups serve as focal points of identity and sociability, but they also serve as points of reference. Groups serve as yardsticks for us to measure our successes and failures in performing our roles. Membership in a group sets the stage for individuals to learn the form and content of attitudes and values peculiar to that group.

Membership in a fraternity or sorority assumes that one has learned the rituals, signs, and formal tenets as well as the style of behavior expected of its members, such as being "brainy," "athletic," or "an animal." Adoption of these beliefs and behaviors distinguishes members and nonmembers. It identifies "ins" from "outs."

Participation in a group often leads individuals to identify with the beliefs and practices of that group. Anthropologists and sociologists must guard against "going native" when doing participant observation. The observer as an active member in the daily flow of activities not only learns about the attitudes and values of group members, but in fact adopts them as part of his or her world

PEOPLE · Striving for Admission into a Reference Group

A study found that Army privates who accepted the formal rules were more likely to be promoted than those who did not. Among privates generally, acceptance of formal rules was by no means complete and usual; in fact, ambitious privates who were "bucking" for promotion by displaying their cooperativeness with superior officers were known as "brown noses." Their reference group was the status group of officers, in which they aspired to membership. This ambition helped to account for their deviation from the informal rules of the status group of privates as a whole, for whom "bucking" was wrong. That the privates in general had informal rules was shown in the unpleasant sanctions they applied to the ambitious. The epithet "brown nose" was one of the milder sanctions.

SOURCE: Harry M. Johnson, *Sociology: A Systematic Introduction* (New York: Harcourt Brace and World, Inc., 1960), p. 40.

view. Membership, however, is not a requirement for adopting attitudes, beliefs, or values of a group or their patterns of behavior. According to Johnson:

> Any group is a reference group for someone if his conception of it, which may or may not be realistic, is part of his frame of reference for appraisal of himself or his situation, aspirations for one of the groups to which he belongs. We take for granted that the groups to which a person belongs will serve as reference groups for him; if they did not, he could hardly be said to be truly a member of them. Therefore, the concept of reference group is perhaps most useful in that it calls attention to the fact that groups to which one does not belong ("nonmembership groups") also serve as reference groups (Johnson 1960: 39).

To ease the transition status of nonmember to member, the outsider learns the views of group members and begins to practice behavioral styles of group members before ever gaining acceptance as a member. In fact, members of a **reference group** are selected as role models and become significant others to the outsider. These actions are undertaken in the hope that membership will be granted in the not too distant future. Upwardly mobile corporation executives mimic the demeanor of their superiors and espouse values of the country club set to which they have not yet been admitted.

Reference group   a group that one refers to in evaluating oneself.

Learning how to think and behave before joining a group may ease and speed the transition from one group to another, since conformity facilitates social acceptance. In some cases, in the effort to be like others in the reference group, the individual may overconform, that is, adhere more strictly to the beliefs and codes of conduct than in fact any member would (Merton 1957).

How do reference groups operate when spies defect?

The Group's Influence on the Individual

Group Pressures to Conform

Individuals in the presence of others become aroused or motivated to perform some kinds of physical and social skills at higher levels of excellence than they would if they were alone. Some athletes, for instance, are known by their team members as "game players" or "crowd pleasers." They are seen as always expending more effort and performing better before the crowd in the heat of competition. Performance also improves when the audience is known to be made up of experts, as when football players put out for "pro" scouts. When the audience is blindfolded, the presence of the audience makes no difference to the athletes. Similarly, students who take exams in class usually do better than those taking the exam alone (Zajonc 1966). A situation in which an individual is stimulated by the presence of others is called **social facilitation.**

Social facilitation a situation in which the presence of others stimulates one's performance.

Under what conditions would students form study groups to prepare for examinations?

Responses need not always be positive. In some cases, the presence of others increases the likelihood of blocking the learning or the performance of certain skills. When experimenters are female, males react more slowly in recognizing four-letter words flashed on a tachistoscope (a screen designed to test subliminal perception) than females. The same hesitancy is found for females when the experimenters are males.

In some cases, the presence of others inhibits the learning of new subject matter; individuals can assimilate information more rapidly by themselves. A situation in which the presence of others blocks or retards performance is called **social inhibition.**

It is interesting to note how ready or disposed persons are to comply with the suggestions of complete strangers. For instance, some people consent to phone interviews conducted by total strangers. Based on a simple phone request, they may allow strangers to go through their house taking inventory of their possessions. Should the request to search their house be preceded by opening comments, the percentage of respondents who permit a search increases (Freedman and Fraser 1966).

Social inhibition a situation in which the presence of others blocks or retards one's performance.

The research of Milgram (1965) on compliance suggests that a large number of people will do what they are told to do without question, as long as they feel the orders come from a legitimate authority. Milgram paired volunteer "teachers" and "informed learners." The "teacher" was instructed to administer an electric shock to the "learner" for not responding to a question or answering improperly. The voltage showing on the generator switch ranged from 15 to 450 volts. The "learner" pretended to experience pain by grunting,

CONTROVERSIAL ISSUES · Social Loafing

When people get together for some group aim, it is commonly believed team spirit can spur individual effort and enhance the productivity of all. Some social-psychological theorists, along with those who advocate reorganizing assembly lines in favor of production by smaller groups, assume that the presence of other people encourages greater output by each one. Not necessarily so. We have found that when the individual thinks his or her own contribution to the group cannot be measured, his or her output tends to slacken. This notion we call "social loafing" . . .

[One] explanation for social loafing is that people may feel, when performing in groups, that any praise or blame received is less contingent on their individual input than when they perform alone. In our experiments, people could hide in the crowd and avoid the negative consequences of slacking off, or they may have felt "lost in the crowd" and unable to obtain their fair share of the credit for working hard.

Since people may feel that any credit that accrues to a group is divided among its members regardless of each one's individual contribution, they may be tempted to become "free riders" and coast on the group's efforts—a temptation that grows stronger when such contributions take more effort.

SOURCE: Bibb Latané, Kipling Williams, and Stephen Harkins. "Social Loafing," *Psychology Today,* October 1979, pp. 104 and 110.

groaning, and screaming each time the switch was thrown for a wrong answer. Over 60% of the "teachers" were willing to give "learners" the maximum voltage. "Teachers" did, however, moderate voltage levels when physically closer to the victim or when the experimenter was not present. Although the procedures are of questionable ethics and have been vigorously debated by social scientists, the results clearly show how persons willingly obey suggestions of others. Many children's games, such as Simon Says, Mother May I?, and One-Two-Three Red Light are based on the principle of compliance or following the instructions of some authority figure.

Because of people's needs for acceptance and for feelings of identification with groups, a group can exert a powerful influence over an individual's beliefs and behaviors. Such influence is demonstrated in a classic experiment by Solomon Asch (1958). Each subject in a group of five persons was given two cards. On the first card a single line was drawn and on the other card were three lines of unequal length. The subject was to select the line on the second card that matched the line on the first. The lines were drawn in such a way as to make the choice an easy one (see Figure 3.1). Through a prearrangement with the investigator, four of the persons in each group were told to announce unanimous but incorrect judgments. The minority of one could either stand by what he or she saw or could follow the majority and give an

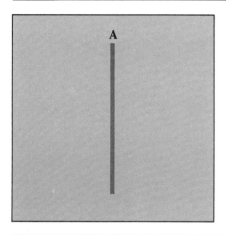 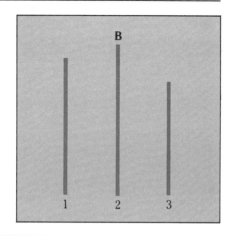

Figure 3.1 Group pressure versus individual judgment.

incorrect judgment. In repeated experiments, the minority of one agreed with the incorrect judgments of the other four members.

Group pressure also exerts a powerful influence on the members' opinions. People tend to be willing to voice the same opinions as others, even though they differ privately. Because of group pressure, people may modify privately held opinions to conform to those of others. Some people go so far as to change privately held opinions, become converts, and proselytize. This push toward conformity of opinions is seen among members of a religious community. The membership publicly adopts a common set of doctrinal beliefs, such as a creed or a code of moral conduct. Some members may publicly espouse commitment to these articles of faith although privately they question selected tenets or interpretations. Others may, through the process of repetition and public profession, come to accept the truthfulness of the tenets. Still others may restructure their beliefs, experience some sort of awakening or conversion, and become vigorous protagonists.

Group discussion plays an important role in shaping attitudes and behaviors. A number of experiments on attitude and behavior change that range across such diverse topics as adding milk to the diet, purchasing name brands, adopting contraception, and trying a new agricultural technique all show that when individuals have a chance to discuss the pros and cons of an idea or action, they are more likely to change an attitude and adopt a new behavior. This process of attitude change is more easily accomplished in a group context than individually. Mao Tse-tung recognized the importance of group discussion in using public confession as a way to punish acts of deviance and publicly recognizing the inviolate nature of the group norms.

Why do persons conform? What are their reasons for not violating the norms? Some social psychologists argue that norms develop and conformity occurs because individuals seek others with similar characteristics. This search for similarity stems from persons' desire for information about similar experiences, actions taken, successes and failures as well as feelings and interests (Schachter 1959). Other social psychologists presume the importance of social affiliation and use a cost-benefit model to account for conformity. This idea is not particularly new. It is a restatement of Aristotle's notion of distributive justice, that is, that rewards in society are passed out according to what one does. A more recent version of the social exchange perspective is that when persons engage in activities, they see that action as an investment or cost. Further, they expect to be rewarded or compensated for their actions proportionally to the expenditure of effort. Presumably if an action is not likely to achieve a profit, that action will not occur.

Conformity is seen to be rewarding because it confers social acceptance, whereas deviancy is viewed as costly because it brings social discomfort and may result in various forms of punishment. In short, individuals in any social interaction behave like calculating machines, seeking to maximize gains and minimize costs. Individuals can define costs and rewards in a variety of ways, depending on the setting in which the exchange occurs, the characteristics of participants, and whether the relationship is short term or long term (Ekeh 1974).

Linkages in Groups

Sociologists also are interested in how people's social ties with one another shape their thoughts and actions. J. L. Moreno earlier in this century was curious about why some adolescent females ran away from a home for girls, while others did not. He found that those girls who took flight were all socially linked to one another.

Diagramming Social Relationships

Moreno contended that social scientists could study the mix of feelings that persons had about one another in any social relationship. This approach was called *sociometry*. He argued that the forces of interpersonal attraction and repulsion, feelings of liking and disliking, of wanting to be with someone or not, could be represented graphically. The graph in which these social choices or ties were diagrammed was called a *sociogram*. When investigating the social ties among individuals in a particular social unit, researchers usually ask each person to list which individual they like best, second best, third best, and so forth. The researcher, then, uses these lists of preferences to draw a map of everyone's choices. This sociogram permits the identification of who are most frequently selected (the stars), who are least chosen (the isolates), and who are linked to one another (mutual choices).

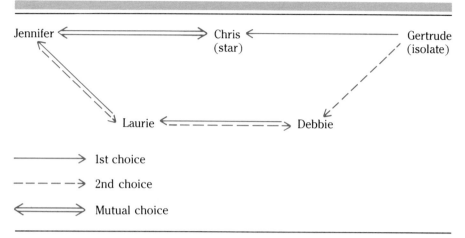

Figure 3.2 Sociogram.

Use the following information about liking and draw a sociogram. Try to arrange the people so that choice arrows do not cross.

Whom do you like best?

	Robert	*Jim*	*Don*	*Tom*	*Neal*
1st Choice	Don	Robert	Robert	Don	Tom
2nd Choice	Tom	Don	Dean	Neal	Robert

PEOPLE · Group Pressure on the Individual

The ultimate sanction on an Amish person is the imposition of the *Meidung* or ban. The Meidung is an extremely potent measure and is imposed only if a member leaves the church, marries an outsider, or breaks a major rule (such as buying an auto) without being repentant. When the presiding bishop places an errant member under the ban, that member becomes persona non grata to all other Amish. No one—including a person's own family—will have anything to do with him. A person's spouse is forbidden to have marital relations with him or her. Moreover, any Amish person who does associate with the shunned member is also placed under the ban. And since an Amish person normally associates only with other Amish, the Meidung effectively isolates the errant member. It is no exaggeration to say that the Meidung is the very heart of the Amish system of social control. So effective is it that it seldom has to be imposed. When it is, the errant member soon recants—or leaves the Amish fold entirely.

SOURCE: Adapted from William M. Kephart, *Extraordinary Groups* (New York: St. Martin's Press, 1982), pp. 49 and 69.

Sociometry helps us understand how people interrelate in social relationships in which everyone knows everybody else. School teachers when arranging seating plans often use this tactic to identify friendships and thereby try to break up unwanted conversations. Other research techniques investigate how people may be linked or tied indirectly, as well as directly, to one another. When we meet new people, we play the game of social location to find out if they know anyone that we know. If they do know someone we know, it gives us a basis for conversation, understanding one another, and figuring out what that person's social standing is.

Social Networks

A number of sociologists and anthropologists are engaged in the study of social networks. A person's *social network* consists of all those people to whom a person is directly and indirectly linked (Figure 3.3). To learn about your social network theoretically a researcher would need to ask who your friends are and then ask your friends who their friends are. If a close-knit group of people know few people outside their group, their social networks could be very similar, whereas people involved in several groups might have very dissimilar social networks. In any case, all the people in a person's social network in our society are not typically acquainted with one another, whereas in less complex societies members of a person's social network may be more intertwined.

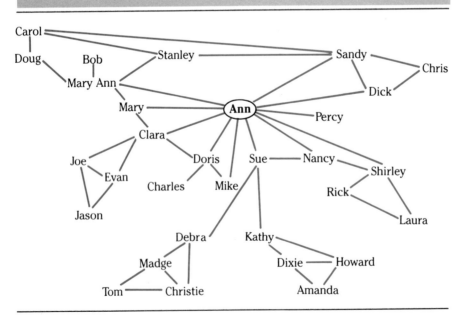

Figure 3.3 Social network. In Ann's social network, she is directly linked to eleven people, but through those people she is indirectly linked to many others.

Sociologists interested in various research topics find social network important. Researchers interested in the adoption of innovations or the transmission of information must consider the linkages between people in order to understand patterns of dissemination. Other social scientists use network analysis to understand which people have power in a community, as well as how corporations are interlocked through the members of their boards of directors. When studying community power structures or corporate elites, researchers must use sophisticated techniques to interrelate information about multiple networks.

Thus for one set of social scientists, social networks can provide data about social structure. For other researchers the social network provides data on people's interrelationships. These researchers argue that the social network provides social and emotional support to people in a complex society. When a person encounters a personal crisis such as divorce, adaptation to the crisis may be facilitated through the efforts of members of his or her support network (family and friends). People who do not have nearby kin to whom they feel close may develop friendship networks that serve some of the functions of kin networks. Granovetter (1973) argued that people who are not closely connected in a small social network may have some advantages over those who are, for they have many more others upon whom they potentially can draw for information or services. He postulates the strength of weak ties. To clarify his argument imagine that you are looking for a job in another city. If all the members of your social network lived in your hometown and have very similar social networks, you would be less likely to know someone who knew someone in that distant city than if your network were more loosely connected.

Sociologists often look at the nature of social ties in a variety of social relationships in order to categorize the societies in which they are found.

Types of Societies

Gemeinschaft and Gesellschaft

The most frequently cited classification of societies is the one offered by the German sociologist Ferdinand Tonnies in 1887. He looked at the pattern of social ties and organizations in order to typify a society as either a gemeinschaft or gesellschaft (Tonnies 1940). In a **gemeinschaft** type of society, social relationships are close, durable, and highly valued by the members. The most important unit in the society is the family, with kinship networks serving as the basis of social organization. Social control is maintained by custom and tradition. Individuals are agents of conformity. Such a set of social ties usually is typical of a preindustrial or communal society in which there is little or no division of labor and only minimal specialization of roles. The Hutterites, a religious group that has established colonies in the United States and Canada, illustrate a gemeinschaft type of social organization in which informal social control is all that is needed.

Gemeinschaft a society based on shared values, norms, and a strong commitment of its members to the group.

The Amish are an example of a gemeinschaft society.

It is no secret that the individual Hutterite tends to have a somewhat passive personality. He "self-surrenders" his own desire for the welfare of the group. Creativity and individuality are sacrificed in favor of the communal concept. Acquisitiveness is constantly played down. [Among the Hutterites] crime and delinquency, divorce and desertion, violence, suicide, alcoholism, drug addiction, sexual problems, and the like are exceedingly rare . . . Hutterian conformity is based on the interplay between conscience and fear of rejection, an interplay which is possible only within a Gemeinschaft type of social structure. Much of the Hutterian youngster's training is devoted to the development of conscience. Ideas of right and wrong are drummed in from all sides, so that by the time he reaches baptismal age his conscience ("feeling scared inside when you do wrong") is finely honed. And since his entire life has been molded by Gemeinschaft relationships, even a mild threat of rejection by the group is likely to bring about the necessary penitence (Kephart 1982: 298).

In contrast to a gemeinschaft is a **gesellschaft** type of society, in which social relationships tend to be impersonal and segmental. Social networks other than the family tend to be pivotal points around which individuals organize the major part of their daily lives. Social ties become associational, springing from an elaborate division of labor. The work environment is governed by contract and highly specialized roles. The locus of social control is

Gesellschaft a society based on impersonality, specialization, and the pursuit of self-interest.

TABLE 3.1   Three Types of Societies

	Preindustrial	Industrial	Postindustrial
Type of social organization	gemeinschaft	gesellschaft	verbindungsnetzschaft
Place of interaction	communities	associations	social networks
Mode of production	agricultural	mechanical	automated
Main means of communication	oral	written	electronic
Main means of transportation	horse and sail	steam-propelled	jet and rocket

Adapted from: Anthony H. Richmond, "The Sociology of Migration in Industrial and Post-Industrial Societies," in *Migration*, J. A. Jackson, ed. (Cambridge, MA: Cambridge University Press, 1969), p. 272.

law with appeal to formal agents of enforcement. Such a mix of social networks and organizations typically is found in societies undergoing urbanization and industrialization (see Chapter 17).

Verbindungsnetzschaft

From the recent technological innovations in electronics and jet and rocket propulsion that are rapidly changing our modes of transportation, production, and communication, a new type of society is emerging, a postindustrial one. To describe the major pattern of social networks and organization in a postindustrial society, Richmond (1969) coined the German term **verbindungsnetzschaft,** which he translates as "social and communication networks." He states: "If gemeinschaft communities were typical of preindustrial societies and gesellschaft associations of industrial societies, then verbindungsnetzschaft are characteristic of postindustrial societies" (Richmond 1981: 300). To paraphrase Richmond, interaction takes place in this type of society through social networks and communication channels that are not necessarily limited to primary or secondary group relations. The electronic church, for example, that televises religious services into one's home, removes the individual from the primary and secondary group interaction that he or she would participate in at a conventional church service (see Chapter 14). These social and communication networks are maintained not only by television but by other means of rapid communication such as the telephone and telex and aided by jet propelled aircraft and space satellites.

> Such interactions are not dependent upon face-to-face contact in a territorial community, nor do they necessarily involve participation in formal organizations. This does not mean that they eliminate communities or associations, but that they compete effectively with them for the individual's attention and involvement (Richmond 1981: 300).

Verbindungsnetzschaft   a society in which interaction takes place through social networks and communication channels.

Summary

The need to be with others and to be part of a group has led to the belief that sociability is part of the human condition. The term "group" has several meanings. For sociologists, what makes a collection of persons into a group is the fact that its members interact.

Sociologists use size and structure to distinguish among various kinds of groups. Voluntary associations are highly structured groups in comparison with a friendship group that has minimal structure.

Groups also vary in the nature of their goals. Some aim at the achievement of specific ends while others are an end in themselves. Other dimensions of groups include identifiability of members, cohesion, and leadership styles.

Primary groups consist of a small number of individuals in close proximity whose relationship is intimate and spontaneous. In secondary groups individuals interact in a limited, impersonal way. Group membership gives the individual a sense of identity and social recognition.

Reference groups serve as yardsticks for individuals to measure their own successes and failures in performing their roles. Groups to which one does not belong also may serve as reference groups. When individuals adopt the values, attitudes, and behavior of a group prior to gaining acceptance as a member, the transition to the new group is eased.

Research on compliance shows that a substantial number of people will do what they are told if they feel the orders come from a legitimate authority. The group can exert a powerful influence on the individual's opinions and behavior because of his or her need for acceptance and a feeling of identification with the group.

A way of classifying societies is by their major patterns of social organization. A gemeinschaft society is characterized by shared norms and values and a strong allegiance from its members; a gesellschaft society is characterized by impersonality, specialization, and individual self-interest. In a third type of society, verbindungsnetzschaft, interaction takes place through social networks and communication channels that are not necessarily linked to either primary or secondary groups.

Suggested Readings

Richard J. Ofshe, ed. *Interpersonal Behavior in Small Groups*, 2d ed. Englewood Cliffs, N.J.: Prentice-Hall, 1973. A collection of articles on group behavior and group problems.

Michael S. Olmstead and A. Paul Hare. *The Small Group*, 2d ed. New York: Random House, 1978. Examines interpersonal behavior in small groups and reviews the research literature in this area.

Charles S. Palazzolo. *Small Groups: An Introduction.* New York: Van Nostrand, 1980. An excellent overview of small group theory and research.

Marvin E. Shaw. *Group Dynamics: The Psychology of Small Group Behavior.* New York: McGraw-Hill, 1976. A summary of small-group research from a social interaction perspective.

Stephen Wilson, *Informal Groups: An Introduction.* Englewood Cliffs, N.J.: Prentice-Hall, 1976. An introduction to the subject of small groups with an emphasis on the concept of solidarity in informal groups.

4

Socialization

Now that you have learned about the social units (groups, societies) in which people live, work, and play, and how shared beliefs, values, and norms (cultures) vary around the world, the processes through which people adopt the behaviors and beliefs considered appropriate in specific groups, societies, and cultures must be considered.

Human infants are born into ongoing social units. They benefit from the activities of members of those units, for more mature humans provide them with necessary protection and assistance. Conversely, societies could not survive if they did not have replacements for members who leave or die. Not only must new people be added, but also they must be taught the rules and beliefs of the society or the existing social order will be destroyed.

As parents and members of older generations in a society know only too well, young or new members of a society do not adopt all of the practices and beliefs that the existing members of the society try to teach them. Human beings can think and therefore can accept or reject what others try to teach them. Social units may undergo gradual or rapid change depending on how extensively and strongly people reject traditional ways. Yet there is generally considerable continuity in society, for people are taught traditions in many different ways and typically are rewarded for following them. Thus it is not surprising that young people find themselves doing things as their parents did them even though they had planned to be different from their parents.

Sociologists emphasize social processes when trying to explain why people are as they are, why they think and act as they do. The learning processes through which human animals become social beings and members of social units are called **socialization.** *Whenever people interact with other people, directly or indirectly, they are undergoing socialization. Thus people are being socialized throughout their lives. But socialization varies over the life cycle, so we need to begin our analysis with the human infant.*

Socialization the learning processes through which human animals become social beings.

Nature versus Nurture

All human beings are biological and social creatures. Social scientists debate to what extent humans are the product of natural, biological processes over which they have little or no control, and to what extent humans are the product of nurturance, social processes over which they may have little or much control (Williams 1983).

When people are very young or old or physically handicapped, we are often more conscious than normal that they are biological creatures because others may have to help them meet physical needs. Human infants, for example, are helpless for a long period of time after birth. Initially, they could not survive without extensive physical care from other members of the species.

Biological processes stimulate children's physical development; coordination and strength gradually improve, so they can feed themselves and

---

CONTROVERSIAL ISSUES · The Importance of Nurturance

Las Vegas, Nev. (AP)—The frail 6-year-old, locked up in a dark room for most of his life with five baby brothers and sisters, now scurries about his playroom, squealing and wailing while reaching for the hugs he craves.

The boy—identified by officials only as "C"—has the mental and emotional development of a 10-month-old, juvenile officials say, the result of a lifetime of incarceration in a rundown home.

"C," a tiny 45 pounds and about 3 feet tall, can't talk now, two months after he and his siblings were freed from seclusion. And officials say "C" may never recover from the neglect.

The others, 4-year-old twin girls, a twin brother and sister 8 months old, and a 3-year-old girl, have fared better, and they are in foster homes. The older twins are speaking short sentences.

But "C" can only say "hi" and "bye" so far, and not always that much. What he wants is to be constantly held or hugged, and he runs from one adult to another, arms outstretched for the affection he apparently missed.

When he is picked up, he shrieks and screams with delight, but the sounds are more like those of an animal than of a little boy.

"C" lives at Child Haven, the juvenile home where he and his brothers and sisters were taken two months ago after a police officer found "C" wandering in a Las Vegas street.

The officer was alarmed because the boy couldn't talk and took him to Child Haven. His mother was found and turned in two children, then three more.

"When they first arrived here they would stand in a group and make noises to each other," Nedra Scott, supervisor of "C's" cottage, recalled Friday. "The way they looked at each other, it was obvious they were communicating in some fashion."

Juvenile officials say the children apparently were locked in a darkened room and bowls of food were slipped to them.

Albiser, deputy director of Clark County juvenile services, said the children did not appear to have suffered physical abuse, although "C" may have suffered neurological damage from being denied environmental stimulation.

SOURCE: *The Knoxville Journal,* April 24, 1982.

---

walk. While these biological developments are occurring, children are talked to and handled by caregivers who provide them with food and protect them from physical harm. Sociologists believe that social interaction with caregivers is essential for normal development.

A classic study by René Spitz (1964) on hospitalism indicates that infants

Human infants are not the only animals who need nurturance to develop into healthy adults. A veterinary assistant provides the necessary attention and affection Kiki's mother refuses to provide.

must have social contact with caregivers as well as physical care from them in order to develop normally. Spitz studied infants in an institutional setting who received adequate physical care (food, clothing, clean bedding) but did not have caregivers who cuddled or talked to them. The children not only lagged behind others of their age in intellectual development, but also suffered impaired physical health, apparently because of their lack of social contact. Such studies indicate that we must examine more closely the role of nurturance, or socialization, in human development, as well as the role of nature, or biological processes.

What is the nature-versus-nurture debate?

Communication

Babies and their caregivers may communicate nonverbally through touching and nonlinguistic verbalizations (cries, gurgles, humming, and so forth), but they cannot communicate as socialized people normally do, that is, through the manipulation of symbols. Human life is quite different than that of other animals because people are able to use languages or symbol systems to communicate.

A **symbol** is anything that is used to represent something else. Symbols may resemble what they stand for (a stick figure may represent a person) or they may be very abstract (H_2O represents water). To use a computer, the user

Symbol a sign used to represent something else.

must learn a set of symbols. The important thing about symbols is that they must be shared. People must learn to assign the same meanings to symbols if they are to communicate or work together.

Early symbolic interactionists such as George Herbert Mead (1934) argued that human beings were the only animals who could manipulate symbols or communicate through language. They argued that other animals' apparent usage of signs was instinctive.

In recent decades new research on animals and new linguistic theories (language acquisition) have generated debate over whether other animals can assign meaning to symbols and communicate by manipulating those symbols. Whatever the relative success of such studies, it appears that no other animals live in a world of symbolic meaning to the degree that human beings do.

If humans could not manipulate complex symbol systems, what would social life be like?

Social Contact

Researchers could not ethically deprive children of social contact with adults to see if they would develop normally without it. Information has been obtained, however, from the intensive study of feral children, children who experienced severe social isolation, lack of social contact (Craig 1978). Sociologists often discuss Anna and Isabel, two classic cases of social isolation (Davis 1948). A recent well-documented case is that of Genie, a woman who was discovered in 1970 in California when she was 13 years old. She had been kept in isolation, restricted by a harness in a small room and had not been spoken to since infancy (Curtis 1977). Even though various people worked with Genie, in her 20s she had not yet developed normal language skills, although she did not lack cognitive (thinking) ability. Her case indicates that social interaction during childhood is important to the development of people's communication skills. The importance of early social interaction is indicated by its designation as primary socialization.

Will human infants undergo normal social development if they are socially isolated?

Primary Socialization

Socialization is a lifelong process because throughout our lives we are changing as we become involved in new social situations. Yet social scientists recognize that early or **primary socialization** differs from other types of socialization (Denzin 1977). Whatever their genetic heritages, newborns differ from other human beings in that they are "social blank slates," that is, they lack

Primary socialization
socialization early in life that begins with a "social blank slate."

Children need love and attention, which can be provided by parents or other adults, male or female.

prior social experiences that may affect their behavior. People responsible for infants—caregivers—are expected to help them learn to function in society. Primary socialization provides the foundation for later learning or socialization.

In our society infants typically are cared for primarily by members of their immediate or nuclear family. This pattern led early sociologist Charles Horton Cooley (1922) to describe primary groups like the family as "nurseries of human nature." He meant by this that the child through interaction with family members acquires the characteristics we associate with social beings. People who object to the development of infant care centers often argue that young children require the care of family members, particularly their mothers, if they are to develop into "good" members of society. Although researchers debate what patterns of caregiving are most desirable, we do know that social interaction is essential to normal development.

Once children acquire language, around age 2, their social development is rapid. This is true, in part, because language permits them to take a more active role in responding to their environment and, in part, because of biological maturation. Various theorists have argued that children must pass through specific stages of development before they are able to function as full-fledged members of society.

Stages of Social Development

One theory of stages that has been disseminated in our popular culture is Freudian or psychoanalytic theory. Sigmund Freud (1856–1939) was an Austrian physician who treated patients with psychological problems. Based on analyses of what they told him, he concluded that what happens to people during childhood affects them later as adults. If problems during early stages (the oral and anal stages) were not satisfactorily resolved, a person could become *arrested* (fixed) at that stage. Although frequent references are made to Freud's ideas in our popular culture, few people today completely adhere to his ideas. Neo-Freudians such as Erik Erikson have identified somewhat different stages of development that are more widely accepted today than Freud's (Erikson 1963).

More recently the work of Jean Piaget has stimulated interest in developmental stages. Piaget has focused on thinking or cognitive development in his numerous studies of children. Through interaction with their environment, children acquire new ways of thinking or new schemes. All children move through stages of cognitive development that involve increasingly greater complexity of thought and shifts from egocentric perspectives to perspectives which take others into account.

The founder of the symbolic interaction perspective in sociology, George Herbert Mead, developed a theoretical scheme for conceptualizing the development of the social being or *self*. His scheme is supported by the data collected by subsequent researchers such as Piaget. Yet unlike some psychological schemes, Mead's stages are not tied to specific ages.

Mead argues as do others that early in life children appear to be unable to understand anyone else's perspective except their own. After acquiring some mastery of language, they learn their names and some of the expectations other people have about how they should behave. Children recognize that they are distinct from other people. Yet it generally is easy to recognize that they have difficulty distinguishing their own perspective. If a little boy named Tommy tells you, "Tommy is a good boy," you recognize that he has not made that evaluation a part of himself as an adult would.

Mead (1934) points out the stages (play and game) involved in being able to maintain a personal perspective and at the same time to take others' perspectives into account. After human beings recognize their own distinctiveness, they begin to recognize the characteristics of others. Children go through a **play** stage during which they act as if they were other people. A child may dress up in her mother's clothes and tell her dolls to "play nice," thereby imitating the behavior of her own mother. In that way children acquire the rudimentary ability to take perspectives different from their own.

Mead (1934) argues that children take an important step toward functioning in larger social units when they are able to participate in a **game.** In our society games are usually packaged with information about the appropriate age level of players. Board games, such as Candyland or Monopoly, require that players take turns and follow various rules to move around the board. Young children often frustrate adult players because they want every "turn" to be theirs and often will not follow the rules if they do not like the consequences, such as losing. To participate in a game, each player has to understand his or her role, the roles of other players, and the rules of the game.

Play early stage of social development when a child can imitate or play at being another person.

Game stage during which a child is able to understand multiple perspectives including the abstract perspective of the generalized other.

To function as a full participant in a social unit or a social activity, we must not only take into account the perspectives of specific other people, but also we must employ an abstract perspective shared by other participants called the **generalized other.** From interacting with others and observing the social world, children learn the general rules and values held by full participants, or, in other words, they acquire the perspective of the generalized other. Often when people make remarks like "we do it this way," "we" does not refer to specific others but rather to the generalized other.

In order for a performance of a symphony to be satisfying to all involved in it, people must take the perspective of the generalized other. Members of the audience must remain seated and quiet during the performance but be prepared to applaud at the appropriate times. Members of the orchestra must be aware of their own musical parts as well as of the symphony as a whole in order to play at the appropriate times. Thus the members of the audience and the performers are aware of how they and others should act during a symphony performance. They all must use the abstract guidelines for behavior which sociologists refer to as the perspective of the generalized other.

Generalized other
the abstract perspective of the social group.

How does the generalized other influence our actions?

Looking-Glass Self

During the years of childhood, children are developing social selves. Interaction with other people is an important aspect of self-development because others' appraisals of us influence how we see ourselves. Charles Horton Cooley (1922) developed the concept of the **"looking-glass self"** to help us see the role of others in our self-development. According to Cooley, we first imagine how other people see us. Based on their responses to us, we try to figure out what they think about us. Second, we imagine how they evaluate or judge our appearance or our presentations of "self." The third and final element of the looking-glass self involves the "self" feelings (such as pride or mortification) aroused as a result of others' presumed judgments of us.

Looking-glass self
sense of self that we experience when we imagine how others judge us.

Underlying Cooley's formulation of the self is an important process, the process through which humans think about themselves or treat themselves as social objects. Mead (1934) discussed this reflexive process by hypothetically dividing the social self into an "I" and multiple "me's."

"I" and "Me"

Every day you carry on conversations with many people, but the person you most frequently talk to is yourself. Typically we do not talk to ourselves out loud, but rather we engage in internal conversations. The concepts of "I" and "me" make it possible for us to analyze how we can carry on these internal conversations.

The **"I"** is continually thinking about the social world. It is considered

I the ability of a person to think reflectively about himself or herself.

to be a social process, for the "I" is continually changing in response to social stimulation. One aspect of the social world "I" can think about, reflect about, is myself. Thus not only can "I" think about other people, "I" can make myself the object of my thoughts. "I" can think about "me."

In fact every person has **multiple "me's,"** for they are perceptions of self developed from interacting with other people. "Me's" are reflected appraisals; they are products of social interaction. *I* may think of *me* as a good student because my teachers and fellow students indicate to me that they think I am a good student. A *me* is a social product, for it is an appraisal of myself gained from social interaction.

If the social self were simply composed of "me's," then a person would simply be what other people thought he or she was like. But we are more than the sum of other people's appraisals of us. The "I" allows us to think about or reflect on "me." I may not like somebody's appraisal of me, and as a consequence construct my future actions to try to change that appraisal. When another person treats me as if I am unfriendly although I believe I *am* friendly, I may make additional efforts to demonstrate my "friendly" self rather than accepting the other person's definition of me as unfriendly. Or I may decide not to associate with someone who does not see me as I see myself.

Multiple me's perceptions of self that we develop from interacting with other people.

Significant Other

The symbolic interactionist formulation of self allows for change throughout a person's life, because some "me's" become past history as we develop new "me's" through involvement with new others. Yet all other people are not equally important influences on our selves. Harry Stack Sullivan's concept of the **significant other** (1964) furthers our understanding of the role of others in our formulation and maintenance of "me's." Our parents, close friends, lovers, and other intimates are people whose perceptions are important to us. Therefore, they are significant others for us. Even if other associates do not support our self-perceptions, we may maintain them if our significant others support them.

Significant others people whose perceptions of us strongly influence how we see ourselves.

Our images of self develop in part because of the roles we play in society. Both symbolic interactionists and structural functionalists turn to the concept of social role to describe human socialization. (See Chapter 1 for a discussion of these theories.)

Who are your significant others?

Socialization as a Lifelong Process

Although we often think of learning as occurring in structured settings such as classrooms, we all learn things whenever we interact with one another.

Social Interaction

Infants are socialized by their caregivers, typically their parents. Their parents attempt to teach them norms appropriate to their group (what a good boy or girl does), social roles (mother, father, child), and social values (what they should believe). Children learn things that their parents did not intend to teach them because any time people interact with one another, they make some impressions on one another. Parents who use swear words around their young children often find to their dismay that the children have learned those words. Socialization is not a single process but an outgrowth of all social interaction.

Socializing Agents

As participants in or observers of social interaction children not only learn things we did not plan for them to learn, but also they learn at times and in situations that were not planned. At one time social scientists emphasized the importance of particular institutions and position-holders, **socializing agents,** to explain socialization. Institutions that served important socializing functions were the family, the school, and the church, because each institution was expected to prepare children for adult life by teaching them norms, roles, and values. Particular roles within these social structures emphasized socialization duties (parents in the family, teachers in the schools). If a child grew into a juvenile delinquent, it was assumed that one or more of these institutions had failed to socialize the child adequately.

Socializing agents social organizations and representatives of those organizations who are assigned the task of training new members.

However, researchers recognized there were other influences, particularly the *mass media* (television, radio, books, magazines, records). Many American children spend several hours every day before and after school watching television. In the past few decades, researchers have found that children become more aggressive if they are exposed to a steady diet of violent television programs. Other researchers examined frequent viewers' gender role stereotypes. Children are apparently socialized by television programs to accept violence and gender role stereotypes. To avoid socialization they disapprove of, some parents have put locks on their television sets to limit the number of hours their children view television; the children must "earn" time for watching television by engaging in other activities. Other parents have joined citizen groups that are trying to regulate what is shown on television (and to eliminate certain types of commercials during children's programs). Since the mass media socialize children, the question is, how should their impact be regulated—by individual parents in their own homes, by citizen groups, or by the marketplace? (See Chapter 18 for further discussion of the influence of mass media.)

The role of socializing agents appears more complex when we recognize that children are simultaneously exposed to different and often conflicting perspectives. Once they reach school age, they must interact with adults other than their parents and with their peers (other children), and they must respond

In schools children are socialized by peers and by what they read as well as by teachers.

to the messages sent through various media (books as well as television). Both cognitive developmental theorists and self theorists believe that interaction with peers is important to development and to the learning of multiple perspectives. During some periods such as adolescence, peers play a very important role, so much so that at times adolescents' fierce adherence to peer group norms is criticized. In adult life, peers (spouses, friends, work associates) may be important socializers when we engage in new activities (marital, career, leisure), but less important at other times.

What people and social institutions play key roles in the socialization process?

Anticipatory Socialization

Through social interaction children and adults learn how others expect them to act. The focus of socialization activities may be upon learning the norms governing behavior in current roles, but it may also be upon preparation for future roles, **anticipatory socialization.** Anticipatory socialization may be focused on preparation for a specific role the person will soon achieve or be assigned (preparing an only child for the role of sibling or a nursing student

Anticipatory socialization training that prepares us to engage in future roles.

for the role of nurse). Or it may involve quite general preparation for roles that most people will play some day (spouse, parent). Anticipatory socialization provides us with some familiarity with the expectations associated with future positions; however, once we occupy those positions and begin to perform those roles, we recognize how much we still have to learn.

Adult Socialization

For many decades theories of human development emphasized the stability of adults' personalities. Many psychological theories assumed that after late childhood or adolescence, the basic nature of a person was established. Even if a person appeared to change later, the basic person would continue unchanged. On the other hand, sociologists believed that people could be shaped by the organizations and institutions that directed adult life. The specific arguments have changed over the decades, but psychologists still tend to believe that *constancy* marks adult life, and sociologists believe that *change* does (Brim and Kagan 1980).

Since people are socialized whenever they interact with one another, sociologists argue that socialization, and therefore personal change, continues throughout life (Becker 1964). Yet adult socialization differs from primary socialization because people have already learned norms, roles, and values. Also they often have some choice about whether they will consider new perspectives. The general process by which we learn perspectives different from those we formerly held is called **resocialization.**

Resocialization the process whereby a social being learns a perspective different from those previously held.

Various kinds of adult institutions seek to resocialize the individuals who enter them as students, patients, clients, inmates, or novices. Colleges and professional schools deal primarily with students who choose to learn new perspectives, although novices entering convents and monasteries perhaps embrace their new perspectives more enthusiastically. On the other hand, mental institutions and prisons often have inmates or patients who are there against their will and are reluctant to adopt the perspectives the institutions' representatives desire them to take (Goffman 1961).

As an aftermath of the Korean War, social scientists began to use the term **brainwashing** (Lifton 1961). Some prisoners of war underwent intensive "reeducation" programs aimed at getting them to disavow their former values, norms, and roles, and subsequently to adopt new values, norms, and roles. In the 1970s the practices of some religious cults, such as the "Moonies," were believed by some to result in brainwashing. Parents of some Moonie converts hired "deprogrammers" to erase the new perspectives learned by their children (many of whom were adults). Although the concept of brainwashing is intriguing, many researchers question whether or not social values can be changed so readily.

Brainwashing the process whereby prior social learning is discredited or erased and replaced by a new perspective.

Can adults be socialized to behave in new ways and to believe in new ideas?

Social Structure and Social Process

The nature-versus-nurture debate persists because we have much to learn about how physiological processes influence our development. Sociologists understand a great deal about the processes of nurturance, socialization, and the structure of society. We recognize that children socialized similarly may develop along very different lines because of multiple influences. But the social structure very powerfully influences each of us.

Ascription or Achievement

Whatever their innate abilities and predispositions, human infants are born into ongoing social units. These social units may be quite small and relatively easy to identify (families or kinship groups) or they may be very large and more abstract (social classes or societies). A child may be assigned permanently to some of those social units (racial or ethnic groups), but other units a child may leave when he or she becomes an adult (a community or a particular social class). If a person cannot enter or leave a social unit freely, the person has an **ascribed position** in that unit. A person can disavow or ignore his or her "blood" relatives, but they remain relatives. On the other hand, a person may have an **achieved position** in other units, gained through his or her own activities. In our society, entrance into most social units is based on choice or achievement rather than ascription.

Ascribed position a position to which a person is permanently assigned, usually from birth.

Achieved position a position a person strives to attain through his or her own efforts.

Social Positions

To understand how social units affect individuals, we must consider the structure of social units. Social units are composed of **positions** or statuses. At the simplest level every person in a social unit occupies the position of a member of that unit. Most social units involve various types of positions, such as the positions of father, mother, and child in the nuclear family unit. Positions in a social unit may be arranged in a hierarchy. In large social units such as colleges the position of college president is higher than that of full professor, the position of full professor is higher than that of associate professor, and so on. Whatever the specific case, a position refers to a location in a social unit.

Position a person's location in a social unit.

Members of a social unit generally have many tasks to perform to keep the social unit going. One way to divide the labor is for everyone to share each of the tasks. However, this division of labor is not always possible or practical. A human infant, for instance, cannot perform many of the tasks confronting a family unit. Another way to divide the labor is to say that whoever wants to perform the task should do so. Unfortunately, some tasks might never be performed if no one had responsibility for doing them or for seeing that they were done. Thus most social units assign tasks among their members, and they do this on the basis of positions.

What positions do you occupy other than college student?

Social Roles

A social unit develops a set of expectations for the occupant of a social position, a **social role.** People who hold the position of parent are expected to perform the role of parent by caring for their children. Thus one set of social role expectations is *duties.* However, roles involve more than duties, because they provide a loose script for how people in a social unit should interrelate. So another set of social role expectations is *rights.* A teacher's role includes the duty of transmitting information to students. One of the rights associated with the student role is the expectation that the teacher will transmit information. Thus the role expectations of teachers and students are interrelated and reciprocal. Some of the many rights and duties involved in the teacher and student interrelation are illustrated in Table 4.1.

Roles facilitate social life since they permit us to expect that occupants of specific positions will engage in the behavior normatively prescribed for them. A woman who gets on a bus expects the bus driver to follow the prescribed route and let her off at a scheduled bus stop. On the other hand, the bus driver expects the woman to pay the correct fare. Every day we interact with many people, some of whom we do not know. The performance of social roles greatly facilitates much of this interaction (Biddle 1979).

Social role   social expectations for the occupant of a particular social position.

Role Performances

Knowledge of social roles gives us some advance ideas about how an occupant of a position will behave. However, the occupant of a social position may not do things we expect and may do other things we do not expect. Thus we must distinguish roles that are sets of expectations for behavior from **role performances** that are the activities of role players. There are many reasons

Role performance the role related activities engaged in by the occupant of a position.

Table 4.1   Interrelated Roles

Teacher Role		Student Role	
Duties	1. Should be prepared for every class meeting 2. Should announce and adhere to the announced grading standards	**Rights**	1. Should receive appropriate educational experience at each class meeting 2. Should receive information about evaluation procedures
Rights	1. Should assume students are prepared for class meetings 2. Should expect students to prepare their own work, unless a team project is involved	**Duties**	1. Should accept responsibility for being prepared for class 2. Should be academically honest, never presenting other people's work as their own

for role performances to diverge from the norms of role behavior. For one, a person may not understand the expectations. A guest at a formal dinner party may try to behave appropriately but not understand the etiquette rules, such as what silverware to use and when. In some cultures dinner guests are expected to belch to show their appreciation of a meal. An American visiting in those cultures might give a faulty role performance by not belching.

Do your role performances always fulfill your partners' expectations?

Role Negotiation

Other kinds of disparity between expectations and behavior lead us to consider the process of interaction. When people interact with one another, roles provide only loose scripts for behavior. Parents are expected to care for their children, but how they should do that on a day-to-day basis and what level of care they should provide are not always clear. Does a person fulfill the parental role by giving a child a candy bar for breakfast or leaving an 8-year-old alone without a baby sitter? When occupants of a position perform roles, they are not only adhering to shared expectations or norms but are also engaging in the process of *role making,* shaping their role-related behavior to suit themselves and the social situation.

Role Taking

Role players engage in a process of negotiation as each person in an encounter attempts to fashion a desired role performance. The negotiation process involves role taking as well as role making. **Role taking** involves our attempts to understand the role the other person is performing (Turner 1962). When two people are interacting, they are thinking about many things: what roles they are playing, how they want to play those roles, how they think the other person will respond to a planned role performance, what role they think the other person is playing, how the other person is playing that role, and whether the role the other person is playing fits with their own role.

Role taking process through which people imaginatively take the perspective of their partners in an interaction.

Impression Management

People continually are negotiating roles with one another, but some situations that call for extra awareness of impression management, such as job interviews, clearly illustrate the process. Before an interview, a job candidate usually carefully prepares a resume to present himself or herself as having performed certain roles and being capable of performing a new role, the potential organizational role. The candidate selects a costume (clothing) that he or she assumes is appropriate for a candidate for the organizational role. Further, the candidate rehearses internally for the job interview—imagining what questions will be asked, preparing responses, and imagining the interviewer's reaction to those responses—through the process of role taking. During the interview, the candidate continues to engage in role taking and role making, trying to get clues from the interviewer about how successful his or her role performance has been. While the candidate is engaging in these activities, so is the interviewer.

Each party makes adjustments based on the other person's actions. If the interviewer indicates the company prefers employees who are good listeners, the candidate may alter his or her performance to demonstrate listening skills. The negotiation involves the participants in **impression management,** a kind of regulation of information.

Impression management processes we engage in to communicate to one another how we would like to be perceived.

The study of impression management leads some to fear that people are cynical and manipulative when interacting with one another; however, impression management is a normal and necessary part of social communication.

Not only does our impression management affect our actions and personal appearance, but we also use the objects we keep in our homes to convey impressions about who we are. Researchers Eugene Rochberg-Halton and Mihalyi Csikszentmihalyi (1981) have studied the objects people keep in their homes to see what is most important to them. They found that mementos of relationships were prominent, but objects associated with social and political causes were not.

The objects we display in our homes may provide us with comfort and happy memories, but they also convey information to others. Many people feel comfortable thumbing through others' record collections to see what taste they have in music and perusing their book shelves to learn their reading habits. Americans are aware that others will form impressions of them based on the objects displayed in the more public areas of their residences, so they may

PEOPLE · Life as Theatre

Sociologist Erving Goffman (1959) proposes that we can use a *dramaturgical perspective* to analyze everyday social interaction. Each person at some time is both an actor and part of an audience. As actors we have a vast repertoire of roles we may perform. We let other people know which roles we are playing through the process of impression management, the presentation of self. The costumes we wear, the props with which we surround ourselves, the postures we assume: all are nonverbal aspects of our self-presentations. In addition we directly and indirectly say who we are today through our usage of language. If our performances are good, our audiences see us as we desire them to see us.

Situations when we are very concerned about our self-presentations, such as job interviews, are called *front stage settings*. In other situations, *back stage settings*, we assume that others will accept our self-presentations even if we do not craft our performances so carefully.

keep trashy novels, pulp magazines, and other objects which do not support their ideal self-presentations in more private areas of their residences. Some oversize books of pictures are called "coffee-table" books because their primary use appears to be as display items for living room coffee tables.

Through our actions, our appearance, and the objects we display around ourselves we communicate information to others. At times we are more concerned about the impressions others form of us than at other times, so we try harder to convey particular information. However, impression management is a natural part of everyday social life. Sociologists have tried to make people more aware of impression management by arguing that social life can be treated as a series of dramatic performances.

In what ways do people engage in impression management whenever they interact?

Social Values

In Chapter 2 you learned that values are a part of culture. Different cultures emphasize different values and, as a consequence, people in those cultures have different ways of acting. The distinctiveness of a culture is maintained through the process of socialization. New people must learn and adopt the cultural values or the culture will change or disappear. Today some values that have been cherished in American society are being challenged. We will consider how these values have shaped individuals' behavior and why they are being challenged.

Self or Society

In Western societies, and particularly in the United States, the individual person has long been considered important. Individuals are encouraged to be independent, self-sufficient, and personally successful. Although a person may be thought "nice" by putting the needs of others (particularly non-family members) before his or her own, such a person may also be thought foolish and naive. Americans often find it difficult to understand people from other cultures who emphasize the group more than the individual.

Eastern societies traditionally place emphasis on the group (society, lineage, clan) and deemphasize the significance of individuals and their desires. During World War II, Americans were shocked by Japanese pilots who flew suicide missions. More recently American business executives have been fascinated by the success of Japanese corporations in which employees are active contributors. Some American executives hope to copy the Japanese style in our own corporations (Ouchi 1981), but others believe that style incompatible with the emphasis on the self and individual success in our society. The

The quest for self-fulfillment may have negative consequences for the individual and society.

Japanese, for instance, do exercises together during work breaks. Many Americans would probably prefer to exercise when they wanted to and how they wanted to, or not at all.

Japanese people endorse different social values and norms for behavior than do Americans. In Japan, rather than competing with one another to attain self-esteem, people work with one another to maintain mutual self-esteem through social rituals. Each person's "face," or personal claim of social worth, is supported by the efforts of other group members (Goffman 1967). Americans might point out and laugh at another worker's embarrassing mistake; Japanese workers would not.

Social commentators have at times applauded the emphasis on self and individual achievement in the United States because they believed it fostered individual mobility and economic growth for the society. In the 1970s some commentators came to believe the emphasis on self was excessively high. Social commentator Tom Wolfe referred to it as the "me decade." Self-help books of many types appeared, telling people how to put themselves first, how to be their own best friend, and how to find themselves. The emphasis on self may have contributed to some extent to the rising divorce rate, because people were encouraged to "do their own thing" without regard to the traditional norms and obligations associated with marital and familial relationships.

Those who share Wolfe's pessimism think that excessive focus on the self leads ultimately to individual self-dissatisfaction and loss of direction for society. Pollster Daniel Yankelovich (1981) agrees that excessive focus on self-fulfillment has negative consequences; however, he argues both that most Americans are not totally caught up in the search for self-fulfillment and that

Social critic Christopher Lasch (1979) believes the United States has developed a "culture of narcissism." Individualistic activities such as jogging are applauded by many but criticized by others as signs of narcissism, love of one's own body. In the 1980s the sight of people engaging in many public activities (jogging, walking, bicycling) while wearing earphones was seen by some as a sign of further retreat into oneself. One question is, when do efforts to attain self-fulfillment and self-actualization (peak self-awareness) become nothing more than selfishness and self-indulgence? Another question is, how can social units survive if their members care only about themselves? What do you think? Are we becoming narcissistic or constructively trying to improve ourselves?

there are signs that people's values are changing in that they are adopting new rules, particularly a new ethic of commitment. Based on a representative survey of working Americans Yankelovich argues that only 17 percent of working Americans have self-fulfillment as their primary life goal. Those who emphasize self-fulfillment tend to be young, professional, and well-educated. During the 1970s, while these young adults sought self-fulfillment, about 20 percent of Americans were not caught up in the search for self-fulfillment. These older, conservative people adhered to traditional values (material success, hard work). Thus the majority of American adults (over 60 percent) have been in transition, adopting the self-fulfillment ethic in part but retaining old values as well. Yankelovich believes that the majority is recognizing the limited satisfaction that comes from total focus on self, as well as the constraints economic conditions place on achievement of greater levels of material success. He optimistically argues that Americans are developing a new ethic of commitment which fits life in the 1980s.

Should individuals give higher priority to personal desires than to anything else?

Cooperation or Competition

The emphasis on self in the United States has been tied to competition. People are supposed to "get ahead" because they work harder than other people. People who do not achieve are losers. If our values are changing, how we socialize young members of society should be changing.

Children learn not only through formal education activities but also through the games they play. Some researchers examine the games children (and adults) play to learn more about the values prevailing in the society. Other researchers observe children and adults playing games to infer their values from their play behavior.

For those social psychologists interested in how people play games, the strategies people choose to follow are important, so they have people play games in which the players have choices. One choice typically involves **cooperation:** If players cooperate they attain game outcomes that benefit most participants. Another strategy is more individualistic or self-oriented: The individual seeks to achieve the best possible outcomes for himself or herself without regard to the outcomes for the other players. Or the game may involve **competition,** trying to maximize one's own outcome while limiting or eliminating rewards for others. Only using the competitive strategy will players try to minimize others' rewards.

Cooperation behavior that produces the most benefits for all participants.

Competition behavior by which each person seeks the best possible outcomes for himself or herself.

The academic setting, although not a game, provides opportunities to observe all three of these strategies. Students in a class may cooperate with one another by sharing notes, studying together, or working on group projects. On the other hand, students may develop their own notes, study alone, and work on individual projects while pursuing individualistic strategies. Some competitive students may even remove crucial reading materials from the library, try to obtain advance information about examinations, or even use other people's work and claim it as their own. The teacher's methods may also affect the student's behavior. For example, if an instructor announces that only the top five students in the class will receive A's, the instructor has created a situation that is bound to be competitive. Further, the structure of the whole educational system may encourage certain strategies. For example, if only the students with the highest grades are admitted to medical school, students in pre-med are in a competitive situation.

Research on children indicates that before children enter school in our society, they have learned to be competitive. Millard Madsen (1967; 1970) has developed a game for children that reveals the children's cultural differences, that is, that children have learned different values. In his studies, four children are seated around a game board, one at each corner. A target circle is marked in the corner in front of each child. Each child holds a string attached to a marking pen positioned in the center of the board. When one child pulls the string and the others do not, the pen moves toward the child and into a target circle.

At the beginning of a session, the children are told that they will be rewarded if they can move the pen through each of the target circles in sequence. Thus they are encouraged to cooperate. Subsequently children are told they will receive rewards only when the pen moves through their own target circles. Children must still cooperate to receive rewards, for if each pulls the string at the same time, the pen will not move, and no one will receive any rewards.

Madsen studied children from various cultures and subcultures and found that children from cultures and subcultures that emphasize cooperation were more cooperative than other children. Children raised in communal settings in Israel (kibbutzim) were more cooperative than urban Israeli children. Poor

---

CONTROVERSIAL ISSUES · New Games

Even though most Americans learn to compete at school, at home, and at games, some people believe that we can teach different values through new games. A nonprofit organization, New Games Foundation, established in the 1970s, promotes alternative forms of physical and emotional outlet. Some of the activities are strictly play (noncompetitive), for they do not have outcomes as games do. These are called "creative games" or "trust games." Other games involving some element of competition are called "soft war" games. In some ways they resemble the activities of young children who have not learned formal games with their "official" rules. Some variations of tag games, such as Keep Away, are new games. To qualify as a new game, all the rules of a game must be modifiable. For example, rather than tagging out and sidelining players, the "out" player may join the other team until everyone is ready to quit playing.

Such efforts are interesting, but most Americans are not likely to play "new games," for they value achieving and winning. As our society is presently structured, competition is routine.

Mexican children, whether rural or urban, were more cooperative than the more affluent, urban Mexican children. Middle-class American children are competitive and become more so at older ages. In fact, children from middle-class American families apparently are so oriented to competition that they compete even in the first trials, when cooperation is clearly the winning strategy.

Consideration of social values such as cooperation and competition leads us back to consideration of how people relate to one another. Our association with other people can lead us to learn new ways of looking at the world, and new ways of behaving, or can give us support for our existing ways of seeing and behaving.

Summary

People become social beings through the process of socialization. The acquisition of symbols through the process of social interaction distinguishes humans from other animals. Biological processes (nature) and social processes (nurture) are both involved in normal social development.

Early in life the family serves as a "nursery of human nature" by providing the primary socialization that establishes a foundation for later learning.

Various theories of human development identify stages we progress through as we mature. Sociologists emphasize the play and game stages that respectively refer to the ability to imitate or play at being another and the more advanced ability to take multiple perspectives into account.

Other people's perceptions of us affect how we see ourselves. We have many different perceptions of ourselves called "me's." Human beings can plan what they are going to do, for they are capable of thinking about themselves. "I" can think about "me."

Although some people may be assigned special socialization responsibilities, whenever people interact with one another socialization occurs. Each person has some impact on how his or her interaction partner views himself or herself.

Through anticipatory socialization we may become prepared for the future. Resocialization provides us with perspectives different from those we held before.

Every social unit has positions. Some positions labeled "ascribed" are assigned to us no matter what we do, but "achieved" positions are assigned on the basis of our actions.

For every position there are expectations for behavior; these expectations comprise a social role. The way a position holder enacts a social role is called a role performance. Through the process of role taking we may imagine how others will act, and we may modify our actions, engaging in role making, in response.

Whenever people interact they form impressions of one another. Impression management is an integral part of social life.

Through the process of socialization not only do we acquire information and skills, but also we learn social values. At present there are debates about whether people in our society value themselves too highly and place too little value on cooperative activities.

Suggested Readings

Daniel Yankelovich. *New Rules.* New York: Bantam, 1982. By using the data from several decades of interviews and questionnaires, Yankelovich attempts to demonstrate how Americans' perspectives on life are changing. He identifies the shift from the self-denial perspective of the 1950s to the self-fulfillment perspective of the 1960s and 1970s. But instead of projecting a pessimistic future, he foresees the development of a new set of rules balancing personal freedom and responsibility.

Maya Pines. "The Civilizing of Genie." *Psychology Today,* 1981, 15:28–34. This article briefly describes Genie's life of isolation before she was "found" at age 13. Then it discusses the ways in which her development appeared to be permanently impaired and the ways in which intensive socialization efforts appeared to be successful.

Morris Rosenberg. *Conceiving the Self.* New York: Basic Books, 1979. A systematic treatment of how people's views of themselves (self-concepts) develop and change. Rosenberg uses research data on children and adolescents as well as adults to formulate his theory of self-concept. He discusses the ways in which society, through units such as neighborhoods, schools, and individuals (e.g., significant others), shapes our experiences and perceptions.

5

Deviance and Crime

A college student sneaks food from the cafeteria; after lunch she goes to the library and secretly removes a book she needs. Is the student a thief or a shoplifter, or is she normal because "everybody" does those things?

A doctor employed by the government has not repaid loans he received while in medical school. Should loan payments be deducted from his salary?

A person leaves a party after drinking and has an automobile accident. Should the driver's license be suspended? Should the party host be sued for damages for permitting the guest to become intoxicated?

A child does not return home from school because she has been kidnapped. Is such a kidnapping a crime if the kidnapper is her father who failed to obtain legal custody of her after his divorce?

A group gathers to protest the operation of an abortion clinic, carrying signs stating "abortion is murder" and blocking the entrance. Are they right? Is their behavior legal?

All of these activities are debated in the media because we do not agree about which of them are crimes. And even if we agreed about which are crimes, we may disagree about which of them should be punished and why.

During tight economic times an increasing number of people are forced to adopt deviant lifestyles, as this homeless woman has.

Sometimes we focus on deviant and criminal acts; at other times we focus on the people whose lives center around deviant or criminal acts. Homeless men gravitate to areas of cities where their deviance is tolerated—skid rows. Old ladies in large cities may live on the streets, carrying all their possessions in bags. These homeless "bag ladies" can be seen picking goods from trash containers. Should these deviant lifestyles be tolerated? Recently officials in some California cities have argued these people will not change but will simply relocate if pressured by police. Rather than trying to ignore their lifestyles, parks were created for their use. What would you do about homeless deviants?

Some people's lives are organized around criminal activities, such as members of organized crime "families." We seem to agree that organized crime should be eliminated, but we have had little success in doing so. How do you think we can prevent people from participating in organized crime activities that provide them with substantial incomes?

In this chapter we consider why some activities but not others are defined as deviant or criminal, and why some deviant and criminal activities but not others lead to punishment.

The Inevitability of Deviance

The question "Why is there deviance?" has a corollary, "Can deviance be eliminated?" Some functional theorists believe that actions can be taken to reduce or eliminate deviance. *Social control* can be exercised over people. People are more likely to deviate if the rewards associated with deviant activities are greater than the probable costs. Therefore such theorists argue that we need to make deviance less rewarding and to convince people that they very likely will receive punishments for deviating that are greater than any possible rewards. Other theorists believe deviance is an inevitable consequence of organized social life. Norms and laws and the mechanisms of social control used to punish those who violate them would not continue to exist if everyone shared the same beliefs about how to behave. Whatever the researchers' specific answers to the question "Why is there deviance?", there appears to be agreement that deviance can be rewarding or fun and monetarily beneficial. Yet researchers give different answers to the question "Can it be eliminated?"

Objective Approach

Structural and functional theorists approach deviance as a phenomenon that can be studied objectively. One of the founders of sociology, Durkheim, argued that suicide rates provide objective measures of social disintegration (1951). According to such theorists we can identify widely shared norms and values and instances of deviation from them.

If a society is functioning well, people who deviate are singled out for punishment ranging from gossip and scorn to excommunication and imprisonment. The punishment of violators or deviants is an important social activity, because it reaffirms the norms and values of a society. Also, social units need to identify and punish deviance to remind other people what happens to deviants. These are some of the ways in which deviance presumably serves the role of maintaining social norms. Sociologists also recognize that deviance may mark social change. As norms lose their functions for people, deviance may be one way to establish new norms.

Those who employ the objective approach try to identify the conditions that lead people to engage in deviance and the mechanisms whereby it is limited or controlled (Merton 1957). If society decreases the rewards for such activities and increases the likelihood of punishment for them, people will stop engaging in deviant activities. Therefore, researchers using the objective approach look at the official records of offenses and the official agents of social control to learn more about the characteristics of offenders.

Subjective Approach

Other theorists believe that deviance will never be eliminated, because nothing is inherently or innately deviant, that is, almost anything can be (and has been) designated as "deviant" by a human society. To support their argument they look at historical changes in activities designated as "deviant" as well as at cross-cultural differences in deviance. When Coca-Cola was originally developed, it contained cocaine. At that time, cocaine usage was not seen as deviant. But in the recent past it was viewed very negatively. Nevertheless today cocaine usage has again become acceptable among certain groups in our society. Examples like this support the idea that deviance is socially defined. A group of people must define an activity as deviant in order for it to be considered deviant. In other words, social norms provide the foundation for social deviance.

Those who believe deviance is subjectively or socially defined argue that deviance cannot be eliminated. In a monastery many deviant acts defined by the society at large may not even occur (getting drunk, reading pornography), but other norms may be violated. The expression "honor among thieves" suggests there are norms that even govern the relations among thieves. Since in any group there are norms, their very existence sets the stage for deviations from those norms.

Conflict Approach

Conflict theorists agree with the subjectivists that deviance is in the "eye of the beholder." However, instead of focusing on social psychological processes (how a person is affected by being categorized as deviant), they focus on why some acts rather than others are defined as deviant or criminal. Drawing on early social theorists such as Marx, these investigators focus on the conflicts between the interests of different groups within a society. Those groups that have power can establish laws and regulations (definitions of crime and deviance) that are to their advantage. As suggested in Chapter 6, Social Inequality, more public attention is directed to alleged welfare fraud than to how wealthy persons "milk the system" through questionable business practices and income tax dodges. Conflict theorists argue that the powerful are able to divert attention away from their activities and to conceal them in part by directing attention to the activities of others.

What can we learn about a society from studying the activities that the society designates as deviant?

Forms of Deviance

To be considered a deviant, a person must be perceived as violating social norms. But if every norm violation led to a person being labeled deviant, everyone would be a deviant in someone's eyes. Various mechanisms or processes govern our perceptions of norm violations and norm violators.

Primary versus Secondary Deviation

Edwin Lemert (1967) distinguishes between **primary deviation,** certain violations that we can overlook or "normalize," and **secondary deviation,** violations that appear to be an integral part of a person's lifestyle. In the case of primary deviation, we recognize what has happened, we see it as undesirable, but we believe it deserves to be excused. Adolescents who break into a community's swimming pool late at night and get caught and "let off" are often perceived as "cutting up"—a primary deviation. However, adolescents who are frequently in and out of reform school are caught up in secondary deviation. Regardless of what those adolescents do, the way people relate to them is shaped by whether society defines their deviance as primary or secondary.

Primary deviation violations of norms or rules that can be overlooked or normalized.

Secondary deviation violations that appear to be an integral part of a person's lifestyle.

Residual Rule-breaking

The norm violations that groups identify are indications of what behaviors they consider important. Designating certain behaviors "sexual misconduct," "insubordination," or "immature" provides group members and others with information about the group's perspective. Yet sometimes people know an act is wrong, a norm violation, although it does not fit into existing categories. Behavior that a group identifies as deviant but for which there is no label is

Gresham M. Sykes and David Matza (1957) propose that delinquents use various techniques to explain away or justify engaging in deviant activities: These are *techniques of neutralization*. Their goal was to show how juveniles can adhere to the values and beliefs dominant in our society and still engage in deviant behavior. Techniques of neutralization are used by all of us. They can be described in terms of the forms of deviance some students exhibit. Three of the techniques involve reinterpretation of the deviance itself: *denial of responsibility, denial of injury,* and *denial of the victim.* A student may explain missing an exam or handing in a paper late by denying responsibility, claiming that external circumstances that could not be controlled were responsible. Students who cheat on exams or assignments may tell themselves and their friends that cheating does not harm anyone, thereby denying injury. Or students may justify cheating by ignoring how it victimizes honest students (since it inflates grading curves) or by claiming that the teacher deserved to be misled for making the tests or assignments so hard.

The other techniques of neutralization consist of condemning the condemners and invoking higher loyalties. Students may focus on how the system presumably operates unfairly: People succeed by "buttering up" teachers, being lucky, and having inside information, rather than by their own actions. The final technique (higher loyalties) works less well with a student example; however, it can give us some insight as to why cheating is so rarely reported. When asked why they do not report cheating when they see it, students often respond that they would not "rat" on a fellow student.

called **residual rule-breaking** (Scheff 1966). Residual rule-breaking may lead to a person being designated mentally ill.

Residual rule-breaking deviance that a group identifies as a violation but for which it has no label.

Norm Variability

Laws specifying criminal behavior are somewhat similar throughout the United States, but there is considerably less agreement about norms. In fact, some behaviors that may be considered deviant in one group may be normative in another. The clothing and behavior normatively prescribed for "preppies" would be considered deviant for "druggies."

If we associate with people like ourselves (those who share our norms), we may be viewed as normal or "straight." But if we associate with other groups, we may be seen as deviant or "crooked." Our behavior must be apparent or known to those who disapprove of it in order for us to be defined as deviant. Therefore, we may avoid being considered deviant by controlling our associations with others. If we do not have the freedom to select our associates, still we may avoid the deviant label through other means.

In San Francisco the gay subculture sponsors parades such as the one in which these bikers are preparing to participate.

Overt versus Covert Activities

We may conceal or reveal our activities or engage in **covert deviance** or **overt deviance.** If some people disapprove and others approve of our activities, we may conceal them from the first set of people but reveal them to the second set. Men who dress as women (transvestites) are generally seen as strange or deviant. Yet research on sexual and gender identity reveals that transvestism is more common than many people would expect; it is simply concealed from them. A male transvestite may tell no one of his "cross dressing," or perhaps only his wife knows. Some transvestites participate in organized activities for transvestites (dress-up contests) that may be more or less hidden from the general public.

If a behavior is strongly disapproved, people may have a greater incentive to conceal that behavior than a less disapproved behavior. Yet to conceal such an activity often makes it more difficult to engage in it. The expression "come out of the closet" is often used to refer to homosexuals who decide to let other people know their sexual preference. Although some people may no longer like them, they also no longer have to worry about being uncovered, and they are free to go out with others of their sex and to openly patronize homosexual establishments. For some homosexuals the solution may be to become overt after moving to an area or community where homosexuality is tolerated or at least less disapproved (such as San Francisco).

Covert deviance violations concealed from those who would disapprove of it.

Overt deviance violations that are generally visible.

Deviant Subcultures

Some theorists propose that societies contain **subcultures** that have norms and values different from those that prevail in the mainstream culture. People who are perceived as deviant by mainstream standards may band together and form a subculture to support or facilitate their activities. Therefore, there may be a homosexual subculture in San Francisco, swinging subcultures in cities of all sizes, and relatively isolated nudist colonies around the country. It is also true that some subcultures may have existed before their members' views or activities were labeled as deviant. Before passage of federal legislation in 1937, people could legally use marijuana in the United States.

At one time some theorists proposed that deviants endorsed the values and norms of subcultures and that subcultures with their deviant norms and values should therefore be eliminated. Other theorists such as Robert K. Merton (1957) pointed out that deviants may share the same goals and values that predominate in mainstream society, but they may lack the legitimate means to attain them. Today the subculture argument is seldom used to explain why persons initially engage in deviant activities. Societal reaction or labeling theorists believe they can account for why deviant subcultures sometimes form specifically through the concept of *deviant career*. According to these theorists people's lives are shaped by how people label them, by social reactions to them.

Subculture units within societies that have some norms and values different from those that prevail in the mainstream culture.

Deviant Careers

Just as people have occupational careers, they may also have **deviant careers.** Analyses of deviant careers often focus on how people get "pushed" into secondary deviance and thus into deviant careers. The difficulties people encounter when they try to disassociate themselves from former deviant careers are examined also. Labeling theorists focus on the limited control people have over beginning and ending their deviant careers.

The *first stage* in a deviant career occurs when people perceive that a person has broken some norm(s). In fact, a person may not necessarily have violated the norm. The key is that people *believe* that a norm has been violated. Therefore, a person may break norms but not begin a deviant career *if* other people are unaware of or choose to ignore the norm violations.

A study of adolescent boys in one community points out the fatefulness of people's perceptions (Chambliss 1973). Boys from respected families were considered "good boys" even though they engaged in many deviant activities to a greater degree than another group of boys labeled as delinquents. The "good boys" missed school but were polite to teachers and provided excuses. Many of their deviant actions were committed in other communities because they had access to cars. On the other hand, the "roughnecks" did not create favorable impressions with the teachers or police, and their deviant activities were visible to the local community because they didn't have cars. One group

Deviant career the stages a person may pass through in accepting the deviant label.

was labeled deviant, but not the other, even though they committed the same kinds of deviant acts.

The *second stage* occurs when a person is stereotyped as deviant. The person is seen not as an ordinary person who has done something deviant, but rather as a deviant person who is expected to engage in all sorts of deviance. In stage one, Mary may be seen as deviant for doing eccentric things. She moves to the second stage if people assume that she is basically eccentric or crazy, and they expect that all or most of her actions will fit the stereotype of deviance.

Once people are typed, they may become more visible to *agents of social control* (social service workers or police) and enter a *third stage.* Identification as a deviant by agents of social control means that official records will be kept and the person's activities will be monitored. Then more people may "type" a person as a deviant once they learn that the person is being observed by the official agents of social control.

Many people are concerned about the effects of record keeping on a person's chances to ever free himself or herself of the deviant label. Juveniles are often treated differently from adult offenders in attempts to keep them from being labeled for life as deviants. When a crime is reported in the newspaper, the names of all adult offenders are listed, but not those of their juvenile accomplices. Some states have procedures whereby records are erased or expunged after a period of time so that there no longer is any record of a person's former deviant activity.

Some people find it difficult to escape the negative consequences of formerly being treated as deviant. Employment applications often ask if a person has served in the armed services and about the nature of his or her discharge. A number of young Viet Nam war veterans received "bad paper" when they left the service. They did not receive a dishonorable discharge, but they did not receive fully honorable discharges either (they received general or undesirable discharges). They believe that this "bad paper" currently limits their opportunities to obtain jobs and are trying to have their discharges upgraded.

In the *fourth stage,* a person's associations with other deviants are increased and those with nondeviants are weakened. One of the reasons juveniles are sent to special detention facilities rather than to prisons is to keep them from being exposed to hardened criminals. However, when persons labeled deviant (delinquent, criminal, mentally ill) enter a "treatment" program, they are thrown into association with other people labeled as deviants, and they have proportionately less time and opportunity to spend with people not similarly labeled.

Organizations such as Alcoholics Anonymous try to make this association with other deviants a strength rather than a weakness. They encourage their members to identify themselves as alcoholics, to recognize they are different from other people (regarding susceptibility to alcohol) and to associate with one another (to provide one another with social support). Harrison Trice and Paul Roman (1970) argue that such activities help members of the organization to delabel or relabel themselves.

For many other deviants, however, being thrown together with other deviants encourages or provides them the means to engage in further deviant activities. Other people not so labeled may shun deviants, leaving them with few "straight" associates. Some parents may not mind their children hanging around with people who are called "wild," but they probably would object to their children being with people officially labeled juvenile delinquents. People who have been in mental institutions often find other people are uncomfortable interacting with them.

The *fifth stage* occurs when the "deviant" person embraces that role and its identity. In other words, an individual decides that he or she *is* that type of person and engages in secondary deviation. The deviant career involves a "self-fulfilling prophecy" through which people's reactions to a presumed deviant lead that person to become what others (the defining group) thought or prophesized.

Theorists who use the labeling perspective emphasize the functions of others' perceptions and actions (the societal reaction in the process of making a deviant), and they also recognize that many people may go through some, but not all, of the stages *and* that some people may pursue deviance because they want to and *not* because others forced them (either purposely or inadvertently). Therefore, societal reaction may explain the career of a young runaway (a status offender) who becomes a member of a deviant or criminal subculture, but it cannot explain as easily why some adults rationally decide to pursue careers as criminals.

So far, we have loosely differentiated deviance (norm violation) from crime (violations of the law). The deviant career framework serves as a bridge, however, because the framework may be used to explain either deviant or criminal careers.

The Prevalence of Crime

The media regularly report that crime has increased or decreased, but sociologists are much more cautious about discussing crime and crime rates. **Crime** occurs when criminal laws are violated. Many crimes are not known because they are well concealed. Other crimes are ignored because the laws do not have popular support or their violation is considered unimportant. Sociologists who study crime, **criminologists,** are interested in how laws are made and enforced as well as in who commits crimes and why. They recognize that the creation and enforcement of laws reflects who does and does not have power in a society.

Yet agencies of social control, the media, and the general public are interested primarily in how much crime occurs and what happens to the people who commit it. Therefore, considerable attention is directed to **crime**

Crime activities that violate criminal laws.

Criminologist a social scientist who studies how laws are created and enforced as well as who commits crimes and why.

Crime rate frequency with which activities defined as crimes occur in society.

CONTROVERSIAL ISSUES · When Is an Act Criminal?

Our society believes people should be held responsible for their acts; however, we sometimes believe people cannot or should not be held responsible for them. Juveniles are treated differently from adults because we perceive they may not have understood the consequences of their actions and we desire to protect them. In general, we believe people must be capable of the rational thought processes of an adult to be responsible for their actions. Thus, people who are severely mentally retarded should not be processed through the criminal justice system for stealing, because they cannot understand abstract concepts like owning and stealing.

At times some cases raise public concern about such differential treatment, such as when adolescents beat elderly people to death. Occasionally such juveniles are tried as adults, thereby making them subject to more severe punishment.

In recent years, public debate has centered on the special treatment accorded adults judged mentally incompetent or insane. Psychologists may be called on to certify whether or not a person is competent to stand trial. A person must be judged capable of understanding the legal proceedings in order for a case to be tried in court.

The question of sanity is raised in terms of guilt or innocence. Defendents may plead guilty or not guilty, or they may try to present a defense that indicates they were "not guilty by reason of insanity." In other words, they argue that they were insane and not responsible for their acts when they committed them. John Hinkley, a man filmed attempting to assassinate President Reagan, was subsequently tried in court and found not guilty by reason of insanity. When that verdict was announced, there was a public outcry about people escaping justice by pleading insanity. Those opposed to the verdict pointed out that after a few years a person formerly judged insane could be judged sane and released. Should such people be released or should they be tried for their crimes when later judged sane? Those who supported the merits of permitting insanity defenses pointed out that only a very small percentage of criminal cases are resolved with verdicts of "not guilty by reason of insanity." Should we imprison disturbed people for activities committed when they were not sane?

rates, the frequency with which crime occurs in a society. The agencies of social control focus on crime rates as evidence that they are doing their job or that they need more money to do their job. And the public wants to know how likely it is that it will be victimized.

In order to discuss crime rates, we must differentiate types of crimes. One distinction is made between less serious law violations, **misdemeanors,** and more serious law violations, **felonies.** Felonies are further divided into

Misdemeanor a less serious crime that results in a sentence of less than one year in prison.

Felony a more serious crime that leads to sentences of more than one year in prison.

property crimes (larceny, burglary, auto theft) and **violent crimes** (rape, homicide, assault, robbery) or crimes against the person. Discussions of crime rates tend to focus on felonies and to use the Federal Bureau of Investigation (FBI) index of major crimes (which includes those listed in parentheses in the previous sentence).

Property crime a crime that involves the illicit taking, removing, or damaging of a victim's property.

Official Statistics

After we decide what acts should be called a crime, we must gather data about them. The FBI produces an annual document entitled the **Uniform Crime Report** (UCR). Individual law enforcement agencies contribute information to the FBI about the incidence of crime in their areas. These are the data frequently reported by the media.

Violent crime a crime in which the victim is physically threatened or harmed.

These statistics are often questioned; the information sent to the FBI is not always completely accurate because of variations in local record keeping and reporting practices. Some agencies have limited funds and staff available for record-keeping activities. Also, there is wide latitude in the reporting, recording, and prosecuting of various offenses. We are all familiar with the discretion exercised in the treatment of minor violations such as traffic offenses. At times the police may engage in slowdowns and issue few citations in order to make a political point, or the police may ticket people for violations they ordinarily would overlook. Regarding criminal offenses, local politicians running for reelection may emphasize the elimination of prostitution and narcotic trafficking. In such communities the reported rates of prostitution and drug arrests may increase temporarily even though there may be no actual increases in prostitution and drug sales.

Uniform Crime Report annual summary of official crime statistics that local agencies report to the Federal Bureau of Investigation.

Another question raised about official statistics is that they reflect biases based on social class. Some researchers believe that lower-class persons' activities are more visible to agents of social control. Therefore, their official rates of crime are higher than those of people from higher social classes. Other researchers argue that police spend less time and energy helping lower-class people settle disputes, and so their criminal activities are underreported. The debate about class differences in delinquent and criminal activities persists because we lack conclusive data to resolve it.

If the official rate of crime rises, has crime necessarily increased?

Self-Reports

Data about crime are collected in at least two additional ways: by asking people what crimes they have suffered and by asking them what criminal or deviant activities they have committed. **Victimization studies** report crimes people may or may not have reported to official agencies generally; such reports usually indicate *higher* levels of crime than FBI statistics. The annual National Crime Surveys produced by the U.S. Bureau of the Census also report

Victimization studies reports based on self-reports of crimes (reported or unreported) by persons who were the victims.

victimization data. **Self-report data** on commission of deviant or criminal activities are usually collected by social scientists who have access to some group of persons. Researchers may ask high school students to indicate which of a wide range of criminal and noncriminal activities they have committed.

Generally researchers believe that crime is underreported by official statistics, and so they often emphasize these other sources of data. However, even these sources have weaknesses or drawbacks. Any time we rely on a person's own reports of activities, we can anticipate errors in perception, problems of recall, and questions about their willingness to be open and honest. Even if researchers assure respondents that the researchers will not let anyone know what illegal activities the respondents self-report, the respondents may be reluctant to disclose them. Presumably victims have fewer reasons to hide what happened to them, so victimization studies are often presumed to be the most accurate indicators of actual levels of crime.

We may question *why* victims do not always officially report crimes. They may not want to spend the time or suffer the publicity. In some cases they may be embarrassed to talk about certain crimes (such as rape or incest). Or they may believe that nothing will happen even if they *do* report the crimes (that the police will be ineffective, local prosecutors will not pursue the case, or the courts will dismiss the case or mete out a light sentence). It is unlikely that all crimes are reported in any society, although some highly visible, serious crimes such as homicide are more likely to be reported than are crimes against property.

Interpreting Crime Rates

For over a decade researchers have attempted to relate crime rates to economic and political conditions. Colin Loftin and David McDowall (1982) recently attempted to specify fully such a theory and to test it with data from Detroit, Michigan. Economic theories of crime assume that people who desire protection from crime desire a state of social optimization in which the losses from crime, including the costs involved in fighting crime, are kept at the lowest level that works. The theory is as follows: Potential offenders are more likely to commit crimes when the rewards from crime appear high and the likelihood of punishment low. Potential victims are moved to action (specifically, efforts to increase law enforcement activities) whenever they perceive threats increasing. The potential victims then seek to elect government officials who promote "law and order" and emphasize more law enforcement. Once these politicians take action by increasing law enforcement activities, potential offenders see the increased likelihood of punishment and do not commit crime. As a result, the crime rate decreases.

Loftin and McDowall compared the number of police per 1,000 residents (a measure of police strength) and crime rates in Detroit from 1926–1977. They did not find support for their economic theory of crime. Although economic factors may be important, this particular theory appears too simple.

David Greenberg and Ronald Kessler (1982) examined a related argu-

Self-report data reports by a sample of people who list deviant activities they engaged in.

ment. Do higher arrest rates deter people from committing crimes? Rather than using data from one city over a long period of time, they examined data from 98 American cities over a specific period of time, 1964–1970. They found that increases in the number of reported crimes cleared by police (those cases closed, typically by arrests) did not lead to lower rates of crime. Greenberg and Kessler suggest that either greater changes in clearance rates or other changes such as the implementation of more severe sanctions may have to occur in order for crime rates to decrease.

Gender and Crime

Overall, rates of juvenile delinquency and criminal behavior are higher for males than for females, although females historically have been more likely than males to be charged with certain forms of sexual misconduct, such as promiscuity. Researchers have frequently asked if males are innately disposed to delinquent activities, if females are socially constrained from engaging in such activities, and if society is less likely to identify most forms of female misbehavior. Self-report studies of youths in the general population indicate that male and female delinquent behavior is more similar than official rates would indicate, although they are still somewhat different (Clark and Haurek 1966).

Sociobiological Explanations

Theorists who believe that there are some basic differences between males and females that account for the differences in their rates of crime focus on sociobiological and in some cases psychological explanations. Some theorists have examined the levels of the male hormone, testosterone, and tried to relate higher levels of this hormone to aggressive behavior. Others seeking sociobiological explanations were intrigued when it was found that some men in prisons were genetically abnormal in that they had an extra Y chromosome (that is, they had an XYY structure instead of XY). Sociobiological explanations of female crime focus on a premenstrual tension syndrome that produces severe symptoms in a limited percentage of women. In two separate British cases reported in the news, charges against women were changed from murder to manslaughter with arguments based on the effects of the premenstrual tension syndrome.

The problem with existing sociobiological explanations is that we do not have adequate data to explain why *all* men with high levels of testosterone or XYY chromosome structures do not engage in aggressive behavior or criminal activities *or* why all women who are afflicted by severe premenstrual tension do not engage in rule violations. Furthermore, many people who *do not* have these physiological characteristics *do* engage in unacceptable behavior: A man with a high level of testosterone may assault someone, but another man with a low level may also assault someone.

Other researchers focus on psychological differences between males and females, arguing that males are more oriented to risk taking and thrill seeking than are females (Sandhu and Irving 1974). The saying "boys will be boys" suggests that boys naturally are going to get into some trouble (that is, it's their nature). Some persons have theorized that girls who get into trouble with the law are probably more masculine than other girls, but they could only explain why *some* girls got into the same kinds of scrapes or trouble as boys. Other researchers point out that girls tend to get into trouble involving different kinds of activities compared with boys; they engage in "feminine" forms of deviance (running away, being incorrigible, or engaging in sexual promiscuity). Therefore, these researchers propose that female criminals and deviants follow the female role when they go wrong, such as being led astray by a man they love or being impulsive shoplifters. In brief, their feminine characteristics get them into trouble. Today, the prevalence of less traditional conceptions of female behavior have led many researchers to seek explanations other than these.

Stereotypes

Justice ideally is blind, but social scientists recognize that all people are not treated the same way by the criminal justice system. These social scientists examine the treatment of people from different groups (socioeconomic groups, racial groups, age groups).

Rates of promiscuity for juvenile females are higher than for males. Are females more likely to engage in sexual misconduct, or are they more likely than males to be reported for such behavior? At every stage of the process, beginning with the likelihood that people will report misconduct, there may be systematic differences in treatment.

If our society as a whole views females as more delicate and in need of greater protection that males, then those people involved in the criminal justice system are also likely to be influenced by those views. Officials would be less likely to suspect a female of engaging in a deviant or criminal activity or to want her to become involved in the criminal justice system. When a female is charged with an offense, are the charges more likely to be dropped? Would a judge dismiss her case or suspend her sentence so that she would not be sent to a correctional facility?

Some persons have argued that females may receive harsher treatment than males. Statutes governing male juvenile offenses concern offenses that would be punishable for adults, whereas female juveniles may be committed to institutions for *status* offenses (such as immorality) that are not offenses for adults (Chesney-Lind 1974). "Bad girls" have violated gender norms, and people may believe they are bad examples who deserve severe punishment. Juvenile females are less likely to appear before judges, but when they do, they are more likely to be institutionalized.

Female Crime Rate Increases

In the 1970s books and articles appeared that directed our attention to changes in the types and frequency of female delinquent and criminal activities. In this literature the women's movement was sometimes seen as stimulating change in the female role and thereby indirectly stimulating women to engage in different behavior, including delinquent and criminal behavior. It is difficult, however, to assign these shifts to a single factor such as the women's movement.

Since World War II women's roles have been changing because of increasing opportunities for employment, the rising divorce rate, and changing attitudes about sexual behavior. The women's movement has generated greater public awareness of the plight of women and their desire for greater changes; but the movement did not initiate those changes nor the observed increases in rates of female criminal behavior.

Changes in females' roles provided them with new freedoms and opportunities to achieve both legitimate and illegitimate goals and to engage in legal as well as nonlegal activities. As it became more acceptable for women to be outside the home (such as going to bars without a male escort), they were less supervised and therefore potentially less constrained in their actions. This argument suggests that women will be as "bad" as men, given the chance. Since females do not engage in the same patterns of criminal activity as males, it cannot account for all rate changes, although females still do not have all of the same opportunities as males.

Other explanations focus on how the changing roles of women have led officials in the courts to treat them in new ways or more like males. If females no longer remain in the home and play the traditional female roles, the "protections" they received from the harsh realities of the criminal justice system may be removed. Police may focus more attention on the criminal activities of women, or they may treat female accomplices as they would male accomplices. Judges may be less inclined to "protect" female defendants, and they may make them subject to the same penalties as males. At least two reasons for rate increases may result from a single phenomenon, namely, the *changed perceptions of females:* (1) law enforcement officials may become more aware of female criminal activities, and (2) the judicial system may no longer protect them by dismissing cases or suspending sentences.

We do not know what will happen to rates of female crime and delinquency in the future, although they probably will increase to some extent because of the changes in females' opportunities and the changes in attitudes toward female offenders. Our theories for the most part are based on male offenders, so until we develop either general theories that apply equally to females and males or better theories of female criminality, our predictive powers will be limited.

The examination of female/male differences points out some of the ways in which perceptions of and responses to criminal activity vary for different categories of persons. Other questions about the operation of our legal system are addressed in Chapter 15.

The Social Costs

Discussions of deviance and crime usually focus on how these activities harm society by threatening the status quo. In other words, they are seen as threatening to the maintenance of social order and organized social life. Yet they do serve to remind people about the rules and in that sense reaffirm the social order. Whatever the positive and negative consequences for the society as a whole, we also need to consider how deviance and crime affect specific individuals or groups.

Crimes without Victims

People in a society may disagree about whether certain activities lead to negative consequences for the society or individuals. Some people who engage in certain activities that carry criminal penalties complain that when there are no victims, when no harm is done to anyone by those activities, those activities are unfairly classified as criminal. Others argue in a practical vein that the activities are not likely to disappear (people value them), and since they only "harm" those who elect to engage in them, why make them criminal? For example, prostitution involves the purchase of a service. Although such transactions are illegal, advocates of **decriminalization** ask, "Who is the victim?" (see Box, p. 112). Other people question laws about pornography, arguing that no one has to purchase it if they do not want to. Still other groups, such as NORML, believe that individuals should have the right to decide about their own use of marijuana. Sociologists refer to criminal activities that people voluntarily do and that allegedly harm no one but themselves as **crimes without victims** (Shur 1965).

Decriminalization removal of criminal penalties for engaging in an activity.

Crimes without victims crimes that the "victim" and "perpetrator" willingly engage in and that involve no loss of property or personal injury.

In some instances, people argue that greater harm is done by maintaining the criminal status of such activities than would occur with decriminalization. In the case of prostitution it is argued that public licensing rather than criminal prosecution of prostitutes would designate the areas in which they could work, limit connections with organized crime, and provide a means for maintaining health standards. Those who resist decriminalization tend to focus on how prostitution undermines the ideal linkages between love-marriage-sexual activity.

Costs to Victims

At times our prosecution and incarceration of criminals seem to serve the society but not necessarily the specific victims of criminal activity. People do not like to think that they may be victims of crime, and so we often do not think about the victim as much as we do about protecting *ourselves* from the perpetrator. Do you believe that a rape victim should have to pay for the medical tests necessary as evidence in a trial? Various legal changes have made it less costly (emotionally) for rape victims to pursue their cases in court, such as exclusion of evidence about prior sexual activity. Yet for the

CONTROVERSIAL ISSUES · Politics and the Decriminalization of Marijuana Use

The debate over decriminalization of individual's use of marijuana points out many of the political and legal questions involved in defining crimes.

When the Committee on Substance Abuse and Habitual Behavior turned in its study of marijuana laws, the National Academy of Sciences president flatly disavowed its recommendations, and the academy brushed it aside in the apparent hope it would fade away for lack of attention. The reason: the committee urged that the possession or private use of small amounts of marijuana should no longer be a crime.

The committee's assignment was to look at the fiscal and social costs of enforcing criminal laws against marijuana use. And it found those costs too high. Tough laws do not appear to deter marijuana use, said the committee, noting that in states without such statutes there seems to have been no "appreciable" increase in pot smoking. In addition, those states have lower costs of enforcement. The committee also cited the contempt that many young people have for the law because it imposes such different sanctions on the use of alcohol and pot.

The report may have ignored the temper of the times. Ten years ago the public was moving toward the idea of lighter punishment for marijuana users. A 1972 study by the National Commission on Marijuana and Drug Abuse concluded that criminal sanctions were failing and counterproductive. Over the next six years, eleven states decriminalized pot possession for individual use, while many others decreased penalties or loosened up their enforcement. But by the late '70s the mood began to swing back. With an estimated 60% of high school seniors having tried pot, and the drug making inroads at elementary schools, frightened parents dissuaded legislators from further liberalization.

Whatever the public climate, committee members stood by their conclusions last week. The official potshot at the report has brought it attention it might not otherwise have received—a self-defeating result that is somewhat analogous to the committee's view that prohibitions on marijuana use are self-defeating for U.S. society.

SOURCE: *Time,* July 19, 1982.

victims of many crimes, the time and emotional stress of participating in the trial is only one set of costs, since the crime itself has already caused them considerable loss—either of property or physical or emotional health.

In many cases there is no restitution, replacement, or return of property. One problem is that the criminal courts only determine whether or not a person is guilty, whereas civil courts provide the setting for adjudicating claims of losses or damages to person or property. Some states have devised **victim**

Victim compensation laws laws that provide that victims should be repaid for their losses suffered in a crime.

compensation laws (see Box, p. 114). But it is difficult to extract compensation from someone who is in prison.

Blaming the Victim

In some cases, victims of crime not only suffer at the hands of criminals but also from the actions and reactions of the justice system and the public at large. In the discussion on gender in Chapter 8, we point out that victims of rape are sometimes considered at fault for being raped. If a woman is out late at night alone and raped, some will argue that the rape was her own fault because she should have known better than to be out late at night. This phenomenon of treating a victim as if responsible for being harmed is called **blaming the victim.** If a person picks up a hitchhiker and is later robbed by that hitchhiker, many people blame the victim for being foolish.

The formulation by Daniel Lerner (1975) of the "just world hypothesis" helps us to understand why we sometimes blame the victims. Many of us like to believe that people get what they deserve. If we were forced to see that anyone could be the victim of some crimes, that there was nothing we could do to protect ourselves, then we could no longer feel secure that this is a just world. Since we prefer to believe our world is fair, we have to explain or account for why bad things happen to people. In the case of the hitchhiker's victim or the rapist's victim, we may argue that the crime could have been prevented by the victims. But, why do we blame the victims rather than those who harmed them?

Blaming the victim the attribution to the victim of blame for letting the crime occur.

Bystander Intervention

In some large cities women stopped in heavy traffic in their cars have become the victims of youths who smash their car windows and grab their handbags. Often people in nearby cars do nothing to aid the victims. Ever since the case of Kitty Genovese was reported in the media, social scientists have been trying to determine whether or when bystanders will intervene to help someone in trouble. (People heard Genovese's screams but did not help her so that her attacker scared off at one time was able to come back and murder the injured woman.)

Various experiments reveal more about why people do *not* intervene than why they do (Latané and Darley 1970; Mynatt and Sherman 1975; Marber and Shaver 1981). If other people are present, such as other people in cars stalled in traffic, each individual is less likely to try to aid someone whose car window is being smashed than when he or she is the only bystander. The phenomenon is called **diffusion of responsibility,** where no one person feels responsible for acting.

Although diffusion of responsibility accounts for many cases of nonintervention, people may also be afraid that they cannot help or that helping someone else will cause problems for themselves. After some cases in which people were sued for damages for problems resulting from their attempts to

Diffusion of responsibility the tendency for no one to feel responsible for acting when there are others present.

CONTROVERSIAL ISSUES · Victim Compensation

"They explained the defendant's constitutional rights to the nth degree. And I, the victim, wondered what mine were. And they told me I haven't got any."

Victims not only suffer financial losses but must often pay for the treatment of injuries. They may be intimidated and threatened by defendants free on bail. They can be browbeaten by defense lawyers, forced to show up repeatedly as witnesses in hearings that are frequently postponed. It may take months to regain stolen—and badly needed—property kept as evidence.

Now the President's Task Force on Victims of Crime has put together a package of recommendations that could begin to redress this unconscionable imbalance.

Among the least controversial proposals, the task force urges state and federal legislation to require that victim impact statements be presented to the court before sentencing. That victims of sexual assault not have to pay for physical exams and medical kits used to collect evidence.

"The state paid for both the defense and the prosecution. I had to find a way to pay the $12,000 this crime cost us."

The task force comes out strongly for federal funding for state victim compensation programs. Thirty-six states now have at least token funds for victims, but almost all are inadequately financed.

Hospitals should be required to give emergency treatment to crime victims without regard to their ability to pay, then collect from state compensation funds, the task force recommends. It says judges should order offenders to make restitution to victims whenever possible.

"The man who molested my little girl shattered our lives. She may never truly recover. He only served 10 days in the county jail."

There should be more referral and counseling services for victims, involving not only social agencies but the mental health community and the ministry, the report says. Victims should get police protection if necessary in instances of harassment.

The task force also makes several highly controversial proposals: That bail be denied to persons judged to be clearly dangerous. That parole be abolished (because it undercuts the courts and is unfair to victims and because parole boards lack accountability).

Finally, the task force proposes an amendment to the Constitution that would add the following to the Sixth Amendment: "The victim in every criminal prosecution shall have the right to be present and to be heard at all critical stages of judicial proceedings."

Congress made a start with its Omnibus Victims Protection Act of 1982. As the report makes clear, much more must be done before our system of justice can claim to be just to those who should be its primary concern.

SOURCE: *Chicago Tribune,* February 7, 1983.

aid victims (as in accidents), some states passed "good samaritan" laws designed to protect people who were trying to be helpful. In cases of domestic disputes, bystanders may be afraid that they cannot help or that they may be harmed by the people engaged in the dispute.

As our society became more concerned about the incidence of child abuse, questions were raised about why other family members, neighbors, teachers, and doctors who saw the child did not report the situation. Since neighbors were sometimes apprehensive about getting in trouble with the child's family for reporting abuse, communities set up mechanisms whereby the identity of the reporting individual could be protected. In the case of professionals, states passed laws requiring them to report cases of suspected abuse.

We are more concerned about preventing some crimes than others, just as we are more concerned about helping some victims than others. These differences reflect perceptions about the threat to others and the seriousness of the offense, as well as the visibility of the offense. Employees who take home supplies from work for personal use may be seen as normal. Employers

CONTROVERSIAL ISSUES · Who Should Have Guns?

Many people argue that Americans have the right to own guns because the Constitution guarantees our right to bear arms. Others believe that the Constitution was intended to protect our freedoms, not to create a country of armed citizens. We generally seem to expect our police, even sometimes our campus police, to carry guns, although in England police officers traditionally have not carried guns.

Those who believe citizens have the right to own guns claim various reasons for their position besides constitutional guarantees. Gun collectors and hunters want to be able to pursue their leisure time activities. Others argue that people need guns to protect themselves, saying that if it were against the law to own guns, the only people who would have guns would be the lawbreakers. Thus, they argue, innocent citizens would be more vulnerable to lawbreakers.

Proponents of gun control argue that many senseless murders could be prevented if there were fewer guns handy. They point out that people can easily purchase cheap handguns, the "Saturday night specials" that are involved in too many murders. They sometimes draw on the police to support their argument that guns kept for protection may lead to harm. The guns may be stolen by criminals and even may be used to murder their owners. Or in the case of a dispute among relatives or friends, people may harm or kill one another if lethal weapons are available.

In the 1980s a Midwestern community and a Southern community both received considerable media attention. One outlawed guns (people had to turn them in), and the other required all its citizens to have guns. What do you think we should do?

may budget for a certain level of employee theft by passing the costs on to consumers. Also, we seem to take for granted that there will be some corruption in government, especially since the Watergate scandal and the Abscam cases. Technological innovations have generated categories of crime that do not fit existing laws, such as the theft of computer time. Criminologists are increasingly studying the phenomenon called *corporate crime.* Although sociologists tend to focus on crimes committed by and for corporations, it appears that corporations are more successful in pressing criminal charges than are individual victims (Hagan 1982).

Corporate Crime

In our postindustrial society people increasingly are employed by large organizations (corporations and governments). Several decades ago sociologists such as Edwin H. Sutherland (1961) argued that criminologists must examine patterned or organized crime within organizations—**white collar crime.** Sociologists have struggled to develop the appropriate tactics (and terminology) for investigating crime within organizations.

White collar crime the term initially used to designate patterns of criminal activity within organizations.

When corporations engage in illegal actions, it is often difficult for individuals to know that they are victims of corporate crime. And even if they do know it, it is legally difficult to pursue such cases. Consumer advocate Ralph Nader first attained widespread public attention in the 1960s for his attack on the automobile industry for producing cars "unsafe at any speed." Subsequent criticisms of the Pinto in the 1970s centered on who knew about the problems that sometimes resulted from rear-end collisions. Did people in positions of power in the company know about the problems and do nothing about them or even conceal them? The Ford Motor Company settled a number of Pinto cases out of court, thereby making it more difficult for the general public to determine guilt or innocence.

Sociologist Harvey Farberman's (1975) study of the automobile industry points out some of the problems we have when deciding who, if anybody, in an organization is guilty of a punishable crime. He utilized the concept of a "criminogenic market structure." Economic policies set at the top of a concentrated industry such as automobile manufacture may push lower-level participants to engage in criminal activities. Car dealers, for instance, may cope with narrow profit margins on new cars by making fraudulent warrantee claims or by engaging in service repair fraud. Those at the top have not violated any laws, but they have created conditions that stimulate illegal activities among those squeezed by their policies.

Conflict theorists such as Richard Quinney (1979) point out that structures, particularly our capitalist economy, produce crime. Of course, white-collar deviance exists in noncapitalistic societies as well, but different conflicts of interest may underlie it.

In any industrial or postindustrial society, whether the crime is called white collar, corporate, or organizational, criminologists focus on law violations that occur within work settings. Increasingly criminologists focus on how criminal actions are learned and reinforced as standard operating procedures

Technological advances have generated new forms of crime, such as the theft of computer time.

within organizations, rather than on how an individual in an organization commits a criminal act such as embezzlement.

Summary

There are two basic approaches to the study of deviance. Objectivists believe certain actions are deviant and that through proper efforts deviance could be eliminated. Subjectivists argue deviance is socially defined and exists in every group, for every group has norms that can be violated (deviated from).

We can engage in some norm violations (primary deviation) without being labeled deviant. If deviant activities appear to be an integral part of our lives, then we are involved in secondary deviation. Sometimes people are labeled mentally ill for doing things that are seen as "just not right," which is called "residual rule-breaking."

Depending on who observes our activities, we may be seen as either normal or deviant.

People sometimes conceal their deviance from those who would disapprove of it (covert deviance). A person may also decide to engage openly in deviant acts (overt deviance). Participation in a deviant subculture may encourage people to be more open or overt in their activities.

People typically do not suddenly engage in full-time deviant or criminal lifestyles. Rather they go through deviant career stages. Societal reaction theorists emphasize the importance of others' perceptions to the evolution of many deviant careers, although they recognize deviant careers may proceed in other ways.

Our legal system differentiates various types of crimes (misdemeanors and felonies). The FBI compiles information about official rates of commission for a set of crimes. Critics believe official statistics do not accurately represent the extent of crime in our society. Victimization studies and self-report studies of deviant or criminal behavior are used to provide a more complete picture of law breaking in our society.

Males consistently have had higher delinquency and crime rates than females, although female rates have increased over the past two decades. Some theorists provide arguments from nature (innate physiological or psychological differences are responsible); others propose arguments from nurture (males and females learn different roles, have different social opportunities, are perceived differently by agents of social control). Female rates probably will continue to increase for a while because of prevailing changes in societal conditions.

Although the literature on deviance and crime focuses on violation of societal norms and laws, deviant and criminal acts may violate specific persons—the victims. Some crimes appear to be victimless, in that there were no unwilling participants. Yet many crimes involve real loss for which victims typically are not reimbursed or compensated. At times victims suffer further when other people blame them for serving as victims.

Social psychologists are interested in factors that keep people from helping one another or intervening in criminal acts. One problem is the diffusion of responsibility.

Criminologists are trying to develop better terminology and procedures for studying patterns of crime in corporations or organizations. In postindustrial society we truly need more information about corporate crime.

Suggested Readings

Howard S. Becker (Ed.). *The Other Side.* New York: Free Press, 1964. A collection of essays which reaffirmed the importance of studying deviance in its social context.

Jack D. Douglas and Frances Waksler. *The Sociology of Deviance.* Boston: Little, Brown and Co., 1982. Various levels of explanation of deviance are examined. And forms of deviance often focused on in our society (sexual, substance use) are analyzed.

William M. Kephart. *Extraordinary Groups,* 2nd ed. New York: St. Martin's, 1982. At the same time members of deviant groups violate the norms of mainstream society, they typically are following the norms of their deviant groups. The beliefs and customs of various extraordinary groups (the Shakers, the old order Amish, the Hutterites) are examined in this book.

PART TWO

Social Inequalities

When sociologists compare different cultures and societies, they find considerable diversity. For example, what may be preferred behavior in one society may be sanctioned as deviant behavior in another. Even though specific features of societies vary, they have some basic features in common. Social inequality is found in all types of societies, although the forms of and extensiveness of social inequality vary from society to society. The next four chapters consider some common forms of social inequality.

Chapter 6 looks at the fundamental processes which lead to social inequality. We differentiate people into a variety of categories on the basis of characteristics they possess. We often compare the categories and rank some categories as better than others. When people agree about the rankings of various categories relative to each other, a social stratification system exists. Social stratification systems vary depending on the complexity of the society and the nature of its economic system.

Some groups in a society may be accorded special treatment because they are perceived to possess characteristics that are particularly valued or devalued. The powerful people in a society may support laws and economic practices that discriminate against members of specific racial or ethnic groups (Chapter 7). Which racial or ethnic groups are devalued in a society depends on historical, economic, and geographic factors.

Two other characteristics used to justify unequal treatment of people are gender (Chapter 8) and age (Chapter 9). In many societies women are assigned subordinate status to men. Social inequality based on age is more variable. In some societies the elderly are accorded high status, but in societies such as our own they are not.

6

Social Inequality: Stratification and Life Chances

Social philosophers throughout the ages have thought about the relationships between people. Are people equal to one another? Political scientists have debated who should be accorded what rights in society. Should every person who lives in a society have the same rights as every other person? Who should rule? Sociologists have examined human social behavior and wondered if there is any social unit in which people do not make comparative judgments. Do people inevitably assume that some people are better than others? Do you assume that you are better than some other people? All of these questions center around social inequality.

The study of organized social life inevitably involves the study of social inequality. The United States Declaration of Independence states that "all men are created equal," but at the time it was written, "men" did not refer to nonwhites (black or Indian) or women of any race. The inferiority of all but white men was taken for granted. But what did the equality of white men mean? Obviously it did not mean that all of them had equal physical health or intellectual ability, because those differences were beyond the control of our country's founders. It has been interpreted to mean that there should be equality of opportunity. Current affirmative action programs attempt to provide the equality of opportunity proclaimed over two centuries ago. In this chapter we examine types of inequality and why inequality is such a persistent aspect of social life.

Basic Concepts of Inequality

Social inequality is studied in many different ways with a variety of concepts. Basically, stratification theorists use **inequality** to refer to the situation in which the economic goods in a society are distributed unevenly among different groups or categories of people. They argue that economic inequality produces or leads to other forms of inequality in society, and that these patterns of inequality, in turn, lead to greater economic inequality. For example, people who possess more economic goods also have access to the "best" schools. Graduates of the "best" schools can more easily obtain better jobs and opportunities to make money than people who cannot afford to attend such schools. Some researchers also identify specific forms of inequality, such as racial or sexual, to discuss how the distribution of earnings (income) varies for different categories of people (blacks or females).

Inequality situation existing when the wealth and power in a society are distributed unevenly among various groups or categories of people.

The Social Psychology of Social Stratification

Research on social stratification systems generally is macro or large scale in focus, but social psychologists also examine how people behave in specific situations. Social psychological theory and research is often used to explain why inequality is such a persistent aspect of social life.

Attributions. Social psychologists recognize that people continually are trying to make sense out of their own lives, the actions of others, and their social worlds (Harvey et al. 1976). Overall, we tend to attribute people's behaviors to either *internal factors* (the person's traits or motives) or *external factors* (things beyond the person's control). Did you do well on the test because you studied hard or because the test was easy? Are people wealthy because they work hard or because they are lucky?

Words do more than differentiate objects. They convey meanings and prompt attributions. People's names are sets of connotations. Surnames often provide clues to a person's ethnic background, and people may be treated differently due to their presumed ethnic characteristics. Further, meanings appear to be associated with first names. Researchers (Garwood et al. 1980) set up a beauty queen contest on a college campus that demonstrated how first names could affect perceptions of physical attractiveness. Students were to select which of six women portrayed in photographs was most attractive. All six had previously been rated by other students as about equally attractive. But for the contest/experiment, three were assigned names that students had previously rated as desirable (Christine, Jennifer, and Kathy) and three names rated as undesirable (Ethel, Gertrude, and Harriet). The three contestants with desirable names received four times as many votes as those with undesirable names. Research such as this suggests that people assign different attributes to one another on the basis of name alone.

Stereotypes. When we first meet people, we often have very little information about them. Yet we cannot wait to interact with them so that we can obtain more information. As a consequence we make guesses about what they are like based on the information we do have—their sex, approximate

Women are often stereotyped in an office "pool" rather than noted for the more prestigious career of a television news reporter.

age, and type of clothing. On occasion we engage in the process of **stereotyping,** by assuming that a person who falls into a particular category because they have certain characteristics also has many other characteristics that we assume belong to people in that category (Lippman 1922). Stereotypes develop because people generalize their observations into patterns that define a whole category, but stereotypes do not necessarily accurately describe any one member of a social category. Further, stereotypes can be harmful because they may lead to unfair treatment of people. In our society some ethnic groups have been stereotyped as lazy. Employers may not hire well-qualified members of those groups because they stereotype them as lazy.

Stereotyping assuming that because a person belongs to a particular category, he or she possesses all the characteristics that are generally assumed to belong to that category.

Self-fulfilling Prophecies.   Once we categorize people through assigning a stereotype, our perceptions of their behavior are filtered through that stereotype. In other words, we pay more attention to behaviors that fit the stereotype, and we act toward the person as though he or she possesses the characteristics included in the stereotype. As a consequence of our perceptions and attendant actions, the person may begin to act as we expect him or her to act (Rosenthal and Jacobson 1968). Thus, assigning a stereotype to a person may result in a **self-fulfilling prophecy.** The attributions we make involve us in making comparisons between people.

Self-fulfilling prophecy when our behavior toward a person causes that person to adjust his or her behavior in accordance with our expectations.

Social Comparisons.   Social scientists find that people need to compare themselves with others in order to establish for themselves what kind of people they are. Social scientists such as Leon Festinger (1954) describe **comparison processes** through which people learn how sociable, friendly, mean, or nasty they are compared with other people. Sociologists discuss comparison processes in terms of specific phenomena, such as using a group as a *negative reference group* (Kelley 1952). In high school and college, students have negative reference groups, the people they do not want to be like ("preppies," "jerks," "frats," "freaks," "hippies," "greasers"). Generally students believe they are "better" than people who belong to their negative reference groups.

Comparison processes when people judge their own worth (such as ability, beauty) by comparing themselves with others.

A Fair World.   Related to the key role of comparison in social life are beliefs about justice or the fair distribution of rewards. We often find that people are more concerned about establishing **equity** (just division of rewards) than **equality** (equal division of rewards). The concept of *distributive justice* or equity refers to outcomes being proportional to inputs (Homans 1974). Recent research and theory suggests desire for justice or equity may affect our perceptions more than our actions (Leventhal 1980).

Equity condition existing when a society's rewards have been distributed fairly.

Experimental research indicates that under some conditions, when people receive more than they should (disproportionate rewards), observers may begin to believe that they deserved the greater rewards compared with their unlucky companions (Lerner 1965). The importance of beliefs in the maintenance of inequality or inequity is suggested by research related to the "just world" hypothesis.

Equality condition existing when a society's rewards are distributed equally.

According to the **just-world hypothesis,** people like to believe that there is justice, that people get what they deserve (Lerner 1980). In some cases, the operation of the just world hypothesis leads people to engage in what is called "blaming the victim." Rather than believing that anyone could be the victim of rape or assault or that poor people do not deserve to be poor, those who believe in a just world blame the people who are victims of crime or inequity. (See Chapter 5, Deviance and Crime, for a description of blaming the victim.)

"Just-world hypothesis" people assume (hypothesize) that people receive the outcomes they deserve.

Therefore, social psychological research indicates that people make attributions about themselves and others, compare themselves with others, form judgments about who is better and who is worse, and develop beliefs that justify inequities. Research on social stratification deals with the consequences of these processes for the society.

Do you believe some people are better than other people? Why?

Social Stratification Systems

In recent years the concepts of social differentiation and social stratification have been clearly separated. **Differentiation** refers to how things or people can be distinguished from one another. We may differentiate people on the basis of hair color (blondes, redheads) or any number of other criteria. Differentiation may refer also to whether the institutions in a society are simple or complex, or how clearly separated institutions are. In small preindustrial societies, institutions may be very simply structured, but in large postindustrial societies, they may be highly differentiated or very complex.

Differentiation separating people (or objects) into distinct categories.

Apples and oranges may be differentiated as varieties of fruit, although typically one type of fruit is not assumed to be better than another. **Stratification** refers to the ranking of things or people. In a **closed stratification system,** people cannot change their rankings, but in an **open stratification system** they can. Often, differentiation and stratification are associated with one another. People can be differentiated on the basis of the work they do (their occupations) and also stratified on the same basis (their occupation's prestige).

Stratification separating people or objects into categories that are ranked as higher or lower.

Closed stratification system system of stratification in which people cannot change their ranks.

One problem for stratification researchers is that the members of a society can be differentiated and ranked in many different ways. Marx (Bendix and Lipset 1966) focused on people's relationships to the means of production. Weber (1946) identified three stratification dimensions: class, status (prestige), and party (power). In the earlier decades of the twentieth century, American sociologists focused more on class, whereas in recent decades attention was directed more toward prestige hierarchies. In the past few years, sociologists have turned to class analysis again (Wright and Perrone 1977). Which stratification dimensions are the focus of research reflects the type of society or societies under examination.

Open stratification system system of stratification in which people can move from one rank to a higher or lower one.

The next section examines the "division of labor" and shows how differentiation and stratification vary in different types of societies. To aid in your understanding of that material, some additional concepts need to be introduced. If people live at a *subsistence level,* they produce only enough goods to survive. As soon as they produce a **surplus,** people may have **wealth** (accumulated money, property, or resources gained through work or inheritance). People who live at the subsistence level do not have earnings or income because they produce whatever goods they need and no more. **Income** or earnings exists in societies in which people work to receive money with which they can purchase the goods (products) they need or desire. If people all do similar work and produce only what they need to subsist, classes do not develop (although there may be some leaders). When economic and occupational differentiation develops (and markets emerge), clearly distinguishable classes appear and differences in occupational prestige become apparent.

Surplus when more goods are produced than are needed for survival.

Wealth accumulated money, property or other valuable resources.

Income what a person or family acquires in return for services or loan of resources.

Is social differentiation inevitable? Is social stratification inevitable?

The Division of Labor

One set of stratification theorists emphasizes the importance of economic systems, particularly modes of production, in shaping other social institutions. Those who base their work on the ideas put forth by Marx believe that the nature and organization of work provides the basis for differentiating types of societies. In the nineteenth century Engels (1972), a theorist who had collaborated with Marx, developed a theory that was both *materialistic* (emphasizing the key role of economic institutions) and *evolutionary* (describing transitions from one type of society to another). Although modern sociologists do not accept Engels' typology of societies (savagery, barbarism), they do continue to differentiate societies on the basis of predominant modes of production.

To differentiate types of societies, social scientists focus on the various types of work that prevail in a society, how the work is organized, and who owns the work equipment and products produced; in other words, the division of labor in the society. Not all theorists who examine the division of labor adhere to materialist conceptions of society. Durkheim (1964) distinguished between organic and mechanical divisions of labor in order to describe how people in a society are bound together. The types of society described below provide a useful framework for those anthropologists and sociologists who address questions about the role of technology in shaping societies.

Hunting and Gathering Societies

People may rely on very simple techniques (digging sticks) or very complex technology (satellites) to produce desired goods. Presumably people who are joined together in social units such as societies will in some way divide the work that confronts them. Although functional theorists debate exactly what functions must be fulfilled in order for societies to survive over time, sociologists recognize that people must obtain food.

The societies using the simplest forms of technology for food production are called **hunting and gathering** or foraging societies. Hunting and gathering societies were more common in past centuries, but over time they have disappeared, and few of them remain today. In these societies people use simple tools such as spears and axes to collect or forage for food products (animal and plant life) that exist in nature around them. Typically people share food in these societies and recognize that with their limited control over food resources, in the future they may need one another's assistance. They do not "sell" goods to one another but rather emphasize sharing or reciprocity. After they have been in an area for a time and have exhausted the food products in the environment, they move to a different location.

In hunting and gathering societies people produce enough to survive and subsist. Since they move around often, they do not create private goods that cannot be moved or that weigh them down in their travels. Without the accumulation of private goods, inequality as we know it is virtually nonexistent. And generally there is a minimal division of labor, so that people cannot be accorded higher or lower status on the basis of the work they do.

There often is some division of labor on the basis of sex. Hunting, particularly of large game, and strenuous deep sea fishing are male activities because of the typically greater strength of males and the limits that bearing and nursing children place on females' mobility and physical resources. The

Hunting and gathering societies societies that employ the simplest forms of technology for obtaining goods needed for survival.

In many hunting and gathering societies women contribute half or more of the food supply.

sexual division of other labor varies. In some societies women may participate in hunting small animals (Mbuti Pygmies) or fishing and men in some gathering and child care. Women contribute substantially to the food supply in most foraging societies through gathering (Tanner and Zihlman 1976). Eskimo societies are an exception because the frozen land does not yield food products for women to gather and the animal products are obtained through strenuous activity. An interesting point about the sexual divisions of labor in hunting and gathering societies is that they do not generally lead to highly developed hierarchical arrangements, **sexual stratification.** Yet since meat is highly valued in hunting and gathering societies, males have advantages because of their hunting activities (Friedl 1975).

Sexual stratification a hierarchical arrangement based on the sex of persons.

Horticultural Societies

In various parts of the world people have learned ways or techniques (slash and burn, hoe cultivation) to obtain some control over food resources. In simple horticultural societies, inequality is limited, because people have fairly equal access to resources (land) and the products of cultivation are shared equally. People are similar regarding their wealth and power, and prestige differences are obtained largely through "giving" other goods that they cannot immediately return in kind.

In **horticultural societies,** more people live in smaller areas than in hunting and gathering societies, because the technology permits them to draw more food products from the same amount of land. Horticultural societies produce *surplus* goods, goods beyond those needed for subsistence. The production of a surplus and the technology that led to metal tipped tools and weapons of warfare provided the basis for the development of classes in advanced horticultural societies. Warfare also leads to the emergence of leader and warrior classes that do not engage in food production, as well as a conquered or slave class.

Horticultural societies societies that employ some forms of plant cultivation.

Horticultural societies develop clear sexual divisions of labor. While the division of other activities varies, in all such societies men do the strenuous and territorial claim staking work of clearing the land. Depending on the society, cultivation may be women's work or shared work or infrequently men's work. Rigid sexual division of labor is often associated with social segregation by sex, which permits little contact between males and females. When women contribute little to the economy and are socially segregated, sexual stratification is pronounced. Among the Bamenda in West Africa male dominance is limited because women control the crops grown on the agricultural land owned by the men (Friedl 1975).

Agrarian Societies

The emergence of settled agriculture is sometimes treated as a turning point in human social life, marking the beginning of "civilization." The "great" civilizations of the past (Roman, Egyptian, Chinese) were agrarian. As we examine the nature of **agrarian societies,** the social losses as well as the gains should be kept in mind. The pyramids of Egypt are one of the wonders of the world, but the lives of countless slaves who built them were probably quite miserable by our standards.

Horticulturalists gained some control over food production, but agriculturalists gained many times greater control through the use of irrigation and fertilization, plows and work animals. Agricultural technology requires much more labor than hunting, gathering, or horticultural technologies. At the same time it allows production of more goods and thus a greater surplus. In agricultural societies large numbers of people can live in smaller areas because the land is more productive. Furthermore, segments of the population are free to engage in activities other than food production.

The abundant goods produced in early agricultural societies facilitated the emergence of distinctive classes. The focus of this discussion will be on well-known agricultural societies of the past, for in the modern world agricultural societies in various ways have been affected by involvement with industrial and postindustrial societies. Accounts of these societies often focus on the lives of governing classes, so that we know much about the lives of Egyptian Pharaohs and nobles, but little about the peasants. Yet the overwhelming majority of people in agricultural societies past and present, were *peasants* who had few rights or duties and few opportunities to improve their class positions. They produced food products, but they had to turn over a substantial portion of these products to the ruling or governing classes. Because of the lack of land, some of their children were forced to move to urban areas to make a living. The urban dwellers often produced goods and services needed by the society, but historically their living circumstances were similar in quality to poor peasants. They were expendable (Lenski 1966). Yet, the *slave class* was even more disadvantaged than peasants or former peasants, because they were almost totally under the control of their masters or conquerors. Other categories or classes of "common" people in agricultural societies were the "untouchables" and the "outcasts" (criminals, beggars). In societies such as India and Japan, people in the untouchable or degraded classes performed the dirty work for other members of the society. They were despised for doing what other members of the society did not want to do but had to have done.

The people in the "common" classes produced goods and services needed for the society and its members to survive. Yet they could retain only some of the goods they produced, received little of value in exchange for their goods and services, and were looked down upon by those in other classes. The *merchant classes* flourished in the urban areas because they negotiated market activity within their area and with other regions. Merchants accumulated wealth, but they were not usually accorded highest prestige. The relatively low prestige of merchants is apparent in Western literature (Shakespeare, French farces), which often depicts them as greedy and craving higher prestige.

Agrarian societies were large and complex, so government became more elaborate. The governing classes were small and the common classes were very large, so an intermediate set of people had to perform many of the day-

Agrarian societies
Societies that practice settled agriculture, which permits greater control over the production of food resources.

to-day governing functions for the rulers. Typically, lower government officials collected taxes and rents from the peasants, and soldiers protected the rulers from threats from outside and within the society as well as conquering new territory for them. Another set of people served the rulers as advisors, attendants, and servants.

The people at the top of the society, the *rulers* or governors, had great wealth and income. Other members of society were expected to "honor" them.

CONTROVERSIAL ISSUES · The British Monarchy

England was the first country to undergo an industrial revolution, yet it retains social classes from its earlier agricultural phase. Most people in England can be ranked in terms of American occupational prestige; those at the top of the stratification system in England are the nobility and royalty.

Families who have passed the honorific titles of lord and lady, duke and duchess from generation to generation originally had (and in some cases still do have) members serving the "rulers," the royal family. The titles provide prestige for their bearers, because they inspire deference from others. Noble families often had great wealth in the past (marked by extensive land holdings and castles), but the modern tax structure and industrial economic system make it difficult for many of them to retain the wealth.

The royal family maintains great prestige and wealth in part through the support of the state (personal allowances, maintenance of yachts and some castles) although it no longer has the power it had in the past. The royal family at one time had extensive powers—to declare war, establish the official religion, and so on. The monarch today has chiefly titular power; the queen is the official head of the church and opens sessions of parliament, and can name the prime minister in case of disputes, but she serves ordinarily as a figurehead rather than as a decision maker.

Entrance into the royal family is limited, because the monarch must give his or her permission for the members to marry. The 1981 marriage of the heir to the throne, Prince Charles, demonstrates how class boundaries are maintained in traditional stratification systems. Given the lack of available marriage partners in European royal families, Prince Charles married a member of a British noble family.

The widespread celebrations over the marriage of Prince Charles to Lady Diana Spencer and the birth of their child are interesting because they occurred when many English workers were unemployed and suffering from the effects of severe inflation. What interests American sociologists is why the English people not only maintain, but for the most part, actively admire a class of people who do not perform what traditionally has been seen as "functionally important" work for the society. Apparently the noble and royal classes serve valued functions in British society, otherwise they would no longer be supported or accorded prestige. Why do *you* think the British maintain their system?

Not only is *class stratification* clearly developed in agricultural societies, but also *sexual stratification* is highly developed. The sexual stratification appears to reflect changes in the sexual division of labor. Agricultural societies require heavy labor in the fields and on the battle fields. The physical strength and endurance required by these activities limit the involvement of women, particularly with the constraints of pregnancy and nursing added to other differences between males and females (in musculature or stature). Women in the common classes engage in the production of necessary goods and services (preparing and preserving food, weaving, making clothing, rearing children, working in the fields when labor is in short supply). Unlike in hunting and gathering and horticultural societies, women do not produce the primary economic goods. This division of labor leads to the perception that their work is of less importance than that of their male counterparts.

How does social stratification become more elaborated in agrarian societies?

Industrial Societies

Just as the agricultural revolution led to massive social change, so did the industrial revolution. The industrial revolution involved the gradual change of Western economies. The slow and small-scale production of goods in homes (cottages) and shops was replaced by much more rapid and large-scale factory production. At the same time that the location and nature of goods production was changing, societies were also becoming more urbanized and centralized. (See Chapter 11, The Structure of Postindustrial Society, for further discussion of industrialization.)

Often, descriptions of the development of Western industrial societies emphasize the role of one type of economic system such as capitalism. Capitalism is an *ideal type*. A specific economic system is unlikely to have *all* of the characteristics used to define capitalism and may have some of the characteristics of other economic systems. "Ideally" a **capitalist economy** is one in which capital goods are owned by individuals or private corporations, decisions about investments are made by individuals rather than some governmental unit (the state), and goods are distributed on the basis of competition in an open (unregulated) market.

Capitalist economy
a system in which the means of producing capital are owned by individuals or private corporations and the operation of the system is essentially unregulated by government.

As industrialization became more prevalent, people's lives were fundamentally altered. More people lived in cities and worked away from their homes. The goods they and others produced in factories did not belong to them, but rather to the people who owned the factories. Workers had no products to trade for other goods but rather received wages for their work. To obtain the goods and services they wanted, workers had to enter into various market relationships. The values of goods and services were established by how much money people were willing to pay for them. This value system is quite different from that in preindustrial societies in which value was established by how useful goods and services were.

The relationships between segments of the population changed. In traditional agricultural societies peasants, slaves, and other "common" people had little choice about whom they worked for. Their governors also had to provide some protection (police, military) for them. In industrial society a free labor market develops in which owners and workers are not tied permanently to one another. A factory owner is not obligated to care for workers no longer needed, and the workers are not obligated to spend their lifetimes working for one factory owner.

In industrial societies a limited number of people become very wealthy. Workers clearly have less income and prestige than those who own capital goods, but there are various groups of workers. Some workers receive better wages, have better working conditions, and are accorded higher prestige than others. One reason some workers are better off is that they have skills that are more valued in the market place.

At one time *functional theorists* such as Kingsley Davis and Wilbert E. Moore (1945) argued that the workers who received the highest rewards were those (1) who performed the work (tasks) most important to the smooth functioning of society and (2) who had the most training or talent. Do you believe rock stars receive high incomes and prestige because their work is more functionally important to society than the work of sanitation department employees? The vigorous debate that followed the publication of Davis and Moore's paper revealed that many sociologists disagreed with their position (Tumin 1953; Moore 1970).

Conflict theorists believe that some workers are given enough rewards to keep them from seeing how all workers are oppressed and joining together with other workers to overthrow their common oppressors—those who own the means of production. Marx studied European societies as they progressed through the social upheavals accompanying industrialization. He theorized that eventually workers would unite and a new and better society would result (Marx 1967). Although Marx's prediction did not come true (Western societies moved from industrial to postindustrial stages), one group of modern stratification theorists (Dahrendorf 1959) accepts at least partially his basic analysis of the plight of workers in a free labor market.

Randall Collins (1971) developed a conflict theory of sexual stratification to explain why there was less developed sexual stratification in foraging societies than in the agricultural societies prevalent before industrialization. He emphasizes how males' size and strength advantage over women and more aggressive behavior, as well as the market resources available to women, led to more or less developed sexual inequality.

Feminist and *socialist* theorists focused on what happened to specific types of workers, such as women, as industrialization progressed. When industrialization began, women and men often worked together in their homes to produce goods. When work became centralized in factories, men left the home to work for wages, and middle- and upper-class white women remained in the homes to produce goods that did not enter the market economy (their families' food, clothing, candles, and so on). Therefore, a form of sex segregation was established in industrial societies.

An ideology asserting that women's primary responsibility was in the domestic sphere developed to justify sex segregation. As a consequence of the emphasis on domestic skills for women, they could not effectively compete with men for jobs having high income and prestige because they lacked appropriate labor market skills. However, women played an important role as **reserve workers.** When needed (as when men were at war) they could be drawn into the labor market and paid low wages. Further, male and female workers would be unlikely to unite, because male workers would perceive females as a potential threat to their jobs, given the females' acceptance of lower wages.

Reserve workers workers pulled into the labor force when the economy requires more labor and pushed out when it is not required.

Some women were in the labor force, particularly the poor, black, and foreign born. These women belonged to groups that fared poorly in the free labor market. Blacks and foreign-born people had few opportunities to obtain the skills needed for good jobs, but they filled an important function. They had to take the undesirable, short-term jobs that other workers did not want. White male workers did not often "take up the cause" of these low-paid workers, for they (1) saw themselves as more deserving than the others and (2) feared that these workers would be willing to take their own jobs for less pay.

In the first part of the twentieth century, workers were stratified as professionals, white collar, skilled blue collar, unskilled blue collar, and unemployed. Sociologists who studied social stratification recognized that it was difficult to group people into classes similar to those that had existed in previous types of societies. Further, people sometimes perceived they were better than others even though their wages were not higher. Therefore, measures of occupational prestige were developed, as discussed later in this chapter.

How did people's work roles change with industrialization?

Postindustrial Society

After industrialization, more people in American society received higher incomes and more education. Mass production of goods not only permits more people to acquire goods, but also requires that people consume more goods in order for the economic system to grow. Some of the marks of being better off in the early decades of the twentieth century (owning an automobile, having running water and plumbing, having a telephone) are now items that most people consider basic necessities. However, inequality continues to persist, because new things are used as indicators of being better off.

As industrialization advanced, fewer people were needed to engage in strenuous labor. Now industrial plants are being developed where physical labor is not required, where industrial robots are programmed to perform chores previously performed by humans. With such developments, the increasing demand in industry is for educated, white-collar workers who can program machines.

CONTROVERSIAL ISSUES · Will Robots Displace Workers?

Imagine the perfect assembly-line worker. Never bored, never sick, the worker never takes long coffee breaks, never comes to work with a hangover, and—best of all from management's point of view—never asks for a raise.

Production workers now make up about 15 percent of the American labor force, but that number may drop to as little as 3 percent as many assembly-line jobs are taken over by this "perfect worker"—the robot.

Although the robot population of the United States presently numbers only 5,000, sales are booming and, according to one estimate, will increase from $100 million in 1980 to $2 billion by the end of the decade.

"We're going to end up producing much of our national wealth without human interference," says Joseph Engelberger, president of a leading manufacturer of industrial robots. "Over the next fifty years, it will be as profound a change as the Industrial Revolution."

SOURCE: The *Knoxville News-Sentinel,* December 16, 1981.

The demand for **service workers** increases in advanced or postindustrial societies. People have the income to buy services and more leisure time in which to utilize the services of other people. Laborers in the textile mills built during the early phases of American industrialization typically worked from dawn to dusk for subsistence level wages. Today many people take for granted that they will work 40 hours (or less) a week and be paid for holidays and a vacation. The increased demand for services and changes in the structure of work contributed to the demand for more service workers.

As the economy shifted more and more toward the provision of services after World War II, and as people expected better standards of living including less time at work, additional workers were needed. Women increasingly were drawn into the labor force because there were not enough men to hold all the jobs, particularly the service jobs, of which many were typically defined as female.

Service workers
people who perform services but do not produce goods.

How has the work force changed in postindustrial society?

Dual Labor Market

Analyses of how various types of people are distributed in the labor force has led to the argument that there is a **dual labor market** (Bibb and Form 1977). The idea of a dual labor market or a segmented market first emerged in analyses of differentials in the earnings (wages) of blacks and whites. As it

Dual labor market
When advantaged workers compete for desirable jobs in one segment of the labor market and disadvantaged workers compete in a second, less desirable segment.

Over the course of the twentieth century the segregation of workers in male-dominated and female-dominated occupations has decreased to some extent. Yet, few women are in the most prestigious occupations or in the most prestigious positions in male-dominated occupations.

has developed, the disadvantaged positions of other minority group members and women also can be explained by the framework. (See Chapter 11 for more discussion on the dual labor market.)

The basic argument is that there is a **primary labor market** and a **secondary labor market** and that the primary market is basically closed to many groups. The primary market contains the jobs that offer higher wages and better opportunities for advancement (managerial and professional occupations). The secondary market involves jobs that offer lower wages and limited opportunities for advancement. The data in Table 6.1 demonstrate that

Primary market consists of jobs that offer high wages and good opportunities for advancement.

Secondary market consists of jobs that offer low wages and few opportunities for advancement.

TABLE 6.1   1981 Median Weekly Earnings of Full-time Wage and Salary Workers 16 Years and Older by Race and Sex for Selected Occupations

Occupation	White		Black	
	Male	Female*	Male	Female*
Professional & Technical	$443	$315 (71%)	$352	$308 (88%)
Managers & Administrators (except farm)	471	282 (60%)	391	303 (77%)
Salesworkers	372	191 (51%)	249	182 (73%)
Clerical Workers	335	219 (65%)	286	220 (77%)
Service Workers	245	165 (67%)	214	166 (78%)

*Percentage of male earnings, same race.
SOURCE: Earl F. Mellor and George Stamas, "Usual Weekly Earnings," *Monthly Labor Review,* April 1982.

whatever the job category, white men earn more than any other group. Women consistently earn less than men whether white or black.

To understand better the stratification in industrial and postindustrial societies, the procedures used to assess *relative social position* require examination.

Measuring Social Position

In preindustrial societies, a person's social position generally reflected the position held by their forebears and the work they did. With the advent of industrialization, societies became much larger, and people moved from where their ancestors had lived to urban areas. As one consequence, a person's social position had to be judged more on what work he or she performed than on what was known about the person's family.

Social Classes in the United States

In the period 1930–1960 various attempts were made to identify and establish the American class structure. Researchers did not rely entirely on people's economic positions or their relationships to the means of production in their efforts to identify classes.

In the 1930s Robert S. and Helen M. Lynd conducted a study of "Middletown" (Muncie, Indiana), which was studied again recently. The Lynds were interested in how Middletown responded to economic boom and bust; their interest in social change required that they also learn about social position and social class. They defined social classes as based on economic power flowing from differences in income, wealth, and privilege. However, they studied social class using what is called the **reputational technique.** The reputational technique involves asking people to rank other people into classes on the basis of their reputations—what is known about them. As a result, they defined six classes. People were differentiated into classes on the basis of perceived differences rather than by measurement of differences in income, wealth, and privilege.

Reputational technique assigning persons to ranks on the basis of their reputations.

1. A very small top group of the "old" middle class is becoming an upper class, consisting of wealthy local manufacturers, bankers, the local head managers of one or two of the national corporations with units in Middletown, and a few well-to-do dependents of all the above . . .
2. Below this first group is to be found a larger but still relatively small group, consisting of established smaller manufacturers, merchants and professional folk and also of most of the better-paid salaried dependents of the city's big-business interests . . .
3. Below Groups 1 and 2 come those who have been identified as Middletown's own middle class in purely locally relative terms; the minor employed professionals, the very small retailers and entrepreneurs, clerks, clerical workers, small salesmen, civil servants . . .

4. Close to Group 3 might be discerned an aristocracy of local labor: trusted foremen, building trades craftsmen of long standing, and the pick of the city's experienced highly skilled machinists of the sort who send their children to the local college as a matter of course.

5. On a fifth level would stand the numerically overwhelmingly dominant group of the working class; these are the semi-skilled or unskilled workers, including machine operatives, truckmen, laborers, the mass of wage earners.

6. Below Group 5 one should indicate the ragged bottom margin, comprising some "poor whites" from the Kentucky, Tennessee, and West Virginia mountains, and in general the type of white worker who lives in the ramshackle, unpainted cottages on the outlying unpaved streets. These are the unskilled workers who cannot even boast of that last prop to the job status of the unskilled, regular employment when a given plant is operating (Lynd and Lynd 1937:458–460).

W. Lloyd Warner and his associates used a definitely **subjective approach** to study social class in various American communities (Newburyport, Massachusetts; Natchez, Mississippi). They focused on the prestige or status accorded various groups in a community by other members of the community. Warner and his associates talked to community members and listened to gossip as part of their research strategy. This was called *evaluated participation* (Warner, Meeker, and Eells 1949). Their studies of "Yankee City" and "Old City" led them to the conclusion that there were six classes: *upper-upper* (well-established families with wealth, prestige, and power), *lower-upper* (similar to the upper-upper class except its members were from newly rich families), *upper-middle* (successful business and professional people with respectable reputations), *lower-middle* (foremen, clerical workers, managers of small businesses and others who were good members of the community), *upper-lower* (people who worked hard but at low-prestige jobs that did not pay well), and *lower-lower* (unemployed people who were seen as "not trying," "lazy," or "no good") (Davis, Gardner, and Gardner 1941; Warner and Lunt 1941).

One of the beliefs from Marxian class theory is that people who belong to the same class eventually develop a sense of **class consciousness,** a sense of "belonging together." Their common economic situation may lead them to adopt similar ways of living (lifestyles), which in turn may increase their sense of belonging together.

Some sociologists have used a subjective approach to social class when asking people to identify their own social class standing. When Richard Centers (1949) asked individuals to place themselves, the majority of people identified themselves as middle class. Decades later, Robert W. Hodge and Donald J. Treiman (1968) gave individuals a chance to choose class labels and found that overwhelmingly people identified themselves as "middle" or "working class" and avoided "upper class" and "lower class" labels. Ultimately what classes people identify for themselves depend, in part, on the choices researchers give them.

Generally sociologists are not confident that there are clear and distinct classes with which people identify. In fact many sociologists question whether

Subjective approach reliance on respondents' perceptions of a situation such as another person's social standing.

Class consciousness the shared self-image of a set of people in similar objective circumstances who perceive their common situation the same way.

there are a set of clearly defined strata or classes in American society, although there appears to be clear recognition of the top class (Abrahamson et al. 1976). Limitations of subjective measures may make it difficult to identify classes. One problem may be the size of modern communities. In towns and cities of large size, respondents cannot make informed judgments about all other members of the community, because they have no knowledge about many of the city residents. Another problem may be the ability of people in various economic groups to maintain what appear to be similar lifestyles (through less expensive versions of clothing and other consumables). Such problems make the delineation of a class structure difficult for those researchers who rely on subjective techniques such as evaluated participation.

In general, sociologists question whether there are clearly discernable classes in our large complex society, although they believe that there are hierarchical distinctions. Some sociologists discuss *socioeconomic status* (SES) instead of social class. The SES concept does not require that all people identify the same set of positions or that people clearly identify themselves as belonging to a specific group or class. Yet the SES concept assumes people are ranked on the basis of economic and other (status) criteria, that there are differences in prestige, privilege, and power related to SES. *Relative social position* becomes the primary issue.

Are there distinct social classes in the United States?

Objective Measures: Occupational Prestige

Sociologists have tried many procedures to assess people's relative social positions, including scales evaluating the possessions displayed in living rooms. Some sociologists have tried to develop **objective measures** of social position. Some of the characteristics that researchers have used as indicators of social position are *education, income,* and *occupation.* Individuals may be assigned different hierarchical positions if several indicators are used, because some people may have high incomes but very little formal education, and others may have extensive formal education but relatively low incomes (Lenski 1966). Therefore, some researchers have tried to develop measures that can rank people in a single hierarchy (Reiss 1961).

Objective measures measures of social position based on quantifiable data possessed by researchers (e.g., occupational prestige).

Occupation is often used to measure social position. In functional analyses occupation presumably reflects an individual's level of skill or intelligence, as well as the length of training needed and the "worthiness" of the activity performed as judged by other members of the social unit. Jobs requiring scarce skills, intelligence, and extensive training, and considered functionally important or meritorious tend to be more highly valued than jobs with few or no requirements or merit.

Various surveys conducted by research organizations such as the National Opinion Research Center have questioned Americans about the relative prestige they accord to various occupations (Hodge, Siegel, and Rossi 1964).

Although the results have varied somewhat over the years (reflecting the emergence of new occupations and the discrediting of some traditional occupations such as politician), respondents' ratings are fairly similar from one period to the next. Judges, doctors, scientists, and governors receive high rankings. Carpenters, plumbers, auto mechanics, and other skilled workers are in the middle. People who perform "dirty work"—street sweepers, garbage collectors, shoe shiners—are at the bottom. Further, Donald J. Treiman (1977) reviewed studies of job prestige in various countries and found the relative prestige of jobs in the United States and other industrialized and developed countries is roughly equivalent.

THE FACTS · Income as an Indicator of SES

People may use income as an indicator of their own and others' socioeconomic status, but social scientists find it difficult to use this objective measure alone. One problem with using income is that there are significant state and regional differences in median family income. These 1979 data are from the 1980 U.S. Census.

States in the Southeastern region tend to have the lowest median incomes, while Far West states, a couple of Mountain states and a few Midwestern states, as well as a few Northeastern states, have the highest median family incomes.

Southeast		*Midwest*		*Rocky Mountain*	
Alabama	$16,602	Illinois	$22,007	Colorado	$21,485
Kentucky	$16,399	Michigan	$21,886	Wyoming	$22,497
Mississippi	$14,922	Minnesota	$21,217		
Tennessee	$16,245				

Far West		*Northeast*	
California	$21,479	Connecticut	$23,038
Nevada	$21,666	New Jersey	$22,830
Washington	$21,635	Massachusetts	$21,329

States Not Listed Above
Alaska $28,266 (highest); Arizona $19,150; Arkansas $14,356 (lowest); Delaware $20,658; Florida $17,558; Georgia $17,403; Hawaii $23,066; Idaho $17,278; Indiana $20,540; Iowa $20,243; Kansas $19,575; Louisiana $17,822; Maine $16,208; Maryland $22,850; Missouri $18,746; Montana $18,839; Nebraska $19,110; New Hampshire $19,796; New Mexico $17,151; New York $20,385; North Carolina $17,042; North Dakota $18,239; Ohio $20,710; Oklahoma $17,846; Oregon $19,837; Pennsylvania $20,259; Rhode Island $19,441; South Carolina $17,340; South Dakota $16,431; Texas $19,372; Vermont $17,549; Virginia $20,423; West Virginia $17,261; Wisconsin $21,113

SOURCE: U.S. Census Bureau.

The studies of occupational prestige in industrial and postindustrial societies suggest that in such societies the organization of job tasks—division of labor—develops on the basis of similar criteria. Specialization of job tasks allows a limited number of individuals to control access to and distribution or allocation of scarce resources. Job specialization also leads to the establishment of skill and training levels that prevent some individuals from obtaining the entry-level positions needed to advance to higher-level job positions. Those positions that provide high power (control over resources) and involve advanced technological skills are consistently awarded high prestige in industrial and postindustrial societies.

The social stratification system in a society is assumed to both reflect and affect other aspects of the society. Therefore researchers use the results of studies of occupational prestige to classify the social position of people in their studies of crime, mental health, fertility, and religious behavior. A key concern is social mobility.

THE FACTS · Occupational Characteristics

Occupation is a key variable for analysts of social stratification in America. Numerous scales exist to rank occupations hierarchically in terms of their overall status (Duncan 1961; Featherman, Jones, and Hauser 1975). Yet many sociologists find these scales inadequate, because they are interested in more than occupational prestige or status (power, authority, market segmentation).

For a number of decades sociologists have derived occupational information from data published by the U.S. Bureau of the Census. Pamela S. Cain and Donald J. Treiman (1981) argue that the *Dictionary of Occupational Titles* (DOT), fourth edition, published by the U.S. Department of Labor, provides information about occupational characteristics that may improve future research on occupations.

The DOT shows an overwhelming expansion of specialized positions in our postindustrial society, and it distinguishes over 12,000 specific occupations (base titles). Also it provides information not often available from other sources. Many reports about occupations rely on what people *say* they do (self-reports), but the DOT provides information about what workers *actually* do (observational data).

In the DOT, occupations are described in terms of the forty-four characteristics listed here. Cain and Treiman suggest that researchers should use statistical procedures to reduce the variables to fewer, more manageable dimensions.

Variable Label	*Description**
Worker functions	
DATA	Complexity of function in relation to data
PEOPLE	Complexity of function in relation to people
THINGS	Complexity of function in relation to things
Training times	
GED	General educational development
SVP	Specific vocational preparation

Aptitudes
    INTELL   Intelligence
    VERBAL   Verbal aptitude
    NUMER   Numerical aptitude
    SPATIAL   Spatial perception
    FORM   Form perception
    CLERICAL   Clerical perception
    MOTOR   Motor coordination
    FINGDEX   Finger dexterity
    MANDEX   Manual dexterity
    EYEHAND   Eye-hand-foot coordination
    COLORDIS   Color discrimination
Temperaments
    DCP   Direction, control, and planning
    FIF   Feelings, ideas, or facts
    INFLU   Influencing people
    SJC   Sensory or judgmental criteria
    MVC   Measurable or verifiable criteria
    DEPL   Dealing with people
    REPCON   Repetitive or continuous processes
    PUS   Performing under stress
    STS   Set limits, tolerances, or standards
    VARCH   Variety and change
Interests
    DATACOM   Communication of data vs. activities with things
    SCIENCE   Scientific and technical activities vs. business contact
    ABSTRACT   Abstract and creative vs. routine, concrete activities
    MACHINE   Activities involving processes, machines, or techniques
                             vs. social welfare
    TANGIBLE   Activities resulting in tangible, productive satisfaction vs.
                             prestige, esteem
Physical demands
    STRENGTH   Lifting, carrying, pulling, pushing
    CLIMB   Climbing, balancing
    STOOP   Stooping, kneeling, crouching, crawling
    REACH   Reaching, handling, fingering, feeling
    TALK   Talking, hearing
    SEE   Seeing
Working conditions
    LOCATION   Outside working conditions
    COLD   Extreme cold
    HEAT   Extreme heat
    WET   Wet, humid
    NOISE   Noise, vibration
    HAZARDS   Hazardous conditions
    ATMOSPHR   Fumes, odors, dust, gases, poor ventilation

*Descriptions are from U.S. Department of Labor (1972), *Dictionary of Occupational Titles,* 4th ed.
SOURCE: Cain and Treiman (1981).

Social Mobility

At the beginning of this chapter, the concept of equality of opportunity was introduced. For many Americans the belief that every person has the opportunity to achieve whatever he or she desires is fundamental to American society. Sociologists have distinguished two basic types of stratification systems, class and caste, on the basis of opportunities to change one's position in the system. In class systems people can change their positions through their own efforts; in caste systems people cannot.

Movement in a society can be of several types. Chapter 16 on population describes movement from one location to another. **Social mobility** focuses on people's movement within stratification systems (Sorokin 1959). People may experience **upward mobility** by improving their positions in a stratification system, or they may experience **downward mobility** by ending up in lower positions. The themes of many novels (such as the Horatio Alger stories), biographies (Abraham Lincoln), and self-help books (how to climb the corporate ladder) focus on upward mobility; nevertheless many people in our society experience downward mobility (Miller and Roby 1970).

Mobility may be **intragenerational,** occurring within specific people's lifetimes, or it may be **intergenerational,** occurring when children achieve higher standing than their parents (Blau and Duncan 1967). Much of the stratification literature focuses on individuals' occupational prestige or status attainment rather than groups'. The United States is perceived to have an open stratification system in which individual mobility is possible, yet, studies of mobility indicate that most people in our society do not experience extensive social mobility during their lifetimes; there are many stories of modest change but few "rags to riches" stories.

Social mobility movement from one position to another in a stratification system.

Upward mobility movement from a lower ranking position to a higher ranking one.

Downward mobility movement from a higher ranking position to a lower ranking one.

Intragenerational mobility movement by a person from one position to another in a stratification system within his or her lifetime.

Intergenerational mobility movement from one rank to another in a stratification system that occurs over generations.

Life Chances

Individuals' life chances are affected by their positions in the social stratification system of their society. **Life chances** refer to a person's likelihood of experiencing some event, such as dying, becoming sick, being committed to a mental hospital, falling victim to a crime, or obtaining a divorce. Babies are not born with equal chances of survival, much less with equal chances for good health and occupational success. Socioeconomic position is associated with the chances of surviving through infancy and childhood. Families with incomes below the poverty level have higher rates of infant mortality and childhood mortality than do families living above that level (Shapiro et al. 1968). Whether because of inadequate resources, lack of knowledge about available medical and health care services, or the dual standard of medicine practiced in American society (one for the rich and one for the poor), lower-income people make less use of prenatal and postnatal medical care and health services than do those who are financially better off (Bouvier and van der Tak 1976).

Lower-income families are less likely to carry insurance to pay for phy-

Life chances likelihood of experiencing some event(s) within one's lifetime

sician and hospital care. They are also less likely to seek such services for preventive reasons (Stockwell et al. 1978). Those with lower incomes have higher risks of job-related accidents and deaths compared with those with higher incomes. The operation of the dual labor market means the poor often must take jobs that are hazardous, because they are generally not admitted to workers' unions that fight to establish safer working conditions.

The poor are more likely to be committed to mental institutions than the wealthy. After exhausting their emotional resources by personally caring for "difficult" family members, lower-class families have to hospitalize them because they cannot afford private psychiatric care. Therefore people who begin life in the disadvantaged strata in many ways have poorer life chances, as measured by the likelihood of surviving to adulthood, having or dying of certain diseases, and being committed to mental institutions (Bouvier and Lee 1976), compared with people whose parents were better off.

Various views of the situation of the disadvantaged predominate at different times. During the Great Depression of the 1930s, when all types of people were out of work, government programs were developed to help people in need. When our society became more affluent in the late 1950s and 1960s, politicians and social scientists believed that programs should be developed to improve the life chances of those born into the disadvantaged strata. Social scientists described the "vicious cycle of poverty," referring to the limited chances poor people had to change their circumstances. In the 1960s President Lyndon B. Johnson declared "war on poverty." Programs such as Headstart were developed to provide the children of the poor an opportunity to succeed in school and thus break out of the poverty cycle. Other programs, such as the Food Stamp Program, were developed to ensure that every American had the basic necessities.

Are there class differences in life chances?

Welfare versus Wealthfare

In the 1970s and 1980s doubts about the assistance programs began to be expressed by various groups. **Welfare** programs were attacked by the general public basically on two grounds: (1) some people cheated, and (2) recipients lost the motivation to improve themselves because they allegedly felt the government would take care of them. The amount of money spent on assistance or welfare programs (Aid for Dependent Children, Food Stamps) was seen as excessive by those with higher incomes and higher levels of education. Public opinion polls reveal that Americans distinguish the poor who cannot control their fate and those on welfare who are unworthy and believed to milk the system (Jaffe 1977). Thus, people on welfare are labeled negatively. Regarding the second criticism, participants in welfare programs support the work ethic as much as other Americans (Goodwin 1971; Kaplan and Tausky 1974).

Underlying the welfare debate are questions about who should receive

Welfare programs that provide benefits to persons disadvantaged by our system of inequality.

Shifts in the economy may force people such as these Detroit residents to seek governmental assistance, such as welfare.

assistance, under what circumstances, and the consequences of such assistance. Some conservatives argue that in a capitalist system some will fail and some will succeed, and that the government should not interfere with "natural" operation of the system. Conflict theorists, on the other hand, point out that we do not have a true capitalist or free market system. Furthermore, they point out that **wealthfare** programs cost our government considerably more than welfare programs, *and* that welfare programs maintain the stratification hierarchy by keeping the poor at the subsistence level (Turner and Staines 1976). By wealthfare they mean programs that assist the wealthy in maintaining and increasing their wealth. Programs that provide tax shelters, investment credits, and other tax advantages for the wealthy as well as programs such as price supports for farmers (dairy, peanut, tobacco) are viewed as components of a system of wealthfare.

Wealthfare programs that provide benefits for those who have advantages (e.g., tax shelters).

Do welfare and wealthfare programs perpetuate inequality?

Analysis of differences in life chances and our dual system of welfare and wealthfare leads to an emphasis on the structural properties of social inequality. Researchers such as G. William Domhoff (1979) argue that a very small upper class (less than 1 percent of the population) rules over the remainder of the society. From his perspective, inequality will persist as long as the ruling class can dominate the vast majority of the population who own no income-producing property.

Researchers such as Domhoff focus on the processes through which structural inequality is perpetuated, whereas those stratificaton theorists who emphasize occupational prestige and status attainment focus on individuals' activities and opportunities for mobility.

Yet other social scientists focus on how beliefs about social stratificaton affect how people see themselves and others. Thus in concluding this chapter we return to some of the social psychological issues with which we began. Many questions can be raised about the criteria we use to judge one another's worth to society. But some of the most devastating consequences of social comparisons follow from people's judgments of themselves.

CONTROVERSIAL ISSUES · Who Should Survive?

In the early 1980s the media reported on some proposals prepared for the government on what should be done in case of nuclear war. One proposal was that older people should be the ones to do the work required in the contaminated world outside the shelters. The authors of the proposal responded to critics by saying that their "suggestion" was based on the premise that older persons would die before they would suffer the long-term effects of radiation exposure. What the proposal did was stimulate questions about who should survive.

Imagine that in the mountains there is a shelter that can protect people from radiation fall-out. The shelter can be used by only a limited number of people because large quantities of food and water must be stored for each person who stays there. You are assigned the task of deciding who will be sheltered there. In making your decisions you must consider what each person can contribute to maintaining the shelter and eventually building a new society after it is safe to leave the shelter. Select *five* of the following people.

1. A 20-year-old white male with an elementary school education who works as a maintenance man
2. A 15-year-old mentally retarded female from a wealthy family
3. A 70-year-old white male who is President of the United States
4. A 45-year-old black priest who has worked in poor neighborhoods teaching people to help themselves
5. A 25-year-old white mother of two children who has never worked outside the home
6. A 30-year-old black female physician
7. A 36-year-old white male "hippie" who has spent the last 6 years "living off the land"
8. A 2-year-old male child of immigrant parents
9. A 30-year-old black army sergeant who is an expert marksman
10. A 40-year-old white male who has earned a great deal of money as a corporation lawyer
11. Yourself

Were the criteria by which you normally judge people's social worth useful in making your decision?

The beliefs about equality of opportunity expressed by the framers of the Constitution encourage people to work hard to get ahead, to achieve "the American dream." These beliefs persist even though sociologists find that most Americans do not experience significant upward mobility and that people who start out in the lower strata of society have limited opportunities to attain higher status or to improve their life chances. Some sociologists have vividly depicted how "the American dream" generates unfulfilled expectations and loss of self-esteem for many working-class Americans (Rubin 1976; Sennett and Cobb 1973). Americans recognize that opportunitites are not truly equal but still berate themselves for not having achieved as much as others have. Inequality hurts, particularly if you are asked to believe that it is your own fault.

Summary

Economic inequality is a key aspect of modern social life that leads to other forms of inequality.

Various social psychological concepts help us to understand how and why people make the distinctions that on a macro or large scale constitute social stratification. We make attributions about others that sometimes are very general stereotypes. By stereotyping people we may produce self-fulfilling prophecies; people may begin to behave in accordance with our expectations.

Human beings continually compare themselves with one another. Sometimes we compare how rewards or outcomes are distributed to see if we and others have been treated fairly. If rewards are distributed equally, equality exists. Often we would rather have rewards distributed on the basis of justness or fairness—equitable division. When we assert that people get what they deserve, we are drawing on the "just-world hypothesis."

These social processes lead to social differentiation, the separation of people into distinct categories. When the categories are hierarchically arranged, a social stratificaton system is formed. An open system exists when people can move from one category to another; in a closed system they cannot change categories or positions.

Social stratification theorists often focus on economic issues, asking whether there is a surplus and who controls it. The ideas of Marx have been very influential in directing researchers to examine the bases of production and who controls it in a society.

In simple societies (hunting and gathering) there is considerable sharing and little stratification. In horticultural socieies, surpluses develop and so does stratification. However, differences in social standing become more pronounced in agrarian societies, which rely on settled agriculture. In these societies distinct classes emerge with clear differences in power, prestige, and privilege.

The shift to settled agriculture was accompanied by tremendous changes in social organization and social stratification, but industrialization led to revolutionary changes in how most people's lives were organized. Most men began to work outside the home for wages with which they could purchase goods or services; most women remained in the home. The organizations people work for are controlled by a limited number of persons who accumulated wealth, prestige, and power.

Industrialization eventually permitted more people to have better lifestyles than before, although the working conditions for early industrial workers often were poor. We are now in a postindustrial stage in which most people do not engage in the production of goods. The service sector of our economy has expanded considerably and in conjunction with that expansion the percentage of women in the labor force has increased. Men and women, whites and blacks do not appear to compete in the same job market because we have a dual labor market that perpetuates sexual and racial inequality.

Sociologists tried to identify a class structure in the United States. Early researchers used people's perceptions, or subjective measures, to identify classes. Researchers found that Americans do not appear to develop strong class consciousness.

Because sociologists question whether there are a set of national social class categories, they focus on socioeconomic status (SES) rankings, or relative social position. Rather than using subjective measures, current researchers focus on more objective measures, such as occupational prestige.

Although our cultural beliefs emphasize that our society provides equality of opportunity, studies of movement from one rank to another (social mobility) reveal overall that individuals have limited opportunities for mobility. Children differ in their life chances according to their parents' social position.

Our society developed welfare programs to assist those with the poorest life chances. The merits of these assistance programs are widely debated. Increasingly wealthfare programs that assist the wealthiest in maintaining and increasing their wealth (as through tax shelters) are being questioned; however, the proponents of wealthfare are those who also have power in our society.

Suggested Readings

G. William Domhoff. *The Powers That Be.* New York: Vintage, 1979. In various works Domhoff has argued that a limited number of people control or rule American society. Domhoff uses reputational, positional, and statistical studies to establish the existence of a ruling class. The essay focuses on the specific processes (candidate selection and policy formation) through which the ruling class promotes its interests and thus dominates.

Phillip Green. *The Pursuit of Inequality.* New York: Pantheon, 1981. In a series of essays Green refutes various arguments justifying social inequality. He attacks the sociological justifications of racial and sexual inequality. And he questions the "new individualism" proposals of neoconservatives. Green questions the "naturalness" of inequality.

Richard Sennett and Jonathan Cobb. *The Hidden Injuries of Class.* New York: Vintage, 1973. The authors' report of their conversations with working people shows that for many people the American dream is the American nightmare. The belief that everyone can make it if only they work hard enough may be scoffed at, yet people question whether or not they could have done more to succeed. The ideology of equality and unlimited mobility leads to hidden injury and self-devaluation.

7

Ethnicity and Race

*Wander through the various sections of New York City and you see highly
visible subcommunities of Irish, Italians, Chinese, Vietnamese, black Cari-
bees, Puerto Ricans, black Americans, Bangladesh, Pakistanis, Greeks, and
varieties of Slavs—to name but a few. In many cases the concentrations of
these people in enclaves are larger than the populations of major cities in
their countries of origin.*

*A trip to Kansas City reveals blacks and whites as visible communities,
while Mexicans go largely unnoticed. A drive through Salt Lake City finds
Danes, Swedes, English, Germans, and some Greeks, but blacks, Japanese,
and American Indians remain almost invisible. Whether communities are
rigidly subdivided into distinct ethnic and racial groups, whether these
groups are large or small, visible or invisible, diversity marks American society.*

Meanings of Ethnicity and Race

From early childhood individuals are sensitized to the amazing diversity in the
way people look, think, and behave. To make sense of this diversity individuals
focus on selected visible physical and cultural characteristics. These features
are used to note who is alike or different and to identify individuals as belonging to particular social categories. These social categories are called race
and ethnic groups.

Which physical and cultural traits are chosen to mark groups differ from
society to society, as does the social meaning of membership in a particular
group. In some societies, ethnicity and race are used simply to distinguish
among various subgroups in the population. Individuals make social distinctions of "we" and "they." Each group maintains its own customs, social institutions, and rhythm of life. The groups remain relatively separate, limiting
social intercourse, and avoiding intermarriage.

In other societies, ethnicity and race not only mark subgroups in the
population, but also become crucial in determining the social standing of one
group relative to others. In such societies, ethnicity and race play powerful
roles in distinguishing rich from poor, powerful from powerless, and privileged
from underprivileged. When such inequalities exist, race and ethnicity are
important criteria in shaping how individuals see and respond to one another.
Racial and ethnic markers trigger expressions of sympathy and antipathy, as
well as acts of preference for or discrimination against certain individuals. The
emphasis given ethnicity and the alleged superiority of one racial or ethnic
group's culture as compared with others shapes the nature of intergroup relations. Alleged superiority serves as justification for claiming that one group
should dominate and others be dominated. It is also grounds for arguing that
one group should maintain its distinctiveness and others should surrender
their identities, adopting the outlook and behaviors of the dominant group.

The importance attached to ethnicity and race is tied to the reactions of the ethnic and racial group members as they struggle for power, seek to assimilate, or strive to maintain their uniqueness.

Ethnicity

There are three principal features of **ethnicity.** First, it is a *socially assigned* or *attributed* identity. Some visible trait or combination of traits is treated as a socially meaningful marker. Some of the markers, socially recognized and used in creating ethnic categories, are physical appearance, religious customs and conduct, nationality, and language. For instance, a necklace with a plain cross, a crucifix, or star of David marks respectively Protestant, Catholic, and Jew. Some markers are pronounced, such as the language difference between Quebecois and other Canadians, or Tex-Mex dialect versus hidalgo Spanish among Mexican-Americans. Other markers are more subtle, such as stylized gestures of greeting, farewell, or affection: European males embracing and kissing on the cheeks versus Americans shaking hands.

The markers and labels affixed to a social category become symbols to which people react in defining "who people are." In cases where distinguishable markers are not immediately apparent, people often invent symbols to

Ethnicity identity based on social or cultural traits used in defining a sense of self and peoplehood.

Potential Klan members in the next generation.

identify groups. The Nazis in Germany during the 1930s and the 1940s marked Jews with armbands bearing the star of David. Moslems in Jerusalem during the later half of the thirteenth century required Christians to wear blue turbans while inside the city gates. Mongols, after defeating the Chinese, required Chinese men to wear their hair in a pigtail.

Second, ethnicity is a *social psychological* characteristic. In some cases, ethnicity is viewed positively. An individual belonging to a particular ethnic category takes both the label and membership to be important. They become symbolic of one's "sense of self" and crucial in denoting "who or what I am." Sometimes the symbols are publicly paraded. In the United States buttons saying "Black is beautiful" and T-shirts emblazoned with "Kiss an Italian American" or "The Pope is Polish" can be statements of a person's personality, group affiliation, and social distinctiveness. Other times, ethnic identity is downplayed and occasionally trotted out during festivals. In some cases, ethnic identity is seen negatively. An individual rejects the label and seeks to sever all claims of membership in a group. In the 1940s and 1950s in some sections of the southwestern United States, Native Americans claimed to be Mexican-Americans to avoid more extreme forms of prejudice and discrimination.

Third, ethnicity is *communal.* Persons identified as distinctive or claiming to be, interact with each other and organize their lives around each other. They develop social bonds and boundaries. They decide who shall be excluded from and included in their social networks and cliques. They create social institutions and beliefs supporting their claims of uniqueness. They share a sense of intimacy, belonging, and peoplehood. They have a sense of history—real or imagined—that emphasizes their common ancestry and destiny (Weber 1968:387–398).

What are the three key features of ethnicity?

Ethnicity, in short, locates people within a community that provides them with a network of social relationships that bind them together from cradle to grave. Children play and go to school together. As teenagers, they date one another. As adults, they choose a spouse from within the community. They often work and worship together. They visit each other, and in times of financial and emotional crises depend on each other for assistance. They frequently are buried next to one another (Gordon 1964:19–59).

Race

Race has the same social meaning as ethnicity. **Race** is some physical characteristic taken as a marker in defining a socially distinctive subgroup in the population. People usually operate *as if* there are genetically based traits that can be universally and accurately applied in designating racial subgroups.

Race socially agreed on identity based on physical traits to mark a subgroup in the population.

A number of different classification systems have been tried, using skin color, hair color and texture, eye color and shape, blood types, even morphological differences in the skull, heart, limbs, and buttocks. None of these efforts resulted in identifying mutually exclusive subgroups. Depending on the combinations selected, classificatory systems include as few as three groups—Caucasoid, Mongoloid, and Negroid—to well over a hundred (Montague 1952; 1972).

Although no scientific grounds exist for claiming a physiological basis for race, social scientists agree that many cultures around the world have constructed socially agreed upon definitions of race (Kaplan and Van Valey 1980). In some cases the markers are clear cut, in others they are quite ambiguous. What is important for sociologists is not the marker per se, but rather the meanings attached and reactions to racial identities that are socially assigned or individually claimed. Race, like ethnicity, differentiates subgroups in the population and serves to structure interactions among individuals and groups. It is a basis for making invidious comparisons and plays a role in channeling people's access to privilege, prestige, and power.

What markers do you use in defining racial subgroups in your community?

In sum, ethnicity and race are socially created categories. The physical and cultural characteristics singled out as important and the meanings assigned to them are socially agreed upon conventions. These conventions vary from society to society. Race and ethnicity are markers used for differentiating subgroups in the population, as well as making invidious comparisons between individuals and sensitizing people to the inequalities that exist between groups.

How people perceive and feel about members of particular ethnic and racial categories depends, on the one hand, on individual beliefs and, on the other hand, on group values. Both individual beliefs and group values reflect the social meanings constructed around identification with or membership in a particular ethnic or racial category. Individual beliefs get expressed as attitudes about oneself and others. Similarly group values are articulated as group norms, that is, shared understandings about how we think and act and how others think and act.

Problems in Race and Ethnic Relations

Stereotypes

Whether attitudes and norms are derived from personal experience or simply taken for granted because people say so, sometimes they contain generalized assumptions about *all* members of a particular social category. These ideas are called **stereotypes.** Stereotypes are assumptions universally applied to racial and ethnic categories that may refer to their physical characteristics, personality traits, mannerisms, and beliefs. Examples include the images of Germans as "industrious," "efficient," "extremely nationalistic," "aggressive," "submissive to authority," and "methodological"; or those of Americans as "materialistic," "ambitious," and "pleasure loving"; blacks as "musical," "happy-go-lucky," "lazy," and "ostentatious"; Jews as "materialistic" and "clannish"; and Mormons as "polygamous" (Karlins, Coffman, and Watters 1969). Sometimes the images contain a kernel of truth that makes it more difficult to show that the statement does not pertain to all group members. Mr. Charley in the movie *Carbon Copy* automatically assumes that his black son, Roger, is a good basketball player without even asking him. Some stereotypes are pure fictions, such as "All Mexicans are Catholics" or "All Irish are heavy drinkers." Stereotypes, in short, are social understandings that reflect judgments made about characteristics supposedly shared by all members of a particular social status category.

List a number of ethnic groups. List three defining characteristics for each group. Are these traits that you have personally observed? Are these images based on things you have heard, read about, or seen on television or in the movies?

Prejudice

An unthinking acceptance of stereotypes blinds people to the actual range of behavior and thought within any racial or ethnic group. Acceptance of these images gives rise to **prejudice.** Prejudice is an inflexible pattern of thinking and rigidity of feeling displayed toward an individual or group of individuals. People literally prejudge others as "different" simply because of the markers they possess and their membership in a group. These prejudgments may be positive or negative. The crucial aspect of prejudice is that images about racial and ethnic groups and attitudes toward them are not modified as new information is presented.

Prejudice inflexible pattern of thinking and rigidity of feeling displayed toward an individual or group of individuals.

The rigidity of prejudicial thinking can be seen in an excerpt from a poolside conversation between two whites on a swimming team. "You know, there is only one black in the league." "Yeah, blacks can't swim too well. They don't have the bodies for it. They're too dense. They sink." "But Jones won the conference championship last year in the 50-yard freestyle." "See what I mean. Blacks can only swim short distances or they'll sink." Prejudicial thinking that relies on stereotypes has ready-made justifications for liking and disliking particular racial and ethnic groups, as well as for using race and ethnicity as grounds for targeting individuals for differential and unequal treatment. Prejudice can rationalize denying to certain groups the rights that normally are accorded to all. It rationalizes hiring and firing of employees, as well as determining with whom to associate or not (Allport 1958).

Ethnocentrism

Prejudicial thinking also may be expressed as part of the normative beliefs of one group compared with other groups. When group members think that their lifestyle, mannerisms, social institutions, and beliefs are "superior" and others are "inferior," this pattern of thought is called ethnocentrism (Sumner 1906:27–28). In effect, a group uses its way of life as a yardstick to prejudge others. The Japanese upon initial contact with Europeans thought them barbarians, since Europeans bathed infrequently, ate meat, and were disrespectful of feudal lords and samurai. Ethnocentrism in its most extreme form leads to mistrust and even hatred of strangers and all things foreign. This pattern of thinking is called **xenophobia.** Idi Amin, former dictator of Uganda, sought to purify the country by driving out "foreign devils." He expelled thousands of Asians, many of whom could trace their ancestry in Uganda back for several generations.

Xenophobia hatred or distrust of all foreign things and persons.

Do you think that a rise in feelings of nationalism is associated with a heightened sense of ethnocentrism? Does war usually increase feelings of xenophobia?

Ethnocentrism provides the rationalization for avoiding, if at all possible, situations in which individuals from two different groups might be forced to interact. Since ethnocentrism stresses the superiority of one group over others, it provides the grounds for singling out particular racial and ethnic categories and treating them as inferior. In short, ethnocentrism justifies maintaining social distance between individuals marked as different, thereby strengthening their sense of in-group solidarity.

Discrimination

How people act toward members of racial and ethnic groupings depends not only on their privately held beliefs, but also on the kinds of discriminatory actions that a society condones. Prejudice is attitudinal and ethnocentrism a group value, but **discrimination** is overt behavior. It is unequal treatment of individuals and groups because they possess a particular physical or cultural marker. Members of a racial or ethnic status category become targets of either favoritism or maltreatment.

Discrimination unequal treatment of individuals or groups based simply on their membership in a given social category.

Racism is both overt and covert. It takes two, closely related forms: individual whites acting against individual blacks, and acts by the total white community against the black community. We call these individual racism and institutional racism. The first consists of overt acts by individuals, which cause death, injury or the violent destruction of property. This type can be recorded by television cameras; it can frequently be observed in the process of commission. The second type is less overt, far more subtle, less identifiable in terms of specific individuals committing the acts. But it is no less destructive of human life. The second type originates in the operation of established and respected forces in the society, and thus receives far less public condemnation than the first.

When white terrorists bomb a black church and kill five black children, that is an act of individual racism, widely deplored by most segments of society. But when in that same city–Birmingham, Alabama–five hundred black babies die each year because of the lack of proper food, clothing, shelter and proper medical facilities, and thousands more are destroyed or maimed physically, emotionally, and intellectually because of conditions of poverty and discrimination in the black community, that is a function of institutional racism.

SOURCE: S. Carmichael and C. Hamilton, *Black Power* (New York: Vintage, 1967).

Forms of discrimination vary in kind as well as degree. Some types of action are performed by individuals acting on the basis of their privately held beliefs. This behavior is labeled *individual* discrimination. Other actions are performed because the rules, regulations, and norms of an institution or the policies of a society dictate that a particular group be treated unequally. This pattern of behavior is called *institutional discrimination.*

The severity of abusive actions taken against racial and ethnic categories varies. The least severe, but most widely practiced, form of individual discrimination is *verbal abuse.* Individuals often call members of racial and ethnic

TABLE 7.1   Selected Forms of Individual and Institutional Discrimination

	Forms of Discrimination	
Actions	Individual	Institutional
Verbal abuse	Ethnophaulism	Stereotype casting (media)
Social distance	Shunning	Segregation
Physical removal	Neighborhood covenants	Transfer of population subgroups
Death	Murder	Extermination (genocide)

groups derogatory names. Labels and epithets are created that play on stereotypical images of these groupings. Blacks are called "spades," "jungle bunnies," "midnight mollies," "niggers," and "coons"; Jews "kikes," "hebes," and "Christ-killers"; Orientals "chinks," "japs," "nips," "gooks," and "slopes"; and whites "flannel heads," "honkies," "mistah Charley," "white devils," and "ofays." This kind of term is called an **ethnophaulism.** The list of groups and ethnophaulisms used as part of everyday speech could easily be extended. The number of terms used indirectly indicates the visibility of various status groups as well as the intensity of prejudice directed toward them. Racial and ethnic jokes also are generated that denigrate the character and behavior of various groups. These jokes and the brand of "humor" serve as "testimony" for the superiority of one group's way of life over those targeted in the jokes (Palmore 1962).

Ethnophaulism verbal abuse based on stereotypical images of racial or ethnic social category.

CONTROVERSIAL ISSUES · Some Definitions

Black is being told you must "earn" the rights that the U.S. Constitution guarantees to all Americans.

Black is going to court to be judged by a jury of your peers and finding that all your peers look bleached.

Indian is watching John Wayne defeat 50 "savage redskins" with a single-shot pistol on the late, late show.

Indian is learning in school that your country was "discovered" by Christopher Columbus.

Chicano is learning in school that the pioneers "settled" the West 200 years after your ancestors were living there.

Puerto Rican is wondering why white tourists get brown on your island's beaches while you get pale in a mainland ghetto.

A racist, southern style, is someone who allows blacks to live close as long as they don't get "uppity."

A racist, northern style, is someone who allows blacks to get "uppity" as long as they don't live close.

ASSIGNMENT

1. Find the accusations implicit in each of the above "definitions." What kinds of racism are being ridiculed?
2. Make up your own definitions of racism beginning with:
   Black is.........**White is**.........

SOURCE: Definitions collected from minority sources. For additional definitions see: Turner Brown, Jr., *Black Is* 1969; Preston Wilcox, ed., *White Is* (New York: Grove Press, 1970).

The use of ethnophaulisms and stereotypes in the mass media is a form of institutional discrimination. For many years newspapers when reporting arrests of individuals for alleged felonies took great pains to include the race and ethnic identity, especially if the alleged perpetrator was not a WASP. Such articles became just another bit of evidence of the need to keep out-group members in their place. Television and movie producers, while increasingly sensitive to the use of stereotypes, still usually cast and portray persons of various racial or ethnic groupings according to popular stereotypes.

Another form of discrimination is maintaining social distance between individuals from different racial and ethnic status categories. When practiced as a form of individual discrimination it becomes *shunning.* It is the refusal to treat another individual as a social equal. It is Orthodox Jewish parents prohibiting their children from dating a gentile; Protestant parents refusing to allow their children to attend a dance at the Catholic Youth Organization; Japanese refusing to sit at the same table with Koreans; Southerners expressing a reluctance to date or wed Northerners.

When groups are set apart and separateness becomes a policy of institutions or society, it is called **segregation.** Segregation may be practiced voluntarily or involuntarily. Voluntary segregation has been a way of life for a number of religious sects. Disenchanted with urban life or fleeing from persecution various groups, such as the Amish, the Hutterites, and the Mennonites have set up communities in isolated rural areas where they might follow the tenets of their beliefs without fear of interference.

Segregation social pattern in which racial and ethnic groups live apart from one another.

Segregation in the American South in the past.

Where separation is involuntarily imposed, it is typically achieved by enforcing separate patterns of residence, such as designating villages, ghettos, or neighborhoods as the legal habitation of certain racial or ethnic groups. Social contact between groups is prohibited or highly regulated by law and custom. Separate facilities may be designated for many aspects of daily life—lavatories, drinking fountains, restaurants, schools, and means of transportation. Travel may be restricted, permitted only with proper documentation. Elaborate "codes of etiquette" are developed dictating how racial and ethnic group members must behave when forced to interact. Racial or ethnic groups targeted for discrimination under a pattern of segregation are relegated to certain jobs, usually inferior ones, and systematically denied equal treatment before the law. Violations of rules that are designed to maintain separation are severely punished (Rose 1948).

Segregation became a way of life in the United States around the turn of the century. Between 1901 and 1910 a series of "Jim Crow" laws were passed that made segregation of blacks and whites mandatory in some states and optional in others. Educational facilities for blacks and whites were established following the principle "separate but equal." Where whites and blacks attended the same school, school activities were separated: Whites entered the school first, blacks entered last, when the "nigger bell" rang; whites attended one assembly, blacks another; school dances and sports were separate. Public facilities also were segregated by race, such as bars, waiting rooms, parks, playgrounds, movie houses, and toilets. Blacks were systematically excluded from industry, denied access to many professions, and relegated to menial service and unskilled occupations. Blacks were subjected to literacy tests and poll taxes in order to deny them the right to vote. Segregation affected all aspects of black-white relations, and reduced blacks to second-class citizens.

A form of discrimination that is individually motivated is removing unwanted racial and ethnic groups from neighborhoods. Sometimes a person in cooperation with other neighbors in a suburb or a restricted enclave in the city puts up the necessary capital to purchase the unwanted person's house. The price sometimes is above market value. Whether the unwanted person sells or remains in the neighborhood the message is clear—you represent a contaminating presence and we would all be happier if you left.

A more dramatic form of institutional discrimination is the physical *transfer* of racial and ethnic groups from their local communities to other areas or their complete removal by means of expulsion. Russia, in its attempt to achieve political, economic, and social control over an ethnically diverse population, from time to time has transferred various nationalities from one region to another. In the early Depression years in the United States Mexican labor came to be seen as no longer an asset but rather a liability. The County of Los Angeles, to reduce welfare rolls and save tax dollars as well as to eliminate foreign competition for local jobs, repatriated thousands of workers. Similarly the State of Texas sent more than 200,000 Mexicans back across the Rio Grande,

Stemming the flow of undocumented Mexicans.

not only to save money but to keep workers from organizing for better wages and working conditions.

During World War II Japanese-Americans, regardless of their patriotism and the number of generations their families had lived in the United States, were suspected of being loyal to Emperor Hirohito. The United States government confiscated their property, systematically rounded them up and sent them to relocation camps located in various states in the Rocky Mountains, Midwest, and Southwest. These strategies of population transfer and incarceration were also used in the early 1980s on a temporary basis to manage the Cuban and Haitian immigrants that came to Florida by sea.

History is filled with examples of ethnic and racial groups that have been expelled from different societies allegedly to purify their culture or eliminate diversity in their populations. Japan during the Tokugawa Period (1600–1868) expelled Spanish and Portuguese priests and missionaries, curtailed foreign trade, and clamped tight regulations on contacts between Japanese and "barbarians."

The most extreme form of individual discrimination is murder. In its institutional form it is called *extermination*. Members of particular racial and ethnic categories systematically are singled out and killed. In ancient times, it was a standard strategy for one tribe or army, after defeating the enemy, to destroy their dwellings, ruin their temples, and kill most of the men, women, and children; the remaining survivors were taken as slaves. A more recent example is the effort of Nazi Germany during the 1930s and 1940s to eliminate Jews and other Eastern European ethnic groups. The word *genocide* was coined

Japanese-Americans
in a relocation camp
during World War II.

to denote the magnitude of that effort, the killing of an entire race, religion, or ethnic group. In 1949 the United Nations defined genocide as an international crime and accepted the principle that individuals, regardless of a nation's policy, shall be held accountable for participation in such activities. Some twenty countries adopted the principle in 1951, although the United States never ratified it (Berry and Tischler 1978:362–366).

Consistency between Attitudes and Behavior

When trying to understand patterns of discrimination, sociologists sometimes examine the connection between attitudes and behavior. Simply put, they assume that if people are prejudiced, their actions will be discriminatory. Conversely, if individuals profess to be without prejudice, they do not engage in discriminatory actions. To understand patterns of discrimination, then, all that needs to be done is probe what people think and how people feel about certain racial and ethnic groups. If people do not wish to maintain social distance between themselves and an out-group, they probably will interact. Where people wish to maintain separateness, they will discriminate. But life is not so simple. For instance, a number of innkeepers were sent letters inquiring about their willingness to register ethnics as guests. Some innkeepers replied that such a request would be honored; others that ethnics would be refused registration. When innkeepers were asked face-to-face to register an ethnic, some acted consistently with what they said they would do; others were inconsistent. Among those who said they would deny registration, some did and some did not. Similar inconsistency was observed among those who stated they would admit ethnics. These discrepancies suggest, on the one hand, that discrimination can occur despite privately held beliefs, and on the other hand, that people may be prejudiced yet not engage in discriminatory action (LaPierre 1934).

These inconsistencies between attitudes and actions suggest that patterns of discrimination may be understood better by looking at the structuring of racial and ethnic intergroup relations in society, rather than by focusing on attitudes.

Equality or Inequality

Two systems of relationships typically are identified when looking at the relative equality or inequality between racial and ethnic groups in a society. These are ethnic differentiation and ethnic stratification.

Ethnic Differentiation

The simpler, and perhaps more rare, of the two systems is **ethnic differentiation.** In this system, people clearly distinguish among racial and ethnic groups, using physical and cultural markers. People recognize that each group has its own culture, forms of social organization, and lifestyle. In some cases, groups even may hold ethnocentric beliefs, but these beliefs do not prevent the groups from coexisting with one another, interacting as social equals, and engaging in simple forms of economic exchange (Banton 1967, especially Chapter 4).

Ethnic differentiation situation in which people recognize racial or ethnic differences and may hold ethnocentric beliefs, but interact as social equals.

Systems of ethnic differentiation typically are found among primitive societies rather than urban industrial societies. Such a system appears to develop when the groups are of roughly equal size; the groups occupy different territories or the same territory, but engage in different and complementary economic activities; and the groups do not compete for the same resources, but rather trade with each other on an equitable basis.

The Tungus and Cossacks were examples of two racially and ethnically distinct groups coexisting as equals without conflict under a system of ethnic

TABLE 7.2 Typology of Prejudice and Discrimination

	Discrimination	
Prejudice	Yes	No
Yes	Individual who acts out beliefs	Individual who does not act out beliefs
No	Individual who is not prejudiced but unwittingly discriminates	Individual who is not prejudiced and acts accordingly

differentiation. The Tungus and Cossacks lived in roughly the same territory along the western border of Manchuria. The Tungus had Mongolian features, were bilingual, illiterate, tent-dwelling nomads, and depended on hunting for their subsistence. The Cossacks had Caucasoid features, spoke only Russian, were literate, lived in villages, and depended on agriculture. Both groups were roughly the same size. They had frequent contact with each other, trading regularly, occasionally hunting together, and sometimes visiting each other for extended periods of time. Both held ethnocentric views. Tungus saw the Cossacks as thieves, yet praised their sobriety; the Cossacks viewed the Tungus as honest and condemned them for their drunken bouts of violence. In short, the Tungus and Cossacks are typical of groups who recognize ethnic differences, but do not use ethnicity as the principal basis for governing intergroup relationships (Lindgren 1938).

Ethnic Stratification

The more complex, and common, of the two systems is **ethnic stratification.** In discussing the nature of social stratification it was earlier noted that in most societies a variety of social characteristics are used to distinguish between individuals and groups, as well as to ascribe social standing. Social rank usually is judged on one of the three major hierarchies—class, power, and prestige—that when combined, form the fabric of any system of social stratification. When an aggregate of individuals shares similarly evaluated positions on a hierarchy, it forms a stratum. Differences between strata identify rich from poor, powerful from powerless, and favored from unfavored. These differences, in turn, influence who will occupy positions of authority, exercise control over society's institutions and resources, and reap the rewards of privilege, power, and prestige. The persistence of strata differences inevitably results in inequalities between individuals and groups that affect their lifestyles and life chances.

> **Ethnic stratification** situation in which people recognize racial or ethnic distinctions and rank one another according to beliefs about the worth of various groups.

Ethnic stratification is simply another hierarchy in the overall process of social stratification. In multiracial and multiethnic societies people often make invidious distinctions among individuals and groups. People have prejudices and preferences for various groups. Groups hold ethnocentric values. Thus, people rank one another based on beliefs about the "worthiness" of traits that mark racial and ethnic group members. These groups also are ranked following assumptions about the "worthiness" of their lifestyles, modes of social organization, and beliefs. Thus, the population is differentiated into a hierarchy of layers with racial and ethnic groups variously assigned to different strata (Jefferies and Ransford 1980:153–177). Although a number of possible layers are found in different societies, racial and ethnic groups are usually judged as superior or inferior.

What are the distinguishing features of ethnic differentiation and ethnic stratification? How is conflict related to the appearance of ethnic stratification?

Jamaica is an example of a society in which skin color was historically important in assigning individuals to strata in the social hierarchy. Jamaica's population was racially and ethnically mixed. It was made up of whites, blacks, and mulattos, people of mixed white and black ancestry, as well as a sprinkling of Chinese, East Indians, and other ethnic groups. Jamaica was first occupied by the Spaniards, then later by the British. As a British colony it was important in the "unholy" triangle of trade involving tobacco, rum, and slaves. Its principal export, grown on plantations, was sugar cane. Blacks were imported from Africa to work the plantations owned by whites. Since many plantation owners left their families in England, a system developed in which white owners took black females as concubines. Over the generations the result was a sizeable number of mulattos in the population. Skin color historically was associated with social class. Whites occupied the upper rungs of the social ladder and blacks the lower rungs; white skins were seen as passports to political influence and social acceptance. Mulattos came to identify with whites and disassociated themselves from blacks. Nowadays occupation and wealth are the major criteria for fixing one's social position in Jamaican society. Skin color is no longer a major factor in assigning people to a position in the social hierarchy.

How ethnicity and race affect both the individual and the group in their social standing in society depends on labor force mobility and the structure of wages in the marketplace, the fluidity of social mobility in society, and policies governing majority-minority relations.

Discrimination in Jobs and Wages

Some sociologists see workers moving from job to job as part of their search for social and economic improvement. When people have adequate transportation, complete information about job opportunities, and the required skills for job placement, then the movement of workers simply reflects changes in the mix of job opportunities in various occupations and industries. Similarly differences in wages reflect varying skill levels of workers. Wages paid to workers presumably rise and fall according to changes in the demand for products and the costs of production. This view of the labor market ideally assumes that no barriers exist to inhibit the free movement of individuals from job to job. In fact there are barriers to both the free movement of labor and the fixing of wages. Barriers are erected in the recruitment of workers, the actual hiring of workers, and the direct and indirect benefits paid.

Some employers prefer to hire workers with particular markers and discriminate against people with other kinds of markers. For instance, individuals who are taller than average, good looking, or trim usually get hired before short, ugly, or fat people. Similarly employers express preferences for recruiting, hiring, and rewarding members of particular racial and ethnic categories. Preferred workers often are paid higher wages than they would be if free and open competition were permitted. Some researchers see this practice as a temporary gain or benefit for those hired. For the employers this practice is detrimental since the costs of hiring preferred labor are higher than normal, whether they realize it or not. Wage discrimination permits members of favored racial and ethnic groups to occupy higher rungs on the social ladder of privilege, prestige, and power than those from less favored groups (Becker 1957).

Sometimes employers operate as if they have a monopoly when filling job openings. They discriminate between various racial and ethnic groups. For groups targeted for unequal treatment employers impose low wages, set rules that contribute to high rates of job turnover, restrict entry into certain jobs, and limit opportunities to obtain funds for more education and other forms of self-advancement. Those receiving favored treatment get high wages, job security, and easy access to money and opportunities for career advancement. These monopolistic practices quickly force individuals and groups that bear the brunt of discrimination into a disadvantaged position. With lower incomes, they cannot compete equally for commodities, luxuries, and services. Without prestige and power, they cannot obtain adequate services, such as medical, police, fire, insurance, and so on. In short, they form an underprivileged class (Thurow 1969).

Another strategy of economic discrimination is to create a double standard of job employment for individuals from different racial and ethnic backgrounds. A job gets defined or labeled in such a way that when a member of an ill-favored racial or ethnic group is employed, the pay is low, there are no benefits, and career advancement is impossible. Should a preferred individual occupy the job, high wages, good benefits, and career mobility are possible. This split labor market permits individuals from various racial and ethnic groups to enter into a variety of occupations in different sectors of the economy, but it prevents them from assuming supervisory responsibilities, achieving any economic advantages, or experiencing upward mobility within their job careers (Reich, Gordon, and Edwards 1973; Bonacich and Modell 1980).

Would business interests be likely to practice wage discrimination under tight economic conditions?

When job and wage discrimination of particular racial or ethnic groups are practiced along with other forms of exploitation, inequalities result. Should patterns of preference and discrimination be repeated from generation to generation, discrimination becomes institutionalized and inequalities rigidly defined. Some groups end up occupying lower positions in social standing, others middle positions, and still others higher positions. In some cases, the concentration of a particular group in an occupation was forced upon them by dominant members of society. Chinese were forced to take menial jobs upon initially coming to the United States. In such an instance, race and ethnicity usually become linked to class standing. Ethnic group status then serves as a good predictor of the job in which its members will be employed or at least within which narrowly defined range of occupations within a segment of the economy they are likely to find employment.

An example of a society in which ethnicity and occupation become rigorously intertwined and justified by religious beliefs is the caste system in India. Although the caste system was outlawed in 1951, it still operates today. Ethnic group members are assigned social rank at birth. Members of the group form a distinct social stratum. Members cannot change their identity nor their social standing during their lives. Members of a caste typically practice the same occupations as their parents and their parents' parents. The occupations performed by a caste tend to be similarly evaluated in prestige or "worthiness." One caste may serve as carriers of human and animal excrement, another as artisans or tradespersons, another as warriors, others as religious dignitaries, and yet others as administrators or educated elites. Caste distinctions in social rank are marked by dress, conduct, and sometimes name. Distinctions between castes are jealously guarded. Castes maintain as much social distance from one another as possible. Members of a caste are expected to marry within their own caste. Elaborate rules of etiquette and deference govern behavior between individuals when members of different castes have to interact. Inappropriate behavior is severely punished. Religious beliefs, legal practices in some cases, and customs serve to preserve superordinate and subordinate positions between castes from one generation to the next (Davis, Gardner, and Gardner 1941).

During the first half of the twentieth century, segregation in the United States effectively created a quasi-caste system. Whites were dispersed on a hierarchy of class from the superrich—Geddes, Rockefellers, Carnegies, and Mellons—to the "down and outs" in shanties; ranged in prestige from proper Bostonian "bluebloods" and "mainline" Philadelphians to poor white trash; and held jobs spanning the spectrum from corporate executives to ragpickers. Whites controlled the seats of power in business, government, the military, the media, and even organized crime. Conversely, blacks were concentrated among the poor with a sprinkling in the middle class. The majority were in jobs such as farming, household service, and other unskilled and semiskilled positions. Few were entrepreneurs or professionals. Blacks were barred from any likelihood of challenging the power of whites. Color blinded the eyes of Americans. Blacks were trapped by accident of birth to an underclass or inferior caste. Whites were free to move up and down the social ladder. No matter how far whites skidded, even at the lowest rung of the ladder blacks were presumed to be inferior and were targets of prejudice and discrimination.

Sometimes an ethnic group may seek to obtain a monopoly in an occupation or a set of related occupations to ensure its economic survival and well-being. In some cases the ethnic group moves to monopolize a particular job so as to establish control over resources, production, and market distribution, thereby gaining superiority in any economic exchanges with outsiders. Jews historically have dominated various sectors of the diamond industry, in occupations ranging from cutting, polishing, and grading, to sales. Armenians briefly established control over window washers in New York. This strategy of monopolization guarantees economic advantage as long as jobs produce goods or provide services that are in demand. Should the market change, the ethnic group risks economic disaster.

How much emphasis to give race and ethnicity as opposed to individuals' actions in determining individuals' and groups' placements is a matter of intense debate among sociologists. What is clear, however, is that a system of ethnic stratification generally occurs when three factors are present. First, groups engage in competition for control over society's resources and the benefits to be gained from doing so. Second, one group has an advantage over others in the competition or conflict over control. Third, by far most important, individuals with particular racial and ethnic markers are singled out for special treatment—those with worthy traits are favored and those with unworthy traits are discriminated against.

Minority and Majority Groups

Minority Group Defined

A racial or ethnic group's overall social ranking—superordinate or subordinate—and relative size are looked at in combination to determine whether a group is dominant or dominated and a majority or minority. If a racial or ethnic group is overrepresented in key positions of authority and power in business, government, the military, and the media, along with other institutions in society, then that group is dominant. A racial or ethnic group whose numbers constitute a plurality in the population is a statistical majority, while groups smaller in size are statistical minorities.

By cross-referencing power and size, four possibilities are obtained for labeling the various racial and ethnic status categories: (1) a dominant majority—white ethnics compared with blacks in the United States; (2) a dominant elite—ruling whites in South Africa; (3) a dominated mass—blacks in South Africa; and (4) a dominated minority—Native American Indians. Group size is important in that sufficient numbers must be present so that a group has visibility. Most sociologists, however, see the relative social power of a group as more important in labeling groups as majorities or minorities. Thus, dominated groups despite their size may be called **minority groups** (Schmerhorn 1978).

Minority group a term used to refer to a group that receives discriminatory treatment and lacks adequate power, privilege, or prestige.

Majority-Minority Relations

The form that majority-minority relations takes depends on three conditions. First, the way racial and ethnic groups come into contact. Second, the

TABLE 7.3 Typology of Size and Power

Power	Population size	
	Plurality	Minority
Dominant	(1)	(2)
Dominated	(3)	(4)

basis for determining who is eligible to hold power, privilege, and prestige—individual merit or race and ethnicity. Third, the beliefs pertaining to absorption—whether a racial or ethnic group should preserve its uniqueness or surrender it.

Conquest-Colonial Model

One pattern of majority-minority relations is the conquest-colonial form. This form is found when one racial or ethnic group is more powerful militarily and economically than another. Contact between the two groups results in the more powerful defeating the weaker. The victors, then, either establish their own system of government and colonize the losers or force the losers to migrate. Members of the minority are stripped of their political rights, exploited economically, and systematically discriminated against socially. The lifestyle, social institutions, and beliefs of the minority are denigrated by the majority and redefined as inferior, if not completely destroyed. Under a conquest-colonial form, race and ethnicity become the grounds for targeting individuals for exploitation. The system is maintained for economic reasons, since the majority enjoys the benefits derived from cheap labor provided by exploited minorities (Jefferies and Ransford 1980: 152–177).

The experience of blacks in the United States has been likened to that of a colonized minority. Blacks were captured by slavers and transported in shackles for sale on the auction block. A system of slavery replaced tribal customs. Every aspect of their daily life was managed by white plantation owners. An elaborate ideology of racial superiority was developed to justify the inferiority of blacks and their subjugation by whites. Segregation merely was another form of colonization of blacks by whites. The struggle of blacks following desegregation to achieve equality of opportunity and establish a viable political and economic base is simply a part of the process to reduce the inequalities inflicted by majority whites (Blauner 1972).

The early experience of Mexican-Americans fits a pattern of conquest-colonial exploitation. Mexican-Americans became an instant minority as territories under Mexican control passed to the hands of Americans (Anglos) following warfare and by purchase. Anglos in a relatively short time achieved economic dominance over Mexican-Americans. In Texas the fencing of rangelands by large sheep and cattle interests squeezed out small-time farmers, many of whom were Mexican-Americans. Later the arrival of King Cotton created demand for cheap field labor. Cheap immigrant Mexican labor and Texas landowners became a pattern that still operates.

In New Mexico an early alliance between Anglos and Spanish-Americans against hostile Indians saw wealthy landowners, bankers, ranchers, and early railroaders from each group controlling Sante Fe politics. The coming of the railroad, heavy in-migration, intrusion of mining interests, and especially the intervention of federal government in public land ownership and control of resources eroded cooperative ties between Anglos and Mexican-Americans in New Mexico and other parts of the Southwest. Anglo enterprises engaged in wage discrimination when hiring Mexican-Americans. In California irrigation agriculture similarly created a demand for immigrant Mexican labor. As long as the demand for labor is high, Mexican immigration, legal or illegal, is supported by agribusiness (large-scale commercial agriculture).

Assimilation Model

A second pattern of majority-minority relations is **assimilation.** It is the process of adjustment and integration experienced by immigrant minorities as they set up residence in a new society and learn to cope with a new way of life dictated by the majority. Immigrants may have fled their homelands to avoid political, religious, or economic discrimination or simply moved to attain a higher standard of living. Regardless of their reasons for emigration, immigrant minorities upon arrival recognize that to obtain jobs, gain social acceptance, and eventually to move up the social ladder of success, they best accommodate to the lifestyle defined by the majority. These processes of social absorption and social mobility take time. More and more members of each succeeding generation of a minority presumably surrender their old racial or ethnic identities, turn away from traditional ways of thinking and behaving, and adopt the outlook and behaviors of the majority. As minorities become more successful politically, socially, and economically and become more like the majority in outlook and behavior, presumably minority-majority distinctions cease to be important.

Assimilation is not a uniform process. Different kinds of assimilation occur and at differing rates. Most immigrant minorities entering the United States initially undergo *acculturation.* They learn to speak English and master a variety of social skills necessary for surviving in an urban-industrial setting. They are resocialized by learning to conform to customs and laws generally taken for granted by majority Americans. When minorities' cultural backgrounds are similar to that of the United States, they tend to acculturate more rapidly than minorities coming from cultures that differ markedly. For instance, immigrants from Wales, Scotland, England, and Ireland melted more rapidly into the American mainstream than did the Slavs.

Most minorities usually experience some *structural assimilation* as they adjust to a new culture and behavioral patterns. This type of assimilation means that minorities enter positions within various clubs, cliques, and voluntary associations as well as the principal institutions dominated by the majority. Their penetration may be into split labor markets, taking low-status, low-income jobs, on the same social footing with majority members. Minorities with small populations, without readily identifiable markers, and with occupational skills needed by the majority usually obtain jobs quickly and rapidly move up the occupational hierarchy. Conversely, mass minorities, with high visibility and without marketable skills, have fewer choices for employment and find upward social mobility more difficult.

Immigrant minorities who have resided in the United States for some time undergo *civic assimilation.* They become citizens and enter the political arena. They exercise their right to vote, become party members and office-holders and establish a power base for representing their interests. Not all

Assimilation process by which persons changing social identities surrender old identities and adopt new outlooks and behaviors of the group they wish to join.

immigrant minorities are eligible for citizenship. In several European countries "guest workers" and undocumented immigrants are denied rights of citizenship and merely allowed to reside in the country as long as there is a demand for their labor.

As minorities become more successful, socially and economically, they experience *identificational assimilation.* They depend less on their ethnic communities for social and emotional support, and increasingly define themselves as Americans. As minorities rise in the majority's eyes, as prejudicial sentiments weaken and discriminatory barriers erode, increased interaction between majority and minority occurs. Minorities gain social entry into the social clubs and networks long the domain of the majority. They interact with members of the majority as status equals. With increased social contact and reduced prejudice and discrimination, *marital assimilation* occurs (Gordon 1964).

Some minorities rapidly "melt" or assimilate into the mainstream of social life, but other minorities are "unmeltable." They remain tied to their own racial and ethnic communities (Hastings et al. 1982). The rapidity or resistance to absorption and social mobility depends on the cultural background of immigrants, their relative visibility, economic conditions in society, and most importantly the ideologies governing majority-minority relations.

The Chinese are an ethnic group that has proven rather unmeltable. With the Gold Rush of the 1850s, Chinese immigrants flocked to California in search of the proverbial mountain of gold. They hoped to get rich quickly and return to a life of leisure at home. Instead they were forced to cull over dead mine tailings, take service jobs as restaurant workers, laundry workers, cigar makers, tailors, and common laborers—coolies. Further they were severely abused, often physically beaten and even murdered. They were swindled through phony taxes and forced to take subsistence wages. To build the transcontinental railroad Union Pacific hired several thousand Chinese despite the resentment of white ethnics like the Irish and German workers. In 1882 labor unrest and the fear of the "Yellow Peril" stimulated passage of the Chinese Exclusion Act, which prevented men from bringing their wives and children to this country. The Immigration Act of 1924 prohibited naturalization of Chinese-American spouses. It was not until the 1940s that immigration policy again was opened up for the Chinese (Berry and Tishler 1978).

Faced with extreme prejudice and discrimination they turned inward for emotional, financial, and social support, depending on families and various voluntary associations that developed in their own communities. They established residentially segregated Chinatowns in cities with large concentrations of Chinese. By the end of World War II they achieved only limited entry into the "better" jobs despite being well educated. They remained socially isolated. They participated only marginally in local politics and remained endogamous. It was not until after the May 1949 victory of Mao Tse-tung and the influx of Chinese refugees that resistance to Chinese was significantly reduced. Many refugees were professionals or skilled workers. Nowadays Chinese-Americans are considered favorably by other Americans. They are moving out of Chinatowns like those in New York and San Francisco, living in suburbs, and gaining entry into professional occupations. They are slowly entering the mainstream of American life.

Pluralism Model

A third pattern of majority-minority relations is **pluralism.** This form of intergroup relations occurs when racial or ethnic groups maintain their distinctiveness. Each group maintains its own sense of identity and community, as well as its own culture and social institutions. Each group is viewed as contributing something special to the overall quality of society. Each group participates in and contributes to the economy, yet is guaranteed autonomy as well as political, religious, and legal freedom (Cross 1971).

An ethnic group falling between assimilation and insularity, therefore typical of pluralism, is the Greek-American. Since the last half of the eighteenth century Greek peasants deserted the poor soil, scanty harvests, and grinding poverty in Greece to flock to the United States in search of wealth. While the United States immigration policy was open rather than restrictive (see Chapter 16), some 400,000 Greeks came to this country. For many their dream was to earn enough money to afford luxurious living upon return to their native villages. Many sought their fortunes in the West working in the mines and on the railroads as laborers and cooks; others settled in New England, taking jobs in textile mills and shoe factories; and still others went to urban centers like Chicago and New York, finding employment as bootblacks, busboys, or peddlers. They endured hardships and privations to accumulate enough wealth to establish lunchrooms and restaurants. This pattern of immigration, finding "soft spots" in the economy as a toehold entry to the middle class, continued until immigration policy became restrictive in 1924. Recognizing that only citizens could bring wives and relatives to this country, Greeks became naturalized citizens. They sent for their families. The volume of immigration slowed until the 1960s when immigration policy loosened up again. Nowadays the volume of Greek immigration both legal and illegal has picked up markedly.

Since the 1920s and 1930s a Greek-American community has developed. Greeks as entrepreneurs and individualists always have had a middle-class model of success and upward social mobility. They easily achieved economic assimilation even though leary of using ethnic solidarity as a political weapon for getting advantages from the state. Despite their reluctance to mobilize politically, they maintained a Greek identity, a Greek social life, and a sense of peoplehood. They rely on family, the Greek Orthodox church, Greek newspapers and journals, and a variety of fraternal organizations. They interact with non-Greeks but sustain communal ties with fellow Greeks. They eat in Greek-American restaurants and celebrate Greek festivals and holidays. Although American born and acculturated, they continue to affirm their Greek heritage and maintain a sense of separateness (Moskos 1980).

Switzerland is perhaps the best-known example of a country following a policy of pluralism. Its population is ethnically mixed. It has four official languages—German, French, Italian, and Romansh—important in identifying ethnic groupings yet defined as equal by the constitution. Its population also is

Pluralism form of intergroup relations in which racial or ethnic groups maintain their distinctive cultures and institutions yet participate in the economy and political activity of the larger society.

divided into Catholics and Protestants, each group guaranteed freedom of expression and conscience. Cantons (political divisions similar to states) tend to have high concentrations of particular ethnic groups. To insure cultural diversity and maintain a balance of power among various groups, strategies such as proportional representation and referendums are used to reduce political conflict.

In sum, each of these three forms of majority-minority relations results from different historical circumstances as well as social, economic, and political factors. Different philosophies arise from various settings and produce various answers to questions such as: (1) whether racial or ethnic differences should be preserved or eradicated; (2) whether individuals should be encouraged to participate in racially and ethnically bound communities or in the larger society; and (3) whether inequalities between groups should be maintained or equality between groups guaranteed.

Under a conquest-colonial system, racial and ethnic distinctions are rigorously maintained. Individuals are forced to exist within rigidly defined communities. Inequalities between majority and minority are perpetuated through social discrimination, ideologically justified through prejudicial theories, and protected through force.

In a society fostering assimilation, racial and ethnic differences presumably wither away simply as a consequence of increasing rationalism in urban and industrial settings. Minorities adjust to and adopt the majority outlook. Inequalities that exist between individuals result from differences in individual merit and achievement and are not based on racial or ethnic criteria. William J. Wilson (1978) and other sociologists contend that being black is less important today than in the past; they hold that in fact, economic factors may have come to override racial criteria in allocating social standing to blacks. Wilson is severely criticized by sociologists who contend the racism of American institutions makes it impossible for blacks to be seen as people. Being black takes precedence over other social characteristics in fixing social position.

Under a system of pluralism, racial and ethnic distinctions are granted official legal standing. Individuals maintain ties with their respective racial or ethnic enclaves. Equality between groups in the political arena is encouraged as formulas are used to insure that each group is adequately represented.

Select a minority group in your community. Which of the three models best describes majority-minority relations? Does the model fit historically? Currently?

Minority Responses

When treated as inferiors and barred from equal access to the social rewards of power, privilege, and prestige minorities often become sensitive to the stigma attached to racial or ethnic identity and concerned with being victimized by the majority. How minorities react to the frustrations of being targets of prejudice and discrimination affects whether they accept or reject their identity as imposed by others. Whether they see themselves favorably or unfavorably in turn influences what strategies may be used in coping with minority status and identity, as well as in reacting to the majority.

Where minorities accept racial or ethnic markers as important in defining a sense of self and community, they develop strategies to build self-pride, to foster group solidarity, and to gain greater independence from majority constraints. To instill a sense of group pride and debunk stereotypes that debase minority culture and character, accomplishments by group heroes are praised. Media practices that portray minorities in a demeaning way are challenged. Educational policies aimed at homogenizing racial and ethnic groups through conformity to majority values and practices are questioned and pressures generated to effect programs that recognize the integrity of minority beliefs and lifestyles. To enhance group solidarity, minority associations are developed so that individuals have the opportunity to participate in a variety of social activities denied them under exclusionary policies of the majority. To gain economic leverage and power, minorities attempt to achieve monopolies in particular jobs or build minority owned and operated businesses. To broaden their political base, minorities band together, vote as interest groups for candidates sensitive to their needs, and agitate for reforms and greater representation in positions of authority.

In early stages of assimilation, immigrant minorities often use the strategy of building local communities. On the one hand, these communities provide newcomers with a "home away from home," a setting within which they can follow traditional customs, practice their rituals, and escape from the daily pressures of conforming to demands and constraints of the majority. On the other hand, as minorities acculturate and gain affluence, these communities provide a base of operation for lobbying for social and political changes to guarantee greater opportunities for minority persons to achieve the social rewards of power, privilege, and prestige.

In pluralistic societies local communities are strengthened to preserve the integrity and continuity of various racial and ethnic groups and their way of life. These communities serve as the base for insuring that the interests of each group are protected and each group has equal access to society's rewards.

In some cases, social and ethnic groups reject assimilation, for it would mean the end of their identity and the destruction of their culture. Similarly they reject pluralism, for they believe it would make them second-class citizens. Instead they prefer *separatism* or *withdrawal*. Separatist movements argue that territory should be ceded to them so that they can establish their own institutions, be free to follow their own lifestyle, believe as they wish, and determine their own fate. In some cases, separatists demand reimbursement for injustices committed against them and demand return to their native lands. Other less militant groups establish isolated communities in rural areas, simply cut their ties, and become self-sufficient, quietly preserving their traditional beliefs and lifestyles.

Marcus Garvey's "back to Africa movement" is an example of separatism.

Marcus Garvey was a black Jamaican, widely traveled and well read, who settled in the United States. He was taken by the absence of black institutions, leaders, dignity, and roots. To redress these omissions he founded the Universal Negro Improvement Association, which was dedicated to black pride, moral and technical education, and nationalism and separatism to be achieved by returning to Africa. As an orator Garvey successfully stirred the imagination of many American blacks. Despite the internal bickering among branch organizations in various cities, Garvey proved successful in getting the movement going. He instituted a number of self-help programs—black business enterprises, lunch programs, and a newspaper—*Negro World.* To reach his goal of returning to Africa he sold stock in a steamship company, the Black Star Line. Garvey was a "grandiose and bombastic" leader—according to W.E.B. DuBois, a bitter foe of Garvey—but a rotten businessman. Also, he was not knowledgeable about the law. He failed to incorporate before selling stock through the mail, which constituted a case of mail fraud. He was charged, pleaded his own case, lost, served time in Atlanta federal prison, and eventually was deported as an undesirable alien. Despite Garvey's failure he sparked a theme that repeatedly has recurred in black protest movements—racial pride and a return to the blacks' true roots. Although separation fires the imagination of some blacks, it often encounters resistance among black intellectuals and middle class, since separatism is antagonistic to goals of assimilation and upward social mobility (Myrdal 1944).

The Present and the Future

Persistence of Race and Ethnicity

Why race and ethnicity persist as important aspects of human behavior and thought is a matter of interest to sociologists. Some sociologists argue that race and ethnicity as social categories are products of human nature. They believe that from birth human beings have both the capacity and the need to distinguish between physical and social objects that make up their environment. Since human beings are capable of learning and manipulating symbols, they come to assign meanings and labels to these distinctions. Further, as creatures capable of self-reflection, they use these symbols to distinguish between "self" and others. Thus, when people who look, think, and behave differently come into contact with one another, social and physical distinctions are marked and racial and ethnic categories are created (Glazer and Moynihan 1963; Greeley 1974; and Gordon 1978).

Other sociologists reject the idea that race and ethnic categories are created in response to some vague "need" to distinguish self from others. Their rejection is based on two points. First, social scientists do not have a set of procedures for demonstrating that a need exists. Such a claim smacks of using instinct to explain the persistence of race and ethnicity, a claim dismissed out of hand. Second, sociologists observe that individuals may mark differences among one another, but racial and ethnic markers are not always the principal criteria for defining self-identity, determining group membership, or organizing intergroup relations. In some societies, for instance, whether one owns land or not is more important in defining personal identity and social worth than race or ethnicity. Even in societies where race and ethnicity are deemed important in defining who people are, sociologists see their importance linked to social, economic, and political inequalities that exist between groups (Hechter 1975). Therefore, to understand why race and ethnicity are treated as crucial issues in a society, we must study the social arrangements of who rules, who controls the wealth and resources, and who is honored.

Do people have an inborn need to make racial and ethnic distinctions? Are racial and ethnic distinctions a result of economic, political, and social competition for privilege, power, and prestige?

Future of Race and Ethnicity

Sociologists are uncertain about how important race and ethnicity will be in the future for shaping social identity, defining group memberships and boundaries, or determining majority-minority statuses. One camp of sociologists argues that modernization fundamentally changes the nature of social relationships, thus undermining the salience of race and ethnicity. Modernization brings the growth of cities, substitution of machines for animal and human power, and expansion of industry, trade, and commercial agriculture. Work becomes specialized, routinized, and bureaucratized. Social relationships, once informal and regulated by custom, become formal and governed by contract and law. As the number and variety of jobs increase, especially in the cities, opportunities for social advancement stimulate rural-to-urban migration. Individuals become more autonomous, and individuals' ties to their families, local communities, and region weaken. Ability and achievement outweigh family background and, more importantly, also outweigh race and ethnicity as factors in assigning social rank in society. Thus, as the world becomes more modern, people should increasingly focus on economic criteria in defining social identity and majority-minority statuses. Conversely, race and ethnicity should become less important as individual or group markers.

Another camp of sociologists counters that as long as majority-minority distinctions persist and race and ethnic markers are used to ascribe social standing, then race and ethnicity will be important as sources of conflict. These sociologists argue that modernization, especially under capitalism, engenders conflict. Owners of production, in their drive for greater profits, increased production, and reduced costs, often resort to exploitation of particular racial and ethnic groups. Discriminatory hiring practices and lower pay and benefits give rise to an underclass made up of disadvantaged racial and ethnic groups. Even in capitalist societies fostering a policy of assimilation, in which minorities experience some degree of acculturation and some upward social mobility, race and ethnicity will persist as grounds for conflict as long as immigrant minorities are exploited as a source of cheap labor.

In pluralistic societies, as long as jobs and state funds are distributed according to racial and ethnic quotas and these groups are guaranteed various freedoms by law, race and ethnicity will continue to be important, both as a source of personal identity and as a basis around which community interests and organizations develop.

In short, the future of race and ethnicity in shaping the nature of majority-minority relations is problematic. As long as the diversity of populations in societies changes, as long as differences are judged important in determining individuals' and groups' social status, and as long as inequalities between majority and minority are shaped by group membership, race and ethnicity will persist as explosive issues in social relationships.

Summary

Visible physical, social and cultural markers—how people look, think and behave—are used to distinguish among racial and ethnic groups. Markers are used: (1) to catalogue "who people are"; (2) to denote an important aspect of one's sense of self; and (3) to locate individuals within communities where they can receive social, emotional, and psychological support.

Some sociologists contend that race and ethnicity persist as important, since individuals have a "need" to distinguish self from others as well as to make group distinctions of "we" and "they." Other sociologists argue that race and ethnicity are important because the social arrangements of who rules, who controls the wealth and resources, and who is honored in a society often depend on an individual's racial or ethnic group membershp.

Stereotypes are employed to typecast how people of particular racial and ethnic groups presumably look, think, and behave. An unthinking acceptance of stereotypes gives rise to prejudice.

Prejudice locks people into rigid ways of thinking about all members of a particular racial or ethnic group. When one group prejudges others as inferior because they see their own way of life as superior, they are engaging in ethnocentrism.

When discrimination is practiced, one group is targeted for unequal treatment by another. Forms of discrimination range in severity from verbal abuse, through segregation and transferal of subgroups, to genocide.

The patterns of intergroup relations found in a society are tied to the importance of race and ethnicity in determining who gets what. Under a system of ethnic differentiation, group differences are noted and groups may hold ethnocentric views, but they get along with one another as equals and without conflict. Under a system of ethnic stratification, prejudices and preferences about the worthiness of each group may lead to inequalities between them.

Three forms of majority-minority relations generally are noted.

Assimilation is the process in which immigrant minorities seek to accommodate to the outlook and behaviors of the majority and take on new identities and lifestyles so as to achieve success. Pluralism is the situation in which differences between various racial and ethnic groups are maintained. Each group is encouraged to preserve its own identity, culture, and institutions, and minority individuals participate as equals in the economic and political arenas of the larger society. Conquest-colonial is a pattern of majority-minority relations in which the identities and cultural tradition of minorities are demeaned and they are exploited as sources of cheap labor.

How individuals respond to their minority status depends on the policies governing majority-minority relations and whether individuals view race or ethnicity as central to their sense of self and their chances for success. Some minorities may espouse ethnic pride and foster ethnic solidarity to improve their social stand-

ing in society. Some may deny their minority status and seek to assimilate or to withdraw from the mainstream of society.

How important race and ethnicity will be in the future is problematic. As long as invidious distinctions are made between individuals and groups by means of physical, social, and cultural markers, race and ethnicity will serve as rallying points for social conflict.

Suggested Readings

Charles H. Anderson. *White Protestant Americans: From National Origins to Religious Group.* Englewood Cliffs, N.J.: Prentice-Hall, 1970. Reviews the patterns of immigration, settlement, and welding of Anglo-Saxons, Dutch, Scandinavians, Welsh, and Scottish together in a Protestant ethnic group.

Marjorie R. Fallows. *Irish Americans: Identity and Assimilation.* Englewood Cliffs, N.J.: Prentice-Hall, 1979. Weaves together oral and documentary sources of history to trace the immigration, acculturation, and assimilation of Protestant and Catholic Irish into the American mainstream.

Joseph Fitzpatrick. *Puerto Rican Americans: The Meaning of Migration to the Mainland.* Englewood Cliffs, N.J.: Prentice-Hall, 1971. Reviews ebb and flow of Puerto Ricans to and from the United States, the importance of statehood versus territorial status, and problems of social adjustment among migrants on the mainland.

Milton M. Gordon. *Assimilation in American Life.* New York: Oxford, 1964. Classic volume reviews literature on assimilation/acculturation and suggests a paradigm for looking at seven dimensions of assimilation. Discusses Angloconformity, melting pot thesis, and pluralism.

Milton M. Gordon. "America as a Multi-Cultural Society." The Annals, vol. 454 (March 1981). Collection of essays on minority groups. Also examines notions of pluralism.

Harry H.L. Kitano. *Japanese Americans: The Evolution of a Subculture.* Englewood Cliffs, N.J.: Prentice-Hall, 1976. Treats pre- and post-World War II Japanese and Anglo relations, focuses on notion of generations in discussing dimen-

sions of assimilation, as well as role of the family.

Helena Znaniecki Lopata. *Polish Americans: Status Competition in an Ethnic Community.* Englewood Cliffs, N.J.: Prentice-Hall, 1976. Focuses on rise of ethnic identity and discusses the concept of Polonia.

Joseph Lopreato. *Italian Americans.* New York: Random House, 1970. Well written. Good review of an ethnic group as it carves out an identity and achieves success.

Rose H. Lee. *The Chinese in the United States of America.* Hong Kong: Hong Kong University, 1960. An oldie but a well-documented reference.

Joan W. Moore, with Harry Panchon. *Mexican Americans.* Englewood Cliffs, N.J.: Prentice-Hall, 1976. Focuses on immigration, economics, and political activities. Good discussion of Chicanos.

Alphonso Pinkney. *Black Americans.* Englewood Cliffs, N.J.: Prentice-Hall, 1975. Profiles blacks, using Gordon's paradigm. Discusses annexation, migration, slavery, and colonialism.

Murray Wax. *Indian Americans: Unity and Diversity.* Englewood Cliffs, N.J.: Prentice-Hall, 1971. Difficult to cover contemporary Indian relations, but is worth reading.

William J. Wilson. *The Declining Significance of Race.* Chicago: University of Chicago, 1978. Argues discriminatory barriers against blacks have weakened. Class is now more important than race in fixing social placement. Needless to say this book has stimulated more than a bit of controversy.

8

Gender

One fundamental way to differentiate people is in terms of gender—male or female. All societies recognize physical differences between males and females, although they do not necessarily emphasize the same differences (such as size of mammary glands). These visible physical differences lead many people to assume that biological explanations of male and female behavior are more important than sociological or psychological explanations. Yet the social and psychological characteristics people believe are inherently male in our society may be considered female characteristics in another society. Men in our society who meet each other are expected to shake hands, whereas women, who are "more emotional," may hug each other. How do we explain why Italian men hug each other? Many decades ago a classic study by anthropologist Margaret Mead (1935) of three New Guinea tribes demonstrated that what was "naturally" male or female in one society was not necessarily true for another society. The recent publication of a book (Freeman 1983) critiquing Mead's conclusions about the importance of nurture (based on her research in Samoa in 1925) indicates that debates over social and biological explanations of human behavior are hard to resolve permanently.

Beliefs about gender are such a fundamental aspect of our culture that sociologists often have failed to study these beliefs adequately, if at all. Many early sociologists apparently saw no need to examine the positions of women and men, and those who did, such as Comte and Spencer, affirmed the view prevailing in nineteenth century America—that a woman's place was in the home. Many early American sociologists continued that tradition by paying little or no attention to gender arrangements. Social Darwinists such as William Graham Sumner believed simply that women were subordinate socially because of their innate inferiority. Others such as Lester Ward and W. I. Thomas believed in male-female equality to a limited extent. But they, too, resorted to psychobiological explanations that assumed that innate biological and psychological differences between males and females accounted for their different positions in society. They accepted such ideas as women's possession of a maternal instinct and men's inherent aggressiveness, while downplaying or ignoring more sociological explanations, such as those that focused on social structural barriers to equality.

Until the 1970s most sociologists paid little attention to the bases of male-female inequality in American society, although a few *functionalists* (Talcott Parsons, for example) noted that the subordination of women in society probably was necessary for the survival of the family, a key societal institution. Sociologists studied occupations, social stratification systems, criminal behavior, and many other topics by looking only at men and their lives, and they often studied the family by interviewing only women.

During the 1960s and into the 1970s, equal rights movements—civil rights, women's rights, homosexuals' rights—emerged, and governmental mandates ensuring equal treatment followed. Social scientists began to study these movements and the *social inequalities* that were being questioned by participants in the movements. Research funds became available to study "new" forms of social inequality, and opportunities to publish research on gender inequality increased.

Today one body of literature provides information about women to parallel the existing information about men. Thus, researchers report on women's criminal behavior and women's political and economic roles.

Another body of literature establishes the importance of studying activities solely or largely performed by women—reproduction and homemaking. Such topics received little attention in the past, because the activities of women were evaluated as trivial and unimportant.

Currently, much attention is given to how society produces males and females and how those distinctions are maintained. Sociologists further examine the structural arrangements that tend to maintain inequality between males and females.

Being Male or Female

Public debate over equality between the sexes in recent decades has stimulated a vast body of research. This new research has led to clarification of the effects of biological and social factors upon human behavior and more precise concepts.

Sex and Gender

One fundamental distinction that researchers make is between biological and social/cultural categories. **Sex** refers to the biological categories of male and female that reflect chromosomal differences: male (XY) and female (XX). Although a few people have chromosomal abnormalities (XXY), only the biological categories of male and female are socially recognized.

Sex the biological categories of male and female based on chromosomal differences.

In the early stages of embryonic development, there are no distinctive male and female characteristics. Although our society tends to assign females a secondary role, biologically the female form appears to more closely resemble the basic embryonic form from which all humans develop.

At birth infants are identified as female or male on the basis of their external genitalia, which developed during the later stages of embryonic development. **Gender** is used to designate the social/cultural categories of male and female to which people are assigned after birth.

Gender the social/cultural categories of male and female to which people are assigned.

Sex Characteristics

Researchers try to distinguish carefully between characteristics of sex and gender. **Primary sex characteristics** relate to the gonads, primary sex glands. Many of the visible differences between males and females (body form)

Primary sex characteristics those relating to the gonads.

are **secondary sex characteristics** produced by the large-scale secretion of gonadal or sex hormones from the onset of puberty. Secondary sex differences do not provide a basis for distinguishing all men from all women. Males in our society tend to be taller than females and to have proportionately less fat for their body weight; however, these are general tendencies. Not all men are taller than all women, and some men have proportionately more fat for their body weight than some women. Also, variations between males and females may be greater in some societies than in others or during some periods in a society. Diet and physical training are important factors. Modern women athletes who train have lower levels of body fat relative to their weight than women who have not had such training.

Many of the characteristics we associate with being male or female reflect our cultural beliefs and practices rather than fundamental differences. Ray Birdwhistell (1972) identifies **tertiary sex characteristics:** body language that people learn is appropriate for a person of their sex. Males and females learn to walk with their pelvises in different positions, to sit with legs crossed or open, and to carry books and packages in different ways.

Secondary sex characteristics those produced by the large-scale secretion of gonadal or sex hormones from the onset of puberty; anatomical in nature.

Tertiary sex characteristics learned movement and communication patterns that signal to others a person's gender.

What are examples of primary, secondary, and tertiary sex characteristics?

Tertiary sex characteristics vary from society to society. In our society males position arms and legs to take up more space than females.

To clarify the effects of social/cultural factors, examination of some people who fall in special categories is useful. Most people are assigned to the same categories for both sex and gender. The very small percentage of people for whom the categories do not coincide point out the differences between sex and gender as well as the need to consider social expectations for behavior. Whether filling out birth certificates or building restrooms, people in our society only recognize two sex categories. **Hermaphrodites** are born with both male and female gonads because of chromosomal abnormalities. The physical sexual ambiguity may be concealed and eventually resolved surgically. For other individuals, pseudohermaphrodites, ambiguous sexual features develop because of hormonal secretions.

Hermaphrodites persons with both male and female gonads due to chromosomal abnormalities.

The persons who have received considerable attention in the mass media are those dissatisfied with their sex category who desire to change it surgically. In other words, although they were born with male or female gonads and assigned to the associated sex and gender categories, these **transsexuals** feel trapped in bodies of the wrong sex. Although they can change their behavior to conform to expectations for the opposite gender, their physical apearance limits acceptance of such behavior. Some transsexuals undergo sex change surgery and hormonal treatments to alter their physical appearance. Tennis player Renee Richards (a male surgically changed to a female) generated considerable criticism when she entered women's tennis tournaments, for some people believed she had the unfair advantage of male strength. Questions about Richards and other transsexuals reflect to some extent people's desire to categorize clearly all individuals as distinctly and irrevocably males or females.

Transsexuals people of one sex who behave as if they belonged in the opposite gender category.

Roles, Statuses, and Identities

Before sex change surgery is performed, an institute or hospital may require a male patient to live as a female for a year to see if the person can function satisfactorily in that role. The person learns about functioning as a male or female by playing the **gender role**—responding to the social expectations for appropriate behavior. People are taught gender roles early in life, for example, when they are told that "little boys don't cry."

Gender role expectations for behavior based on one's gender.

All roles reflect the statuses or positions that people occupy. Occupancy of some statuses limits attainment of others. Gender status differs from most social statuses because it influences behavioral expectations in almost all social situations. Gender, race, and age form **master statuses.** They determine which other statuses typically may be occupied and how the roles associated with those statuses should be performed. The use of gender labels illustrates that the master status of gender affects role designations. A gender label is often used when the performer of a role is expected to be a certain gender but is not. People usually speak of a male nurse but a female doctor, a male telephone operator but a female telephone installer, a female household head but a househusband, indicating that these people are expected to perform their occupational roles somewhat differently because of their gender.

Master status a limited number of statuses (racial, sexual) that affect what other statuses people may attain.

In addition people learn to think of themselves and to see themselves as male or female, that is, to assume **gender identities.** Not only do people identify themselves as male or female, but also other people assign gender identities to them. People learn male and female social psychological characteristics and assign themselves and others gender identities based on perceived exhibition of those characteristics. People who desire sex change operations typically have assumed the gender identity for a person of the opposite sex. Furthermore, perceiving themselves to have unfortunately been given a body of the wrong sex, they may encourage others to cross-identify them. But transsexuals' gender identities are not in accord with "social facts" until they are surgically modified. Medical centers such as the one at Johns Hopkins have discontinued transsexual surgery because adjustment appears to be tied to social and psychological factors more than to physical ones.

Gender identity how a person thinks of himself or herself in terms of gender or how other people categorize a person.

Traditional Conceptualization

very
masculine   ⟵――――――――――――――⟶   very
feminine

For many decades social scientists accepted the commonsense notion that men and women were fundamentally different. Masculinity was placed at one end of a continuum and femininity at the other. People could be located at one point on the continuum; they could not be both masculine and feminine. Recently, social scientists have argued that not only can people have both masculine and feminine characteristics, but also they are better off if they do have both (Bem 1975; Buck 1977). A person who possesses positively valued masculine and feminine social psychological characteristics (showing both independence and compassion) is called **androgynous.**

Experimental studies suggest that those people who are androgynous are more flexible and adaptable than those who have traditionally masculine or feminine characteristics (Bem 1975). Androgynous people given a choice of performing a traditional gender task for less money or an opposite gender task for more money choose to perform the better-paying task. Yet a traditionally

Androgynous having both male and female positive social and psychological characteristics.

TABLE 8.1 Androgynous Conceptualization

		Positive Masculine Characteristics	
		Few	**Many**
Positive Feminine Characteristics	Few	Undifferentiated Person	Traditional Masculine Person
	Many	Traditional Feminine Person	Androgynous Person

Male transvestites enjoy dressing up as women.

feminine person would be likely to select a lower-paying task such as "preparing a baby bottle" over a higher-paying masculine task such as "oiling squeaky hinges" (Buck 1977). Also, research indicates people who hold stereotypical views of males and females have more difficulty than androgynous people do relating to people of the opposite gender.

Proponents of the androgyny concept argue that individuals who avoid assuming the stereotypical male and female roles and identities may be more socially flexible and adaptable compared with those who closely adhere to gender stereotypes. Sociologist Joseph Pleck (1981) agrees with them in part but provides a somewhat different analysis. He agrees that masculinity and femininity are *stereotypes* but argues that the real problem is the conflicting expectations for behavior (traditional versus modern). As a consequence, males experience *strain* (feelings of inadequacy) because if they conform to some expectations they fail to meet others.

Are masculinity and femininity stereotypes?

Before concluding the discussion of roles and identities, one other type of identity must be presented. A person's sexual preference for a partner of the same or the opposite sex reflects the person's **sexual identity.** Social norms prescribe that we should develop sexual preferences for people of the opposite sex, or heterosexual orientations. People who have homosexual identities or orientations prefer partners of their same sex. Homosexuals at some times and in some societies may be viewed as a threat to the survival of the family and ultimately society. As a consequence they may suffer various forms of discrimination. In the past decade, various groups have attempted to eliminate forms of discrimination against homosexuals (in housing, employment). Another interesting development in the 1970s was the discussion of bisexuality. Some theorized that we are taught to identify ourselves as heterosexual or homosexual, but that in fact we are all ambisexual. Both homosexuals and bisexuals argue that the heterosexual identity is forced on people. Yet the heterosexual orientation remains dominant in our society.

Sexual identity preference for a sexual partner of the same or opposite sex.

Sex/Gender Differences

Numerous researchers have attempted to learn in what ways males and females differ from one another. In some areas of study, there is a great deal of confusion, because some studies report one type of difference, some report the opposite pattern of differences, and some report no differences (Maccoby and Jacklin 1974). Such confusion reflects measurement problems and differences in the groups studied, but the confusion also occurs because often researchers are searching for ways in which males and females are totally different from one another. Many sex and gender differences do not separate *all* females from *all* males, but rather distinguish *most* males from *most* females. Sex differences in intelligence do not appear to be supported, but some differences (longevity, verbal ability, physical aggression) may be generated by both social and biological factors.

One of the striking differences between males and females in our society is the greater *average* longevity—7 years—of females. Although males born in 1979 could expect to live 69.9 years, the average expectation for females is 77.8. Women in past centuries did not enjoy greater longevity because the maternal mortality rate was very high. Changes in medical practices, health care, and average family size lowered the incidence of maternal mortality. In 1910 there were 106 males for every 100 females. The pattern steadily changed until it was 94.5 males to 100 females in 1980. Such shifting in the relative longevity of males and females indicates that researchers must examine social as well as biological factors to understand longevity patterns.

Nature

Although females commonly are designated "the weaker sex" because males on the average are physically stronger, in several ways males are more

THE FACTS · Male or Female?

Biological

Chromosomes	Primary Sex Characteristics	Secondary Sex Characteristics
Male (XY)	Male (testes)	Male (more muscular, angular, taller)
Female (XX)	Female (ovaries)	Female (softer, rounder, shorter)
Other (XXY, etc.)	Hermaphrodite (testes and ovaries)	Pseudohermaphrodite (inappropriate form)

Sociological

Statuses	Roles	Gender Identity	Sexual Identity
Male	Male (husband, father, breadwinner)	Male	Heterosexual
Female	Female (wife, mother, homemaker)	Female	Homosexual, lesbian
		Transsexual	Ambisexual

Psychological

Masculine (independent, aggressive)
Feminine (dependent, passive)
Androgynous (both positive masculine and feminine)
Undifferentiated

---

vulnerable than females. More males are conceived than females, but fewer male conceptions result in live births, and slightly more males than females are born (Rubin 1967). The chromosomal structure of males may account for some of these differences. Various hereditary problems occur primarily among males (color-vision defects, blood clotting disorders).

Nurture

Social factors may account for higher male mortality in later years—adolescence and adulthood. A few researchers have described the male role as "lethal." Rates of accidental deaths, suicides, and homicides provide support for this view. Males are several times more likely than females to die from accidental causes (motorcycle and car accidents, sports accidents). The stereotype that depicts men as daring and adventuresome may lead men to prove they are masculine by engaging in activities that are inherently risky or by taking unnecessary risks when engaging in other types of activities. Males are the victims of homicide about five times as often as females, perhaps also as a consequence of engaging in activities designed to prove their masculinity. There are higher rates of suicide for males and of institutionalization of boys for mental problems, which suggests that meeting the expectations for males

The brother pictured above not only is assisting his younger sister, but also facilitating her development as an androgynous person.

in our society creates unmanageable stress for some of them. One social factor that is related to rates of mental illness is marital status. Automobile insurance companies whose rates are lower for married than for single males are correct. Marriage appears to exempt males from some of the pressures that make the male role "lethal."

Learning To Be Male or Female

Nature versus Nurture

Sociologists emphasize the importance of socialization processes and social learning in the acquisition of identities and behaviors appropriate for one's gender. Before we examine modern sociological views of gender learning, we should review the nature-versus-nurture debate that persisted in sociology for many decades (see Chapter 4, Socialization, for an overview of nature versus nurture debate).

Early sociologists (Comte and Spencer) shared the beliefs about the inherent differences between men and women that prevailed in the societies in which they lived. They believed that the fundamental *natures* of men and women were different. They assumed that biological factors disposed women to be more passive and nurturant than men. Some later sociologists argued very strongly that the differences are consequences of *nurturance* or socialization. For them, the different treatment that girls and boys receive from birth produces gender differences.

The nature-versus-nurture debate was relatively quiet during the mid-twentieth century, because most sociologists accepted the key role of nurture in explaining human behavior *and* believed that biological explanations were not within the domain of sociology. In recent years **sociobiologists** have renewed the debate by arguing that biological factors do explain why, for example, males often are reported to be more aggressive than females. Opponents of sociobiology argue that because human beings can think about and control their behavior including responses to physiological phenomena (such as changes in hormonal levels), strict biological explanations are too simplistic and deterministic.

Sociobiologists those who believe that much social behavior is in fact a product of biological processes.

Why have sociologists been unable to put the nature/nurture debate to rest? From the moment of birth, children are bombarded by external stimuli. Human infants cannot survive without the assistance of other human beings or caregivers. These caregivers, directly and indirectly, intentionally or unintentionally, shape the infants' behaviors and thoughts. We can never observe what a male or female would be like without social influences, and therefore, we can never thoroughly disentangle the effects of physiological (natural) and social (nurturant) processes upon a person.

Learning Processes

Social scientists use three basic theories to explain the specific ways in which children learn the male or female identities appropriate to their gender (categories: identification, social learning, and cognitive). In addition, sociologists use the symbolic interaction perspective to discuss the processes involved in gender role and identity learning.

Identification theories emphasize the importance of the same-sex parent. The child *identifies* with the same-sex parent and as a consequence acts and thinks like that parent.

Identification process through which a person learns by identifying with another person.

One of the best-known identification theories was developed by Sigmund Freud (1965). The identification process is stimulated by children's recognition of anatomical differences, basically the presence or absence of penises. As a result the assertion "anatomy is destiny" became popular.

According to Freud both very young males and females depend upon and identify with their mothers until such time as they recognize genital differences. Males' attachments to their mothers develop sexual overtones that produce Oedipal struggles; boys perceive themselves as competitors with their fathers for their mothers' affection. The boy is fearful that his father would punish him if he knew of the boy's desires, and so the boy develops castration anxiety. In order to protect himself (avoid castration) the boy engages in defensive identification with his father. The process for females also emphasizes anatomy, the penis, because girls are struck by penis envy. The girl blames her mother for her lack of a penis and focuses on her father. As her desire to have a penis is replaced by a desire for what she ultimately may have—a baby—her original identification with her mother is reinforced.

Although Freud's views were widely accepted for some time in the twentieth century, they were based not on studies of children but rather on Freud's therapy sessions with adult patients. More recent identification theories emphasize love and learning rather than fear as the basis for identification (Sears 1955), but they too have limited empirical support.

Social learning theorists (Bandura 1969; Mischel 1970) argue that general learning principles can explain how "appropriate" male and female behavior is acquired. The child does not have to have any special internal arousal state (fear of castration) to learn. The social world of the child provides many opportunities to observe what kinds of people do what kinds of things and how they are rewarded or punished as a consequence. Learning theory stresses the importance of reinforcements (positive and negative) in shaping the probability that a child will repeat a behavior. And it also emphasizes the *imitation* or observational learning process through which the child practices observed behaviors and adopts them for himself or herself. Thus, according to this perspective, learning of gender appropriate behavior is contingent upon reinforcement.

> **Social learning** process emphasizing the importance of reinforcement in shaping what a child learns.

Cognitive developmental theory emphasizes forces within the individual, internal motives. Jean Piaget, a well-known cognitive theorist, believes that children pass through various stages of understanding as they mature (1960). Physical and mental maturation help move the child through a set of developmental stages; but other factors (greater experience with the physical and social world) are identified in his work, also. Lawrence Kohlberg (1966) drew upon Piaget's framework in developing a set of six invariant stages of children's moral development.

> **Cognitive developmental** a framework emphasizing that changes in internal states occur in stages.

Gender researchers are interested in Kohlberg's view of gender learning, which emphasizes self-socialization. Kohlberg begins his analysis with children's recognition that there are two basic categories—female and male—and that they and others are categorized as belonging in one group or the other. Once children acquire these mental categories of gender identity, they try to fit themselves into one of them. Kohlberg argues that children like or value themselves and, as a consequence, they positively value what is similar to them—same-sex parents. Thus, children identify with same-sex parents. Children socialize themselves by adopting characteristics of their same-sex parents.

Others have modified Kohlberg's theory by arguing that societal influences should also be recognized. They point out that children are influenced by the male/female stereotypes prevalent in society (as in the mass media).

The sociological theory most often used to describe gender role and identity learning is *symbolic interaction*. From this perspective, development of gender roles and identities is an integral part of *self*-development. Interactionists stress the importance of social interaction in shaping, maintaining, and changing roles and identities. Every episode of interaction has some impact upon how an individual sees herself or himself, negligible as that impact may be in some cases. Interaction with *significant others* such as parents presumably has greater impact than interaction with more transient or less important others.

Compare and contrast the different perspectives on learning.

Gender Socialization

To demonstrate the key role of social interaction, sociologists draw on various forms of evidence to illustrate that from the time of birth, gender socialization is underway. In fact, some parents prepare to begin gender socialization prior to the baby's birth. Women at baby showers play games to ascertain the sex of unborn infants. Various beliefs—"old wives' tales"—about a pregnant woman's experiences persist. For example, one folk belief is that if a fetus kicks a great deal it is male, because males are more active than females.

Births are proclaimed with "It's a boy" or "It's a girl." Clothing, toys, and nursery furnishings are color-coded to emphasize the fact that the infant is a female or a male. Parents and other infant caregivers are often unaware of the many other ways in which their actions are guided by gender assignments.

Mothers and fathers of newborn infants interviewed within 24 hours of their babies' births were asked to describe their children for relatives or close friends (Rubin, Provenzano, and Luria 1974). The parents tended to choose adjectives expressing sex stereotypes. Males were portrayed as stronger and hardier; females were described as smaller, prettier, and more delicate. The parents' word choices reflected their expectations for males and females, since the male and female infants did *not* vary in average length or weight.

Adults offer different toys to an infant identified as male than they do to the same infant when identified as female (Will, Self, and Datan 1976). And researchers have found that parents are more likely to handle and talk to female infants than to male infants. Michael Lewis (1972) reports that observations of 3-month-old infants and their mothers revealed that the amount of response mothers gave their children did not vary by sex, but the *types of responses* did. Male infants received more touching and holding; female infants were looked at and talked to more often.

The problems involved in resolving the nature-versus-nurture debate are numerous. Female infants may stimulate more talking by their mothers because they develop somewhat earlier (producing vocalizations) than male infants. Mothers may find it rewarding to talk to female infants who are able to respond to them at earlier ages. In any case, female infants tend to begin talking earlier and to score better on early verbal tests than males. These findings may reflect both the effects of differential rates of maturation and differential socialization practices.

When does gender stereotyping begin?

Media Influences

From very young ages, children are exposed to mass media, particularly books and television programs. Various studies of children's picture books have revealed that these books present primarily male characters—be they humans or animals. A study by Lenore Weitzman and others (1972) of award-winning picture books revealed that male pictures outnumbered female pictures by a ratio of 11:1. Whether portrayed as girls or women, females were portrayed as passive. When shown as active, they typically were providing services for males (helping brothers or fathers, cooking). Males were leaders who pursued adventure. They performed the roles that are assigned higher value in our society.

Children's documented capacity to learn from films (Bandura 1969) suggests children may learn gender stereotypes from television programs, if the programs present consistent views. Studies of television programs reveal that females and males are presented quite consistently in stereotypical roles. Thus, children probably receive support for stereotypical views of males and females when they view television. Even such innovative shows as "Sesame Street" have been criticized for the consistent dominance of male characters.

Research by Paul McGhee and Terry Fuchs (1980) on middle-class elementary school children who are frequent viewers of television (25 hours or more of viewing per week) reveals they have more stereotypical perceptions of adult males and females than infrequent viewers (10 hours or less of viewing per week). Their study participants (grades 1, 3, 5, and 7) had reported similar levels of viewing 15 months before, so the impact of frequent viewing over time could be assessed. Such findings support the view that mass media often reinforce gender stereotypes. (See Chapter 18, Mass Behavior, for further discussion of how television and other media may shape beliefs and behavior.)

Do we all learn gender stereotypes from the mass media?

The Educational System

No one requires children to watch television for a certain number of hours each year, but they are required to attend school. In school, children are exposed to the perspectives of teachers, counselors, and other students, as well as to the perspectives presented in their reading material. Parents, particularly middle-class parents, often are very sensitive about what the public schools in their communities are teaching, for they want their children to hold the same values they do.

One outgrowth of the public debate about gender equality in the 1970s was closer examination of the reading material children received in school. As a consequence, new materials were developed, because investigators found very stereotypical presentations of males and females. Information about occupations was often presented in stereotypical fashion; that is, doctors were male and nurses were female.

Other researchers focused on the more subtly transmitted messages.

Patricia Sexton (1969) argued that schools inadvertently taught males to be feminized. According to her, the elementary school system is dominated by females because the majority of the teachers in the system are female. (However, the majority of administrators are males.) And the emphasis in classrooms is upon "propriety, obedience, decorum, cleanliness, silence." Sexton argues that schools emphasize feminine behavior and that boys can either rebel and do poorly in school or become feminized. Critics of Sexton's work point out that both females and males would be disadvantaged if they learned the values she believes the schools are teaching, because success in adult life depends upon characteristics traditionally assumed to be masculine.

Another concern focuses on the **channeling** of students in schools. Teachers and counselors may unconsciously reinforce traditional roles by encouraging males to take courses in science and mathematics and to consider careers as scientists or doctors, but directing females into practical courses that prepare them to be good wives and mothers. Various tests that measure students' interests have been criticized as biased, because males and females who express the same interests are encouraged by test interpretations to pursue different (gender stereotyped) occupations.

Channeling directing students to follow stereotypical career paths.

Legislation and executive orders enacted in the 1970s (such as Title IX of the Education Amendment of 1972) mandated that schools provide equal opportunities for all students. Athletic programs at many schools were traditionally quite different for females and males. Numerous schools had no interscholastic athletic activities for females. Others had programs that were perceived to be disadvantageous for females, such as basketball programs that required females to play only on half of the court. Programs have been changed to a greater or lesser extent in the various states; however, athletic program equality has yet to be fully achieved.

As advanced education becomes almost a requirement for pursuit of many occupations, attention increasingly has focused on college and university programs. In the nineteenth century, women were denied advanced education at many colleges because they did not need such training and because it was assumed the mental strain would lead to poor physical health. Many early programs for women prepared them in the domestic sciences (Degler 1980).

In the twentieth century, women encountered somewhat different barriers when seeking advanced levels of education. Some universities even into the 1950s maintained quotas for female students, thereby limiting the number that could enter. Women were openly discouraged from enrolling in professional schools (law or veterinary medicine) and were clearly discriminated against since males with lower grade point averages and examination scores were admitted when they were not.

Today women are entering school with new goals. According to the American Council on Education, in 1980 only 10% of the college-bound female high school seniors planned to major in education, and over 25% of freshman women planned careers in business, engineering, law, or medicine. In 1966 only about 6% of freshman women had such career plans. In the 1980s a number of entering classes in schools of veterinary medicine were over half

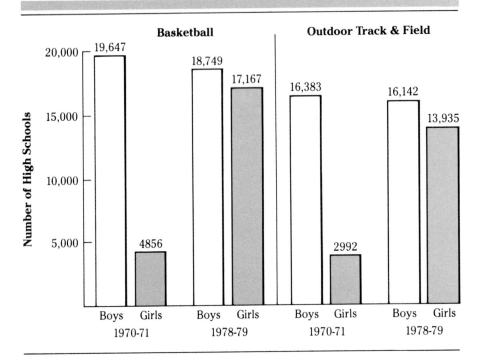

Figure 8.1 Number of high schools offering interscholastic basketball and outdoor track and field to boys and girls, 1970–1971 and 1978–1979. Data from National Federation of State High School Associations, *Sports Participation Survey*, 1971 and 1978. From "More Hurdles To Clear: Women and Girls in Competitive Athletics," United States Commission on Civil Rights, Clearing House Publication #63, July 1980, p. 14.

female. However, men far outnumber women when all graduate degree programs are considered, even though more than half of all undergraduate students today are women.

Once we begin to look at how the mass media and educational institutions shape people's lives, we have begun to consider how male-female inequality is maintained or structured. To understand how deeply rooted this inequality is, we need only look in a new way at some things ordinarily taken for granted, such as the words we use.

Language

Generic or Biased

Is "he" male? Of course, unless the writer learned to use what is called the generic male pronoun. One of the English language rules taught in schools of all levels in our society is that female terms only refer to females, but male terms may refer to males or to both males and females. Students learn that words such as "mankind" are **generic words,** or general words, and refer to both men and women.

Does it matter which words are used as long as we all understand what they mean? In the past decade women and men, social scientists, and members of the general public have all argued that it does make a difference. Linguistic scholars argue that language shapes how we see things. When a female student reads what a "he" must do to qualify for a job, how can she be sure that "he" refers to her too?

Researchers have investigated how children respond to usage of generic words. Third-grade children were asked to choose the drawing appropriate to a hypothetical situation described to them (Harrison and Passero 1975). When a generic term (one using "man") was employed, 49 to 85% of the students chose drawings of males. On the other hand, when a gender-neutral term was given, only 3 to 31% chose drawings of males. Junior high school students display the same tendency to think of males when generic terms are used (Harrison 1975).

Many people object to attempts to eliminate usage of generic male words, often saying that it is a silly or unimportant issue. Others, proponents of change in language usage, believe that words are very important and have pressured publishers to stop producing books with sex-biased language. Major publishers today have guidelines for nonsexist language usage for their textbook authors, because they became convinced that educators would not select textbooks that used sex-biased language. Sociology textbooks whose titles included such phrases as "Man in Society" were retitled in the 1970s so that their titles were sex-neutral.

Government agencies and various work organizations have attempted to remove gender references from job titles, terms used in business letters, and in discussions of the labor force. What words could you use instead of those listed in the left hand column?*

housewife   _____

policeman   _____

manpower   _____

chairman   _____

Sandra Bem and Daryl Bem (1973) demonstrated the importance of job titles in a research project that asked students to indicate their relative interest in twelve jobs. They varied the wording for various telephone company jobs by using traditional terms (frameman), neutral terms (sales representative), or reversed terms (line-woman). When the descriptions used traditional terms, students of the opposite gender were unlikely to say they were interested. When the wording was neutral or reversed (opposite of the stereotype), men

Generic words those used to refer to general categories rather than specific cases.

*Homemaker or housekeeper, police officer, human power, chairperson.

and women were both more likely to express an interest in jobs not traditional for their gender.

Names and Social Status

One custom widely followed in our society is for women to assume their husbands' names when they marry. Samantha Loki becomes Mrs. Robert Jones. But no laws require that a woman's name be changed when she marries. However, if she uses her husband's name, a woman must go to court to resume usage of her own name. Some men and women believe that this custom denies married women their status as independent persons. Thus, when they marry, some couples assume a joint last name, such as Loki-Jones, or continue to use their individual birth names. Some societies have naming customs different from ours. Spanish societies combine the husband's and wife's family names, and oriental societies place family names first rather than last. The prevailing custom in our society may reflect the traditional conception that a woman becomes her husband's property upon marriage (Spender 1980). Those who do not follow the prevailing custom argue that naming is important.

Many judgments about people and their activities are influenced by attributions made on the basis of their names. Use of female or male names has significant consequences for appraisals of literature and art. Researchers (Deaux and Taynor 1973; Goldberg 1968; Morris 1970) have demonstrated that literature and art identified as the work of males is valued more highly than works that are attributed to persons with female names; both female and male subjects assigned higher value to the works presumed to be produced by males.

The tendency to use *gender attributions* when "objectively" appraising persons and their activities has serious consequences for persons' life opportunities. Subjects in one study recommended hypothetical female candidates for lower-rank positions than they did hypothetical male candidates, when the only differences in the candidates' resumes were the names (Fidell 1970).

Talk and Power

Analysis of interaction episodes between males and females reveals that a number of our stereotypes are faulty, such as the one that portrays the husband quietly suffering while the wife talks incessantly. Gender stereotypes fail to acknowledge that women have a structural disadvantage, or power disadvantage, when interacting with most men and that interaction is not always smooth and effortless but rather can be hard work. Couples on dates may recognize that interaction involves work as they struggle to think of something interesting to say that will induce their partners to converse with them. Yet they may not recognize power differentials, because they are both on their best behavior. Employees who learn that they must "read" their employers' moods before talking with them likely understand that people whose roles accord them more power can determine when an interaction will occur, how long it will last, and what it will involve. With the generally greater power men have over women, they often leave to women the work of striking up and maintaining conversation. But they retain the power to control conversation by ignoring or responding to women's conversational activities (Spender 1980).

A young married woman once told the author that one of the advantages of being married was that she did not have to talk when there was a silence. She was unknowingly reflecting the view of Pamela Fishman (1978) that interaction is the work of women. Fishman left tape recorders from 4 to 14 days in the homes of three white couples between 25 and 35 years old. Some of her findings from the transcribed conversations confirm the results of other researchers, for example, that women ask more questions than men (Lakoff 1975). She argues that question asking reflects differences in social power. Women have less social power than men. One way women try to insure that their conversational efforts obtain a response is to ask questions, because interaction partners are supposed to respond to questions. Contrasting "question asking" with "statement making" further clarifies the underlying processes at work. Men made over twice as many statements as women in Fishman's study. Although the women virtually always responded to the men's statements, the reverse was not true. Thus, if women want to interact with men, asking questions appears to be a better conversational strategy than making statements, which may be ignored or only recognized by a distracted "Oh?"

Men are probably not aware of how they exercise control over conversation. In fact, males are as restricted by gender roles as females. However, males generally are not concerned about those restrictions, because the activities males are expected to perform are valued more highly than those expected of females.

The sexual division of labor, socialization practices, and societal beliefs all place women in a subordinate position in our society. Men may demonstrate their masculinity, their power over women, by taking sexual license. Or they may exercise power over women every day by choosing how and when they communicate with them. Whichever of these phenomena we are examining, we must remember that individual men and women may not see their behaviors in terms of superordination-subordination, or power. Sociologists consider the behavior of many individuals in order to see how social behavior is structured and maintained by social institutions and organizations. Institutional patterns and individual behaviors that result in the unfair treatment of people on the basis of their sex or gender are **sexist.**

Sexist institutional patterns and individual behaviors which result in the unfair treatment of people on the basis of their sex or gender.

Inequality and Power: Sexual License

The relationships between men and women in our society generally reflect the relative power they are accorded, with men being superordinate and women subordinate. Many sexist social customs and activities support this power differential. The maintenance of the superordinate/subordinate relationship is particularly apparent in two kinds of sexual license—rape and sexual harassment. To different degrees, both involve a person's taking sexual license with another.

Rape

Why do men rape? *Individualistic* explanations focus on a man's personal characteristics (personality, sexual outlets) or those of the victim (appearance, behavior, reputation). Studies of convicted rapists provide little support for individualistic explanations. Rapists often are married men who have legitimate sexual partners. Psychological profiles of rapists reveal that they differ from others basically in only *one* way: their tendency toward violence and aggression (Selkin 1975). Blaming rape victims for provoking their attackers can be questioned for many reasons, including the following: rape victims are of all ages (ranging from preschool age to over 100 years of age); rapists frequently plan their attacks rather than impetuously responding to a woman's costume or actions; and rapes serve as a sign of conquest during wars and in prison settings.

If sexual gratification is not the goal of rapists (Burgess and Holmstrom 1974), why do men rape? Sociobiologists suggest that men instinctively desire to reproduce themselves, and, therefore, they may rape to insure reproduction of their genetic material. No irrefutable evidence supporting this position exists.

Sociological explanations of rape focus on the patterned social arrangements that may generate rape and the consequences of rape for social arrangements. The key issue for sociologists is *power*. In our society a few individuals have a great deal of power over their own and others' lives, but most people have quite limited power. Those who lack legitimate power may try to use illegitimate means to control others. As a consequence, some men may coerce women into sexual contacts that the women do not desire in order to demonstrate to themselves and others that they possess power. The physical strength advantage of many men and the learned passivity of many women facilitate this coercion.

Although men rape men in certain settings, such as prisons, and a few women have been accused of raping men, **rape** typically involves a man's coercing a woman to have sexual contact she does not desire. But if women are a subordinate group, what do men gain by demonstrating their power over them in this way? Many current explanations of rape assume that through rape some men demonstrate their individual "masculinity" and by their actions make *all* women aware of the subordinate position of women in society.

In some societies, including our own in the past, women were classified as property. Early in life they were the property of their fathers, who could give them away (transfer ownership rights) to other men—their husbands. Marriage gave men sexual access to women, and provided women with someone to support them and their offspring. Fathers controlled sexual access to their daughters, so that husbands would receive desirable (unused) property. When

Rape involves coercing a person to have undesired sexual contact.

Women who are the victims of rape at times receive blame from other people rather than the support they need.

such views prevail, men who rape women actually exercise power over other men because they are violating another man's property. Even today some rape victims in our society report that their parents and husbands react very negatively to them (the victims), apparently because they are tarnished (defiled) property. In any case, rape today is primarily an exercise of power over women.

Sexual Harassment

Unlike rape, sexual harassment often is perceived as unimportant and of concern to only those parties directly involved in the incident. **Sexual harassment** involves one person forcing undesired sexual attention on another person. Some forms of sexual harassment are very physical and obvious; others are verbal and more ambiguous. All forms, however, may be devastating to the victim. The federal government studied sexual harassment in federal workplaces (U.S. Merit Systems 1981). The subsequent report defines *less severe* forms of sexual harassment as "pressure for dates," "sexually suggestive looks or gestures," and "sexual teasing, jokes, remarks, or questions." *More severe* sexual harassment involves "pressure for sexual favors," and "touching, leaning over, cornering, or pinching." The *most severe* forms of sexual harassment are "actual or attempted rape or assault." Figure 8.2 graphically presents the extent of sexual harassment in the federal workplace.

Sexual harassment involves one person forcing undesired sexual attention on another person.

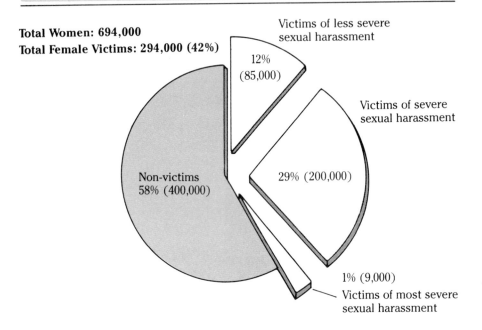

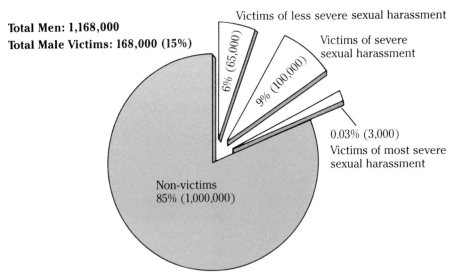

Figure 8.2 These figures indicate the number of people harassed, classified by their most severe experience. Since many people reported that they had more than one experience, the number of harassment incidents is considerably larger. From *Sexual Harassment in the Federal Workplace: Is It a Problem?* Washington, D.C.: U.S. Merit Systems Protection Board, 1981, p. 35.

Obviously, people usually do not continue to associate with others who press unwanted sexual attention on them. Thus, sexual harassment usually involves taking sexual license of someone who is in a less powerful or subordinate position and cannot readily terminate social interaction. Unwanted sexual attention is a serious problem in organizations because people in organizational situations have less freedom to choose with whom they interact, and negative reactions to a superior's behavior may threaten the victim's organizational position. Employers may harass employees, teachers may harass students, customers may harass servers—all these relationships are asymmetrical or unbalanced ones in which one role performer has power over the other role performer. Sometimes victims of harassment appeal to higher authorities. Female students at the University of California and Yale University openly protested the behavior of male instructors that they believed to be sexual harassment. Investigations resulting from such protests either support or refute the claims. Unfortunately, many women silently suffer undesired sexual attention or quit their jobs because they perceive that alone they cannot stop the harassment.

Presumably those in more powerful positions believe they have the right to use subordinates sexually, or at least that they can do so without penalty. Less powerful persons know that they have little recourse because often it is one person's word against another's and the more powerful individuals have status in the organization. Also, some people do not see anything wrong with bestowing sexual attention freely, even if it is unwanted, as long as the target is young and attractive.

Both men and women may be victims of sexual harassment, most often by a person of the opposite sex. The United States Navy prohibits sexual harassment, and it has charged both men and women with sexual harassment. Newspaper and magazine articles as well as television programs have picked up on the problem of sexual harassment. The television program "One Day at a Time" portrayed a character, Ann Romano, harassing a young man who worked for her in one episode. Although women's harassment of men may draw more people's attention because of the apparent reversal of power, women are more often the victims of sexual harassment than men, for they are more likely to occupy the less powerful positions in our society.

Is sexual harassment a consequence of people in power viewing subordinates as sexual objects rather than persons?

Inequality: Men, Women, and Work

For many years sociologists who studied people's work lives focused on men's activities, and those who studied family life primarily examined women's activities. Such research reflected societal beliefs about the kinds of behavior that are gender appropriate, as well as about the greater participation of men in the work world and women in family life.

Before our society industrialized, work was not defined as it generally is today (activities performed for pay). Both males and females worked on family farms producing goods needed for their families, although males did more work with large livestock and crops and women produced household goods (candles, clothing, soap) and cared for gardens and chickens. In the preindustrial phase, people worked in homes producing goods (cottage industries). As industrialization progressed, people left their homes to work in factories for wages. Sometimes people point to this shift to work outside the home as marking the time when men's and women's lives took divergent paths, as men entered the outside world of work and women remained in the domestic world. In fact men and women engaged in somewhat different work before the industrial revolution, and not all women remained at home as the industrial revolution progressed.

Women and Work

The concept of work as what a person does to earn wages is so powerful that other activities are ignored. Full-time homemakers have responded to the question "What do you do?" with "Oh, nothing, I'm just a housewife."

As our country industrialized, the image of women as delicate creatures who required protection became prevalent. However, if a woman remained at home not producing goods (making food and clothing) needed by the family or wages with which they could be purchased, then someone else had to support her. Yet some women have always been in the labor force. Early female industrial workers tended to be single, widowed, or married to disabled men. Also, they were often members of disadvantaged groups, such as blacks or recent immigrants. These women worked because they had to support themselves and their relatives. Women in the labor force were not put on pedestals; they worked longer hours for lower wages compared with men.

During the first decades of the twentieth century, women workers who were young and single were preferred. Husbands of women in the labor force were seen as failures. When the United States was in the midst of "the Great Depression" of the 1930s, married women were pushed out of the labor force because men were seen as needing the jobs more (female teachers who married were forced to resign).

Women were encouraged to be patriotic and leave their homes for the workplace during World War I and World War II; however, they were expected to leave those jobs when the soldiers returned. It is interesting that since the end of World War II, the participation of females in the labor force has steadily increased. More and more of these women workers are married women with children at home. Both during the world wars and in recent decades, the growth of female labor participation reflects increased demand for women workers. During the wars the lack of males created the demand, but in recent

Housework has changed in many ways, but it is still perceived as women's work.

decades the jobs stereotyped as female have increased in number, and that generated the increased demand.

In the past 30 years, males' and females' attitudes about women working have been changing. In the 1950s a man might be seen as a poor provider if "his wife had to work," whereas a woman who wanted to work might be seen as a neglectful wife and mother. Yet in 1950 32% of all females 25 and older were in the labor force. A woman's employment was often described as temporary (to facilitate some purchase or until she married) or out of necessity. By the 1970s women began to report in increasing numbers that they received satisfaction from working. And the percentages of women who were employed kept increasing. By 1981 half of all women 25 and older were in the labor force.

Women apparently do not work to escape housework, because very few of them pay anyone to do their housework. And although there have been some changes, children and husbands generally do very little of the housework.

Men and Work

Although it seems reasonable to ask why women work in our society, it may seem silly to some people to ask why men work. Men are expected to support themselves and be the primary but not necessarily sole source of support for spouses and children. In the late 1940s almost 90% of all men 25 and over were in the labor force. By the 1980s the rate had dropped to slightly less than 80%. Yet men's work activities remain an important part of how they see themselves and how other people see them.

When children are questioned about what they would like to do "when they grow up," girls may talk about family or about work and family plans, but boys must talk about work. If an adult male is not employed, we expect an explanation (he was laid off, he is disabled). We expect all able-bodied adult men to be employed, but it is not clear how important work activities are to men.

One way to ascertain the importance of work to men is to examine their interest in working when they do not have to. A nationwide survey of households conducted by Louis Harris and Associates indicates how working men respond when asked whether they would work if they were guaranteed a living as comfortable as they would like (General Mills 1981). Half of the men indicated they would work full time even with a guaranteed adequate income. Another 28% would work part time. About 10% would work at home, and 9% would do volunteer work. In comparison only 17% of the working women (19% of those classified as executive/professional/manager) would work full time. Another survey of American men also conducted by Louis Harris and Associates revealed that men rated such things as family life and health as more important to a happy life than work (Playboy 1979). But apparently for many men it is not simply an activity performed for money, since three-fourths of these respondents would still work if guaranteed an adequate income.

Women who are not employed outside the home are called "homemakers" or "housewives." Although some people believe that women should not be full-time homemakers, most people recognize homemaking to be a legitimate full-time occupation for women who choose it. Males who are not employed outside the home have not been viewed in the same light.

Various national polls that the Roper organization conducted for Virginia Slims, particularly "The 1980 Virginia Slims American Women's Opinion Poll," highlight changing views about men who are homemakers instead of participants in the labor force. In 1970 one-eighth of the women and one-fifth of the men surveyed indicated they would *not* lose respect for a male homemaker. By 1980 two-fifths of both the women and the men interviewed said they would *not* lose respect for a male homemaker. Thus, during the 1970s attitudes toward the male homemaker became less negative. These attitude changes must be interpreted with caution. Those surveyed were not saying they wanted men to be homemakers or that they would accept being married to a male homemaker or being a male homemaker themselves. In fact, the husband who remains at home and assumes all the traditional duties of the housewife while his wife works is still rare. Surveys of adolescents reveal that males' adult life plans do not include aspirations to be homemakers.

Inequality and the Future

Adolescents, the adults of the future, apparently have been socialized to hold values and beliefs very similar to those that have prevailed in our society for some time. Lloyd Lueptow (1980) compared the life goals, work values, and achievement orientations of Wisconsin high school students in 1975 with those of students in the same high schools in 1964. Female valuation of religion was substantially lower in 1975 than in 1964, but other life goals (making a contribution to society) thought to be traditionally feminine were highly valued. Further, in 1975 women indicated stronger preference for working with and helping people than did males, whose occupational values included leadership and freedom from supervision. Although the women indicated they generally valued liberation from traditional institutions, they did not assume traditional male values. Thus, traditional male and female roles continue to influence people. Work will continue to be important to men's lives, and men and women will "select" different occupations.

Some proponents of gender equality emphasize altering the messages girls and boys receive through the socialization process, although others argue that inequality will persist until the organization of family life and the structure of work change. As long as women are seen as the primary caregivers in the family, they will be expected to deemphasize personal goals for the sake of the family. Opponents of gender equality believe that women should put their families' interests before their own. At times the debate between the proponents and opponents has been quite heated (as on ratification of the Equal Rights Amendment). It is not likely that it soon will be resolved.

Will gender roles change dramatically in the next decade?

Summary

We must differentiate biological (sex) categories from sociocultural (gender) categories. Characteristics used to describe or differentiate males and females may vary from society to society because they reflect social rather than biological processes.

Sociologists focus on how statuses and roles shape how we see ourselves and how others see us (our identities). Some researchers argue that androgynous people are more socially flexible than people who play more traditional male and female roles.

There is conflicting research about many differences between males and females. We do know that during the twentieth century the pattern of greater male than female longevity was reversed, and social factors must be cited to explain the reversal. Further, many presumed sex/gender differences (such as in sociability) depend upon researcher's definitions. Few characteristics seem to be entirely male or entirely female.

Social scientists have debated the relative importance of biological and social processes in "determining" differences between males and females in what has been called the nature versus nurture debate. The debate was renewed recently by sociobiologists.

Three basic learning theories are used to describe how children acquire gender behavior: identification, social learning, and cognitive development. In addition, sociologists draw on various symbolic interactionist concepts.

Gender socialization begins at birth. Parents, the mass media, and schools contribute to the gender socialization process. Gradually, perceptions of males and females are changing, so that both males and females are becoming interested in pursuing activities previously stereotyped as exclusively male or exclusively female domains. And barriers to their nontraditional pursuits are being removed (through legislation).

Our language usage and conversational patterns continue to reflect and reinforce traditional perceptions of males and females.

Inequality between males and females is perpetuated by differences in power. Forms of taking sexual license such as rape and sexual harassment can more accurately be viewed as exercises of social power than as examples of extreme sexual desire.

In our society participation in the labor force provides people with income that is often used to measure their social worth. Men are expected to be in the labor force. Historically, women have been constrained from entering the labor force and have earned lower wages than men when working. Men and women entering the labor force tend to pursue different occupations, and the ones the men pursue tend to be higher paying and more prestigious. Inequality in the labor force will disappear slowly.

Suggested Readings

Rosabeth Moss Kanter. *Men and Women of the Corporation.* New York: Basic, 1977. Kanter focuses on the work roles of women and men in a corporation. She points out why the characteristics often attributed to secretaries are a product of the structure of their work. And she describes how women's career advancement may be limited because they are not integrated into the male corporate structure.

Joseph Pleck. *The Myth of Masculinity.* Cambridge, Mass.: Massachusetts Institute of Technology, 1981. Although much of the literature on gender focuses on the barriers women encounter, Pleck points out how the myth of masculinity constrains men. Some men react to the strain of trying to live up to the masculine ideal by overconforming to the ideal. Others behave in inconsistent fashion trying to adhere to the traditional masculine ideal and more modern ideas.

Marie Richmond-Abbott. *Masculine and Feminine: Sex Roles Over the Life Cycle.* Reading, Mass.: Addison-Wesley, 1983. Richmond-Abbott demonstrates how sex/gender expectations influence males' and females' behaviors as they move through the life cycle. New models of adult life (permanent singlehood, childless marriage, single parenthood, and dual-career marriages) are examined.

9 Aging

At what age is a person considered to be old? Recently when an introductory sociology class was asked this question, answers ranged from age 40 to 85. A survey done by Louis Harris and Associates in 1975 found that about half of the American public feel that there is some fixed age at which a person becomes old, but there was no clear-cut agreement as to what this age is. A popularly held belief is that 65, the age arbitrarily chosen and originally set for social security payments to begin, is the beginning of old age. Some say the start of old age is 60 or 62, and still others maintain it is 70. Actually, no one birthday serves as a definite marker for the onset of old age. This is because aging is subject to a wide range of variations among individuals: People age in different ways and at different rates. How one ages is also shaped by the experiences he or she has had in the preceding stages of the life cycle. In addition, aging is such a slow, gradual process that it can only be viewed as a continuous part of the life cycle.

An Historical Perspective of the Life Cycle

All societies divide the life cycle into stages, varying from the simple distinction between children and adults to delineating as many as ten or more age strata. Some societies extend the life cycle to include the unborn and the dead. In such cases the unborn child becomes part of the social world from the moment pregnancy is detected, and the dead are regarded as active participants in societal activities the same as the living. In our society, the life cycle is divided into at least four major stages: childhood, adolescence, adulthood, and old age. Strange as it may sound in our child-centered society of today, throughout much of history "childhood" was not even recognized as a part of the life cycle. The concept of adolescence did not come into being until the nineteenth century. Unlike childhood and adolescence, old age has always been viewed as a stage of life, but it has undergone considerable change in the last few centuries.

Childhood

In Europe during the Middle Ages, adults thought of children as identical to themselves, differing only in size. This lack of distinction is reflected in Medieval art, where children are often depicted as miniature adults and given the same features and proportions as adults. According to Philippe Ariès (1962), around the age of 7, children were ushered into adult society, going from swaddling clothes to grown-up attire and sharing the work and social activities of adults.

In western Europe, not until about 1600 was childhood seen as a separate stage in the life cycle and children were dressed differently from adults. Ariès attributes this change largely to the churchmen and moralists of that period, who felt that children needed to be safeguarded and reformed. Their teachings

THE FACTS · Childhood in the Past

A child's life prior to modern times was uniformly bleak. Virtually every child-rearing tract from antiquity to the eighteenth century recommended the beating of children . . . The beatings described in most historical sources began at an early age, continued regularly throughout childhood, and were severe enough to cause bruising and bloodying . . .

The baby was tied up tightly in swaddling bands for its first year, supposedly to prevent it from tearing off its ears, breaking its legs, touching its genitals, or crawling around like an animal. Traditional swaddling, as one American doctor described it, "consists in entirely depriving the child of the use of its limbs by enveloping them in an endless bandage, so as to not unaptly resemble billets of wood, and by which . . . the flesh compressed, almost to gangrene." Swaddled infants were not only more convenient to care for, since they withdrew into themselves in sleep most of the day, but they were also more easily laid for hours behind hot ovens, hung on pegs on the wall, and, wrote one doctor, "left like a parcel, in every convenient corner." In addition, they were often thrown around like a ball for amusement . . . Doctors complained of parents who broke the bones of their children in the "customary" tossing of infants.

SOURCE: Lloyd DeMause, "Our Forebears Made Childhood a Nightmare." *Psychology Today*, April 1975, pp. 85–88.

---

stressed the responsibility of parents to care for and protect their children as well as to prepare them through education for their future life as adults. This was a totally new concept. Until that time the parent's responsibility had entailed only the transmission of a name and an estate. As the attitudes of parents toward their offspring began to change, the child was given a central place in the family. The concern about education led to the development of the school, which isolated children for a period of time from adult society in a world of their own. Since the seventeenth century, childhood has become undeniably enshrined as a stage of life.

Adolescence

The word "adolescence" was coined by G. Stanley Hall in 1904 when he wrote his classic work on the subject (Hall 1904). Since then, adolescence has become a recognized stage in the life cycle as well as a household word. Prior to the twentieth century, children went directly from puberty, which occurred several years later than it does today, into the adult world.

Although the interest in education led to the creation of childhood, adolescence was created when America changed from an agrarian to an industrial society. Industrialization brought about increased productivity and economic surpluses that freed teenagers from work in the fields and factories. At the same time, because of the need for extensive education and specialized skills in an industrialized society, many more years of schooling were required. This postponed teenagers' transition to adult society until their 20s. This prolonged period of formal education, together with the economic dependency of the student, gave rise to a new stage in human development—adolescence.

The increase in educational attainment since the turn of the century has been phenomenal. In 1900 only 6.4% of the population completed high school, whereas currently it is about 80%. There were only 238,000 college students in 1900 compared with nearly 10 million today.

Old Age

Growing old in earlier times was quite different from what it is today. First of all, old age was rare. In the past, the average life expectancy in most places was about 25 years. Few persons lived to 50 and even fewer to 65 or older. By 1790, when the first United States census was taken, only 2% of the population was 65 and over (the census definition of elderly).

Between 1790 and 1860 the elderly were highly exalted (Achenbaum 1978).* It was believed that they had important roles to play and constructive contributions to make. There was no such thing as mandatory retirement or age discrimination against the elderly in any job or profession. The only exception to this was an upper age limit that about half a dozen states imposed on the holding of judicial office. W. Andrew Achenbaum notes that the aged served as oral historians during this period, and their experience, wisdom, and advice were highly valued by a young republic:

> It should not be altogether surprising, therefore, that early Americans chose the image of a sinewy old man with long white hair and chin whiskers to symbolize their new land. Dressed in red and white striped pantaloons and a blue coat bespangled with stars, and sporting an unabashedly old-fashioned plug hat, "Uncle Sam" seemed to personify the honesty, self-reliance, and devotion to country so deeply cherished in the early decades of our national experience. . . . Uncle Sam not only epitomized the hopes of young America but he also seemed to demonstrate that the nation could be wise and experienced even in its formative years (Achenbaum 1978:25).

Devaluation of the Elderly.   After the Civil War, the attitudes toward old age underwent a radical transformation. The role of the elderly in society changed from being useful to being obsolescent. Several factors are responsible for this reversal. Previously, the elderly were valued for their insight into the sources of longevity. They were regarded as the sole possessors of the types of behavior that led to a long life. But this changed after the Civil War, when medical advances in scientific knowledge led to an increase in life expectancy. These advances occurred mainly through the combating and prevention of communicable diseases and the establishment of more sanitary

---

*This section is based largely on the work of W. Andrew Achenbaum, *Old Age in the New Land* (Baltimore: The John Hopkins Press, 1978), pp. 23–54.

THE FACTS · Old Age in the Past

In older times, age was revered, not despised, because there was so little of it. . . . In a world without the printed or electronic word, the few old people who lingered were the treasured resources of society, the repository of tradition, the only sure link with the past. They were the logical judges and rulers, the respected accumulators of wisdom into whose hands and brains the Church and State could safely be placed. So it was that churches, tribes, cities and even empires were ruled by "elders." The word "priest" comes from the Greek word for "elder" and the word "senator" from the Latin word for "elder."

SOURCE: Isaac Asimov, "The Pursuit of Youth." *Ladies' Home Journal,* June 1974, p. 155.

living conditions. Americans began to rely more on the knowledge of scientists and other professionals for increasing their longevity and less on the advice of the elderly themselves. As a result, the value of the elderly as models of healthful living declined. In addition, medical specialists at that time began identifying a host of incurable diseases that they convinced the public were associated with the aging process, even claiming that old age itself was a disease.

> Contrary to previous judgments, attaining old age no longer seemed either re-markable or a desirable achievement . . . The ultimate result of living a long life, medical evidence confirmed, was often more deleterious than useful. Conse-quently, new scientific theories and data forced people to reevaluate their opin-ions about the elderly's value in other capacities (Achenbaum 1978:45).

Another factor that contributed to the devaluation of the elderly was the belief that old age was a period of economic obsolescence. The idea of man-datory retirement gained much support in the latter part of the nineteenth century in both the public and private sectors. The trend toward mandatory retirement led to a derogatory attitude toward old age that was reflected in a change in the meaning of the words "retire" and "superannuate." In the 1828 edition of Webster's American Dictionary "retire" was defined as "withdrawing from public notice." By 1880 this definition became obsolete, and "retire" meant among other things " 'to designate as no longer qualified for active service; as to *retire* a military or naval officer.' An additional definition was added to the verb 'superannuate': 'To give pension to, on account of old age, or other infirmity' " (Achenbaum 1978:50).

Finally, the idea of progress as the notion that human beings and their societies are forever improving was a widely accepted belief during this period. The theorists of the nineteenth century felt that civilization was moving toward an ever-increasing enlightenment. They based their evolutionary concept of social change and progress on the rapid technological advancements that were being made at that time.

The elderly were viewed as being in a state of physical and mental decline and no longer able to keep up with a rapidly changing society. Their experience and knowledge were considered outdated and obsolete, and their former role as a link between the past and present had little value in a future-oriented society. The elderly's qualitative wisdom and experience were replaced by youth's resourcefulness, enthusiasm, and inventiveness. The exaltation that the elderly once enjoyed had now shifted to the exaltation of youth.

Myths about Old Age. Many of the beliefs that led to the steady devaluation of the elderly are inaccurate and have been dispelled by recent research. The following quiz concerns some of the more widely held beliefs about aging. On the basis of your present knowledge, decide which statements are true and which are false. After you have finished, look below for the correct answers.

True-False

_____ 1. Senility is to be expected in older persons.
_____ 2. Intelligence declines with age.
_____ 3. Older people cannot learn.
_____ 4. All older people are alike.
_____ 5. Retirement brings poor health and an early death.
_____ 6. Older workers have high accident and absentee rates.
_____ 7. Older people are not interested in sex.
_____ 8. Most elderly live in institutions.
_____ 9. Most older people prefer to live with their children.
_____ 10. People tend to become more religious with age.

If you found all ten statements to be false, you made a perfect score.

1. Senility is not an inevitable accompaniment of aging. Only a small percentage of older persons show overt signs of mental deterioration or senility.
2. There is little or no decline in intelligence as one ages. In fact, in some areas intelligence actually increases.
3. The old adage, "You're never too old to learn," is true. Older people can learn things about as well as younger persons, but it may take them a little longer.
4. There is as much, if not more, variation in the attitudes, abilities, and physical capacities of the elderly as there is among the young. Actually, as people age they become less alike.
5. Research shows that retirement does not mean an earlier death but often a longer life and in some cases improved health.
6. Younger workers tend to be more accident prone than older workers. Absenteeism is also less for older workers than for younger workers.
7. The majority of older persons maintain sexual interest and activity well into their 70s. Many people are sexually active into their 80s and beyond.
8. Only about 4% of the elderly live in institutions at any one time. Most of

Individuals live longer today and can remain active participants.

the others are relatively healthy and are living in their own homes or with their families.

9. Most older people prefer to live near their children but not with them.
10. Studies show that there is no change in religious interest or religious activities with age. People who were religious when young continue to be religious when old, and vice versa.

Some Demographic Aspects of Aging

American society contains an ever-swelling number and proportion of older people. Today 25.5 million Americans or over 11% of the population are age 65 and over. Since 1900, when the elderly population was 3 million, their number has increased over eightfold. Projections for the year 2000 place the number of elderly at 31.8 million (see Figure 9.1). Each day about 5,000 Americans turn 65 and about 3,400 persons aged 65 and over die. The net increase is approximately 1,600 per day or nearly 600,000 per year.

What accounts for this rapid growth in the older population? Primarily it is due to several factors: the high birth rate during the nineteenth and early twentieth century, the high immigration rates before World War I, and the gains made in life expectancy during this century.

Life expectancy (remaining years of life) at birth for Americans has increased 25 years since 1900. Then a person could expect to live 48.3 years. By 1979, the average life expectancy was 73.8 years, 69.9 for males and 77.8 for females. Since 1920 the gap between the sexes in life expectancy has been widening so that today women in this country outlive men by nearly 8 years.

Life expectancy the remaining years of life that a person has at a specified age.

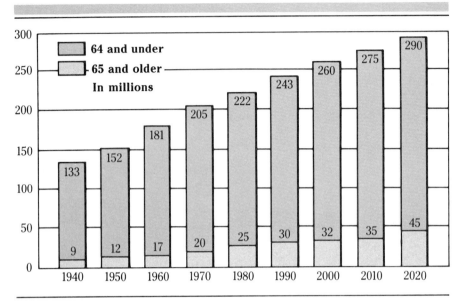

Figure 9.1 The elderly—a growing population. Data from the U.S. Bureau of the Census.

Because of this difference, as well as the fact that most men marry women younger than themselves, about 52% of older women are widows. In 1979 there were over five times as many older widows as widowers.

Although life expectancy has dramatically increased, enabling more people to reach old age than ever before, the **life span** (the biological age limit) for humans, which is approximately 100 years, has remained unchanged since earliest times. Most biologists see no major scientific breakthrough in the near future that will produce an extension of the life span. The Fountain of Youth appears about as distant today as it was when Ponce de Leon started his quest. Nevertheless, men and women throughout the ages have continued to search for ways to extend youth and increase longevity. Methods for achieving a longer life have varied by time and place and appear to be endless. The box on page 215 shows some of the ways that people in various cultures have tried to increase longevity.

Life span   the biological age limit.

The Social Structure and Aging

Age Norms

In Chapter 2 we discussed how norms shape our behavior and provide us with guideposts for living. Some of these norms apply to an entire society, others only to certain groups within the society. One of the factors that determines whether or not a given norm applies to a particular individual or group

1. Bathe in urine, ice, or snow. The Kwakiutl and Hopi Indians felt that these elements promoted longevity.
2. Tell the truth. The Berber believed that a person who was always truthful lived longer.
3. Avoid your mother-in-law. The Dieri, an Australian aborigine tribe, felt that this would prevent gray hair.
4. Be kind. The Hopi said that "whosoever is not mean will live long."
5. Cultivate body lice. The Yukaghirs of Siberia would keep a few lice on their bodies to prolong life.
6. Get a fetish. The Arunta would make a long-life potion from particles that they scraped off their fetish objects. The Crow used a rattle that gave them the power to reach old age.
7. Remove all gray hairs. The Xosa of Africa thought that getting rid of the gray would keep old age away.
8. Be brave. "He who encounters head winds will live a long life," according to the Labrador Eskimos.

SOURCE: Leo W. Simmons, *The Role of the Aged in Primitive Society* (New Haven, Conn.: Yale University Press, 1945), pp. 220–224.

---

is age. We require young people to begin attending school at a specified age; we expect a person of 65 or 70 to retire, but not a 25-year-old. Expectations about behavior that is appropriate for people in a given age group are called **age norms.** What is proper behavior at one age might be improper at another. We would not expect a college professor to skip into class, suck his thumb, and speak in monosyllables. By the same token, we would not expect a 4-year-old to come into a college classroom and give a lesson in sociology. The familiar phrase "Act your age" reflects our concern for age-appropriate behavior.

Age norms expectations about the behavior that is appropriate for people in a given age group.

How often have you heard someone ask, "Are you *still* in school?" Once out of school the question changes to: "Haven't you found a job *yet*?" or "Isn't it *time* you got married?" Later in life the questions asked are: "Don't you have any grandchildren *yet*?" and "Shouldn't you be retired by *now*?" These are examples of age norms that govern the timing of our adult behavior and have been referred to as "social clocks." These clocks operate to speed up as well as to slow down major life events. "Men and women are aware not only of the social clocks that operate in various areas of their lives, but they are aware also of their own timing and readily describe themselves as 'early,' 'late' or 'on time' with regard to family and occupational events" (Neugarten et al. 1965: 711).

A high degree of consensus concerning age-appropriate behavior was found in a survey of middle-class, middle-aged people (Neugarten et al. 1965).

"Gee, Grandma, what big eyes you have!"

According to the respondents, the best age for a man to marry was from 20 to 25, and for a woman, 19 to 24; the best age to finish school and go to work was from 20 to 25; and most people should retire between 60 and 65.

Like other norms, age norms are constantly changing. Bernice Neugarten points out that in the past decade or so, age has become a less significant dimension of the life cycle:

> The whole internal clock I used to write about that kept us on time, the clock that tells us whether we're too young or too old to be marrying or going to school or getting a job or retiring, is no longer as powerful or as compelling as it used to be. It no longer surprises us to hear of a 22-year-old mayor or a 29-year-old university president—or a 35-year-old grandmother or a retiree of 50. No one blinks at a 70-year-old college student or at the 55-year-old man who becomes a father for the first time—or who starts a second family (1980:66).

Neugarten refers to this trend as the emerging of an age-irrelevant society and claims that age, like race or sex, is declining in importance as a regulator of behavior.

Although our society may have become less age-conscious in recent years, a double standard still prevails in relation to the age of marital partners. If a man of 65 divorced his 60-year-old wife and married a young woman of 25, people might raise their eyebrows but nothing more. In fact, they probably would admire such a man and explain the relationship by attributing to him some special charm, virility, or other qualities. But when the situation is reversed and an elderly woman marries a young man, people become outraged and hostile because she has violated one of the mores of our society. "Far from being admired for her vitality, she would probably be condemned as predatory, willful, selfish, exhibitionistic" (Sontag 1972:37).

What mainly accounts for this different standard of aging is that aging

In our society people have various images of the elderly. We admire those who are still active, especially those in public life, such as actress Helen Hayes and Representative Claude Pepper. However, many of us think of the elderly as a group that no longer has anything useful to offer society, or is a burden on family or society. The fact is, many old persons are self-sufficient, happy, and productive. Some have retired and have taken up the traditional roles of older people, but others keep on with the work they have always enjoyed.

One of our nation's greatest—and often overlooked—resources is the accumulated experience of its older citizens. In our fast-paced, technology-oriented society, we often value theoretical knowledge over practical know-how. But many skills can be acquired only by years of practice. One of the greatest contributions older persons can make in any society is to teach others what they have learned. They can share their skills with other old people, who sometimes need the help of someone who understands their special needs. And perhaps even more important, they can pass the fruits of their experience on to the younger generation. We can never afford to waste the skills of our elderly.

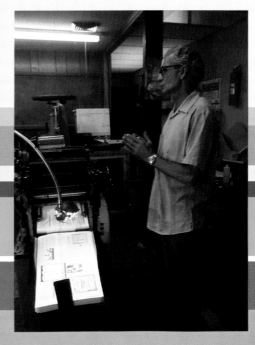

After retirement, people find many different ways to enjoy themselves. Some return to school, either for the education they missed before or just for the fun of trying something new. Their success puts to rest any myths that older persons cannot learn as well as the young. Other older persons take up a new career, perhaps doing something they never even thought of before, perhaps doing something they always wanted to, deep down, but never had the chance. And many older persons are happy to be footloose, maybe for the first time in their adult life, free to see the world and take part in its pleasures.

Older people may derive a deep satisfaction from using skills that recall their roots or the ways of their youth. Part of the pleasure in keeping up traditional pursuits comes from affirming your own role in a culture, but part also comes from the sense that you are ensuring the continuity of the culture. Minority groups—such as Navahos, Hasidic Jews, or Chicanos—sometimes feel the need for a special effort to maintain their identity in the face of pressure from the majority culture. Practicing traditional skills can enhance our sense of who we are by helping us see what we have come from. And often we need the elderly to show us the way.

takes different forms for men and women. Society defines women as "old" five or ten years sooner than men, giving men a decided advantage over women. As Susan Sontag (1972) points out:

> Women become sexually ineligible much earlier than men do. A man, even an ugly man, can remain eligible well into old age. He is an acceptable mate for a young, attractive woman. Women, even good-looking women, become ineligible (except as partners of very old men) at a much younger age. . . . Thus, for most women, aging means a humiliating process of gradual sexual disqualification . . . . On the contrary, getting older tends (for several decades) to operate in men's favor, since their value as lovers and husbands is set more by what they do than how they look. Many men have more success romantically at forty than they did at twenty or twenty-five; fame, money, and, above all, power are sexually enhancing (31–32).

It is somewhat ironic that in our society we believe that women age faster than men and become sexually unattractive earlier, although women continue to outlive their male counterparts and are able to remain sexually active longer.

Age-related Roles

Closely associated with age norms are *age roles.* Similar to other roles, age roles are made up of sets of norms, and these norms define the appropriate and expected behavior for each age group. Age norms often determine when one is considered eligible or ineligible to perform certain roles. A person must be at least 18 before he or she can acquire the role of voter; an employee often must leave the work role by age 70.

Age-related roles usually proceed in some sequential order, such as a high school student, college student, worker, and retiree. As we move through the life cycle, we continually acquire new roles and discard old ones. When we take on the role of spouse, for instance, we relinquish the role of single person. The number of roles we possess usually peaks at middle age and then begins to decrease as we reach old age. A unique characteristic of old age is that it is the only stage in the life cycle in which we lose more roles than we gain.

Two major age-related role losses in old age come with retirement and widowhood. The loss of the roles of worker and spouse signify that one's participation in the occupational structure and the nuclear family has ended and the central tasks of life are finished. These losses are largely irreversible, for seldom do retired persons resume full-time employment and few widows remarry.

Work, Retirement, and Leisure

Retirement is unknown in many places throughout the world. Abkhasians of the Caucasus Mountains of Russia believe that "without rest, a man cannot work; without work, the rest does not give you any benefit" (Benet 1971). As a result, these people continue to work until the end of their lives at whatever tasks they are capable of performing. Retirement as we know it is a new phenomenon found in industrialized societies. Past societies had aged people but no retired ones. It is only recently that retirees have constituted a distinct social category. Up until only 50 years ago, most men in the United States age 65 and over were still in the labor force. Today the proportion of men still working over the age of 65 has dropped to about 19%.

The transition from the world of work to the world of leisure is one of personal as well as social significance. Some workers eagerly anticipate retirement, but others view it with considerable reluctance or even dread. For some, retirement is the fulfillment of a lifelong dream; for others the idleness and boredom of retirement is a nightmare. A survey conducted by Harris and Associates reveals that nearly 4 million, or about 30%, of those now retired would prefer to work (Harris 1975). The following case illustrates the plight of one retiree:

> Charlie had looked forward to retirement so that he could spend his time hunting, fishing, and traveling. But after a while he grew bored and disillusioned. He felt that he was not doing anything worthwhile and that his life was totally useless and unproductive. He missed his work and the feeling of accomplishment that it brought him and he desperately wanted to return to it.

The Retirement Event

Retirement can be viewed as an event, a role, a process, or all three. When seen as an event, it is sometimes marked with a farewell dinner for the retiree or a group of retirees. After some speech-making and a few jokes, there is the presentation of a gift such as a watch, luggage, or a plaque for long and devoted years of service to the company. Sometimes the event is reported in the newspapers.

The Retirement Role

As a role, retirement represents what Burgess has called a "roleless role." There are no clearly defined norms and widely shared expectations about the proper role for a retiree. As a result, the lives of the elderly are socially un-structured and unchartered. Since our society does not specify an aged role, it is up to the individual to carve out a new role at retirement to replace the interests and activities of former years. Irving Rosow (1973) points out that in old age life is largely shaped by one's own personal choices and initiative:

> Because many people lack the interest and initiative to fashion a satisfying ex-istence independently, life patterns range from the highly active and imaginative to passive vegetation. To be sure, almost the entire spectrum of possible social styles is socially acceptable. But this broad range of permissible alternatives simply documents the role vacuum: there are few prescriptions, norms, and expectations; weak definitions of what an old person should be like and how he should spend his time; and only a clouded picture of the good life in old age (83).

On the other hand, Vern Bengtson (1976) argues that the lack of a definite role for the elderly can also have positive consequences because it represents a gain in freedom. For those elderly who have the capacity and motivation to exploit this freedom, it affords a wide variety of behaviors and lifestyles from which to choose.

The Retirement Process

Lastly, retirement may be thought of as a process. Ideally, this process should begin early in the work career so that one may begin to cultivate interests, develop hobbies, and make plans for the retirement years well in advance. For most persons, however, the retirement process does not begin until a few years before retirement, when one becomes increasingly aware that the time of retirement is approaching. To heighten this awareness and to help facilitate the transition and adjustment to retirement, today many businesses and industries are sponsoring preretirement preparation programs for their employees. These programs provide the preretiree with some knowledge about retirement, what problems to anticipate in retirement, and how to prepare for them. One approach to accomplishing these objectives is through group ses-sions.

> Group sessions are considered by many to be the most effective method of retirement preparation. They give employees the opportunity to exchange ideas and information freely and to discuss retirement problems with one another. Each session, which usually lasts about two hours, focuses on one major topic involved in retirement preparation. These topics generally include finances, health,

Through contact with older persons, children gain a continuity and a link with the past.

the sociological and psychological aspects of retirement, and the use of leisure time. Most group programs schedule weekly meetings, ranging anywhere over a period of from 6 to 12 weeks; employees are given time off during working hours to attend the sessions. Some firms hold their meetings in the evenings to enable the employee's spouse to attend (Harris and Cole 1980:118).

After the event of retirement, many persons go through a period of adjustment consisting of the following phases, which represent an ideal type (Havighurst 1955). The period immediately following retirement is usually characterized by some activity or activities that one has been looking forward to and has not had time for previously. These activities may include extended travel, extensive household chores, or prolonged visits with one's children who live in far-off places. In the second phase, the retiree begins to seek out new roles and searches for ways to use his or her free time. Usually the first two phases of retirement adjustment are reached by the end of the first year. In the next phase, a period of stability is attained as the retiree puts in action the roles that he or she has chosen. By this point, new routines and patterns have been established, and life in retirement becomes reasonably self-fulfilling and satisfying. However, the process of retirement is never quite completed, because as time goes on and as new problems arise, new adjustments are required.

Mandatory Retirement

Mandatory retirement has long been the subject of much heated debate. Although some argue that it cannot be considered as firing or dismissal, the results are the same, since it denies people the right to work and forces them into unemployment. The decision to base retirement on the age of 65 dates back to the Social Security Act of 1935. At that time 25% of the work force was unemployed and it made sense to remove older workers from the labor market. Since social security was originally intended for industrial workers, no distinctions were made in the differing mental and physical requirements of various occupations. A far-reaching consequence of the social security legislation was that age 65 became firmly established in the minds of business and industrial leaders as the time for retirement. The general population also began to accept retirement at 65 as the right and proper thing to do (Woodring 1976).

Since 1935, many argued against the unfairness of basing mandatory retirement on age alone and not taking performance into account. The lack of any age distinction between jobs requiring brains and those requiring brawn was another point of contention. Finally, opponents of mandatory retirement pointed to the unnecessary waste of human resources and talent. Employers rallied to the support of mandatory retirement on the grounds that it was

An increasing number of older persons are seeking further education. At the age of 80, Claire Jacobs received her bachelor's degree.

impartial and eliminated the need of having to evaluate employees on the basis of merit.

In 1978, 43 years after the passage of the Social Security Act, the mandatory age of retirement was raised from 65 to 70. It is predicted that during the next decade, the age will be raised again or that mandatory retirement will be eliminated altogether.

The case against mandatory or compulsory retirement is slated to gain even more support in the future, as Peter Drucker (1980) explains:

> The resistance to compulsory retirement is going to be greatly accentuated by the educational shift in the work force. Eight out of every ten people who reach the traditional American retirement age of sixty-five these days had only a junior high school education, whereas six out of every ten new entrants into the labor force from now on will have had formal schooling beyond high school. The people who retire have largely worked in manual jobs all their lives. Manual workers, by and large, are content to retire at age fifty-five or sixty after thirty-five years in the steel mill . . . For knowledge workers, however, the need to keep on doing something productive is overwhelming. This need on the part of the knowledge worker not to "retire" at any given age will lead to seeking a second career in his or her forties or fifties (128–129).

Leisure

At retirement the worker loses his or her occupational identity and an economically productive role in society. To compensate for this loss, the retiree is offered leisure. But a career of leisure goes against our cultural values and is not considered a socially recognized virtue, placing the elderly in a social dilemma. Full-time leisure activities do not successfully substitute for the meaningful activity and functionality related to the work role. According to Stephen Miller (1965):

> A career of leisure (play) is characteristic of the socially immature (children) or the socially superannuated. For the aging individual, it can only serve to add to his social loss, negating any social benefits that might be derived from remaining active by serving to reinforce a definition of him as superannuated (79).

In an attempt to identify how older people spend their leisure, Robert Havighurst and August de Vries (1969) have delineated seven patterns of free-time activity.

1. *Challenging new experiences.*   Older persons in this pattern vigorously pursue their own interests and pleasure in such a way that it results in their coming in contact with a variety of new people.
2. *Instrumental service.*   These persons devote large amounts of their time and energy to their church, community, or occupational group.
3. *Expressive pleasure.*   In contrast to serving others or self-improvement, this pattern consists solely of indulging oneself and seeking pleasure.
4. *Mildly active time filling.*   In this pattern, the person exercises some initiative by doing a routine leisure activity that takes several hours a day,

CONTROVERSIAL ISSUES · The Detroit Syndrome

I'd like to elaborate just a little on the wastefulness of our society, what I call the "Detroit" syndrome. The Detroit syndrome builds obsolescence into all our thinking and production. Only the new model is desirable, marketable, profitable. The "Detroit" mentality has taken us over as a society. We are a wasteful society. We've been wasting people who cannot produce at what we consider to be productive peaks. They're surplus, they're scrap. We as a society, for all our protestations of compassion and humanity, have never come to grips with dependency and been able to deal with it in any human, compassionate way. We make the people who are dependent non-people. We throw away people, and before we throw them away we warehouse them in institutions. We make them vegetables, fit for nothing but scrap piles.

SOURCE: Dieter T. Hessel, *Maggie Kuhn on Aging* (Philadelphia: The Westminster Press, 1977), p. 15.

such as going to the library, taking a long walk, or going to a senior citizens center.

5. *Ordinary routines expanded to fill the day and week.* The person with this pattern does nothing but the usual activities that expand to fill time. A 72-year-old retiree who goes to the store every morning with his wife remarks, "By the time you shop and come home and put your purchases away it seems to be a day's work" (Havighurst and deVries 1969).

6. *Apathetic.* This pattern consists of the "rocking-chair" approach to life. The person has no new interests, does not initiate any activity, and is quite passive.

7. *Literally has no free time.* This pattern is somewhat uncommon and would apply to those older persons who have little time or energy left for leisure activities. A person may continue to work full or part time in addition to having household chores and various other duties to perform.

A study by Louis Harris and Associates (1975) reveals that there is a great disparity between how persons under 65 think the elderly use their leisure time and how the elderly actually use it. In addition the involvement of the young and old in many activities is not as different as one might think. Over ⅔ of those under 65 believe that most older people spend their time "watching TV a lot." Yet only 36% of those 65 and over said they watch TV frequently, compared to 23% of those under 65 who do so. A majority of younger persons think that older people "spend a lot of time just sitting around and thinking." But only 31% of older people say they do compared to the higher percentage (37%) of those under 65 who report that they just "sit around and think a lot." A large number of persons under 65 believe that older people spend a lot of

TABLE 9.1   Activities of Persons 18–64 and 65 and Over

Activity	Percent Spending a "Lot of Time" Doing Activity	
	18–64	**65 and over**
Socializing with friends	55	47
Reading	38	36
Sitting and thinking	37	31
Gardening or raising plants	34	39
Participating in recreational activities and hobbies	34	26
Watching television	23	36
Going for walks	22	25
Participating in sports like golf, tennis, or swimming	22	3
Sleeping	15	16
Participating in organizations or clubs	13	17
Just doing nothing	9	15
Doing volunteer work	8	8
Participating in political activities	5	6

SOURCE: Adapted from Louis Harris and Associates, *The Myth and Reality of Aging in America* (Washington, D.C.: National Council on the Aging, 1975), p. 57.

their time sleeping. However, the percentage of older people that reported they do indeed "sleep a lot" was almost identical to the percentage of younger people who said that they spend much of their time sleeping.

As one might expect, one of the greatest differences between the two groups involved participation in sports. In comparison with the elderly, a much higher percentage of the younger group participated in such activities as golf, tennis, or swimming. Overall, however, the Harris study found there were more similarities than differences between younger and older people. The results of the study reveal that both the younger and older age groups spend their leisure time in similar ways. (See Table 9.1.)

Death and Dying

Most people believe that the elderly fear death and dying more than any other age group. A number of studies have shown that just the opposite is true: Older persons tend to find death and dying less frightening or stressful than do younger persons. Several reasons may account for this. First, having lived a long time, it is likely that the elderly think they have had their fair share of time and do not feel cheated. Second, the lives of elderly persons are less valued by the elderly themselves as well as society. Finally, with age, people become socialized to their own death as family members and friends begin to die.

One of the most influential books on the subject of dying in recent years was written by Elisabeth Kübler-Ross (1969). The book contains interviews with over 200 dying patients from which she developed a view of the dying process that involves five stages. The first stage is *denial.* The patient refuses to believe that he or she is dying and usually reacts with the statement: "No, not me, it cannot be true." *Anger* is the second stage in which the dying person asks, "Why me?" This anger may be directed toward medical personnel, friends, family, or life in general. The third stage is one of *bargaining* in which the patient attempts to bargain with God to postpone death. The patient may promise to make a contribution to charity if only he or she can live long enough to attend the wedding of a favorite grandchild. At the fourth stage, *depression,* the person begins to mourn his or her own death and the losses that ensue. The last stage is *acceptance.* At this point the patient has become more tolerant, devoid of feelings, and is resigned to his or her fate.

Kübler-Ross's theory of stages has never been tested empirically or carefully evaluated. As yet, there is no evidence to support the existence of these five stages of dying or any stages for that matter. Also, as Robert Kastenbaum (1978) points out, Kübler-Ross's theory does not take into account the patient's "particular illness, mode of treatment, environmental pressures, ethnicity, and lifestyle." (6)

In the past, old persons lived and died at home. Today most old persons live at home but eventually die in hospitals. Robert Blauner (1968) describes how death has become bureaucratized by the hospital staff:

> The modern hospital as an organization is committed to the routinization of the handling of death. Its distinctive competence is to contain through isolation and reduce through orderly procedures, the disturbance and disruption that are associated with the death crisis . . . Hospitals are organized to hide the facts of dying and death from patients as well as visitors. Personnel in the high-mortality wards use a number of techniques to render death invisible. To protect relatives bodies are not to be removed during visiting hours. To protect other inmates, the patient is moved to a private room when the end is forseen (535).

In studying death in modern hospital situations, Barney Glaser and Anselm Strauss (1965) have distinguished four types of awareness situations. In the first type, *closed awareness,* the patient does not know about his or her impending death. The secret is well guarded by the doctors, nurses, and family members. In the second type, *suspicion awareness,* the patient suspects what the others know and attempts to confirm or negate his or her suspicions. In the third situation, *mutual-pretense awareness,* the patient knows he or she is dying and the medical staff and family members know, but everyone pretends that it is not true. Lastly there is the *open awareness* situation in which all concerned are fully aware of the fact of terminality.

Although there is some evidence that patients want to know about their terminality, most American physicians do not believe that this is the case and attempt to maintain a closed-awareness context.

> Physicians, like other Americans, shy away from the embarrassment and brutality of making direct reference to another person about his impending death. They also undoubtedly would rather avoid the scene that an announcement of impending death is likely to precipitate (Glaser and Strauss 1965:31).

A patient may go from closed, suspicion, mutual pretense to open awareness. An open-awareness context has the advantage of affording the patient an opportunity to get his or her affairs in order and "to close his life in accordance with his own ideas about proper dying" (Glaser and Strauss 1965:103). An aware patient may also make his or her death easier for the family by reducing the strain of maintaining closed or suspicion awareness and allowing family members to share in his or her confrontation of death.

Summary

Childhood did not become recognized in Europe as a separate stage of life until the seventeenth century, and the concept of adolescence as a distinct period of life did not come into existence until the nineteenth century. Old age as a stage in the life cycle has undergone considerable change in this country. Following the Civil War, the status of the elderly shifted from their being highly valued to being considerably devalued.

Today more people are living longer than ever before. At present, there are 25 million persons in the United States age 65 and over, and by 2000 there will be about 31.8 million. Life expectancy has increased dramatically since the turn of the century (from 48.2 years to 73.8 years), but the life span has remained the same since earliest times.

Our expectations about the behavior that is appropriate for people in a given age group are called age norms. A different standard of aging exists for men and women in our society. Women become "old" and sexually ineligible earlier than men. As we go through life, we give up old roles and acquire new roles, but in old age we tend to lose roles without having new ones to replace them. Two major role losses in old age are retirement and widowhood.

Retirement is a recent phenomenon that is occurring in all industrialized societies like our own. Being unstructured and ill-defined, the retirement role can have negative as well as positive consequences for the retiree. It can be viewed from several perspectives: as an event, role, or process. Mandatory retirement deprives many persons of the right to work. In 1978 the age of mandatory retirement was raised from 65 to 70.

The transition from full-time work to full-time leisure can be difficult. For many, leisure activities are a poor substitute for the economic productivity and meaningful activity that work provides. Leisure activities can assume a number of patterns ranging from "challenging new experiences" to "apathetic." According to a Harris survey, older and younger people share many similarities in their use of leisure time.

Research reveals that most elderly persons fear death less than any other age group. Kübler-Ross identifies five stages through which dying persons typically pass: denial, anger, bargaining, depression, and acceptance. Many doctors do not tell their patients that they are dying and prefer to keep them in a context of closed awareness instead of open awareness.

Suggested Readings

Zena Smith Blau. *Aging in a Changing Society,* 2d ed. New York: Franklin Watts, 1981. Explores the problems faced by older people in our society and offers some recommendations for solving them.

Robert N. Butler. *Why Survive? Being Old in America.*

New York: Harper & Row, 1975. A highly readable overview of the problems and experiences of older people.

Alex Comfort. *A Good Age.* New York: Crown, 1976. A clear, concise book on the basic facts about aging.

Diana K. Harris and William E. Cole. *Sociology of Aging.* Boston: Houghton Mifflin, 1980. A comprehensive text on aging and the aged in our society.

Arlie R. Hochschild. *The Unexpected Community.* Englewood Cliffs, N.J.: Prentice-Hall, 1973. A participant observation study of the social integration of elderly residents in a San Francisco apartment building.

Irving Rosow. *Socialization to Old Age.* Berkeley: University of California Press, 1974. A concise discussion of adult socialization theory.

PART THREE

Social Institutions and Organizations

Human beings are social animals. To maximize satisfaction of individual and collective goals, people form social organizations. Involvement in a social organization limits an individual's freedom, but typically provides the individual with greater rewards than he or she could obtain by functioning alone. A society is one type of social organization, but there are many others—families, work organizations, schools, churches, social groups, political parties, prisons—some of which are considered in Chapter 10.

The social organizations called societies are categorized in terms of their economic systems. Our society is described in Chapter 11 as a postindustrial society because our economic system emphasizes technology and services. Formerly we were an industrial society which focused on manufacturing.

Even though sociologists can analyze individuals' actions and values as societal products, individ-

uals do not typically think of themselves as societal members or products. People ordinarily think
of themselves as members of particular organizations or groups. Specific organizations and
groups may have unique characteristics just as
individuals do, but sociologists are interested in
characteristics groups and individuals have in
common. For example, family life is organized differently in different societies and even among
subgroups within a society. Chapter 12 considers
what functions families in general serve for societies and individuals. In that way the family is
treated as a societal institution.

Complex societies such as our own have a number of other institutions. Three others are the educational, religious, and political institutions.
Chapters 13, 14, and 15 discuss the functions of
these institutions. For example, we consider how
societal beliefs and values are transmitted from
generation to generation and how institutional
practices often promote stability or the status quo.

10

Organizations

Two couples are seated at a booth in a restaurant discussing where to spend their two-week vacation. They debate the merits of the beach, the mountains, the desert, a trip to various cities, an ocean cruise, and so forth. After some two hours of talk they decide that an ocean cruise to the Yucatan after a visit to EPCOT at Disneyworld would be the best way to satisfy each person. They split up tasks to prepare for the vacation: writing for cruise information, making reservations, purchasing supplies, and notifying their relatives of their plans.

Eight hunters hide behind scrub brush waiting for the leader to select an antelope from the herd. A hand is raised and points toward a buck with broken antlers. The hunters fan out in a long line. As the herd drifts along grazing, suddenly the men jump up and shout. The herd leaps off in a stampede, but the men have separated the buck from the herd. The men form a large circle. The leader pursues the buck, chasing and driving him toward the next hunter. As the first hunter tires, the second picks up the chase, driving the buck toward the next hunter. The leap-frogging pursuit of the buck continues until the antelope is winded and staggering. The best hunter springs forward and makes the first spear thrust. If the thrust is clean, the animal drops instantly. If merely wounded, the others thrust repeatedly until the animal is dead. After the kill, the heart is cut out and left for the wandering spirits to insure a good hunt next time. The liver is removed and eaten by the hunters while it is still warm. The hunters skin the buck, removing the haunches. They sew the skin into crude carrying pouches, distribute the meat among them, and trek back to camp. Upon reaching camp they divide the meat, with each hunter's share governed by custom. The women prepare a meal, and the tribe celebrates its good fortune and safe hunt.

A data processor operator enters the office, pauses by the door long enough to remove his card, punch in, and pick up his work assignments for the day. He heads for his desk, where he sits down before his data processor. Thirty-five other data entry operators occupy the room. This department is one of some forty responsible for handling domestic and foreign inventories. Each worker is assigned one particular product and a particular country where the company has divisional offices. All persons are expected to complete their daily assignments. All are on weekly salaries with the pay scale fixed by seniority. All are sworn to secrecy on matters pertaining to input data; disclosure of secrets brings immediate dismissal.

Each of these settings depicts people involved in some form of collective activity. The activities range from free-flowing discussion and decisions reached through conversation, to acts based on customs, to work highly regulated by contract and rules. In each situation people are cooperating to accomplish some common goal. The couples want to share a vacation. The hunters want meat for survival. The workers want to earn their pay. In each setting people

Increased
specialization
sometimes allows
workers to conduct
the activities of their
jobs either alone or
interacting with a
machine.

decide who does what. Roles are assigned. In effect each collectivity is structured, since individuals occupy particular positions and are responsible for
particular obligations and duties. The couples agreed on which of them would
write for information, get supplies, make reservations, or notify relatives. The
hunters knew who was to lead the hunt. Each hunter's position in the circle
was fixed by skill and tradition. The data entry personnel had job descriptions
assigning particular tasks and responsibilities. In each situation individuals
gain benefits from participating in the collective action. The vacationers got
to spend at least a portion of their time doing what they wanted. The hunters
got meat to eat. The data entry personnel received their salaries. In each
situation individuals surrender something they want for the good of the collectivity. No one vacationer was able to spend all the time at the "best spot."
The hunters risked danger. The data entry operators experienced frustration at
not being able to discuss job-related matters with their co-workers (McCall
and Simmons 1982).

Each of these settings represents different kinds of **social organizations,** ranging from informal to formal. In informal organizations, joint actions
tend to be influenced by the personalities of the individuals involved; in formal
organizations, joint actions tend to be shaped by the arrangement of relation-

Social organization
a group of people in-
volved in joint activity
pursuing a common
goal.

ships between positions. In informal organizations, who you are shapes how you relate to and act with others. In formal organizations, the position with its role assignment dictates how you relate to and act with others. Individuals deciding on where to vacation reached an agreement after considering the wants of each personality. Data processors have little if any concern about the personalities of their co-workers. They are forced to interact with their machines.

Social organization is essential to everyday existence, for joint activities take into account the interests of the collective. People may share common goals, as a sports team desires victory in a game or law partners want a favorable verdict. People may have complementary goals or interests. One person may want his lawn mowed, another his house painted, and still another her car fixed. To achieve these ends, they form a work group and help each other. Social organizations, then, define what the purpose of being together is and what ends are sought collectively. Social organizations also define what things need to be accomplished and who is responsible for doing them. This means social organizations have a division of labor. Social organizations regulate our collective actions. They set guidelines for coordinating our actions with others (Barnard 1938). Social organizations establish rewards and penalties for successfully and unsuccessfully working with others. In short, organizations help to make life predictable.

Roots of Formal Organization

Recorded human history provides testimony for the increased importance of social organization in people's lives and, more especially, for the importance of formal organizations as major social forms. With the agricultural revolution and the urban revolution, the size of communities increased (see Chapter 17). Organizational arrangements developed to take care of a variety of demands for goods, services, and individual or group needs. Economic organizations coordinated the production and distribution of necessities and luxuries. Political organizations emerged to administer the government, control the military, levy taxes, provide direction for the construction and maintenance of public works such as irrigation systems, roadways, and postal services (Wittfogel 1955). Religious organizations evolved to lead the faithful in worship, ritual, and sacrifice as well as to instruct the uninitiated in the mysteries of magic, the meanings of scriptures, and the awe of the unknown (Parsons 1956).

The change from relatively simple forms of communal and kin-based organizations to increasingly complex forms was accelerated by the Industrial Revolution. (For a discussion of the transition from gemeinschaft to gesellschaft-type societies, see Chapter 3.) The use of energy sources other than human and animal power, the growth of mass production, and the increase in job and task specialization led to new definitions of work and new modes of decision making. The Machine Age with the interchangeability of workers and the spread of mass markets was accompanied by the emergence of formal organizations, especially bureaucratic organizations.

Bureaucracies are large, special-purpose organizations, geared for efficiency whether in the production of goods or the provision of services. Such organizations were ideal in an age of modern capitalism (Blau and Myer 1971), rapid industrialization, and urbanization.

Nowadays formal organizations in various guises are omnipresent and, many fear, omnipotent. Corporations are formal organizations. Some corporations extract resources (Atlantic Richfield, Oxy, Alcoa, Amax, Kaiser), some convert raw materials into finished products (Burlington, Levi Strauss, Genesco, Scovill), and others generate the new technologies (IBM, Xerox, Control Data, Texas Instruments). Still others create and manipulate money markets (Continental, J. P. Morgan, Aetna, Prudential). Organizations also exist to coordinate other organizations—the mighty conglomerates. Organizations even act as watchdogs over other organizations (Federal Trade Commission, Federal Communications Commission, Environmental Protection Agency).

Formal organizations exist for many purposes besides business, such as the military, religious, service, and special interest organizations such as clubs. Formal organizations vary in size and degree of formalism. But the tone of modern society is heavily influenced by formal organizations.

What social, economic, and historical factors were associated with the growth of formal organizations?

Organizational Structure

A **formal organization** is a network of individuals who follow rules and regulations that prescribe and proscribe actions to be taken in the production of goods, the offering of services, or the pursuit of particular goals. Formal organizations differ from other social organizations in their size, complexity, centralization, and degree of formalization (Hall 1982).

Formal organization a network of individuals who follow rules and regulations that prescribe and proscribe actions to be taken in the production of goods, the offering of services, or the pursuit of particular goals.

Size

As communities increase in **size,** formal organizations are developed to solve problems of adapting to the environment (government), handling survival needs (sanitation), and providing social services (welfare). In large communities it is impossible for each person to relate to every other person. Channels of interaction are established to direct who interacts with whom. Which individuals interact is determined by what kinds of activities they perform as well as whether the activities need to be coordinated with one another. As activities interlock and tasks are more sharply defined, channels of commu-

Size the number of persons or subunits in an organization.

nication become more circumscribed. In sum, increased size leads to formalization and specialization of positions and roles in a community. Size is not only a condition that sparks the growth of formal organizations, but also a feature of organizations. As the size of organizations increases, the processes of formalization and specialization are duplicated.

Formal organizations tend to be large, such as the Roman Catholic church, the National Rifle Association, or the Democratic party. Among formal organizations of a business type, size is indicated by the number of persons on the payroll. Some large corporations have over 100,000 employees. Hospitals mark their size by the number of beds, or schools by the number of students.

As organizations increase in size, the number of social units or subunits in the organization also increases. A large organization may be highly subdivided. These subunits may be called wards, departments, branches, bureaus, agencies, or parishes.

Some resource extraction companies are formal organizations with many subunits around the world. Amax mines coal, molybdenum, tungsten, aluminum, iron ore, and even pumps gas and oil. Not only does it extract these resources, it also refines them and markets the products around the world. This scope of production requires various divisional operations throughout the United States, Europe, and Africa. Amax also has financial ties with companies in Japan, France, Botswana, Zambia, South Africa, Canada, Australia, and the United States (Moskowitz et al. 1980). Other formal organizations may be even more highly subdivided, such as the United States government. The federal bureaucracy is a labyrinth of departments, divisions, branches, bureaus, and agencies.

How does size affect interaction in organizations?

Complexity

In formal organizations **complexity** refers to the arrangement of subunits as well as to the **division of labor.** Whether a formal organization has branches, divisions, departments, wards, or agencies, each subunit has different tasks and amounts of responsibility. Subunits may be vertically linked with subunits that rank higher or lower. Higher-level subunits usually have more tasks and broader sets of responsibilities than subunits in subordinate positions. This type of arrangement is a hierarchy of authority. On a university campus the president's office has a broader range of decisions to make than the dean's office or a department office. The total number of levels in an organization or in all subunits in the organization measures the complexity of the organization (Hall, Haas, and Johnson 1967).

A **chain of authority** or **line of command** is created among the occupational positions in the organization. Each job is specialized, and job descriptions vary in their specificity. Superordinates' job descriptions are broader in scope. They have more latitude in decision making, and their responsibil-

Complexity arrangement of subunits in an organization; may be vertical or horizontal.

Division of labor distribution of positions in an organization or proliferation of various kinds of jobs.

Chain of command, chain of authority, line of command a hierarchy of authority with differing amounts of responsibility and power assigned to superordinate and subordinate positions.

In highly centralized organization, subordinates must follow the directions provided by their supervisors.

ities are more diffusely defined. Subordinates tend to have more delimited job descriptions, with little freedom in decision making and tasks that are defined specifically. A college president may be responsible for fund raising, academic standards, and other matters pertaining to the state of the institution, whereas a secretary is required to type a certain number of words per minute, prepare specific reports, and schedule appointments. Perhaps the best example of an organization with an elaborate chain of command, as well as with specific job descriptions for each rank and grade, is the military services.

Subunits and positions in formal organizations also are arranged *horizontally*. That is, some subunits are assigned similar degrees of responsibility. They occupy the same rank of power. In a college each academic department has roughly the same sets of responsibilities. Departments may vary in size and budget, but their faculties are expected to teach, conduct and publish research, and engage in service to the academic community and the larger community. Research suggests that organizations involving several kinds of professions tend to become horizontally arranged, since the professionals define their jobs as fairly broad in scope (Blau and McKinley 1979). In many hospitals, specialty units such as pediatrics or obstetrics and gynecology wards are at the same level in the organization.

The arrangement of subunits and jobs within an organization often is presented in an organizational chart. Sometimes job candidates may ask to see a copy of the company's chart to orient themselves on where they fit in the hierarchy. In some cases the company may not be able to produce an up-to-date plan because the organization frequently revamps its system of duties and responsibilities.

As an organization increases in size, the number of recognized positions increases. For example, the rapid growth in colleges and universities in the 1960s and 1970s triggered topsy-turvy additions of departments and programs. With declines in enrollments and smaller budgets of the 1980s, faculty and administrative positions are being cut, along with some programs.

What aspects of organizational complexity can be studied by looking at an organizational chart?

Centralization

As organizations increase in size and the tasks increase in variety and number, problems of communication within and between subunits at different levels may increase. As size increases, it becomes increasingly necessary to take steps to coordinate activities throughout the organization. In response to these problems organizations often centralize their authority hierarchies. They may set up new regulations governing incentives and disincentives to encourage desired behavior and discourage nonconformity. Responsibility for important decisions is concentrated in fewer and fewer hands. Concentration of power is called **centralization.** Occupants of the powerful central positions become the ruling elite in the organization.

Centralization concentration of power.

Centralization has advantages and disadvantages. From an organizational viewpoint, limiting major decision-making duties to a few persons may increase efficiency, if communication channels are adequate. Also decisions may be carried out more efficiently when the number of people who report to the administrator is not too large.

Should an organization become too centralized, it may become autocratic. The distance between superordinate and subordinates becomes greater. In some cases this distance creates new problems of communication and coordination of activities. Supervisors may not learn about subordinates' problems, and instructions may become garbled as they pass down the chain of command. Workers may not understand directives, organizational goals, or policy changes.

For an organization to be maximally efficient, a delicate balance between centralization and decentralization must be maintained. **Decentralization** involves a dispersal of authority throughout the organization as well as a reduction in the number of individuals and tasks for which each superordinate is held accountable (Van de Ven and Ferry 1980). An organization long noted for its high degree of centralization is IBM. Organizations in which decentralization has been tried are Polaroid and Xerox. Employees of these organizations find work a less demoralizing and a more democratic experience. Also, decentralization permits greater flexibility in the organization's efforts to meet such external demands as changes in the market or new technologies (Hage

Decentralization dispersement of authority throughout more positions and subunits in the organization.

and Aiken 1967). Too much centralization cuts down on communication and innovative problem solving.

What kinds of problems may be found in an organization when it becomes too centralized?

Formalization

Closely related to size and complexity is the characteristic of formalization. As a formal organization increases in size and expands the number of subunits, formalization increases. **Formalization** means that the formal norms—policies, rules, regulations, and memorandums—tend to grow faster than informal norms—the understandings shared between people who interact with one another on a daily basis. The more formal an organization, the greater the reliance on written directives for behavior. They allegedly insure that everyone will be treated evenhandedly.

Formal norms or rules govern who can be hired and fired, how people should dress, who may interact with whom, what is received as rewards as well as punishments. Rules define the scope and interconnections of job activities, so that each job is coordinated with others. Ideally, formal norms make the flow of activities predictable.

Formalization and decentralization go together more typically than do formalization and centralization. In fact, formalization increases predictability. Thus by knowing the rules, people can spend their energies elsewhere, such as in problem-solving activities (Blau 1970).

Formal organizations vary in the degree of formality found in their regulative system. Bell Telephone, with a work force covering virtually every job defined in the *Dictionary of Occupations*, has a high degree of formality. Even the type, shape, and color of tissue paper holders on executive desks are spelled out in the regulations (Hage and Aiken 1967).

Administrators also vary in how they choose to implement the regulations. Some go by the book, others keep the book on the shelf. In general, the larger the organization and the more diversified its activities, the more complex and more formal the organization becomes.

> **Formalization** expansion of formal norms—policies, rules, regulations, and memorandums.

What are some of the purposes that formalization serves in an organization?

Informal Structure

Information on how complex, centralized, or formalized an organization is may be gathered by looking at its organizational chart and by reading its rules and policies. But to understand an organization in its daily operation, sociologists must learn about its **informal structure.** The hierarchy of authority may spell out who is supposed to control whom, but often managers,

> **Informal structure** development of groups among coworkers, emergence of norms, channels of communication, and leadership.

secretaries, or workers within each of the various subunits informally agree or understand that a particular person is really in charge, no matter what the chart says. Other workers turn to that person for information or supplies, to express requests or problems, or for approval or disapproval. A secretary, for example, may be the key person in an office for getting things done, and may be recognized as a major power factor.

Similarly organizational members develop their own channels of communication to subvert, bypass, or ignore certain officials or offices in the hierarchy. Experiences teach the members that informal channels of communications may be more effective than formal ones in getting action without a hassle.

Organizational members find satisfaction with each other and form groups. Informal norms develop on what constitutes a fair day's work, how rapidly tasks should be accomplished, and what tasks are important or unimportant. Students often agree how long papers should be or how much reading they should do. Sanctions are developed to insure conformity to group norms. Mild forms are ridicule or failure to share in group gossip or to share needed information to get a job done. Sometimes ostracism is used to stop people from producing too much during a work period. Workers who violate the social pecking order of prestige may even suffer physical reprisals (Roy 1952).

Organizational members also may generate norms about which pieces of equipment (typewriters, tools, books) may be borrowed for home use, what kinds of supplies (stationery, raw materials, machines) and how many may be taken as fringe benefits of the job. Cutbacks or official actions against the persons who follow these informal practices may cause labor unrest with slowdowns, sickouts, and strikes.

Informal norms may enhance the efficiency and effectiveness of the organization. Office workers, for example, may cover for a fellow worker who is absent for a reason acceptable to the group but not to management. Co-workers may work harder to cover the absent person's output. The worker is then obligated to return the favor at a later time. In some cases norms develop that do not fit the aims of the organization. Coaches and graduate assistants in athletic departments in universities or colleges may express sexist views and discriminate against female athletes even though university and federal policies prohibit such actions.

How does the informal group modify the formality of the formal organization?

Organizational Control

Formal organizations sometimes are classified by how they structure authority relationships and allocate work tasks. **Authority** is the right to exercise power or use force. Sometimes legitimate and illegitimate authority are distinguished.

Authority right to exercise power or use force.

Legitimate authority implies that the actions taken by an individual occupying a position are seen by others as acceptable and proper. For instance, a doctor in a hospital has the right to write prescriptions or draw medical supplies. **Illegitimate authority** implies that actions taken by an individual are unacceptable and improper for someone in that position. It was improper, for instance, for former President Richard M. Nixon to withhold evidence on the Watergate break-in under the guise of executive privilege.

Weber was interested in accounting for authority relationships as modern life became increasingly rationalized (Gerth and Mills 1958). When societies were transformed from fiefdoms and estates to states, from rural-agrarian to urban-industrial economies, and from family-based enterprises to those managed by nonrelatives, the patterns of authority were shifted too. Weber outlines three types of authority: charismatic, traditional, and legal-rational. Each type is a model or ideal type. Thus in actual organizational settings, elements of more than one type may be present at the same time. Under each type of authority, the bases for leadership and acceptance by others have different social roots.

Charismatic Authority

Charismatic authority is based on the personal qualities of an individual. A charismatic leader commands by virtue of his or her magnetism of character and social vision. People either love or hate these leaders. There is no middle ground. Followers will sacrifice personal property, friends, and family in order to serve. Disbelievers denigrate such leaders, using ridicule and ostracism. In more extreme cases, such leaders are targeted for assassination. Charismatic leaders may become the focal point around which cults develop (see Chapter 14, Religion).

Charismatic leaders delegate tasks following personal preferences. To effectively control their followers, the leader must be recognized as important. Typically the followers offer undying loyalty to the leader. The bond is fragile, however, and only as strong as the successes achieved by the leader. Conquering heroes such as Alexander the Great, Genghis Khan, and Napoleon are often cited as charismatic persons, but so are religious visionaries such as Jesus, St. Francis, and Ghandi. More recently, political leaders such as John F. Kennedy and Martin Luther King, Jr. were seen as having charisma.

Traditional Authority

Traditional authority is rooted in custom. A chief assigns the various jobs or grants power of commission. For instance, a lord may ask a knight to escort family members on a journey or commission an artist to paint a family portrait. The chief as well as other household officials make decisions following precedents, traditions, and sometimes whim. Elaborate codes of etiquette are followed in rendering judgments affecting matters of state. The chief typically recruits persons from within the kin group or household when assigning tasks or bestowing certain powers. Sons of nobility may be eligible for mem-

Legitimate authority
actions taken by leader seen as acceptable and proper by others.

Illegitimate authority
actions taken by leader seen as unacceptable and improper by others.

Charismatic authority
leadership based on individual's personality, magnetism of character, and social vision.

Traditional authority
leadership based on household or family ties and rooted in custom.

bership in elite groups (knighthood), but sons of peasants are not, although exceptions may be made. When the chief selects someone from outside the kin group or household, the act is seen as a favor.

Individuals sometimes are trained in traditional beliefs, rules of conduct, and skills, although such training is not usually systematic. The leader takes care of appointees by equipping them from the household stores. The leader may provide clothes, uniform, shelter, weapons, food, and even money. Such gifts are fixed by rank and stereotyped by tradition.

The right to rule depends on kin ties, whether they are fixed by blood, or marriage. In cases where a ruler has been recently deposed, the claimant's authority is initially backed by force. Once the claimant is seen as legitimate, precedence is again established, and tradition takes over.

In sum, charismatic and traditional authority systems of control emphasize an individual's personality or tradition as the bases for leadership.

Legal-Rational Authority

In opposition to these two types of authority, Weber postulated a third type—**legal-rational.** Legal-rational or bureaucratic authority is impersonal instead of personal; regulated by rules rather than whim and precedent. Leadership is assigned on the basis of technical competence rather than personal character or family ties. In short, the aim of legal-rational bureaucracy is to create decision making that is predictable, routine, and systematic.

Legal-rational authority leadership based on administrative position responsibilities and tasks governed by contract and law.

In the legal-rational bureaucracy, officials occupy administrative positions. Authority is vested in the position, not in the individual office holder. The position persists even if the incumbent leaves it. In short, officials are substitutable. The emphasis on position highlights the impersonal character of the bureaucratic organization.

Appointment to an administrative post is based on technical merit. Ideally it is "what you know, not who you know" that counts. Technical training and prior experience provide the basis for defining technical merit. The kinds of training and experiences needed as well as the conditions for appointment are set forth in detail in contractual agreements, policies, and sometimes law.

What is expected from the leaders and the workers is often defined in written regulations—the job description. A system of incentives, salaries, bonuses, and fringe benefits is laid out in contracts and policy statements. These rules are ideally applied systematically, thus eliminating favoritism and nepotism.

A clearly delineated hierarchy of authority exists between positions in the organization. The scope of authority for each position also is delimited. Decisions are made in accordance with the regulations and policies defining who has responsibility and control. The arrangement of divisional units also is articulated, and the coordination of various social units defined.

Weber emphasized those aspects of organizational structure that lead to impersonality, elimination of favoritism and nepotism, increased competency, and greater uniformity and routinization of action. More recently, sociologists have noted that these ideals are rarely obtained in practice.

What are defining characteristics for each of the three types of authority?

No organization possesses all of the characteristics of any single ideal type, whether it is charismatic authority, traditional authority, or legal-rational bureaucracy. Most organizations have some of the features of one type but not all of them. Sometimes a mix of characteristics of different types is present. Although the cases that Weber analyzed in presenting his ideal types suggested that bureaucracies were typical of modern societies, and traditional authority structures were typical of nonindustrial societies, research shows that a mixture of authority types is found in each setting. The worth of these ideal types is not their empirical accuracy, but rather their quality of sensitizing us to look at the features of organizations and how they change over time.

Bureaucratic emphasis on the impersonal nature of relationships between members and the ease with which employees, students, and clients may be substituted for one another are associated with the beliefs that people are simply cogs in a machine or just statistics to be processed by the organization's computer and accounting office. Students sometimes are frustrated when they are treated as a number when they register or change courses. To counteract this feeling of impersonality, employees find ways to express their individuality. The older view of management was to fit the individual to the job, but a more recent view of management is to modify the job and enhance individual performance.

Similarly the bureaucratic emphasis on competence serves as a double-edged sword. Competence as a basis for hiring and incompetence as a basis for firing can protect both administrators and employees from capricious actions by superiors. But also, the moves by workers to guarantee job security by elaborating the grounds for dismissal can lead to protectionism and undue difficulties in eliminating workers who are incompetent or "burned out." The Civil Service System is charged with such shortcomings, as is the tenure system for faculty used in many colleges and universities.

The bureaucratic emphasis on routinization and specialization of job activities may lead to standardized products, but it also leads to trained incapacity. Workers become so specialized they do not know who does what in other divisions of an organization. Nor could the workers perform other activities unless they were trained for them. Such specialization leads workers to disassociate themselves from the product produced or the service offered. To counteract this incapacity and overcome workers' lack of involvement in the overall production process, management sometimes moves workers from one task to another. This shifting of jobs lets the workers learn new skills and develop an understanding of the entire production process. They recognize how each activity is coordinated and what their own contributions are, as well as their importance.

Organizations and People

The sociological dictum of W. I. Thomas, "If people define situations as real, they are real in their consequences," aptly applies to the discussion of both management's and workers' adjustment to organizational life. Douglas McGregor (1957, 1960, 1967), after analyzing the role of management and its tasks and the prevailing images of people in organizations, suggested two models of management: Theory X and Theory Y.

Theory X—Scientific Management

In Theory X, management is responsible for looking after capital, plant, and people, with the economic aim of maximizing profits and minimizing losses. Management is responsible for motivating people to work, to conform to organizational rules, and to fulfill the goals of the organization. Management must take an active role, for if it does not, people become passive and do not actively work to achieve the aims of the organization. Presumably the worker is lazy, doing only what needs to be done and nothing more. The worker lacks ambition and would rather be told what to do than be a self-starter. The worker is more interested in fulfilling personal wants than those of the organization. The worker resists new methods of operation and job assignments.

Managers operating with this view of workers see themselves as actively responsible for establishing organizational goals; they set up strong rewards for work and punishments for failure to work or to conform to organizational rules. One consequence of this perspective is that the interests of management and workers are seen as in conflict. Management adopts a paternalistic stance and often becomes autocratic. Workers become hostile toward management and turn to their own informal groups for mutual support and security.

Early studies of organizations conducted in the **scientific management** tradition often reflected the management's view of the worker. Frederick W. Taylor developed the idea of scientific management that was adopted widely in the major centers of heavy and light industry during the 1920s and 1930s. These were called "time and motion" studies. He concentrated on eliminating inefficiency in movements associated with a task, thereby reducing fatigue, increasing production, and lowering costs. Taylor and others in this tradition had the ideal of social reform. They assumed that scientific management would help workers work more efficiently, earn more pay, and thereby improve their social standing. In fact, the movement prohibited the workers' economic gain. It merely increased units produced, lowered pay scales, and often, through increased efficiency, eliminated workers from the job.

Some of these studies also analyzed the composition of management in

Scientific management research tradition with the aim of eliminating fatigue in order to increase production and lower costs; assumes managers are responsible and workers are irresponsible.

Whether they work in white-collar or blue-collar settings, many people perform the same specialized tasks day after day.

bureaucratic organizations. They searched for the characteristics that suited individuals to work as executives and become successful career administrators.

Studies of scientific management were based on three assumptions. First, people are basically substitutable and can move into and out of an organization easily. Second, to be efficient, organizations must find ways to select people who can fit into a job and, once on the job, can be motivated to work diligently simply by manipulation of the reward system. Third, the organization is the best way to achieve success and move toward a better quality of life in society.

Theory Y—Human Relations

McGregor's second model—Theory Y—is less pessimistic about the innate nature of people. Under Theory Y, management is still responsible for looking after capital, plant, and people to make profits. But it assumes that unless people have already learned otherwise, they are not passive and self-centered by nature. Instead they learn these behaviors and attitudes if the organizational structure encourages such a view. Basically people have the motivation to learn, are capable of directing their own lives, and can be creative when given the opportunity. Management, then, is responsible for establishing procedures, work conditions, and rules so the workers can maximize their own potential (McGregor 1957).

CONTROVERSIAL ISSUES · Hawthorne Effect—Fact or Fantasy?

Representatives of the human resources tradition long pointed to a series of experiments (1927–1932) conducted in the Hawthorne plant of Western Electric Company near Chicago. Management wanted to identify which working conditions could be manipulated to reduce fatigue on the assembly line and increase production. Researchers in a series of experiments manipulated the lighting, physical working conditions, length of work intervals, and pay scales for individuals and groups. In one experiment on the amount of lighting in the relay assembly room, no matter how much the illumination was increased or decreased, productivity increased. The experimenters concluded that the female workers saw themselves as an experimental group and as members of a special group receiving attention other workers did not receive, and this perception motivated them to work harder with each change in illumination levels. In the bank wiring room experiments, wages were manipulated. Although various incentives were tried, workers maintained the same levels of production. Presumably informal groups developed among co-workers, and norms evolved that regulated the amount of production.

These earlier studies did not rely on statistical techniques to analyze the data to test whether the alleged patterns actually existed. A reexamination of the Hawthorne data suggests that what affected productivity was the (1) exercise of managerial discipline—firing workers who were disagreeable, (2) workers' awareness that a depression was in effect and their fear for their jobs, and (3) introduction of rest periods that alleviated fatigue and increased hourly production. Some evidence exists for use of group incentives to increase production, but its impact is minor compared with the other three conditions.

SOURCE: Richard Herbert Franke and James D. Kaul, "The Hawthorne Experiments: First Statistical Interpretation," *American Sociological Review* 43, October 1978, pp. 623–643.

Several studies have been conducted in this **human relations** tradition. Their aim is to find ways that management can fit the job to the person. Should this match be achieved, workers will be happier, production higher, and conflict between management and organizational members lower. In effect, the job setting will be an arena in which the worker can become self-actualized, reaching his or her potential (Maslow 1954).

This tradition flows from early work done by Elton Mayo, who was dedicated to solving problems in business as well as industrial civilization. Although he studied the psychological states of workers, he eventually recognized that workers could only be understood within the context of their work group. Work groups, and by extension society, were cooperative systems that supported the individual. As group morale improved, production would rise. Thus, attention should be focused on ways to structure the work environment to enhance group morale and cohesiveness (Mayo 1933; 1945).

Human relations research tradition with aim of studying development of informal groups and understanding their impact on organizational efficiency; assumes workers have needs beyond economic goals.

Workers sometimes are more satisfied with their jobs if they have an opportunity to participate in decision making.

This human relations tradition rests on three assumptions. First, people should not have to fit into a job; rather, jobs should be molded to fit people's needs. Second, to be efficient, organizations must find ways to restructure the work tasks and environment to capitalize on human resource and potential. Third, both the organization and its goals become ends in themselves, with work being a positive rather than a negative experience. Subsequent research suggests that this humanistic assumption requires modification. Given the choice between a well-paying job or one that offers a challenge and provides self-enrichment, some workers opt for the dollars (Champagne and Tausky 1978). Although some workers profess that challenge is important, personal fulfillment is not always as important a factor as was earlier assumed.

What are the assumptions of the scientific management approach and the human relations approach to the study of formal organizations?

The optimism of the humanist is again popular. William Ouchi (1981) has lauded the Japanese for integrating worker and management into a highly successful and productive relationship.

Theory Z

Ouchi (1981) describes a model of management presumably found in some companies in the United States (Hewlett Packard, Eastman Kodak, IBM), which is called Theory Z. This model allegedly builds on the work of human

---

THE FACTS · How To Succeed in Business

Kanter (1977) studied the relationships between executives and lower-level office workers in the Indsco organization. She found that the success or failure of executives in the organizations often was linked to actions of secretaries. Some secretaries intentionally or unintentionally withheld information on important meetings or urgent matters. Given the competitive nature of the organization, failure to be properly informed put some executives in a disadvantaged position relative to others.

The mobility of secretaries also was affected by actions of executives. Given the executives' uncertainty of their positions, they tended to engender feelings of loyalty and dependence from their secretaries. Actions viewed as being dependable, subservient, and trustworthy were rewarded, but requests for personal advancement were viewed as tantamount to desertion. Executives regularly failed to post announcements of job openings and tended to underestimate the skill levels of the office workers.

Kanter suggested that to improve work relationships, jobs should be evaluated for actual skills required, work performances evaluated by co-workers, job announcements posted, jobs redesigned, and workers rotated. These actions would improve workers' attitudes and more especially serve to break the stranglehold of executives over lower-level office staff.

Rosabeth Moss Kanter, *Men and Women of the Corporation* (New York: Basic Books, 1977).

---

relations theorists such as Chris Argyris (1957; 1959; 1964). Relationships between people in the work setting are supposed to be holistic. People should relate to one another as total personalities rather than simply cogs in the machine. The work milieu should be arranged to integrate employer and employee fully into a set of relationships and behaviors that facilitate trust, loyalty, and commitment. The style of interaction fostered offsets organizational tendencies toward depersonalization, autocracy, and excessive supervision. Instead, patterns of interaction should be encouraged that facilitate free-flowing communication, openness, and honesty between superordinate and subordinate, and an autonomous style of work. Ouchi fails to recognize that Japanese employer-employee relations are governed by tradition. In Japan loyalty between boss and worker is an extension of Confucian rules of respect between master and subject. Failure to conform brings loss of face (shame). Japanese workers are committed not because of desires for personal fulfillment, but rather because they do not want to bring shame on their families.

Contingency School

Another approach to management is the **contingency school,** which sees organizations as handling two types of problems. First, managers must handle internal problems of taking care of capital, plant, and people. Second,

Contingency school assumes organization must maintain flexibility to handle internal and external problems, especially changes in personnel and changes in technology.

managers must address such external problems as dealing with the larger community, delivering product and service, as well as responding to shifts in consumer demand, pressures generated by changes in legislation, and new technologies.

To be effective the management must develop mechanisms for adjusting to both types of problems. In reacting to these problems management likes to identify a course of action that reduces uncertainties, eliminates crisis, and makes organizational actions predictable.

Internally, people who best fit the role of administrators like to create order out of chaos, to reduce uncertainty, and to set up routines. These kinds of people usually are highly motivated, assertive, physically active, and are perfect candidates for coronaries. But they make excellent career executives. This type of personality was the "man-in-the-gray-flannel-suit" of the 1950s and is the blazer-and-briefcase type of the 1980s. Individuals who are less compulsive and who can more readily leave the planning to others fit better in the lower rungs of the organizational ladder.

Externally, Toffler (1970) argued that rapid social change and the development of new technologies require alternative organizational forms in order to survive. With greater management emphasis on reducing long-range costs in plant and personnel, as well as an increased demand for flexibility in mobilizing personnel and resources to create new products and to advertise, distribute, and market them, we find another form of organization occurring. This form of organization is a *contract team of professional specialists*. A team of professionals is hired to address a particular problem. The team may be asked to develop a limited set of proposals for generating a new technology, product, advertising campaign, or distribution strategy. A team's strength lies in its collective form and the professionals operate as status equals. They brainstorm ideas. Success or failure of an idea depends on its technical merit, not on the organizational status of the person who puts forward the idea. Individual esteem is linked to professional stature. Decisions are reached through consensus. The team exists only as long as the life of the project. Once a contract package is completed and accepted by an employer, their involvement ends until their services are again needed.

This style of management enhances flexibility in selecting personnel, reduces long-term personnel costs, and guarantees high levels of profit margin. It also facilitates organizational response to the vagaries of the market.

For the professionals competing for employment, it places a premium on high-quality performance, demands geographic mobility, eliminates job security, fringe benefits, and predictable work schedules. With increased reliance on electronic forms of communication and data processing, these losses may not be as important as they were in an earlier period. Individuals may interact with one another using telecommunication videophones, electronic mail, or interactive computers. What was once a condition giving rise to formalization in the workplace, that is, the need for a number of workers to gather in one spot, no longer is required to conduct work. Place of residence and place of work may once again coincide. Similarly, work routines no longer need be constrained by bureaucratic rules. All that is required is that a limited number of colleagues coordinate their work schedules. In effect, this type of organization is a product of changing technology and the demand for flexibility.

Other Organizational Forms

Thus far we have focused primarily on formal organizations, looking at their internal arrangement and classifying them by size, complexity, centrality, and formalization. We also have looked at how authority and work relationships are set up. Another scheme for analyzing organizations is offered by Blau and Scott (1962). They examine the makeup of the people involved in the organization—its membership.

Four basic categories of persons are involved with organizations: (1) members or rank-and-file participants; (2) owners or managers; (3) clients, technically outside the organization, who have regular, direct contact with it in various ways (patients, customers, welfare recipients, prisoners, ex-convicts, students); and (4) the general public, members of the society in which the organization operates.

All organizations may be defined on the basis of who benefits: (1) mutual benefit associations in which the prime beneficiary is the membership; (2) business concerns in which the owners receive the rewards; (3) service organizations for which the clients are the beneficiaries; and (4) commonweal organizations that mainly benefit the general public.

Mutual Benefit Associations.   The category of mutual benefit organizations includes professional associations (American Medical Association, AFL-CIO), fraternal organizations (fraternities, sororities), and clubs (bridge, sports, social). The Fraternal Order of Police or Rotary are mutual benefit associations from which membership derives the most value. The American Farm Workers is a union organization that benefits its membership.

Business Organizations.   The Bank of America, J.C. Penney's, and the John Hancock Life Insurance Company are examples of a host of retail stores, mail-order houses, and financial or industrial firms defined as business organizations. Such organizations are operated for a profit, and generally their owners (including shareholders) receive the rewards of the organization's activities.

Service Organizations.   Service organizations include public health clinics, social work agencies, nonprofit hospitals, schools, and other organizations aiding or providing for clients. St. Jude's Hospital, The University of Tennessee, and the Cincinnati Board of Health provide service to clients of various kinds. Although such organizations profit to some extent from fees paid by clients for services rendered, the client is the major beneficiary.

Commonweal Organizations.   Commonweal organizations benefit the general public. Highway departments, police departments, and the Center for Disease Control are organizations that exist to safeguard society. The entire community benefits from the activities of commonweal organizations. Workers at the Center for Disease Control may like their jobs and receive benefits from performing them, but the prime beneficiary of their investigations of toxic shock syndrome, legionnaires' disease, and AIDS is the community at large.

Another way to classify the variety of formal organizations is suggested by Etzioni (1961). He suggests at least two types categorized by how members are recruited and participate: voluntary and coercive organizations.

Voluntary Organizations attract members to join and participate. Often the activities and goals of an organization selectively attract a membership, since particular groups cater to specialized interests. Groups that fall in this category would typically include political parties, hobby clubs, sports associations, action groups. The memberships vary in size from small groups in a particular locale, like a drama club in a local high school or a neighborhood Dungeons and Dragons Club, to national organizations like U. S. Swimming or the Sierra Club, or to international groups like the Girl Scouts. Many social commentators have noted that Americans have a penchant for joining clubs. Most high schools incorporate a variety of extracurricular activities. The joiners may rise in the pecking order of high school status depending on which clubs they belong to and hold office in, although some clubs have prestige among only a few people (chess). Patterns of joining carry over into adult life. Affluent people tend to join voluntary associations more than lower-class and working-class people.

Coercive organizations are at the opposite end of the continuum of how members are recruited. Individuals usually have no choice about participating or, once they have joined, on the style of participation. People typically are conscripted or assigned to such an organization by other persons or agencies in society. People housed in prisons and mental hospitals may have been placed there by family members or an agent of the law courts. These types of settings are called total institutions (Goffman 1961b). They are separated from the community. Prisons, TB sanitoriums, leper colonies, concentration camps, or mental hospitals initially were constructed to maintain maximum physical and social distance between inmates and community members. This distancing was presumably to protect the community from the inmates, who were seen as a potential source of disruption, contamination, or physical injury. Inmates are cared for, guarded by, or treated by a staff. Staff members are often responsible for establishing a routine that facilitates rehabilitation, recovery, or readjustment of the inmates to a point where they can fit into the mainstream of everyday life. Such organizations tend to be coercive. Inmates are reduced from total personalities to numbers or cases to be processed. Inmates are forced to undergo a process of socialization to learn how to get along with other inmates and follow the rules set up by institutional staff. If it is a mental hospital inmates have to learn a jargon to engage in self-diagnosis and convey symptoms and recognition of cure to doctors, nurses, and aides.

If it is a prison, convicts must learn an argot to communicate among themselves, to convince staff of their remorse and willingness to go "straight" upon release. Failure to learn the rules of the game leads to increased restrictions or prolonged incarceration. Some individuals spend so much time in these settings they cannot relearn how to cope with society at large. They become institutionalized.

Whether people are housed in total institutions, participate in voluntary associations, work in bureaucracies, or cooperate in informal groups among co-workers or friends, interaction is oriented toward achieving personal and collective interests. Further, organizational norms pattern people's interaction and make life predictable. Organizations large and small are fundamental building blocks of social life.

Summary

Social organizations involve people in joint activities cooperating to reach some common goal. People become responsible for performing particular actions to accomplish those goals. Individuals derive benefits from collective activity as well as experience personal costs in order to share in the collective good.

Social organizations are efficient ways of getting things done. The patterning of activities, the structure of who does what, and the development of rules guiding joint activities makes life predictable.

Informal organizations have joint activities shaped by the personalities of individuals involved, whereas formal organizations tend to have joint actions shaped by the arrangement of relationships between positions.

Formal organizations have arisen to provide central control for economic, political, and religious activities. The transformation of social life that accompanied the urban-industrial revolution and the rise of modern capitalism accelerated the growth of formal organizations. Formal organizations exist in many forms.

Formal organizations emphasize conformity to rules and coordinated activity as people produce goods, offer services, and pursue common ends. The distinguishing traits of the formal organization are its size, degree of complexity, centralization, and formalization.

Despite the elaborate rules and regulations in formal organizations, informal groups develop. Organizational members develop their own norms, mechanisms of enforcement, authority, and channels of communication.

Various systems have developed historically to handle authority in organizations. Weber identified three types: charismatic authority (leadership based on the magnetism of personality), traditional authority (leadership based on custom), and legal-rational bureaucratic authority (leadership based on executive administrative position).

Styles of management–worker relations depend on assumptions about people's innate nature. Optimistic and pessimistic styles have guided researchers and managers in their study and treatment of workers. Pessimistic views infused the scientific management approach, whereas optimistic views form the basis for the human relations approach. More recently, sociologists have emphasized that the worker is neither completely motivated by economic incentives and disincentives nor desires for self-fulfillment. Rather the worker is motivated by both kinds of rewards. Organizations to be efficient must maintain flexibility, accommodating jobs to workers as well as finding the right person for the job. Organizations also must maintain flexibility in meeting changes in the market and technology.

Although organizations are often catego-rized according to management–employee relations, other ways of typing them have been suggested, such as who is benefited by the organization, how the members are recruited, and members' styles of participation.

Suggested Readings

Erving Goffman. *Asylums: Essays on the Social Situation of Mental Patients and Other Inmates.* Garden City, N.Y.: Anchor, 1961. Discusses the notion of total institutions.

Richard H. Hall. *Organizations: Structure and Process.* Englewood Cliffs, N.J.: Prentice-Hall, 1982. Excellent summary of literature on formal organizations.

William Ouchi. *Theory Z. How American Business Can Meet the Japanese Challenge.* Reading, Mass.: Addison-Wesley, 1981. Looks at Japanese employer–employee relations and the response of Japanese industry to foreign competition. Provocative but open to criticism among more serious students of Japan.

Curt Tausky. *Work Organizations: Major Theoretical Perspectives.* Itasca, Ill.: Peacock, 1978. A readable review of perspectives and review of findings on behavior in formal organizations.

11

The Structure of Postindustrial Society: The Economic Order, Technology, and Work

*Three of the main components of the **social structure** are the economy, the technology, and the occupational system. The **economy** is the institutionalized system for producing and distributing goods and services. The technology refers to the sources of innovation and the means of production within a society. The occupational system reflects the division of labor within a society that is necessary for the pursuit of its economic activities.*

The terms "industrial" and "preindustrial" refer to a society's mode of production and the social relationships and the social structure based on it. These terms reflect the importance that modes of production have for almost every area of social life.

Many students of society have discerned changes in the economy, the technology, and the occupational system of the United States since World War II. These changes are often perceived as significantly differentiating our society from its recent industrial past. Our current society has been called "postcapitalist," "postmodern," "postcivilized," and "deindustrialized," among other descriptions. The term most frequently used, "postindustrial," is attributed to sociologist Daniel Bell (1973). The term "postindustrial society" and some of Bell's ideas provide a framework for discussing changes in the economy, the technology, and the occupational structure in this chapter. We also examine here criticisms of what these changes mean for the world in which we live.

Social structure the organized interactions among basic components of a society.

Economy the institutionalized system for producing and distributing goods and services.

The Economic Sector

Colin Clark in *Conditions of Economic Progress* (1940) outlined three areas of economic activity. These terms have gained acceptance as popular labels. The *primary sector* includes agriculture, and the extraction of natural resources, such as mining, fishing, and forestry. The *secondary sector* is manufacturing, the conversion of raw natural resources into finished products. The *tertiary sector* consists of services. Although the economy of any society contains all three sectors at any time, one way to distinguish among types of societies is to ascertain which sector dominates the economy. According to Bell (1973), one major dimension of the postindustrial society is the change from a manufacturing economy to a service economy.

Preindustrial Society

In Chapter 6 we discussed several kinds of preindustrial societies. In preindustrial society the primary sector of economic activity dominates. Most of the countries in the world today—in Asia, Africa, and much of Latin America—are predominantly preindustrial, although they are in the process of industrializing. The bulk of the jobs in those economies are in agriculture or the ex-

traction of natural resources. The United States was predominantly a preindustrial society until roughly the middle of the nineteenth century (Gutman
1976).

In preindustrial societies communities are typically small, and most of
the population lives in villages or in the countryside. Social relationships are
personal and intimate, often involving kinship ties or participation in other
primary groups. There is a relatively simple division of labor. Most people are
farmers, artisans, or merchants. The technology is primitive, based mainly on
human and animal power. In such societies, the rate of social change is slow
and social values tend to be shared not only among contemporaries, but also
are largely transmitted orally from generation to generation. The community
is predominant over the individual; people tend to think of themselves primarily as members of a group and secondarily as individuals.

Industrial Society

In an industrial society the secondary sector of economic activity dominates. In such societies the majority of the labor force is concentrated in
manufacturing and industry. As the farm is at the heart of preindustrial society,
the machine is at the core of industrial society.

In the late eighteenth century the invention of mechanical devices far
superior to those of previous centuries, combined with the development of
steam power, ushered in the Industrial Revolution, bringing in its wake the
most radical social changes the world had ever seen. England, where that
revolution began, became in the nineteenth century the most industrialized
country in the world. The United States developed an industrialized economy
during the second half of the nineteenth century, and in the first half of the
twentieth century became the leading industrial society.

The introduction of sophisticated machinery and more dependable sources
of energy had three major effects on the economic and social structure. First,
there was a massive increase in efficiency. Machines run by steam power (and
later electricity) could produce goods much more rapidly than machines powered by animals, air, or water.

Second, there was an increase in the division of labor and a concomitant
increase in specialization. A single craftsperson or artisan was replaced by
semiskilled or skilled workers as mass production was introduced.

In a preindustrial society a tailor would measure a client, draw the pattern, cut that pattern, and sew the garment by hand. From bolt of cloth to
finished garment, there was no social division of labor; one tailor produced
one garment. That labor, although highly skilled, was specialized only in comparison to, say, a stonemason's. But in an industrial society, in a clothing
factory, one set of people drew patterns, another group cut material (with the
aid of machines), and yet another group sewed the garment (also on machines). From bolt of cloth to finished garment, the division of labor required
several specializations. The principal source of employment in society was the
manufacturing sector, with its proliferation of skilled and semiskilled jobs.

The efficiency of machines plus the division of labor resulted in a massive increase in **productivity**—the ability to gain a more than proportional output from a given expenditure of capital or exertion of labor, that is, the ability to produce more goods at less cost. With more goods available at lower prices, markets for goods expanded. More people could afford to buy them.

Growth in productivity made possible a situation in which everyone could end up a winner. The level of productivity strongly affects the standard of living. With high productivity, more people can buy a wider range of necessities and luxuries.

The third major effect of the Industrial Revolution was the economic changes associated with the increase of investment in fixed capital, such as machinery and buildings, which keep the same form over a long period of time. In preindustrial societies, the basic source of wealth was land that produced crops or contained coveted natural resources, from gold to timber. In preindustrial societies people who made money in nonagricultural activities usually did so in trade, where the essence of the capital was its fluidity. With industrialization, investment took the form of fixed capital, necessary to the manufacturing process that built up a nation's industrial capacity and formed the core of a nation's strength.

As productivity continued to grow and industrial enterprises increased in size and complexity, the corporation—a fictitious "person" set up by law to own property or conduct business as a collective entity—came to replace private ownership of the means of production. Collective ownership allowed the investment of more money than one person might possess and minimized personal financial risk.

Although the manufacturing sector predominates in an industrial society, the primary sector (agriculture and resource extraction) and the tertiary sector (services) are also represented. Because food remains a basic human necessity, agriculture must exist. It is a transformed agriculture, however, mechanized and commercial. The introduction of farm machinery increased food production with less manpower. As fewer agricultural workers were needed, many of them had to leave the farms to seek work in the secondary or tertiary sectors.

As industrialization increased, two major parts of the tertiary sector expanded. First, as manufacturing grew, auxiliary services in the form of transportation, communications, and utilities also grew. Goods had to be moved, energy to run the machines had to be harnessed, and producers of interdependent goods had to communicate with one another and with their markets. Second, as business corporations grew, they also needed auxiliary services in the areas of banking and finance, real estate, law, and insurance.

Industrialism wrought changes in the social structure as vast as those in the economic order. As mechanization reduced the need for agricultural labor, industrial cities, the sites of large factories with numerous employees, came to predominate over villages and small towns. (See Chapter 17.) The importance of family and kinship ties declined, and other institutions, such as schools, arose in an attempt to make social life orderly and predictable. General agree-

Productivity the ability to gain a more than proportional output from a given expenditure of capital or exertion of labor; the ability to produce more with less.

ment about cultural values declined, as differing lifestyles and subcultures developed. The pace of social change accelerated. Change was welcomed as progress. The locus of responsibility switched from the group to the individual, as custom and tradition lost much of their force and as increasingly individualized specializations formed a web holding society together.

The strength of U.S. industry in the first half of the twentieth century is indicated in several ways. The United States had the highest gross national product (GNP) per capita and the highest standard of living in the world. Every year the United States had a trade surplus, meaning that Americans exported more goods than they imported. Further, until the 1950s the United States produced more steel than all other countries combined. Steel production is one foundation of a modern, industrial society, for it is used in the production of numerous goods as well as the fixed capital goods—machinery and buildings—necessary for the production of the other goods. Steel has become the symbol as well as the bedrock of industrialism.

In the wake of World War II, however, profound changes began to take place in the American economy. The postwar years saw the birth of postindustrial society.

Postindustrial Society

In a postindustrial society the tertiary sector dominates the economy. In the early 1970s almost 70% of the United States labor force was employed in jobs contributing to the service sector. Growth in manufacturing continued but at a slower pace than in the past. Long a mainstay of the American economy, "old line" manufacturing showed job losses in such categories as processing minerals, making furniture, and producing and finishing leathers and metals. The shift in the mixture of important industries and jobs reflects fundamental changes in society (Steinlieb et al. 1982).

Growing efficiency among manufacturing corporations, higher wages, and rising standards of living stimulated a wave of consumerism. As industrialization became more efficient, productivity rose. More goods were available to the general public. High wages paid to the workers allowed them to maintain high standards of living. Higher incomes also meant more disposable income. No longer did the public need to be careful in purchasing the necessities—food, housing, clothing, and transportation. A greater ability to buy meant that people could go out to eat instead of cooking at home. The large-scale entrance of women into the labor force since World War II also clearly reinforced the habit of eating out. The demand for fast-food services is seen in the expansion of eating and drinking places. From 1976 to 1981 these places increased by 44%.

Not only did Americans spend more of their discretionary income on food, they also spent more on travel, recreation, and leisure. Between 1969 and 1979 wholesale and retail trade and hotels and restaurants increased by 34.7%. Transportation, storage, and communication increased by 18.3% in the same period (Steinlieb et al. 1982).

The rise of multinational corporations also contributed to the shift away from an industrial-based economy. *Multinational corporations*—companies conducting business in more than one country—often set up factories outside the United States in order to minimize costs of labor, plant construction, and production, to avoid heavy corporate taxes, to maximize access to resources and labor, and to earn higher profits. Corporations often feel constrained by U.S. domestic labor costs. Higher wages are expected by American workers. They feel that they won higher wages through difficult collective bargaining and that they deserve them because they have higher educational levels than foreign workers. Corporations that operate abroad need not pay higher wages or get involved with unions, or submit to increasing government intervention. Jobs previously held by American workers have been moved abroad. In effect, the manufacturing sector increasingly is moving to countries with a cheaper labor force.

As the society becomes increasingly sophisticated technologically, the labor force moves from low-technology to high-technology jobs. Low-tech jobs are replaced by automation. People who earn low wages and whose skills are easily performed by machines are replaced. This process of automation is more easily carried out in the manufacturing sector of the economy than the service sector. Service industries generally involve relationships between people, processing of information, or transfers of funds. Despite the push toward automation, these kinds of activities have resisted the intrusion of machines. The movement out of low-tech jobs also creates demands for government services at the state and federal levels to help displaced workers and to administer programs of social reform.

Since World War II government has expanded rapidly. Bureaus, agencies, departments, and institutes have expanded to carry out the reforms, social programs, and watchdog activities legislated by Congress. By 1968 approximately 8 out of 10 government employees worked for state and local agencies. One of the principal areas of expansion was the educational wing of state and local governments, with approximately 50% of government employees employed there (Bell 1973).

The expansion of state and local government continued during the late 1970s. Between 1976 and 1981 state and local government increased 8.9% and 8.0% respectively (Steinlieb et al. 1982).

In an advanced industrial society, industries and businesses are marked by increasing sophistication in technology. International competition requires a skilled labor force. High-technology businesses demand a sophisticated and well-educated labor force to draw upon for filling jobs. Science and engineering graduates are in great demand. The high-tech and energy industries have grown by leaps and bounds. From 1976 to 1981 industries such as offices and computing machines grew 57.4%, electric and electronic equipment grew 19.3%, aircraft up 35.8%, and instruments and related products 39.5% (Steinlieb et al. 1982).

In advanced industrial societies, industries and businesses are marked by increasing complexity and differentiation of work tasks (see Chapter 10,

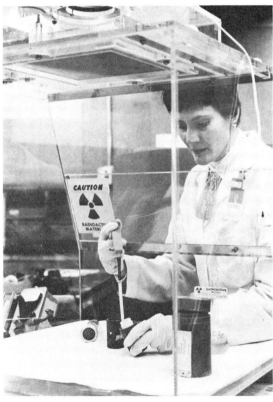

As technology advances,
demand for worker safety
has changed.

Social Organization). As a society moves from the advanced industrial to the postindustrial stage, differentiation and specialization begin to mark intellectual spheres as well as the institutions that house the pursuit of knowledge. As educational institutions such as universities become more complex and divide into nonteaching units—administration, finances, student services and development—the academic disciplines they exist to teach also subdivide into specializations unknown a quarter of a century ago.

In an economy whose decisive growth is in service areas such as health, education, research, and government, the major resource is in neither land (as in preindustrial societies) nor in machines (as in industrial societies), but in knowledge. Preindustrial societies confront nature, and industrial societies confront machines. The design of postindustrial society, according to Bell (1973), becomes a "game between persons" as an "intellectual technology" based on information rises alongside machine technology.

Our world has been technologically shrunk since World War II by the enormous advances made in transportation and communications—a process leading to what some have called the "global village" (Marshall McLuhan). Such advances, combined with the rebuilding and revitalization of the economies of Japan and Western Europe in those same years, resulted in an increased rate of diffusion of knowledge and technological developments. Such diffusion has been speeded by the willingness of some American firms to sell new technological developments, what is called front-end technology, to foreign companies.

In addition, as the preindustrial societies in today's world—the so-called developing nations—undergo the process of industrialization, they have increasingly monopolized labor-intensive industries, such as fabrics and apparel, because of their supply of cheap labor.

Finally, the United States no longer leads in technological development in many areas associated with industrialism, such as steel, where Japanese technology has far outstripped American developments. Although the United States spends an enormous amount of federal and corporate money on research and development (R&D), 80% of that money between the end of World War II and 1972 went into defense and atomic energy (Blumberg 1980).

Many question the trade-off of funds for defense over domestic programs, since the dissemination of benefits beyond the corporations is not immediately obvious. The space program stimulated indirect gains, such as computer development and scientific knowledge, and although questioned for its cost, it is generally seen as a positive operation.

As economic interdependence becomes worldwide, and as the United States becomes postindustrial, this country is no longer preeminent as an industrial nation. By 1978 the U.S. per capita GNP fell to fourth place, behind Sweden, Switzerland, and Canada (Blumberg 1980). In world steel production, the United States' percentages declined from 55% in 1950 to 16% by the late 1970s (Blumberg 1980).

In 1971 the United States had its first trade deficit since 1893, and it did also for 6 of the subsequent 8 years. Those areas in which the United States

If you're not primed and ready, finding a job in the future may be even harder than it is now. The world is changing faster than any of us dare imagine, and a job seeker must do everything in his power to adjust to those changes before he is left in the wake of untold technological breakthroughs. After all, who wants to be outproduced and outwitted by a computer less than one-sixteenth his size?

At no other time is long-range career planning so crucial. In this high-tech, supersonic world of ours, strategy, focus, direction and acquisition of skills are mandatory. Above all, you must understand the givens of the marketplace. A few of those are:

• High unemployment. Unfortunately, high unemployment is going to be with us for a while. The national unemployment rate is hovering at 10%, with some forecasters predicting continued increases. Even if the unemployment rate drops a bit, all indicators point to an uncomfortably high unemployment rate for some time.

• The automated work place. Remember joking about machines replacing men? It's no laughing matter anymore. Machines—actually sophisticated computers that can do just about anything short of breeding other computers—are replacing people in a variety of heavy industry, assembly-line jobs.

• A changing work force. In 1900 there were 4.9 million women in the labor force; in 1950 it was 18.4 million; and in the summer of 1982 the figure jumped to 43.5 million. The Bureau of Labor Statistics reports that by the time we reach the 21st century, women will make up an additional 4 percent of the labor force.

• The explosion of white-collar information jobs. In 1977 the United States became a white-collar economy, with white-collar jobs outdistancing blue-collar jobs for the first time in history. White-collar employment is expected to account for 60.7 million out of a total 119.5 million workers by 1990, according to Bureau of Labor Statistics projections. Almost a third of the projected growth throughout the remainder of the 1980s will be due to the creation of new jobs. Through technological evolution we've become an information society. At the moment five out of ten jobs are information jobs; in the next two decades, seven out of ten jobs may fall into the information category.

• Growth of the service sector. Within the 35 to 45 age range, which is considered the high-earning period of people's lives, there are approximately 12 million families with two full-time adult workers in each. Over the next decade this group is expected to increase by 50%. They'll be busy, hard-working and aggressive, and they'll depend more on others to provide basic services. Hence, the growth in the service sector.

Medical-care expenditures accounted for 8.4% of personal-consumption expenditures in 1972 and 8.7% in 1979. By 1990 the figure will escalate to better than 10%. The most dramatic reason for the continued growth of medical-care expenditures will be an aging population. In 1979 the number of persons age 65 was 24.7 million, or 11.2% of the total population. By 1990 29.8 million, or 12.2% of the total, will fall into this age group. So from any number of career perspectives, geriatrics offers an exciting future. There will be a continuing need for geriatric physicians, psychologists, psychiatrists; support, social and recreation workers; as well as physical therapists, employment specialists and an army of clerical workers.

Aside from the anticipated demand for health-care services, there is going to be an increasing need for child care and food-industry workers. Many individuals and families will be eating out far more than they are now. Career possibilities start at the small local eatery and extend all the way up to the giant hotel chains.

The key question you have to ask yourself is: "Will there be a strong demand for my particular expertise in the future, taking into consideration the givens of today's marketplace?" The all-important given is—you guessed it—technology. Realistically, we can expect technological advances for as far as we dare forecast the future. Each change will have either positive or negative effects on the workers within that industry. The savvy jobholder thinks like a futurist, evaluating his job against technological breakthroughs in his industry. If computers are coming dangerously close to putting you on the unemployment line, it's time to bail out and move to an allied field or another industry altogether. Below is a random list of careers to avoid. Note that every field has been affected by technology (computerization) in some way.

Farming: At present one out of 36 works the land. By the 21st century it may be one out of 60.

Industry: Automatic equipment has decreased the need for boiler tenders, core makers, electroplaters, electrotypers, machine-tool operators, machine set-up workers, printing compositors, photoengravers, press operators and production painters.

Office: Use of computers has severely dampened future employment prospects for bookkeeping workers, cashiers, file clerks, keypunch operators, office-machine operators, postal clerks, shipping and receiving clerks, stock clerks, etc.

Service: Similarly, use of computerized equipment offers a cloudy employment picture for gas-station attendants, motion-picture projectionists and telephone operators.
In sum, as the job market changes, you must change with it. In the end, it's the person whose heart and soul are totally committed to succeeding in a rapidly changing world who will reap the biggest rewards.

SOURCE: Robert V. Weinstein, *Family Weekly,* July 17, 1983.

---

holds a trade surplus are the typical areas of a postindustrial society—sectors dominated by high technology and intensive R&D, such as machinery, chemicals, aircraft and parts, and professional and scientific instruments (Blumberg 1980).

Science, Technology, and Education

Technology is "the methods, processes, devices, knowledge, and facilities that are used in the completion of work tasks" (Woodward 1965). As the plow had made possible the agricultural revolution and new machines powered by new energy sources made possible the Industrial Revolution, vast changes in science and technology (microchips) since the end of World War II have marked the beginning of what is called the information revolution.

Technology the methods, processes, devices, knowledge, and facilities that are used in the completion of work tasks.

In the early twentieth century, science was perceived as an exhaustible field that would eventually be fully explored (Bell 1973). There was no scientific establishment or institution as we know it today. Science training constituted a minute part of academic curricula, and practicing scientists were not only relatively few—90% of all scientists who have ever lived are alive today—but relatively isolated from one another.

Many of the inventions of the nineteenth and very early twentieth centuries were the creations of "inspired tinkerers" (Bell 1973). Thomas Edison, Alexander Graham Bell, and Wilbur and Orville Wright all worked independently of, sometimes even in hostility to, theoretical research in their fields. But further developments in the fields pioneered by these men—electrodynamics, satellite communications, jet engines—could be made only through the application of theoretical, abstract scientific knowledge. Postindustrial society is marked by the centrality of theoretical knowledge as a source of innovation, that is, the joining of science to invention (Bell 1973).

Merging of Science and Technology

For further technological development, there must be increased scientific research. In response to this need, since World War II science has undergone an increased organization and institutionalization. The National Science Foundation, which funds various scientific projects, was a postwar creation. The economic strength of a postindustrial society depends on research institutes, universities, and corporate and governmental R&D.

The development of the atom bomb showed the potential of nuclear energy for peacetime use, and the development in 1946 of UNIVAC, the first digital computer, brought a heightened awareness of the power of science. Thus began an increased emphasis on scientific R&D.

As the social organization of science has contributed to further scientific development, so has each scientific discovery. There is a branching effect. Each scientific advance opens up new fields, which then sprout their own branches. Like the manufacturing and corporate sectors in industrial society, science has become more specialized and interdependent. For example, the National Register of Scientific and Technical Personnel, a federally sponsored inventory of all persons competent in scientific work, listed fifty-four scientific specializations immediately after World War II; twenty years later, it listed more than 900 distinct specializations (Bell 1973).

In industrial society, the development of industries such as steel, automobiles, and telephones, followed from key inventions. In postindustrial society, the development of such dominant industries as computers, electronics, optics, and chemicals is based on scientific breakthroughs. Postindustrial manufacturing is a prime example of the incorporation of institutionalized research into the structure of the economy. In these science-based areas much nonmilitary R&D takes place. The United States maintains a significant trade surplus in these areas.

"Hey, man, can you spare a quarter for a game of Space Invaders?"

Electronic junky in the post-industrial age.

Computers and Society

Although R&D may be the core of postindustrial society, the most visible symbol of the technological age is the computer. Made possible by research in solid-state physics and developed through R&D, the computer deals chiefly with information: storing it, codifying it, and performing complex multivariate analyses on it.

The computer is everywhere in American life, from science to business, from government to education, and of late, making major incursions into our leisure and recreation.

The seeming omnipresence of the computer as symbol and reality raises issues well beyond those of the workplace that have only recently begun to be studied by sociologists. Paul Blumberg (1980), writing of the centrality of theoretical knowledge in postindustrial society, claims it might just as well be called the "centrality of theoretical ignorance."

The social consequences of computers are being investigated from two perspectives (Kling 1980). The first is the social problems approach. This approach deals with real or potential harm to people caused by unreliable or error-prone information systems that include computers as components.

In a survey of people likely to have had dealings with government systems, banks, and department stores—and thus, with computer systems, Theodor Sterling (1980) found that 40% of the sample had encountered one or more errors during the preceding year. He found that errors occurred in every type of computerized transaction, that it took an average of 8 weeks to correct the error, and that 7% of those who attempted to have the error corrected did not succeed.

In postindustrial society, people are encouraged to learn more about computers, to acquire computer literacy.

For 4 years in the mid-1970s an experiment with a computer ombudsman—a person mediating between computerized systems and citizens experiencing errors with them—was undertaken in Vancouver, British Columbia. The ombudsman functioned in three areas: assisting in individual cases; identifying recurring problems in need of further study; and making recommendations to consumer, governmental, and business groups about further action or reports (Sterling 1980). The computer ombudsman exemplifies the social problems approach, which seeks technical or social solutions to computer problems while accepting the legitimacy of the ends to which computing is put.

The second approach to computer-caused problems is the institutional approach. This approach analyzes the relationship between computing and the social arrangements in which the computer is embedded. Such analysis does not necessarily accept the legitimacy of the ends to which computing is applied. There is growing concern, for example, about proposed federal data banks and the threats they might pose to privacy and civil liberties. The institutional approach is less concerned with the technical manipulations of the computer per se than with social organization and political choice about the uses of computers. Systems should not be built without statutory provisions for independent audit to allow Congress and the public to monitor their operations; they should not be built without statutory guidelines that establish responsibility and authority and thus accountability (Laudon 1980). Computers stimulate questions about fundamental social beliefs and structures, questions that must be dealt with by social and political choice.

Education

Postindustrial society is based on acquiring and handling information; science and technology play key roles, and education becomes more essential and specialized.

One major function of education is the transmission of skills demanded directly or indirectly by the economic order. In preindustrial society education was the prerogative of the elites. Most of the skills demanded by such an economy were passed from parent to child or artisan to apprentice, with no need for an intervening educational institution. What we today consider basic skills, those implicitly needed to function in society and the labor market, were not at all basic in a preindustrial society. In present-day rural India or in an American village before the Revolution, a person could function quite well without being able to read and write. But in our contemporary society, a person cannot apply for the most menial employment without reading and writing.

In 1940 there were less than 3.5 million college graduates over the age of 25 in the United States; by the late 1970s, there were 18.5 million college graduates in the same age group, and over 43 million persons had had at least one year of college (Blumberg 1980). In 1946, 22.1% of the population aged 18 to 21 had been enrolled in college, but by 1964 the figure had risen to 43.9% (Bell 1973).

With the increased college enrollments, the United States has an abundance of people with degrees (law and business). Some of these people will not be able to get the jobs for which they were trained. Table 11.1 shows the decreasing job availability in numerous fields, including highly scientific and technological ones.* For those who do get jobs in their chosen fields, Table 11.2 shows the change in purchasing power of salaries offered.

Thus an old word has become a buzz word of our time: *underemployed,* referring to those whose skills exceed their job tasks. The cabbie who drives you from a metropolitan airport into town just may have a Ph.D. degree in English or anthropology.

At the same time, a form of educational inflation ironically makes having a college degree increasingly necessary. As college degrees become more and more prevalent, high school diplomas mean less and less. Educational requirements for employment have been raised as much to eliminate some applicants as to guarantee acquiring more skilled workers.

---

*This job decline is generally regarded as temporary due to economic problems, with a continued need for technically skilled people foreseen.

TABLE 11.1   College Graduates' Opportunities, 1983

Degree	Average Annual Salary	Job Outlook for 1983 Graduates (compared with 1982)
Chemical engineering	$27,083	Job offers to fall by 16%
Electrical engineering	$26,031	Big decrease in hiring
Computer science	$24,485	Drop of 12% in offers forecast
Civil engineering	$22,473	Hirings to plummet sharply
Physics	$20,076	Steep decline in opportunities
Mathematics	$17,660	Modest decline expected
Marketing, sales	$16,941	Small cutback in jobs ahead
Business administration	$16,419	Large cutback in job offers
Personnel administration	$15,931	Big slide in work opportunities
Communications	$15,606	Modest cutback in hirings
Hotel, restaurant management	$14,699	Small drop of 7% in jobs
Social sciences	$13,835	Decline of less than 10%
Education	$13,358	About one-tenth fewer jobs

SOURCE: *U.S. News & World Report,* December 13, 1982.

Education, however, serves purposes other than vocational or professional training. One of its major functions is the transmission of values. Social values, like the skills demanded by the economic order, were transmitted largely through the family and other primary groups in preindustrial society. In industrial society, one of the institutions that assumed some of the functions of kinship groups was the educational system. Postindustrial society has inherited and intensified this dependence on institutional education.

TABLE 11.2   Declining Values of Salaries, 1967–1976

Major	Salary Offered		1976 Salary in 1967 Dollars	% Change in Purchasing Power, 1967–76
	1967	1976		
Business	$613	$ 872	$518	− 15.4%
Accounting	637	1,028	605	− 5.0
Humanities and social sciences	589	804	478	− 18.8
Chemical engineering	733	1,279	760	+ 3.6
Civil engineering	706	1,108	659	− 6.7
Biological sciences	543	810	482	− 11.3

SOURCES: College Placement Council, "Salary Survey: A Study of 1966–67 Beginning Offers, Final Report," and "Salary Survey: A Study of 1975–76 Beginning Offers, Final Report," reprinted in Neale Baxter, "Payoffs and Payments: The Economics of a College Education," *Occupational Outlook Quarterly* (Summer 1977). [In Paul Blumberg, *Inequality in an Age of Decline.*]

Distribution of Occupations

Of the many statuses each of us occupies, our occupational status is one of the more important in industrial and postindustrial society. One can observe this in operation at any party, when strangers strike up a conversation. One of the first questions they ask about each other is usually, "What do you do?" On any college campus, when students meet, the usual introductory question is, "What's your major?", which is another way of asking what kind of work a person does or intends to do.

Occupational status reflects the simple fact that a great portion of our lives is spent working and that therefore our occupation is a central part of our lives. A more complicated fact of occupational status is that in industrial and postindustrial society, most of our social relationships take place in secondary groups and many of these secondary relationships develop in the workplace. It also reflects the increased division of labor in industrial and postindustrial society.

In industrial and postindustrial society we see the phenomenon of social mobility, the movement from one status to another, within status systems determined by various criteria (political, economic, and cultural). Wealth, power, and education are typical criteria of status. But, according to Bell (1973), "In large part, occupation is the most important determinant of class and stratification in society." Thus occupation determines not only our status in the economic system, but also our place in the system of social stratification.

White Collar–Blue Collar

Almost 7 out of 10 Americans in today's labor force are employed in the service sector of the economy. The expansion of the service sector, which includes office work, education, and government, has meant an increase in white-collar occupations. In 1956 white-collar workers for the first time outnumbered blue-collar workers in the labor force (Bell 1973); by 1979 white-collar workers comprised slightly more than half the total American work force—50.9% (see Table 11.3).

Observing this trend, Bell (1973) states:

> By the end of the century the proportion of factory workers in the labor force may be as small as the proportion of farmers today [2.8%]; indeed, the entire area of blue-collar work may have diminished so greatly that the term will lose its sociological meaning.

Several sociologists have taken issue with Bell's observations and implications about the white-collar/blue-collar situation as well as with the terms themselves.

Blumberg (1980) points out that the number of manual workers increased from 10 million in 1900 to 31 million in 1979 and fell only a few percentage points—from 35.8% to 33.1%. (See Table 11.3.) He also points out, as Bell

CONTROVERSIAL ISSUES · Displaced Workers

As manufacturing industries decline, many workers are losing their jobs. Some have lost their jobs when plants have been closed or work forces reduced because of decline in demand for products. Others have lost jobs because technological advances made it possible to replace assembly line workers with robots and other machines.

At times the situation of displaced workers has been questioned. Some argue there are jobs—just look at the want ads. Yet if you look at the want ads, it is apparent that many available jobs are in the rapidly growing service and technology sectors. Well-paid assembly line workers may be reluctant to take poorer paying service jobs (as nurse's aides, orderlies, janitors, salesclerk, or secretaries). Even moderate-paying technological jobs require training that most displaced workers lack.

Retraining is one proposed answer. Corporations such as General Motors have offered training for positions in the aerospace and data processing industries to laid-off automobile workers. The federal government has set aside modest sums of money for worker retraining programs.

But workers live in communities. They have homes, friends, and children in school. Communities dominated by a single manufacturer or single industry such as steel or automobiles have encountered severe economic problems when local plants have been closed. If a high percentage of local workers lose their jobs, the local economy suffers because the displaced workers cannot purchase goods (furniture, clothing, cars) and services. If the displaced workers are retrained, there are still no positions for them in the local community. Thus some economists have argued that displaced workers should be relocated to communities where jobs exist and then retrained. The financial and social costs of moving workers are high, but so are the costs of their continued unemployment.

Beginning in the early 1970s there has been a wave of employee buy-outs of companies. About 10% of them have occurred when the company was on the verge of being closed down or bought out (*Time,* March 28, 1983). The town of Weirton, West Virginia, is working on buying the Weirton division of National Steel with an employee stock ownership plan. Such buy-outs are not feasible in very many cases. Most workers cannot avoid unemployment or relocation in this way.

acknowledges, that the sharp rise in white-collar growth came about largely through a sharp contraction in agricultural labor, from 37.5% of the labor force in 1900 to 2.8% in 1979. Additionally, he points out that although the percentage of blue-collar workers has decreased, the percentages of male blue-collar workers among working men has increased from 37% in 1900 to 46% in 1979, when male white-collar workers were only 41.3% of all male workers.

TABLE 11.3　Occupational Distribution of the Employed Labor Force, 1900 and 1979 (in thousands)

	Men				Women				Total			
	Percentage		Number		Percentage		Number		Percentage		Number	
	1900	1979	1900	1979	1900	1979	1900	1979	1900	1979	1900	1979
WHITE-COLLAR WORKERS	17.6%	41.3%	4,166	23,241	17.8%	64.3%	949	25,694	17.6%	50.9%	5,115	48,935
Professional & technical workers	3.3	15.3	800	8,630	8.2	16.5	434	6,590	4.3	15.8	1,234	15,220
Managers & administrators (nonfarm)	6.8	13.9	1,623	7,809	1.4	6.3	74	2,503	5.8	10.7	1,697	10,312
Sales workers	4.6	6.1	1,079	3,425	4.3	6.6	228	2,647	4.5	6.3	1,307	6,073
Clerical workers	2.8	6.0	665	3,378	4.0	34.9	212	13,942	3.0	18.0	877	17,331
BLUE-COLLAR WORKERS	37.6	46.3	8,924	26,042	27.8	14.6	1,477	5,817	35.8	33.1	10,401	31,859
Craft & kindred workers	12.6	21.4	2,985	12,038	1.4	1.8	76	726	10.5	13.3	3,062	12,764
Semiskilled operatives	10.4	17.4	2,456	9,791	23.8	11.4	1,264	4,543	12.8	14.9	3,720	14,332
Unskilled nonfarm laborers	14.7	7.5	3,482	4,215	2.6	1.4	137	548	12.5	4.9	3,620	4,762
SERVICE WORKERS	3.1	8.5	740	4,783	35.5	19.9	1,886	7,945	9.0	13.2	2,626	12,728
FARM WORKERS	4.17	3.9	9,880	2,214	19.0	1.2	1,008	486	37.5	2.8	10,888	2,698
Farmers & farm managers	23.0	2.3	5,451	1,278	5.8	.2	311	99	19.9	1.4	5,763	1,376
Farm laborers & foremen	18.7	1.7	4,429	936	13.1	1.0	697	387	17.7	1.4	5,125	1,322
TOTAL	100.0%	100.0%	23,711	56,280	100.0%	100.0%	5,319	39,941	100.0%	100.0%	29,030	96,220

SOURCES: Computed from U.S. Bureau of the Census, *Historical Statistics of the United States, Colonial Times to 1970, Bicentennial Edition,* Part 1 (Washington, D.C., 1975), pp. 139–140; *Employment and Earnings* 26 (June 1979), pp. 35–36. Percentages may not add to 100 due to rounding. All subtotals do not add to totals due to minor errors in government data. [In Paul Blumberg, *Inequality in an Age of Decline.*]

The "white-collar revolution," Blumberg claims, has really been a "white-blouse revolution," as hundreds of thousands of women have entered the work force, largely in low-level, ill-paid clerical, sales, and semiprofessional work.

Several sociologists have asked whether the terms *"white-collar"* and *"blue-collar"* actually tell us anything meaningful about the U.S. labor force. Andrew Levison (1974) claims that the categories into which workers are classified give a false impression of the American labor force. Many service workers—hair stylists, salesclerks, waiters, bartenders—closely resemble blue-collar workers in their working conditions, education, and income, which are major criteria of status in American society. Further, as Table 11.3 indicates, if service workers were reclassified as blue-collar workers, the combined total for the blue-collar segment of the working force would then rise to 46.3%, and the blue-collar percentage of male workers would rise to 54.8%. If such occupations as shipping clerk, messenger, and baggage handler were also reclassified from white-collar to blue-collar, the blue-collar percentage would climb even higher.

Stanley Aronowitz (1973) argues that the term "white-collar" obscures more than it illuminates because it refers to the type of work rather than to the type of authority relations. Does a stenographer (white-collar) in an insurance company have more in common with the manager (white-collar) of that insurance company or with a factory foreman (blue-collar)? Aronowitz claims that the concept "white-collar" reflects an ideology of privilege based on the type of work and its relative status rather than on social power, which at least ought to be considered.

Whence comes the higher status relegated to white-collar workers? It derives in part from intangibles. A person does not get dirty doing the job and is more likely to wear "dress up" clothes. Before colored shirts became acceptable, most nonmanual workers did indeed wear white collars. The status of such work derives also in part from the assumption that it requires higher-level (mental) skills than does manual labor. But the primary source of status is the traditionally higher earnings of white-collar workers.

The rapid inflation that began in the late 1960s, however, produced some dramatic shifts in these income differentials. Between 1967 and 1978 prices doubled in this country, according to the consumer price index. Only workers belonging to strong unions, which achieved substantial cost-of-living adjustments, were protected in their real spending power. The overwhelming majority of white-collar workers have not been unionized. If we compare the average earnings of automobile workers as a percentage of the average earnings of various white-collar employees, we would see that in 1967 auto workers made 178% of the salary of nonsupervisory department store employees and 214% in 1978; 102% of the salary of a school teacher in 1967 and 121% in 1978; 44% of the salary of full professors in 1967 and 61% in 1978 (Blumberg 1980).

It must be remembered, however, that blue-collar workers receive hourly wages rather than salaries; they are more subject to being laid off than are most white-collar workers; and they can lose their jobs completely when plants close. (See Table 11.4.)

Some segments of the white-collar work force have responded to such income trends by increasing unionization; today many teachers, health workers, and municipal employees belong to strong unions.

Person to Person

Bell (1973) describes two conditions that increasingly mark the workplace in the service sector and thus are significant factors in postindustrial society. The first is the decreasing population size of the workplace. Some extremely large corporations still exist in parts of the service sector (such as American Telephone and Telegraph in utilities and Metropolitan Life in insurance), but many firms in such services as retail trade, personal and profes-

TABLE 11.4   Unemployment Rates, 1980–1981

Unemployment Rates by Occupation	Sept. 1981	Sept. 1982	In 10 Largest States	Sept. 1981	Sept. 1982
White-collar workers	4.1%	4.8%	California	7.4%	10.1%
Blue-collar workers	10.2%	15.6%	Florida	7.3%	7.5%
Service workers	9.0%	10.7%	Illinois	8.5%	12.5%
Farm workers	4.0%	5.1%	Massachusetts	6.6%	7.2%
			Michigan	11.9%	15.9%
by Industry			New Jersey	6.8%	9.2%
Construction	16.3%	22.6%	New York	17.0%	8.6%
Manufacturing	7.0%	13.8%	Ohio	10.3%	12.5%
Transport, public utilities	4.2%	6.9%	Pennsylvania	8.5%	11.3%
Trade	8.5%	9.8%	Texas	15.5%	8.4%
Finance, services	6.0%	6.8%			
Government	4.7%	4.9%			

SOURCE: *U.S. News & World Report,* October 18, 1982.

sional services, finance and real estate, and hospitals employ fewer than a thousand persons. And even when the size of the operation is large—such as a hospital or school—it is frequently broken down into departments or sections of much smaller size with relatively large degrees of autonomy.

Second, central to the new working relationships is interaction or communication, "that individuals now talk to other individuals, rather than interact with a machine, is the fundamental fact about work in the postindustrial society" (Bell 1973). In the world of services, teacher interacts with student, salesperson relates to customer, welfare client talks with social worker. Of course, such encounters are not always mutually enjoyable—but they are encounters.

There is, however, another side to the service sector. For Aronowitz (1973) the most important development among traditional white-collar sectors of the economy is the mechanization of the office, evoking the image of industrial society, a minute division of labor and standardization of the work task. The white-collar woes join the blue-collar blues as office machines and computers of various sorts proliferate, and with them, the subdivision of office labor.

Harry Braverman (1975) claims that it is incorrect to assume that any kind of white-collar work, such as routine clerical tasks, demands a higher degree of skill or training than any kind of manual work. His observation not only questions white-collar status based on skill differentials but calls attention to the fact that routine, boring work is not the exclusive province of blue-collar labor.

Robert Blauner (1964) has written extensively about the alienation experienced by workers in highly routinized, specialized jobs. **Alienation** is perceived powerlessness and meaninglessness associated with one's work and work quality. Marx, writing largely about nineteenth-century factory workers, observed that the further removed employees are from the actual product, the more alienated they become. Blauner has observed such alienation among white-collar as well as blue-collar workers.

Alienation perceived powerlessness and meaninglessness associated with one's work and work quality.

As perceived status differentials between blue-collar and much white-collar work appear to shrink, difficulties associated with the workplace appear to be growing.

Central Occupations

Bell (1973) points to an immense growth in postwar America of professional and technical employment. At the turn of the century, 4.3% of the American work force were in the professional and technical category; by 1979 that share had grown to 15.8%. (See Table 11.3.) Since 1940 the growth rate in the professional/technical category has been twice that in the labor force as a whole and the growth rate for scientists and engineers has been triple that of the working population.

Blumberg (1980) points out that five professions—all low-paid, low-status, and female-dominated—comprise over a third of the professional category: school teachers, librarians, social workers, nurses, and dieticians. He also points out that scientists, engineers, technicians, and computer specialists—the classic occupations of postindustrial society—comprise only 20% of all professionals and 3% of the entire labor force.

Aronowitz (1973) paints a bleak picture even for many of these elite 3%, at least those in the corporate sector. He claims that technical labor has moved from independence to dependence and is marked by a contradiction between high expectations students acquire during training and the routine boredom of the actual work tasks. The technician and scientist have become a new version of the front-line production worker, performing routine work and possessing no power over the conditions of their own labor.

Computers facilitate typesetting in the newspaper industry.

There are, therefore, two sides to the story of work in postindustrial society. There is excitement or boredom, routine or creativity, jobs held for need of a paycheck or love of the work, challenging or dulling interactions of person and machine, rewarding or harassing relations between persons.

The move from preindustrial to industrial society was marked by numerous shifts in culture and society. One of these was a move from low to high productivity. Another was the move from a communal to an individual ethos.

As our society becomes increasingly marked by the threat of fragmentation and group hostility in competition for shrinking economic rewards, we hear more and more talk of the public good from all points on the political spectrum. We may find ourselves forced to move from our individualistic ethic to a new, communal one. The complexity of modern life may compel choices made for social rather than individual purposes.

Summary

The economy can be divided into three sectors: agriculture and extractive activities (primary), manufacturing (secondary), and services (tertiary).

The primary sector is dominant in preindustrial society; the secondary, in industrial society; the tertiary, in postindustrial society.

A goods-producing (industrial) economy has a high level of productivity; an economy dominated by services has a decreased level of productivity.

An industrial society is marked by its quantity of consumer goods; a postindustrial society is marked by its quality of life provided by services and amenities.

A major resource of postindustrial society is its knowledge and information.

Postindustrial society is characterized by the centrality of theoretical knowledge as the source of innovation, that is, the joining of science and technology.

The social problems of computer use are approached from two primary perspectives. First, the social problems approach accepts the legitimacy of the ends to which computers are put and deals with real or potential problems caused by unreliable or error-prone computer systems. Second, the institutional approach does not necessarily accept the ends to which computers are put but analyzes the relationship between computing and its social milieu.

Education assumes greater importance in postindustrial society, and the economic value of academic degrees is simultaneously deflated.

As the service sector of the U.S. economy includes almost 70% of the labor force, white-collar workers comprise over half the work force.

The status of white-collar workers has been undermined by inflation and decreasing earning differentials relative to the blue-collar work force.

Central to the work relationships of postindustrial society is the encounter of persons with other persons rather than with machines.

An important development in some traditional sectors of white-collar work is the mechanization of the office and the alienation that results.

The development of postindustrial society also involved a growth in professional and technical employment, especially of scientists and technicians; such categories, however, form a small proportion of the entire labor force relative to services.

Suggested Readings

Barry Bluestone and Bennett Harrison. *The Deindustrialization of America.* New York: Basic, 1984. An examination of how U.S. corporations are shifting their investments from older manufacturing ventures into mergers and new acquisitions, speculative ventures, and foreign operations. The resulting deindustrialization of various communities has produced displaced workers and reduced tax base. Bluestone and Harrison advocate legislation or plant closings and an industrial policy for reindustrialization.

12

The Family

In the 1950s and 1960s television situation comedies presented idealized versions of the "typical" American family. For example, on "Ozzie and Harriet" the Nelsons' lives with their boys, David and Ricky, were portrayed, and on "I Love Lucy" Desi and Lucy Arnaz were the parents of little Ricky. The husbands were employed and the wives were full-time mothers and homemakers. While Dad ruled the family, Mom and the kids often manipulated Dad to get what they wanted.

By the 1970s situation comedy home and family life had changed. Lucille Ball no longer had a spouse. "The Mary Tyler Moore" show focused on the work and social life of a single woman past the typical age of marriage. "Maude" could laugh about her multiple marriages and about having her divorced daughter and grandson live with Maude and her latest husband. "All in the Family" dealt with many controversial issues. In the early years of the show Archie, a traditional working-class man, and his wife Edith, a homemaker, shared their home with their married daughter and her student husband.

By the late 1970s "Three's Company" emerged showing three unmarried adults living together (two females and a male). A standard comedy focus was the landlord's belief that the male roommate must be gay. In the 1980s "Love Sydney" portrayed a single older male living with an unmarried mother and her child. The show discretely skirted the issue of the male's sexual preference. Divorced women forming households on their own with their children and struggling to have careers were presented on "Gloria" and "One Day at a Time." Comedian Bob Newhart starred in two programs on which he and his wife were apparently happy childless couples.

The changes in the television situation comedies reflected to some extent the changes occurring in our society. People are marrying later than they did in the 1950s. The number of couples postponing childbearing or opting to be childfree is on the increase. Gays are demanding recognition of their relationships. The number of unmarried mothers is rapidly increasing. There are increasing numbers of nontraditional households—single persons, single parents, unrelated adults.

Is the traditional family losing its functions and disappearing? Are changes in the family and households signs of progress? The family institution is so important to so many of us that we find it difficult to consider changes without making value judgments of good or bad. Sociologists do not believe that the family will disappear but, rather, that it will adapt to changes in society, taking new forms and performing new and different functions. Because almost every society has a unit that can be defined as a family, sociologists regard the family as a cultural universal. (See Chapter 2, Culture, for a discussion of cultural universals.)

Family Forms

Depending on the society in which they live, people have different conceptions of a family. In our society, for instance, when people talk about their "families," they usually mean a **nuclear family,** a unit composed of husband, wife, and children. The nuclear family unit in which a person was reared is called the **family of origin** or orientation, and the unit a person forms through marriage and reproduction is called a **family of procreation.** In other societies families of origin and procreation from the same kinship line may be united into **extended families,** multigenerational family living units. In an extended family, grandparents form a nuclear family from one generation and parents head a nuclear family of another generation.

Some people believe that extended families were common at one time in our society. Television programs such as "The Waltons" influence people's perceptions of family life in the past. At times people idealize the American family of the past as typically an extended family household in which people shared work and felt greater emotional closeness than families do today (Goode 1963:6). Yet three-generation households were never the norm in our society, nor were they always free of conflict. Today, even as people age they do not typically move in with their adult children (Neugarten 1978), for our society stresses independence and privacy (Davis 1980:125). Most people in our society prefer to live in nuclear family units or nuclear family-like arrangements.

In contrast, various societies have or have had the extended family as their ideal family form. Even in these societies many people do not live in such households, whether by choice or economic necessity. In recent decades very few societies, including India, have had significant proportions (over 20%) of their populations living in extended family arrangements (Burch 1967).

The multigenerational family may be preferred by people who desire more frequent contacts, greater cooperation, and closer relationships with relatives, but extended families have various problems. Interpersonal conflicts may exist. The multigenerational family has greater economic needs than smaller family units. In modern industrial and postindustrial societies, in which families depend primarily on wages for their economic survival, extended family living arrangements may be impractical. Researchers note that nuclear families are commonly found in societies that require their members to be relatively mobile. Nuclear family units are characteristic of relatively simple societies in which people are nomadic and engage in hunting and gathering. They are also characteristic of industrialized societies. Extended families are more commonly found in societies in which people rely on the food they cultivate—agrarian societies.

Nuclear family traditionally a unit composed of husband, wife, and their children.

Family of origin the nuclear family unit in which a person was raised.

Family of procreation the nuclear family a person forms through marriage.

Extended family related nuclear families who live in the same household.

Which type of family do you think of as normal? As ideal?

Marriage Patterns

The survival of a family or kinship group requires that new members be added to replace those who die. Young members are encouraged to mate and reproduce. In our society people are born into specific family and kinship units, but affiliate with others when they marry later in life. Our society enforces **monogamy,** limiting people to one marital relationship at a time. The high divorce rate in our society allows some people to enter into second or third marriages. This pattern has led some observers to argue that at least some people are practicing *serial monogamy,* having multiple spouses but one at a time. Other societies permit people to have two or more marriage partners at the same time, a practice called **polygamy.** In some societies, polygamy is not only permitted but is the ideal. In American society polygamy is not legal, and people who marry without dissolving previous marriages are charged with bigamy. Mormons who practiced polygamy as part of their religious beliefs were forced to stop the practice when Utah was considered for statehood; the United States made this condition one requirement for admission to the union.

Studies of cultures all over the world reveal that **polygyny,** or the mar-

Monogamy marriage to only one partner at a time.

Polygamy marriage to two or more partners at a time.

Polygyny marriage of one man to two or more women.

Nuclear Family   **Extended Family**

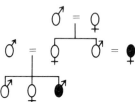

Polygamy

Polygyny   Polyandry   Serial Monogamy

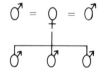

straight lines designate consanguine relatives: children, brothers and sisters

♀ – female   ♂ – male   = – connects marriage partners

● – deceased female   ● – deceased male   ≠ – marriage ended by divorce

Figure 12.1 Marriage and family forms.

riage of one man to two or more women, is the common form of polygamy (Murdock 1949). In societies where polygyny is the ideal, however, the most common type of marriage may be monogamous. Several factors may account for this. If a man has several wives and these wives all bear children, he would have a very large family to support. If women and children provide useful labor, the husband and the wives (Ware 1979) may benefit economically from polygamy. However, the practice of polygyny often is limited by economic resources. Also, most human populations are about equally divided between females and males, although wars or other events temporarily may change the sex ratio for a specific population. Consequently, if some men have several wives, other men will encounter a shortage of potential wives and may not marry or have only one wife.

Because of their religious beliefs, Muslim societies held polygyny to be the ideal form of marriage for many centuries. Yet as societies industrialize, polygyny becomes more difficult to practice, because women and men are increasingly able to pursue new social and economic roles.

Polyandry involves the marriage of one woman to two or more men. This marriage form has not been widely practiced throughout the world.

Polyandry marriage of one woman to two or more men.

Recently it has been suggested that polygyny should be approved for the elderly in our society (Kassel 1970). The tendency for men to marry women younger than themselves and the differences in mortality rates for males and females in our society result in a proliferation of widowed females with few possibilities for mates. Regardless of the merits of such arguments, monogamous marriage undoubtedly will continue to be the preferred and typical form of marriage in American society. Although monogamous marriage will predominate, it is likely that many people will marry more than once and the nature of the husband and wife roles will continue to change.

In addition to having rules governing the number of marriage partners a person may have, societies also have rules about who may marry whom. Some societies prefer **endogamy,** marriage within one's group. In the United States people often marry others with similar religious, racial, educational, and socioeconomic characteristics, but there are no societal rules requiring that they do so. A religious group may expel a member who marries outside the faith, but this type of sanctioning reflects the group's rules, not societal rules. At one time there were state laws and rules prohibiting blacks and whites from marrying, but those laws were invalidated by the U.S. Supreme Court. In spite of legal safeguards, the vast majority of marriages in our society today are not racially mixed.

Endogamy marriage within one's group.

Sometimes societies require **exogamy,** or marriage outside the group. A social unit may find it possible to build ties to discourage warfare with other social units through such marriage rules. In our society we have *incest* laws forbidding marriage within family groups or between close blood relatives. It may be argued that incest laws may prevent potential genetic defects due to inbreeding, but some societies even have incest laws that prohibit marriages between people who are not blood relatives. Therefore, some persons theorize that incest laws serve to prevent the development of sexual relationships that

Exogamy marriage outside one's group.

might undermine preferred family arrangements: a father-daughter relationship might disrupt the husband-wife relationship and the father's relationship with other children (Murdock 1949).

Are people in the U.S. free to marry whomever they wish, whenever they choose?

Familial Roles

For much of the twentieth century in American society the idealized family consisted of a husband/father "breadwinner," a wife/mother full-time "homemaker," and dependent children. Resistance to married women working outside the home reflected various attitudes or beliefs about the nature of men's and women's roles, the structure of the family, and the appropriate treatment of children. At the beginning of the twentieth century, Victorian beliefs about men and women prevailed. Men and women were assumed to make distinctly different contributions to society. Men were considered naturally oriented to the world outside the home, and women especially suited to domestic life because of their social and physical delicacy and nurturant natures (Douglas 1977). A good husband was expected to provide sufficient economic goods so that his wife did not need to work outside the home.

For much of this century, the prevailing attitude was that a woman should not work, especially if her husband could provide for her. A Gallup poll in 1938 reported that 78% of the people surveyed agreed that women should not be employed outside the home, if their husbands could support them. During and after World War II, married women's participation in the labor force increased, although many people continued to believe that a wife should not work if her husband could support her.

Breadwinners and Homemakers

The *functionalist* perspective argues that the idealized family system of husband/father breadwinner, wife/mother full-time homemaker is desirable for the smooth functioning of society. Talcott Parsons (1949) proposed that keeping women out of the labor force served to eliminate competition between the sexes. Parsons argued that the husband/father role was **instrumental,** relating the family to the world outside the home, whereas the wife/mother role was **expressive,** focusing on the internal social and emotional needs of family members.

People were socialized to believe that a man had failed in his role as a husband if his wife were a part of the labor force. Also, mothers who worked were stigmatized, because full-time motherhood was advocated during the early twentieth century. In our society women who did not want to make mothering a full-time occupation were seen as abnormal and unconcerned about their children.

Instrumental functionalists' view of the "traditional" husband/father role: relating the family to the outside world.

Expressive functionalists' view of the "traditional" wife/mother role: focusing on the internal social and emotional needs of family members.

CONTROVERSIAL ISSUES · Attitudes about Women Working, 1936–1943

During the later years of the Great Depression:
Should a married woman earn money if she has a husband capable of supporting her? (August 1936)

	Total
yes	18%
no	82%

Do you approve of a married woman earning money in business or industry if she has a husband capable of supporting her? (October 1938)

	Total	Males	Females
yes	22%	19%	25%
no	78%	81%	75%

During World War II:
Females: Would you be willing to take a full-time job running a machine in a war plant? (December 1942)
Males: Would you be willing to have your wife take a full-time job running a machine in a war plant? (December 1942)

	Males	Females
yes	30%	40%
no	50%	40%
qualified answer	11%	17%
don't know	9%	3%

After World War II:
Female workers: After the war, do you plan to go on working? (March 1943)

	Total	Single	Married
yes	56%	75%	35%
no	31%	14%	49%
no opinion	13%	11%	16%

SOURCE: George H. Gallup, *The Gallup Poll: Public Opinion,* 1935–71 (New York: Random House, 1972).

Care Giving

Another prevailing belief is that women have a **maternal instinct** that "naturally" makes them better able to care for children. Although so-called instinct theories of all types have been discredited by social scientists and the public over the years, some people continue to argue that women are naturally better suited to care for children. Thus the instinct view was replaced by belief in natural aptitude and the argument that women are better suited for caring

Maternal instinct presumed innate nurturant behavior of human mothers.

Family roles have changed. Relatively few families today are headed by a father who is the sole breadwinner and a mother who is a full-time homemaker.

for children compared with men. Furthermore, children will be harmed if they do not receive adequate care from their mothers. For a number of years, researchers attempted to link children's delinquency with mother's employment. Eventually, they acknowledged that other variables would be necessary to explain delinquency.

In other societies and at previous times in our own society, the biological mother of a child has not been assigned almost exclusive responsibility for familial care giving. Instead of relying entirely on mothers for care giving, some societies have relied on older female relatives who could no longer do hard labor, older children, and child-care specialists (wet nurses, nannies). In experimental communities such as the kibbutz in Israel, some individuals are designated to care for all of the community's children in central facilities. In ghetto areas people may rely on domestic networks of kin and friends living in separate households for child care and other domestic assistance (Stack 1974).

As more research has focused on the interactional needs of young children, it appears clear that infants should experience a high degree of continuity in their experiences with their care givers. Yet interactions with children can be of varying types and frequencies, differing in both quality and quantity. Various forms of care giving may be equally successful in the socialization process.

Advocates of change in gender roles believe that both females and males should have the opportunity to be involved in rearing young children. Societies such as Sweden have established social policies to allow fathers as well as mothers to care for their young children (Melsted 1980). Sweden has a parental insurance system that permits one parent at a time to earn 90% of his or her normal salary while remaining at home to care for an infant during the first 9 months after birth. Egalitarian parents may take turns remaining at home or both may work part time or both may choose to continue working full time.

Is everyone equally able to care for children?

Husband-Wife Relationships

Since the beginning of our society, marital roles have changed considerably. John Scanzoni (1981) identifies four types of husband-wife relationships: *property-owner, head–complement, senior–junior partners,* and *equal partners.* When a woman has no independent legal standing (when she cannot own property, enter into contracts, or vote), she is effectively the property of her father who may "give her away" through marriage to a man who becomes her husband or her new owner. This is the **property-owner** type of husband-wife relationship. The emphasis on romantic love as the basis for marriage in modern Western society is incompatible with this type of relationship.

The three other types of husband-wife relationships that currently appear in our society involve more rights for women and fewer rights for men. The **head–complement** relationship occurs when the man is the breadwinner and final decision maker and the woman is the full-time homemaker whose activities complement those of her husband. Although she is clearly subordinate to him, he is expected to have affection toward her. The instrumental/expressive roles depicted by Parsons, including what are often referred to today as "traditional" husband-wife roles, fit into the head–complement category. By 1980 less than 7% of American households fit the pattern of full-time breadwinners and full-time homemakers raising their dependent children.

As increasing numbers of married women entered the labor force after World War II, many men no longer were the sole breadwinners. Rather they were the *primary* breadwinners for their families. As lifestyle expectations changed, more couples became dependent on a second income. Today about half of all married women are employed. Married women appear to be gaining some rights as they are employed, thereby improving their status to that of junior partners in a **senior–junior** partnership. Unfortunately, many employed married women experience **role overload:** This occurs when they enter the labor force but continue to perform all the duties of their traditional family role as well.

Scanzoni argues that married couples can be called equal partners only when they have similar rights and duties or when they both pursue jobs that are seen as equally important and perform equivalent care giving and housekeeping functions. If the husband's job is assumed to be no more important than the wife's, the couple may be **equal partners.** In recent years, the equal partnership notion has been discussed primarily for the **dual-career couple,** particularly when one professional is married to another. The ways such couples cope with the demands of traditional roles may not be available to less

Property owner relationship in which the husband/owner has legal rights and the wife-property has few or none.

Head–complement relationship in which the husband/head is in charge of the family but he expresses concern for his wife/complement.

Senior–junior partners the husband/senior partner is assisted in his breadwinning duties by the wife/junior partner.

Role overload situation that occurs when a person takes on an additional role or roles without being relieved of any existing role responsibilities.

Equal partners marriage in which both spouses equally share the economic and domestic responsibilities and rewards of family life.

Dual-career couples marriage in which both spouses pursue demanding occupational careers that they value highly.

Traditional child-care
arrangements sometimes
create strain for mothers.
Company child-care facilities
provide opportunities for
working fathers and mothers
to spend more time with their
children.

affluent couples (paying for many of the housekeeping and child-care activities associated with the traditional wife role) or may be unacceptable (living in different cities).

Female and male roles have been changing for some time in our society, but still most marriages are not equal partnerships. Some individuals and groups oppose change in gender roles for fear that the family will be changed as a result. As yet these roles have not changed as much as might be expected, considering the increases in the employment of married women, particularly those with young children.

At present Americans do not appear ready to institute governmental policies like those in Sweden. Yet work organizations are recognizing that roles are changing. Some companies now provide child-care facilities to provide employees (female *and* male) with quality child care. Employees may also have opportunities to interact with their children during work breaks. Other organizations permit their employees to adjust their work hours to their particular lifestyles by instituting flex-time schedules. Typically, **flex-time** requires workers to be present at work during specific hours but allows them to start work either earlier or later. In a few organizations paternity leaves are available for men, but few men have elected to take them.

Flex-time system that permits workers to adjust their working hours with their employers' consent.

How would current family and work arrangements have to change for spouses to have an equal partnership in marriage?

When people live in social units, their behavior is shaped by the rules of those social units in several ways. Depending on the society in which they live, when people marry, their relationships may undergo a variety of changes. The most common result of entering into this kind of legal contract in our society is that the marriage partners are no longer free to terminate their relationship without appealing to judges and courts. Also, each state has many other laws that pertain to marriage. Since these laws tend to reflect the preferred societal practices and are changed very slowly, an examination of them can tell us much about the traditional functions of marriage in society.

Sexuality and Reproduction

The survival of a society requires that new members be socialized to replace members who die or leave. *Reproduction* is the primary process for adding new members, although at some times, societies may acquire new members from other societies. Human infants are a valuable resource, ensuring the continuation of a society. But infants are also a tremendous drain on resources because they are so dependent on others for many years. Most societies develop means for regulating reproduction and assigning responsibility for the care of the infants who are produced by their members.

There are many ways of regulating reproduction. Human beings typically become capable of biological parenthood as preteens or young teenagers, but they do not typically reproduce as soon as they are capable of doing so. Societal rules and practices often prevent such early reproduction by regulating sexuality or sexual activity.

Dating

A society may limit contact between males and females, and therefore restrict opportunities for sexual exploration, activity, and reproduction. In rural Ireland prior to World War II, opportunities for young men and women to interact were limited basically to church supervised dances. The young men could socialize with one another at pubs, but they could not meet young women there because the women were kept at home on the farmsteads. Many of these young people were economically dependent on their parents and could not afford to break away from their families. The parents had considerable control over their lives and in a number of cases arranged matches for their adult children. Often, the parents were reluctant to let their sons marry, because the parents would lose control of the family farm at that time. As a consequence, many men married for the first time in their 30s and 40s.

In Ireland today, the younger members of society no longer are as restricted in their opportunities to meet one another. Rural pubs make accommodations for females. Automobiles provide greater mobility and freedom from parental supervision. And some youths are taking advantage of job opportunities in urban areas. As a consequence, people are marrying and having children at comparatively younger ages.

Islamic societies demonstrate another pattern. For centuries they rigidly regulated opportunities for males and females to be in contact with one another. After the 1979 revolution in Iran, females changed from wearing Western-style clothing to wearing traditional costumes that conceal all but a woman's eyes. The change in dress symbolically represented a reemergence of long-standing views about the need to restrict female sexuality in Islamic societies. Women must be chaste when they marry, and so the males of their family must make certain they are supervised closely. In traditional Islamic societies, a young person's family arranges where, when, and to whom he or she will be married.

Although some societies, such as the traditional Irish and Moslem, severely limited contact between unmarried males and females, other societies permit supervised opportunities for males and females to become acquainted before marriage. In traditional Spanish societies, males and females can be together if an older woman, a duenna, is present to supervise their activities. Until recent decades, dances and parties for young people in the United States had to be chaperoned in order to be respectable. Parents or other relatives were expected to supervise contacts between young males and females in their homes by staying in the next room when the young couple was together.

The widespread availability of the automobile in our society and others (as in post-World War II Ireland) has dramatically affected opportunities for sexual exploration. Currently, young people are highly mobile, and they can quickly and easily move away from the eyes of relatives and other community members. Today in American society young people are brought into frequent contact with one another in our educational system. Beyond mid-adolescence when they are together they are often free from direct adult supervision.

Premarital Sexual Intercourse

Some societies (South Sea) do not limit young people's opportunities for interaction and sexual exploration, because they believe it is natural and acceptable for the young to engage in sexual activities. On the other hand, our society increasingly deregulates interaction between males and females after puberty, but premarital sexual intercourse is not officially sanctioned.

Many religious groups in the United States emphasize that sexual intercourse and reproduction should occur only when people are married to each other. Furthermore, young people are taught that they should not marry until they are "responsible" and "mature." In fact, most states prohibit marriage until both the male and female are well past puberty (specifying they must be 18 or even 21 years of age to marry without parental consent). Yet our culture, through the media (television, newspapers, magazines), emphasizes the importance of sexual experience for personal fulfillment.

Increasing percentages of teenagers are engaging in sexual exploration at relatively younger ages than they did in the past. Most teenagers are aware of the facts of reproduction but do not consistently practice contraception. Some are not able to easily obtain contraceptives, while others are too embarrassed or fearful of discovery or stigmatization as "not nice" to use contraceptives (Scharf 1982). Proposed government regulations that require that parents be informed if their children seek contraceptives might lead to more pregnancies rather than the intended chaste behavior.

One consequence of early sexual exploration is that increasing numbers of young teenage girls are becoming pregnant. Melvin Zelnik and John Kanter (1980) report that approximately 16% of metropolitan teenage women in 1979 acknowledged having been pregnant without being married compared with about half that percentage only 8 years earlier (Table 12.1).

In most societies, children born to unmarried parents do not have the same social position as children born to married parents. Such children may not be recognized as heirs, as having rights to the father's family name, property, or social position. In our society such children have been called "illegitimate" and stigmatized for life by being so identified on birth certificates.

TABLE 12.1. Metropolitan Teenage Women Premaritally Pregnant

	Percent Ever Pregnant Before Marriage	Pregnancy Outcome			Marriage		
		Give Birth	Induced Abortion	Other (e.g., Spontaneous Abortion)	Before Pregnancy Resolution	Remain Unmarried After Pregnancy Resolution	Other
1971	8.5	67.1	23.4	9.5	32.7	57.5	9.8
1979	16.2	49.4	36.6	14.0	15.5	70.2	14.3

SOURCE: Melvin Zelnik and John F. Kanter, "Sexual Activity, Contraceptive Use and Pregnancy among Metropolitan-Area Teenagers: 1971–1979 *Family Planning Perspectives* 12 (September/October 1980): 230–237.

Consequently women have been encouraged to identify the fathers of their children conceived "out of wedlock" so that the men could be pressured to marry them and assume responsibility for the children. Although the connection between marriage and reproduction can be maintained by such "shotgun" marriages, these marriages are more likely to end in divorce than other marriages.

As more teenagers engage in sexual intercourse at younger ages in our society, greater numbers of them are becoming pregnant because of their failure to practice contraception. In the late 1970s a *lower* percentage of teenagers resolved their premarital pregnancies by entering into marriage compared with previous years (Table 12.1). One reason for this is that a lower percentage of teenage pregnancies are resulting in live births. In addition, more people of all ages are choosing to be unwed parents. In 1940, 1 in 30 children's parents were unwed, the rate rose to 1 in 20 in 1960 and further jumped to 1 in 6 by 1977 (Nye and Lamberts 1980). Therefore, the association between marriage and reproduction appears to be weaker in our society today than it was in the recent past.

How likely is it that young teenagers will engage in sexual intercourse in the future?

Cohabitation

Some men and women not only engage in sexual relations, but further, live together without marrying. Although people had noncontractual marriage-like arrangements in past years, **cohabitation** became more common and less stigmatized recently.

Cohabitation increased in the 1960s and rapidly increased in the 1970s. By 1978, 2.3% of all couples living together were cohabitants (Glick and Spanier 1980). As this practice became more common, behavior formerly called "shacking up" was termed "living together" or "cohabitating." States eliminated common-law marrige regulations which typically had treated as legally married those who had lived together (for 7 years) and had been treated as husband and wife.

Cohabitation may be a prelude or an alternative to marriage. Particularly for young adults it may be an additional step in the process of selecting a suitable marriage partner (casual dating—serious dating—marriage). Although particular cohabitants may not ultimately marry one another, cohabitation does not signify a permanent rejection of marriage either. Research on cohabitation by university students has revealed that most cohabitants expect to marry someone someday and that they would not have children unless they were married (Bower and Christopherson 1977). In fact, the increase in cohabitation in the past decade primarily involves couples without children (Glick and Spanier 1980).

For formerly married people, cohabitation may be an alternative to mar-

Cohabitation involves living together in a "husband-wife" relationship without a marital contract.

riage. In the 1970s, in order to preserve their individual social security benefits, some elderly couples lived together without marrying. Divorced people may try to avoid the legal and social entanglements of marriage by living together. They are more likely to say that cohabitation is a satisfactory alternative to marriage than the "never marrieds."

Beginning with the widely publicized Marvin v. Marvin "palimony" decision in 1976, cohabitants became potentially subject to certain legal obligations similar to those for marrieds (Kay and Amyx 1977). One of the emerging issues is economic responsibility. Usually state laws obligate the husband/father to provide the basic necessities for his wife and dependent children. Such laws keep the community from having to support its dependent members. Currently, some females who have depended on their male cohabitants for economic subsistence while performing the traditional tasks associated with the wife role are suing for support. In some cases cohabitants are seeking rights ordinarily limited to married persons. In the 1980s the city council of San Francisco debated whether or not benefits provided to city workers' spouses should be available to workers' long-term cohabitants (homosexual and heterosexual).

Is cohabitation a threat to the family institution?

**CONTROVERSIAL ISSUES · Husband Sent to Jail
in Rape of His Wife**

Redding, Calif. (UPI) — A man who pleaded guilty to raping his wife has been sentenced to eight months in the Shasta County jail and also placed on three years probation.

Superior Court Judge Joseph Redmon imposed the sentence yesterday for Hughlen Watkins, 24, of Redding, who pleaded guilty yesterday to breaking the state's new spousal rape law, which went into effect on Jan. 1.

The maximum sentence for misdemeanor spousal rape is one year in the county jail.

In March, Watkins' wife, Catherine, 23, told police her husband choked her and forced her to have sex. She said he told her to "call the cops if you want," then fell asleep.

"I filed for divorce the same day I called the police to report my husband had raped me," Mrs. Watkins said last month.

SOURCE: *Knoxville News-Sentinel,* September 3, 1980.

Regulating Sexuality

In our society sexual intercourse is only officially approved within marriage. Sexual intercourse between unmarried individuals, legally termed *fornication,* is against the law in many states, as is adultery or sexual intercourse involving a person who is married to someone else. Since homosexuals are not permitted to marry legally, their sexual relationships are not approved, and in some states there are laws against homosexuality. Legal authorities typically do not enforce laws governing fornication, adultery, and homosexuality when consenting adults engage in sexual activities, but the laws do reflect how our society viewed these activities in the past.

Not only is sexual intercourse officially approved only for marital partners, but for many years it was virtually mandated for them. A marriage may be dissolved easily if the partners never engaged in sexual intercourse. In the past husbands had the lawful right to their wives' sexual services. Recent laws recognizing that a husband may be guilty of raping his wife reflect the belief that sexual relations should involve *mutual consent.*

Should the government regulate the sexual relationships
of consenting adults?

Parenthood

One conceptualization of the family is as a *biological unit*—mother, father, and their offspring. Our laws and customs support this biological definition by encouraging people to marry before they have children and requiring them to care for their offspring. But although natural or biological parenthood is emphasized, legal and social definitions do not entirely coincide with the biological facts and are subject to change over time.

Sample survey data indicate that most people in our society plan to marry and have children—to form families in which the biological facts and social definitions are in agreement. However, today there are many conflicts over social values and beliefs, patterns of divorce and remarriage, standards of child care, and new medical procedures that have generated numerous questions about the assignment of parent status as well as the rights and duties of parents.

The Biological Relationship

One set of questions on parenthood concerns the rights of the biological parents. Various groups in our society disagree about when an unborn child, a fetus, acquires the status of a societal member. The debate centers around the legality of *abortion,* or induced pregnancy termination. One group takes the so-called pro choice position and argues that "would be" parents, particularly mothers, should have the right to choose whether or not they should have children. A group opposed to abortion argues that from the moment of conception, when the sperm unites with the egg, a human being exists with full legal rights. They argue that societal regulations are needed to protect the rights of unborn members of society. The conflicting values and beliefs involved in the debate over abortion will continue to raise questions for some time about the rights of biological parents, about whether parenthood is an individual's choice or a social obligation.

The rights and obligations of biological fathers are also the subject of debate. A few teenage males have tried to assert their rights as the biological fathers of unwed mothers' babies. Some teenage males have gone to court to try and prevent "their babies" from being adopted. They argue that they should be given custody of their infants. Other men have gone to court to prevent women from aborting "their babies." The legal system has not clearly resolved the rights of unwed fathers. As paternity tests become more accurate, medical scientists can more accurately determine whether a man is a biological father of a particular child, but the legal and social rights of unwed fathers remain less clear.

Social Definition

Other questions about parenthood are raised when parents voluntarily or involuntarily relinquish the rights and responsibilities of parenthood. Some parents who are physically, emotionally, or economically unable to care for their children permit their children to be adopted. People who are unable to have children may go through legal proceedings that transfer other people's children to their own legal custody. Unfortunately, some children eligible for adoption remain wards of the state, because many people want to adopt only healthy, newborn babies.

Other children whose biological parents do not relinquish their legal rights as parents become temporary members of other family units as **foster children.** Children may be assigned foster parents because their parents perceive they are temporarily unable to care for them or because courts temporarily remove their children from their care. Foster children are the responsibility of social service agencies that pay people specified amounts to care for them. Foster parents have neither the rights nor the responsibilities of other parents, because the expectation is that foster children will either be returned to their natural parents or be adopted should their natural parents relinquish their legal rights. Unfortunately, contrary to the expectations that foster care should last only a brief time until more permanent arrangements can be made, a number of children grow up living in a series of foster homes. A *Better Homes and Gardens* survey (1980) indicates that many Americans believe that if incompetent parents are unwilling to release their children for adoption, courts should be able to terminate their parenthood rights.

Foster children children assigned temporarily to the care of adults who perform parental functions.

Legal Custody

The high rate of divorce in our society has introduced other questions about parental rights and responsibilities. In many traditional societies children are their fathers' heirs. In cases of divorce, they are placed in the **custody** of their father. Until the early 1900s children in our society were considered the property of their fathers. Today courts determine custody on the basis of what is best for the child. Because of our emphasis on the importance of a mother's care during the child's "tender years," judges have tended to award custody to the mother unless there is strong evidence she is not fulfilling the prescribed mother role or she does not want custody. In recent years, the number of fathers receiving custody of their children has increased. This is a result of changing social attitudes about what makes a good parent, increasing numbers of women who feel free to acknowledge that they do not want custody, and more interest in fathering among some men.

A parent who does not receive custody of a child often finds it difficult to be as involved in the child's rearing as he or she was before the divorce. The parental role sometimes is limited to occasional visits and child support payments. Many noncustodial parents cease child support payments after a relatively brief time and many who pay attempt to renegotiate (eliminate or decrease) obligations for such items as college tuition.

Both the father and mother may desire to remain active parents, and, with the consent of the court, they may agree to do so by sharing the custody of their children. In a unique case, the teenage sons of a Traverse City, Michigan couple remained in the family home and the parents shared custody by alternating the months of living with the sons in the house. Data from Los Angeles County indicate that families with joint custody (a form of shared custody) are half as likely to be back in court as those families where one parent has exclusive custody. Nevertheless in most cases of divorce one parent is awarded custody of the children, usually the mother.

Parental roles may undergo further change if there are remarriages. If the custodial parent remarries, the noncustodial parent may perceive that he (or she) will no longer be as involved and release the children for adoption by the stepparent. Researchers exploring stepparent/stepchild families report that no specific types of problems differentiate these families from other types (Wilson et al. 1975).

In some cases two formerly married persons with children marry and form *blended* or *reconstituted* families. People who form such families have few established norms to guide them and find they lack kinship terminology appropriate for their multiple sets of relatives. While a remarried woman may refer to her former or ex-mother-in-law and ex-father-in-law, her children retain them as biological grandparents. Some children end up with four or more sets of grandparents with no terms to distinguish them from each other. Of course, our conventional kinship terminology may be strained even further by new *reproduction technology.*

Custody assignment of authority over and responsibility for the welfare of a child to a specific adult or adults.

CONTROVERSIAL ISSUES · Child Custody Rights

Jersey City, N.J. (AP) — Edward Lucas, who has been blind since he was 12, has gained custody of his two sons after a year and a half of legal wrangling with his ex-wife.

"If I could see for five minutes, I would want to see my boys," said Lucas.

Lucas and his wife separated in 1971 and the boys have lived with their father since 1972, when Eddie was 4 and Christopher was 2.

Their mother saw them periodically until 1979, when she began court proceedings. He finally gained legal custody in late September.

Lucas taught the boys to read with children's books with print on one page and Braille on another.

"I taught my boys, 'This is an A, this is a B.' And we used to play games. They'd read one page of a book and I'd read the next page," he said Friday.

"I could read to them in bed with the lights out. They got a kick out of that."

The boys learned how to play ball from their baseball fan father. Lucas would pitch to his sons as they stood in front of a wall that served as a backstop. Eddie suggested pitching, while his dad batted. "He'd tell me when to swing. If I missed it, he made me find it," Lucas recalls.

He took them to the movies. "Once, we went to a Walt Disney picture. I was sitting there, and the music was going on and on. Finally I asked Christopher, 'When is it going to start?' Well, it had already started — it was "Fantasia," which is all music. He always kids me about that."

The couple divorced in 1973 and when his ex-wife began custody proceedings last year, she tried to use his blindness to get their sons.

The blindness stems from a premature birth. He was in an incubator and received too much oxygen which, doctors discovered years later, can cause eye weakness. He had congenital cataracts, which led to secondary glaucoma.

When he was 9, a fellow Cub Scout accidentally hit his glasses. The blow detached the retina and left him blind in his left eye. When he was 12, a rubber ball hit him in the right eye, which hemorrhaged. The last thing he saw was the World Series in October 1951.

Lucas works as an agency aide, helping patients in the activities center at Meadowview Hospital in Secaucus.

Eddie began school this fall in St. Peter's Prep and Christopher attends St. Aloysius. Lucas said, "My main goal is to see them do well in education. I help them with their homework."

SOURCE: *Knoxville News-Sentinel,* October 19, 1980, p. B-7.

Technological Intervention

Other questions about parenthood reflect the development and increased usage of medical technology to assist people in becoming parents. Some couples marry and find that medical problems prevent them from becoming parents. For many years medical practitioners have been able to artificially inseminate a woman's uterus. If a wife has no fertility problem but her husband does, his semen or that of another man could be introduced. For some time men have been permitted to sell their semen for artificial insemination. Con-

---

CONTROVERSIAL ISSUES · Sperm Bank for Gifted Announces Its First Birth

Escondido, Calif. (AP)—The Depository for Germinal Choice, set up in 1979 to make available the sperm of Nobel prize winners and other "creative, intelligent people," announced its first baby Monday.

A spokesman said a girl was born with the sperm of a man he would identify only as "a mathematician," a university professor in his 30s.

The baby is "a healthy, 9-pound daughter born in April in a rather small town in a sparsely populated state," he said without identifying the parents or the state "at their request."

The sperm bank had been named in honor of the late Indiana University geneticist Hermann J. Muller, a Nobel prize winner in 1946 for discoveries of the effect of X-rays on genes. But founder Robert K. Graham deleted the reference to Muller at the request of Muller's widow.

Graham has said the repository was intended to bring into the world "a few more creative, intelligent people who otherwise might not be born."

A former optometrist, Graham made a fortune after pioneering techniques to develop shatter-proof plastic eyeglass lenses.

Nobel Laureate William B. Shockley, physics winner in 1956, said he contributed to the sperm bank, but Graham has declined to confirm reports that other Nobel Prize winners also have been donors.

The spokesman declined to identify himself so he won't be recognized when he calls on potential donors. He did say he is the repository's medical geneticist and its only full-time employee.

The first mother, he said, "has a high IQ but is not a member of Mensa," a club for people in the top 2 percent of measured IQ, or intelligence quotient.

Although he hasn't met her—the sperm was delivered by Greyhound bus—he described her as "quite charming."

SOURCE: *Chicago Tribune*, May 25, 1982.

troversy emerged when because of a wife's infertility, another woman, a **surrogate mother,** was inseminated with the husband's semen. Two issues appear to concern people: payment for providing the baby and the "unnaturalness" of a mother giving up her biological baby. Of course, there are questions about legal rights also, particularly if the surrogate mother should decide to question the contract she entered into with the "parents."

      Recent medical developments have focused on problems of female infertility, particularly involving blockage of the passageways (Fallopian tubes) through which eggs must partially travel before they can be united with sperm. Scientists in a number of countries have successfully fertilized an egg taken from a woman with her husband's sperm and then implanted the fertilized egg in her uterus. The resulting children have been described as **test-tube babies** in media reports of their births, because fertilization occurred in laboratories. For many infertile couples such procedures provide new hope, although other people are concerned about where such developments might lead in the scientific manipulation of reproduction.

Surrogate mother a woman who agrees to have a child for a couple by being artificially inseminated with the husband's semen.

Test-tube baby an embryo that is conceived (egg fertilized by sperm) in a test tube and then implanted in the mother's uterus.

Should reproduction be limited to those with "desirable" genes?

Conflict, Violence, and Abuse

We idealize the family as a social unit in which people provide one another with emotional support and in which harmony prevails. So people feel disappointed when they experience conflict and unhappiness in their family lives. In the 1950s sociologists emphasized the importance of harmony in the family and the negative consequences of conflict. Since then, however, family sociologists have recognized that conflict is not only inevitable in close personal relationships, but also can have positive consequences. If we find that our goals and values are not compatible with those of our casual associates, we may decide to spend less time with them or ignore the differences. When parents and children disagree about goals and values they neither can freely terminate their relationship nor, usually, agree to disagree, since it is difficult for people closely tied to one another to ignore such differences. When parents and children engage in conflict over values and goals, they may learn to understand better one another's positions and take the first step toward resolving their problems. If people do not face up to conflict, problems do not go away but rather quietly erode relationships (Scanzoni 1982).

      Conflict should not be confused with violence. Conflict involves people disagreeing with each other. Violence occurs when one person harms another. Today violence in the family is receiving more media coverage and governmental attention than it has in past years. As a consequence, more information is available about child abuse, spouse abuse, and "granny bashing," or the

Massachusetts, 1646: If any child[ren] above sixteen years old and of sufficient understanding shall curse or smite their natural father or mother, they shall be put to death, unless it can be sufficiently testified that the parents have been very un-christianly negligent in the education of such children, or so provoked them by extreme and cruel correction that they have been forced thereunto to preserve themselves from death or maiming. . . .

If a man have a stubborn or rebellious son of sufficient years of understanding, viz. sixteen, which will not obey the voice of his father or the voice of his mother, and that when they have chastened him will not harken unto them, then shall his father and mother, being his natural parents, lay hold on him and bring him to the magistrates assembled in Court, and testify to them by sufficient evidence that this their son is stubborn and rebellious and will not obey their voice and chastisement, but lives in sundry notorious crimes. Such a son shall be put to death.

SOURCE: Elizabeth Douvan, Helen Weingarten, and Jane L. Scheiber, *American Families* (Dubuque, Iowa: Kendall/Hunt, 1980), p. 291.

abuse of elderly relatives. Unfortunately, abusive and violent behaviors are not new phenomena within the family.

Defining Violence

One thing that has happened is that people increasingly are unwilling to ignore or passively accept certain behaviors. Values have changed. Now each family member is believed to have rights. In our society wives and children had very few rights in the past, and so husbands and fathers had considerable power to "correct" them. Most wives and children probably were not violently abused, but those who were had no legal recourse.

Another value change involves our perceptions of acceptable behavior. In societies where there were limited resources, people sometimes limited the number of mouths to feed in ways that we would find unacceptable. As people aged in Eskimo societies, they drained rather than contributed to the group's resources. When a group moved to a new area, the elderly were expected to remain behind and die for the good of the group. In some European societies when there were too many babies to feed, babies would not be fed or were thrown over cliffs to die. More often female infants were the victims of infanticide, because male children had more important roles to play in the family and society than females. By the standards of acceptable behavior in our society, such behavior is inhumane.

Child Abuse

Despite value changes, newspapers regularly report cases of **child abuse,** sexual molestation, and neglect. One problem is to determine what is regarded

Child abuse behavior that causes a child a degree of harm that is not socially acceptable.

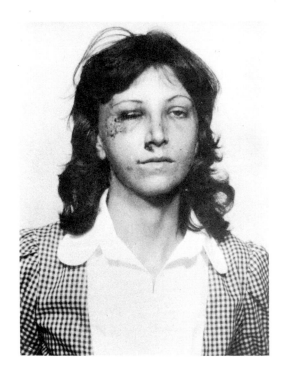

As awareness of family violence increased, programs were developed to help battered spouses and abused children.

as acceptable treatment of a child. Richard Gelles and Murray Straus (1979) have reviewed various studies revealing that between 84% and 97% of parents had at some time in their children's lives physically punished them. Other research by Gelles indicates that physical punishment of children (except extreme behaviors such as those involving usage of a knife or gun) is patterned, that it is not a unique event. Apparently most people believe that physical punishment is appropriate under certain circumstances (Table 12.2).

In our own and other countries, the treatment of children is being reevaluated. The adage "spare the rod and spoil the child" is being questioned.

TABLE 12.2   Parents' Attitudes toward Physical Punishment

QUESTION: Do you think children should be disciplined by physical punishment?

		Age of Respondent			Education of Respondent			Who Filled Out the Questionnaire?		
	Total	Under 35	35–54	55 & Over	H.S. Grad. or Less	Attended College, Graduated	Graduate Work	Man of the House	Woman of the House	Both
Yes, whenever necessary	77%	82%	74%	72%	79%	78%	76%	82%	76%	86%
No, not at all	20	16	23	24	19	19	21	17	21	13
Did not answer	3	2	3	4	2	3	3	1	3	1

SOURCE: *A Report on the American Family.* The Editors of *Better Homes and Gardens* (Des Moines, Iowa: Meredith Corp., 1978), p. 66.

Among other things the 1974 Child Abuse Prevention and Treatment Act has called for the systematic study of child abuse and neglect. Defining emotional and psychological abuse has been an even greater problem for researchers and social service workers than identifying when physical punishment constitutes abuse. In 1979 Sweden prohibited spanking and other forms of humiliation by parents in an attempt to change both parents' attitudes and behavior.

Spouse Abuse

Although wives may abuse husbands, more attention has focused on the abuse of wives by husbands. This reflects the greater risk the wife typically experiences due to lesser physical strength and greater economic dependence, as well as beliefs about the absurdity of any husband "letting" his wife physically harm him.

When wives were viewed as their husband's property, husbands had the right to regulate their behavior by correcting them. A significant minority of men and women today believe that it is acceptable for wives and husbands to slap one another (Gelles and Strauss 1979).

For those not involved in physically abusive relationships, it is hard to understand why any adult would remain in such a situation. Richard Gelles'

Most couples strive to resolve family conflict without violence.

(1976) research provides some answers to the question of why wives remain in marriages where they are physically abused. First, women who experienced violence in their families of procreation, as victims or observers, are less likely to seek external assistance than those who had experienced less violence. Second, women whose spouses engage in less severe and less frequent abusive acts are less likely to seek external assistance than those experiencing frequent, violent attacks. Third, women who are less able to provide adequately for themselves, because they do not have jobs or have less education, are more likely to remain with abusive husbands. Fourth, people who are victims of violence at the hands of their spouses often do not know whom to call for assistance. Often, the police, court officials, and social service agents are not well-prepared to handle cases of domestic violence.

Responses to Abusive Behaviors

As a society we have ambivalent views about abusive behavior in the family. One set of beliefs emphasizes the sanctity of family life, another set emphasizes the need for society to protect children and people who cannot care for themselves from inhumane treatment. Americans tend to believe that whatever people do in their homes is their own business, that they have a right to privacy. In the case of children, however, states have enacted laws to encourage or even require nonfamily members to report suspected cases of child abuse. Yet often people are reluctant to report their neighbors for suspected child neglect or abuse. Many people including the police and social service workers are hesitant to become involved in disputes between husbands and wives. They believe that such disputes will blow over or the couple may unite against those who interfere in their private lives. Police officers argue that many wives fail to press charges against their husbands after the police have been called to intervene. Official statistics reveal that police officers run greater risks of personal injury answering domestic disturbance calls than with other calls such as robbery.

Another belief is that children are better off living with their natural parents. Courts may remove children from their parents' homes if the parents have been maltreating them, but usually the children are returned to their parents after a short period of time (after some counseling of the parents). In some instances, some children return home to experience further abuse and neglect, because the parents have not learned how to manage better the stresses and strains of family life.

Divorce

Societies usually develop mechanisms for dealing with marriages that fail. In some societies a marriage is a failure if no children (or at least no *male* children) are produced. Such societies permit a husband to return a barren wife to her family and terminate the marriage. If the woman's family received payment from the man or his family for taking her (and for her family's loss of her services)—a bride price—her family would be obligated to return the bride price (goods, livestock). In our society, some people may officially stop living with one another by obtaining a legal separation. Other people may choose to officially end their marriages by obtaining divorces.

Individuals' rights to divorce are regulated by the societies in which they live, specifically by social institutions and social organizations. In traditional Moslem societies, only men had the right to divorce. In traditional Chinese society there was a high suicide rate among young wives whose only alternative to an unhappy marriage was death. The Catholic church, an important social organization for people in many societies, also does not recognize divorce.

Divorce Rates

Generally, as societies emphasize individuals' rights to choose their own marriage partners, those individuals' opportunities to dissolve their marriages appear to increase. Industrialized societies tend to have higher **divorce rates** than traditional societies. Recently the United States has had the highest divorce rate in the world, although other societies such as Israel and the Soviet Union have had higher rates at times. In 1979 there were 5.1 divorces per 1,000 population in the United States compared with only 1.6 divorces per 1,000 in 1930. Comparing the number of divorces to the general population is a *crude* measure of divorce, for when there are a lot of young people in the population many members of the population are not married and thus not at risk. Another way to measure the rate of divorce is to consider the number of divorces per 1,000 married persons. This is called the *refined* rate. There were 22.8 divorces for every 1,000 U.S. married women in 1979 compared to 11.2 per 1,000 married women in 1967. Whatever measure we use, the percentage of marriages in our society ending in divorce has increased in recent decades.

Divorce rate crude divorce rate—the number of divorces per 1,000 persons; refined rate—the number of divorces per 1,000 married women.

Divorce as a Legal Proceeding

In our society individuals may socially terminate their marriages by no longer living together. However, they are legally married until they go to court and have the dissolution of their marriages officially sanctioned. The system of divorce prevalent in our society for some time has relied on an adversarial procedure, in which one spouse sues the other for divorce. The spouse who begins the divorce action specifies certain complaints about the other spouse. Each state recognizes certain complaints as legal **grounds** for divorce (adultery, desertion, mental cruelty). In the 1970s various states passed laws permitting husbands and wives to obtain divorces without making specific complaints about one another. Such divorces are labeled "no-fault," because neither party is seen as being solely at fault for the failure of the marriage. In some states individuals may receive a divorce by citing mutual incompatibility. This procedure also avoids the assignment of fault to either spouse.

Grounds the behavior recognized by a state as legal reason for divorce.

Divorce and the Family

In the 1970s divorce rates rose very rapidly in our society. This led some people to view as detrimental to marriage the changes in laws and policies that made divorce more accessible and less emotionally trying for many people. In addition to the institution of no-fault divorce and other new grounds for divorce in many states, funds for legal aid were made increasingly available to poor people who sought divorces. Critics fear that more people are terminating their marriages simply because it is easier to do so and that as a consequence the American family and American society are threatened.

Others have interpreted the rising divorce rate less pessimistically. When divorce is difficult to obtain because of legal or financial constraints, people may be forced to remain in unhappy marriages, or they may "socially" divorce through the processes of desertion or separation. Such alternatives are seen by some as less desirable than divorce, particularly for those who believe that family life is better when individual family members are happy. When women are better able to provide for themselves (through paid employment), they may not remain in unsatisfactory marriages. Willie Pearson and Lewellyn Hendrix (1979) studied a number of tribal societies and indeed found that when women were less dependent on their husbands, when there was greater sexual equality, societal divorce rates were higher.

Does an increase in the divorce rate mean that more people are unhappily married?

Remarriage

Those who argue that a high rate of divorce does *not* mean that family life is less important to people point out that the majority of divorced persons remarry. For a period of time, the remarriage rate rose with the divorce rates, but today it seems to have stabilized. Furthermore, a comparison of the marital happiness between "never divorced" and "ever divorced" respondents has revealed that remarriages are generally about as successful as intact first marriages (Glenn and Weaver 1977).

Female-Headed Households

One consequence of many divorces is the creation of **female-headed households.** Such households may occur as the result of death, marital separation, desertion, or out-of-wedlock births. Women are less likely to remarry than men, and they are more likely to be awarded the custody of dependent children. The number of families headed by females increased dramatically during the 1970s, from 1 out of 9 families in 1970 to 1 out of 7 families in 1979. The large number of female-headed households means not only that fewer people are living in the ideal intact family, but also that a substantial percentage of women and children are living in dire economic circumstances. These are the households most likely to be below the poverty level, compared

Female-headed household   a family living unit that is headed by a female.

with any other category of households (Wattenberg and Reinhardt 1979). Analysis of detailed census questionnaires from 1980 shows that family composition is the key factor in poverty regardless of race. Whether black or white, single women with children tend to have the poorest families.

Households headed by females are more often poorer than others for several reasons. On the average, women make a little more than half of what men do in the labor force. Furthermore, women from lower socioeconomic levels are more likely to be divorced than women from higher socioeconomic levels. These women are unlikely to obtain jobs that pay well. In addition, they are caught in the double bind of working fewer hours in order to provide for their children or paying considerable sums for child care.

Our government has developed several programs to assist these mothers with their problems. One program provides financial aid for dependent children. Other programs have focused on improving the job skills of displaced homemakers. In any case, many female-headed households continue to remain below the poverty level.

Why are female-headed households more likely to be poor than any other type of household?

Summary

The term "family" can refer to different sets of persons: nuclear family or extended family, family of origin or family of procreation. Generally, Americans think of nuclear families as composed of husband, wife, and children; however, as our society has changed, more arrangements are considered to be nuclear families.

Americans are limited to one marriage partner at a time, a practice known as monogamy. In other societies people may be permitted to have or prefer to have more than one spouse, a practice known as polygamy. In modern industrial societies people tend to live in nuclear family units and to practice monogamy.

In the first half of the twentieth century societal attitudes opposed the employment of married women. Women were assumed to have a natural role in the home because of their special nurturant abilities, their maternal instinct. In the second half of the twentieth century increasing numbers of married women including mothers of young children have entered the labor force, and alternative forms of care giving have been considered.

The husband-wife relationship may take several forms. When our society began women had little or no legal recognition, leading to a relationship in which the husband could be considered as owner and the wife as property.

In contemporary American society three types of husband-wife relationships prevail. The head–complement relationship represents the "traditional" form of marriage roles. The senior–junior partner and equal-partner forms are increasingly more common, for they usually occur when women enter the labor force.

In our society families are the units in which sexual expression in the form of sexual intercourse is permitted, and they are responsible for reproducing new societal members through reproduction and socialization (parenthood).

Societies vary in the extent to which they

restrict contact among unmarried youth of the opposite sexes as well as their sexual activity. In our society premarital contact is not restricted and premarital sexual activity is increasing, although it is not universally approved.

More pregnant unmarried women are keeping their babies, loosening the preferred linkage between marriage and reproduction. At the same time more heterosexual couples are openly cohabiting, violating the preferred linkage between marriage and sexual activity. Homosexual relationships and "marriages" also weaken traditional linkages.

Medical technology now permits people who could not become biological parents in the past to do so. Although such advances are her-alded by many, others have reservations about where the scientific manipulation of reproduction will lead us.

Family violence and abuse are more widely publicized today than they were in the past, but it appears that such behaviors today are not more frequent, but rather less tolerated. Abusive behavior is difficult to eliminate because abusers have to learn new modes of behaving.

Divorce is becoming more frequent in our society. Changes in divorce laws have made it easier for couples to obtain divorces, but the underlying reasons for more divorces appear to be greater emphasis on individual happiness and greater opportunities for independent economic survival.

Suggested Readings

Christopher Lasch. *Haven in a Heartless World: The Family Besieged.* New York: Basic, 1977. In this controversial book Lasch argues that we need to put more emphasis on family life. In the interests of avoiding conflict, parents have relinquished responsibility for training children to others (peers, teachers, and other professionals). He argues that although feminists correctly point out the economic inequalities women experience in the work place, economic equality for women achieved under the present system would be at the expense of quality family life.

Lillian Rubin. *Worlds of Pain.* New York: Basic, 1976. A portrayal of life in white working-class fam-ilies. Rubin argues that class differences lead to significant differences in the attitudes and behaviors of family members. Taught to believe in the American Dream, these people find their lives do not live up to their expectations; they live in worlds of pain.

Carl N. Degler. *At Odds.* New York: Oxford University Press, 1980. Degler examines the joint history of American women and the American family. He argues convincingly that despite various changes in the family since the founding of our society the rights of individual women have been at odds with their roles in the family.

13

Educational Structures

"Your honor, the prosecution contends that the defendant failed to perform the services promised the client. Because of this obvious case of malpractice, we ask the court to award our client damages of $1,000,000, which will only partially offset the irreparable harm and injury sustained to our client's career and livelihood."

The setting could be any federal, state, or local court in the land. The case could involve anyone performing services to a client. The most common reaction we might have to such a statement would be to envision a doctor sued by a patient on the grounds of malpractice. But in this legal case, a doctor is not involved. The prosecution is suing on behalf of a client, but the defendant is the school system. *The client is a student poorly trained and ill-equipped to deal with the complexities of everyday life. Lacking the skills necessary to compete in the economic marketplace for scarce jobs, the client is clearly at a disadvantage.*

The legal incident described above may be imaginary, but it is increasingly commonplace to see various school systems sued by students. More and more cases of "malpractice" are appearing on court dockets as students and parents are forcing schools, teachers, principals, and other educators to account for their actions in the educational institution. Some observers believe that "legal questions about teaching methodologies, learning environments, and the degree to which an individual learner has acquired certain basic skills will increasingly be raised" (Hughes and Gordon 1978:356). Accountability is moving into the courts as parents and students sue schools for malpractice (Lewis et al. 1978a:20).

The sociologist views education and the educational system as basic to the perpetuation of society. It is one of the chief socializing agents, rivaled only by the family and the religious institutions as major agencies of socialization. In the United States, citizens are required by law to attend an educational institution for a fixed period of years. Thus, it is compulsory for most children in our society to have a minimal amount of educational experience. Our economic and political institutions further enhance the power of the educational systems by requiring holders of certain jobs to have degrees or certificates of advanced learning. In short, most of us are locked into the educational system at an early age and leave it only when we reach early adulthood.

The costs associated with higher education in the United States have increased 77% between 1970 and 1980. Several of the leading schools in the nation are charging five-figure fees—more than $10,000 per year for tuition and living expenses. Projections for 1990 place average tuition, room, and board costs at over $16,000. With these astounding increases in costs, the pressure is mounting on educators to provide an equally high-level education to the students exposed to so pervasive an institution.

In this chapter, we consider some of the issues and problems associated with education at the elementary, secondary, and postsecondary levels. We also examine some of the more important characteristics of education in the United States. Finally, we discuss important trends in education at all levels, illustrating some of the more important linkages between the educational system and the larger society of which it is a part.

THE FACTS · Who Can Afford College?

Do you have any idea what it costs to attend one of our most prestigious private colleges or universities as an undergraduate? The fee schedules for the 1982–83 school year have been announced. Glance at the table:

School Name	1982–83 Fees	Up from 1981–82
MIT	$12,250	15.7%
Harvard	12,100	14.8
Yale	11,790	14.0
Stanford	11,643	15.2
Brown	11,562	12.8
Princeton	11,468	14.6
Dartmouth	11,447	14.1
Northwestern	11,205	15.6
Wesleyan	11,030	8.9

These are basic fees for tuition, room, and board. To them add the cost of clothes, books, transportation, and entertainment, and you come up with an additional $1000 or more. And that's just for one year!

Even if inflation is reduced to 5% a year—an unlikely prospect—it will cost $20,000 a year by 1990 to send an undergraduate to any of the listed institutions. Tuitions increase at about the same rate at all such private schools, since they are usually caught in the same cost-rise vise.

Fortunately, many of these schools maintain a policy of "aid-blind" admissions. Students are admitted without considering their economic circumstances and are assured that they will be able to attend regardless of financial need. Without such student aid, these institutions would be unable to maintain an open-door policy for young men and women from all socioeconomic levels.

At Harvard, for example, about 65% of the 6500 undergraduates receive financial aid, including employment and bank loans.

The median charge for residents attending state and land-grant universities during the 1981–82 school year is $2905—up 14.3% from 1980–81. It costs, on the average, about three to four times as much to attend one of the selective private schools as it does for a student to attend his or her own state university.

SOURCE: *Parade,* April 25, 1982.

Some Functions of Educational Institutions

Among the most important functions performed by our educational structures are: dissemination of our culture, societal assimilation, provision for tracking of skills, building of personal character, and stimulation of social change.

Dissemination of Our Culture

Schools are the primary bastions of our culture and cultural heritage. History courses impart significant developments in our past that made it possible for present conditions to exist. It is not uncommon for schools to present particular versions of our national culture and ignore other aspects. Predominantly white schools, on the one hand, have usually omitted references to the significant contributions of many black Americans in the history of the United States. Predominantly black schools, on the other hand, have often presented a version of certain aspects of our history quite different from that of many predominantly white schools.

There is not much variation from one school system to the next or from one part of the country to the next, relating to school curriculum. Each state has standards for accepting teaching credentials from teachers in other states, and few teachers find this transition from one school system to another very difficult. Our institutions of higher learning—the colleges and universities responsible for turning out teachers for lower education—are reasonably similar in the way in which they fulfill their training functions. No accredited university seriously drops below national averages when it comes to general teacher competence (measured through achievement tests and qualifying examinations for teaching credentials). Of course, there will always be individual differences in teaching quality when individual comparisons are made.

Culture is also transmitted informally in school systems. In school yards, lunch rooms, hallways, and other locations on every campus, students group together in more or less constant social arrangements. They exchange the latest information or gossip. They learn from one another about various things they have experienced. In this fashion, socialization occurs, and culture and cultural values are transmitted. This informal, casual cultural transmission parallels—at times rivals—the traditional socialization medium of the classroom.

Societal Assimilation

A high degree of social integration is established through students' normal progress through the lower educational system. We are taught respect for the law and various reasons for obeying the law. We are also made aware of persons who deviate from the law, and we learn to label these persons as deviant or in some respect different from ourselves.

We learn the same language (although pronunciation varies noticeably from one part of the country to another), and in many respects, we learn to value the same things. We respect or come to respect achievement and competition as primary values. In turn, we learn to admire those who achieve and to despise failure. Although we all differ in appearance and behavior, we share sufficient similarities to cause us to feel that we fit in or belong to society. We sing a common national anthem, whether in Alaska or in Florida. We use similar verbal expressions to describe our experiences. The relatively high degree of continuity in our early educational experiences tends to yield a high degree of uniformity and similarity among us as adults.

Provision for Tracking of Individual Skills

Our school systems fulfill a selective screening function for society. The best students are advanced or promoted, encouraged into careers or onto professional "tracks" that can eventually lead them to the higher rewards our society has to offer. Students who do not achieve as well throughout their school years are, in turn, discouraged from following the lines or tracks leading to the careers or professions that are rewarding in terms of prestige or income.

Since high school attendance is usually compulsory in our society, the screening function of education usually is not clearly apparent until the student enters higher educational systems, if he or she enters at all. Not all persons who graduate from high school enter college. Furthermore, not all persons who enter college ultimately graduate. Many persons "drop out," or discontinue their formal education before graduating.

The advice of teachers and counselors may have tremendous impact on students' adult lives, for the tracks they enter will affect their opportunities for both jobs and further education.

TABLE 13.1   Cost per Pupil by State

Expenditures per pupil in average daily attendance in public elementary and secondary day schools, 1979–80.

	Expenditure per Pupil					Expenditure per Pupil			
State	Total[1]	Current[2]	Capital Outlay[3]	Interest on School Debt	State	Total[1]	Current[2]	Capital Outlay[3]	Interest on School Debt
United States	$2,494	$2,275	$170	$49	Missouri	2,071	1,936	98	37
Alabama	1,741	1,612	115	14	Montana	2,882	2,476	363	43
Alaska	5,146	4,728	151	267	Nebraska	2,403	2,150	199	54
Arizona	2,433	1,971	398	64	Nevada	2,553	2,088	356	108
Arkansas	1,839	1,574	224	41	New Hampshire	2,069	1,917	115	37
California	2,376	2,268	89	19	New Jersey	3,379	3,191	116	72
Colorado	2,826	2,421	330	75	New Mexico	2,396	2,034	339	23
Connecticut	2,520	2,425	47	48	New York	3,681	3,462	134	85
Delaware	3,019	2,868	55	96	North Carolina	1,871	1,754	104	[3]13
District of Columbia	3,265	3,259	6	0	North Dakota	2,071	1,927	121	23
Florida	2,082	1,889	160	33	Ohio	2,208	2,075	94	39
Georgia	1,833	1,625	181	26	Oklahoma	2,176	1,926	229	21
Hawaii	2,528	2,322	204	2	Oregon	3,104	2,692	355	58
Idaho	1,914	1,659	215	40	Pennsylvania	2,742	2,535	101	106
Illinois	2,778	2,587	140	51	Rhode Island	2,670	2,601	17	52
Indiana	2,166	1,910	248	7	South Carolina	1,996	1,752	209	35
Iowa	2,552	2,340	177	35	South Dakota	1,932	1,911	1	19
Kansas	2,422	2,205	175	42	Tennessee	1,825	1,635	175	14
Kentucky	1,847	1,701	91	55	Texas	2,309	1,916	316	77
Louisiana	2,017	1,794	172	52	Utah	2,208	1,657	491	60
Maine	1,947	1,824	82	41	Vermont	2,240	2,049	137	55
Maryland	2,843	2,598	204	41	Virginia	2,211	1,970	191	51
Massachusetts	2,952	2,819	54	79	Washington	3,073	2,568	446	58
Michigan	2,873	2,640	151	82	West Virginia	2,160	1,920	219	21
Minnesota	2,686	2,457	221	9	Wisconsin	2,693	2,495	145	53
Mississippi	1,788	1,664	124	1	Wyoming	3,326	2,527	698	101

[1]Includes current expenditures for day schools, capital outlay, and interest on school debt.
[2]Includes expenditures for day schools only; excludes adult education, community colleges, and community services.
[3]Estimated by the National Center for Education Statistics. NOTE: Because of rounding, details may not add to totals.
SOURCE: National Center for Education Statistics, U. S. Education Department.

Some writers have referred to the selection function of higher education as "cooling out" (Clark 1960). "Cooling out" is a term that has been used by con men to help their "marks" or victims develop a rationale for not reporting them to the police. A con man might say to a victim, "Report me to the police, and you'll be humiliated for what you let me do to you." The "mark" or victim often does not contact police because of this fear of humiliation. In education a different form of "cooling out" takes place when students are informed that their progress in a given academic area (such as nuclear engineering or physics) is not satisfactory, and perhaps they ought to consider changing majors. Eventually the student opts for an easier curriculum and may remain in the system until graduation, although the student's sights have been lowered drastically in the process. Or the student may receive a continuous barrage of

TABLE 13.2 Educational Attainment by Age, Race, and Sex

Race, Age, and Sex March 1980	Years of School Completed					Percent				
	All Persons	Less than High School, 4 Years	High School, 4 Years	College, 1 to 3 Years	College, 4 Years or More	All Persons	Less than High School, 4 Years	High School, 4 Years	College, 1 to 3 Years	College, 4 Years or More
All races										
18 to 24 years	29,118	6,667	13,329	7,157	1,963	100.0	22.9	45.8	24.6	6.7
25 years and over 130,409		40,902	47,934	19,379	22,193	100.0	31.4	36.8	14.9	17.0
25 to 34 years 36,615		5,357	14,481	7,942	8,836	100.0	14.6	39.5	21.7	24.1
35 to 44 years 25,426		5,579	10,456	4,109	5,280	100.0	21.9	41.1	16.2	20.8
45 to 54 years 22,698		7,194	9,128	2,834	3,542	100.0	31.7	40.2	12.5	15.6
55 to 64 years 21,476		8,431	8,065	2,521	2,459	100.0	39.3	37.6	11.7	11.4
65 years and over . . 24,194		14,340	5,804	1,973	2,076	100.0	59.3	24.0	8.2	8.6
Male, 25 years and over.	61,389	18,885	20,080	9,593	12,832	100.0	30.8	32.7	15.6	20.9
Female, 25 years and over.	69,020	22,018	27,854	9,786	9,362	100.0	31.9	40.4	14.2	13.6
White										
18 to 24 years	24,717	5,246	11,466	6,207	1,796	100.0	21.2	46.4	25.1	7.3
25 years and over 114,763		33,803	43,149	17,350	20,460	100.0	29.5	37.6	15.1	17.8
25 to 34 years 31,435		4,160	12,449	6,855	7,969	100.0	13.2	39.6	21.8	25.4
35 to 44 years 22,129		4,425	9,193	3,633	4,878	100.0	20.0	41.5	16.4	22.0
45 to 54 years 19,971		5,730	8,385	2,597	3,258	100.0	28.7	42.0	13.0	16.3
55 to 64 years 19,331		6,990	7,601	2,374	2,365	100.0	36.2	39.3	12.3	12.2
65 years and over . . 21,898		12,495	5,521	1,892	1,989	100.0	57.1	25.2	8.6	9.1
Male, 25 years and over.	54,389	15,756	18,026	8,609	11,998	100.0	29.0	33.1	15.8	22.1
Female, 25 years and over.	60,374	18,047	25,124	8,741	8,462	100.0	29.9	41.6	14.5	14.0
Black										
18 to 24 years	3,711	1,257	1,598	733	123	100.0	33.9	43.1	19.8	3.3
25 years and over 12,927		6,306	3,980	1,618	1,024	100.0	48.8	30.8	12.5	7.9
25 to 34 years 4,097		1,007	1,712	868	508	100.0	24.6	41.8	21.2	12.4
35 to 44 years 2,677		1,003	1,080	380	215	100.0	37.5	40.3	14.2	8.0
45 to 54 years 2,257		1,308	597	186	165	100.0	58.0	26.5	8.2	7.3
55 to 64 years 1,855		1,298	363	125	70	100.0	70.0	19.6	6.7	3.8
65 years and over . . 2,040		1,688	229	59	65	100.0	82.7	11.2	2.9	3.2
Male, 25 years and over.	5,717	2,797	1,706	774	440	100.0	48.9	29.8	13.5	7.7
Female, 25 years and over.	7,209	3,509	2,274	844	583	100.0	48.7	31.5	11.7	8.1

TABLE 13.2   Educational Attainment by Age, Race, and Sex (*Continued*)

Race, Age, and Sex March 1980	All Persons	Years of School Completed				All Persons	Percent			
		Less than High School, 4 Years	High School, 4 Years	College, 1 to 3 Years	College, 4 Years or More		Less than High School, 4 Years	High School, 4 Years	College, 1 to 3 Years	College, 4 Years or More
Spanish Origin[1]										
18 to 24 years	1,954	854	751	304	44	100.0	43.7	38.4	15.6	2.3
25 years and over	5,934	3,291	1,586	603	454	100.0	55.5	26.7	10.2	7.7
25 to 34 years	2,227	971	730	326	198	100.0	43.6	32.8	14.6	8.9
35 to 44 years	1,454	748	432	146	128	100.0	51.4	29.7	10.0	8.8
45 to 54 years	1,036	638	237	88	72	100.0	61.6	22.9	8.5	6.9
55 to 64 years	643	456	120	34	32	100.0	70.9	18.7	5.3	5.0
65 years and over . .	574	477	67	8	23	100.0	83.1	11.7	1.4	4.0
Male, 25 years and over.	2,825	1,556	677	332	261	100.0	55.1	24.0	11.8	9.2
Female, 25 years and over.	3,109	1,736	909	271	193	100.0	55.8	29.2	8.7	6.2
March 1970 **All races**										
18 to 24 years	22,494	5,732	9,996	5,392	1,374	100.0	25.5	44.4	24.0	6.1
25 years and over	109,310	48,948	37,134	11,164	12,063	100.0	44.8	34.0	10.2	11.0
25 to 34 years	24,865	6,517	10,929	3,491	3,926	100.0	26.2	44.0	14.0	15.8
35 to 44 years	23,021	8,216	9,325	2,523	2,958	100.0	35.7	40.5	11.0	12.8
45 to 54 years	23,298	9,735	8,875	2,352	2,336	100.0	41.8	38.1	10.1	10.0
55 to 64 years	18,413	10,347	4,905	1,567	1,594	100.0	56.2	26.6	8.5	8.7
65 years and over . .	19,713	14,134	3,100	1,230	1,249	100.0	71.7	15.7	6.2	6.3
Male, 25 years and over.	51,784	23,311	15,571	5,580	7,321	100.0	45.0	30.1	10.8	14.1
Female, 25 years and over.	57,527	25,638	21,563	5,584	4,743	100.0	44.6	37.5	9.7	8.2
White										
18 to 24 years	19,536	4,496	8,865	4,886	1,289	100.0	23.0	45.4	25.0	6.6
25 years and over	98,112	41,789	34,493	10,452	11,380	100.0	42.6	35.2	10.7	11.6
25 to 34 years	21,887	5,222	9,828	3,204	3,633	100.0	23.9	44.9	14.6	16.6
35 to 44 years	20,392	6,756	8,541	2,319	2,776	100.0	33.1	41.9	11.4	13.6
45 to 54 years	20,961	8,134	8,392	2,209	2,227	100.0	38.8	40.0	10.5	10.6
55 to 64 years	16,731	8,960	4,719	1,526	1,527	100.0	53.6	28.2	9.1	9.1
65 years and over . .	18,141	12,716	3,013	1,193	1,218	100.0	70.1	16.6	6.6	6.7
Male, 25 years and over.	46,606	19,963	14,410	5,259	6,972	100.0	42.8	30.9	11.3	15.0
Female, 25 years and over.	51,506	21,825	20,083	5,191	4,408	100.0	42.4	39.0	10.1	8.6

TABLE 13.2   Educational Attainment by Age, Race, and Sex (*Continued*)

Race, Age, and Sex March 1980	All Persons	Years of School Completed				Percent				
		Less than High School, 4 Years	High School, 4 Years	College, 1 to 3 Years	College, 4 Years or More	All Persons	Less than High School, 4 Years	High School, 4 Years	College, 1 to 3 Years	College, 4 Years or More
Black										
18 to 24 years	2,713	1,158	1,076	419	61	100.1	42.7	39.7	15.4	2.2
25 years and over	10,089	6,686	2,358	592	452	100.0	66.3	23.4	5.9	4.5
25 to 34 years	2,651	1,237	1,018	237	161	100.0	46.7	38.4	8.9	6.1
35 to 44 years	2,347	1,372	690	164	122	100.0	58.5	29.4	7.0	5.2
45 to 54 years	2,128	1,509	422	117	81	100.0	70.9	19.8	5.5	3.8
55 to 64 years	1,545	1,284	165	38	59	100.0	83.1	10.7	2.5	3.8
65 years and over ..	1,417	1,290	64	35	28	100.0	91.0	4.5	2.5	2.0
Male, 25 years and over...............	4,619	3,120	1,025	261	212	100.0	67.5	22.2	5.7	4.6
Female, 25 years and over...............	5,470	3,565	1,333	330	240	100.0	65.2	24.4	6.0	4.4

[1]Persons of Spanish origin may be of any race.
SOURCE: U.S. Bureau of the Census (number of persons in thousands).

academic probation notices or warnings of poor academic achievement or scholarship. Failing to improve his or her marks appreciably may eventually provoke a student to consider dropping out of school. But the time interval between receiving warnings and actually "dropping out" may be sufficiently long that the student is able to justify the action.

No one likes to fail. Almost everyone wishes to achieve the ultimate, the American Dream, whatever they think that might be. The average student is prepared mentally for a variety of events that may occur throughout a venture into higher education. The gradualism of failure experiences and the suggestions by counselors to seek alternative careers or academic programs seem to operate fairly effectively in "cooling out" those students "destined" to fail or do poorly in higher education.

In some respects our educational institutions are molded in the image of the bureaucratic model, where the most qualified persons gravitate to those positions suited for their interests, abilities, and skills. To this extent, the screening function of higher education is performed admirably.

Building of Personal Character

Throughout a person's schooling, he or she acquires a sense of "self" or personal identity. "Who am I?" is a question answered in part by one's peers and teachers in the school system. We learn to evaluate ourselves relative to others on achievement tests of various kinds. We learn about good personal qualities and bad ones. We come to define ourselves as "good" or "bad" relative to the definitions of behavior and achievement that we have learned.

We are taught to value integrity, not to cheat on exams, and to uphold the honor systems of the schools we attend. We learn how to fit in with others socially. We learn about manners and social etiquette.

Stimulation of Social Change

Schools and particularly colleges are often regarded by the society at large as the pioneers or catalysts for innovation and change. Many colleges and universities are endowed by the government and various foundations with financial backing for innovative experimentation and research. Many of our societal achievements were pioneered in university research centers. Placing astronauts on the moon was accomplished largely because of research conducted at universities.

Our society *expects* education to answer technical questions, to provide panaceas or "cure-all's" for society's ills. We are tuned in to expecting results, and we expect the results to be satisfactory for problem resolution. We marvel at technological innovations and changes, but we accept as commonplace the fact that many of these changes occur in educational settings.

In lower education, however, many people have mixed feelings about innovation and change. When schools want to innovate with teaching methods or curricula—such as new math—we have ambivalent feelings regarding these innovations. This is in part because people are unfamiliar with the innovations proposed. Parents do not like to be asked questions by their children that they

Traditional classroom settings may not be as effective as open classrooms for special students such as these learning disabled children.

cannot answer. Many people only grudgingly accept innovation and change in the lower educational system, preferring to see our children receive the standard "three R's"—reading, 'riting, and 'rithmetic.

Education in the United States

When you hear or use the word "education," what do you mean? **Education** is a deliberate, systematic, and sustained effort to transmit or acquire knowledge, skills, attitudes, and values (Lewis et al. 1978b:2).

    Education may be informal; children learn from parents or other children. Education may be formal as well. Public and private elementary, secondary, and postsecondary schools, with a fixed number of grade or year levels, are typically what we associate with the term "education."

Education the deliberate, systematic, and sustained effort to transmit or acquire knowledge, skills, attitudes, and values.

Formal Education

    Formal education in the United States comprises a set of processes that are purposefully directed toward the accomplishment of learning. **Learning,** in turn, is a product of socialization, in which our culture is transmitted from one generation to another. Generally, learning is the alteration of behavior resulting from informal or formal education.

    The members of our society generally believe that an educational institution is an important contributor to the socialization of the young. In postsecondary education, the belief also persists that utilitarian skills or talents and knowledge will be imparted, and that persons so trained will emerge as "specialists" in chosen professions or occupations. At least they will be capable of learning more advanced skills in addition to those they acquire through their college or university experiences.

Learning the product of socialization, in which our culture is transmitted from one generation to another; also the alteration of behavior resulting from informal or formal education.

The Transition from Elite to Mass Education

    Education is no longer the exclusive province of the wealthy and well-to-do. In the early 1900s, it was most common for persons in the upper socioeconomic classes to attend colleges and universities and obtain first-class educations. Those persons could afford the high costs of education, whereas those in the lower socioeconomic classes could not. As a result, education was viewed as a luxury, as a privilege of the wealthy. Many poor persons simply had to be content with little or no formal education. A status system was being perpetuated in the United States with education as a great dividing line between the "haves" and the "have nots."

    Over the years, it became evident that for most persons to cope and survive in an increasingly competitive economic environment, they had to have greater amounts of formal education. High school education was adequate for many jobs at one point in our history. In the 1980s many more jobs require persons with some postsecondary education, if not a college degree. Even masters' degrees are increasingly necessary in our increasingly complex work world.

Our society is strongly committed to education on a mass basis. We have instituted various laws and requirements that set *minimal* levels for various learning achievements. These minimum standards in several achievement areas are relatively similar in most states, although each state adds special stipulations that have federal endorsement. There are also stipulations that specify penalties against persons, states, or school systems in which these standards are not regulated or upheld. The fact that legal machinery exists for reinforcing the educational standards of society further insures the perpetuation and relative uniformity of the educational system at the different grade and year levels.

The Uniformity of Education and the Education Process

In spite of the uniformity that characterizes most of our educational systems from one state to another, fluctuations do occur from one school system to another even within the same state. Such fluctuations reflect the fact that a certain amount of community control exists. Various forms of community control express the traditions and values of a particular community. The community insures that certain values will be imparted to the young by maintaining a degree of control over the school superintendent, the principals, and the teaching staff in these schools. Any teacher or principal who deviates too far from community values and informal guidelines (informally established within each community by its leadership) is sanctioned (positively or negatively) by some higher authority or organization, usually a school board. Of course, school personnel who conform to recommended community guidelines and standards are frequently rewarded by the significant figures of the community with various teaching achievements and related awards. Little latitude is permitted in teaching basic subjects in school curriculums on the elementary and secondary levels. But enough uniformity exists within and between states that we can still label this process as mass education.

Students go to school to learn specific facts about this society. They are also taught how to behave properly around others. Of course, instilling obedience to authority and work discipline in children and young adults in the various school grades is not a manifest function of school systems; rather, it is a *latent function*. Some persons regard these achievements as the "real goals" of schools. Other people want school systems to generate conforming products: If some students are rebellious, delinquent, and in other ways deviant, the school system is often blamed for not carrying out this "function." Note that such a function is also shared by the institutions of the family and religion, although those institutions are not liable to be attacked to the same degree as education. It seems to be the line of least resistance to attack the educator rather than the church or the family. If a student breaks the law, fails to get a job or hold it, or in any other way fails to perform in a manner expected of him or her by society, the blame is usually placed on the doorstep of the educational institution.

Frequent controversies also arise when a teacher or a school library obtains a book that the community-at-large finds offensive. Again, conflicts develop between basic community values and the values imparted by the schools (as seen through the eyes of community officials).

In the following discussion of educational issues and the educational system, we refer to "lower education" and "higher education." Lower education encompasses grades K-12 (kindergarten through the 12th grade or high school); higher education comprises community colleges, 4-year colleges, and universities. Considerably more emphasis is here placed upon educational systems in the public sector than the private sector.

It is beyond the scope of this chapter and this book to describe fully the processes, problems, and trends of education in the United States at all levels. Rather, we highlight here some of the more important characteristics that are particularly relevant and interesting to the sociologist. Probably no other single social institution receives as much criticism and is rewarded so little for its role in the socialization process.

Lower Education in the United States

Lower education consists of elementary and secondary schools. Perhaps the greatest uniformity occurs within the lower education years. Since public lower education is generally available to all who desire it, some writers have labeled it "massified."

One problem that has arisen in recent years pertains to the children of migrant workers in the Southwest and in other agricultural areas of the United States. As the cost of education at all levels has soared, many citizens have had substantial increases in their city and county property taxes. Angered by a greater tax burden, Americans in some parts of the country have demanded that children of migrant workers not be allowed to attend local elementary schools and high schools. Their belief appears to reflect the idea that many of these migrant workers are not citizens and have in fact entered the country illegally; and as illegal aliens, they should not be allowed to participate equally in our educational system. The Supreme Court of the United States heard a case involving the children of migrant workers in 1982. The result was a ruling by the Supreme Court that children of the migrant workers, regardless of their parents' alien status, could and should be extended all rights and privileges of the education process, the same as any United States citizen's children. This controversial ruling has not been favorably received by many dissident taxpayers.

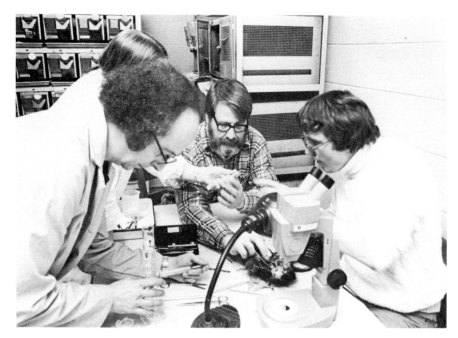

The more prestigious and complex the task performed in the workplace, usually the more education was demanded of the worker. This is increasingly the case today in our complex work world.

Lower education is financed by city and county property taxes in large part. State and local agencies regulate the curriculum and organizational structure of schools and school districts within the various states. Although there are differences within school systems and specific schools regarding faculty composition, ethnicity, race, and socioeconomic status, all of the schools are generally committed to insuring that a fairly uniform set of skills and educational principles are transmitted to the children processed by these institutions. These commitments are especially difficult to fulfill in systems that enroll large numbers of children from migrant families. The problem of dual-language schools arises as schools search for bilingual faculty who can teach in other languages as well as in English. The costs of operating dual-language schools are high and have no doubt contributed to the rising taxes necessary to offset such costs.

But state and local controls over public education do not insure that the same level of quality is sustained within all schools in a district or within all districts in a state. Each state allocates different dollar amounts for educational expenditures. New York spends considerably more per pupil than Mississippi or South Dakota. Generous educational budgets—which usually mean salaries—are likely to attract better teachers. One result appears to be a better education for students processed by certain schools (Wellisch et al. 1978).

These differences in funding from state to state in lower education have prompted some critics to complain that not all children subsequently graduating from high school have an equal footing for success in college. Children

THE FACTS · School Spending State by State

About $3 of every $10 spent by state and local governments last year went for education.

According to the Census Bureau, public-education spending rose 9.4% to a total of 145.8 billion dollars—an increase that occurred before President Reagan's slowdown in federal aid to education. Public grade schools cost 100.5 billion. Public colleges and universities cost 38.1 billion.

A state-by-state look at what was spent on public education, from kindergarten through college—

	Total Spent	Per Capita
Alaska	$0.8 bil.	$1,896
Wyoming	$0.5 bil.	$1,014
Washington	$3.4 bil.	$824
New Mexico	$1.0 bil.	$795
Oregon	$2.1 bil.	$788
Utah	$1.1 bil.	$756
Delaware	$0.4 bil.	$753
Michigan	$6.9 bil.	$748
Colorado	$2.2 bil.	$747
Wisconsin	$3.5 bil.	$743
North Dakota	$0.5 bil.	$733
Arizona	$2.0 bil.	$731
New York	$12.7 bil.	$724
California	$16.9 bil.	$716
Iowa	$2.1 bil.	$716
Montana	$0.6 bil.	$715
Minnesota	$2.9 bil.	$713
Maryland	$2.9 bil.	$688
Vermont	$0.4 bil.	$686
Nebraska	$1.1 bil.	$679
New Jersey	$5.0 bil.	$674
Kansas	$1.6 bil.	$669
Rhode Island	$0.6 bil.	$645
Oklahoma	$1.9 bil.	$637
Virginia	$3.4 bil.	$628
Hawaii	$0.6 bil.	$625
Louisiana	$2.6 bil.	$624
Texas	$8.7 bil.	$614
North Carolina	$3.6 bil.	$612
Illinois	$7.0 bil.	$609
South Carolina	$1.9 bil.	$604
Indiana	$3.3 bil.	$603
South Dakota	$0.4 bil.	$599
Connecticut	$1.8 bil.	$593
Massachusetts	$3.4 bil.	$593

Ohio	$6.4 bil.	$592
Idaho	$0.6 bil.	$587
Nevada	$0.5 bil.	$585
West Virginia	$1.1 bil.	$583
Dist. of Columbia	$0.4 bil.	$564
Pennsylvania	$6.6 bil.	$557
Mississippi	$1.4 bil.	$553
Alabama	$2.2 bil.	$553
New Hampshire	$0.5 bil.	$547
Georgia	$2.9 bil.	$531
Florida	$5.1 bil.	$527
Kentucky	$1.9 bil.	$525
Missouri	$2.6 bil.	$524
Arkansas	$1.2 bil.	$522
Maine	$0.6 bil.	$522
Tennessee	$2.2 bil.	$479
U.S.	**$145.8 bil.**	**$644**

SOURCE: *U.S. News & World Report,* December 13, 1982.

from less endowed schools may not read as well as children from so-called better schools. And there is the very real possibility that because better schools attract different teachers, the same kinds of values are not imparted from teacher to student in the lesser-quality schools. Some children may not be as highly motivated to achieve or to compete as those exposed to other educational environments.

Some critics of public schools in the United States contend that the teachers are drawn predominantly from the middle classes. Indeed, there is much evidence to support this criticism in the educational research literature (Williams 1976; Richer 1974). One result of this feature of lower education in the public sector is that middle-class values are imparted to children. In actual practice, middle-class values of competition and achievement tend to be more familiar to middle-class children, whereas these values operate *against* lower-class children who perhaps might not learn as well under conditions of competition and constant evaluation.

Lower education is conceivably perpetuating existing social inequality by ensuring that the prime beneficiaries of education are middle-class children who are rewarded by successful classroom experiences. Children from lower social classes perhaps do not do as well and may come to define themselves as unsuccessful, resenting their public education experiences. In the current job market, where increasing amounts of education are desired or required, a bias definitely exists in favor of middle-class and upper-class children, thereby placing lower-class children at a competitive disadvantage. The more financially rewarding positions are more likely to be filled by persons with greater amounts of education. It may be argued also that students are more inclined to pursue education if they find their early educational experiences satisfying and rewarding.

In 1980 about 86% of all children ages 5–17 in the population were enrolled in public elementary or high schools. Although the United States government has no clear national educational policy, system of financing, or administration of lower education, some striking similarities among elementary and secondary schools have come to be identified as characteristic of our public educational system.

Tracking

Tracking, or systematically placing children into one of several alternative "tracks" or curricula based on their educational achievement, is more the rule today than the exception.

Achievement tests administered to students at intervals during the years of lower education prompt school counselors to encourage (or discourage) certain students into (or away from) particular achievement goals. Some schools have "college prep" and "general" alternative programs. On the basis of their test scores, some children are encouraged to choose college preparation courses that usually involve a more difficult curriculum. Children who are encouraged to elect "general" courses gravitate toward easier curricula. If children who follow a "general" curriculum decide to enter college at a later point, they often find that they have skipped certain courses that are required for admission to higher education. The necessary remedial work can slow or hinder their progress and sometimes deter them from pursuing higher education. These students sometimes adopt a defeatist perspective: "Why bother going to college—I have too much course work to make up to make it worth my time and effort."

Tracking is commonly practiced in all educational years. Students who demonstrate more promise in academic areas such as liberal arts or general education are tracked into community colleges or four-year colleges. Students who demonstrate greater proficiency in mathematics or with figures in general may be "tracked" into commercial fields such as banking or business. Yet other students who seem to be skilled with their hands or appear to have a fairly good and quick grasp of mechanical devices are tracked into various vocational fields where such skills are assumed to be useful.

Some critics feel that tracking begins too early in a student's academic career. How is a student supposed to know whether or not he or she will like to be a businessperson or a lawyer or a lathe operator? In the 7th and 8th grades, where tracks are firmly established, students are encouraged to pursue certain vocations and occupations and discouraged from following others in which they may have an interest. On the other hand, some critics note that some students get to college without a clear perspective as to what they want to do and the courses they should take. These critics blame high school administrators for not tracking the student earlier.

The fact is that tracking is here to stay. The student is not obligated by

Tracking the process of channeling students into one type of curriculum or another depending on their skill level as determined by achievement tests and aptitude examinations.

law to stay in one track or another, but the pressures of the educational system are definitely weighted in favor of persons remaining in one track or another. Some critics have compared the American tracking system to the Indian caste system. James E. Rosenbaum observes that "the most effective weeding-out system in the schools is tracking. . . . tracking procedures produce a highly rigid stratification system much like that of a caste structure" (Rosenbaum 1975).

Making education available to the masses and insuring that most persons in our population receive at least a high school education has been and continues to be an American objective. For many years education has been seen by many idealists as the "great leveler," the institution destined to bring about equality of opportunity in the economic sector as well as in the pursuit of happiness. But considerable evidence exists to illustrate that education is not living up to the expectations people have of it in this respect.

Although not conclusive and most certainly controversial, the report directed by James Coleman (1966) offers an illuminating view of our lower educational system insofar as it affects students' life chances in the occupational sector. Coleman headed a research effort that was perhaps the largest ever undertaken: Over 600,000 students in elementary and secondary schools throughout the United States were studied. Among the variables investigated by Coleman and his associates were the extent to which educational facilities (libraries, financial expenditures) affected students' performance on standardized tests.

Several prevalent beliefs about our system of lower education were challenged and disputed by the Coleman report. One of the more profound results of the study revealed that differences in educational facilities or quality had virtually no impact on a student's success in academic achievement. Rather, it seemed more likely that students' socioeconomic background accounted for their success (or lack of success) in career attainment. Coleman found that middle-class values of teachers were consistent with the values of middle-class and upper-class children, and that children from these socioeconomic levels generally achieved significantly greater amounts of education (and better occupations and professions) than lower-class children.

Subsequent research has supported the original investigation by Coleman and his associates. Christopher Jencks (1972) conducted an extensive study of lower education and found that large appropriations and educational expenditures in various school districts had no effect upon student achievement and subsequent life chances. His studies again revealed that persons' middle-class or upper-class values tended to bias them toward achieving higher education. Students from lower socioeconomic strata tended to do less well on achievement tests and to be less inclined to pursue college or university work.

Although these studies are inconclusive regarding the true impact of educational environment on student achievement, they do nevertheless underscore the dilemma of whether schools can operate to eliminate inequality of educational and occupational opportunity in America today.

It is increasingly clear that family background and general socioeconomic condition are greater determinants of one's academic success than the quality of educational facilities. Some well-equipped schools have been made available to children from the lower socioeconomic segments of society. These superior educational surroundings failed to have the desired effect of raising general achievement levels of pupils. Curricula continued to be geared in favor of middle-class youths, and teachers with middle-class orientations continued to reflect latent biases toward such students in the classroom.

The "Self-Fulfilling Prophecy" and Labeling

Closely related to the matter of equality of educational opportunity in America and the middle-class bias of teachers in lower education is the extent to which teachers themselves perpetuate inequality through projective differential treatment of students from different social classes. Trevor Williams (1976) studied 10,500 high school students in an effort to determine the extent to which the "self-fulfilling prophecies" of teachers were instrumental in perpetuating social class differences in educational achievement.

The notion of **self-fulfilling prophecy** means, in effect, that whatever situations persons define as real will be real in their consequences (Merton 1957:421). (See Chapter 6, Social Inequality, for a more thorough review of this and related phenomena.) Applying the concept to the educational setting, Williams observes that "if teachers prophesy that students will do well (or poorly) in school they will, in fact, do well (or poorly) as a result" (Williams 1976:223). Williams believes that teachers are influenced in their treatment of students by the students' manner of dress and mode of behavior. In many respects, this notion is consistent with the belief that middle-class teachers tend to reward middle-class and upper-class students more than lower-class students.

Williams found that teachers' expectations of student achievement had little or no effect on actual material learned. However, such expectations did seem to matter when teachers themselves evaluated student performance and assigned grades. Williams observes that "given the importance of grades for a student's status within the school, and for ultimate certification by the school, this finding assumes some importance. Teacher prophecies do not affect so much what is learned, but affect instead the certification of this learning within the school" (1976:234).

Some persons refer to this phenomenon as "labeling." Teachers often label students by their appearance or behavior. Students who conform to middle-class expectations in dress and behavior are labeled as "more successful" and "better fitted" to school life and work. Students who do not fit these behavioral expectations as well (typically students from the lower social classes) are less likely to receive approval and rewards from their teachers. A vicious cycle is instituted, therefore, in which better students are aided by more positive definitions of their performance by teachers, and the poorer children receive no such reinforcements and rewards.

The middle-classness of American lower education also tends to operate against minorities. In the Southwest, persons of Hispanic or Indian origin may use English as a "second language." This characteristic of some students handicaps them in fulfilling the expectations of their teachers, who tend to be predominantly white and middle class.

Busing

Blacks as a minority have endured a variety of problems over the years. In education, blacks have been segregated by various local laws in the past (*de jure segregation*), although such laws have now been determined to be unconstitutional. Community segregation in housing has led to a different type of segregation in schools, *de facto segregation,* in which the racial composition of schools is determined by residential housing patterns. If a neighborhood's housing is segregated racially, schools in that neighborhood are probably segregated racially too.

In the late 1960s and early 1970s, massive efforts were undertaken by federal, state, and local governments to ensure equality of educational opportunity for persons of all races through **busing,** or physically transporting children who live in one neighborhood to schools in another neighborhood, often many miles from their home. This busing policy often meant that black students would be "bused" to predominantly white schools, although some white children have been bused to predominantly black schools.

The objective of busing was to promote equal educational opportunity by insuring that members of all races would have access to education in so-called better schools. The studies by Coleman (1966) and Jencks (1972) have tended to discount and discredit the value of busing and its potential effect of attaining educational equality for the children involved. Their findings were and still are the subject of criticism and debate, but the social effects and the educational impact of busing have been inconsequential as well. A proportion of white parents in areas where busing has occurred have transferred their children to private schools, where available. In some instances legal means have been sought to prevent busing in particular neighborhoods. Critics of busing continued to question whether it positively affects the equality of educational opportunity for students involved in it. If Coleman and Jencks are on target with their findings, we must seek answers to differential educational attainment beyond the classroom.

Another question raised by the busing controversy is whether it has led to higher levels of social acceptance between whites and blacks. Given the fact that the social impact and effect of busing was not assessed by the research of Coleman and Jencks, the question remains unanswered at present.

Busing the physical transporting of children from one neighborhood to schools in another neighborhood in an effort to achieve racial balance.

Higher Education in the United States

Today there are approximately 3,100 colleges and universities in the United States. Almost one million bachelor's degrees were conferred in 1978, more than double the number of degrees awarded in 1950. With an ever-increasing number of persons attending colleges and universities today, our attention has focused more and more upon the role of higher education in our society, its functions and its overall effectiveness.

Higher education is perceived by society as one of the most important (if not the most important) means of acquiring high status, professional and occupational rewards, high income, and certain recognition. Business and industry have come to rely increasingly upon colleges and universities as "feeder" facilities, supplying a stream of adequately trained graduates to take positions in those fields.

Universities and colleges are regarded as bastions of creativity, invention, and innovation. Social changes of both small and large magnitude are seen as occurring first within the educational realm, and then within the society at large. Changes in technology have caused many persons to embark upon courses of study in our institutions of higher learning in order that they might secure employment in an expanding technical world.

Higher education, like lower education, includes public and private institutions. Two-year community colleges and junior colleges offer students an opportunity to obtain college experience without having to endure a 4-year tour of duty, as well as a stepping-stone to senior colleges. Colleges offering a 4-year course of study typically award bachelor's degrees of various kinds. Universities offer additional education beyond bachelor's degrees, such as master's degrees and doctor's degrees. Some universities also have law schools, medical schools, and other professional schools.

Each type of institution of higher learning has different priorities or em-

Members of minority groups may seek advanced education in order to increase their opportunities for social mobility.

phases. Junior colleges and community colleges often emphasize a liberal arts curriculum, close teacher/student contact, smaller student bodies, and preparation (potentially) for further higher education elsewhere. In some community colleges, two-year vocational programs are offered. Universities emphasize research and innovative investigations. Quality teaching is desirable, but publishable results are more highly prized. University faculty members who publish or who do research of one sort or another usually receive more recognition by the university administration; they are often promoted more rapidly and are rewarded more highly than faculty members who emphasize quality teaching at the expense of research efforts.

Different educational environments tend to attract different kinds of students with a variety of educational objectives. Although the standards for admission to many universities and colleges are similar, small 4-year colleges and community colleges attract some students who want to see what college is like and who may or may not like it. Accordingly, they may or may not continue their education at a large university when they have completed their shorter curriculum requirements. Clark Kerr, a former chancellor of the University of California system, has observed that junior colleges and community colleges are often effective as "cooling out" institutions. That is, they lead to a greater number of **drop-outs** or persons who discontinue their educational work after they find out that college life is not for them.

Drop-out a person who leaves school without completing a degree program.

Many college students are in college (or in a university environment) because they have been told (by counselors or other significant persons) that a college degree is the key to a good job and upward social mobility. They also know that they need to acquire numerous skills to be economically competitive in the job market in our increasingly sophisticated technological society.

Whatever the motivation of today's college and university student, entry into some of the largest universities in the country means entering a "multiversity," a small metropolis of anonymity and impersonality. Student schedules are increasingly computer-determined, and in many large classes students have no direct contact with a faculty member. Some faculty utilize closed-circuit television services as a means of communicating with thousands of students at one time. Exams are often machine-scored.

Universities are increasingly bureaucratic institutions, governed by rules and regulations, procedures and protocols, and by large, business-like administrations. In fact, many universities have taken on a "big business" character or atmosphere. As "feeder institutions" to business and industry, universities are training areas for successive waves of students on their way up the mobility ladder.

Assisting in this transition is the federal government. Over the years the federal government has made available to many colleges and universities research funds. To a great extent, many colleges and universities have come to depend upon the federal government for monetary support in the form of grants and research contracts. This has only served to increase the dependency of institutions of higher learning upon the federal government.

Faculty in the larger universities have become increasingly specialized and segmented into various departments. As the university system has become increasingly bureaucratized and specialized, faculty members have begun to act like employees in a large bureaucracy. To this extent, many faculty members have lost sight of the original goals and purposes of the university as a learning facility. Some faculties have organized unions and have emulated more and more their counterparts in the blue-collar segments of industry.

As universities and colleges have grown in size and complexity, faculty are no longer able to maintain a personalized relation between themselves and students. It is rare to find a close teacher/student learning relation on today's college campuses. The mounting pressure on faculty to publish and to be "productive" has been aggravated by numerous evaluation studies of the quality of higher education in America. Many schools have been lured to participate in a national ranking game where the prestige of each institution is assessed in faculty prestige, which is in turn assessed by how "productive" faculty have been. Productivity invariably has been measured by quality and quantity of research publications and books, grants awarded, and other visible educational accomplishments (Cartter 1966).

During the latter 1970s, many schools experienced (and are continuing to experience) financial difficulties. Particularly affected were many small liberal arts colleges whose support depended largely upon contributions from alumni and friends. Priority shifts in federal government agencies caused many larger schools to reexamine their existing needs and requirements as federal funds were gradually removed. The fact that today comparatively few grants of any kind are awarded for pursuing pure knowledge for the sake of knowledge means that many departments with liberal arts affiliations are suffering from a general lack of funds.

In the 1980s academic circles have felt a stress on utility and technological preparedness. For many professors, the shift away from theory and toward hard scientific inquiry in the university setting has led them to reevaluate their place in higher learning. Some professors have left the university for positions in the business world. Others who have remained with their colleges or universities have been obliged to alter drastically their professional objectives toward more practical ends.

We are in an "age of accountability," where students are demanding better services than have been provided to date. Higher education, to some critics, has not been doing an effective job of preparing graduates for jobs in our increasingly technical work environment. More professors are being called upon to account for their actions in terms of the utility and practical value associated with their teaching and research activity.

At the beginning of this chapter, a hypothetical case was being heard in a court of law. A student was suing an educational institution for damages, for failure to perform services (malpractice) that in turn adversely affected the student's life chances and ability to realize certain occupational and professional goals. This sort of case is rapidly becoming a fact rather than an isolated instance of a student activist or malcontent desiring publicity through legal channels.

For some persons, our higher educational system is out-dated and based upon a false image of what the future has in store (Toffler 1970). Instead of perpetuating a rigid learning atmosphere, academics are encouraged to modify existing learning arrangements to be more flexible and adaptive to anticipated rapid social changes and technological developments. Americans continue to view our higher educational establishment as critical to the preservation and perpetuation of a healthy society.

Future Trends in American Education

It is difficult to forecast trends in any field, especially one in which changes have been occurring over the last 10-year period at an ever-increasing rate. But certain developments on our technological fronts and economic horizons have made it possible to anticipate certain things. Among the more important changes in the educational system over the next two decades are the following: (1) declining enrollments in both lower and higher educational institutions; (2) advances in technological hardware and software that will make possible improved instruction and more flexibility in quality and quantity of teaching; (3) increased federal, state, and local control over both lower and higher education, with accountability emerging as a chief concern at all governmental levels; (4) a growing rate of conferring tenure upon college and university faculty; and (5) a greater importance of continuing education, particularly for older persons in the population.

Declining Enrollments

As families in the United States continue to limit the number of children and postpone having children until later in their careers, the numbers of students in both lower and higher education will decline appreciably. It may be argued that such reductions in enrollments will reduce the need for more teachers. But it may also be argued that smaller class sizes will improve teaching quality and provide students with more personalized instruction, a condition many students do not currently enjoy.

Technological Advancements

The increased use of closed-circuit television in classrooms will make it possible for teachers to provide more flexible instruction to more students and to attempt new and different educational innovations. Students may be able to replay earlier lectures that they may have missed because of illness, or they may repeat lectures for greater learning retention.

The growing use of high-speed retrieval devices in libraries will facilitate a student's ability to study certain subjects more effectively. Rather than seeking help from a librarian or card catalog, a student will merely program a display board in the library with information requested. In seconds the information needed will be displayed. Entire books may be stored in such computer systems for instant retrieval by anyone. The library as we knew it is rapidly becoming a historical relic, gradually replaced by computers with vast memory capacities and retrieval capabilities.

Increased State and Local Control

Society is demanding a greater voice in the sorts of courses and materials taught in contemporary classroom settings. As taxpayers are called upon to provide more funds for "quality" education (whether this comes about through greater expenditures or not is unclear at present), they will demand a greater voice in the kinds of educational experiences their children will have. More and more we will come to rely upon and demand from our educators greater efforts in teaching effectiveness and greater accountability and responsibility regarding practical curriculums.

Many universities and colleges are continually striving to eliminate from their curriculums duplications of courses or areas of study that have small enrollments and that serve little function. The true functional importance of each field is going to be increasingly scrutinized by state legislators and boards of higher education. Many schools will be hard-pressed to justify the continuation of programs regarded as frivolous or as luxuries. In 1982 a professor at Long Beach State University became the subject of controversy when he conducted a course in psychology permitting college credit to be obtained for in-class sexual experiences in the name of "sexual awareness." Even the otherwise liberal society of southern California found such a course offensive and moved to have it discontinued. The professor resigned shortly after it was canceled.

Growing Rate of Tenure

More educators will expect greater job security from their respective educational institutions. During the latter part of the 1970s and continuing into the 1980s, many professors left university settings to pursue careers in business or industry. Such career moves often mean considerably more money and greater job security beyond what is available in academia. In response to such an exodus of faculty, many universities and colleges are finding it necessary to make the academic setting more attractive to faculty.

One method of making the university setting more attractive for faculty is to award *tenure* to them at an increasing rate. **Tenure** is in effect a guarantee from a university that a professor will not be fired or dismissed except under circumstances of dire economic emergency or for moral violations. Today, tenured faculty at many colleges and universities make up a large proportion of those faculties.

The more prestigious universities and colleges do not necessarily follow the lead of less prestigious institutions in the granting of tenure. Harvard, Yale, Columbia, and other established universities are probably able to retain most

Tenure a guarantee to a faculty member, usually by a college or university, that the institution will not fire him or her except under circumstances of dire economic emergency or for moral violations.

of their faculty because of their reputation. Less well-known universities often have to use tenure as well as other rewards to retain faculty who threaten to resign. One such tactic to entice faculty to stay with the system is to offer a lucrative early retirement benefit. The University of Florida is currently offering faculty the opportunity of retiring at age 55 at 110% of their base salary. Although this may sound unusual, the Florida university system is considering the fact that they will be able to hire two or three other faculty for much less money to replace the higher paid retiring persons. This is one way of reducing education costs.

Greater Importance of Continuing Education

One indication of the growing flexibility of institutions of higher learning is the development of programs of continuing education. Continuing education is specifically designed to offer college courses to persons who cannot enroll in on-campus classes, who have been out of school for many years, or who have never had an opportunity to earn any college credits. It is also used for recertification of professional personnel.

Senior citizens, persons who have retired early, persons suffering from disabilities, handicapped persons, and parents who no longer have the responsibilities of rearing children have been reentering universities and colleges at an increasing rate to learn new subjects or to learn new skills. Many of these older persons returning to higher education are responding to the economic demand for more technical education and to the need for greater skills in order to become more occupationally competitive. Others are reflecting early retirement or growing amounts of leisure time, and they seek meaningful and fruitful ways of filling their time. Certainly the reentry of older persons in school settings is giving current educators a new perspective on their own roles.

Summary

The sociologist views education and the educational system as basic to the perpetuation of society. It is one of the key socializing institutions.

Between 1970 and 1980, educational costs rose by 77%.

The functions of education include transmitting culture, integrating society's membership, and facilitating the development of personal qualities.

Education also screens and selects certain persons to perform particular roles in society. This is called "tracking" and is part of the "cooling out" function performed by higher education.

Education is the deliberate, systematic, and sustained effort to transmit or acquire knowledge, skills, attitudes, and values. Education may be either formal or informal.

During the past 25 years, education has shifted from an elite institution to a mass institution, available to almost anyone who desires it.

Lower education in the United States is highly standardized. There is also evident a middle-class bias operating in many classrooms to the benefit of students of middle-class and upper-class backgrounds and to the detriment of students from lower-class backgrounds.

Lower education has faced a number of problems during the last several decades. Among these is busing of students from one school district to another school district. Busing is seen as one way of restoring racial balance in schools. Some persons view busing as a form of forced integration.

Higher education is undergoing numerous transformations at present. Declining enrollments and technological advancements are making it possible to offer a higher quality education to students with smaller class sizes and to increase technical innovations in the teaching process.

More of the older adults in the population are reentering schools to achieve the education they missed as young adults.

Continuing education is growing to meet the needs of older persons who seek higher education.

Suggested Readings

Randall Collins. *The Credential Society: An Historical Sociology of Education and Stratification.* New York: Academic Press, 1979. This very readable book examines changes in the educational institution over time that parallel our social class structure. Shows the interplay between social stratification and the role of education in society.

A. V. Cicourel and J. I. Kitsuse. *The Educational Decision-Makers.* Indianapolis, Ind.: Bobbs-Merrill, 1963. An examination of values in conflict as curriculums are determined and educational priorities are established. The vested interests and bureaucratic powers are described that control a principal socializing medium in our social system.

Paul Goodman. *Compulsory Mis-Education.* New York: Vintage Books, 1962. Argues that some school curriculums and lines of coursework do not meaningfully relate to current labor demands and employer expectations; our educational priorities need to be reexamined in view of the rapidly changing quality of our division of labor.

Ronald P. Dore. *The Diploma Disease.* Berkeley and Los Angeles: University of California Press, 1976. Partly the fault of our major industries and businesses and partly a result of the processes of social stratification, increased importance on degree attainment forces people into degree programs that are not relevant to their career interests. Highlights the preoccupation of our society with advanced degrees.

John Holt. *How Children Fail.* New York: Dell, 1970. A critical examination of our educational system and the factors that lead to differential rates of learning and achievement.

Henry M. Levin. "Schooling and Inequality: The Social Science Objectivity Gap." *Saturday Review,* November 11, 1972, pp. 49–51. A critical analysis of the inequality of educational opportunity in America.

Jerome Karabel and A. H. Halsey (eds.). *Power and Ideology in Education.* New York: Oxford University Press, 1977. The interplay between societal values and education as an instrument of power.

14 Religion

Americans in general emphasize rationality, but some people believe that certain objects bring them good luck (rabbit's feet, four leaf clovers, clothing worn at a certain event) or that some actions bring bad luck (breaking mirrors, walking under ladders, opening umbrellas indoors) and other actions ward off bad luck (throwing salt over the shoulder). Superstition about the number thirteen may be laughed about, but many tall buildings do not have a thirteenth floor.

Can we know the future? For some time newspapers have printed horoscopes. In the 1960s and 1970s interest in astrology increased. Some people believe that they "know" someone's personality if they learn the person's zodiac sign. Fortune tellers continue to make a living predicting people's destinies. The Ouija board is used at least half seriously by some for spiritual communication.

People in postindustrial societies tend to pride themselves on their rational and sophisticated thought processes; they may even scoff at beliefs endorsed by people at other times and in other societies. People who consider themselves modern expect science to provide answers to questions about this world; even if scientific answers are not available now, such people expect they will be in the future. Nevertheless, for many Americans, theology provides answers to the questions that science is not expected to answer, questions of otherworldly affairs.

The Nature of Religion

Religion has been studied by sociologists since the discipline was founded, for, in one form or another, religion plays a role in all known societies. Sociologists who focus on the study of religion do not define a single set of fundamental characteristics of religion, since religion takes many forms. Most sociologists, however, use the term **religion** to refer to a belief system that emphasizes the supernatural. Some sociologists examine belief systems to see if they endorse the existence of a god or gods. Others examine belief systems that include any acceptance of, or commitment to, an awe-inspiring object or idea.

Religion a belief system that emphasizes the supernatural.

In his classic study, *The Elementary Forms of Religious Life*, Emile Durkheim defined religion as "a unified system of beliefs and practices relative to sacred things" (Durkheim 1915:62). Religious symbols and meanings shape the world views, thoughts, and beliefs of their adherents. Sociologists are interested in how believers' actions are related to their commitments to any given system of meanings. Durkheim and later sociologists recognized that people who share common beliefs and practices form moral communities or religious groups and that religions are tied to communities of believers.

Durkheim used anthropological reports on the Zuni Indians and Australian aborigines in his search for the fundamental characteristics of religion. After examining religious forms of expression in these primitive societies, he concluded that the source of religion was society itself. Objects held to be religious or awe-inspiring were actually symbolic manifestations or expressions of social arrangements among members of the society or between them and the physical environment.

In Australia, for instance, aborigines were organized into clans. Each clan used some object in the environment as a symbolic representation and extension of their shared or collective conscious. These objects became synonymous with clan identity. Such objects are called *totems.* When clan members gathered they engaged in rituals that expressed their sense of awe for the totem, as well as bonding with it. In short, a totem was **sacred.** Clan members interacted with the supernatural by performing clan rituals. The social function of religion or totem worship was in creating and maintaining a sense of social belonging. The social order and the religious or moral order were one and the same. A person excluded from clan rituals was an outsider, and to live outside this social and religious circle was to be **profane** (Durkheim 1915).

Sacred   what people hold to be awe-inspiring, worthy of religious worship.

Profane   all that is not worthy of religious worship.

The degree to which religion is either central or peripheral in a society depends on how interwoven religious beliefs and activities are with the society's other social institutions.

In some societies, such as post-revolutionary Iran, religious thought, rules, and rituals dominate all aspects of social life. Religious thought becomes the framework even for decisions shaping foreign policy. Shadings of interpretation of various religious tenets and doctrines affect political organizations. The moral (religious) order may also shape the system of law and punishment, as in Hammurabi's Code of Laws, the oldest known example. These same codes of conduct structure the interactions between various groups within society (young and old, male and female, rich and poor). In short, in some societies the moral order defined by the prevailing religion is the foundation of the social and political orders.

In societies such as the United States, religion is merely one of many social institutions. Structural functionalists argue that religion interrelates with politics, the economy, and the family. Each of these institutions contributes rules, standards, beliefs, and goals in the elaboration of society's moral framework. However, the religious institution performs primarily integrative functions.

In countries such as the USSR, religion is an institution officially separate from the basic rules, beliefs, and goals of society. Religion does serve a role in shaping the values and identities of members of various subcommunities, but the government emphasis on nonreligious interpretations of life is antithetical to religious emphasis on the supernatural and the sacred. The United States emphasizes separation of church and state, but the USSR officially opposes religion.

When examining religion as a societal institution, sociologists often focus on one of three components: beliefs, rituals, and religious organizations.

Features of Institutionalized Religion

Beliefs

Sociologists have analyzed both the content and structure of various belief systems. Groups have myths and folk legends that explain the origins of the world, the nature of god or gods, and humans' genesis and struggles for survival as well as their particular group's greatness. In Western societies theologies developed that explained the meaning of god and the mission of believers to fulfill god's universal plan (Georges 1968).

Primitive Religions.   One of the ways to classify belief systems comes from the efforts of anthropologists to distinguish between various types of primitive religions and to distinguish between advanced and primitive religions (Lowie 1924). The term **primitive religion** is used simply to designate the belief system of nonliterate tribes or groups (Goode 1951). Many anthropologists distinguish two types of primitive religion: preanimism (sometimes called supernaturalism) and animism. **Preanimism** holds that the world around people is in flux. A force or fluid spirit moves about. This force may invest itself in objects thus giving them a potency they otherwise would not have. Objects invested with this potency evoke a sense of awe or admiration, if not fear among believers. People occasionally may be touched by the force.

Societies assign various terms to signify what they believe is the force or fluid spirit and call upon it in different ways. Japanese sometimes express this extraordinary quality as *kami*. Polynesians call it *mana*. Its presence affects

Primitive religion the belief system of a nonliterate tribe or group.

Preanimism a religious belief system that emphasizes the importance of a force or fluid spirit.

A few sects believe that being able to handle poisonous snakes or to drink poison and survive demonstrates that a person is "right with God."

social events, and believers engage in rituals and ceremonies to insure its presence. Cheyenne warriors before going into battle prayed, fasted, and abstained from sexual intercourse to ensure the spirit force would be strong and their chances of victory increased. In the movie *Star Wars* the phrase "may the Force be with you" referred to the hope that a person would be touched by a force or spirit and have greater powers as a consequence.

Closely akin to preanimism is animism. **Animism** holds that the social and physical world is inhabited by spirits. These spirits may or may not be the spirits of deceased group members. Spirits are capricious and must be humored, for they are capable of striking out from the spirit world to harm the living. The spirits control sickness, health, and death, so they are very important.

Animism a religious belief system that holds that the social and physical world is inhabited by spirits.

Spirits may reach the living when they are conscious or when they are dreaming or hallucinating. To avoid interference from spirits, group members must perform rituals to propriate and supplicate them (Tylor 1871). The Kung, an African tribe, after a successful hunt leave a portion of their kill to feed the spirits and insure good hunting in the future. In other tribes the names of the dead are taboo (never mentioned), for the people fear that the spirits will awaken and cause harm to the living.

Give some examples of superstitions rooted in animistic thought.

Advanced Religions.   A social group that is literate or at least has an educated subgroup of religious leaders is said to have an **advanced religion.** The mythologies and theologies of advanced religions may be classified as theistic or abstract. A theistic religion involves belief in a being or beings who are greater than mortals—a god or gods. The supreme being or beings are assigned somewhat different characteristics by practitioners of different religions.

Advanced religion a belief system maintained by a literate population or an educated subgroup of religious leaders.

Believers in Christianity, Judaism, and Islam recognize one god; that type of religion is called **monotheism.** Yet their conceptions of the supreme being vary.

Monotheism a religious belief system that recognizes one god.

Another type of religion is called **polytheism.** Such religions recognize a pantheon or a number of gods. Typically each god controls some specific aspect of nature. For the ancient Romans, Mars was the god of war and Mercury the god of trade and good gifts. For the ancient Greeks, Pan was the god of hunters and shepherds and Hermes the messenger of the other gods. The Greek gods were shown falling in love and having families. Zeus was the king of Greek gods, and Hera his sister and wife. Thus mythological beliefs in some ways paralleled social arrangements in the society.

Polytheism a religious belief system that recognizes a number of gods or goddesses.

The other form of advanced religion is the **abstract.** The abstract position asserts that a force stands in total transcendence to humans and nature. The abstract force is timeless, eternal, and may only be understood if people reach an extraordinary state for humans, that is, true enlightenment. Buddhism, some forms of Hinduism, and mysticism are examples of abstract religions.

Abstract an advanced religion that asserts that a force stands in total transcendence to humans and nature.

Assuming one of the many yoga positions is part of the ritual associated with meditation.

These various systems of religious beliefs provide people with means of understanding the world and human existence, and provide people with guidelines or motives for action. Statements of faith serve to shape individuals' thoughts and behaviors when dealing with religious objects (objects of awe) as well as with nonreligious objects (including other people). Some religions provide guidelines even for specific everyday behaviors. After the revolution in Iran, the people were encouraged to follow traditional religious prescriptions for behavior. In the United States some people use religious guidelines extensively in planning their daily behavior, but many use them much less extensively than in previous eras. At one time stores were closed on Sunday in the United States in recognition of Sunday as the Christian sabbath. In most areas of our country, Sunday "blue laws" are no longer in effect, so those who treat Sunday as a complete day of rest do so voluntarily because of their beliefs.

Interplay of Belief Systems and the Social Structure. The meanings and motives in religious belief systems serve as cultural guides for individuals' daily actions. These meanings and motives are part of the symbolic frameworks that people use to interpret human relationships and the cosmos. Sociologists seek to account for the emergence of particular types of religious orientations. Some sociologists emphasize economic aspects, the mode of production. Others stress the importance of authority relationships.

Sociologists who emphasize modes of production note that gathering

People who profess belief in a religion may vary considerably in how knowledgeable they are about the doctrines of their religion. Larger religious groups (churches) may establish special schools (seminaries) to instruct those planning to pursue religious leadership roles (priest, rabbis, ministers). Small religious groups (sects) tend to deemphasize special training; all adherents are expected to be knowledgeable. Still other religious organizations (cults) may rely on a charismatic leader who passes on to followers divine messages. Those who constitute the general membership in any religious organization receive continual indoctrination through participation in religious services and the reading of religious publications.

Many children receive some religious training during their socialization within family units. Religious organizations often provide special training for children in the form of Sunday school or Hebrew school. Children often are required to demonstrate knowledge of their group's religious beliefs before they can become full-fledged members of the religious organization (through confirmation, adult baptism, or bar mitzvah). If people continue to belong to their parents' religious organization when adults, their knowledge of religious tenets may be taken for granted.

Rodney Stark and Charles Glock (1968) surveyed northern California adults to find out among other things if church members could articulate the tenets and doctrines of their religion. Respondents often could not recite all Ten Commandments. Christian groups apparently vary in how well they teach the commandments or how much emphasis they place on them, for members of some religious organizations consistently performed better than others. While 34% of the Roman Catholics could recite them, among Protestants the range was from 27% for Missouri Synod Lutherans to 1% for Congregationalists. Can you remember all Ten Commandments?

One reason people may not be knowledgeable about religious doctrines is that some of them do not fit with their personal belief systems, and those they deemphasize— or forget. Stark and Glock found that some Christians did not endorse statements of presumably core Christian beliefs. The percentage stating that they had no doubts that God exists ranged from 99% for Southern Baptists to 41% for Congregationalists. "Belief in life beyond death" was endorsed by 94% of Southern Baptists and 36% of Congregationalists. "Belief in the existence of the devil" ranged from 92% of the former to 6% of the latter. Apparently Congregationalists diverge more from traditional Christian beliefs than Southern Baptists do.

---

and hunting, horticultural, and agrarian societies (preindustrial agricultural) often treat nature as mechanistic. The nineteenth century conception of theism incorporated this idea. People in such societies are much more subject to the vagaries of nature than people in postindustrial societies. All elements are tied to one another, and changes in one aspect of nature affect others. People living directly off the land must learn to accommodate to the endlessly recurring seasons. They must learn when to sow and when to reap. They must recognize what kinds of crops flourish and which do not. Past experience is important. Members of the society must carefully follow traditions and respect nature, or it is assumed they will fail.

The world views in such preindustrial societies tend to resist change and experimentation. People rely on what worked in the past because they know from the elders in their societies that such practices worked. If people fail whether they attempt new practices or not, their failures are viewed as proof that they did not achieve harmony with nature. Some classic examples of such world views were peasant farmers' practices of divination and geomancy in China and Japan before industrialization (Fung 1960).

In industrial societies, people are encouraged to adopt world views different from those of earlier kinds of society, for old ways of doing things often do not work any more and new ways get quickly replaced by even newer ways. Greater percentages of populations in these societies are literate, and many more activities require literacy.

People in industrial societies tend to view nature as ordered but constantly unfolding, always changing. To adapt to such a world, people must discover principles that describe and explain the changing world. People believe they can structure how they relate to nature rather than adapting blindly to changes. Explanations that work are added to the body of technological knowledge, and those that fail are rejected and forgotten. Failures lead to new strategies rather than to retreat to the old ways. Thus change and experimentation are fostered. Once new ways are found to be successful, people believe they have gained some mastery over an aspect of nature. The Western European and American ethos during the heyday of industrialization typified this world view (Kallen 1965).

How may religious beliefs relate to various economic systems?

Societies with traditional authority systems (see Chapter 10) tend to endorse religious myths and maxims that justify the superiority of their rulers, the beneficence of the rulers' actions, and the rewards subordinates achieve by carrying the twin mantles of duty and indebtedness to the rulers. In some instances myths trace the rulers back to gods and goddesses, thus defining the rulers as different from other mortals. Shintoism asserts that the Japanese emperor is a direct descendant of the sun god and goddess (Tsunoda et al. 1958). In Japan, Buddhism stressed the notion that acts of giving obligate the receiver (engender indebtedness). The receiver must strive to repay the giver, but the indebtedness can never be erased if the giver is of superior rank. In China a ruler received a mandate from heaven. When a dynasty was overthrown, the ruler simply lost the mandate. In Western societies the concept of the "divine right" of kings developed. These societies are usually *agrarian.*

In societies with more representative forms of authority systems, leaders may try to demonstrate that they are faithful religious adherents, but attempts to claim a divine right to rule would not be accepted.

How do rulers benefit from legitimation of their authority by religious belief systems?

Rituals

Another key aspect of institutionalized religion is ritual. As religious systems differ in content and structure of beliefs, so they also differ in the content and structure of rituals. **Ritual** is a set pattern of behavior or activity rooted in tradition and symbolism. Rituals relate to beliefs, as shown by rituals that mark the beginning and end of addresses to the force, the spirits, or the gods; such as Catholics' dipping fingers in holy water and crossing themselves upon entering a church, or Moslems' bowing to Mecca when praying to Allah, or Hindus' assuming a yoga position when meditating. Also, rituals mark various points in worship, supplication, and meditation, for example, chanting, singing, ringing bells, lighting incense, eating or drinking special substances. The diversity of rituals is of less concern to sociologists than when and why people engage in them.

Rituals serve not only as signs of faith among religious adherents, but mark off believers from nonbelievers. Rituals become visible professions or acts of faith, as well as public statements of moral commitment. In some instances the practice of a ritual is more important as a public sign of commitment than as a personal commitment to a system of beliefs. Religious leaders become concerned when people appear to engage routinely in rituals without thinking about the symbolic meaning of the ritual.

Tension in many religious organizations revolves around the need to maintain both continuity *and* vitality of rituals. The problem is, can religious leaders eliminate rituals developed under different historical conditions that now appear to be followed merely by rote, while still maintaining a sense of continuity with a long religious tradition? Orthodox, Conservative, and Reform Jewish congregations long have debated changes in ritual. Similarly, changes in the Catholic mass, such as the switch from Latin to vernacular languages, generated intense debate both before and after adoption. Debates about rituals and their meanings sometimes lead some groups to break away from traditional religious organizations and form new or schismatic organizations.

Ritual   a set pattern of behavior or activity rooted in tradition and symbolism.

Identify some of the rituals practiced by a religious group you know.

Types of Religious Organizations

People whose religious beliefs are similar may nevertheless form different religious organizations. Ernst Troeltsch (1960), when attempting to untangle the historical splintering of various protesting groups that broke away from the Roman Catholic church, identified two types of Christian religious organizations: church and sect. We examine these as well as two additional types of organizations: denominations and cults. These religious organizations vary in size, mode of organization, stability of membership, ties with the secular world, nature of doctrine, and style of ritual. Table 14.1 presents information on the size of various U.S. religious organizations.

Church. A **church** has a large membership. Individuals are usually born into the faith and follow it because their parents did. The clergy is organized into a rigid hierarchy. Clergy and church officials are specifically trained or socialized for their occupations. Doctrine is systematized; religious tenets and credos are developed to address problems the faithful encounter in the profane world outside the church. The congregation participates minimally in services (rituals) that are conducted by religious specialists, the clergy.

A religious organization that includes all or most of the people in a society may become an **ecclesia,** the religious body officially recognized by those who govern. During the Middle Ages the Roman Catholic church operated as the official religion in European societies. The early Protestant churches also became the officially recognized religious bodies in many parts of Europe. During various Chinese dynasties different religions served as state religions: Confucianism, Taoism, and legalism. Today Islam is the official state religion of such countries as Iran and Saudi Arabia.

Church a religious organization with a large membership, formal clergy, systematized doctrine in which membership is ascribed.

Ecclesia a religious organization that includes all or most of the people in a society.

What is a church? an ecclesia?

Sect. In contrast to churches and state religions, **sects** have fewer members. Individuals do not become members by accident of birth, but rather by conversion. Conversions involve such activities as the giving of personal testimony. Religious leaders are not specially trained; they are "called" from the laity (the membership at large). Members join with leaders in following mostly literal interpretations of scriptures. Sects deemphasize ritual and mystery. Members participate actively in religious services.

Holy Ghost people form sects. Their clergy are "called" untrained from the congregation. Religious leaders may have full-time secular occupations because the organizations neither believe in nor have the means to support a special category of religious leaders. Fundamental interpretations of Biblical passages are endorsed. Strong emotional outbursts from members of the congregation are expected and greeted with approval, for they are signs of true religious participation (Watterlond 1983).

Sect small religious organizations with a clergy drawn from the congregation, emphasizing literal interpretations of the scriptures and conversion experiences.

What are the characteristics of a sect?

Denomination. Intermediate in size to the church and the sect is the **denomination.** A denomination has a larger membership than a sect. Over time, denominations have relatively stable memberships, and they exercise some form of organizational control over who can become members. The

Denomination a religious organization intermediate in size to a church and sect with a stable membership and established theology.

TABLE 14.1   Adherents of Selected Religious Faiths in the United States, 1980

Religious Organization	Number of Congregations	Number of Adherents*	Percentage of U.S. Population
African Methodist Episcopal Zion	1,801	1,092,723	0.5%
Catholic Church	22,348	47,502,152	21.0
The Church of Jesus Christ of Latter-Day Saints (Mormons)	6,771	2,684,744	1.2
Christian Methodist Episcopal	1,780	681,391	0.3
Judaism—Conservative	793	240,097	0.1
Judaism—Reform	708	562,629	0.2
Lutheran Church—American	4,845	2,361,845	1.0
Seventh-Day Adventist	3,676	668,611	0.3
Southern Baptist Convention	35,552	16,281,692	7.2
United Methodist	38,465	11,552,111	5.1

*The religious organizations provided data for this report. For some organizations the number of adherents was projected from data on the number of communicants or confirmed members, using 1980 U.S. Census data. Included in the report is an evaluation of the quality of the religious organization's data.
SOURCE: Bernard Quinn, Herman Anderson, Martin Bradley, Paul Goething, and Peggy Shriver, *Churches and Church Membership in the United States, 1980* (Atlanta: Glenmary Research Center, 1982).

theology and credos are agreed on by the membership. The organization has established relationships with institutions in the society, but is not sanctioned by the state. In the United States there are a number of denominations, but many more sects.

Religious organizations begin as religious movements. One view is that religious movements are seen initially as deviant because they profess divergent beliefs. If a religious movement and its members are seen as highly deviant, the group exists in a state of high tension with the society. If the adherents adopt more conventional beliefs and behaviors, they may reduce the tension and more people may be drawn to membership. Some sects may become denominations. Some of the denominations we recognize today began as sects in Europe, such as the Methodist denomination. The process of transformation from sect to denomination takes time. Five large and distinctive religious movements originated in the United States: Mormonism, Seventh Day Adventists, Jehovah's Witnesses, Christian Scientists, and Pentecostalism. They exist in varying degrees of high tension with the overall society. Many sects do not grow larger but gradually die out, such as the Shakers.

There are other religious groups that do not fit in any of the above categories. One type that often draws considerable public attention is the cult.

Cult. A **cult** arises in response to a strong leader or to a novel idea. They may be religious or secular in orientation, but here we focus on religious cults. Various conditions appear to facilitate the emergence of cults. When traditional premises for interpreting the world seem inadequate because of changes (social, political, environmental, or economic), cults emerge. Rodney Stark and William Sims Bainbridge (1981) argue that people are apparently more receptive to cults when traditional religious organizations are weak.

Cult an organization that arises in response to a strong leader or a novel idea when some people find conventional organizations unsatisfactory.

The Hare Krishna is one cult that proselytizes openly to attract new members.

CONTROVERSIAL ISSUES · Conversion: Acquisition of a New Perspective

In the 1970s public attention was drawn to the phenomenon of conversion to cults. Parents and friends of individuals who converted to new religious perspectives became concerned about the changes they observed in the converts. Conversion involves "a radical reorganization of identity, meaning, life" (Travisano 1970:594). Former associates who recognize changes in converts' lifestyles and beliefs sometimes claim that converts have been "brainwashed" or programmed. Parents in some cases have sought legal control (conservatorship) of their adult children in order to remove them from cults. Other parents have simply had their children "kidnapped" or employed the services of "deprogrammers" who attempt to make converts disavow cult beliefs. Cult members argue that they have the right to religious freedom as guaranteed by the U.S. Constitution. Sociologists cannot answer the legal questions; however, they have tried to understand the processes through which people become members of cults or marginal religious movements (Harper 1982) and the rise of an anticult movement (Shupe and Bromley 1980).

John Lofland and Rodney Stark (1965) identified steps that people generally go through before becoming converts to a deviant religious perspective, such as the "world saving" Unification Church (Moonie). When people are comfortable with their current belief systems, they are not likely even to consider new perspectives. Thus Lofland and Stark identify a series of predisposing conditions that make some people open to a new perspective. Potential converts experience *tension* because their present life circumstances are far from what they ideally want. To deal with such tension, potential converts might adopt a *religious perspective* rather than a political or psychiatric one. These individuals find old answers, including those available from conventional religions, unsatisfactory, so they actively *seek* new answers. The persistence of these conditions leads people to *turning points* at which they are ready to adopt new beliefs and lifestyles.

Situational contingencies influence whether people who are generally open to a new religious perspective will adopt a particular one. Potential converts must learn about the new perspective. They interact with people who have already converted. The social interaction facilitates socialization to the new perspective and the formation of social ties, *cult affective bonds.* Preexisting relationships with people who do not support the cult's beliefs, *extracult affective bonds,* are weakened as converts no longer see those people frequently and may see them as hostile to the cult's beliefs. Finally, a person has completed the conversion process when all of his or her life is bound up in the new perspective. This *intensive interaction* phase is the key to conversion (Snow and Phillips 1980).

The criticisms of cults often focus on the intensive interaction phase. Former "Moonies" report long periods of sleep deprivation and schedules that permitted them no time to be alone and think about the new perspective (Lenz 1982). Cult members argue that people are free to join or leave their organizations, and that attempts to "deprogram" them are violations of their right to religious freedom. Do you believe people would object to cult involvement if they found cult beliefs acceptable?

For at least some people, old accounts or explanations of why the world is as it is no longer seem adequate or fair. New views or interpretations may be presented by individuals with personalities that fire the imaginations of the disaffected. As noted in Chapter 10, these leaders are called *charismatic.* Groups led by charismatic leaders are the Unification church (Reverend Moon) and Scientology (L. Ron Hubbard).

Many people may attempt to get others to follow them and to endorse their ideas. The promoter of new ideas must get at least a loose collection of followers. Once there are followers, rituals and symbols are generated to mark the membership as different from other people.

Cults draw attention to themselves because their ideas are not only a reaction to old ways, but also a challenge. The old order must accommodate to change or be ready to respond to a new system of beliefs, ethics, and ways of thinking about the world. Although cults begin with small, loosely organized memberships, they may become quite large. In some instances, cults have aligned themselves with forces of protest in society. In Japan, for example, when agricultural crises occurred during the Tokugawa regime, a segment of the peasantry would on occasion band together with a dissident priest (a charismatic leader) and march on some feudal lord or attempt insurrection against the shogunate. Such attempts were usually dealt with summarily and quickly stamped out before they could become more powerful threats to the existing social order.

Cults evolve in various ways. In some societies cults have developed that stress discipline, allegiance to the group, a recognition of the mastery of the group's claims over members' lives, and periodic challenges to the individual that test personal commitment to the cult's beliefs.

The Functions of Religion

Religion serves purposes somewhat different from other social institutions, although similar functions may be fulfilled in institutions such as the family. Some of the important functions are: accounting for the mysterious and unknown, providing answers about life and death, comforting people facing tension and stress, and providing people with a sense of identity.

Religion and the Individual

The language, imagery, and meanings that constitute a religious belief system provide people with shared ways of viewing the world. An individual learns a set of answers for life's problems. The social support derived from belonging to a group, interacting with others who are seen as similar to oneself, is also very important. Undesired events—illness, death, divorce, bankruptcy, crop failure—each become interpretable as part of a larger fabric of events explained by the religious belief system. Those who share the belief system offer a person social support as well as ideological support in such times of crisis.

Recognition of the relative importance of crises judged from the perspective of a "divine" plan in effect reduces anxieties generated by disturbances in the daily rhythms of life. A crisis or unexpected event becomes relativized and put in perspective. It becomes understandable, for meaning is assigned to it. In other words, one function of religion is to make familiar and understandable the mysterious and unknown (Berger and Luckman 1967).

All human beings die. Death leads many people to question the meaning of life. Most religions offer explanations for life and death. In some religious groups, funerals are festive occasions, for the deceased person embarks on a trip to some envisioned paradise and will no longer experience the pain and suffering of the living. Other groups may not treat funerals as festive occasions, but survivors are consoled by the belief that the dead are in a superior state and the survivors will some day rejoin those who died. In other religions it is believed that the dead have another opportunity to enhance themselves in the wheel of being by returning to life, perhaps even in nonhuman form. Religions that emphasize the other world may provide hope for people whose lives are marked by degradations and deprivations. According to Marx, "religion is the opiate of the people" and provides justification for inequalities and exploitation. The belief in a better life after death may keep people from actively attempting to change their lives in this world.

Religion also serves as a *social marker.* It operates like ethnicity or race (see Chapter 7 for further discussion of markers). Many religious organizations, as well as congregations of organizations, are racially and sometimes ethnically distinct. As a consequence, people may categorize or stereotype others on the basis of their religious beliefs. People may use their own religious beliefs as a mark of who they are and what they stand for.

For many people in the United States, religious identity is important. When social surveys are conducted, most Americans claim a religious affiliation, typically Protestant, Catholic, or Jewish. Although relatively few people identify themselves as Muslim, with the influx of immigrants from the Middle East, Islam is one of the fastest growing religious bodies in the United States.

Although people identify themselves as affiliated with religious groups, religion may or may not be important in how they organize their daily lives. Sociologists have attempted to measure **religiosity,** a person's involvement in religious activities and commitment to religious beliefs, to learn more about the importance of religion in people's daily lives.

Religiosity level of involvement in religious activities and degree of commitment to religious beliefs.

Why do people who are not religious identify themselves with a religious group? The religion may provide them with a general belief system that they can turn to in times of crisis, or it may be a part of their ethnic or family heritage. It is also generally expected in this country that people have some religious identity. People who profess to be doubters, agnostics, disbelievers, or atheists are criticized by many Americans. Those who seek public office in our society usually identify themselves with some religion, even if it appears not to be very important to them. But, by the same token, some Americans are skeptical of people who openly and frequently profess their beliefs. When President Jimmy Carter publicly affirmed his identity as a "born-again Christian," some were concerned about the effect of his religious beliefs on how he governed the country.

Religion and Group Behavior

People are aware that various societal institutions affect each other. In some societies religious values predominate in the family, political, and educational institutions, but in other societies quite different relationships may prevail. In American society the Supreme Court has enforced the doctrine of separation of church and state; in other words, the political/legal institution is officially separate from the religious institution. Yet groups within our society continually are trying to eliminate the distinction between the moral order and the social order. Some argue that there should be prayer in public schools, although a 1963 decision of the U.S. Supreme Court ruled that religious ceremonies in public schools are unconstitutional. Some argue that the biblical version of creation should be taught in public schools instead of evolutionary theory. Some religious groups oppose all killing on moral grounds and want to change the political/legal institution accordingly. Interestingly, various groups appear to be outraged by different forms of killing: some by war, some by abortion and euthanasia, and others by capital punishment.

Religious organizations in many societies seek to make the moral and social orders more similar. Religious organizations actively endorse economic policies and political candidates and platforms. One way to influence government is through lobbying activities that require substantial sums of money. Organizations need members who will contribute or raise money, and they also need members to argue that they are a large group that deserves recognition.

Thus religious organizations need to recruit and socialize members. Religious organizations sometimes offer programs of instruction to insure not only that individuals learn the proper beliefs but also that they can spread them to others directly or indirectly through changing the social order. Religious instruction occurs not only in religious organizations but in families. In the USSR, where religion was for some time suppressed and currently is barely tolerated, people who often could not attend religious services persisted in their beliefs, perhaps because of early religious indoctrination. Family and ethnic group ties probably also helped them to maintain their religious beliefs in the face of official opposition.

Religious Institutions and Society

Sociologists have spent considerable effort looking at how the **Protestant ethic** (a religious belief system) may have affected the development of American society. The interaction between religious values and other institutions, as well as the processes of assimilation and social mobility, can be seen by looking at the role of the Protestant ethic in the history of the United States.

Protestant ethic a religious belief system that emphasizes the importance of good work.

Weber studied religions in China (1951), India (1958), and western Europe, as well as ancient Judaism (1952). He noted that the value orientation of Calvinistic Protestantism was well suited to the emergence of successful entrepreneurs in a capitalist, industrial society, for it provided a set of "moral" motives that emphasized the ethic of individual success. Calvinists adhered to the notion of predestination, that is, the belief that some individuals were bound, predestined, to be among the elect and sit at the right hand of God after death, whereas others were bound to go to hell. However, people could not be certain of their destiny. Believers hoped that there were signs of being elected by God. Doing good works perhaps could demonstrate their likelihood of being among the saved, the elect. The signs of salvation were usually the results of materialistic acts, that is, spending money to help the poor or other philanthropic gestures. To achieve this goal, hard work and the accumulation of wealth were prerequisites. Thus these religious beliefs led Calvinists to work hard and seek to accumulate wealth, and thus fostered the expansion of a middle class deeply involved in seeking control over the economy and creating concentrations of capital and power (Weber 1958).

The United States was settled by groups who endorsed the values generally called the Protestant ethic: Anglicans, Presbyterians, Congregationalists, Methodists, and Lutherans. In the Northeast these people eventually established control over the political and economic sectors of society. Their beliefs and lifestyles set the standards of social acceptance and economic success for later immigrants.

Most sociologists argue that those immigrant groups who had or quickly adopted the values embodied in the Protestant ethic assimilated more rapidly and more quickly climbed the social ladder of acceptance and respectability than racial and ethnic groups who maintained their own cultural heritages and whose orientations were more *communal* than individualistic.

Weber did not argue that the Protestant ethic *caused* developments to occur as they did, but rather that it was an important factor. Today sociologists recognize that there are groups of immigrants who have been successful but have not adopted Protestant religious beliefs. Jews from many different countries have achieved considerable success, as have Japanese and other Asian peoples of diverse religious backgrounds. The Jewish people tended to emphasize the importance of education (a route to upward mobility), honoring contracts, self-improvement, and other values that are counterparts of those emphasized by the Protestant ethic. Among the Japanese, the belief in hard work, self-discipline, honoring contracts between supervisor and subordinate, and a recognition of the importance of self-improvement dovetailed with values of the Protestant ethic. Yet the bases for similar actions are not necessarily the same. For many Asians, individuals strive hard not to prove something about "self" but to honor the family.

Religious Trends in the United States

The role of religion varies from society to society and also may be quite different at various times within one society.

Civil Religion

Since the founding of the United States, religion has been invoked in civil contexts. References to religion have been abundant in political and social life. Presidents swear their oaths of office using a Bible; other oaths are followed by the phrase "so help me God." The patriotic hymn "America the Beautiful" has religious allusions, and the popular patriotic song "God Bless America" has an even more directly religious tone. Sociologists use the term **civil religion** to refer to this kind of incorporation of religion into nonreligious spheres of activity (Bellah 1970).

During time periods when the nation is more religious (church attendance is higher), civil religion also may be emphasized. After World War II our nation became more religious. In 1954 the Pledge of Allegiance was modified by Congress to include the phrase "under God," and in 1956 "In God We Trust" was adopted as the official national motto.

Civil religion the elements of religion incorporated into non-religious spheres of activity.

Civil religion in the United States tends to reflect traditional Protestant beliefs (Wimberly, et al. 1976), so some groups object to it. Atheists and adherents to dissenting religious organizations (Jehovah's Witnesses) object to religious symbols in public life. In some school districts Christian songs cannot be sung in December during the pre-Christmas period. Songs about snowflakes and snowmen are acceptable, but not those about Jesus.

Other critics of civil religion argue that at times Americans have apparently believed that they lived in God's chosen nation. As a consequence of such a belief, our country adopted policies of expansion such as manifest destiny.

What are some aspects of civil religion in the United States or other countries you know?

Women's Movement

During the 1960s and 1970s the women's movement raised questions about women's political, familial, and economic roles. Within some religious organizations women raised questions about internal issues (religious doctrine

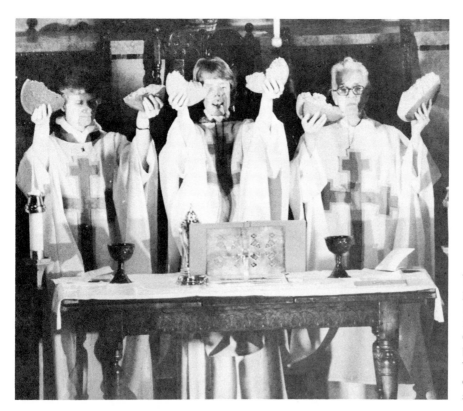

Women Episcopal priests only recently led the congregation in celebrating Holy Communion since being ordained. Women's roles in official religion are still being debated.

and rituals) and about external issues (such as support for the Equal Rights Amendment). Members of fundamentalist groups did not raise these questions and organized in opposition to changes proposed in the society at large. Women theologians addressed issues such as barriers to female ordination and the subordinate state of women in religious teachings (Daly 1975; Christ and Plaskow 1979). Judaism was the subject of feminist scrutiny (Koltun 1976), as well as Christianity.

Today women are ordained as ministers and rabbis, but not as Catholic priests. Debates about the position of women in religious organizations persist. Religious organizations continue to take opposing positions on women's role in society.

The Electronic Church and the Moral Majority

In the past decade the phenomena of the electronic church and the moral majority have emerged. Various evangelists who appear on television have claimed that they have vast listening audiences of people opposed to changes in our society—a moral majority. Evangelists such as Jerry Falwell and Oral Roberts present political messages as well as religious messages on their

The Rev. Jerry Falwell has promoted the idea that there is a "moral majority" which endorses traditional religious, social, and political values.

programs. Pat Robertson of the Christian Broadcasting Network is recorded as saying, "We have enough voters to run the country."

The transmission of religious messages over the electronic media is not a new phenomenon. Regular religious programs were first aired over radio in the 1920s. The "radio priest" Father Charles Edward Coughlin broadcast from Royal Oak, Michigan during the 1930s. Gradually regular religious programs were adopted by radio stations throughout the country. And as television broadcasting expanded, Sunday morning Christian religious programs were offered by local stations.

In the 1970s religious programming dramatically expanded; by the end of that decade, over 25 television and 600 radio stations were airing religious programs almost exclusively (Armstrong 1979; Mariani 1979). Also, the Christian Broadcasting Network emerged and seemed to experience considerable success. The expansion in programming was aimed at evangelical Christians more than at non-Christians or more traditional Christians. Thus the expansion of the electronic church appeared to be tied to an increased interest in evangelical Christianity.

The claims for a moral majority are based on a presumed listening audience that is large and that endorses certain political views, chiefly conservative. Some estimates of the number of viewers of Jerry Falwell were as high as 20 and 30 million during the 1980 elections, although Arbitron ratings indicated that Falwell had fewer than 1.5 million viewers. Indeed for all syndicated religious programs (66) at that time, viewership was approximately 20 million.

The claim that the moral majority represents a powerful political force assumes that people who watch certain television programs also endorse the political messages presented on those programs. Past history suggests that people may listen to a religious program and not endorse political views presented on it. Father Coughlin broke with President Franklin D. Roosevelt during the 1930s and endorsed another candidate in 1936, yet Roosevelt won by a landslide. A study of Georgia church members (Rice 1983) found that family members, friends, politicians, and local clergy were perceived as having more influence on voting behavior than television evangelists. Apparently people listen to media religious programs for their religious messages, not their political ones.

Religion and Social Conflict

Conflicts in a society may lead to conflicts within religious organizations. In the period before the Civil War various religious organizations split into Northern and Southern organizations because of disagreement over issues such as slavery. Most of the organizations eventually reunited, but some did not.

Some conflicts may appear to be due to religion. Hostilities between Catholics and Protestants persist in Northern Ireland. Catholics make up the majority, but they are economically disadvantaged compared to the Protestants. Religion apparently marks some people for unequal treatment. And disagreements between advocates of two religious organizations have produced a historical social conflict that has led to many deaths.

Northern Ireland is not alone. Lebanon has been turned into a shambles by combatants representing different religious groups. Holy wars have been fought in the past and apparently will be fought in the future. Leaders such as Adolf Hitler may arise again to persecute people for their religion.

Because belief systems provide people with strong motives for action, both great good and great evil may occur in the name of religion.

Summary

A religion is a belief system that differs from other belief systems in its emphasis on the supernatural. Sociologists examine the different types of religious organizations and religions to understand their roles and functions for individuals and social groups. The analysis of religion in social life requires that people suspend evaluations of religious belief systems as good or bad, right or wrong.

According to Durkheim the source of religion is society itself. Each religion defines some things as sacred or awe-inspiring, and all else as profane.

Religious belief systems are different in literate or advanced societies and illiterate or primitive societies. In primitive societies two types of religious belief systems prevail: preanimism and animism. Both emphasize forces or spirits. The religions in many advanced societies are theistic, emphasizing the powers of a god or various gods and goddesses. In some advanced societies the religion is abstract, recognizing a force that stands in total transcendence to humans and nature.

Different types of religions tend to prevail in different types of societies. Agrarian societies with traditional authority systems tend to have religions that justify the rights of rulers.

Rituals, patterns of behavior rooted in tradition and symbolism, provide believers with a sense of continuity: that is, people do today what they did in the past and will do in the future.

Religious leaders try to maintain ritual continuity, yet they modify rituals to fit modern society better.

Historically, religious organizations were classified as a church or a sect. Today Christian and non-Christian religious organizations are classified as churches, sects, denominations, or cults. Churches are the largest organizations in societies and the most stable. Next in size and stability are denominations. Sects that emphasize literal interpretations of scriptures are next in size. Cults are typically the smallest religious organizations. All religious organizations began as religious movements. Some religious organizations have undergone a transformation from sect to denomination, while others have not.

From time to time people make proclamations such as "God is Dead." Yet religion persists because it serves important functions for individuals and for society. Religion provides people with answers, with reasons for living and dying. Religion can motivate people to work hard and do good deeds, or it can lead them to fight other people who disagree with them.

Although American society emphasizes separation of church and state, many have argued that we have a civil religion, that there are religious elements in our nonreligious institutions and practices. Some evangelists have attempted to use the electronic pulpit to shape people's political beliefs, to create a "moral majority." They appear to have had limited success.

Proponents of women's rights also have attempted to alter religious organizations and rituals. Some women have now been ordained as ministers and rabbis in religious organizations that formerly did not permit women clergy.

Other institutions and organizations in society will continue to try to change the religious institution and the organizations that comprise it. At the same time various religious organizations will continue to try to make other organizations and institutions more "moral" in the future.

Suggested Readings

Sydney E. Ahltsrom. *A Religious History of the American People.* New Haven: Yale, 1972. An award-winning historical depiction of religion in the United States through the 1960s. For information about the more than 1,000 religions in the United States, J. Gordon Melton's work *The Encyclopedia of American Religions* (Wilmington, N.C.: McGrath, 1978) is useful.

Peter Berger. *A Rumor of Angels: Modern Society and the Rediscovery of the Supernatural.* Garden City, N.Y.: Doubleday, 1969. At times sociological analyses of religion are seen as antagonistic to religion, particularly in postindustrial societies. Berger argues religion has a meaningful place in modern society and that the sociological study of religion does not preclude maintaining one's religious belief.

Barbara Underwood and Betty Underwood. *Hostage to Heaven.* New York: Clarkson N. Potter, 1979. A daughter who joined the Unification church and her mother who went to court seeking conservatorship provide parallel accounts of what happened. Appendixes provide additional information about the doctrines and terminology of the Unification church.

Michael Watterlond. "The Holy Ghost People." *Science 83*, May 1983, 50–57. For those not familiar with the Holy Ghost people or other pentecostal groups that emphasize literal interpretation of scriptures and speaking in tongues (glossolalia), this article provides an interesting introduction.

15

Political and Legal Institutions

Two major structures in American society are the political and legal institutions. These institutions closely resemble each other in their respective organizations and functions. In a sense, the political institution created the legal institution, although they are independent of one another. In America, the judiciary was created as a part of the overall organization of federal government. The broad powers of the judiciary, however, extend to cover most actions by states or any governmental body at any level.

Political Institutions

Political institutions are the configuration of organizations, agencies, and behaviors having to do with the production, distribution, and control of social power. These include various political organizations that exercise authority within the political system, such as the Republican and the Democratic parties. Terms such as "government" and "political institution" are often used interchangeably, not only in our everyday language but also among political scientists who study the development and perpetuation of political and governmental systems.

> **Political institutions** the configuration of organizations, agencies, and behaviors having to do with the production, distribution, and control of social power.

The political institution is made up of a wide variety of organizations and agencies relating to rule making and enforcement; but the legal institution operates to enforce the legal norms and resolve disputes between various parties. Its agencies include those that detect, enforce, prosecute, judge, and award or punish in legal disputes.

Models of State and Law

Two models for understanding and analyzing the political and legal institutions are the functionalist model and the conflict model.

Functionalist Model

This model is often designated as "value-free" because it considers only the functional aspects of the institutions. Its main premise is that the state is a value-free entity, representing the will of the people governed by it. Also, the law is the means whereby rules are enforced and disputes settled. According to this model, the origin of values is found in custom, natural laws, and the will of the people governed. Once formed, the state becomes the general apparatus representing a working consensus of all of the interests of the people.

The U.S. Congress is a rule-making body.

Conflict Model

Some social theorists argue that legal structures involve many value choices. Society is seen as consisting of various competing interest groups. According to this model, some conflict between competing groups is inevitable. The state makes value choices by determining whose interests are satisfied. This model views the value-free or functionalist model as unrealistic. The argument is that no system exists without some kind of value choices by those persons holding positions of power and authority. Although many sociologists would probably agree that those in positions of power frequently make value choices, others would observe that political institutions vary considerably regarding the number of persons and groups that participate in the decision-making process. Therefore, even within the conflict model of society, there are many alternatives regarding how political choices are made.

Political Bases of Social Organization

All forms of social organization have a political component, the power and authority to make decisions over all those who fall within the boundaries of any given system. Even disputes over the jurisdictional boundaries of a system may occur. The settlement of such disputes depends to a great degree on who has the legitimate power in the system.

Power

Power is the ability of a person or group to impose its will on others. Power is central to any discussion about the political institution. It is both a property and a process. It is the property of being able to guarantee that others conform to certain expected behaviors. It is a process, also, for it brings sanctions to bear on those who do not conform and also confers favors and rewards upon those who do conform.

Power takes many forms. Some of the types of power involve the political, economic, and social dimensions. In political systems, power tends to be concentrated or consolidated among persons in a very small group. In American society, there is a separation of certain kinds of power, such as the separation of powers between church and state. Yet, in some instances, close relationships exist between leading religious and governmental leaders.

Power the ability of persons or groups to impose their will on others.

Authority

Social scientists acknowledge the close connection between power and authority. **Authority** is the legitimatization of power. In the United States the President has both the power and the authority to command the armed forces. But only the U.S. Congress has the authority to declare war. From time to time in our nation's history, there have been situations in which disputes have arisen between the President and Congress over who has the real authority to make certain decisions regarding the deployment of our military forces. In Viet Nam in the late 1960s it was unclear as to precisely how much authority Presidents John F. Kennedy, Lyndon B. Johnson, and Richard M. Nixon had to engage in various military actions. Many vested interest groups attempted to sue the government in the federal courts for so-called illegal actions, contending that only Congress had the power to declare war. Even when Congress passed the "Gulf of Tonkin" resolution, a declaration that gave the President certain powers to take military actions in Southeast Asia, there remained many unresolved legal questions concerning the apparent overlap of powers between the President and Congress. Therefore the matter of "legitimatization of power" of the President of the United States becomes an important issue at times.

Authority the legitimatization of power.

Power and authority are closely related terms. But we should not automatically assume that persons who exercise power always have the authority to do so. Former President Richard M. Nixon argued he had the authority to withhold documents related to the Watergate scandal because of "executive privilege." The courts ruled against him and the documents were subsequently made available to the public. Often there are disputes in groups and organizations over who has power or who has the authority to exercise power. In the United States, one group or another is always attempting to change existing institutional arrangements, possibly the entire federal governmental system, and replace it with some alternative organizational arrangement.

The Political Institution of the United States

The political institution of the United States is an elaborate and complex **representative democracy.** Elected officials represent various constituent interests, and these same officials may be removed from public office for failing to represent their constituents' interests adequately. A wide variety of laws at the federal, state, and local levels make up the United States political institution.

     A major feature of the American political system is that of a multilayered government, with local and state control over the many social, political, and economic activities. A second premise is the separation of powers between the various governmental agencies. This means that the executive branch directs the daily activities of government and enforces the laws of the land. The legislature creates laws and appropriates funds for the operation of government. The judicial branch interprets the law. On occasion, the judiciary creates law through its many court decisions. Also, Congress declares war, approves treaties with other countries, approves presidential appointments, and conducts investigations including the impeachment of various public officials.

     Our political system traditionally involves two political parties, although more than two parties can be identified during the state and national elections. Ideological differences often exist between members of various parties, and, to some extent, this reflects the conflict model of organization. The Republican party, for instance, usually favors less governmental control, slower change, and tighter economic policies. The Democratic party is usually concerned with the rights of the working class and various minorities, a greater degree of social legislation, and a greater role for government in overseeing economic and business programs.

Representative democracy a system in which elected officials represent various constituent interests.

Functions of the Political Institution

Some of the more important functions that the political institution performs are maintaining order and control, allocating and distributing society's valuable resources, overseeing the nature and direction of social changes, as well as fostering individual freedoms and resolving disputes.

Maintaining Order and Control

     The political institution creates the mechanisms for establishing order and control throughout the society. Police departments, National Guard units, civil defense organizations, and the military exist to maintain order both in and out of the system.

The powers of government are such that information available to the public about the affairs of state may be expanded or limited. The Federal Communications Commission regulates the air waves and all forms of video and telephonic communication. Rules are created whereby orderly relations between persons and groups are established and maintained. The government enforces the rules for the benefit of all members of society.

Allocating and Distributing Society's Resources

The government, through treaties and international agreements of trade, obtains scarce resources from other countries in exchange for materials that are abundant here. Welfare systems are created to assist the needy. Food resources are allocated to society's members as well as to other parts of the world where disease and famine exist.

The government oversees the production and distribution of the society's coal and oil reserves, crop and dairy yields, and numerous other resources. Governmental agencies are created to manage the fair allocation of scarce resources.

Overseeing the Nature and Direction of Social Change

Our society is in a constant state of change. Each year, new and different products are available to consumers. Technological changes are drastically changing the automobile industry, for instance. Cars are being designed that run on resources other than gas and oil in order to relieve our dependence on oil. The government regulates the pace of change in automobile manufacture as well as in other economic sectors.

The Food and Drug Administration tests and retests new drugs and foods proposed for human consumption. The controversy over the drug Laetril, presumed to eliminate certain forms of cancer in the human body, is a classic case of governmental control. Before any drug is certified as safe, it must be subjected to stringent analyses and examinations by appropriate governmental scientists and researchers. After a reasonable period of analysis, the item is then certified as either safe or unsafe, and the public eventually has access to it or is prevented from using it.

Fostering Individual Freedoms and Resolving Disputes

As a part of the objective of establishing and maintaining social control, the government supports individual freedoms and strives to guarantee everyone the right to pursue happiness without infringing on the rights of others.

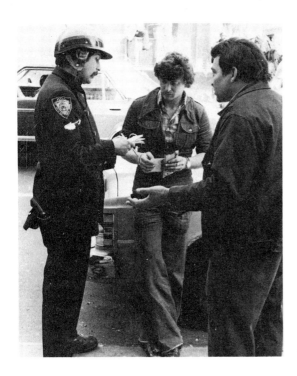

Persons who infringe on the rights of others are often dealt with through the legal system.

The courts act to punish those who infringe on others' rights. The legal machinery exists for achieving justice in disputes between parties.

Theories of the Distribution of Power in the United States

Several theories exist concerning the distribution of power in the United States. Three of the more popular views include: the pluralist theory, the power elite theory, and the Iron Law of Oligarchy.

Pluralist Theory

The **pluralist theory** of the distribution of power holds that power is concentrated in the hands of various competing interest groups. Each group exercises a certain amount of power capable of canceling or counteracting the power exerted by other interest groups. Various groups exercising power within the United States include the American Bar Association, the American Medical Association, the National Council of Churches, the National Association for the Advancement of Colored People, and the National Organization for Women. Each of these organizations has a certain amount of power. Usu-

Pluralist theory that power is concentrated in the hands of various competing interest groups.

ally these associations and organizations lobby in Congress and in other branches of government in an effort to achieve their objectives.

Preceding the decision to use busing as a means of overcoming racial inequality in the schools, many vested interest groups demonstrated in the streets and lobbied before Congress to insure that their interests would be served. Some persons were against busing (see Chapter 13, Educational Structures, for a discussion of the busing issue) and sought to prevent it from occurring. Others were in favor of busing to achieve equal opportunity in education. Subsequently, busing was supported by those in power as a means of overcoming discrimination in education. The wheels of political machinery move slowly and deliberately, in response to the many opinions expressed by the population concerning critical issues.

The various interest groups that exercise power are perceived by the pluralist theory as being in conflict. Only through continual conflict are laws made and arguments over policy resolved.

Power Elite Theory

C. Wright Mills (1959) used the term **power elite** to refer to three interlocking elites at the highest levels of government. These elites included the leading persons in the military, in large corporations, and in Congress. Rather than visualizing a situation involving competing interest groups, Mills projected a condition in which a convergence of the interests of these groups would occur. Certain large corporations frequently engage in business with the federal government through lucrative contracts, for instance. Members of Congress and holders of other governmental positions covertly obtain sizeable contributions from these corporations. The Federal Bureau of Investigation revealed through the "Abscam" operation that some members of Congress were secretly accepting money from domestic and foreign business representatives in exchange for favorable voting in crucial legislation involving these business interests. In the early 1980s, several members of Congress were obliged to resign their posts when their illicit money schemes were exposed by the FBI.

Power elite a system of interlocking elites at the highest levels of government including the military, large corporations, and Congress.

The power elite is also seen as self-perpetuating. Through marriage, informal social exchange, club memberships, and positions on boards of directors, many persons in the power elite preserve their power and perpetuate it. Decisions made by the government reflect the interests of the power elite rather than the interests of the people or masses.

Iron Law of Oligarchy

A view similar to Mills's power elite is set forth by Robert Michels (1915). Michels was a German political sociologist who believed that any organization at virtually any level would automatically lead to a concentration of power in the hands of a few. This compares favorably with Mills's notion of the power elite, although there is no attempt in Michels' scheme to show that interlocking elites exist in the military, politics, and the economy.

Michels specified simply that any organization tends toward a condition of **oligarchy,** or power concentrated in the hands of a few. Through the creation of administrative positions and various leadership roles, followers in any organization give up certain rights to be led by others. Michels saw oligarchy as an inherent feature of organization. He believed that continuous checking would be necessary to minimize the chances of a strong oligarchy developing.

All three theories of governmental power explain some of what goes on in our government. We can certainly see the existence of competing interest groups daily in various controversies concerning abortion laws, the right to life or death (in the case of the terminally ill), and the environment. We can also appreciate the existence of a power elite of sorts by examining the affiliations and board memberships of various persons in higher echelons of government and business. There appears to be plentiful evidence to support the notion of a concentration of power in the United States.

Oligarchy a system in which power rests in the hands of a select few.

Forms of Political Participation

Americans participate in the political arena in a variety of ways. Some of the forms of political participation include lobbies, vested interest groups, political parties, and the media.

Lobbies

Lobbies are organized factions of individuals dedicated to promoting or curbing specific legislation in Congress and in other decision-making political bodies. A lobbyist approaches specific representatives or senators and asks them to support one view or another, depending on the interests of the lobbyist. The lobbyist attempts to "sell" the government official on the merits of certain legislation. Or, if the legislation proposed is unfavorable to the lobbyist, the lobbyist attempts to convince the legislator that such legislation should not be supported. There are numerous active lobbyists at virtually all levels of government—national, state, and local.

Lobbies organized factions of individuals dedicated to promoting or curbing specific legislation in Congress and other decision-making political bodies.

Vested Interest Groups

The term **vested interest group** refers to a group or an organization organized around a particular set of positions on an issue that involves them directly. The American Medical Association is a vested interest group, or special interest group, since it supports laws and federal policies that are consistent with the well-being of the medical profession. "Antinuclear" groups are organized around the issue of preventing nuclear proliferation. Other groups argue that nuclear development is essential.

The list of special interest groups is virtually endless and involves almost every aspect of American life. Vested interest groups have always been an

Vested interest group a group or an organization organized around a particular set of positions on an issue that involves them directly.

integral part of the American political process. What makes them more visible in recent decades is in large part their growing power to influence legislation. They are visible because they frequently receive coverage by the media, conduct widespread advertising campaigns, and demonstrate in Washington, D.C.

Political Parties

The most usual form of participation in political activity is through membership in a political party. Democrats and Republicans are the dominant parties and are the referents in the phrase "two-party system."

The Media

The media, particularly television, have emerged as the major force in the American political scene. Presidents now have their images created for public consumption. (See also Chapter 18, Mass Behavior.)

Presidents now have "media specialists" whose sole job is presenting the chief executive in the most favorable light to the public. Since the Nixon-Kennedy election of 1960, the role of the media has grown in importance. In 1976 Gerald Ford and Jimmy Carter spent more than a third of the $21.8 million allotted each of them in federal subsidies directly on television advertising. Today almost all presidential candidates and other aspirants or hopefuls for state offices plan their campaign schedules around broadcast deadlines in an attempt to reach more "media markets."

What are some of the major forms of political participation?

The Legal Institution

In contemporary industrialized society, there has been an increasing concern for and reliance on law as the major form of social control. As societies throughout the world become increasingly differentiated and complex, an enforceable and normative system that cuts across all class, ethnic, religious, and cultural lines becomes more necessary. The legal institution fulfills this important function.

Four major elements of a rational legal system have been identified (Sutherland and Cressey 1978): politicality, specificity, uniformity, and penal sanction. **Politicality** refers to the condition that a politically recognizable body creates law. Whether the political body is a county, state, or nation, the political authority exists to create and enforce laws within the specific political boundaries. **Specificity** refers to the condition that laws should be able to differentiate between behaviors that are permissible and those that are not. Laws must be detailed enough to provide recognizable guidelines for shaping

Politicality the condition that a politically recognizable body creates law.

Specificity the condition that laws can differentiate between behaviors that are permissible and those that are not.

behavior. Vague, ambiguous laws create problems for compliance and enforcement. **Uniformity** refers to the condition that laws will be applied and enforced equally on all those within a given jurisdiction. Discriminatory enforcement generally serves to undermine public confidence in the legal system and may therefore lead to less compliance. **Penal sanction** refers to the power of the political body to punish those who do not comply with the law and who are detected and processed by legal authorities. The threat of punishment, either by fine or incarceration, may be used to encourage the public to conform to recognized legal standards.

Uniformity the condition that laws are applied and enforced equally to all those within a given jurisdiction.

Penal sanction the power of the political body to punish those who do not comply with the law and who are detected and processed by legal authorities.

Why is uniformity an important component of the legal institution?

The Rational Basis of Law

Weber suggested in the early part of the twentieth century that law was a desirable form of social control because of its *rational basis.* He suggested that societies based on a reasoned legal system, unlike those that relied on vague conceptions of natural law, would likely meet with greater success.

Weber also identified two forms of rationality: substantive and formal. **Substantive rationality** is the logical application of the law to a particular case at a particular time. **Formal rationality** speaks to the rationality and logic of the legal system in general. It is possible to have a legal system that is formally rational, or logical and reasoned, but also to have situations in which substantive rationality may be absent. This might be a situation in which an exceptional case occurs that calls for punishment less severe than the laws require. In the United States, many lawmakers have pointed to the need for ensuring that the law is flexible enough in its application so that within the bounds of uniform application, the doctrine of fairness is upheld.

Substantive rationality the logical application of law to a particular case at a particular time.

Formal rationality the rationality and logic of the legal system in general.

What is the difference between substantive and formal rationality in law?

Functions of Law

As with many other forms of social control and social processes, law performs several important functions. Some of the functions may, in fact, be in conflict with one another. Given the nature of the legal institution, such an occurrence is not infrequent. The law has been characterized as a double-edged sword, working for and against certain principles, groups, and goals.

Generally we can identify four major functions of law: regulation of social conduct, social engineering, fostering individual freedoms, and dispute resolution. Although there are conflicts between these functions, each plays a critical role in maintaining social continuity.

The Regulation of Social Conduct

The regulation of social conduct is probably the most obvious and familiar function of the legal institution. As noted earlier, law provides a recognizable standard of conduct that, in theory, applies to all persons equally. The legal institution has grown in importance and pervades almost every aspect of social life, including public and private matters. Not only do laws tell us what will or will not be allowed under the threat of punishment, but they also tell us the minimum educational level we must meet, when we can marry, how fast we can drive our cars, and a virtually endless list of additional behaviors.

Social Engineering

The social engineering function of law centers on directing social change, both its direction and pace. At the turn of the twentieth century, several legal scholars argued that the law provided the forum for bringing about the most desirable form of social organization. Law was to be the mechanism that effected constructive and planned social change. The critical issues are determining what kinds of directions are desirable and who gets to make these various decisions. In the civil rights movement, legal change, primarily through the efforts of the United States Supreme Court, pushed the country toward desegregation. Without such efforts, the civil rights movement would not have been as successful as it has been. Again, however, the key element in the notion of social engineering is whose concept of desirable change is recognized and implemented.

Fostering Individual Freedoms

Related to the concept of social engineering is the function of fostering individual freedom. Basic rights such as freedom of speech, religious practice, and freedom of assembly are established in the Constitution. The law performs the function of assisting the less powerful and the poor in exercising their rights. Small claims courts, for instance, as well as consumer protection agencies, provide individuals with recourse against business.

Ultimately the exercise of individual freedom and the regulation of social conduct tend to come into conflict. In the late 1960s and early 1970s, numerous ideological and sometimes physical battles were waged involving such diverse groups as students, workers, farmers, draft resisters, teachers, and those charged with maintaining order (police, National Guard). Some groups stressed the right of the state to maintain order and peace, whereas others argued that individual freedom as guaranteed by the Constitution was of the greatest importance. The existing legal structure is the result of a continuous tension between these two ideologies.

Dispute Resolution

Law also serves to resolve disputes. The law is designed to provide a relatively peaceful and impartial method of resolving disputes, whether they involve individuals, corporations, or the government. Some sociologists argue that the legal system is neither peaceful nor impartial, and that by definition it does what is necessary to ensure the continuation of the status quo, particularly in the area of criminal law. However, impartial or not, the legal system is the method used by many individuals and organizations to work out their differences. Each year the number of suits increases. Today a major threat to the legal system is the tremendous work load that has been created by more people relying solely on the courts for the settlement of their disputes with each other.

What are some social engineering and social conduct functions of law?

Political Aspects of the Legal Institution

It is difficult to distinguish clearly between the political system and the legal institution. Our legal system was created through a political process and is perpetuated and changed by that same process. Political elements are part of the entire legal structure, from the creation of laws to the enforcement and interpretation of them.

To most persons, the process of creating laws is complex, and it is often unclear even to those inside the government. On a state or federal level, the legislatures must draft and pass bills that are sent to chief executives for approval or rejection. For there to be new federal legislation on the use of energy by private homeowners, a bill would first have to pass both houses of Congress by a majority vote. It is then presented to the President for approval. If the President signs the bill, it becomes law. If the President vetoes the bill, Congress can override the veto with a ⅔ majority vote. This formal process seems straightforward enough. However, the process by which a bill develops, the way it is worded, the money appropriated to enforce the proposed regulations (should they become law), and how the money is dispersed are matters that are determined to a great extent by those who have access to Congress.

There are numerous special interest groups whose lobbyists are registered with Congress. The lobbyists keep a close watch on pending legislation. In many instances, lobbyists participate in drafting legislation that directly affects their interests. Some powerful groups, such as the American Bar Association, have influenced legislation at both the state and federal levels on matters such as criminal law and legal assistance. The American Medical Association wields power in the areas of health care and medical insurance. Some groups of people such as the poor, the unemployed, children, the undereducated, or persons confined to mental institutions have a great deal at stake in the legislative process, but they do not have access to the political machinery that creates law. Their interests, if they are considered at all, must be represented by other organizations. The legal system is more attuned to individuals and groups who can politically and economically influence those who create and enforce the laws.

In the area of law enforcement, the principle of uniformity of application of the law is an expressed ideal, but it is not always realized in everyday life. Political considerations influence the kinds of laws enforced, the targets of enforcement, and the intensity of enforcement. In our legal system, violations of the law committed by the less powerful in our society—the minorities and the poor—are more likely to result in convictions compared with violations committed by the more affluent. Crimes such as burglary, robbery, and theft are more likely to be dealt with effectively, given the nature of our existing police and prosecutorial resources. To investigate and prosecute white-collar crime violations such as corporate price fixing, stock fraud, and income tax evasion, the skills of several accountants and attorneys are likely to be required. The laws are exceedingly complex, and evidence is often difficult to detect and collect. Successful prosecution is not assured because the affluent, white-collar defendants can afford the best legal defense talent available.

For several reasons, the poor are more often targets for law enforcement than middle-class or upper-class persons. Crimes of the poor such as snatching purses and stealing cars, are more visible than certain types of crimes committed by middle-class persons (embezzlement). In the case of middle-class and upper-class crimes such as price fixing and income tax evasion, there are no immediately identifiable victims to complain to the police.

The poor usually are forced to rely on court-appointed public defenders for legal assistance. Given the limitations of time, money, and support services usually available to attorneys performing these services, the poor are far less likely to be able to exercise their entire range of legal rights under the due process of the law. Usually, only those persons with sufficient financial resources to obtain private counsel are in a position to obligate the prosecution to go through the full process of jury trial. In short, the less powerful and the poor are more likely to become targets of the enforcement of the laws.

Selection of Legal Officials

One of the ways that the political process can directly affect the legal institution is through the election of criminal and civil justice officials. In most states, local prosecutors, sheriffs, and judges who preside over both civil and criminal trials are elected. Furthermore, even those persons in the legal institution who are appointed are not far removed from the political process. Chiefs of police are usually appointed by mayors who, in turn, are elected. On the federal level, U.S. attorneys, trial and appellate judges, including the Supreme Court, are appointed by the President. The legal system is staffed throughout as a result of the political process, whether people are appointed or elected.

Interpretation of the Law

One additional aspect of the political process concerns the ways in which the various forms of law are interpreted. Presidents appoint federal judges and governors appoint judges in about a third of the states. The political ideology of a candidate may be considered in the appointment process. Whether the candidate is liberal or conservative, probusiness or proconsumer, may enter into determining whether a particular person is appointed. All of the candidates for judicial appointments must have minimal qualifications, but the range of their abilities or interest within the legal profession is vast. President Ronald Reagan has stated that, for the Supreme Court appointments, he favors individuals who take a strong stand on the issues of abortion and federal interference in local school issues, including the busing of children to achieve educational equality.

Less conspicuous is the way in which other sociopolitical factors enter into how the law is interpreted. Judges are often concerned that their decisions might open up the courts to additional litigation. Among judges who are elected, they might also consider the political implications of any given decision or ruling. Will they be forfeiting future contributions to their political campaigns and their aspirations to higher political offices? Having a tremendous impact on judicial decisions are whether legal principles such as freedom of speech, press, and assembly are viewed from a perspective of individual freedom or power of the state. This is particularly relevant for decisions relating to unreasonable search and seizure, due process of law, and cruel and unusual punishment. In the final analysis, the decisions are made not only on the basis of legal principles, but also on ideological and political ones.

Why do the poor and minorities seem to be frequent targets of law enforcement? What do you think this says about our legal system?

The Criminal Justice System

Our system of justice is based on the presumption that people are innocent until proven guilty, and that all people should receive equal treatment under the law. Formally, all accused persons are presumed innocent, but social scientists suspect that people with wealth and good reputations are more likely to be considered innocent than less respectable defendants, at least regarding certain crimes.

The criminal justice system (CJS) comprises several autonomous agencies with different responsibilities, and, to some extent, different goals. Binding these agencies together is the processing of criminal defendants. Five major agencies may be identified: police, prosecutors, courts, corrections, and parole.

THE FACTS · Federal Bureau of Investigation

The Federal Bureau of Investigation (FBI) is the investigative arm of the Department of Justice, and is located at 9th Street and Pennsylvania Avenue, Northwest, Washington, D.C. 20535. It investigates all violations of Federal law except those specifically assigned to some other agency by legislative action, such violations including counterfeiting, and internal revenue, postal, and customs violations. It also investigates espionage, sabotage, treason, and other matters affecting internal security, as well as kidnaping, transportation of stolen goods across state lines, and violations of the Federal bank and atomic energy laws.

The FBI's Identification Division houses the largest fingerprint repository in the world, with over 175 million fingerprint cards on file. The file is utilized by law enforcement and other governmental authorities throughout the nation to identify persons having arrest records. The file is also available for humanitarian purposes, such as the identification of persons suffering from amnesia and the victims of major disasters.

The FBI has 59 field divisions in the principal cities of the country. (Consult telephone directories for locations and phone numbers.)

An applicant for the position of Special Agent of the FBI must be a citizen of the U.S., at least 23 and under 35 years old, and a graduate of an accredited law school or of an accredited college or university with a major in accounting. In addition, applicants with a four-year degree from an accredited college or university with a major in other academic areas may qualify with three additional years of full-time work experience. Specialized need areas include languages, science, and financial analysis. Those appointed to the Special Agent position must complete an initial training period of 15 weeks at the FBI Academy, Quantico, Virginia.

SOURCE: Federal Bureau of Investigation.

TABLE 15.1   U.S. Crime Reports

Offense	Number 1980	% Change over[1] 1979	% Change over[1] 1976
Murder	23,044	+7.4	+22.7
Forcible Rape	82,088	+8.0	+44.7
Robbery	548,810	+17.5	+30.6
Aggravated Assault	654,957	+6.6	+33.4
Burglary	3,759,193	+13.9	+21.7
Larceny-theft	7,112,657	+8.1	+13.4
Motor Vehicle theft	1,114,651	+1.6	+16.4

[1]Percent by which the rate of crime per 100,000 population changed in 1980 as compared with 1979 and 1976.
SOURCE: 1980 Uniform Crime Reports, Federal Bureau of Investigation.

TABLE 15.2   Crime Index Trends by Geographic Region 1980 over 1979 (rates per 100,000 population)

Region	Total	Violent	Property	Murder	Rape	Robbery	Assault	Burglary	Larceny	Auto Theft
Total	+6.9	+ 8.5	+6.7	+ 5.2	+5.5	+ 14.8	+4.1	+ 11.3	+5.6	− .8
Northeast	+7.8	+ 11.9	+7.3	+ 7.9	+4.2	+ 19.3	+3.8	+ 14.1	+4.7	+2.7
North Central	+7.0	+ 5.9	+7.1	+ 2.6	+2.7	+ 10.8	+2.8	+ 12.4	+6.5	−4.0
South................	+7.1	+ 7.5	+7.1	+ .8	+6.4	+ 14.4	+4.0	+ 11.5	+5.7	− .1
West	+5.0	+ 7.8	+4.7	+ 10.8	+5.7	+ 13.4	+4.3	+ 6.6	+4.7	−1.8

SOURCE: 1980 Uniform Crime Reports, Federal Bureau of Investigation.

Police

The police component constitutes the largest and most pervasive of all criminal justice agencies. There are an estimated 50,000 law enforcement agencies at the local, state, and federal levels. The number of law enforcement personnel is estimated to be in excess of 500,000. They are the persons most likely to come into direct contact with us compared with any other criminal justice officials. This is because the role of the law enforcement officers places them at the very front of the system.

Most police work consists of routine activities rather than the exciting adventures portrayed on television or in the movies.

Many police functions may be identified, but the major ones center around keeping the peace, deterring crime, and enforcing the law. The state empowers the police to investigate crimes and, where there is probable cause, to arrest suspects. The police are also responsible for numerous other activities including traffic control, public assistance, maintaining local jails, and regulating parades, funerals, and other public occurrences. Although the public usually views police work as exciting, in reality most of an officer's day is spent on routine matters and paperwork. Many police officers go for long periods without making arrests. Administrative matters and increasing paperwork occupy a considerable amount of their time. The television program "Hill Street Blues" more realistically portrays the routine nature of much police work than earlier television shows such as "Kojak."

Police officers have the responsibility for making many basic decisions that set in motion the wheels of the justice system. They determine whether to respond to citizen complaints, to investigate, to arrest, and to collect and analyze evidence. How these decisions are made often depends on the organizational goals of the police department, the ideological goals and positions of the heads of the law enforcement agencies, the training of the officers making the decisions, and the resources of the department. From a sociological point of view, numerous organizational, social psychological, and institutional factors play a direct role in determining the kinds of decisions that are made by the police.

Prosecutor

The prosecutor has the primary responsibility of representing the state in processing criminal cases.

The prosecutor's primary responsibility is to determine whether a suspect should be formally charged with an offense, and if so, the level and number of crimes to be charged. A relatively small number of cases go to trial compared with the number of cases coming before prosecutors.

Right to Counsel

The treatment of the accused as innocent until proven guilty is perhaps less questioned than the concept of equal justice for all. Every criminal defendant has the right to counsel, and so those who are too poor to pay for a lawyer's services are frequently represented by public defenders. In a society that emphasizes the idea that "you get what you pay for," many people question whether court-appointed attorneys can or will do as thorough a job of defending a client as lawyers who are well paid for their services. Well-known lawyers such as F. Lee Bailey and Melvin Belli receive very large sums because their services are seen (at least by their clients) as extremely valuable. And an affluent defendant also has the money for a lawyer to build a better defense, as by hiring expert witnesses or reconstructing the scene of the crime.

David Sudnow (1965) observed the activities of public defenders and concluded that many offenses are treated as "normal" crimes. Based on their past experiences, public defenders stereotype some crimes and the persons accused of committing them. Cases of normal crime receive so-called standardized treatment. The public defender and district attorney generally work together in a system that encourages the defendant to plead guilty to a lesser offense and thus avoid a trial.

When there is an option for a trial by a judge or a jury, lawyers usually recommend a decision to their clients. Lawyers estimate that some judges and jurors are likely to be more desirable than others for their particular clients. A study has revealed considerable variation in how judges react to cases (Rhodes and Conley 1981). Over 250 federal judges were asked to indicate their attitudes about sentencing and to assign sentences to hypothetical offenders. The researchers varied the ages, criminal records, and roles (leaders and accomplices) of the offenders, as well as the use of weapons and amounts stolen. As expected, different case specifics resulted in variations in the punishments (prison sentence, fine, probation, or parole); however, a considerable amount of the variation observed in the sentences remained unexplained.

Judges' views on the criminal justice system apparently accounted for many of the differences remaining. A judge who believed that people were imprisoned to protect society gave a 25-year sentence to the same hypothetical defendant to whom rehabilitation-minded judges had awarded sentences of 2 to 4 years. Also, judges varied in what they perceived to be moderate sentences for the same hypothetical crime. These differences between judges could not be explained by the judges' political views (conservative or liberal) or by their regional location, because those factors accounted for only a small percentage of the differences. Some observers of our CJS believe that the answer to such disparities is to reduce the amount of discretion judges have in setting sentences. Others believe that judges should be free to take into account specific aspects of each case. What do you think?

Plea Bargaining

The process of plea bargaining or plea negotiation is an integral feature of the CJS. About 90% of all felony convictions in the United States are the result of plea bargaining. **Plea bargaining** is a system whereby the defendant pleads guilty to a criminal charge in exchange for some concession on the part of the state, usually in the form of a reduction in the seriousness of the original charge or the length of the sentence.

From a sociological perspective, plea bargaining fulfills not only the function of a rapid method of disposing of a large number of cases, but also provides a forum for the resolution of disputes in a way that allows individuals and groups in society with different values, attitudes, and behaviors to negotiate over their respective interests.

Plea bargaining the system whereby the defendant pleads guilty to a criminal charge in exchange for some concession on the part of the state.

Courts

The courts comprise an agency of the CJS that provide a forum wherein disputes of a criminal or civil nature are resolved. Judges are usually viewed

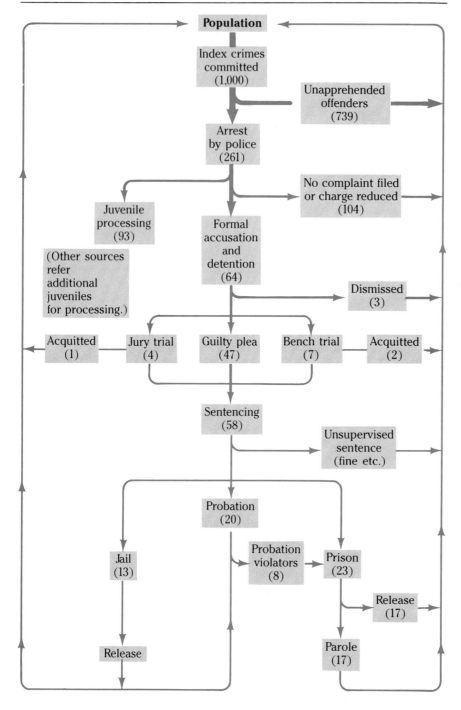

Figure 15.1 Model of criminal justice system (typical flow of offenders for *Index* crimes, per 1,000 offenders). Adapted from *The Challenge of Crime in a Free Society,* A Report by the President's Commission on Law Enforcement and Administration of Justice (Washington, D.C.: Government Printing Office, 1967), pp. 262–263. Reprinted with permission of Harper & Row from *Major Social Problems* by Earl Raab, 1973.

as referees to insure that due process is applied to all parties and that adherence to the law is maintained.

Impartiality of Juries

A jury trial involves the judgment of guilt or innocence by a panel of one's peers. Both the prosecution and the defense can question potential jurors and decide that specific jurors may not be impartial. In addition, both sides may dismiss some potential jurors without stating a reason.

Research on hypothetical juries suggests that people try to be fair jurors. But the composition of a jury is increasingly viewed as possibly influencing its verdict. A black defendant might argue that an all-white jury is not a "fair" trial by his or her peers. Would a male rapist receive a fair trial from an all-female jury? Some lawyers are hiring social scientists to help them identify the social and economic characteristics of people most likely to view their clients' cases favorably, and they use such information to guide their selection of jurors.

Lawyers often encourage their clients to dress well and behave properly in order to increase the likelihood that the judge and jurors will perceive them to be respectable, law-abiding citizens.

Corrections

The fourth major agency of the CJS is corrections. The administration of jails and prisons is the primary responsibility of this agency.

Despite a lawyer's best efforts, if a defendant is found guilty, the judge pronounces sentence. At times, criminologists have supported **determinate sentences** (those of clearly specified lengths); at other times, **indeterminate sentences** (those of discretionary length) that permit consideration of special circumstances. Those who believe that penalties deter potential offenders support more clearly specified punishments (sentences), whereas those who believe in rehabilitation support the notion of indeterminate sentences.

Unless a judge in some way suspends a sentence (probation), the person judged to be a criminal is incarcerated in a correctional institution.

Determinate sentences sentences of a fixed or prescribed length.

Indeterminate sentences sentences of unprescribed or discretionary length.

Parole

The parole agency is the last cog in the CJS. **Parole** refers to a conditional release from prison in the community, usually with some sort of supervision by a parole officer. Parole officers have the responsibility to oversee the readjustment of former inmates to community life. They are also charged with ensuring that parolees adhere to the conditions specified in the parole agreement. It is the responsibility of the parole board in each state to determine who will be released from prison.

The foregoing discussion only outlines briefly the major agencies of the CJS. Clearly the CJS functions as a major form of social control in our society.

Parole a conditional release from prison into the community, usually with some sort of supervision by a parole officer.

During the past 50 years, the CJS has expanded its services and interests considerably. Accordingly, as our society becomes more complex and more differentiated, we will likely become more dependent upon the legal institution for resolving conflicts and mediating disputes between individuals and groups.

What are the principal agencies and organizations that make up the criminal justice system?

Problems Confronting the Criminal Justice System

Institutionalization

Societies have not always had institutions in which they imprisoned criminals, the mentally ill, and other rule-breakers. In traditional Moslem societies, the "eye for an eye" code meant that justice was swift and direct. A person who stole lost a hand; a man who killed lost his life. These forms of punishment served as lessons to the offender and to others. During the early years of our society, public punishment was meted out by placing people in stocks. Religious dissenters were expelled from communities. During some periods, women thought to behave strangely were persecuted as witches and sometimes were even burned at the stake. Therefore, people can be punished or kept from threatening the community through means other than institutionalization.

One reason often given for institutionalizing rule-breakers is to protect other people from their activities. According to this line of thought, rule-breakers who commit crimes against people may make us their next victims. Sending people away to banishment or exile to remote areas constitutes another way that a community protects itself. Accordingly, in the eighteenth and nineteenth centuries the English sent certain of their criminals to form colonies in America and Australia.

Yet a society may want to punish someone publicly for rule-breaking because of the offense to members' sensibilities and as a lesson to potential rule-breakers. Therefore, punishment may serve a vengeance or revenge function as well as an educational function. Denying persons their rights and freedoms through institutionalization may accomplish these purposes and at the same time protect the community from harm.

Some people see institutionalization as less drastic and more humane punishment than cutting off their hands or beheading. But there is a continual tension in our society concerning how comfortable people's lives should be in institutions, particularly in prisons. Newspaper reports of "country club" prisons often arouse public outcry.

In twentieth century America, many people have argued that institutions (prisons and mental asylums) should do more than just hold people for a period of time. They should *rehabilitate* prisoners so that they can function as normal members of society. At one time, mental asylums were described as "snake pits" because of the unbelievably poor conditions that existed in them. Reformers pushed for better living conditions and the development of programs to help inmates become more "normal."

As researchers and reformers looked more closely at what was occurring in institutions such as prisons, they argued that *treatment programs* should be developed for the good of society as well as the inmates. Our CJS assigns offenders sentences that presumably reflect the seriousness of their offenses. After serving their "time," offenders are released. Reformers point out that if no efforts are made to treat or rehabilitate people in institutions such as prisons, why should we expect their behavior to be better when they are released? They point out that in some cases, we should expect their behavior to be worse, because while in prison, people are socialized by other prisoners and learn more about how to perform criminal activities.

One early prison reform program involved separating juvenile offenders from adult offenders. Separate facilities for juveniles were designed to keep them from being thrown in with hardened criminals and presumably from being led into lifelong criminal careers.

Recent reforms have taken various approaches. Additional facilities have been developed to help people leaving institutions learn how to cope as "normals." We recognize that people who have been in institutions may never have learned to cope well with life on the outside or may have adopted ways of behaving appropriate in an institution but not in other settings. Therefore, *halfway houses* provide a means for gradually reintegrating former inmates

---

CONTROVERSIAL ISSUES · Total Institutions

Psychologists (Haney et al. 1973) ran a mock prison study with Stanford University students. Students were assigned the roles of prisoners and guards in a mock prison setting. As the experiment progressed, prisoners became more passive and guards became more abusive and aggressive toward the prisoner. Researchers had to stop the experiment earlier than planned because of serious changes in the behaviors of the guards. This study indicates how institutional settings may influence people to behave in ways they normally would not, such as being more aggressive.

Sociologist Erving Goffman (1961) studied how people behaved in a real mental institution and found other ways in which people may respond to such settings. He found inmates tended to develop an inmate perspective (ways of dealing with what was happening to them).

into the community. "Halfway" signifies that they are somewhere between institutional life and life on the "outside."

Such programs serve the society as well as the individual because they help the person to adjust and protect us by preventing recurrence of deviant or criminal activities (recidivism). Critiques of our system point out the high rates of recidivism as measured by the number of convicted criminals subsequently convicted of other crimes. The problem that continues to confront us in changing our treatment of criminals is that we do not agree on which goals are most important (deterrence, punishment, protection, or rehabilitation). The debate over capital punishment is further evidence of these conflicting beliefs and goals.

Debate over Capital Punishment

Some crimes are seen as so serious by people that they receive harsher responses than others. The harshest response in our society is death, *capital punishment,* and it can only be assigned for crimes such as murder and kidnapping. People who believe that penalties deter others from committing criminal acts argue that penalties for acts such as murder are important in preventing others from committing similar acts. Others believe that these acts (murder, kidnapping) are so antisocial that the perpetrator deserves the most severe punishment. Yet, others argue that we must be protected from people who would engage in such actions and that their deaths provide the only certain form of protection. Finally, some argue that civilized or humane people should not commit murder in the name of justice, that we should try to rehabilitate all offenders.

The people who approve of capital punishment argue that if the death penalty is eliminated, the most serious penalty is life imprisonment; and if people are given life sentences the society has to pay a lot of money for their care. Of even more concern to them are policies that permit murderers to be released eventually. In the 1980s the California criminal justice system received considerable attention because the convicted assassin of a presidential candidate, Sirhan Sirhan, was up for parole consideration and Emily Harris, the kidnapper of Patricia Hearst, was paroled.

Those who oppose capital punishment draw on recidivism rates and point out that most murderers, if released, are not likely to engage in criminal activities. They note that we are more likely to be murdered by friends and family members than by strangers. Therefore, murderers are not a general threat and are good parole risks.

The most recent arguments over capital punishment involved questions of justice. "Death rows" in prisons where people assigned the death penalty are kept have larger numbers of blacks than whites. State laws and procedures have been challenged in courts because all people are not equally likely to be assigned the death penalty. After court rulings that invalidated state capital punishment laws, many states passed new capital punishment laws.

Most people on death row appeal their convictions and sentences. These prisoners may remain on death row for many years while they exhaust their channels for appeal. Many of those prisoners are reaching the end of the appeals process, and so there may be many more executions in our society in the 1980s than in previous decades. If this occurs, the debate will be renewed over capital punishment and the legitimacy of our criminal justice goals.

Regardless of the amount and nature of change in our CJS, arguments about it will continue for many years to come. Under our system, efforts are made to ensure that people are not unjustly accused (by requiring formal charges), unfairly treated (by requiring that people be read their rights), or improperly convicted (by presuming innocence and providing channels for appeals). Jurors are asked to use the standard of "reasonable doubt" in decisions of acquittal.

Do you think that capital punishment is fair? Do you think that juries can be totally impartial in capital cases?

Summary

Political institutions are the configuration of organizations, agencies, and behaviors having to do with the production, distribution, and control of social power.

Power is the ability of a person or group to impose its will on others. Authority is the legitimatization of power.

The functions of the political institution include maintaining order and control, overseeing the nature and direction of social changes, and fostering individual freedoms and resolving disputes.

Theories of the distribution of power include the pluralist theory, the power elite theory, and the Iron Law of Oligarchy. The pluralist theory holds that power is concentrated in the hands of various competing interest groups. The power elite theory suggests that military, corporate, and congressional leaders form an interlocking directorate of the major businesses and industries in our society. The oligarchy theory is similar, for it states that power is always concentrated in the hands of a few.

Americans participate in political activity through lobbying, joining political parties, and through the media.

The legal institution is based in rational law, the legal-rational authority described by Weber.

Law functions to regulate our social conduct, foster individual freedoms, and resolve disputes.

The criminal justice system, an integral part of the legal institution, involves the police, the courts, corrections and penal institutions, and the parole system.

Some problems confronting the legal institution include the lack of uniformity of laws from state to state and jurisdiction to jurisdiction. Some persons feel that our justice system responds to class differences. Persons who are too poor to afford a good defense in a criminal prosecution are more often placed in penal institutions and given stiffer sentences than persons who are wealthy or influential.

Suggested Readings

William J. Chambliss and Robert B. Seidman. *Law, Order and Power.* Reading, Mass.: Addison-Wesley, 1971. A comprehensive text on the sociology of law and the relationship between the political and legal institutions.

David Halberstram. *The Best and the Brightest.* New York: Random House, 1972. A thorough and penetrating analysis of the decision-making process during the Kennedy and Johnson presidencies.

Donald J. Newman. *Criminal Justice,* 2d ed. Phila-delphia: Lippincott, 1978. A complete review of the criminal justice system.

Richard Quinney. *Critique of Legal Order: Crime Control in Capitalist Society.* Boston: Little, Brown, 1974. A critique of the legal system from a Marxian perspective.

Bob Woodward and Scott Armstrong. *The Brethren.* New York: Simon & Schuster, 1979. An informative look at the inner workings of the Supreme Court and how it makes important decisions.

PART FOUR

Social Dynamics

In earlier parts of this text we looked at how people see themselves and their respective social worlds; how individuals learn to become social or to shift membership from one group to another or from one culture to another; how individuals coalesce into various kinds of groups and organize themselves to handle major problems of survival; and how individuals and groups stand relative to each other. In this last part we take a macroperspective and look at major features of society and how they change.

In Chapter 16 we focus on population as a way of understanding society. We look at the population variables of fertility, mortality, and migration. We sketch historical and regional trends in population growth and look at the consequences of increased human numbers on the ecosystem. Shifts in population structure and composition are discussed as they relate to various aspects of social life. Finally, we review various approaches used by students of population to explain how social, economic, and biological determinants affect fertility, mortality, and migration.

In Chapter 17 we move from population as a unit of analysis to cities. We look at the various conditions required for urban life to evolve and explore the preindustrial, medieval, and modern industrial cities as typical urban forms within the urban revolution. The forms that urbanization took in developed and developing nation states are discussed as is the history of urban development in the United States. How sociologists and urbanologists look at various aspects of city forms and living are reviewed. Finally, we consider the range of responses individuals express about city life, whether in the inner city or in the suburb.

In Chapter 18 we alter our perspective once again, moving from cities to how people form and act in larger collectivities such as crowds and mass movements. We discuss the processes whereby individuals move from isolated entities to crowds, adopt a new behavior, become part of a fad, and become recruited, committed, or converted to a social movement. The role of the media in facilitating formation of larger collectivities and shaping popular culture also is examined.

In Chapter 19 we look at social change. Our perspective derives from the various theories that sociologists offer to account for the transformation of society. We review the ways in which individuals, institutions, and societies organize themselves in response to a shifting combination of circumstances.

16

Population Parameters and Processes

Have you ever asked what it would have been like to live in London while the Black Death raged? Have you speculated on what would happen if everybody suddenly achieved immortality or cancer was eradicated? What if you heard on the six o'clock news that for some mysterious reason women were having twelve children at each delivery? Is it possible that the earth will become so crowded that daily lotteries will be held for food and water, or that governments will encourage "death games" to cull excess numbers of people? What does it portend for the future that astronauts now report that the earth is increasingly covered by a darkening cloud of pollution?

If you have had any of these thoughts or similar ones, then you are interested in some of the issues and questions that concern demographers when they look at records of numbers of people in earlier centuries, probe reasons for changes in population, or attempt to analyze the impact of population changes on social institutions and everyday lifestyles.

From early records demographers estimate that at the time of Christ some 250 million people lived on the earth. By the industrial revolution—some seventeen centuries later—the world's population reached a half billion. By the mid-nineteenth century the one billion mark was topped. In the twentieth century each billion has been added more rapidly: 1930, 2 billion; 1960, 3 billion; and in the 1970s, 4 billion. According to some estimates of world population growth we can expect some 6 billion people to be living on the earth in the 1990s.

Today with the growing crush of people many believe that spaceship earth is in danger. Energy supplies are dwindling and food supplies are stretched thinner each year. Water for drinking, cooking, agriculture, or industry is diminishing. Added numbers of people similarly challenge the capabilities of governments and social organizations to provide needed services and opportunities for simply maintaining the quality of life, much less improving it.

Demography Defined

Demography is the systematic study of population. Demographers typically focus on two aspects of population: its structure and its dynamics of change. The structural aspects include: *size,* number of individuals; *composition,* distribution of individuals among age, sex, income, occupation, education groupings, and so on; and *geographical* distribution, people's dispersion and density. The dynamics of change include the three processes of **fertility** (births), **mortality** (deaths), and **migration** (moves). These three processes are called the basic demographic variables, since births and in-moves add to the population, and deaths and out-moves subtract from the population. Some demog-

Demography the systematic study of population focusing on population size, composition, density, and dispersion as well as fertility, mortality, and migration.

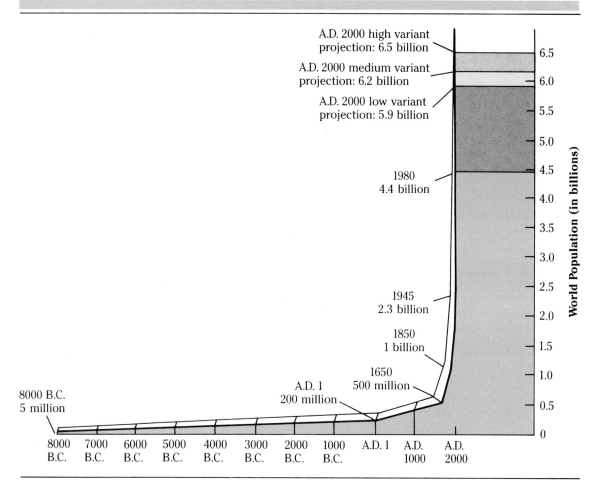

Figure 16.1 The difference in numbers of people added to the world's population by 2000 will depend to a significant extent on the actions taken by governments to modify birth rates. The difference between the high and low projections—about 650 million persons—is equivalent to the addition of three times the current U.S. population within 20 years. SOURCE: *Popline, 4*(4): 1.

raphers also consider *nuptiality* (marriages) and *social mobility* (changes in social statuses) among the dynamics of change (Petersen 1969:1–4; Hauser and Duncan 1959:2; Bogue 1969:1–2). Being married or not is studied since it affects so many aspects of individuals' lives, from their economic and social well-being to their mental and physical health. Similarly shifts from one social category to another, such as employed to unemployed or high school student to college student, are investigated, since they change the social makeup of the population.

Some demographic analysts look at how changes in the patterns of child-bearing, dying, or moving affect the structural aspects of population. They try to express these relationships using mathematical formulas. Their goal is to create a body of techniques that permit accurate estimation and projection of population trends. Other analysts are less concerned with mathematics and more with the effects of population on society (Bean et al. 1971). They address such questions as: Does the aging of the population lead to a more conservative or more liberal voting public? Does the flow of illegal aliens from Mexico change the job market for native-born United States citizens? Is it more difficult for a member of the "baby boom" generation to get a well-paid job than for a

TABLE 16.1 Characteristics and Examples of Formal Demography; Population Studies, Type I; and Population Studies, Type II

Type of Study	Independent Variables	Dependent Variables
	Demographic Variables (examples)	**Demographic Variables (examples)**
Formal Demography	Age composition	Birth rate
	Birth rate	Age composition
	Age composition of in-migrants	Birth rate of the total population
	Nondemographic Variables (examples)	**Demographic Variables (examples)**
Population Study, Type I	Social class (sociological variable)	Birth rate
	Attitude toward maternal role (social-psychological variable)	Number of children
	Incidence of venereal disease (medical variable)	Number of children
	Cigarette smoking (medical variable)	Death rate
	Economic opportunities (economic variable)	Out-migration
	Demographic Variables (examples)	**Nondemographic Variables (examples)**
Population Study, Type II	Age composition	Voting behavior (political variable)
	In-migration	Social disorganization (sociological variable)
	Birth rate	Economic growth (economic variable)

SOURCE: Kenneth C. W. Kammeyer, *An Introduction to Population* (San Francisco: Chandler, 1971), p. 4.

member of other generations? They may also ask how nondemographic factors affect population dynamics. Does the building of a textile mill cause job seekers from outside the region to move into the area, or does it simply recruit from a local labor pool? Does catching a case of herpes simplex virus increase the likelihood of eventually developing cervical cancer?

Whether demographic variables are treated as independent variables and nondemographic variables as dependent variables (Population Study—Type I), or vice versa (Population Study—Type II) (Goldscheider 1971), demographic analysts agree on their general tasks. (See Table 16.1.) They are interested in collecting accurate population statistics, describing and reporting population events and trends, and building a body of knowledge that explains how population and society influence each other (Bogue 1969:vii–viii).

Data Sources

Throughout history people have gathered information on the numbers of individuals and the social makeup of populations living inside their borders. Documents often mention population counts taken by monarchs, patriarchs and officials in Egypt, Rome, Ancient China, and Babylonia. These counts were used to assess potential military strength and sources of conscriptive labor, as well as to identify heads of households to be taxed and individuals eligible for election to political office (United Nations 1953; U.S. Bureau of the Census 1973). Catholics, Anglicans, and other religious denominations concerned with the size and composition of their congregations have kept records on baptisms, marriages, and burials. These early censuses and church records, along with such other documents as tax listings, legal records, and genealogies, permit historical demographers to examine early trends in population and the social and economic factors affecting them (Hollingsworth 1969). Nowadays population information generally is gathered through the census, sample surveys, vital registration systems, and the population register.

A **census** is a nationwide counting (enumeration) of all persons present in a country. It is usually taken by the government and administered in a particular year. Some countries take a census every 5 years, others every 10 years, and still others less regularly. In the United States, the Constitution, Article 1, Section 2, requires that a census be taken every 10 years for the purpose of determining representation and apportionment of Congress. Congress also has passed a number of laws requiring that census information on a variety of characteristics be used in calculating how federal dollars are to be distributed to the states, cities, and rural areas. Questions asked in the census generally cover information on selected personal characteristics, relationships between household members, and household characteristics. The amount of information that persons filled out for the census of 1980 depended on whether they received the short or long form of the questionnaire.

The *sample survey* is like the census in its format. Some part of the population, either individuals or households, is selected as representative of the larger population. Respondents are asked questions about their attitudes

Census nationwide counting of all persons present in a country, usually administered by a recognized government agency.

"Boy, did *I* have an afternoon!
The census man was here."

and behaviors linked to demographic events. Special surveys have been taken on women's fertility histories, on individuals' job careers and migration histories, and on their health-care practices.

A **vital registration** system is an on-going collecting and recording of information about vital events. When a birth, death, marriage, or divorce occurs, a certificate is filed with the county clerk. A variety of personal, legal, and medical facts pertaining to the event are recorded. The state and federal governments cooperate in compiling these statistics and publishing annual reports.

Some demographers also include the population register as a data source. A *population register* provides for continuous collection of information on inhabitants of a geographic unit. Demographic events such as births, deaths, and changes in residence or marital status are recorded as they occur. Some demographers feel that this system, since it covers migration, produces the most detailed record on population events of the four methods. However, it is not widely used and is limited mainly to smaller European countries. It is difficult to establish and administer effectively as well as very expensive.

Vital registration ongoing collection of information about vital events such as births, deaths, marriages, and divorces.

What are the principal sources of information used by demographers?

Demographic Equation

To understand the dynamics of population change, demographers use a simple accounting formula called the **balancing equation** or the **demo-**

Balancing equation (demographic equation) $P_2 = P_1 + (B - D) + (I - E)$.

$P_{t2} = P_{t1} + (B - D) + (I - E) + e$

where P_{t2} = population size at end of observation period

P_{t1} = population size at beginning of observation period

B = sum of births occurring during observation period

D = sum of deaths occurring during observation period

I = sum of in-migrants during observation period

E = sum of out-migrants during observation period

e = measurement error

Using the values for the United States and substituting them into the formula, we obtain:

226,505,000 = 203,235,000 + (33,499,000 − 19,322,000)
　　　　　　 + (3,585,000) + (5,508,000)　(1980 figures)

Notice that 3,585,000 is net migration and 5,508,000 represents an error due to undercount in 1970 and improved count in 1980.

SOURCE: Jeffrey S. Passel, Jacob Siegel, and J. Gregory Robinson, *Coverage of the National Population in the 1980 Census by Age, Sex and Race: Preliminary Estimates by Demographic Analysis. Current Population Reports–Special Studies P-23, No. 115.* U.S. Bureau of the Census (Washington, D.C.: G.P.O., February 1982).

graphic equation. It neatly summarizes additions (births and in-moves) and losses (deaths and out-moves) to the population between two points in time.

For the balancing equation, numbers for population size are taken from two consecutive censuses. Similarly, annual numbers of births and deaths for the years between the censuses are drawn from vital registration reports. Numbers of in-migrants and out-migrants may be available from immigration records, such as port, frontier, or passport statistics (Thomas 1959). When actual statistics on migration are missing, estimates are used. After gathering the numbers and substituting them in the formula, one sees whether the population is increasing or decreasing, as well as the sources of gain and loss.

The difference between births and deaths is called **natural increase.** For most countries of the world, it has been the major source of population gain. The difference between in-moves and out-moves is called **net migra-tion.** Ireland is a famous case of a population losing numbers due to the exodus following the potato famine. When demographers look at sources of population change in a single country, they study both natural increase (or decrease) and net migration. When they try to assess trends in world population growth, they emphasize natural increase.

Natural increase births minus deaths.

Net migration immigration minus emigration, or in-migration minus out-migration.

Which factor is more important for population increase in the
United States—natural increase or net migration?

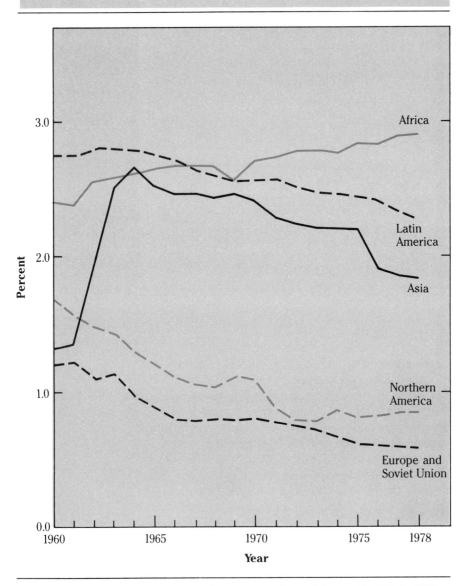

Figure 16.2 Annual population growth rates for regions of the world, 1960 to 1978.
SOURCE: U.S. Bureau of the Census, *World Population 1979—Summary Recent
Demographic Estimates for the Countries and Regions of the World.* ISP-WP-79(B)
(1980).

World Population Growth

Estimates of world population size and annual growth rates are at best guesses. Many poorer and less-developed countries do not systematically gather population statistics. To fill this data gap, the United Nations and other organizations interested in population occasionally release estimates for various countries. Even among countries that do take censuses, some, such as China, do not regularly report results. Thus, a simple fact like population size is a matter of debate (Brown 1977).

From censuses and estimates, the world's population size in 1980 is placed around 4.4 billion people. The annual growth rate is roughly 1.65%. Looking at the pattern of world population growth we see its pace has not been uniform across regions. (See Figure 16.2.) Rapid population growth was triggered by reductions in mortality and high levels of fertility. This population explosion started in Europe in the eighteenth century when the economy developed, better agriculture increased food supplies, and public health practices and sanitation were improved. At the end of the nineteenth century and into the twentieth century the lessons learned in Europe for reducing mortality were imported by developing countries and rapid population growth began in them. As population growth slowed in developed countries in Europe, North America, and Oceania, it gathered speed in developing countries in Africa, Asia, and Latin America. Nowadays developed countries generally have low annual growth rates; some countries in western Europe show negative growth rates—deaths exceed births. Developed countries will grow, but very slowly.

Although the world population continues to increase, the rate of growth has slowed. The peak was reached in the mid-1970s. This turnaround is mainly due to declines in fertility. Some demographers suggest that slight increases in mortality occurring in some countries also have contributed to the turnaround, but how much these contribute is still a matter of debate.

When did the world's population reach 1 billion? What was the world's growth rate as of 1980? Which regions of the world are growing fastest? slowest?

Trends in Fertility and Mortality

The decline in fertility generally is worldwide. According to Parker Mauldin (1980:156): "The crude birth rate of the world population was about 36 per 1000 population per year in 1950" and declined to below 30 in 1980. In developed countries crude birth rates fell sharply, by almost one-third. Although in developing countries rates dropped less sharply. This downswing is due to many factors, including: later age at marriage; growing acceptance of the smaller family as a norm; abandonment of government policies en-

THE FACTS · Crude Rates

Demographers use rates to analyze components of population change. To calculate crude rates, values for an event, such as birth and death, are taken from vital registration statistics and values on population size from the census. The basic formula for constructing a crude rate is:

(1) Crude rate $= (E / P_t) \times 1,000$
    where $E =$ number of events during period of observation
    $P =$ number in population at midpoint of observation

Examples of crude rates are:

(2) Crude birth rate (CBR) $= (B / P_t) \times 1,000$
    $3,598,000 / 227,100,000 \times 1,000 = 15.8$ U.S. Births per 1,000 population in U.S. 1980
(3) Crude death rate (CDR) $= (D / P_t) \times 1,000$
    $1,986,000 / 227,100,000 \times 1,000 = 8.7$ U.S. Deaths per 1,000 population in U.S. 1980
(4) Crude rate of natural increase
    increase or growth (NI) $=$ CBR $-$ CDR
    $15.8 - 8.7 = 7.1$ or .7% per annum in 1980

The growth rate usually is expressed as natural increase per annum. It is calculated in formula (4) to the base 1,000. To convert to a percentage, simply shift the decimal point one place to the left.

SOURCE: National Center for Health Statistics, *Births, Marriages, Divorces, and Deaths, U.S., 1981.* Monthly Vital Statistics Report 30, 12 (March 18, 1982) DHHS Pub. No. (PHS) 82-1120. Public Health Service, Hyattsville, MD.

---

couraging large families; spread of family planning assistance programs; increased use of contraceptives, including vasectomies and tubal ligations; and liberalization of abortion and divorce laws.

The decline in world mortality continues although its pace is far from even across regions. Developed countries, with already low crude death rates, generally had additional declines. Improvement in survival resulted from new ways to lower deaths of infants. A few western European countries (East Germany, West Germany, Luxembourg, and Austria) with high percentages of people age 65 and over had slight increases in mortality as more people lived longer only eventually to die from degenerative diseases like heart failure and cancer.

In some developing countries the crude death rates fell sharply; in others, the rates declined slowly; and in still others, the rates actually increased. Mortality dropped sharply in Taiwan, South Korea, Hong Kong, and sections of Africa and Latin America. The drop in mortality came by cutting deaths to infants and children. Developing countries with increases in mortality include: in Asia—Bangladesh, Cambodia, Vietnam, and various states in India; in Africa—Ethiopia, Senegal, Mauritania, Niger, Upper Volta, Chad, and Mali; and in Latin America—Haiti. These countries had crop failures, flood, drought, or civil unrest that proved disastrous, resulting in malnutrition and starvation, claiming infants, children, and elderly as victims (Brown 1977:237–251).

Even though the world's population growth rate has declined, human numbers will continue to increase. Optimists see a lower limit of 8 billion— four times the current mark; moderate estimates range between 10 and 13 billion (Maludin 1980:156). No one will bet when the world population will stop growing. Most demographers forecast slower growth in developed countries and rapid growth in developing countries, with their already large populations doubling by the year 2000. Among the developing regions of the world, Africa will grow most rapidly, followed by Latin America, South Asia, and East Asia.

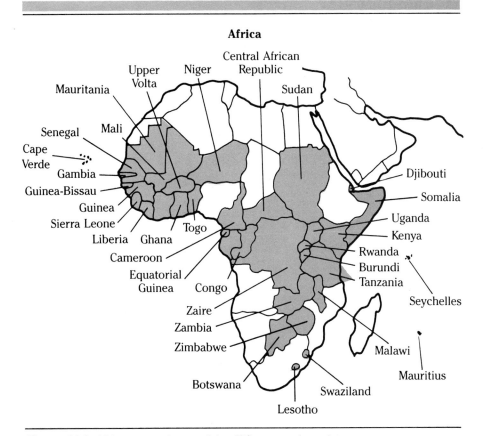

Africa

Figure 16.3 African countries receiving U.S. economic assistance.

THE FACTS · Africa Falling Further Behind

Sub-Saharan Africa Facts

Current Population Estimate: 392 million
Crude Birth Rate: 45 per 1,000 people
Crude Death Rate: 17 per 1,000 people
Number of Years To Double (at current rate): 27
Population Projected for 2000: 678 million
Infant Mortality Rate: 143 per 1,000 infants
Average Number of Children of Women in Reproductive Age: 6.0
Population under Age 15: 44%
Life Expectancy at Birth: 48 years
Persons per Sq. Kilometer of Arable Land: 167
Per Capita Gross National Product: $592

During the past two decades, economic development has been slow in most of the countries of Sub-Saharan Africa. Despite significant long-term potential, most of Africa is falling further behind the rest of the developing world.

This disappointing economic performance can in part be attributed to:

• The region's per capita food production is now declining by 1.4 percent annually, a rate of decline exceeding any other developing region. A deficit of 23 million tons of food grains in Sub-Saharan Africa is forecast by 1990 unless production is significantly increased.

• Fifty two percent of Africa's land is desert or undergoing serious desertification. More than any other Third World area, the natural resource base in Africa is threatened by severe damage.

• The 3% population and 11% urbanization growth rates are among the world's highest.

• About three-quarters of Africa's population remains illiterate and an equal percentage have no access to health services.

• Wholly inadequate transportation systems prevent agricultural and social services from reaching isolated rural people and prevent food from reaching markets and food deficit areas.

• With the rapidly rising cost of oil and other imports and with stagnant export markets, Africa today suffers from its worst balance of payments deficits.

• Energy shortages seriously affect prospects for rapid economic growth and the quality of life for Africans. Increasing demands for firewood are causing massive deforestation.

• Africa has more refugees than any other region of the world. Conflict in several parts of Africa along with projected food deficits portend growing movements of displaced persons and refugees.

SOURCE: Population Reference Bureau.

Examine the data in the box on Sub-Saharan Africa. Is there any chance for this region of Africa to lower fertility and avoid increases in mortality?

Growth and Resources

Population growth affects global economics and politics, the quality of daily life, and likelihood of the individual's survival. As human numbers increase, so does the demand for life's necessities—food, water, energy—and the resources to supply them. Pressure increases to expand the sources of supply. The costs of buying necessities rise, as do the costs of extracting and processing resources and transporting goods. Thus population growth is a major factor in the worldwide cycle of inflation that will not ease until the increase in human numbers is halted.

Food

The relationship between population and food is critical. Each year between 65 and 75 million new mouths are added to the already 4.4 billion that must be fed. The pressure mounts on small farmers and agribusinesses to increase annual harvests. Cereal grains, starchy crops, dry beans, and vegetable yields per unit of land planted must be increased. Poultry and livestock herds must be expanded and fish harvests increased.

Total world production of food generally continues to grow, but its rate of growth is unevenly distributed across developed and developing regions. In developed countries with temperate climate, such as Europe and North America, agricultural output typically grows about 2% per year (Wortman 1980:160). In developing countries, many in tropical and subtropical or arid and semiarid areas, annual agricultural output generally is lower and more variable.

From 1950 to 1970 farms and fisheries of the world produced sufficient harvests, and food per capita increased. In the 1970s the trend reversed and food production fell, although population continued to increase. Developing countries in Africa, Asia, and Latin America that once had been grain exporters suddenly became dependent on imports from developed countries. Overplowing and shortening the fallow periods eroded the soil's fecundity. Expansion of croplands and harvesting of trees for cooking, heating, and building led to deforestation and loss of watersheds. Drought and flood tipped the already precarious balance toward disaster. Civil unrest in some countries, such as Haiti and Bangladesh, reduced planting, harvesting, and distributing of meager supplies to city dwellers (Brown et al. 1976:177–202). World grain production levels fell and grain reserves sharply declined (Brown 1963). Developed countries with surpluses were reluctant to assist countries without adequate supplies through gifts and donations. Their reluctance was due to the increased costs of fertilizers, equipment, and gasoline brought about by the inflationary effect of reduced oil flow from the Middle East. The world price of grain soared.

The consequences of overgrazing and drought.

Overgrazing of grasslands that support cattle, sheep, and goats as well as drought in several places decimated herds. Declines in grains available for feeding livestock also reduced herd sizes. Meat prices rose.

In the 1970s declines in fish harvests also gained international attention. Haddock, herring, cod, and anchovy catches fell below earlier bumper seasons. Overfishing of the coastal banks was the culprit. Countries in which fish is a major source of protein in the diet were hard hit by shortfalls in supplies.

Food prices rose on the world market. In rich nations people who could afford to pay higher prices did so, grumbling about inflation. In poorer nations the rich survived and the poor paid with malnutrition. Many of the young and old died—the lingering death of starvation.

Water

The balance between population and water resources is becoming increasingly delicate. Clean water for drinking and cooking is mandatory for adequate health and survival. Supplies of potable water limit the densities of human settlements. Large amounts of water are required for agriculture: "To produce a pound of wheat requires some 60 gallons of water; a pound of rice

200-250 gallons; a pound of meat, 2500-6000 gallons; and a quart of milk about 1000 gallons" (Ehrlich and Ehrlich 1970:64). In arid and semiarid areas choices sometimes must be made whether to use water for drinking, crops, or live-stock.

Industrial production, like steel manufacturing and petrochemicals processing, uses vast quantities of water. A single car requires 100,000 gallons of water for its production.

As population increases and cities become denser and more numerous, water tables are shrinking. Streams, rivers, and lakes increasingly are being fouled with raw or partially treated human sewage and agricultural runoff from animal wastes and chemical fertilizers. The industrial dumping of toxic and carcinogenic pollutants also aggravates the situation. The availability of clean water is becoming more problematic in both rich and poor countries. "Two thirds of the population in poor countries lack access to safe water, and con-struction of pure water services lags behind growth in demand" (Brown et al. 1976:184). In developed countries water already is in short supply; future needs will increase. For many rivers in the United States the peak demand for water use in summer months exceeds the minimum flow, as in the Salt River in Arizona and the Colorado River. Recreational uses of water are being curtailed in some states as water is reserved for drinking and commercial use.

With continued population growth, shortages will increase in frequency. The costs of cleaning polluted water supplies will be high. Competition over rights for water use between agriculturalists, industrialists, and environmen-talists will be bitterly fought.

Energy

As population growth continues, the demand for energy climbs (Ploch 1980). Energy is required for cooking, heating, and transportation, as well as for agricultural and industrial production. Energy sources may be categorized in three ways: *nonrenewable*—fossil and nuclear fuels; *renewable*—varieties of biomass, that is, wood and cellulose by-products and animal and human wastes; and *constant*—wind, water, solar, and geothermal.

Energy uses in various societies depend on available combinations of sources. These combinations have changed over time. Before the Industrial Revolution and in its early stages, people relied on wood for cooking, heating, and making charcoal. Wood was replaced by coal and water power as indus-trialization quickened its pace. Coal, water, and other energy forms declined in relative importance with the discovery of oil. "Black gold" became the major source for meeting energy needs in developed countries. More recently coun-tries without wood, fossil resources, or hydroelectricity have placed their hopes on nuclear power and alternative energy forms such as wind, solar, geother-mal, and even the harnessing of tidal flows.

In developing nations the principal source of energy is biomass. Nine-tenths of the poor countries of the world are wood-based economies. Defor-estation looms large as a threat to future energy needs. In developing countries where deforestation already is severe, such as India and Africa, animal dung is dried and burned for heating homes and cooking. Reforestation programs to halt soil loss, prevent climatic changes, and replenish wood supplies are being instituted in a number of countries—India, Brazil, and the Philippines. Signs are hopeful for using trees that mature quickly and yield many cuttings from the same root system; however, program successes so far have been limited (Revelle 1980:164–174).

In developed countries heavily dependent on oil for meeting residential, commercial, and transportation energy needs, the bubble burst in the 1970s. World oil supplies no longer were easily accessible. The nations of OPEC (Organization of Petroleum Exporting Countries) reduced supplies and raised prices. Political turmoil in Iran, producer of 10% of the world's supply, further reduced the flow of black gold. Newer finds in Alaska, Mexico, Nigeria, and China, seen as symbols of hope, are under tight political and economic controls and have had little impact on world supplies.

Coal is again being pushed as an energy source to substitute for oil, particularly as a source of electricity. The pace of mining coal has quickened. In the United States the expansion of stripping operations in western states and stripping and tunneling operations in eastern states are underway. Growth, however, has not been as rapid as policy makers had hoped. Miners are uncertain about regulations governing reclamation, and steam plant operators, the major consumers of coal, are wary about regulations limiting sulfur dioxide and flyash emissions. Nuclear power, once seen as the solution to energy needs, is no longer popular. Nuclear plants no longer are being built because of the time involved in the certification process, problems of ensuring environmental safety, costs of plant construction, and increasing public resistance.

Alternative forms of energy—wind, solar power, harnessed tidal flows, and geothermal heat—are found only in limited regions. Even in areas where conversion from finite energy sources to renewable or constant sources is possible, the short-run costs of conversions are seen as higher than potential long-run benefits. Synthetic fuels obtained from processing varieties of biomass—such as gasohol from grain—although signs of hope for the future, presently play but a minor role in meeting current world energy needs.

Various combinations of energy will have to be employed. The mix will be determined by local resources and the available technologies best suited to environments. Moving from one mix to another will be expensive and require people to change their beliefs and habits. As population growth continues and energy demands mount, costs for fuels will add to world inflation. The inequalities between nations with and without resources will sharpen. The inequalities between rich and poor within nation-states will also sharpen as their relative abilities to purchase life's necessities change.

What regions of the world are rich in food, water, and energy sources? What regions require imports? Do you think that the gap between energy-rich and energy-poor countries will widen? narrow? Discuss.

Reactions to Population Growth

Whether solutions for adjusting the imbalance between population and resources are proposed depends on a person's beliefs. Some believe the problem can be solved by the actions of people; others do not. Pessimists believe population growth eventually will outstrip natural and social resources. No matter what action is taken, either by governments or individuals, such actions will be futile. Tinkering will simply generate new problems. In the long run population will exhaust food supplies, destroy the bases of social organization, and natural forces will come into play, resulting in severe population losses through famine, starvation, and death. The balance is then restored and the cycle begins again (Malthus 1960; McNamara 1969; Ehrlich and Ehrlich 1970; Meadows et al. 1972).

Optimists claim that the earth's resources are infinite. Human beings possess the capabilities to invent new technologies to handle problems as they arise. To redress inequalities in food and resources, all that is needed is redistribution, with those nations with surpluses trading or donating them to nations in want (Davis 1963: 62–71; Kahn et al. 1976).

Both approaches share the assumption that the balance between population and resources is largely self-regulating. Strategies for modifying imbalances are irrelevant. In the long run a balance will be maintained.

Another group of theorists believe that change can be instituted, but the debate focuses on the "chicken-egg" dilemma, that is, demographic versus nondemographic factors. Both sides agree that population variables affect nondemographic variables, and vice versa, but they disagree on the priority to be given to one side of the equation or the other. Those who contend that nondemographic factors are more important argue that economic development must be stimulated, since one of its major consequences is the reduction of the rate of population growth. They point to the experiences of western European countries as proof for their position. Opponents contend economic development cannot occur until reductions in the rate of population growth are achieved so that resources are freed for economic expansion.

In both camps there is intense debate over the kinds of strategies needed to effect change. Some persons argue that population is a societal problem, thus actions must be collective. Only by modifying the values that serve as guidelines for individual actions and by rearranging the institutions that serve the major needs of the people can policies and programs be introduced that will be successful. Debate also rages over whether policies should be proposed and carried out by public (government) or private (nongovernment) agencies, as well as whether programs should be national, regional, or local in scope (Coontz 1957:102–134; Meek 1971).

Other theorists contend population changes really are the sum of individual decisions and actions. Thus, to effect changes, efforts must be directed to altering individuals' beliefs and modifying circumstances, so that the individual has the opportunity to translate belief into action (Bogue 1969).

A theme that runs through these debates is how much time does the world or a particular nation have, before it is too late. Some forecasts stress that dramatic change must be instituted and bear results in one generation, others are less urgent, saying two generations. Regardless of one's assessment of the deadline, the message that change must occur is crystal clear (Hernandez 1974:145–172).

Are you a pessimist or an optimist? Do you believe individual or governmental action is needed to control population? Do you believe control of population is out of people's hands?

Common Good versus Individual Freedom

Population growth has created demands for services of such magnitude that governments can no longer effectively respond. Sufficient resources for education are not available to stem the rising tide of illiteracy in India and Bangladesh. Adequate materials are in short supply for building construction to replace the sprawl of slum barrios in Latin American cities. Money is not expanding quickly enough to fire economic development and generate jobs to reduce unemployment and underemployment. Personnel are needed for staffing health and medical systems to cope with infectious diseases in crowded and impoverished environments.

As the crush of numbers continues and demands mount for living space and for resources to insure individual survival, governments might have to instigate controls on access to, allocation of, and use of resources. Regulations might limit personal choices now taken as freedoms; actions will be licensed in the name of promoting the common good and guaranteeing survival. Who gets to define the common good has a tremendous effect on the nature of social inequalities, either reducing them or sharpening them. (See Chapters 6, Social Inequality, and 7, Ethnicity and Race.)

Population Structure

To understand the social makeup of a particular society as well as to compare different societies, students of population examine a variety of measures besides crude and detailed rates of fertility, mortality, and migration. These statistics, when combined with an understanding of the social processes at play in a society, allow users of population data to assess what changes may take place in the immediate future. The most basic feature of a society is its population structure. *Population structure* is the breakdown of the population into age and sex categories.

Sex

The importance of sex norms in defining responsibilities and obligations for individuals in social relationships is widely recognized. (See Chapter 8, Gender.) When we know the relative balance of males and females in the population, we can anticipate the kinds of activities that are likely to be found in a society.

The **sex ratio** is a simple measure of the relative balance between males and females. It is the number of males divided by the number of females multiplied by 100. A value of 100 shows an equal number of the sexes; values above 100 indicate a majority of males; and values below 100, a female majority.

Sex ratio   number of males divided by number of females times 100.

Biological factors affect the sex ratio. More males are conceived than females, and more males are born than females. More males die at each age than females. Thus the sex ratio changes from male to female as a function of age and differences in the pattern of dying.

Social factors also affect the sex ratio, such as the nature of work and the job mix of a region. Economies that are agricultural or deal with extraction of natural resources, such as fishing, mining, and lumbering, have an excess of jobs filled by males, as in California during the Gold Rush or Alaska when the pipeline was constructed. Conversely, economies that are commercial or administrative have more jobs traditionally filled by females, as in Washington, D.C.

Demographic factors also influence the sex ratio of an area. Migration over long distances usually involves more males than females. Thus, regions that are destinations for long distance moves tend to be predominantly male.

Age

Age also is important in defining expectations and obligations in a wide range of social activities. By knowing what these age norms are in a society, we can anticipate how social practices and institutions may change as the age composition of a population shifts over time.

Age usually is counted as of a person's last birthday or reckoned from date of birth. Ideally age information is reported in single years, but often intervals of 5 or 10 years are used. The simplest way to study the age structure of a population is to look at percentages of persons in each age group.

Certain ages are studied since age norms mark them as important stages in persons' lives. Persons under age 15 are the youth of a country. From the percentage of youth, inferences are drawn about the level of demand for children's health care, day care centers, schools, and the kinds of products children need. Similarly persons over age 65 are defined as "old" or "elderly." The percentage of elderly suggests potential demands for retirement centers, special services, and costs to private and public pension programs. The work force is made up of persons 15 to 64 years of age. By adding the totals for the

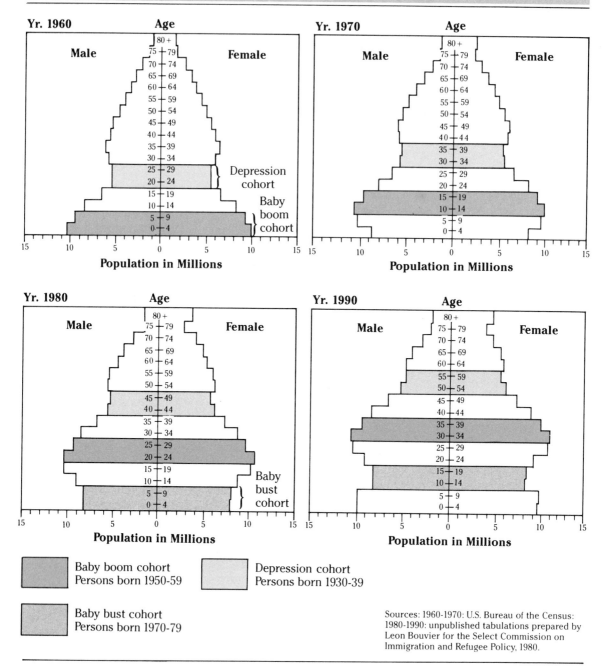

Figure 16.4 U.S. population age-sex pyramids: 1960–1990. This is an executive summary of a briefing by five population experts before the Congressional Advisory Committees to the President's Commission for a National Agenda for the Eighties. The briefing was organized by the Population Resource Center with technical assistance from the Population Association of America. This summary was prepared by the Population Reference Bureau, Inc., Washington, D.C.

old and young age groups, then dividing by the number of persons in the work force, we obtain an **age dependency ratio** or **burden ratio.** This measure shows how many dependents—people typically not working—are supported by workers in a society.

Measures of central tendency, **mean** and **median**, also are used for comparing age distributions. In the United States, following the baby boom of the 1950s, the median age of the population declined. This process is called the "younging" of the population. In the 1960s Americans' anxiety about a youthful population was seen in novels and movies that portrayed a society with "teenie boppers" in control and persons over 30 placed in concentration camps. Now with the fertility declining, the median age has increased. For the first time in 30 years in the United States, half the population is older than 30 years; and if no migration occurs, the **population pyramid** will assume a fixed shape. This is called a **stable population**. When birth, death, or migration rates change, the population pyramid assumes different shapes.

In Figure 16.4, in the population pyramid for 1980, the bulge between ages 20–29 represents the baby boom generation. The indentation from ages 0–9 represents a smaller generation resulting from declines in fertility. By looking at this pyramid we can anticipate how these two generations may affect social institutions in coming years. As the baby boom generation moves into middle age, we would expect an increased demand for housing. As they age further and move toward retirement, the demands on retirement pension plans and recreation facilities will increase dramatically. Similarly as the younger generation ages and moves through high school and college, enrollments will shrink; and high schools and colleges will face retrenchment and financial difficulties. The smaller younger generation may find getting a job easier than the baby boom generation.

Age dependency ratio (burden ratio) number of persons under age 15 plus number of persons age 65 and older divided by number of persons 15–64 times 1,000.

Mean the average of a set of values; found by dividing the sum of values by the number of cases.

Median a value such that 50% of the cases lie above and 50% lie below.

Population pyramid bar graph displaying percentage of population in each age and sex grouping.

Stable population population with constant birth and death rates and no migration, which, after a period of time, results in a population pyramid of fixed shape.

TABLE 16.2   Median Age of the Population, by Sex: United States, 1920–1980.

	Median Age in Years		
Year	Total	Males	Females
1980	30.0	28.8	31.3[a]
1970	28.1	26.8	29.3
1960	29.5	28.7	30.3
1950	30.2	29.9	30.5
1940	29.0	29.0	29.0
1930	26.4	26.7	26.2
1920	25.3	25.8	24.7

SOURCE: U.S. Bureau of the Census. *Census of Population: 1970, General Population Characteristics, Final Report PC(1)-B1, United States Summary, Table 53.*

[a]Phone conversation: J. Gregory Robinson, U.S. Bureau of the Census. Preliminary figures for 1980.

Components of Change

Mortality

Of the three demographic variables, mortality was the first to be studied systematically. John Graunt (1939), using mortality lists and parish records from London and Hampshire in the late 1600s, observed regularities in the patterns of dying. In his classic work, *Observations,* he reported differences in numbers of deaths by age, season, and sex, as well as for urban and rural areas. He attempted to separate causes of death into acute and chronic and to calculate the risks of dying using basic actuarial statistics.

Students of population today, like Graunt, are interested in various patterns of dying and changes in the major killers over time. The most fundamental fact linked to death is age. Demographers divide the life span into age groups and look at the relative risks of dying.

Infancy is the most problematic stage for survival. The chance of dying is highest in the first hours of life following birth, then declines steadily through the first birthday. Death in early childhood is less likely than in infancy, reaching a low point in later childhood, until the middle forties when it accelerates for all but the last few ages (after 80).

These risks are calculated using death rates for each age group and a mathematical model called the *life table.* The model presents not only the likelihood of dying age by age, but also that of surviving age by age. Estimates on longevity express the average number of years of life from birth—*average life expectancy at birth*—as well as the average number of years remaining to individuals for any given age. These estimates are used to determine the premiums individuals pay on life insurance. The human **span of life**—oldest reported age—has remained approximately the same for many years. However, the average life expectancy at birth has increased markedly in the last 130 years. Prior to 1850 a baby could be expected to live about 35 years; by 1850 about 40 years; by 1950 about 68 years; by 1977 roughly 73 years. Increases in longevity are due to dramatic declines in infant and childhood mortality and a shift in the major causes of death brought about by improvements in sanitation, public health, and nutrition (U.S. Bureau of the Census 1973:338–339).

Since 1900 increased longevity has favored females more than males. The gap in average life expectancy has widened since the 1930s. Three reasons are generally offered for this sex-related difference. First, females are biologically superior to males in resistance to diseases. Second, females have benefited from improved obstetrical practices during pregnancy, childbirth, and postnatal recovery, all of which have sharply reduced maternal mortality. Third, females traditionally maintain lifestyles with lower levels of risk than males. Females generally are employed in less hazardous work than males, and are less likely to have personal habits, such as smoking and drinking, that increase risks of death. However, as more females work in jobs traditionally held by males, and as more females smoke and drink, some of the sex-related differences in mortality might get smaller.

Marital status and mortality are associated. At all ages married persons have lower chances of dying than singles. Singles have the second lowest set of age-specific death rates, followed by divorced and widowed persons. Two explanations are offered for mortality differences by marital status. First, norms encourage people to marry spouses who are physically fit so they may fulfill social, sexual, and economic obligations and responsibilities. Persons with poor health, mental or physical, are less likely to wed. Second, lifestyle differences between married and unmarried presumably favor the married. Married people are more likely to live a regular life, eat regularly, and have someone to care for them in the event of sickness.

Age, sex, and marital status are only a few of the factors associated with differences in mortality. Population analysts examine a broad range of environmental, societal, and individual factors that influence patterns of dying and surviving. Environmental factors include the *physical*—terrain, water, and climate; and the *biological*—distribution of flora and fauna as food sources or carriers of disease. Societal factors include the *modes of social organization*—agriculture, industry, and commerce; *value systems*—religion and education; and *support agencies*—family, public health, and medicine. Individual factors include *genetic and physical* makeup—susceptibility to disease; and *lifestyle*—risk-taking behaviors. By understanding how any single factor or combination of them influences mortality, population analysts may suggest policies to lengthen human longevity.

Migration

Second of the basic demographic variables is migration. It involves movement of people across politically defined boundaries and a change in their usual place of residence. Migration affects the size, density, distribution, and composition of both the communities or countries that people leave, as well as those they enter.

The places people leave are the *sending* or *origin* areas; the places they enter are the *receiving* or *destination* areas. Movement between origin and destination is called a migration *stream* or *flow*. The numbers of individuals in various streams determines its relative importance. Large streams in American history include the exodus from European countries to the New World in the 1800s and early 1900s; the westward expansion and settling of the frontier; the black migration from urban and rural areas in the South to the urban and industrial centers in the North; the flight from cities to the suburbs; and more recently the movement from northern regions to the Sunbelt.

Population analysts study three types of migration: international movement between countries; internal movement from one area to another within a country; and local change in residence within a city or county. People who leave one country for another are emigrants. Upon arrival, they are immigrants. People who leave a state are out-migrants; arrivals are in-migrants. Demographers try to account for factors that "push" migrants from one setting or "pull"

Migration movement of population across a politically defined boundary, usually involving a change in place of residence.

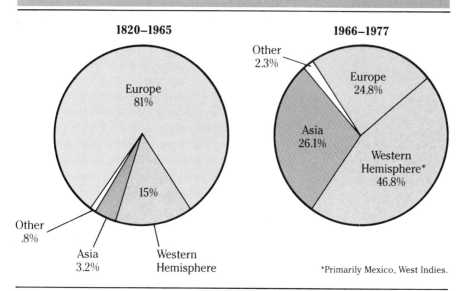

Figure 16.5 Legal immigrants by region of origin. SOURCE: Population Reference Bureau, Inc., Washington, D.C.

them to another. Absence of political and religious freedoms pushes people to emigrate; guarantee of freedoms in another country are pull factors.

The flow between sending and receiving areas often meets barriers. Policies governing legal immigration may be open, restrictive, or regulatory. During the era of *open* immigration in the United States before 1882, immigrants came to this country principally from northwestern European countries, later from southern European countries and parts of Asia. In the *restrictive* period, 1882–1929, barriers were erected. Laws were passed prohibiting Chinese and Japanese immigration (see Chapter 7). Quotas also were established in the Congressional Acts of 1921 and 1924, which respectively fixed immigration levels at 3% and 2% of nationals resident in the United States based on the 1910 and 1890 population figures for racial and ethnic groups already in the United States. The current phase of *regulated* immigration started in 1929, when the National Origins Act limited total immigration to 150,000 a year, with each country's allotment determined as a percentage of the white population in 1920. In 1952 the McCarran-Walter Act restated the principle of quotas based on national origin to perserve the "cultural and social" composition of the United States population. Under President Lyndon B. Johnson in 1965 a preference system was established. Up to 170,000 immigrants were permitted from outside the Western Hemisphere, with 20,000 from any single country as a maximum. Preference was given to relatives of U.S. residents, professionals, skilled workers, and refugees from communist countries, the Middle East, and disaster areas.

Immigrants coming to
America, about 1890.

Illegal immigration is difficult to study. Illegal aliens come to the United States from countries in Latin America, Canada, parts of Asia, and the Middle East. Some estimates place the number of illegal aliens around 2 million persons annually. About 50%, or about 1.3 million, are Mexican. Estimates of the number of undocumented migrant workers who enter and stay in the United States range from about 82,300 to 234,000 each year (Heer 1979:417–423).

In the past, what part of the world was the principal source of immigration to the United States? Currently what parts of the world are the areas of origin for immigration to the United States? What will the racial and ethnic composition of the United States be when the baby boom generation dies?

To explain regional differences in migration flows, demographers study economic factors, such as job opportunities, relative costs of living, nature of the tax base, availability of services, and overall quality of life. Individual career decisions and desired lifestyles also are used to explain why individuals and families move.

The consequence of migration on social composition of a region concerns policymakers. As governmental support for research and industrial development drops in one country and rises in other countries, people move to take advantage of new opportunities. When industries move, local and regional economists and politicians raise a hue and cry over loss of income and jobs, and ask for assistance to offset losses. When scientists move from country to country, one country claims a "brain gain," and the other bemoans a "brain drain." Since migration changes the economic composition of the population, migration policies always are controversial. Questions asked include: Should we modify immigration laws to prevent foreigners from entering the United States and competing with citizens for jobs? Do foreigners fill jobs that United States citizens normally avoid? Should we increase quotas to encourage immigration from countries that traditionally have sent large numbers to the United States, or establish new quotas to stimulate immigration from countries with lower standards of living, thereby providing our economy with cheap labor? (Answers to these questions depend on economic conditions as well as policies concerning race and ethnic relations. See Chapter 7.)

Fertility

Although mortality received the lion's share of attention in the past and migration will likely receive it in the future, fertility currently occupies center stage. It is the most explosive factor in population growth. Persons migrating add to or subtract from the population once. Individuals die but once. But human beings have the capacity to replace themselves many times. The impact of women adding one birth to their current family size has a dramatic effect on population increase.

Fertility is the actual performance of bearing children. It is not to be confused with **fecundity**, the biological capacity for bearing children. If **menarche**—onset of menstrual periods—occurs at age 12 and **menopause** at age 49, a healthy woman could have approximately 44 single births, assuming an interval of 10 months between children. Even in natural fertility populations—societies where no contraception is practiced—no woman produces at her biologic maximum. The highest median number of children per woman at the end of her reproductive years is the 10.9 reported among the Hutterites.

Fertility actual performance of childbearing.

Fecundity biological capacity to bear children.

Menarche onset of menstrual periods.

Menopause cessation of menstrual periods.

Distinguish between fecundity and fertility. What is meant by the term "natural fertility population"?

Since people are capable of reproducing many times, population analysts investigate the direct and indirect impact of environmental, societal, and normative factors on fertility decisions and behaviors. The goal is practical: to reduce fertility, halt population growth, and achieve population stability.

Environmental factors, such as clean water, adequate food, public sanitation, and medical care, increase the efficacy of the reproductive process. With good diet, deaths from malnutrition and anemia to mother and infants are lower. Clean water and good sanitation eliminate cholera, dysentery, and typhoid—major killers of infants. Adequate medical care controls diseases such as gonorrhea and genital tuberculosis that cause infertility. Thus, when women can give birth to healthy babies that survive, they no longer need to have lots of children to replace those that die, to ensure that some will survive to old age.

Societal factors also influence fertility. Fertility is higher in developing countries than in developed countries. In developing countries most of the population works in agriculture. Women are usually poorly educated, if not illiterate, and do not work outside the home. Women's prestige is tied to marriage and childbearing. The more children they have, the better, since many hands are required for farm work. As the society industrializes, farming moves from family-run operations to commercial agriculture, and there is less need for many hands to produce a crop. Women become better educated and often enter the labor force. As their prestige becomes less tied to marriage and childbearing, they can escape the biological tyranny of continued child-bearing.

Normative factors operate directly on fertility behaviors. Group norms shape individuals' decisions and actions by answering such questions as: At what age should one start having sexual intercourse or enter wedlock? Should one use contraception or not? Should one rely on abortion? Should couples remain childless or have children? How many children should one have and how rapidly? Should infants be breastfed or bottlefed? Are boys preferred or girls? (Cox 1970) The way individuals act in conforming to these group norms influences how many years females face the risk of childbearing and how rapidly each generation is added to the population.

Demographic Transition

Students of population, in their attempt to understand the interrelation-ship between demographic and nondemographic variables in an historical and developmental context, use the "theory of the demographic transition." This theory is primarily based on what occurred in western European countries as they modernized. Various transition theories have been suggested, but the simplest is the three-stage (or category) model. Each stage—category—iden-tifies the relationships between birth, death, and growth rates, as well as the social and economic conditions associated with the rates (Weinstein 1976).

Stage 1: High Potential Growth. Fertility is encouraged. No con-traception is practiced. Crude birth rates are high—40 or more per 1,000. Mortality also is high—crude death rates 30 to 50 per 1,000, frequently going higher because of epidemics, famines, natural calamities, and war. Infant mor-tality is high—200 to 300 deaths per 1,000 live births. One-third of all deaths occur among children under age 5. Maternal mortality—the numbers of women dying in childbirth—is high. Life expectancy at birth hovers between 20 and 40 years of age. Natural increase is low and cyclical. Any gains in population size are wiped out by mortality. The population is young, with a large per-centage under age 15. It is predominantly rural, although a few small and medium-sized cities exist. (See Chapter 17 for a discussion of preindustrial cities.) Society is traditional, emphasizes custom, and has a fatalistic outlook;

people rely on folk medicine and witchcraft. Living standards are abysmal. Unsanitary conditions are rampant. Water is contaminated. Sewage is dumped in the streets. Subsistence agriculture is practiced, labor is largely manual. Available food is poor in quality, and frequently chronic or acute shortages occur.

Stage 2: Transitional Growth.   Fertility initially remains high. Crude birth rates start at 40 per 1,000, then slowly decline to the low 30s and high 20s. Infanticide, abortion, and withdrawal are practiced. Many women remain single or marry late in life. Mortality declines at first slowly, then more rapidly; crude death rates hover in the 40s per 1,000 and then drop into the low 30s. Plague disappears. Epidemics become less frequent. Infant mortality drops below 150 deaths per 1,000 births. Deaths of children under age 15 decrease. Maternal mortality decreases. Life expectancy at birth climbs above 40 years. Natural increase becomes explosive. The size of the population rises rapidly. The age of the population becomes younger as more babies survive. The population is predominantly rural, although urban areas increase in numbers and densities. Society is less traditional. Lower classes remain provincial. The elites accept a "faith in reason" and a middle class emerges. Living standards improve as nutritional resources expand. Personal hygiene is upgraded. Technological breakthroughs in agriculture, such as crop rotation, use of fertilizers, and some mechanization produce food surpluses. Transportation and communication become more efficient. Industrialization begins to take off; extractive industries flourish; and manufacturing that involves the processing of raw products expands.

Stage 3: Incipient Decline.   Fertility declines—with the crude birth rates falling below 20 per 1,000. Contraception is increasingly adopted and used more effectively. Mortality reaches new lows; the crude death rate is less than 20 per 1,000. Major killers are degenerative diseases, such as heart diseases, cancer, stroke, and man-made causes such as automobiles. Infant mortality falls below 25 deaths per 1,000 births. Risks of dying in childhood are minimal. Maternal mortality is at a minimum. Life expectancy at birth jumps quickly to above 70 years of age. Natural increase again declines; in some cases natural decreases occur; the population becomes older. The urban way of life pervades the social institutions in the society. Society is industrialized. Agribusiness produces foodstuffs for export. Nutritionists worry about diets with excessive calories, high fat content, and food preservatives. Public sanitation provides clean water and adequate sewage treatment. Medicine stresses preventive health care (Omran 1971:509–538).

In each of the three stages of the demographic transition, what happens to fertility, mortality, natural increase, and the age composition of the population? What are the major killers in each stage? What is the dominant form of economic production?

Students of population use this typology not only to understand the correlations between demographic and nondemographic factors over time, but also to learn how they affect one another. Based on this understanding, policies may be formulated that might overcome problems faced by developing countries as they modernize and undertake to check the consequences of excessive fertility and rapid population growth.

The framework of the demographic transition is thus used as a standard against which to compare the experiences of nonwestern countries that experience economic development. From these comparisons it is clear that not all countries undergo economic development at the same pace. Great Britain moved from stage one to stage three in roughly 150 years, whereas Japan accomplished that feat in roughly half the time. Not all countries must industrialize before fertility begins to decline. It is not clear whether economic development precedes demographic changes, or vice versa. In short, the ability of the theory of the demographic transition to predict the sequence of events when changes occur is questionable.

The framework suggests a number of possible explanations accounting for demographic and social change. Some demographers focus on whether the urban lifestyles have values that discourage childbearing and childrearing and encourage leisure, entertainment, and self-expression. Others ask whether the pursuit of upward social mobility, prevalent in urban and industrial societies, leads couples to have smaller families.

Whether the framework of the demographic transition attains the status of theory remains a moot point. Clearly it is useful as a framework for comparing the experiences of the developed and developing nations. It also serves as a framework for examining the problems faced by countries where the population bomb is still ticking.

Summary

Demography is the systematic study of population. Analysts look at population structure and the dynamics of population change—births, deaths, and movement. How additions and losses affect the composition of the population and the institutions of society, as well as how social and cultural changes affect population, are the twin concerns of students of population.

Demographic data are obtained from censuses, vital registration systems, and sample surveys, along with surviving historical documents. State governments and federal agencies cooperate in collecting, analyzing, and publishing population statistics. Estimates and projections for countries without systematic data collection agencies are published by the United Nations.

Of major interest to demographers are the topics of population size and growth. Population size and the components of growth are examined using the demographic equation. Natural increase, the excess of births over deaths, accounts for rapid increase in world population. Rapid growth in population started in Europe about the time of the Industrial Revolution, caused by improvements in agriculture and food distribution, sanitation, public health, and medicine, which lowered mortality. As European nations modernized and their growth rates slowed, the lessons learned in lowering mortality were imported by other countries. Rapid population growth was triggered in developing countries. Nowadays developing countries have high growth rates and are faced with the task of lowering their birth rates.

Continued population growth threatens the balance between human numbers and natural resources. With increases in population, the demand for food, clean water, and energy has soared. Population growth also threatens the ability of governments to provide basic services, such as educations, housing, public health services, and medical care. Unless steps are taken to reduce fertility and halt population growth, conflicts might develop between the "haves" and the "have nots" over access to and use of natural resources.

To understand population structure, demographers examine the age and sex composition of the population. The sex ratio reflects the relative balance of males and females in the population. It is affected by biological, economic, and social factors. The population pyramid is a bar graph for displaying the percentages of population in various age and sex groupings. Its shape reflects past changes in births, deaths, and migration. By looking at the percentages of persons in various groupings, such as young, old, and working ages, some idea is obtained of how many dependents are likely to be supported by workers. It also gives

some idea of the resources a society must expend to meet various social objectives.

To understand the dynamics of population, demographers study the relations between nondemographic factors and births, deaths, and movement.

Mortality was the first of the demographic variables to be studied. The age at which people die, and from what, is affected by factors related to the environment, the society, and individual lifestyles.

Migration, the shifting of people across borders, is affected by factors pushing people from one setting and pulling them to another. The flow between countries is tied to migration policies as well as to economic opportunities at place of origin and destination.

Fertility is the most explosive of the components of change. It is affected by environmental factors, as well as by individuals' conformity to group norms on issues related to marriage and family. To halt population growth, fertility must be controlled through establishing policies and programs that encourage smaller families yet maintain a desirable quality of life.

Some understanding of how population growth has slowed in the past and the factors associated with its decline is obtained by considering the demographic transition. Although economic development is not a prerequisite for reduced fertility, many of the lessons learned in modernized countries may be transferable to developing countries in order to defuse the population bomb.

Suggested Readings

Paul R. Ehrlich and Anne H. Ehrlich. *Population/Resources/Environment*. San Francisco: Freeman, 1972. Examines nature of various biosystems and social systems as impacted by population growth, declining resources, and growing pollution.

Demographic Dynamics. Ithaca, NY: American Demographics, Inc. Monthly journal aimed at

readership without technical training in demography. Articles cover population issues and trends within United States.

Donella H. Meadows et al. *The Limits to Growth*. New York: Signet, 1972. Presents computer projections on various scenarios of linkages between population and future of industrialized society.

William Ophuls. *Ecology and the Politics of Scarcity:*

Prologue to a Political Theory of the Steady State. San Francisco: Freeman, 1977. A provocative analysis of how current political values are no longer compatible with the realities of ecological scarcities.

Robert H. Weller and Leon F. Bouvier. *Population: Demography and Policy.* New York: St. Martin's, 1981. A readable introduction to demography. Focuses on people as "population ac-

tors" making decisions related to having children, moving, or dying.

U.S. Commission on Population Growth and the American Future. *Population and the American Future.* Washington, D.C.: U.S. Government Printing Office, 1972. Reviews research and testimony of scholars in a variety of disciplines. Makes general policy recommendations on limitation of population growth to enhance the quality of life.

17

Urbanization and Urban Life

We live in an urban world. A lobsterman in Cundy's Harbor, Maine, chats with the bank teller about his daughter's progress at Brown University in Providence. A widow in Spencer, Iowa, calls her broker in Chicago to check on the prices of wheat and soybean futures. A blood technician in Knoxville punches up computer code numbers to check the results of a laboratory test run in San Diego. An airline ticket agent in Pittsburgh tells a customer wanting to fly to Birmingham that she has to fly through Atlanta.

Guerrillas plotting to effect a coup stress the importance of sealing off the capital city by capturing the airport, taking over the radio and TV stations, and shutting down public utilities until the new regime is recognized. Farmers in India dream of all the rupees paid to street vendors. A peasant in the campo plans a pilgrimage to the shrine in Buenos Aires.

People throughout the world turn to cities to obtain gratification of their economic, political, cultural, and spiritual wants. Despite the fact that much of our life is shaped by forces emanating from urban populations and we take them for granted, this ascendence of the city is really quite recent in the affairs of people.

For much of history human life was rural in character. With the agricultural revolution, urban settlements developed and the urban revolution began. The urban revolution was accelerated with the onset of the Industrial Revolution. Nowadays the city is fast becoming the major social form of human settlement. In the 1950s less than 20% of the world's population lived in large cities. By 1970 almost 25% inhabited large cities. By the year 2000 over half of all people on the earth will reside in urban settlements (Davis 1952). Science fiction writers foresee a future world with "megacities"—huge cities of a half billion to a billion people living on top of one another. Whether such a future is possible, clearly the numbers of people living in cities will increase, as will the number of cities. (See Figure 17.1, p. 418)

The Urban Revolution

According to archeologists, people have existed on earth for more than two million years. For most of history people were nomadic, living off the land—hunting for game and gathering edible plants. They lived in small bands. Living sites often were temporary with the time spent at any site shaped by the rhythm of the seasons and the availability of food and water.

Permanent urban settlements, large populations or densely inhabited population living in a circumscribed area, first appeared between 10,000 and 5,000 B.C. The shift from a nomadic to sedentary way of life and from small to larger groups radically changed the physical and social environment of human beings. It altered people's relationship to nature, the way they thought,

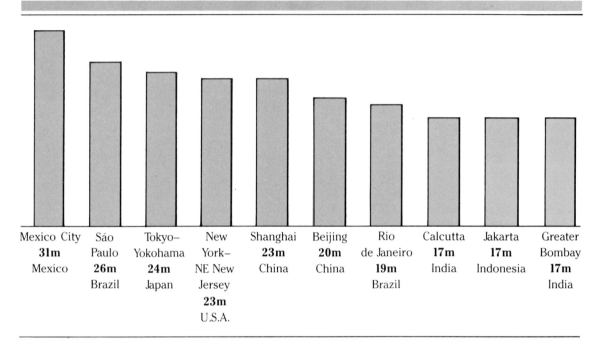

Figure 17.1 Tomorrow's giants. In the year 2000 the biggest cities in the world will be those shown here. SOURCE: *Popline,* *4*(5): 8.

the quality of their interpersonal relationships, and the arrangement of their social institutions. It was called the "urban revolution."

Although the urban revolution started thousands of years ago, the spread of cities initially was slow. As conditions became favorable, cities increased in numbers and their populations grew. As conditions deteriorated, some cities declined in size; others disappeared. Only with the onset of the Industrial Revolution did large-scale urbanization occur and the effect of cities on social life became pervasive. The variety of forms that the patterning of urban settlements has taken as well as the importance of cities have interested sociologists (Davis 1955). By looking at the preindustrial, the medieval, and the modern industrial city, we can gain some understanding about different types of urban forms that developed during the urban revolution.

The Preindustrial City

Four conditions generally are recognized as necessary for the development of a **preindustrial city:** an adequate population base, a favorable ecology, adequate technology, and some degree of social organization (Hauser 1965). The first condition required for urban settlements to develop was a population large enough to supply sufficient labor to produce the food, goods, and services needed by urban dwellers and people living in areas outside the

Preindustrial city
early urban settlement, usually found along rivers, dependent on agricultural hinterland and trade.

cities—the **hinterland.** As food surpluses grew, more people could live in cities and work in nonagricultural jobs. There are various ideas of the minimum size that qualifies a settlement as urban. Most students of the city agree that early settlements with a population between 5,000 and 10,000 were urban (Sjoberg 1960).

Second, favorable ecological conditions were necessary for urban settlements to develop. Preindustrial cities often were located in regions with a moderate climate, arable soil, and sufficient water for people, animals, and crops. Many of these early cities were located on silted flood plains and along valleys of major rivers, such as the Tigris, Euphrates, Nile, Indus, and Yellow rivers.

Third, a technological base was necessary for urban settlements to expand in area, size, density, and importance. The discovery of irrigation and hydraulics—ways of moving water from rivers inland—extended croplands. Domestication of plants (grains) (Harris 1967) and animals, along with the invention of the plow, the yoke, and the wheel, increased the efficiency of agricultural production. The introduction of pottery permitted storage and transportation of foods, leading to the development of trade networks between urban settlements. The extraction of metals, the discovery of metallurgy, and the rise of metal work, with the fashioning of weapons and ornaments, stimulated trade, both between regions and within the cities. The development of writing and the calendar permitted an expansion of commerce, centralization of administration and record keeping, as well as the planning of harvest times and religious rituals.

Fourth, as preindustrial cities grew in size and density their social organization became more complex and stratified. A two-class system of rich and poor existed. A small aristocratic or priestly elite was responsible for city administration, supervision of agriculture in the hinterland, construction of religious centers, and protection of the population during conflicts. The elite was supported by taxing the poor. The poor were the farmers (peasants), artisans, merchants, and outcasts. Artisans and merchants scratched out a living from the sale of artifacts to the elite and occasional trade with other urban settlements.

What were the four conditions necessary for growth of urban settlements?

Preindustrial cities, whether in Mesopotamia, Egypt, India, China, or Mesoamerica, displayed a typical pattern of land use. The city center was dominated by administrative headquarters or religious ceremonial sites and buildings housing the elite. Dwellings of elites and other officials were larger than those of poorer urbanites. Spreading outward from the city center along narrow unpaved alleyways were smaller buildings containing shops and dwellings of merchants and artisans. Each craft occupied its own territory or alleyway.

Hinterland countryside surrounding a city.

The streets of this city have not changed in hundreds of years.

Alleyways were noisy, congested with merchants hawking their wares and children playing. In dry weather the dust was choking; in wet weather alleyways were mires of mud, excrement, and offal. Water supplies often were contaminated. Crowding fostered the rapid spread of disease. On the periphery of the city along the city wall or beyond lived the more destitute of the poor. Farmers usually lived beyond the wall.

Regardless of the size of the preindustrial city, a rural flavor was noticeable. Livestock roamed the alleyways. Markets selling food dotted alleyways. The rhythm of business and religious rituals often was tied to cycles of sowing and harvest. The quality of life in the city, however, differed sharply from the hinterland. The city was the center of art, law, education, and trade. It dominated the hinterland (Sjoberg 1960). The fate of the preindustrial city depended on the ability of the elite to maintain military, political, religious, and economic control over its territories (Wittfogel 1955).

The Medieval City

The fall of the Roman Empire in the sixth century marked the end of the empire's cities in western Europe. By that time, towns had become fortifications for the protection of feudal lords or for clergy and Church properties.

Manorialism and feudalism were the pillars of life for several centuries thereafter. By the eleventh century food production increased as larger farms developed. Revival of trade in luxuries and commodities between Europe and the Byzantine Empire during the eleventh through thirteenth centuries stimulated trade centers in Mediterranean seaports and in river towns along trade routes. The **medieval city** came of age (Sirjamaki 1964; Weber 1962; Pirenne 1925; Gies and Gies 1969; Rorig 1967).

With new wealth a merchant class developed. Merchant guilds and associations were formed. Merchants appealed to the king to secure privilege, rank, and protection from feudal lords and the church. The king relied heavily on merchants to increase his region's wealth and power. Manufacturing developed in silks, woolens, and linens. Handicraft production expanded. Guilds maintained monopolies over occupational specialties, recruiting workers, setting up apprenticeships, controlling social lives of members, fixing standards of production, and resisting government interference. Administrative councils formed to protect trade interests of the city, provide services, pass ordinances, and collect taxes. Cities became centers for education and the arts. Teachers and artists were sponsored by patron merchants and nobles.

Medieval cities were stratified into two classes. The rich included nobles, merchants, wealthy manufacturers, and lesser officials. The poor included the artisans, shopkeepers, liberated serfs, manual laborers, thieves, and riff-raff.

Land use in the medieval city was similar to that of the preindustrial city. The city was walled, with the city center containing a square facing the church or the residence of the ruler. Next to these buildings, or separated by an inner

Medieval city urban settlements, usually seaports or sites on trade routes, dependent on agriculture, luxury trade, handicrafts, and manufacturing.

An example of a walled city.

wall, were multistoried buildings of wood and stone with gabled roofs. Buildings closely spaced on narrow streets made up the remainder of the inner city. The rich lived in the more spacious houses. Farther from the center of the city were one- and two-storied houses where the more well-to-do among the poor lived. Housing was crowded. The downstairs or front portion of the dwelling served as the work area, and the upstairs or back was the living quarters for the family. The destitute lived in poverty either next to or beyond the outer walls. Life in medieval cities for the wealthy was luxurious; for the poor it was miserable. But both rich and poor faced the problems of congestion, filth, contaminated water, and occasional epidemics. Deaths exceeded births. Only through migration from the rural countryside could cities survive.

The Modern Industrial City

From the late fifteenth century to the middle of the eighteenth century towns and cities were born and died in response to changes in commodity markets, trade routes, occasional wars, and crop failures. As nation-states achieved relative peace and political stability and the Industrial Revolution began, capitalism matured and the **modern industrial city** came into being.

Modern industrial city urban settlements usually sited near energy sources or raw materials, dependent on manufacturing, banking, and transportation.

Between 1750 and 1900, a series of technological advances in agriculture, transportation, communication, manufacturing, and banking altered the character of society. Agricultural advances—such as new methods of swamp and land drainage, intensive cultivation, new fertilizers, better seed selection, and animal breeding—increased the quantity, quality, and variety of foods. More food enabled the urban populations to increase. Demand for food led to enclosures and conversion of pastures and woodland to farmland. Small farms gave way to commercial agriculture.

Water and land transportation improved. At sea the steamship replaced the sailing ship and cargo space expanded, thereby increasing tonnage hauled. Inland water transport spread as networks of canals were dug. On land, highways were improved and tollroads constructed. Railroads replaced barge traffic after the 1850s, providing more efficient movement of manufactured goods and raw materials to and from cities.

Communication improved. Newspapers increased their circulations. Postal services improved as highways and rail systems expanded. The telegraph greatly facilitated information flow for business.

Manufacturing dominated the economy. Coal and ore extraction increased. Metallurgy led to advances in iron and steel production. Inventions in one industry were borrowed and adapted for use in other industries. Light industries, especially textiles, reaped the benefits of an ever-expanding technological base.

As agriculture, manufacturing, and commerce boomed, the demand for capital to finance land, plant production, and marketing stimulated banking. The system of credit was extended. Joint-stock companies developed. Futures in commodities and currencies were traded.

In short, the Industrial Revolution in Europe changed the fundamental nature of social relationships. Manual labor and animal power were replaced as energy sources by water, wood, and coal. Craftsmanship fell victim to the machine. Local markets became extended to regional and international markets. The dormitory and factory system replaced handicraft production. Place of work became separated from place of residence. The corporation took over for the family in financing work, recruiting workers, and marketing goods. Specialization of jobs and routinization of work fostered the growth of elaborate networks of economic exchange and the rise of bureaucracy. Management and worker became divided by class interests. Manufacturing replaced agriculture as the main source of employment for the population.

Modern industrial cities were stratified into three classes: the wealthy, the middle class, and the working class. Social distinctions were based on wealth and power. Social mobility was gained through initiative and individual merit.

Land use in the modern industrial city in Europe was unique. The city's area was expansive, its inhabitants numerous, and its density high. Commercial activities, such as banking and retail trade, occupied a central business district. Another section of the city, usually close to a source of energy or a transportation terminal, was dominated by manufacturing. As trolley and train replaced carriages, residential areas for middle and upper classes sprang up on the fringes of the city. Workers lived near the factories in substandard housing. Working-class sections of the city often were without paved streets, public services, or adequate water.

The modern industrial city in Europe was noisy, congested, and dirty. The air was fouled by smoke, soot, and ash emitted from factory and chimney. Work hours were long, tasks monotonous; and vacations a rarity. Despite the ugliness of urban life and the lack of amenities for many urbanites, the modern industrial city thrived as a center for manufacturing, business, and commerce.

What are the essential features of preindustrial, medieval, and modern industrial cities?

In sum, the three types of cities differed in their quality of life. They differed in size, in the principal kinds of economic activities, in their social stratification, and land-use patterns (see Table 17.1).

Although the three types of cities have been discussed here in a historical framework, a few words of caution are needed. First, urban settlements that attained the character of preindustrial cities did not necessarily develop into medieval cities, then later into modern industrial cities; for example, Katmandu. Some cities, Carthage, for example, came into being when social and economic conditions were favorable, then as circumstances changed faded into oblivion. Other cities that started out as preindustrial or medieval maintain much of their original character even today. Venice is one such city. Still other cities have changed their basic nature, as conditions changed.

Second, much of the discussion of modern industrial cities is based on the experiences of cities in European countries where urbanization and industrialization occurred as twin processes. The experiences of these countries were not necessarily the same as those of many developing countries.

World Urbanization

Urban settlements have been part of human history for thousands of years, but the Industrial Age marked the beginning of the rise in the proportion of the world's population living in urban areas. Since the nineteenth century the pace of world **urbanization** has quickened. At first, the smaller urban areas— places of 5,000 or more—contained the lion's share of the world's urban population. Since World War II, cities of 100,000 or more have been increasingly the localities where urbanites live. (See Table 17.2.) Should present trends

Urbanization increase in the number of localities called urban, as well as the proportion of the population living in urban areas.

TABLE 17.1. Summary of Selected Characteristics for Preindustrial, Medieval, and Modern Industrial Cities

Characteristics	Preindustrial	Medieval	Modern Industrial
Population size	5,000 to 30,000	8,000 to 100,000	30,000 and larger
Main economic activities	Agriculture Trade in farm goods, metal goods	Agriculture Trade in luxuries Handicrafts Textile manufacturing	Commercial agriculture Wholesale and retail trade Banking Light and heavy manufacturing
Class system	Military or priestly elite Artisans, traders, and peasants	Kings, nobility, wealthy manufacturers, and merchants Working class, guild members, poor, and farmers	Wealthy Middle class Poor
Land use	Religious or administrative center Shops and residences Agricultural hinterland	Church or royalty in center Wealthy residence Guild territories and housing Agricultural hinterland	Central business district Transportation terminals and manufacturing zones Residential areas Suburbia Rural farm

TABLE 17.2.   Percentage Estimates of World's Population in Cities

	Rural	5,000 or more	100,000 or more	1 million or more
1800	97.0	3.0	1.7	—
1850	93.6	6.4	2.3	—
1900	86.4	13.6	5.5	—
1950	71.8	28.2	16.2	7.3
1970	61.4	38.6	23.8	12.4
1985	53.7	46.3	30.3	15.4
2000	46.4	53.6	40.0	26.5

SOURCE: Kingsley Davis, "The Role of Urbanization in the Developmental Process," *International Technical Cooperation Centre Review* (Tel Aviv) 1:1–13 (July, 1952). Figures for 1800–1950 cited from Table 2; figures for 1985 and 2000 from Table 3.

continue, cities of one million or more, megacities, will house larger shares of the world's population.

Although urbanization has touched all continents except Antarctica, its pace has not been constant over time nor its spread uniform throughout the world. Two general models of urbanization describe its history and spread— a mature model for developed countries and a late model for the developing countries. The **mature model** focuses on selected aspects of urbanization in western European countries. In contrast, the **late model** highlights various conditions found in many countries in the process of modernizing. For each set of countries there are different demographic factors, sources of growth, and potential for future urban growth.

Mature Model

Western Europe was the first region in the world to modernize. Within this region some countries began the process earlier than others, and some countries progressed more rapidly than others. Various paths of development were followed, depending on available resources, political ideologies, and economic conditions. Despite differences within the region, sufficient similarities exist to identify three conditions that typify the urbanization of this region and other countries that followed the European model of urban development.

First, the shift in population from rural to urban and the economy from agriculture to industry generally occurred as twin processes. The technological base expanded and became more complex over some 200 years. As technical advances spread from one area of activity to another—agriculture, manufacturing, banking, communication, and transportation—changes occurred in the institutional arrangements and lifestyles of the population. Altered economic and social relationships fostered the rise of cities. Conversely, city growth generated greater demand for goods and services, as well as providing labor for the expansion of industry and other segments of the economy.

Second, the Industrial Revolution fundamentally changed demographic conditions that in turn modified the character of urbanization in western European countries. Prior to the industrial take-off, most countries in the region demographically were in the stage known as "high potential growth"—namely,

Mature model of urbanization model based on developed countries, involving both urbanization and industrialization, with slow urbanization accomplished by rural to urban migration; most countries in this category have over 70% of population in urban areas.

high levels of fertility and mortality, with minimal growth rates. Their populations were largely rural with a few larger cities and a scattering of smaller urban settlements.

As the Industrial Revolution gained momentum the countries progressed through the stage of "incipient growth"—namely, high levels of fertility, slowly but steadily falling levels of mortality, with high rates of natural increase. Populations continued to be mostly rural, but the number of urban areas increased as did the size and density of larger cities.

By the end of the Industrial Revolution and the onset of the postindustrial era, these countries entered the stage of "incipient decline"—namely, low levels of fertility and mortality, with low, if not negative, growth rates. (For a discussion of major trends in fertility and mortality in developed and developing nations as well as the demographic transition, see Chapter 16.) Over half of the population lived in urban areas, with many persons dwelling in intermediate or large cities and their suburban fringes. This process of urbanization was relatively slow, taking some 200 years to complete. The process passed through two periods.

In the early period, "incipient growth," cities did not increase as rapidly in size as might be expected given the high rates of natural increase. Although births generally exceeded deaths, cities were more deadly places to live than the countryside. If cities had depended solely on natural increase for their survival, they would have lost numbers. It was only by tapping the reservoir of the larger rural population that the cities replenished their losses through migration.

In the later period, "incipient decline," urban areas have expanded principally through natural increase. The rural population has shrunk in size. Proportionately it is smaller than the urban population. No longer can cities turn to the rural reservoir as a source of sustained growth.

Third, the potential for further urbanization in many developed countries is fast approaching the upper limit. By definition, only 100% of the total population can live in urban areas. Today, many countries already have 70% or more of their populations residing in urban areas. Given the reduced importance of rural-to-urban migration and the lower growth rates in developed countries, the pace of urbanization will probably continue to slow.

Late Model

Developing countries are dispersed throughout the world, but chiefly in Africa, Asia, and Latin America. They differ greatly in their available resources, political ideologies, and strategies for modernizing. They differ widely in the relative degrees of modernization achieved. Despite these differences some points of similarity are apparent when their experiences are compared with those of the developed countries.

First, the historical association of industrialization and urbanization, so strong in developed countries, is not universally found among developing countries. In many developing countries much of the technological base has

Late model of urbanization model based on countries with absence of industrialization, with relatively rapid urbanization, accomplished through natural increase plus rural to urban migration; most developing countries have high potential for further urban growth.

been imported rather than discovered and developed autonomously. Such imports include sanitation and medical strategies reducing sickness and mortality; the "green revolution," that is, principles of scientific agriculture; capital-intensive manufacturing supplanting animal and manual labor; bureaucratic principles of organizational management substituting for traditional authority rule; and capitalistic market principles replacing adventuristic capitalism. (For a discussion of social organizations see Chapter 10.) In a relatively short time, developing countries have experienced a "knowledge implosion." Institutions have not had the opportunity to adjust fully to new technologies. If the pace of change in the modernization of western European countries is like a walk, then its pace in developing countries is that of a gallop.

In many developing countries, cities that are centers of administration, trade, or extractive industries have been testing-grounds for imported technologies. Some cities have industrialized successfully. Others have not and are **over-urbanized.** Such cities contain massive numbers of people, as in Calcutta, Buenos Aires, Kampala. So many people live in these cities that neither job opportunities nor services can be expanded rapidly enough to meet the demand.

Over-urbanized cities growing so fast in size and density that governments cannot provide jobs or basic services to take care of population.

Engineers are continually developing and testing alternative forms of energy such as this wind turbine.

Second, as in the developed countries, the character of urbanization in developing countries has been dramatically shaped by demographic conditions. About a fourth of the population of developing countries live in urban areas. Many of these countries are at the stage of "incipient growth." Their fertility levels are high, though showing signs of decline. The importation of public health and medical technologies caused mortality levels to fall sharply. Both countryside and urban areas have high rates of natural increase. In contrast to the medieval and early industrial cities of western Europe, the urban areas in developing countries are relatively healthful places to live. In fact, natural increase is conservatively estimated to contribute slightly over one-third of the increase in city size.

Third, the potential for future urbanization in developing countries is high. Most of the populations are largely rural. Cities still have a large reservoir from which to draw in the future. Rural to urban migration contributes heavily to growth in urban areas. The pace of urbanization is rapid and will continue to be so. From 1950 to 1970 the rise in the proportion of population living in urban areas in developed countries rose about 30%. Thus, developing countries are experiencing urbanization almost twice as fast as developed countries (Davis 1952).

In sum, in developed countries urbanization and industrialization were twin historical processes. The pace of urbanization was slow. Urbanization was achieved principally through rural-to-urban migration. Developed countries currently are heavily urbanized, approaching the upper limit of full urbanization.

In developing countries urbanization and industrialization are not necessarily interdependent processes. The pace of urbanization is rapid. Urbanization is due to rural-to-urban migration, as well as a marked excess of births over deaths. These countries are lightly urbanized. They are far from the upper limit of full urbanization.

How did the process of urbanization in western Europe differ from what is going on today in the developing countries?

Urbanization in the United States

Urbanization in the United States has followed the mature model. Our history of urbanization has three periods: the colonial era (1652–1840), with a mix of backcountry agriculture, inland towns, and seaport cities; the manufacturing era (1840–1930), with cities where a single industry or a number of highly related industries dominate their economies; and the metropolitan and megalopolitan era (1930 to present), with cities of millions of people, highly diversified occupation structures that dominate regions of the country economically, socially, and demographically.

The Colonial Era

The early phase of urban growth in the American colonies witnessed the rise of an urban frontier on the fringes of the wilderness. Colonials came from countries already undergoing urbanization and rapid technical changes. They represented all classes and a variety of occupations. Immigrant farmers, displaced by enclosures or denied inheritance of family farms, settled in the "back country." An agricultural mix developed of self-subsistence farms, general-purpose farms geared to local markets, and cash-crop farms run by tenants or plantation owners (Johnson and Kross 1960). Artisans, craftspersons, manufacturers, and workers drawn from European shops and industries were knowledgeable of technical advances in their various specialties. They located inland and in seaport towns and set up shops, forges, and mills. Village industries produced the textiles, flour, lumber, brick, rope, and iron that were needed by local farmers and traded regionally. In seaport towns, craftspersons created clothes, furniture, pewter, glass, and silverware for wealthy merchants, ship-owners, and gentry.

Seaports, such as Newport, Boston, New York, Philadelphia, Baltimore, and Charleston, S.C., with deep water access, sheltered anchorage, plentiful freshwater, and defensible positions grew into cities. These ports became focal points for finance and commerce, trade with inland economies and exportation of tobacco, lumber, fish, rum, and iron to foreign countries. Also, these ports were entry points for immigrants and supply centers for migrants moving inland to settle in villages or to stake out homesteads. These cities were compact, dense with wharves, markets, shops, and residences scattered throughout. Workplaces and residences usually were separated, but within easy walking distance.

As the colonial population increased, inland towns became more numerous and seaport cities grew larger. Small towns previously on the periphery of cities were annexed. By the early 1800s, despite long distances between settlements and poor transportation, an elaborate trade network linking farm, village, and city was firmly established. American urbanization had begun, although it was not until the manufacturing era that large cities came to dominate the hinterland (Gilchrist 1967; Bridenbaugh 1955).

The Manufacturing Era

The middle phase of urban growth in the United States was one of dramatic technological and social change, as well as rapid population growth. American industry moved from dependency on European know-how to a position of world leadership. Stealing British textile technology in the late 1700s and early 1800s and using Yankee ingenuity, woolen and cotton manufacturing quickly became competitive with European mills. Textile cities, where water drove the looms, sprang up along New England streams and rivers.

The mass production of interchangeable parts revolutionized industry. Armament manufacturing centers grew in New England and Middle Atlantic states. Mass production, using specialized machines and tool-making techniques, turned out products ranging from sewing machines to bicycles and farm equipment. As the demand for more complex machines and specially designed tools increased, metallurgy advanced, metal working skills became more sophisticated, and engineering came of age.

Iron and steel production led to the growth of heavy manufacturing cities located near limestone, coal, and iron ore deposits in the Appalachian region. The move from light industries to heavy manufacturing required more efficient power sources. Steam replaced water as the reciprocating engine shut down the water wheel. Industry, no longer dependent on rivers, dispersed. Manufacturing cities spread even farther following the invention of the transformer, which made possible long distance distribution of electricity.

Sectional rivalry between the North and South and competition between major cities on the seaboard for financial control over commercial and manufacturing interests in the West spurred advances in transportation and banking. Turnpikes and toll roads laced the countryside. Canals linked the Midwest

Traffic jam at Randolph and Dearborn Streets, Chicago, 1905.

and the East. Railroads connected manufacturing centers and seaport cities and spanned the continent. With the spread of transportation the urban corridor advanced steadily westward.

Population concentrations clustered along transportation routes. Cities such as St. Louis, Chicago, and Buffalo developed at points where transfer from one mode of transportation to another was required. The continuous influx of immigrants provided cheap labor for manufacturing. Large cities constituted ready markets for manufactured goods.

The modern industrial city became the major urban social form. Cities were identified by products produced: Pittsburgh—steel, Troy—textiles, Buffalo—flour, Detroit—automobiles, Akron—tires. By the end of the manufacturing era the spread of urban settlements ranged from coast to coast and major cities in various sections of the country had established regional economic dominance.

The Metropolitan and Megalopolitan Era

The last phase of urban growth in the United States marked the emergence of metropolitan areas and the rise of the megalopolis. Several cities passed the million mark, their populations swelling from natural increase, rural to urban migration, and immigration. Cities once densely inhabited and compact became even denser and began to spread outward. The spread of highways and motor vehicles permitted the population to move farther from the city center. Commuting long distances between places of residence and work became a way of life. Trucks replaced barges and rails, and trucking lessened the importance of central terminals in cities. The ability to move goods with greater ease stimulated the dispersion of manufacturing, industrial, wholesale, and retail sites in cities and in satellite communities.

Communication systems also changed dramatically. Expansion of industry and business was bolstered by advances in communications. The telephone permitted decentralization of purchasing, production, and marketing activities, yet promoted easy coordination between people widely separated from one another. Suburbs developed. Better transportation and communication led businesses and industries to move from larger cities to the suburbs or to smaller cities on the fringes of large cities. Chain stores, branch offices, and shopping malls developed, allowing corporations downtown to expand their services to the suburbs. Decentralization extended the regional influence of cities as networks of economic exchanges covered larger and larger geographic regions.

Public health and sanitation, water, fire, and law enforcement were upgraded and extended. Regional agencies developed to coordinate efforts between cities and satellite communities and states to guarantee delivery of services to urbanites. Agribusiness squeezed out unprofitable farms. Agribusiness became highly specialized, and its markets were increasingly protected by state and federal legislation or international agreement.

The growth of American metropolises in number, size, and density and the expansion of their cultural and economic influence continued until the territory of one urban giant touched that of another. There developed corridors of metropolises, intermediate sized cities, and suburbs, as well as occasionally interspersed recreational areas and farmlands. Such a corridor is called a **megalopolis** (Gottman 1964). On the eastern seaboard of the United States, the megalopolitan corridor stretches from Portland, Maine, to Alexandria, Virginia. This is one of the most urbanized regions in the world. It is economically interconnected to a degree that has never before been achieved in human history. It is within this and other megalopolitan settings that the postindustrial society has developed.

Megalopolis a corridor of interconnected metropolises extending over a large area.

In sum, urbanization is a process with two basic features. First, it is an increase in the number of localities defined as urban. Second, it is an increase in the proportion of the population residing in urban localities. Urbanization started slowly at first, gaining speed as population grew and technical advances permitted more and more people to work in nonagricultural jobs. Its pace varied in different countries of the world, depending on whether cities grew as modernization occurred or did not occur. Urbanization took place slowly in the currently developed countries, but in developing countries it is moving more quickly. Urbanization in the United States followed the same path taken by developed countries in Europe. Should the world see the continued urban growth, by the twenty-first century the city will be the dominant pattern of human settlement.

Urban Structure

To understand the variety of patterns in the urban environment, sociologists pay attention to various aspects of urban structure and process. These structural features include: *size* and *areal* characteristics—how geographic units are classified as urban, as well as the concentration of social and economic activities in these localities; *compositional* characteristics—the population's racial, religious, and ethnic diversity, its educational and income levels, its makeup by marital status, and its patterns of labor force employment by occupation and industrial groupings; *organizational* characteristics—its tax structure, political forms, and range of services offered; and *lifestyle* characteristics—its climate, recreational and cultural opportunities, as well as such disadvantages as blighted housing, crime, and pollution.

Two systems are used to identify geographic units and classify them as urban localities. The first system uses political and geographically defined areas such as towns, cities, townships, and incorporated and unincorporated places. These are classified as "urban" depending on their *size* and *density*. Categories of size considered "urban" vary from as small as 250 persons in

THE FACTS · Definition of Urban in the United States

In general, the urban population comprises all persons living in urbanized areas and in places of 2,500 inhabitants or more outside urbanized areas. More specifically, ... the urban population comprises all persons living in (a) places of 2,500 inhabitants or more incorporated as cities, boroughs, villages, and towns (except towns in New England, New York, and Wisconsin); (b) the densely settled urban fringe, whether incorporated or unincorporated or urbanized areas; (c) towns in New England and townships in New Jersey and Pennsylvania which contain no incorporated municipalities as subdivisions and have either 25,000 inhabitants or more or a population of 2,500 to 25,000 and a density of 1,500 persons or more per square mile; (d) counties in states other than New England states, New Jersey, and Pennsylvania that have no incorporated municipalities within their boundaries and have a density of 1,500 persons or more per square mile; and (e) unincorporated places of 2,500 inhabitants or more. The population not classified as urban constitutes the rural population.

SOURCE: U.S. Bureau of the Census, *U. S. Census of the Population: 1970 Number of Inhabitants.* Final Report PC (1)—A1 U.S. Summary (Washington, D.C.: U.S.G.P.O., 1971), p. ix.

Denmark to 40,000 in Korea. In the United States any locality with less than 2,500 persons is categorized as rural (Schmeckebier 1925; Holt 1929; Alterman 1969).

To identify localities that are suburban or unincorporated but socially and economically dependent on larger urban areas, a new category called "urbanized area" was created by the census bureau. This definition classifies areas that are neither urban nor rural. Sometimes these areas are called "suburbs" (Dobriner 1958; Wood 1958; Farley 1964; U.S. Bureau of the Census 1969) or "rurban" (Firey 1946; Kurtz and Eicher 1958) or "urban fringes," since they are located near central cities of 50,000 people or more and have an urban lifestyle.

The second system of classifying localities uses statistical criteria. Sometimes states, but more frequently counties, are the areas used. A set of economic, social, and population statistics is used to identify counties that are alike and combine them into regional areas. When defining regional areas, the census bureau is interested in two issues. First, to what extent is a region economically integrated? Second, to what extent is a region dependent on a large metropolitan city?

Although a number of different definitions have been suggested, such as State Economic Areas, Metropolitan Economic Areas, or Standard Metropolitan Areas (U.S. Bureau of the Census 1973; Bogue and Beal 1961; U.S. Bureau of the Census 1969), the most widely used term is Standard Metropolitan Statistical Area (SMSA). In 1960 there were 212 SMSAs in the United States and 3 in

---

THE FACTS · Definition of Urbanized Area

1. Incorporated places with 2,500 inhabitants or more.
2. Incorporated places with less than 2,500 inhabitants provided each has a closely settled area of 100 housing units or more.
3. Towns in the New England states, townships in New Jersey and Pennsylvania, and counties elsewhere classified as urban.
4. Enumeration districts in unincorporated territory with a population density of 1,000 inhabitants or more per square mile.
5. Other enumeration districts provided that they serve one of the following purposes: (a) to eliminate enclaves, (b) to close indentations in the urbanized areas of one mile or less across the open end, (c) to link outlying enumeration districts of qualifying density that were no more than 1½ miles from the main body of the urbanized areas.

SOURCE: U.S. Bureau of the Census, *U.S. Census of the Population: 1960 Selected Area Reports, Size of Place,* PC (3)—1B (Washington, D.C.: U.S.G.P.O., 1964), p. xxvi.

Puerto Rico; in 1970—243 SMSAs and 4 in Puerto Rico; and in 1980—288 SMSAs.

Sociologists interested in urbanization often use statistics reported by SMSAs to trace the development of metropolitan growth. These statistics reveal the U.S. population is not only urban but also metropolitan. Of the approxi-

---

THE FACTS · Definition of SMSA

For an area to be designated an SMSA: (1) the area must include one city of at least 50,000 inhabitants or more, or two cities with contiguous boundaries with a combined total population of a minimum of 50,000 inhabitants and which basically comprise a single community; (2) an SMSA may be made up of two or more adjacent counties containing cities of 50,000 or more if the cities are within twenty miles of each other and if the entire area is economically and socially integrated. The criteria of metropolitan characteristics include: (1) at least seventy-five percent of the labor force of the area be nonagricultural plus one of the following; (2) fifty percent of the population residing in densities of 150 persons per square mile or more, or (3) the proportion of nonagricultural workers equal to at least "ten percent as many nonagricultural workers residing or working there as reside or work in the county containing the largest city in the metropolitan area," or (4) at least 10,000 employed in nonagricultural pursuits.

SOURCE: U.S. Bureau of the Census. *U.S. Census of the Population: 1960 Detailed Characteristics.* United States Summary. Final Report PC (1)—1D (Washington, D.C.: U.S.G.P.O., 1963), p. ix.

---

mately 203 million Americans counted in 1970, some 69%—139 million—lived in SMSAs. Between 1960 and 1970 the population increased roughly 13%, but in that decade the metropolitan population increased 23% (*The Report of the Commission of Population Growth and the American Future,* 1972).

Much of the metropolitan growth occurred through suburbanization. Suburbs are smaller areas outside of or on the periphery of urban areas. As the number of suburbs increase and the proportion of the population living in these areas increases, the urban or metropolitan sprawl becomes more extensive, as in Atlanta, for example. Some central cities, such as New York City, have lost population as residents moved to previously rural areas on the urban fringe. New metropolitan areas were added as mid-sized cities attained SMSA standing in the southern and western portions of the country. Albuquerque, Salt Lake City, and Denver are examples. Generally metropolitan areas became larger in population through natural increase and in-migration and expanded in territory through annexation. Should present trends continue, by the year 2000 over 85% of the American population will live in SMSAs and about one-sixth of the U.S. land area, excluding Alaska and Hawaii, will be metropolitan.

The use of regional areas is important not only for the study of urbanization but also for planners and politicians. Many federal, state, and local agencies are required by law to use statistics reported for regional areas and smaller units in their population projections and their estimates for targeting subgroups who qualify for government funds and services. States with areas that qualify as SMSAs are eligible for a variety of funding for urban development programs. Thus, criteria for defining SMSAs are of particular interest to politicians lobbying for federal funds and planners in agencies competing for their share of tax dollars.

Functional Classification of Cities

By focusing on selected characteristics, singly or in combinations, we can define classes of urban areas with similar features as well as describe unique forms that develop at different points in time.

Relying on popular impressions, cliches, or personal experiences, many people at one time or another have attempted to categorize various cities. Generally these attempts are not systematic. When classifying cities, sociologists choose some important characteristic that permits systematic comparison among hundreds of cities (Atchley 1967).

The simplest approach for classifying cities examines the pattern of labor force employment using industrial groupings: extractive activities, manufacturing, transportation-communication, wholesale trade, retail trade, personal services, professional services, and public administration. With the use of census data, sociologists can identify a city's single most important economic sector of activity; the relative concentration or diversification of a city's economy; and the economic status of a city relative to other cities in a nation, region, state, or class of similar sized cities (Wilkinson 1964; Hadden and Borgatta 1965).

Cities in which a single sphere of the economy dominates all others include: Detroit—manufacturing, Washington, D.C.—public administration, Las Vegas—personal services (entertainment and recreation), Cheyenne—transportation. In contrast, diversified economies are found in New York, Philadelphia, and Seattle. In general the degree of economic specialization and the nature of specialization are associated with the city's population size and its past history of economic development.

Occasionally, a city contains a disproportionately large share of a nation's population and attains a position of supereminence. It is the political seat of power, and it culturally and economically dominates the country. This type is called a **primate city** (Jefferson 1939). Examples include Bangkok, Mexico City, Paris, and London.

Cities smaller in size, but nonetheless influencing large surrounding territories and acting as the cultural and economic hub for other communities in the region, are called centers of **metropolitan dominance** (Bogue 1949). Examples include Salt Lake City, Denver, Phoenix, and St. Louis. The magnitude of influence that primate cities and metropolitan centers have on territories beyond their city limits is linked to the size of the city, the diversity of the city's economy, and the accessibility of the hinterland's population to the city, or vice versa. As larger cities increase in number, the more likely it is that there will be multiple centers of urban dominance rather than a primate city (Stoeckel and Beegle 1969).

Primate city a single city in a country that contains a disproportionate amount of urban population and share of economic, political, and social power.

Metropolitan dominance city's cultural, political, and economic influence on other communities in region.

Urban Ecology

Another perspective for examining urban structure and the processes shaping the city is **urban ecology.** Robert E. Park and his colleagues at the University of Chicago in the 1920s recognized that the modern industrial city was an ideal subject for study. With the use of census tract information they mapped the characteristics of populations making up local communities in Chicago. The city's shape as well as the distribution and concentrations of social and economic activities in various geographic units were identified. Researchers of the "Chicago School" recognized that patterns of land-use— where people worked and the type of work, as well as where people of differing class and cultural heritage lived—changed over time. These land-use patterns changed as cities increased in size and density, as various classes and groups moved into and out of the city, and as economic forces and preferences shifted.

Several ecological processes were defined as factors in the shifting patterns of land-use: concentration, centralization, segregation, invasion, succession, and decentralization. *Concentration* refers to people congregating in a specific area. *Centralization* occurs as communities form social, cultural, and economic ties to achieve their common goals. When identifiable subgroups reside in separate areas, that is *segregation.* As areas once homogeneous on some characteristics become mixed, *invasion* is said to occur. Once the area completes the shift from mixed to homogeneous, *succession* has occurred.

Urban ecology study of the distribution of people and their activities in space, focusing on land-use patterns and factors causing such patterns.

Decentralization is the move of activities once concentrated in a particular area of the city to several other areas. Underlying each of these processes is the continual economic struggle and competition for space.

Ernest Burgess discussed Chicago's areal configuration of activities as a series of concentric circles in the "Concentric Zone Theory." Its core—zone 1—is the central business district (CBD), Chicago's downtown Loop. This is encircled by zone 2—an area of transition—comprising business, light manufacturing, homes of the poor. Farther out is zone 3 where residences of workers and factories are located. Zone 4 contains single-family dwellings and high-rent apartments. Zone 5 contains suburban residences housing commuters who travel into the city to work in the downtown loop. Various zones also have "natural areas," subcommunities residentially segregated, voluntarily or involuntarily, by class and cultural heritage—Skid Row, the Gold Coast, Italian or German neighborhoods (Park 1967). (See Figure 17.2.)

Ecologists sometimes could not reproduce the concentric configuration of zones in other cities. They proposed alternative models. Homer Hoyt studied small, medium, and large cities and suggested that cities developed along arteries of transportation. His "sector theory" suggests that zones of specialized activity and residence were pie-shaped sectors rather than concentric circles.

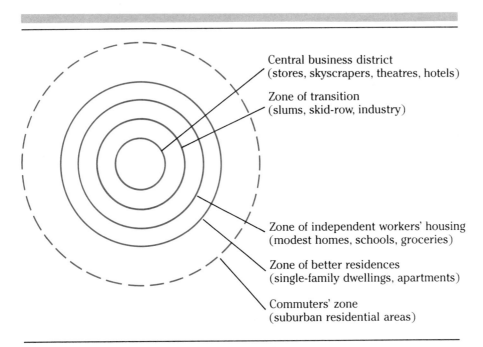

Central business district
(stores, skyscrapers, theatres, hotels)

Zone of transition
(slums, skid-row, industry)

Zone of independent workers' housing
(modest homes, schools, groceries)

Zone of better residences
(single-family dwellings, apartments)

Commuters' zone
(suburban residential areas)

Figure 17.2 Concentric zone pattern of urban spatial organization. SOURCE: Samuel E. Wallace, *The Urban Environment* (Homewood, Ill.: Dorsey, 1980.), pp. 54, 57.

Low-income residences were located closer to the central business district, and high-income residences were found on the periphery of the city (Hoyt 1943). (See Figure 17.3.)

Edward Ullman and Chauncey D. Harris offered a "multiple nuclei theory," which states that cities contain not one central business district (core) but several. Zones of activity and residence assume various shapes. Locales depend on resources available, nearness of markets, topography, and the city's past history of settlement and development (Harris and Ullman 1945). (See Figure 17.4.)

Early ecologists in the Chicago School tradition were criticized for over-emphasizing the importance of economic competition for land as the principal determinant of spatial distribution and concentration of activities. Firey's study of Boston attempted to reproduce the patterns noted by Burgess and Hoyt. Firey found that in many areas of the city patterns of land use remained unchanged despite the economic value of the land. These areas of persistence— the Boston Commons, Beacon Hill, and the North End—were important symbolically to Bostonians, valued as areas of prestige, as landmarks, or as recognized communities of long standing. He also found that the distribution of income by area—judged by rental costs of housing and apartments—was not homogeneous. Many critics of the Chicago School note that geographic units frequently lack homogeneity on a given characteristic (Firey 1945).

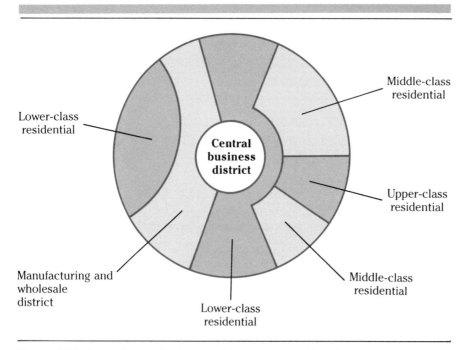

Figure 17.3 Sector theory of urban spatial organization. SOURCE: Samuel E. Wallace, *The Urban Environment* (Homewood, Ill.: Dorsey, 1980), pp. 54, 57.

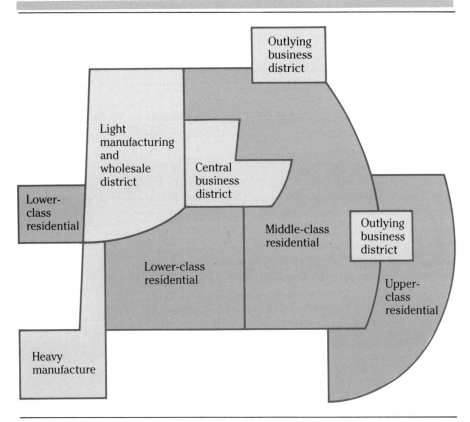

Figure 17.4 Multiple-nuclei pattern of urban spatial organization. SOURCE: Samuel E. Wallace, *The Urban Environment* (Homewood, Ill.: Dorsey, 1980), pp. 54, 57.

Social Area and Factor Analyses

Recognizing that types of urban society differ in the degree of complexity of structure, Eshref Shevky and Wendell Bell (1955) suggested three indexes for comparing a variety of social characteristics for geographic units. These indexes include: *social rank* (or "economic status") measured by occupation, education, and income; *urbanization* (or "family status") measured by child/ women ratios, proportions of working women, and percentages of single-family dwellings; and *segregation* (or "ethnic status") measured by proportions of population in minority groupings. As used by some investigators, each census tract is scored on each of the three indexes, the tract is coded as a particular social type, and then a map is drawn for the city (Shevky and Bell 1955).

Proponents of this method—*social area analysis*—claim that it is useful for delineating neighborhoods and capturing the variability in the mixture of characteristics found in different areas of the city. They also contend that the method is useful, since it permits researchers to select areas for sampling in order to investigate the attitudes and behaviors of residents.

Critics of social area analysis argue that if complexity in urban structure is the subject of inquiry and its detail is to be understood, then it is a mistake to limit unduly the number of characteristics to those specified in the three indexes. A larger number of characteristics should be studied (Abu-Lughod 1969).

Thus some sociologists have used *factor analysis* to examine the dimensions of urban structure. Factor analysis is a statistical procedure that examines a large number of characteristics and sorts interrelated characteristics into sets or clusters called "factors." A profile of characteristics clustered into factors—dimensions of urban structure—is obtained for each area of the city. This approach has at least two advantages over prior approaches: It permits the researcher to look at large amounts of data; and the dimensions of urban structure thereby obtained describe more fully the variety in patterns of characteristics by areas for which data are available.

Factor analyses of data in the United States and in other western nations suggest that urban structure is differentiated by social rank, by family status, and by ethnic status. These dimensions parallel those suggested by Shevky and other social area analysts, but include a longer list of characteristics within each dimension. Similar studies of non-Western cities reveal that areas differ by social rank and ethnic status. The dimensions of social rank include characteristics that are socioeconomic and are linked to family lifestyle traits (Hunter 1977; Berry and Kasarda 1977).

Regardless of the strategy used in studying the ecology of urban areas and the type of city examined, sociologists agree that residential segregation and centralization of activities occur in all cities. The bases for residential segregation are socioeconomic status, race, and ethnicity. The superrich, the well-to-do, the workers, and the down-and-outs find their respective habitats in various parts of the city and suburbs. The ethnics, the immigrants, and the rural-to-urban migrants similarly find their territorial niches. Also, whether the city is preindustrial, medieval, modern-industrial, or a megacity, activities such as business, industry, recreation, entertainment, the arts, and vice are centered in particular locales. How this sorting process gets worked out over time depends on a city's particular topography, availability of resources, types of power, economic arrangements, and modes of transportation and communication.

Individual Responses to the City

Images of the Countryside and the City

Throughout much of the historical transition from rural-agrarian to urban-industrial society, there has been a marked ambivalence in attitudes toward the countryside. Some protagonists of rural life hold a romanticized image about living in the country and in rural farm communities. Rural life allegedly is simple and quiet. People know one another, are bound to friends, family, and relatives. People work close to nature, identify with their community, and have a sense of self-worth. This image is the standard by which satisfied rural folk and disgruntled urbanites assess what is desirable.

Antagonists of rural life see it as dull and unexciting. Individuals allegedly are overwhelmed by a "sense of community," and an insistence on conformity impinges on their personal freedoms. Work is seen as arduous and monotonous, and country life has few opportunities for upward social mobility.

Images about the city also are mixed, containing pro-urban and anti-urban beliefs. Whether the city is praised or condemned, in making the case, various characteristics of rural life are used as comparative points of reference. The city is praised for its diversity in population, its vitality in the arts, availability of recreation and alternative lifestyles, and its opportunities for upward social mobility, whereas rural areas lack these benefits. The city also is condemned for its ugliness, its overcrowding, its alienation, and its degrading routinized work.

Pro-urban and anti-urban biases were less sharply defined in the colonial era than in the manufacturing era and later in the metropolitan and megalopolitan era. As the nation became more urbanized and industrialized, increases in size and density of city populations altered the physical environs of the cities. The lifestyle of the city stood in sharp contrast to the single farm houses, clean air, and the pastoral peacefulness of the country.

The megalopolitan era has sharpened the negative image of the city. Inner cities became wastelands with slums, abandoned housing, and burned-out tenements, as businesses and the more advantaged blue-collar and white-collar families fled to the suburbs. Remaining behind were the "trapped" (the old), the "deprived" (the poor, the minorities), the "single" and "childless," the "ethnics" tied to their enclaves, and the "professional elite." The exodus was too great to prevent the erosion of the tax base (Gans 1962). Thus, rising costs of government and shortfalls in basic services accelerated the flight and the spread of blight; crimes against persons and property increased. Apartments became chained fortresses against rape and rip-off. The daily trial of hitting the streets to shop for necessities or trek off to work stood in sharp contrast to the idyllic images of rural life or its modern substitute—suburbia.

The Myths of Suburbia

Two opposing myths characterize suburbia, although the reality lies somewhere in between. On the one hand, in suburbia a family could escape from the towers of concrete and glass, see grass and trees, and more importantly, own their piece of America—a single-family home. Children had easy access to schools, and a variety of recreational opportunities were available. Wives had quick access to shopping malls and the chance to participate in numerous voluntary associations and self-improvement activities. Husbands had easy commutes to the city and work as well as the healthy enjoyment of

cultivating the "lawn." Social life allegedly was vibrant with community organizations and visiting between neighborhoods. Suburbs were free of drugs,
crime, and pollution and had adequate fire, police, and sanitation.

On the other hand, suburbia was far from idyllic. Not all families could
afford their piece of America. It was often cheaper to rent an apartment than
to buy a house. Teenagers opted for pot, cars, and sex instead of scouts, choir,
and sports. Children had to be bused to school or taxied by carpooling mothers. Shopping mall parking lots were traffic jams with fenderbenders common.
Commuting to the city was a tension-filled "white knuckle" experience. Family
life responsibilities made wives into weekday household managers and husbands into recreational partners on weekends. Social life often settled into a
dull routine of cards, booze, and gossip about occasional extramarital affairs.

Not all communities are "bedroom" communities for city workers. Some
develop their own character, such as the "mainline" in Paoli, Pennsylvania;
"upper class" in Scarsdale, New York, and Lake Forest, Illinois; "industrial" in
Portchester, New York, and Dearborn, Michigan; and the "black" in East Orange, New Jersey, to note but a few. Not all suburbs are exclusively private
houses with lots of acreage and greenery, nor are all just endless subdivisions
with houses cloned by the thousands. Not all are inhabited by middle-class
couples with children, pets, station wagons, and riding lawn mowers.

People that moved from the city to suburbia generally are happier in the
suburbs than they were in the city. People who have not been torn from ethnic
communities in the inner cities generally find living in suburbia a positive
experience, but persons who miss the support of social and emotional ties in
the ethnic community feel a sense of loss and want to return. Just as large
cities are part of American life, so is suburbia. Parents may age and children
may leave, the mix of population may become more diversified as minorities
climb the social ladder of success and move into the suburbs. The sprawl may
extend farther and farther from the core city, but suburbia remains an integral
part of the urban experience.

Perspectives on the City

Whether the city is praised or condemned depends on how we view the
way the city's physical environs, institutions, and lifestyle affect urbanites. It
also depends on what our past experiences have been, whether we have lived
in the country, suburbia, or the city, as well as what we want our future to be.
One perspective argues that the increased size, density, and diversity of city
populations leads to a mass society that is the opposite of life in rural communities. Life in the urban mass is marked by participation in secondary associations. Individuals are stripped of ties with kith and kin and ethnic enclaves. Interpersonal relationships are formal, superficial, and transitory. People
may have greater personal freedom, but the gain is illusory, for they have lost
their social anchorage. Such a loss gives rise to feelings of anonymity, alienation (anomie), and rootlessness. The city is inhabited largely by automatons

and strangers. As a consequence social pathologies result, for urbanites are preoccupied with their own inadequacies and torn by individualism and the relativism of group-determined morality (Simmel 1971).

An alternative perspective sees the city not as a mass society, but rather a mosaic of subcommunities. Each community has its own particular institutions and social organizations. Each is a separate social world with its own beliefs, language, art forms, codes of conduct, and so forth. Although each community takes pride in its uniqueness and sense of peoplehood, they may participate with the city's network of political and economic structures. Sometimes they cooperate with one another, sometimes they become vested interest groups that compete for resources. These communities may derive their identities from common nationality, language, religion, race, even class. As new migrant groups move into the city and others, because of their changing political and economic fortunes, move out, the mix of subcommunities and neighborhoods changes.

This latter view sees the city population as a composite with many individuals and groups electing to live in the city rather than being victims of urban pathology. It focuses on the heterogeneity of population and its diversity of lifestyles. For some it is the variety of behaviors that make a city unique.

The Future of the City

The continued urbanization of the world's population is inevitable. In developing countries, the base of urbanization will expand as the number and size of cities increase and the proportion of population residing in cities rises. Urban growth will be sustained by an excess of births over deaths and rural-to-urban migration. In developed countries, the base of urbanization is already broad. Urbanization will continue with the increase in megalopolitan regions metropolitan areas, and suburban sprawl. Annexation and interregional and interurban migration, along with some natural increase, will feed further urban growth.

Both developing and developed countries will witness more and bigger cities, but the future of cities is questionable. Developing countries with rapidly expanding populations face shrinking supplies of food, water, and energy. Without a broad, diversified economic base, they cannot produce the commodities needed for their growing populations nor provide enough jobs for ever-increasing urban populations.

In developing countries, administrators in government agencies do not always have the technical skills, funds, or personnel needed to guarantee delivery of health care or protective services, much less oversee coordinated programs for future urban growth. The leaders' inability to lessen the effect of inflation on urbanites; to meet demands for jobs, commodities, and services; and to offer opportunities for attaining a better quality of life seriously undercuts the credibility of officials and threatens the political stability. The quality of life, already at best marginal, will deteriorate further unless population growth is checked, new technologies expand agriculture, alternate energy sources are discovered, new sources of wealth are developed, and social institutions rooted in tradition are revamped to accommodate the pressures of rapid urbanization.

Developed countries face problems that result from the stage of modernization achieved as well as from pressures of the world economy. Most developed countries already have highly diversified economies with varying degrees of specialization in selected sectors. Large commitments of technology, labor, and capital support these specialties. To gain a competitive edge in world markets and domestic markets as well as to achieve continued growth, developed countries need investments in new technologies and expansion of organizations and personnel. In these countries economic growth historically has been steady without serious long-term interruptions.

Recent evidence suggests that some developed countries are experiencing a slower rate of economic growth, and their competitive advantage in the world is weakening. The slowdown results in part from worldwide inflation and shortages in energy resources, food, and capital. It also results from difficulties faced by public and private corporations in finding sufficient funds to replace outmoded technologies with newer ones that are environmentally safe, energy efficient, and cost competitive. Dislocations in specialized sectors of

---

CONTROVERSIAL ISSUES · Urban Renewal

Planners and politicians are apt to mark ethnic neighborhoods as slums and classify them for renewal because they do not see the order behind what appears to be disorder. Live, vital, cohesive ethnic communities are destroyed. To make way for a university in Chicago, planners wiped out a Greek and Italian neighborood, over strong protests. The scars haven't healed yet. It is important to stress that when you scatter such a community, you're doing more than tearing down buildings; you're destroying most of what gives life meaning, particularly for people who are deeply involved with each other. The displaced people grieve for their homes as if they had lost children and parents . . .

Take a good look at any neighborhood that's been hit by urban renewal. It's like a European city after a bombing raid. Furthermore, wasting communities is the first step in a chain of events that ends in destroying our cities. As a last resort and if absolutely necessary, neighborhoods should be relocated en masse. The whole community should be moved together—local policemen, streetcleaners, shopkeepers, and even postal clerks should be moved as a unit. Of course it will never happen. It would make too much sense.

SOURCE: Edward T. Hall, "How Cultures Collide," *Psychology Today,* July 1976, p. 97.

the economies in developed countries have repercussions on the cities as conditions shift in the world market.

Governing metropolises with diverse populations, maintaining social control, preserving aesthetic advantages of the urban setting, and refurbishing deteriorated downtowns and blighted areas—these are merely some of the problems to be confronted in larger, older urban concentrations in developed countries. For cities to survive, national urban policies are needed that address questions such as: What are the acceptable limits to metropolitan growth? Should cities be centralized or decentralized? How should residential and nonresidential land use be arranged? What new technologies should be given priority for solving problems of housing, transportation, and energy consumption? What services are best handled by the private or public sectors of the economy? Should regional or metropolitan governments be created to coordinate and plan for urban development? Unless priorities are fixed and strategies for achieving goals are established, crises are likely to follow one after the other. Partial solutions will probably prove ineffective, and the erosion of the urban environment might continue.

Summary

The urban revolution has fundamentally altered the living patterns of human beings. Urban settlements and cities were made possible by favorable climate, arable soil, sufficient water, and a variety of advances in technology.

Preindustrial cities developed as centers of religion and trade and depended on their agricultural hinterland.

Medieval cities grew as luxury trade and textile manufacturing of woolens, silk, and linens expanded.

Large-scale urbanization accelerated with the onset of the Industrial Revolution. As modernization accelerated, the modern industrial city developed. It was dependent on manufacturing, commerce, and transportation.

In developed countries urbanization and industrialization were twin processes. Cities grew slowly. Rural-to-urban migration accounted for their increased size. Living conditions in cities improved as the developed countries passed through the stages of the demographic transition. Nowadays most developed countries are heavily urbanized with over 70% of their populations living in urban areas.

In developing countries urbanization occurred in a relative absence of industrialization. Importation of advanced technologies radically reduced mortality levels. Urbanization occurred swiftly because of both high growth rates and rural-to-urban migration. Developing countries will continue to become more urban as populations continue to grow and rural areas continue to send people to the cities.

Urbanization in the United States started in the colonial era when inland villages and seaports dotted the eastern seaboard. As the country turned from agriculture to industry, manufacturing cities spread. With the rise in motor vehicle transportation, metropolitan growth boomed. Metropolises now are the dominant form of urban settlement. Many anticipate that megacities may well be the major form of urban settlement in the future.

The urban environment and how it is structured—its size, patterns of land use, population makeup, economic composition, and impact on lifestyles—are topics of study for urban sociologists.

Urban ecology examines the pattern of land use, the shape of cities, and the social processes that give rise to various urban forms. Such efforts range from mapping people's activities, to delineating the boundaries and composition of neighborhoods, to searching for social, economic, and demographic causes of residential segregation and variations in social institutions.

How individuals respond to the city is tied to their past and present experiences with the city, suburbia, or rural areas. Those persons disenchanted with the negative aspects of city life dream about a better life in either suburbia or a rural setting. Those overwhelmed by a dull rural life and small town conformity view the city as vibrant, filled with freedom and opportunities for social advancement.

Whether the city survives in the future and what forms it will take are problematic. Cities throughout the world face problems of sustaining the quality of life and adjusting to dislocations in their economies, as new technologies evolve and population growth pressures the available resources. Only through imaginative planning can deterioration of the city as a major organizational form of human settlement be forestalled.

Suggested Readings

Jean Gottman. *Megalopolis: The Urbanized Northeastern Seaboard of the United States.* Cambridge, Mass.: MIT Press, 1961. A work detailing the rise and complexity of the urban corridor stretching from Maine to Virginia.

Shirley Bradway Laska and Daphne Spain, eds. *Back to the City: Issues in Neighborhood Renovation.* New York: Pergamon, 1980. A collection of essays on social, political, and economic issues linked to the back-to-the city movement.

Henri Pirenne. *Medieval Cities.* Garden City, N.Y.: Doubleday Anchor, 1952. A classic on trade cities in Europe, their origins, class structures, institutions and lifestyles.

Gideon Sjoberg. *The Preindustrial City: Past and Present.* New York: Free Press, 1960. A classic discussion of the nature of early cities, their patterns of land use, and various facts of social life.

Max Weber. *The City.* Translated and edited by Don Martindale and Gertrud Neuwirth. New York: Collier, 1962. An essay examining the roots of early cities in Western civilization.

18

Mass Behavior

In other chapters we have examined how people are affected by their various interpersonal relationships, social groups, social organizations, and social institutions. This chapter focuses on social behaviors that do not fit neatly into any of those categories, although these behaviors are an integral feature of everyday social life.

During the 1970s people began to pay more money for clothing that identifies the designer or maker on the outside than for clothing without such external markers. Before then most people did not believe they should pay more for clothing and other goods that carried such blatant advertisements. Why did this happen?

For decades the stock market in our society has fluctuated immediately after Presidents were inaugurated, when rumors about new government policies surfaced, or when news of events in other societies was announced through the media. Various stockholders subscribe to newsletters that tell them when to buy and sell stocks and bonds. Why do people readily risk their money on the basis of speculations about the future, after carefully accumulating the money to purchase stocks?

Periodically we read in the news about people who believe that a holocaust is about to occur or that the world is going to end on a certain date. In the 1980s people known as "survivalists" began preparing for life after a holocaust has destroyed society as we know it. They are buying or building homes in remote areas, stockpiling food, and learning how to shoot weapons so they can kill people who attempt to steal their food, water, and housing. Why do only some people hold these survivalist views?

Although there is considerable diversity in these examples of mass behavior, there are also some commonalities. **Mass behavior** exists when the activities of a number of people reflect shared perceptions of the social world, *if* these activities are less regulated and organized than those occurring in established organizations and institutions.

The least organized form of mass behavior is collective behavior. **Collective behavior** occurs when for a limited period of time a number of people behave in similar ways. Therefore, it is not *unorganized*, but is *less* organized and *more* transitory than behavior within enduring social structures (groups, organizations, institutions).

The popularity of clothing with labels or logos on the outside ("designer" jeans and shirts) is a fashion trend, one form of collective behavior. At one time the Izod logo, an alligator, was only available on clothing sold in expensive stores. When Izod clothing subsequently was introduced into the mass market, many people purchased it perhaps believing that it signified achievement of a higher status level. *Fashion* reflects the process through which taste periodically changes. People seeking to be fashionable are part of a diffuse

Mass behavior behavior of a number of people (mass) that is less regulated and organized than social behavior that occurs in established organizations and institutions.

Collective behavior transitory forms of mass behavior (riots, crowds, panics, fads, crazes, demonstrations).

Rumors, for example, about government decisions to buy wheat, quickly influence decisions to buy and sell commodities at exchanges such as this one in Kansas City.

crowd whose members are seeking the prestige associated with being in the know—in fashion.

Rumors, like fashion, are a form of collective behavior that does not fit the negative stereotype of collective behavior as random, unorganized irrational behavior. When people have no reliable source of information in an uncertain situation, they will rely on rumors (Shibutani 1966). The stock market fluctuations may dramatically affect an individual investor. Individual investors rely on rumors and tips because they are uncertain about what will happen on the stock market and they lack better sources of information.

More enduring forms of mass behavior, *social movements*, involve people who share a common perspective about how the social world should be changed, such as the "survivalists" who believe that they know what is going to happen in the future and are behaving in accordance with their beliefs. Other people also fear nuclear war, but they are involved in social movements with quite different goals (such as the world peace movement). At times participants in social movements may engage in other forms of mass behavior; peace demonstrations, for example, are a form of collective behavior.

We are aware of instances of collective behavior and social movement activities largely because of the mass media. The *mass media* are an important aspect of our culture. They give us images about what the world is like and they entertain us. The media may accurately reflect the social world, but they may sometimes present distorted images of reality as well as projections about what the media controllers believe the world *should* be like. Some commentators believe that the media may be ends in themselves: "the medium is the message," as Marshall McLuhan said. Various media forms are examined here in order that you may draw your own conclusions about the role of the media in mass society.

Collective Behavior

Sociological discussions of social behavior focus on how social structures (groups and organizations) affect individuals and in turn how those individuals contribute to changes in the organization of social life. Social theorists have long recognized that people sometimes become involved in less organized forms of social behavior of short duration—collective behaviors. In fact, some early social theorists believed that collective behaviors should not be called social behavior, because people were not rationally thinking about what they were doing when engaged in episodes of collective behavior (LeBon 1897).

Many different phenomena are called collective behavior (fads, fashions, crazes, panics, riots, mobs, rumors), making it difficult to discuss its specific characteristics. Some forms of collective behavior are encountered less frequently in our society (riots, mobs, panics) but are often emphasized more in discussions of collective behavior than other forms of collective behavior (rumors, fads) that occur more often. Riots, whether in prisons or urban ghettos, receive more attention, for they pose short-term threats to life and property and long-term threats to existing social arrangements. Yet, if our definition of collective behavior emphasizes the characteristics of riots, it is difficult for us to analyze fads such as riding mechanical bulls, talking "valley speak," or playing videogames.

Often reports of collective behavior emphasize the negative consequences of it. In part this is because "bad" things appear more newsworthy than "good" things. Normally American newspapers do not report that Londoners gather in Trafalger Square on New Year's Eve; however, they did report that event in 1982, for the usual celebrants were pushed by drunken young adults and two women were crushed to death.

In fact, people who participate in collective behavior may express various emotions ranging from the less pleasant (fear, anger) to the very pleasant (joy, ecstasy). Also, collective behavior may be positive in its basic aim: Crowds may enthusiastically support certain religious beliefs or artistic performances, and rioters may want to improve their social environment. Further, all people participating in collective behavior may not experience the same degree of involvement or the same emotions.

Crowd Formation

Some of the best-known discussions of collective behavior pertain to crowds, so we can identify characteristics of collective behavior by focusing on crowds.

Contagion.   Early collective behavior theorists developed what became known as a **contagion perspective** (LeBon 1897). Perceptions of events in Europe, particularly the negative views of public behavior during the French Revolution, influenced the concepts these theorists developed. Gustav LeBon believed that whenever persons formed crowds, they would no longer think rationally. Rather, they would be overtaken by a "crowd mind." This "crowd mind" was believed contagious; thus people could infect one another with crowd thinking.

> **Contagion perspective**   situation in which people in crowds stimulate one another to engage in extraordinary behavior.

In the mid-twentieth century, symbolic interactionist Herbert Blumer (1951) developed the idea of **circular reaction**. He detailed how people might lead one another to become more excited or agitated. One person at a sports event might start shouting, or someone at a concert might stand up and clap loudly and whistle. Other people would use these persons as models and imitate their excited actions. In turn, the crowd's behavior would stimulate the initiators to greater levels of reaction, becoming less and less inhibited regarding things that ordinarily would concern them. Spectators at a football game may spill their drinks on other people because they become so involved in cheering that they do not pay attention to the consequences of their actions.

> **Circular reaction**   situation occurring when one member of a crowd imitates another's actions, thereby stimulating the person imitated to engage in higher levels of activity and excitement.

The contagion perspective assumes that crowd participants are "not

Spectators at athletic events sometimes feel free to express emotions because other crowd members are doing so.

themselves" when participating in collective activities. Analyses of negative episodes of collective behavior, those that result in physical harm and property destruction (riots, lynch mobs, panics), are often shaped by the contagion perspective. Contagion analyses assume that people only engage in such behavior because they feel anonymous, caught up in an event, and not responsible for their actions.

Various researchers have found that the contagion perspective does not fit their own observations and interpretations of collective behavior. Historian George Rudé (1964) argued, for instance, that although the crowds during the early modern period in Europe were violent and often stimulated by rumors, they were not necessarily irrational. Researchers who have examined people's behavior when confronted by fire have found that they behave rationally when they know how to escape the fire scene safely. In other words, panic occurs only when normal forms of behavior no longer appear to work. Such questioning of the general utility of the contagion perspective permitted the development of the convergence perspective.

Convergence. According to this perspective, persons do not become involved in collective behavior simply because of chance association with excited people. Rather, the **convergence perspective** proposes that crowds consist of people with specific characteristics (goals, beliefs) who are drawn together because they share these characteristics or qualities.

Convergence perspective situation in which members of crowds are drawn together because they share common characteristics.

The convergence perspective is useful for explaining such diverse events as the formation of hostile mobs and the congregation of sports fans. However, in many instances, crowd members do not all participate in the same activities. A few of them may get very excited while others are less active or even simply passive onlookers, and these different types of participation may reflect crowd members' different personal characteristics (Snow, Zurcher, and Peters 1981).

Emergent Norm. Ralph H. Turner and Lewis Killian (1972) argue that both the contagion and convergence perspectives assume that there is more similarity and commonality in crowds than there really is. Recognizing that crowd members may have different predispositions or characteristics and engage in dissimilar actions, they question why this illusion of similarity or unanimity exists.

Collective behavior is less organized than everyday social behavior. Yet participants in such behavior look for norms to guide them in much the same way as they do when engaging in other social activities. In crowds the behavior of a limited number of highly visible people serves as the acceptable standard of behavior for others. This standard is known as an **emergent norm**. Once the emergent norm is adopted by some crowd members, they act to spread its adoption and enforcement to other members. Eventually the emergent norm may create the illusion of unanimity or uniformity that was often perceived as real unanimity or uniformity by early collective behavior researchers. Recent research (Snow, Zurcher, and Peters 1981) suggests that in many crowds there may be multiple emergent norms just as there are different levels of partici-

Emergent norm behavior of a few visible people that is adopted by crowd members as a norm.

In the past decade proponents of equality for women have organized episodes of collective behavior such as this parade to draw attention to their cause.

pation. This is because different types of crowd members are not necessarily subject to the same influences.

Today researchers try to utilize the parts of all three perspectives that fit the collective behavior they are studying. Also, current researchers emphasize the careful observation of crowds. Media reports and even crowd participants' accounts provide very limited views of what happened. These selective accounts are useful, but they should not be relied on exclusively. A spectator at a football game or a rock concert can see only a limited amount of what is occurring. To surmount some of these problems Richard Wohlstein and Clark McPhail (1979) advocate the use of film recordings to gather more complete collective behavior data. Recorded visual portrayals of crowd events also can be reexamined at a later date for closer scientific scrutiny.

Diversity of Collective Behavior

Since Robert E. Park and Ernest W. Burgess (1921) established the concept of collective behavior in American sociology and the importance of collective behavior in social life, new information has stimulated theoretical development in the area. The study of crowds has directed much collective behavior theory and research, although *diffuse crowds*, those in which participants do not gather together at the same location (fads, crazes, fashion), have received less attention than *focused crowds*. Some theories focus on collective behavior in general compared with those that pertain primarily to focused crowds. (See the box below.) Yet phenomena such as rumors may be explained better using general sociological theories such as social exchange than by general theories of collective behavior (Rosnow and Fine 1976). Turner and Killian (1972) argue that it has been difficult to develop a general theory of collective behavior because there are few confirmed generalizations and many divergent ideas.

Researchers find that collective behavior is often linked to more ordinary social behavior, regardless of whether disasters, rumors, riots, or fashion are investigated. Disaster researchers have refuted the myth that people automatically behave irrationally and antisocially when confronted by floods, earthquakes, and other natural disasters (Militi, Drabek, and Haas 1975). People who converge on the site of a disaster are doing such things as checking on their own or friends' and relatives' possessions or seeking reassurance. Fashion is often pursued to establish or reflect differences in socioeconomic status or social awareness. Confronted with the difficulties involved in building a general theory of collective behavior, one theorist recently suggested that emotional arousal may be one of the key differences between collective behavior and ordinary social behavior (Lofland 1981). John Lofland suggests episodes of collective behavior can be differentiated by the kinds of emotional states that predominate (fear, hostility, joy). Although all participants in an epsiode may not experience the same degree or kind of emotional arousal, emotional arousal may be an important defining characteristic of collective behavior. In

---

PEOPLE · A Theory of Collective Behavior

Neal Smelser (1963) developed a six-stage theory of collective behavior that is often called a "value-added approach." He argues that after each stage, the likelihood of collective behavior increases as alternative actions become less likely.

1. *Structural conduciveness:* the structure of the social unit must lend itself to occurrence of collective behavior. In the early 1980s collective action was permitted in Poland.
2. *Structural strain:* the parts of the social system are not in harmony and strain exists as a consequence.
3. *Generalized belief:* people share a belief about how things should be changed when normal procedures seem inadequate.
4. *Precipitating factors:* events seem to happen that lend support to the generalized belief.
5. *Mobilization of participants for action:* people begin to act collectively (forming crowds, calling for social revolution); leaders may stir them.
6. *The operation of social control:* factors that operate to deter or deflect, prevent, or end collective episodes.

any case, whatever the researcher's focus, collective behavior must be understood by how it relates to other forms of social behavior.

Why do people participate in crowds and other forms of collective behavior?

Social Movements

Collective behavior is analyzed by identifying time-bound episodes, but another form of mass behavior—the social movement—persists over time. Frequently people are confused over the differences between two broad types of mass behavior. This is because certain episodes of collective behavior may be visible components of a more general social movement. Several recent episodes of collective behavior have had "the environment" as their theme. On both the east and west coasts, people are concerned about the safety of nuclear power plants and have gathered in the vicinity of these plants to protest their construction and operation. These incidents have often resulted in the arrests of demonstrators who have refused to leave the plant sites. These instances of collective behavior are highly visible activities of "the environmental movement," which is an example of a social movement.

Many people know about the anti-nuclear movement only because of the publicity given to demonstrations such as this one in Washington, D.C.

Social movements are somewhat abstract in nature and difficult to define concretely. Most sociologists agree that one important characteristic of a **social movement** is that people share a common set of beliefs about the need for society to change and the type of change needed. Typically there is general consensus of belief among social movement participants (Mueller and Judd 1981). Some social movements push society to develop in new ways (revolutionary social movements). Others (regressive social movements) want society to return to its previous form. Often, **countermovements** develop from belief systems that conflict with those of social movements. The opposing belief systems of the pro-choice and pro-life movements were described in Chapter 12, The Family. In the 1970s the feminist and antifeminist movements frequently opposed one another. Periodically, communist and socialist movements have arisen in our society, and various movements in opposition to them have quickly formed.

In any society, social movements occur because there is some disagreement about the way society should be. In complex industrial and postindustrial societies with large populations, there may be more frequent instances of social movements than in more homogeneous societies where less change occurs. Many things we regard as natural today are often the result of past social movements. A social movement was the basis for the American Revolution. The American labor movement fought to achieve recognized unions, better working conditions, shorter working hours, and other things we currently take for granted.

Sociologists are also interested in the kinds of conditions that lead people to seek change. Do people want change when they believe that their present circumstances could be better? The concepts of *rising expectations* and *relative deprivation* suggest that they do, for people's judgments are based on perceptions of well-being rather than concrete conditions. In recent years many people have felt deprived. Based on past indicators people expected to get well-paying jobs, and when they had to settle for less attractive jobs, they felt relatively deprived.

The following section addresses the questions: What are the general factors that lead people to become involved in movements? How are social movements organized?

Social movement
actions of people who share a common set of beliefs about the need for society to change and the type of change required.

Countermovements
movements formed in opposition to other social movements.

Participation in Social Movements

Many *potential* social movements fail to form because they do not stimulate enough interest or attention among the general population. Social movements can develop and persist only if sufficient numbers of people support them. Therefore, our attention is directed toward why people become involved in movements to the extent that they will continue to support them.

Have you ever participated in a social movement? Some people never participate in social movements, while others participate in many of them. Some people are inclined to become members of social movements because of their particular emotional or social psychological states. For example, in modern industrial society some people are searching for beliefs that they can totally embrace. Yet, their movement participation cannot be explained by social psychological states alone (Hoffer 1951).

Recruitment.   From a practical standpoint, most people do not have the *resources* (time, energy, money) or *information* to be members of social movements. Most social movements in the United States attract principally middle-class members. While many poor people would likely benefit from social changes in society, they frequently lack the necessary resources and information to participate in change-oriented groups. And the wealthy people who benefit from existing social arrangements have no interest in changing the status quo. The anti-nuclear movement is an example of a social movement drawing its membership largely from the middle class. People who have trouble paying their bills and worries about their future employment are not likely to be as concerned about nuclear contamination problems compared with people who have no day-to-day survival worries. Furthermore, appeals about improving the environment are less important to them in contrast to arguments about cheap energy from nuclear plants.

In the 1980s the Ku Klux Klan is part of a countermovement that opposes the goals of the civil rights movement.

In fact, many people are not directly exposed to information about social movements and would not know how to become involved in particular social movements even if they desired such membership. Therefore, *social networks* play a critical role in the recruitment of social movement participants. Social networks are chains of people connected with one another as explained in Chapter 3, Groups and Society. A person involved in a social movement may draw friends into attending its meetings and thus into the movement by providing them with information and convincing them of the movement's importance.

Ideology is another element of recruitment. Smelser (1963) argues that participants must share a "generalized belief." A person may be psychologically ready to participate in a social movement, have adequate resources, know movement members, and yet not be recruited by a movement. This is because he or she may not share a common belief system with other movement members. Movement participation depends upon people sharing a common perspective, a vocabulary with which they may analyze the social world. Often people in social networks share similar perspectives. As a result, the ideology and social network factors may work together to recruit participants (Orum 1974).

Commitment.   The initial recruitment of participants does not insure that they will continue to be involved in a movement or that they will become active movement members. Participation in social movements requires that people use their time and energy previously used in other ways and direct it toward movement goals. If a demonstration is to be effective or a newsletter is to be published, people have to expend their resources voluntarily.

Rosabeth Kanter (1972) conceptualized *commitment* as involving oneself in social relations that serve as expressions of oneself. A person with a high degree of commitment to a social movement would be expected to embrace the role of movement member, seeing the role of movement member as expressive of his/her "real" self. Within one movement some people exhibit higher degrees of commitment compared with others. For example, one person may simply attend monthly meetings of a movement organization, while other people may spend all of their leisure time making phone calls, writing letters, attending meetings, and preparing newsletters and flyers. Not only are there differences within movements, but there are considerable differences in the *degree of commitment* required by movements. People who participate in millenial movements that predict the end of the world may be expected to get rid of their worldly possessions, quit their jobs, and in other ways prepare themselves for the "end." In June 1981 members of the Lighthouse Gospel Tract Foundation in Arizona prepared to be lifted into heaven like balloons. Some sold their homes and cars, while more cautious members told their employers they would be "raptured," but did not go so far as to quit their jobs.

Conversion.   Although a few people may rapidly become totally absorbed in and committed to a social movement, *conversion* to a social movement's perspective is usually gradual. People gradually learn the perspective of movement members, find answers to their questions, and adopt the movement's perspective as their own. The process of conversion depends both on potential converts interacting with movement members who teach them the perspective and reward them for adopting it *and* on conducive structural arrangements (those facilitating continued involvement).

Why are some people more likely than others to become movement members?

Social Movement Careers

Social movement researchers not only look at how individuals become involved in social movements, but also at how movements change over time. Once movements become established (acquire enough members and/or attention to be recognized by other members of society), they tend to grow and flourish for a time. Eventually, they decline or become transformed into something different compared with what they were at the outset. These various stages in the life of a social movement are know as its **career**.

Social movement career stages in the life of a social movement.

When movements originate, they tend to have fewer participants and less well-defined ideologies than they acquire later. They also may be less organized or organized differently at the beginning compared with later. During the formative phase some people may separate themselves from the group and form other groups because of disagreements over movement organization and/or ideology. When the women's liberation movement was developing in the late 1960s, various groups splintered off from the initial organization because of such ideological disagreements.

Gradually some organizations or groups are viewed as representative of the social movement as a whole and/certain individuals emerge as *the* leaders or chief representatives of a movement. The media often try to identify movement leaders for selective coverage on television or in newspapers. This promotes the leadership roles of these particular individuals. The early sociologist Weber (1968) argues that some people seem to emerge naturally as leaders because they possess *charisma*. A charismatic leader is one who appears to have exceptional qualities, who clearly distinguishes himself or herself from other people. People who advocate radical religious or political positions have often appeared to be charismatic leaders (Adolph Hitler, Malcom X, and Martin Luther King). Not all social movements have charismatic leaders (the pro-choice movement), and it is quite difficult for these types of leaders to exert substantial influence in some of the later stages of a movement's career.

As a movement becomes better known and increasingly accepted, different kinds of people may become involved compared with the early converts. Some early converts may believe that the newer members are not as committed as they are to the cause. They may become dissatisfied as the movement organization grows, because as movement organizations increase in size, so do their complex bureaucratic activities. Weber's ideas about charismatic leaders suggest that they may not be as effective as other types of leaders after movements become more organized and routinized.

An important concern of any movement is the achievement of social change. Many movements do not accomplish the changes they originally proposed and they eventually die out. In some cases a faithful few may continue to believe in the movement's perspective no matter what happens. For example, members of some millenial groups continue to believe that the world is coming to an end even though the original date it was to have occurred has passed. Other movements experience some degree of success. The feminist movement of the late nineteenth and early twentieth centuries achieved the right to vote for women in the United States, after which it seemed to disappear although a few faithful members of the National Women's Party persisted. The "March of Dimes" once focused on the eradication of polio in our society. Once polio was no longer a threat to the population, the large organization that had developed redirected its goals from eliminating infantile paralysis to the treatment of birth defects. Therefore, movements may end rather abruptly (at least in the public eye), but may persist over time in skeletal form or may redirect their energies toward new goals.

Do all social movements have similar careers?

To understand why some movements succeed and others fail, we need to consider the importance of resource mobilization.

Resource Mobilization

Resource mobilization involves the study of social movement organization. This social movement perspective depends heavily on economic theory and political sociology to explain the "success" of certain social movements. Rather than focusing on individuals' emotions or sentiments, resource mobilization advocates regard them as unimportant, as they assume behavior is economically rational (people behave in their own best economic interest). Social movements and their countermovements are defined by people's beliefs about the social world. According to this perspective, we should examine organizations that have goals tied to the belief structures of specific movements (McCarthy and Zald 1977).

Whether a movement flourishes depends on what resources need to be mobilized, the extent to which "outsiders" must contribute, and how the social movement relates to other social movements and regulatory agencies. The resource mobilization perspective discourages the treatment of social movements and collective behavior as basically different from other forms of social behavior.

Some critics of the resource mobilization perspective agree that organization is important, but they argue that symbols that arouse emotion and

Resource mobilization the process through which social movements obtain resources necessary to further their activities.

stimulate people to identify with a movement should not be neglected (Zurcher and Snow 1981). We should not discard or neglect ideas gleaned from earlier perspectives after new ones are adopted.

Do all social movements engage in some forms of resource mobilization?

Mass Media and Popular Culture

In our postindustrial society the media strive to attract our attention. They influence how people dress, act, or think by presenting to them images of what is popular. We are increasingly interested in learning the extent to which the media reflect traditions and customs and the degree to which they cause persons to behave in new ways.

Print Media

Research analyses of the media often focus on visual media such as television and movies. This is because many adult Americans rely on television as their sole source of news. But the print media (newspapers, books, magazines) are equally important. It is clear that children learn many appropriate behaviors through the books they read as well as through the programs they view. (See Chapter 4, Socialization.)

As one consequence of the Civil Rights Movement of the 1960s, the portrayal of blacks in the print media has been increasingly examined. The Uncle Remus children's stories have been criticized because they have perpetuated certain stereotypes about blacks. Schools can no longer use the *Little Black Sambo* storybook. Textbook publishers are encouraged to include pictures of blacks in nonstereotypical roles. Newspapers have adopted policies that make the reporting of race less apparent (stories about crimes should make references to the race of the criminal only if race is germane to the crime). The race of black criminals should only be mentioned under the same circumstances as the race of white criminals.

Various researchers have studied gender role stereotypes in the print media. These researchers typically assume that the media are going to reflect traditional views of males and females. As a consequence, the media will help to perpetuate traditional views of gender roles. A recent study of descriptions of males and females in "male-centered" and "female-centered" stories has revealed the tendency (both in locally written and national wire service stories) to report about females' personal appearance, marital status and spouses more frequently than for males (Foreit et al. 1980). Such practices are believed to perpetuate the traditional views of women as sex objects and having no status separate from that of their husbands.

Researchers interested in early socialization have also examined children's storybooks. McArthur and Eisen (1976) examined preschool children's behavior after the children heard stories about achievement by a same sex or opposite sex storybook character. Both girls and boys persisted longer at tasks after they heard a story about achievement by a "same sex character" than by an "opposite sex character." This finding suggests the importance of providing positive role models for all children in storybooks.

Sharon Knopp (1980) has questioned whether gender stereotypes have appeared in the pictures in children's readers from other countries. She examined books from East and West Germany equivalent to those used in our grades 1–4. She looked at the ratio of male to female pictures, the body language of the people in the pictures, and the characters' clothing (did girls wear pants?). The West German books presented stereotypes similar to those found in our society. In fact, the books published in the 1970s were *more stereotypical* in their treatment of males and females than those from the 1960s. In contrast, East Germany considers itself to be a socialist society with the federal government regulating many aspects of it including the publication of textbooks. The East German books were not as stereotypical as the West German books. This may be because socialist countries profess the equality of females and males and oppose stereotyping on the basis of gender.

Other researchers have examined media reports of events and compared these with actual behaviors to see if the media reports exerted any effects on behavior. For example, David Phillips (1974; 1982) observed when sensational accounts of suicides appeared in specific newspapers. Then he looked at the suicide rates in the newspapers' circulation areas. The number of suicides in those areas increased after the suicide reports. While he could not prove that the newspaper stories caused more persons to commit suicide, the evidence did suggest that the media contributed to people's decisions to commit suicide.

Studies of *public opinion* reveal that researchers generally have had difficulty "proving" that the media directly influence people's opinions (Lang and Lang 1981). Researchers might possibly benefit from using new approaches (looking for cumulative rather than direct effects, focusing on individuals in a social context rather than in isolation). A study of the effects of the media presentation of Germans' feelings about the 1973–1974 oil supply represents a more fruitful type of approach. Kepplinger and Rote (1979) have indicated that media reports about the oil supply may have stimulated a "spiraling cycle of fear" which led to behavior that worsened the oil supply situation (panic buying).

An alternative perspective focuses on how the media create "products" and what is the nature of those "products." This is in contrast to the approach described above detailing how the media reflected social traditions. Both journalists and the general public tend to believe that stories in newspapers are factual accounts unless they are clearly labeled as editorials, commentaries, or satire. The concept of media "product" enables us to look critically at "facts" as well as commentaries.

Gaye Tuchman (1980) argues that newsworkers define the "frames" within which events are interpreted and reported. Journalists learn ways of "knowing" what are facts and which of them deserve to be reported. Tuchman describes this way of knowing as a "web of facticity." Individual journalists cannot freely modify the "web of facticity," for they often work in bureaucracies which exercise bureaucratic control over their activities. Gladys Lang and Kurt Lang (1981) identify some members of media organizations as **gatekeepers**, because they have the authority to select those stories that will be covered and those that will subsequently be featured.

Media gatekeepers people who have the authority to select which stories will be covered.

Recently, the production of journalistic facts has been examined in specific news stories and in fictional depictions of the newsmaking process. The *Washington Post* newspaper has received considerable favorable publicity for acquiring "facts" about the Watergate Conspiracy. These revelations ultimately contributed to the resignation of then President Richard M. Nixon. The fact-finding process has been dramatized in the film *All the President's Men*. A popular television series, *Lou Grant,* further dramatized newsgathering procedures.

By the early 1980s the activities of the print media were less favorably viewed compared with the past. For instance, a *Washington Post* reporter received a Pulitzer Prize for reporting on an interview with a boy whom she later admitted did not exist. The movie *Absence of Malice* depicted how the reporter could be "fed" incorrect information. And there was more open discussion of how media representatives have "understandings" with politicians in order to obtain information. As the Langs (1981) indicate, the majority of daily news stories are prepared by reporters who have regular "beats" or assignments. Much of their information has an establishment slant. It is obtained from official handouts or from communication with official representatives to the press.

Why do the print media tend to present stereotypes?

Sound Media

While television is taken for granted today, it was not available to large segments of our population until the early 1950s. Before then, people relied on radio and motion pictures (newsreels) for their news and entertainment.

The role of radio is less frequently examined today than it was in the past, although many people hear about key events first on the radio (assassination attempts). There are occasions when people do not critically evaluate what they hear. In 1938 the news and entertainment functions of radio were confused by some people who listened to a program called the "War of the Worlds." They believed that an invasion by Martians was underway. The Mercury Theatre program was described clearly as a drama at the beginning of the presentation, but some people who tuned in late went so far as to pack up their belongings to escape the invading Martians (Cantril 1940). While we may scoff at the susceptibility of people to radio broadcasts today, a radio broadcast about a fictitious 1982 disaster at a nuclear power station in Barseback, Sweden, produced emotional reaction in 1973 (Rosengren et al. 1980). About half of the people who listened to the nuclear disaster program believed it to be factual for at least part of the time they listened. Approximately 70% of those who believed it for a time became distressed, although only a few did anything in response and they primarily made telephone calls.

While both programs had elements of authenticity (having "professors" make authoritative comments, sounding sirens) including being well dramatized, both were clearly identified as fiction at the time they were broadcast, and both contained "unbelievable" elements. Not surprisingly those people who listened to both programs from the beginning were far less likely to misinterpret what they heard than people who tuned in after the programs were in progress. Most people who checked the programs against available information (about the specific nuclear power plant or about the radio programming schedule) were able to interpret the broadcast correctly.

These two famous radio broadcasts of fictitious disasters have been studied because of their relevance for collective behavior, particularly panic, and for the production of news. After both broadcasts, the media reported that people panicked. However, careful research of the responses to the broadcasts revealed that about 2% of the adult population in the listening area panicked in response to the "War of the Worlds" program. There was virtually no collective panic in response to the nuclear disaster broadcast. The primary active response in Sweden was to telephone either the authorities—the police or the radio station—or close associates—family and friends. Research on actual disasters indicates that these responses were not unusual, and that typically there is not widespread panic in the face of disaster. Yet, the media may report that there is panic. This misreporting occurs because of the necessity to rapidly obtain information that often cannot be verified. Sometimes the extreme responses of a few are more visible than the more conventional responses of the majority.

At times the broadcast media are criticized for focusing on negative events as the important news. Russell Veitch and his colleagues (1977) have compared the effects of good news and bad news radio broadcasts. In their study, one set of subjects heard primarily good news, while another set heard primarily bad news. Those subjects who heard the good news broadcast demonstrated more positive feelings and greater degrees of "helping" behavior after the broadcast compared with those subjects who had heard the bad news broadcast. Therefore, the news we hear may influence us in many ways other than those that are the most apparent to us.

Another medium, *records,* is often linked with the radio medium. The sales and popularity of records are directly related to songs being played on the radio. At various times the record and radio industries have been jolted by "payola" scandals, where record companies bribe disc jockeys to play particular songs to improve their record sales. Besides being big business, songs also have social significance.

Adoring fans may reach high emotional pitch when they see their favorite rock star.

For centuries, human beings have used songs to express various emotions (love, despair), to foster a particular behavior or feelings (national anthems), to profess religious beliefs (religious songs), to try to encourage social change (peace songs and other social movement songs), and to tell about everyday life (hopes, dreams, and disappointments). In recent decades advertisers have developed songs to help sell products (the McDonald's jingle).

While the themes of songs in many instances reflect the traditional values and beliefs of members of a society, they also provide the opportunity to express "deviant" or nontraditional values. It is believed by some that changes in songs may indicate that more general changes in society are occurring. During the 1960s and 1970s songs made increasingly explicit references to sexual intercourse and drug usage than ever before in our society. At times groups have been organized to try and restrict what types of songs are played or how they are promoted. In the 1970s a group called Women against Violence against Women (WAVAW) actively opposed the representation of women in chains and other forms of bondage appearing on the covers of numerous records.

By far the largest proportion of record purchases today occurs among young people. Both the type of music they listen to (hard rock, country) and the type of content or lyrics they endorse serve as statements to the "older" generations as forms of protest. Parents who listened to the Beatles to the displeasure of their own parents may now object to their own children listening to hard rock or country music. The fad of carrying large tape players blaring loud music while walking down the street and tiny players with earphones can be seen as ways of creating privatized worlds through the use of sound.

How do the sound media both reflect and shape our perceptions of reality?

Visual Media

Television is an integral feature of American life. U.S. government statistics indicate that only a very small percentage of homes that are wired for electricity do not have *at least one* television set. People who do not have television sets are pitied or thought of as weird or unusual. People who claim that they never watch television generally are not believed.

Television has numerous critics, but it continues to be extensively viewed. As with the other media, television is criticized for presenting stereotypes (people are white, mothers are housewives, all children have two parents at home). Joseph Dominick (1979) analyzed the contents of *TV Guide* for a 25-year period, from 1953 to 1977. He focused particularly on the starring characters of prime-time television programs. The ratio of female to male starring characters remained about the same, or about 3 out of every 10. And most of the females appeared in situation comedies. But perhaps the most important question had to do with the occupations of the female characters. After all, from 1953 to 1977, the profile of female labor force participation changed considerably. Dominick found that the number of housewives and housekeepers declined, while the characters' occupations bore no relation to the actual patterns of the female occupational distribution. Of course, the males' occupations were also unrepresentative of the actual male labor force with a disproportionate number of actors being detectives and policemen.

One implication of studies such as this is that no one believes television represents reality; apparently, it does not make any difference. But those researchers interested in the socialization of children believe that television as well as books provide many ideas about the social world that may shape children's goals and aspirations. A study by Greenberg and Reeves (1976) has indicated that *young* children may have difficulty separating reality as presented on television (fantasy, dreams) from reality, and that they may indeed accept the televised depictions as accurate. Other research indicates adults may believe there are higher levels of violent crime than exist due to viewing television shows that emphasize violence.

Much research has focused on whether television stimulates children and adults to engage in behavior similar to what they view. A primary interest has been the depiction of violence on television. Frederick Elkin and Gerald Handel (1978) reviewed the literature on children's behavior and concluded that viewing violence on television does *not* necessarily cause aggression. Yet, for some people it apparently does. In 1982 the National Institute of Mental Health released a report which concluded that viewing of violence on television leads to aggressive behavior. The report's conclusions, based on a review of 2500 recent studies of television viewing and behavior, perhaps not surprisingly were criticized by the major networks.

Specific groups object to the presentation of material on television that conflicts with their values and beliefs. Various religious groups and television evangelists encourage their followers not to watch or permit their children to watch programs that emphasize sexuality or endorse cohabitation. Some groups have attempted to pressure the sponsors of various programs to cease their support of them. Opponents of such efforts argue that these activities are censorship and that people should have the right to view or not view programs on the basis of their own values and beliefs.

Do we need or want television censorship?

Another set of questions about the effects of television involves its effects on social life. While television networks are interested in having more people view their programs (market, shares), various educators and concerned parents believe that television is watched too much.

Researchers know at least some of the factors that affect television viewing. For example, in cold weather areas of the country, television is watched more frequently in the winter. Jack Lyle and Heidi Hoffman (1972) studied 6th and 10th graders in 1959 and another set of them in 1970 and found that children from blue-collar families tended to watch television more frequently than those from white-collar families. Yet, considerably less is known about how *attentive* people are to what is played on the television. In some homes television sets remain on while people are not even in the room.

Many parents and social critics believe that excessive television viewing keeps children from participating in more desirable activities (reading, exercising) and leads them to become too passive. As a consequence, some parents place locks on their televisions sets. Children may earn "television watching credits" by participating in certain constructive activities. Other parents simply limit the frequency and nature of programs their children watch. In other families, children have their own television sets and are free to make their own decisions.

In the 1950s it was suggested that television viewing was not necessarily a totally passive event, but rather constituted **parasocial interaction** (Horton and Wohl 1956). Rather than detaching people from social life, it may involve them in a new form of interaction. There is no doubt that people can develop a sense of involvement with characters portrayed on television. Some actors and actresses become frustrated when fans of their television characters refuse to recognize them as people different from the characters they portray. Many newspapers carry accounts of the daily events portrayed on soap operas for fans who may have to miss their favorite programs. In the early 1980s, the lives of the characters on the program "General Hospital" were a major topic of concern for many college students.

Critics of television indicate that the parasocial interaction function of

Parasocial interaction an indirect form of interaction.

Political leaders increasingly rely on the broadcast media to communicate messages to the public. In the 1930s and 1940s President Franklin Delano Roosevelt conducted "fireside" chats over the radio to reassure the American public during periods of crisis. British Prime Minister Winston Churchill frequently relied on radio broadcasts to encourage Britons to work together to fight an outside menace (the Axis countries) during World War II. During the 1970s President Jimmy Carter tried a version of a fireside chat on television to encourage conservation. President Ronald Reagan used television coverage to stimulate public support for his budgetary programs in the 1980s. Today we are not surprised that government leaders hire media consultants to help them present their messages to the American people through the usage of the latest technology and communication techniques.

People who desire to be political leaders rely heavily on the broadcast media first to generate "name recognition" and then to establish particular types of images. Potential candidates for the Presidency are beginning to announce their intentions long before the elections, in order to get media coverage for themselves and to generate funds for their media campaigns. Candidates believe they need large campaign funds in order to pay for expensive television coverage.

Critics question what we learn about potential candidates from their paid television announcements. The videotaped announcements often do not tell how a candidate stands on issues, but rather focus on image management. Candidates are shown walking through the woods with soft music playing in the background, petting dogs, playing with children, shaking constituents' hands, or attending celebrations. In different areas of the country, the scenes and words may be altered to "fit" the presumed views of the viewers, the mass market.

Television debates between candidates often do not clarify political differences between candidates either. The first televised debate between candidates Senator John Kennedy and Richard Nixon apparently did not shape the public's views about their political positions, although Kennedy apparently appeared to be more physically attractive than Nixon, who was seen as having a "five o'clock shadow." In more recent elections the "underdogs" in an election have apparently been more interested in televised debates than the leading candidates, for they potentially have more to gain from appearing on the television screen.

In other countries such as Great Britain, election campaigns are considerably shorter, and voters are expected to identify more with political parties than with individual candidates.

television viewing is no more desirable than its tendency to produce passivity and inactivity. However, programs such as *Sesame Street* that are designed to involve children in learning are favorably judged by other critics.

The final set of concerns about television has to do with its function as the primary source of news and information for many people. Many Americans are highly dependent upon nightly news broadcasts for their current information. At times the presenters of the nightly news become father-type figures whom the public can trust. This perception is not necessarily desired by the news presenters themselves. Tuchman's analysis of the news production process pertains to television as well as to newspapers. Very few stories are selected for coverage, and reporters follow particular procedures to obtain the "facts."

Politicians frequently use the media to shape their public images. Presidential press representatives provide "beat" reporters with "photo opportunities," so that the pictures the general public sees of the President are restricted to those which presumably project a desirable image.

Organizations and individuals may sometimes stage events for the purpose of having them reported in the media. These are called **pseudo-events** (Boorstin 1961). Daily news programs focus on these events in part because of the limited time allotted for such programs. There is simply not enough time to cover the *process* of social change. If members of a social movement want to draw attention to their cause, the staging of events (e.g., demonstrations and other collective behavior episodes) will generate publicity more often than other forms of activity. During the time Americans were held hostage in Iran (1980-1981), American television crews filmed scenes of Iranians engaging in what appeared to be collective behavior (shouting slogans, raising arms) in front of the American Embassy where the hostages were held. Subsequently, television commentators said that these activities appeared to be staged for the benefit of the American nightly news programs, for these incidents did not occur when the camera crews were not present. While the staging of pseudo-events may be a very useful technique for individuals and groups who desire greater media coverage, the creation of pseudo-events creates serious credibility problems for people who rely on the television for "correct" and "representative" information.

Pseudo-events events staged chiefly for the purpose of having them reported in the media.

To what extent does television "tell it like it is"?

Films are another visual medium receiving attention from social researchers. At one time in our history, people turned to movies or "newsreels" for news. However, in contemporary society they are seen primarily as an art form or entertainment. While the government and various other agencies produce educational films, these films are less frequently studied scientifically, because they have smaller, often involuntary, audiences. Hybrid forms of films have appeared in recent years, so-called "docu-dramas" and "made-for-television" movies.

Similar to the record industry, the primary audience for the movie industry is the youth. Adolescents and young adults have lifestyles that perhaps stimulate their interest in movies. They are often the "target" audience with movies geared to appeal to their interests. However, in the past, movies played a more central role in adult popular culture when other forms of entertainment were not as readily available.

Struggles and debates over what should appear on television parallel earlier concerns about "talkies," or motion pictures with sound. In 1933 the movie industry adopted a Production Code which affected the content of movies for three and a half decades through the use of censorship. Censorship activities involve the belief that the media *should not reflect* some activities because that may condone and encourage them. Exposure of sex organs, the use of double beds, and the treatment of "perversion" were expressly forbidden. The Production Code tried to limit the presentation of violence, but it was not as restricted as the presentation of sexuality. Although the Code remained in effect until fairly recent times, television has been seen as the more family-oriented medium, while movies have become more controversial. Of

CONTROVERSIAL ISSUES • Subliminal Techniques

Our brains can absorb an incredible amount of information at a given time, although we may not be consciously aware that we have assimilated the information. In discussing an event with friends, they may talk about something that occurred that you were not aware of or had not noticed until they mentioned it. Or, you may act in a certain way not realizing that your actions are in response to a message you received subconciously.

On occasion people may deliberately send you messages through the usage of *subliminal techniques* that you are not aware of receiving. At one time some movie theatre operators would insert pictures of food (popcorn) to stimulate theatre patrons to buy food. The brief pictures would be carefully spliced into the films so that theatre patrons would not be aware that they had seen them. Such usage of subliminal techniques is seen as inappropriate because people are being manipulated without their knowledge.

In recent years media critic Wilson Bryan Key has produced a series of books (*Media Sexploitation* 1974, *Subliminal Seduction* 1973, *The Clam-Plate Orgy* 1980) in which he attempts to warn the public about the usage of subliminal techniques in advertising. His books include various pictures of advertisements, some of which are blown up to show greater detail. He argues that through the positioning of certain barely recognizable body parts, sexual messages are being sent subliminally. Yet, psychologists who have experimented with subliminal perception question whether subliminal messages have any impact on us, particularly of a long-term nature.

course, television has caught up with the movies in the presentation of controversial material in recent years.

While the debate over what should appear in the more widely available media (such as television or movies) will undoubtedly continue (although our definition of what is inappropriate may change), the usage of *subliminal techniques* that may influence people has received less attention. The government has been asked to regulate some forms of advertising, particularly the types of advertisements that appear on programs for young children.

As we have seen, the media reflect what is happening in society, although that reflection is often distorted. Some fundamental questions that continue to be asked about the media in a "free society" are: Should the media be completely unregulated? Should each medium regulate itself? How much should the government regulate the media? Should consumer groups and political groups try to regulate the media through consumer boycotts and other forms of pressure? Who will regulate the regulators?

Summary

Many different phenomena can be called mass behavior. Mass behavior is less regulated and organized than behavior which reflects the norms in established organizations and institutions. It occurs when a number of people's behaviors are shaped by similar perceptions of the social world.

Collective behavior is a short-lived form of mass behavior. Some forms of it are very common (crowds, fads), while others occur less frequently (panics, riots).

Three basic perspectives are used to study crowds: the contagion perspective, the convergence perspective, and the emergent norm perspective. These may be used singly or together to account for specific crowd behaviors.

Social movements may include episodes of collective behavior; however, they are more enduring forms of mass behavior. Participants in social movements share ideas about how the society should change, and they work to accomplish their change objectives.

Some people are more likely to become involved in social movements than others. Differential access to resources and information as well as differences in social networks partially explain the likelihood of a person's becoming a participant in a movement.

Social movements change over time. They have careers. The resource mobilization framework tries to explain why some movements fail and others flourish.

The mass media are an important part of our popular culture. The print, sound, and visual media all shape the way things appear to us.

Critics of the media are concerned about how the media influence our behavior and attitudes. They also want to know who controls the content presented through the media.

Suggested Readings

Herbert J. Gans. *Deciding What's News.* New York: Random House, 1979. Based on years of study of the operation of news magazines (*Time* and *Newsweek*) and television networks, Gans argues the media present a conservative picture of American political, social, and economic life. What is called "news" reflects the interests and views of the powerful (elite individuals and institutions). Gans's proposed remedy is presentation of "multiperspective news."

Gary T. Marx and James Wood. "Strands of Theory and Research in Collective Behavior." In Alex Inkeles, James Coleman, and Neal Smelser, *Annual Review of Sociology,* Vol. I. Palo Alto, Calif.: Annual Review, 1975, pp. 363–428. Marx and Wood provide a thorough review of past and current research directions in the field of collective behavior.

Charles Tilly, L. Tilly, and R. Tilly. *The Rebellious Century, 1830–1930.* Cambridge, Mass.: Harvard University Press, 1975. The Tillys examine civil discontent in a set of European countries. They suggest that people's feelings of deprivation and frustration did not cause the civil protests. The importance of the processes of industrialization, urbanization, and particularly state building are emphasized as instigators of civil disturbances, collective behavior.

19

Social Change

As previous chapters have indicated, industrial and postindustrial societies undergo more rapid change than nonindustrial societies because of rapid changes in technology and diffusion of information. Many things you use today were not available to your parents when they were college age (hand calculators, personal computers, cassette recorders). Yet your parents have learned to take them for granted just as you have.

Occasionally people who have been isolated from a society return to it after a period of time and report shock at how the society has changed (how noisy and fast paced life is and how customs have changed). In the late 1970s people in many societies were shocked to learn that a Japanese soldier had been found on a remote Pacific island. What shocked people was that he had remained in hiding there since World War II.

Newspaper reporters tried to present what it was like for someone to return to Japan after three decades of isolation. The soldier was bewildered by many of the technological gadgets taken for granted in postindustrial Japan that were not generally available in the industrial Japan of the 1940s. Jets screeching across the skies, traffic jams, television sets all made the world a lot noisier than he remembered it. But not only did he have to adjust to technological changes, he had to adjust to changes in how people led their lives. The former soldier cherished the values of the Japan of the 1940s and was unhappy with changes in people's values and behavior. For example, women no longer behaved in the traditional way.

Most of us are aware of the vast number of changes that occur in society during our lifetimes. One major difference between us and people who are isolated is that we have been living in the midst of social change and have not been prevented from seeing it occur. We are not as likely to find changes as dramatic as an isolated person would, because we adapt and adjust while change is occurring. But **social change,** *defined as the alteration of patterns of social organization, structure, institutions, and intergroup or intragroup behaviors over time, is pervasive in our society and affects all of us in one way or another.*

Social change the alteration of patterns of social organization, structure, institutions, and intergroup or intragroup behaviors over time.

Reasons for Studying Social Change

All of us are a part of an ever-changing world. Our personal circumstances and social situations are continually changing as we migrate from place to place, as we perform new and different work, as we take part in new social situations, and enter new businesses.

Some of the many aspects of change in our social world are changes in institutions, changes in material culture, cultural diffusion, and changes in population.

Changes in Institutions

Institutions are regarded by many social scientists as relatively permanent, enduring structures. Although not impervious to change, institutions are
regarded as the sorts of social structures least likely to change quickly. Early
Japanese society, for instance, was fairly static; influences from outside were
severely restricted. In the mid-1800s Commodore Perry secured trade agreements between Japan and the United States. Westerners visiting Japan shortly
thereafter often remarked that Japanese culture seemed not to have changed
for hundreds of years. During the next hundred years, and, particularly after
World War II, Japan experienced many changes in its basic institutions. Traditional Japanese families were upset by the "Westernization" of their culture
and sought to prevent it from occurring (Muramatsu 1971).

Although isolationism may have characterized the United States at the
turn of the twentieth century, in the 1980s many Americans take a more liberal
view of social and institutional change. Some social observers even coined
the phrase "institutionalization of innovation" to indicate our conscious and
deliberate action to promote innovation and change in our basic institutions
(Lenski and Lenski 1982:261–262).

Our basic institutions, including religion, family, politics, and education,
have been undergoing gradual change. In Chapters 10 to 15, where these
institutions were examined in some detail, a consistent finding was that each
of our basic institutions has been subjected to changes of various kinds over
the years.

Relative to the family, new forms of birth control and the legalization of
abortion have made it easier for parents to plan the size of their family. The
responsibilities of parents and of children have also changed. Dual-career
families, together with greater availability of day-care and preschool facilities,
may signal a major new shift in child-rearing responsibilities from parents to
institutions outside the family.

The traditional church wedding, complete with bridesmaids and other
attendants, is sometimes challenged by new and alternative marriage forms.
Some couples are wed during a free-fall from an airplane. Others are married
in large groups with other couples in mass-weddings.

Many husbands and wives are likely to see more of their co-workers than
they see of each other or their children in a typical day. Bronfenbrenner (1976)
reports that working fathers of one-year-olds saw their offspring no more than
an average of twenty minutes a day.

As we saw in Chapter 15, Political and Legal Institutions, changes in our
political structure have occurred partly because of advances in our computer
and media technology. The televised debates between Richard Nixon and John
F. Kennedy were said to have crucially influenced the 1960 election. Later
debates on television between Jimmy Carter and Ronald Reagan also attested
to the power of television in politics (White 1969).

Some theorists assume that institutions are interrelated. The general educational level of the work force has increased markedly over the past fifty
years. Fifty years ago we would have found most blue-collar workers consid-

erably less educated than their white-collar counterparts. Today the average American receives more schooling, and there is less difference in educational level between blue-collar and white-collar workers. (See Chapter 11.)

The foregoing paragraphs illustrate the reciprocal effects of various institutions upon one another. The educational institution produces changes in the economic institution. The economic institution, in turn, produces changes in the family and political institutions. Other institutions also are involved in this complex network. More women are entering the work force today, performing such traditional "male" occupations as telephone linepersons, machinists, pilots, jockeys, managers, lawyers, and administrators.

Changes in Material Culture

The most obvious changes in our society are probably the innovations in material culture. The invention of the automobile and the airplane drastically changed how we live and how we relate to others. These new forms of transportation have made it possible to travel long distances rapidly; they "shrank" our world.

Another technological advance that has had numerous effects on us is the mass production of goods. The Industrial Revolution brought in the assembly-line method of production. Rather than a single individual constructing an entire product, several individuals were positioned along a moving belt that transferred the unfinished product from one person to another (see Chapter 11). Previously most products were manufactured personally by a skilled craftsperson, but in assembly-line production numerous people were brought together in one shop, each working on one aspect of the finished product. Each person became a specialist as a consequence. Pride in one's crafting often became a thing of the past. However, more units of product could be produced during the normal workday than in earlier, single-individual operations. Assembly-line production made it possible for more people to make and to buy more things more cheaply than they could under the previous hand-made production system.

In the United States, industrialists introduced assembly-line methods in the early nineteenth century, especially in New England. In the early twentieth century, Henry Ford applied these methods on a large scale in his automobile plant in Detroit.

Inventions have been significant at critical periods in our history of wars with other countries. The atomic bomb, an overwhelmingly destructive device capable of eliminating entire cities and killing hundreds of thousands, was instrumental in ending World War II after several years of intense fighting. Had German scientists succeeded in perfecting certain rockets and weaponry earlier during the war, the outcome might have been quite different. Likewise, the invention and use of radar and sonar effectively protected many ships from aircraft and submarines during World War II.

Transformation in mass production from automation to robotics.

Of course as developments on these technological fronts transpired, they affected other sectors of our society. The use of nuclear energy, both for weapons and for energy, has created an environmental problem of proper disposal of the radioactive wastes. Fallout from nuclear bombs is potentially hazardous to friendly populations as well as to enemy populations. Radioactive wastes in some areas of the world continue to threaten living things with destruction or harmful mutation.

But nuclear energy has constructive aspects as well. Nuclear reactors provide energy for many areas throughout the country. Medical research is facilitated through nuclear devices of various kinds. In a period in which the world is facing an energy crisis, nuclear reactors were initially seen as a positive solution to our growing energy needs. However, anti-nuclear groups protest the erection of such nuclear power plants as ecologically harmful. Critics point to the likelihood of nuclear "melt-downs" in which a nuclear facility would "self-destruct." Such nuclear accidents could endanger entire cities and whole regions, making them uninhabitable perhaps for generations.

The Diffusion of Change

We are often called a "melting pot" nation, with peoples from many nations, ethnic backgrounds, races, and cultural practices. We have undergone profound changes in our cultural activities as we have interacted with persons

Technological developments may improve the quality of life in some ways, but they may produce undesirable changes as well.

in other social systems throughout the world. The blending of cultural patterns from different societies is termed **cultural diffusion.**

The influence of blends of contrasting cultures may be seen in the construction and style of our "contemporary homes," in the different kinds of furniture selected to put in them, and in new religiophilosophical doctrines. Transcendental meditation, yoga, and other philosophies of the East have been adopted by some Americans. Dress styles also have been influenced by so-called cultural "mixing" or blending. Such diffusion may in fact be one manifestation of what W. I. Thomas referred to as "new experience" or the "wish" to engage in new activity, to behave and to think differently. There is obvious pressure in any society to conform to specified patterns of behavior and dress, and deviations from the so-called rules may be the "new experience" that W. I. Thomas described.

We are brought into contact with the ideas of persons in other lands through our reading or direct contacts in various social settings. Foreign exchange programs operated by high schools and universities permit students to become familiar with the life patterns of other peoples. Likewise, many persons from other countries come to the United States where they learn our way of life and our general psychological and social orientations.

Gradually, through education and exposure to persons from other lands, we have learned to accept persons who are different. This awareness has not been a particularly rapid process, but it has occurred over time.

All of our institutions have been affected through cultural diffusion, usually in the form of modifications rather than drastic transformations. We are

Cultural diffusion
the blending of various cultural patterns throughout a social system; also the processes by which elements or systems of culture are spread.

often unable to specify to what extent a change in a given institution has brought about change in other institutions. It is apparent, however, that the changing educational institution has affected the institutions of the family, politics, and the economy. In the religious institution, for instance, our definitions of right and wrong have changed in response to what persons from other social systems consider right and wrong. Certain churches in our country are adamantly opposed to euthanasia or the mercy killing of persons who are terminally sick. Yet in some countries this practice has existed for centuries. Many peoples of the world look upon the American ethic of prolonging the life of critically ill and suffering persons as sadistic and cruel, whereas Americans generally hold the opposite position.

How has cultural diffusion stimulated social change?

Changes in Population

For the past hundred years or more Americans have witnessed the rise of population concentrations in large city centers such as New York, Chicago, Los Angeles, Detroit, and Philadelphia. Over the years American society has changed from predominantly preindustrial to industrial or "postindustrial." (See Chapter 11, The Structure of Postindustrial Society.) Living and working in large urban centers has increased the importance of adhering to rigid time schedules, particularly related to transportation (mass transit) systems, appointments with persons in various service capacities (doctors, lawyers, dentists, hospital personnel), as well as routine, work-related activities. Increased membership in organizations of various kinds has also contributed to the complexity of our urban lives. Every time we join a new organization, we take upon ourselves new expectations embodied within the roles we perform. In fact, "joining behavior" has appeared to increase drastically with the concomitant increase in urbanization.

Explanations for Change

How does social change occur? Students of social change have posed at least six theories to explain social change. These include the cyclical, evolutionary, functionalist, conflict, and spontaneous theories of change.

Theories of Change

Cyclical Theories of Change.   Those who hold to the theory of cyclical change tend to view social systems or societies as living entities. Biological organisms are born, live in a given environment facing threats to their existence, and eventually die. The rise and fall of the Roman Empire is often cited by these theorists as evidence of the cyclical nature of social change. Other societies are also offered as proof that the cyclical theory of change has a basis in fact.

The German historian Oswald Spengler was a well-known cyclical theorist. In his book, *The Decline of the West,* published in 1918, he argued that most civilizations have gone through both low and high points in their development as societies. Wars and other times of crisis in each civilization pointed to what Spengler labeled societal "decay," and he predicted that each social system was "doomed" to ultimate extinction. His views were primarily speculative. Also, theorists who rely heavily on the biological analogy draw fire from critics because there are far more discrepancies between a society and a biological organism than similarities.

Evolutionary Theories of Change.   The evolutionary doctrines of Charles Darwin have had a significant influence on the development of evolutionary theories of social change. Darwin argued that organisms gradually change from a simple structure to a complex one. He assumed that human beings evolved from some lower form of animal life. In the course of hundreds of generations of human life, the complexity of human thought and behavior increased.

The English sociologist Spencer stated in 1870 that societies are subject to the same laws as those governing the evolution of living organisms. Where Darwin argued that only the species of living things most successfully adapted to their environment would survive over time, Spencer argued that only the most competitive societies would survive over time. His work was popular, particularly during the rapid expansion of the British Empire. The British found in such ideas a justification for their colonial rule over the "less advanced" societies that they had conquered.

The evolutionary view has not been particularly well accepted as a consistent explanation for social change. Not all societies change at the same rate, nor do they all necessarily change in the same directions. Evolutionary theorists also rely heavily on the organic analogy to illustrate the similarity between living organisms and the development of society over time. Again, such a view is not generally accepted in scientific circles.

Functionalist Theories of Social Change.   A relatively widespread theory of social change is functionalism. One of the prominent functionalists who has dealt with societal change is Parsons. Parsons views society as a system consisting of several interdependent parts. Each part, perhaps each institutional arrangement (religion, family, law, education), performs unique functions in relation to the whole. Therefore, a system is always in some sort of equilibrium, with each part of the system functioning in special ways to maintain the system over time.

Change is generated from within the system itself. As the laws in society change, the religious, educational, or other institutions also change in an effort to maintain or to reestablish the equilibrium of society. A law to incorporate busing as a means of establishing equality of educational opportunity for members of different racial groups may cause alterations in the educational institution. Then as the educational institution changes, so do other institutions, such as the tax structure or the political structure.

The functionalist perspective directs our attention to each institution and the functions it performs in the society at large. This perspective does not deny that social systems become increasingly complex, because the functionalist simply notes the increase in the number of institutions created by the system to perform more complex and specific functions.

Conflict Theories of Social Change.   A discussion of the conflict approach in sociology was presented in Chapter 1. The conflict theory of social change holds that society is composed of various competing interest groups. These interest groups engage in continuing conflicts or struggles for advantage, and the resolution of conflicts produces change.

Marx, one of the chief formulators of the conflict perspective, believed that all history is a history of class conflict. He viewed society as divided into two basic classes: those who own the means of production and those who work for those who own the means of production. The interests of the owners are always at odds with the interests of the workers. Profit interests compete with survival interests. This simplified view highlights the continual conflict or struggle between these classes.

Vested interest groups often lobby in Washington, D.C., to achieve their particular aims. Competing interest groups and organizations all contribute to the nature and course of changes in our society over time. Whether or not legal rights are extended to unborn children may depend upon the strengths or weakness of competing groups and their influence on the voting patterns of significant politicians. Changing divorce laws will no doubt change marital arrangements and family forms. Conflict theories are probably among the most accepted today for explaining how changes in history occurred.

Almost all of the theories treated thus far have failed to accomplish perhaps the most crucial function of theory-prediction of future events. A good theoretical scheme not only explains; it must predict as well. Conflict theories have consistently failed to predict future events.

Why are evolutionary and cyclical change theories less valuable to us in explaining change than the conflict view?

Spontaneous Change.   Probably the least useful, as well as the least fruitful, view of social change is that it occurs spontaneously. According to this theory, most social change is traceable to one factor or event as significant in altering the course of a society's destiny. The eruption of a volcano can obliterate a society totally or seriously hinder its cultural development. Natural disasters can generate changes in society that appear to be spontaneous.

The major criticism of the spontaneous change view is that it cannot successfully be linked with any existing theory of social change. It is impossible to predict really spontaneous events and, as a result, theories about spontaneous change are impossible to construct.

Planned Social Change

Planned social change is the conscious application of knowledge to reshape social behaviors, institutional patterns, and goals to fit a predetermined desired state or condition. Any time we discuss planned social change, we inevitably talk about those who make the change (change agents) and those who are changed (targets of change). **Change agents** are persons or groups who develop strategies and tactics whereby a successful change may be accomplished (Bennis, Benne, and Chin 1962:7–17). Change agents might be psychiatrists in the case of individuals seeking to change their lives or self-concepts. They may also be consultants to industry or business.

Consultants to organizations are often viewed as helpers who attempt to establish a learning situation or climate within which changes of various kinds can occur. In some respects a change agent's role in relation to a client system or a target of change is similar to the teacher-student relationship. The question to be answered is, "How can a desired change be brought about most effectively and in a way that will help the client benefit from the newly acquired behaviors without relying further on the change agent?"

Targets of change may be individuals, groups, organizations, communities, or total societies. Marx, for instance, advocated changes in societies. Carl Rogers, a well-known psychologist, is concerned with changes in individuals' self-concepts, and he deals with persons on a one-to-one basis. Both theorists fill the role of change agents in relation to their respective client systems.

In organizations, targets of change may be administration, policies, practices, attitudes of subordinates, communication networks, and authority hier-

Planned social change the conscious, deliberate application of knowledge to reshape social behaviors, institutional patterns, and goals to fit a predetermined, desired state or condition.

Change agents persons or groups who develop strategies and tactics to accomplish a successful change.

Targets of change individuals, groups, organizations, communities, or total societies whose form or behavior other individuals or groups seek to alter.

Habitat, an innovative concept at Canada's Expo '67, has been followed by other types of planned communities, such as Reston, Virginia, and Sun City, Arizona. (Martin J. Dain, Photo Researchers, Inc.)

archies. The variables that are manipulated include labor turnover, absenteeism, organizational productivity, the reward structure, and size of work groups.

Planned social change involves targets of change, change agents, and change goals. Change can occur on various levels of social organization—individual, small group, organizational, or societal. At the societal level (including not only communities and cities but also nations), ideas about social change are understandably more abstract. Broad questions about cultural change are raised. For the societal level, Moore (1963:2) has indicated several characteristics of contemporary change, including the following:

(1) For any given society or culture, rapid change occurs frequently or constantly. (2) Changes are neither temporally nor spatially isolated; that is, changes occur in sequential chains rather than as temporary crises followed by quiet periods of reconstruction. (3) Since contemporary change is probable "everywhere" and its consequences may be significant "everywhere," it has a dual basis. (4) The proportion of contemporary change that is either planned or issues from the secondary consequences of deliberate innovations is much higher than in former times. (5) Accordingly, the range of material technology and social strategies is expanding rapidly and its net effect is additive or cumulative despite the relatively rapid obsolescence of some procedures. (6) The normal occurrence of change affects a wider range of individual experience and functional aspects of societies in the modern world—not because such societies are in all respects more "integrated" but because virtually no feature of life is exempt from the expectation of normality of change.

Sources of Change

Washburne (1964:17) has described several sources of change that have implications for existing social systems. Some of these include mechanical inventions, population changes, natural occurrences, physiological changes, and the interactions of neighboring societies (acculturation and assimilation). In addition to these sources of change, we might consider cultural response to technology as well as revolution.

Mechanical Inventions

High-speed computers and other technological innovations have altered significantly the type of work performed in offices. Accountants and bookkeepers regard mechanical adding machines as relics of the past. Many corporations have produced a wide variety of technical gadgetry now affordable by individuals as well as companies.

Computers are used increasingly to diagnose patient illnesses in medical clinics. High-speed computer systems can process enormous quantities of personal and physical data and print out diagnoses of probable illnesses or infections.

THE FACTS · High Tech: The Career Impact

The buzzword for the 80's is technology. But contrary to popular belief, technology doesn't mean fewer jobs. More accurately, it points to a whole battery of new, exciting jobs.

Even after doubling in the 1970's, overall employment in the technological fields is expected to almost double again by 1990, with continued growth projected into the 21st century. One of the hottest areas is *computers.* Topping the list of fast-growing jobs is computer-service technician, with a projected growth rate of 93.2 percent through 1990. Systems analyst will grow by 67.8 percent. Computer and peripheral-equipment operator, the largest occupational group in the computer field, will more than double. Job openings should average 53,000 a year.

As forecasters predicted, the computer industry is in the process of giving birth to subindustries, which will grow and prosper as the cost of manufacturing advanced systems comes down. One such mini-industry is *telecommunications.* Simply defined, telecommunications takes in many of the latest technological developments, such as data and facsimile transmission, office automation, as well as data-processing equipment, all of which facilitate the transmission and reception of messages over great distances.

According to the International Communications Association, there are approximately 4,000 telecommunications professionals working for some 500 corporations. The field is growing rapidly, and future needs call for qualified people to design, maintain and service telecommunicating systems.

Robotics is another exciting high-tech field that is just erupting in ground-floor opportunities at virtually every level. Japan is currently the world leader in robot technology, with the United States hell-bent on sprinting into first place. Robotics offers lucrative career possibilities for designers, technicians and computer specialists, as well as sales and marketing people.

Solar energy: When industry decides to manufacture and distribute solar parts and accessories on a significant scale, as opposed to channeling token sums into research and development, the solar industry will move into high gear. That day is not far off. There will be opportunities galore, specifically a constant demand for engineers, architects, surveyors, insulation workers, welders, painters, general-construction people, contractors, sales and marketing people, etc.

Conservation-related jobs: Government and industry are fast approaching the day when decisive plans will be made for ridding the environment of pollution and industrial wastes. Soil conservationists, scientists, technicians and skilled and semi-skilled workers will be needed to do the job.

Ergonomic specialists: Ergonomics is a fancy word for biotechnology, which neatly describes the man-machine relationship. Ergonomics specialists or designers search for that happy medium where man and machine can work harmoniously and productively together.

Demand for *engineers* stems from the continued development of synthetic fuels, greater defense spending and the increasing use of cost-effective technologies, such as microprocessors, fiber optics, satellite transmission and computer-aided manufacturing.

Among the high-demand areas are mechanical, computer, science, electrical, electronics, industrial-management, chemical, civil, information science, engineering physics and systems engineering—and that's only the tip of the iceberg. There will also be a demand for environmental, biomedical, fire protection, energy, ocean, ceramic and plastics engineers.

The job outlook for the *health-care industry* is excellent. Since progress within this broad-based field is intimately entwined with technological advances, we can look forward to new careers and accompanying technologies.

Within the *entertainment* industry, cable television in particular offers interesting long-term employment possibilities for technicians at all skill levels, as well as positions in marketing, advertising, public relations and sales. Despite setbacks and losses, each month the industry continues to add 1,000 new jobs, 250,000 subscribers, and at least one more satellite service.

The video-computer-game craze continues to get bigger and bigger each year, pointing to an expanding market with thousands of new openings at the design, manufacturing, sales and distribution levels.

As we head for the 90's, we can look forward to more leisure time, increased productivity, shorter working hours and new technological advances, and this means more jobs within the broadbased *service* sector. The Bureau of Labor Statistics reports that the service sector is expected to increase faster than any other occupational group through the 80's and 90's and well into the 21st century. For the 1980-90 period, projected increases range from 2 percent to 49.6 percent.

How the Hot Jobs Pay

Here is a list of the average salaries in 1982 for some of the best jobs of the 80's. They'll go up as the decade goes on.

aeronautical engineer	**$41,150**
chemical engineer	**$38,890**
electrical engineer	**$37,480**
industrial engineer	**$29,950**
mechanical engineer	**$38,100**
computer operator	**$31,100**
word-processing operator	**$14,000**
systems-analyst manager	**$40,000**
telecommunications manager	**$41,600**
telecommunications analyst	**$28,100**
solar engineer	**$22,000**
robotics specialist	**$30,000**

SOURCE: Robert V. Weinstein, *Family Weekly,* July 17, 1983.

Mechanical inventions have changed how we define our work, how we look at the world around us, and how we relate to other people. Transportation and communication facilities have improved our capacity to carry on business activity in virtually any part of the world at any time we wish. Improvements and developments in teaching aids have modified our classrooms and the way we orient ourselves toward education.

Natural Occurrences

Natural occurrences such as volcanic eruptions, floods, tornados and the like may require entire communities to rebuild themselves totally. Often, during periods of reconstruction, vast changes in the social, political, economic, and educational structure of the social system are instigated. Disasters often cause persons to reevaluate their plans in the light of possible future disasters. New organizations may be created to assist the potentially homeless and to provide economic aid and medical care to persons who may require it. These new organizations within the system may necessitate a redefinition of earlier responsibilities among the various institutions in the communities affected.

Interactions of Societies and Cultural Exchanges

Cultural exchange programs, usually for students and teachers, permit people to see how persons live in other countries. Learning the customs and values of persons in other cultures helps to promote better international relations. Throughout history, contacts between peoples of different cultures have usually fostered assimilation of one degree or another. Cultural diffusion, or the process by which elements or systems of culture are spread, occurs universally.

Cultural Response to Technology

Inventions, especially those contributing to technological changes in our everyday life, usually require some adjustment on the part of the members of a society. William Fielding Ogburn developed a theory of **culture lag** in 1922 to account for the time interval between the development of new technology and the public's acceptance of it (Ogburn 1957).

Culture lag the time interval between the development of a new technology and the general public's acceptance of it.

The development of airplanes was a major technological breakthrough, but it took people some time to get used to the idea of flying from one place to another. Some persons have never flown and will never fly in an airplane for a variety of reasons. Fear of flying is one explanation; religious beliefs might be another. The Amish in Pennsylvania reject mechanical gadgetry of any kind to accomplish their farming tasks, including even electricity. The lag between new developments—whether new technology, new fashions, or new behaviors—and their subsequent adoption and acceptance by the populace of society is evidence of cultural lag.

Revolution and Social Change

In Chapter 18 social movements were examined in some detail. Social movements are responsible frequently for large-scale societal changes. In pre–World War II Germany, for instance, economic strife and war debts imposed by the victorious French, British, and Americans created social discontent, which in turn provided conditions ripe for Adolf Hitler to gain power. The Nazi party was in some respects a sociopolitical movement that unified the German nation. The Nazis instituted large-scale reforms, and the people willingly went along with most of these changes. In some respects, the Nazis' changes at first led the German people to recapture national dignity, although they ultimately contributed to the disasters of World War II. German society was changed dramatically within a relatively short space of time.

Revolution is a sudden or extreme political, social, or economic change in a society, often by force of arms or a threat of force. Since the end of World War II, numerous countries have gone through revolutions to some degree. In the late 1970s the shah of Iran was opposed by various factions, including the religious, and was eventually overthrown. On the heels of his ouster, the new leaders instigated extensive social reforms as well as repression of opposing groups. El Salvador and other Latin American countries have undergone internal strife through revolution. These countries have been torn apart by various warring factions seeking to further the interests of their adherents.

Revolution sudden or extreme political, social, or economic change in a society, often by force of arms or threat of force.

Social changes may be both the reason for and the result of political struggles.

Summary

Social change is pervasive in our society. All of the major institutions are constantly undergoing changes of one type or another and to varying degrees.

Social change is the alteration of patterns of social organization, structure, institutions, and intergroup or intragroup behaviors over time.

Changes in our culture are reflected in part by changing technology, the tools and methods we use to accomplish tasks. The rapidity of change has modified substantially our relationships with others, our self-concepts, and our values.

Various explanations for social change have included cyclical, evolutionary, functionalist, and conflict theories. Planned social change is a deliberate modification in the patterns of social relationships with specific targets for change. Change agents facilitate such change.

Various sources of change include mechanical inventions, natural occurrences, and relations with other societies. Technology and cultural reform also contribute to change.

Changes of a more dramatic form and against the wishes of the ruling elite in society include political or social revolution and the violent overthrow of a government.

Suggested Readings

Daniel Chirot. *Social Change in the Twentieth Century.* New York: Harcourt Brace Jovanovich, 1977. An analysis of how the world system changes in response to shifts in the balance of cultural, economic, and political factors.

Gerald K. O'Neill. *2081: A Hopeful View of the Human Future.* New York: Simon & Schuster, 1981. Optimistic projections about social life a century from now, focusing on five key elements: automation, communication, computer development, energy, and space colonization.

Socialization to gender roles—like other aspects of our current society—has taken on new complexities. Little boys are usually urged to play with "male" toys like cars, but parents have become aware that boys need to play with other kinds of toys too. For girls a typewriter might be presented as a symbol of a subservient "female" role or as a ticket to self-sufficiency. Little League baseball and other sports were male-only not long ago, but today many women have proved their sports talents. Women athletes' efforts have now shifted to a demand for equal resources as well as equal rights. But many children—like the daughter of migrant workers—need encouragement to seek broader horizons and higher expectations for life in general.

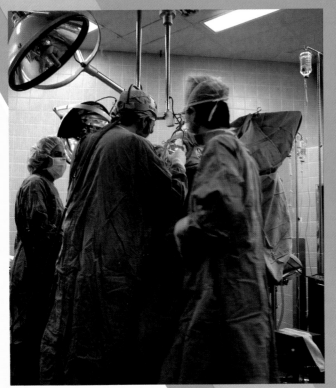

Advances in surgery, together with an amazing array of new drugs and medical equipment, have produced astounding medical achievements in our era. But there is another side to this success story: as more people—especially women—live longer, we may run short of funds for medical care and facilities. The question is whether the nation can afford the level of health care we have come to expect—and extend it to all citizens. And the answer will be dictated more by political than medical concerns. For the mentally ill or handicapped, modern medicine has found no easy or sure cures, and our institutions usually provide inadequate support systems. We need a major effort in this area, but again, can—or will—our nation pay for it?

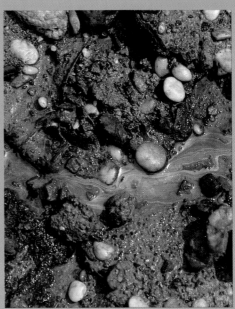

In the last decades of the twentieth century the United States faces a series of conflicts between expanding our economy and protecting our environment. Smokestacks in the great industrial centers of the Midwest must start smoking again to rev up the nation's economy. But emissions from those smokestacks add to the deadly acid rain falling on the Northeast. Full automation—or robotization—is one of the automobile industry's answers to the challenge of foreign imports. But every robot takes a job away from one or more human workers. Oil is still basic to our economy and will be for years to come. But even with more regulations and better technology, we cannot seem to avoid oil spills, such as one that devastated a New Jersey beach.

Equal opportunity for minorities is a major goal of our society, but progress toward it has been slowed by problems arising from education, housing, and welfare cut-backs. Drug-related problems—including alcohol abuse—continue unabated and now affect all ages and all levels of society. In most of our great cities—once portals to a better life for millions of immigrants—the urban core has decayed alarmingly, trapping recent arrivals in mazes of physical and social ugliness. Our present social ills have often suffered from too much mindless activity and too little serious thought. For any future progress we need to know more clearly both *where* we want to go as a nation and *how* to get there.

References

Abrahamson, Mark, Ephriam H. Mizruchi, and Carlton A. Hornung. *Stratification and Mobility.* New York: Macmillan, 1976.

Abu-Lughod, Janet. "Testing the Theory of Social Area Analysis: The Ecology of Cairo, Egypt." *American Sociological Review,* 34:198–212, 1969.

Achenbaum, W. Andrew. *Old Age in the New Land.* Baltimore: Johns Hopkins University Press, 1978.

Allport, Gordon W. *The Nature of Prejudice.* Garden City, N.Y.: Doubleday Anchor, 1958.

Allport, Gordon W., and Leo J. Postman. *The Psychology of Rumor.* New York: Holt, Rinehart and Winston, 1947.

Alterman, Hyman. *Counting People: The Census in History.* New York: Harcourt, Brace and World, 1969.

Argyris, Chris. "The Individual and Organization: Some Problems of Mutual Adjustment." *Administrative Science Quarterly,* 2:1–24, 1957.

———. "Understanding Human Behavior in Organizations: One Viewpoint." In Mason Haire (ed.), *Modern Organizational Theory.* New York: Wiley, 1959.

———. *Integrating the Individual and the Organization.* New York: Wiley, 1964.

———. *Organization and Innovation.* Homewood, Ill.: Dorsey, 1965.

Aries, Philippe. *Centuries of Childhood.* New York: Vintage, 1962.

Armstrong, Ben. *The Electric Church.* Nashville, Tenn.: Nelson Publishers, 1979.

Aronowitz, Stanley. *False Promises: The Shaping of American Working-Class Consciousness.* New York: McGraw-Hill, 1973.

Asch, S. E. "Effects of Group Pressure upon Modification and Distortion of Judgments." Pp. 174–183 in E. E. Maccoby, T. M. Newcomb, and E. L. Hartley (eds.), *Readings in Social Psychology.* New York: Holt, Rinehart and Winston, 1958.

Asimov, Isaac. "The Pursuit of Youth." *Ladies Home Journal* (June):155, 1974.

Atchley, Robert C. "A Size-Function Typology of Cities." *Demography,* 4:721–733, 1967.

Bandura, Albert. "Social-learning Theory of Identificatory Processes." Pp. 213–262 in David A. Goslin (ed.), *Handbook of Socialization Theory and Research.* Chicago: Rand McNally, 1969.

Banton, Michael. *Race Relations.* New York: Basic Books, 1967.

Barnard, Chester I. *The Functions of the Executive.* Cambridge, Mass.: Harvard University Press, 1938.

Bates, Alan P. *The Sociological Enterprise.* New York: Houghton-Mifflin, 1967.

Bean, Lee L., Richmond K. Anderson, and Howard J. Tatum. *Population and Family Planning Manpower and Training.* New York: Population Council, 1971.

Beck, Joan. "To Be a Victim is a Nightmare." *Chicago Tribune,* Feb. 7, 1983.

Becker, Gary. *The Economics of Discrimination.* Chicago: University of Chicago Press, 1957.

Becker, Howard S. "Becoming a Marihuana User." *American Journal of Sociology,* 59:235–242, 1953.

———. "Personal Change in Adult Life." *Sociometry,* 24:40–53, 1964.

Becker, Howard S., Blanche Geer, Everett C. Hughes, and Anselm Strauss. *Boys In White.* Chicago: University of Chicago Press, 1961.

Bell, Daniel. *The Coming of Post-Industrial Society: A Venture in Social Forecasting.* New York: Basic Books, 1973.

Bellah, Robert N. "Religious Evolution." *American Sociological Review,* 29:358–374, 1964.

———. *Beyond Belief: Essays on Religion in a Post-Industrial World.* New York: Harper & Row, 1970.

Bem, Sandra L. "The Measurement of Psychological Androgyny." *Journal of Counseling and Clinical Psychology,* 42:155–62, 1974.

———. "Sex Role Adaptability: One Consequence of Psychological Androgyny." *Journal of Personality and Social Psychology,* 31:634–643, 1975.

Bem, Sandra L., and Daryl J. Bem. "Does Sex-biased Job Advertising Aid and Abet Sex Discrimination?" *Journal of Applied Social Psychology,* 3:6–18, 1973.

Bendix, Reinhard, and Seymour Martin Lipset. "Karl Marx's Theory of Social Classes." Pp. 6–11 in Reinhard Bendix and

Seymour Martin Lipset (eds.), *Class, Status and Power.* New York: Free Press, 1966.

Benet, Sula. "Why They Live to be 100, or Even Older, in Abkhasia." *The New York Times Magazine* (December 26):3, 1971.

Bengtson, Vern L. *The Social Psychology of Aging.* Indianapolis: Bobbs-Merrill, 1976.

Bennis, Warren G. (ed.). *American Bureaucracy.* New Brunswick, N.J.: Transaction Books, 1970.

Bennis, Warren G., Kenneth Benne, and Robert Chin. *The Planning of Change: Readings in the Applied Behavioral Sciences.* New York: Holt, Rinehart and Winston, 1961.

Berger, Peter L. *Invitation to Sociology.* Garden City, N.Y.: Doubleday Anchor, 1963.

Berger, Peter L., and Hansfried Kellner. *Sociology Reinterpreted.* Garden City, N.Y.: Doubleday Anchor, 1981.

Berger, Peter, and Thomas Luckman. *The Social Construction of Reality.* Garden City, N.Y.: Doubleday, 1966.

Berry, Brewton, and Henry L. Tischler. *Race and Ethnic Relations.* Boston: Houghton-Mifflin, 1978.

Berry, B. J. L., Peter Goheen, and Harold Goldstein. *Metropolitan Area Definition: A Re-evaluation of Concept and Statistical Practice.* Working Paper No. 28 (June), U.S. Bureau of the Census. Washington, D.C.: Government Printing Office, 1969.

Berry, Brian J. L., and John D. Kasarda. *Contemporary Urban Ecology.* New York: Macmillan, 1977.

Better Homes and Gardens. A Report on the American Family. Meredith Corp., 1978.

Better Homes and Gardens. Is Government Helping or Hurting American Families? *Better Homes and Gardens,* Meredith Corporation, 1980.

Bibb, Robert, and William Form. "The Effects of Industrial, Occupational, and Sex Stratification on Wages in Blue-collar Markets." *Social Forces, 55:*974–996.

Biddle, Bruce J. *Role Theory.* New York: Academic Press, 1979.

Birdwhistell, Ray. *Kinesics and Context.* Philadelphia: University of Pennsylvania Press, 1970.

Bishop, Lloyd. "Bureaucracy and Educational Change." *The Clearing House, 44:*305–309, 1970.

Blau, Judith R., and William McKinley. "Ideas, Complexity, and Innovation." *Administrative Science Quarterly, 24,* 2 (June):200–219, 1979.

Blau, Peter M. "Decentralization in Bureaucracies." In Mayer N. Zald (ed.), *Power in Organizations.* Nashville, Tenn.: Vanderbilt University Press, 1970.

Blau, Peter M., and Otis Dudley Duncan. *The American Occupational Structure.* New York: Wiley, 1967.

Blau, Peter M., and Marshall Meyer. *Bureaucracy in Modern Society.* New York: Random House, 1971.

Blau, Peter M., and W. Richard Scott. *Formal Organizations: A Comparative Approach.* San Francisco: Chandler, 1962.

Blauner, Robert. *Alienation and Freedom.* Chicago: University of Chicago Press, 1964.

———. "Death and the Social Structure." Pp. 534–540 in Bernice L. Neugarten (ed.), *Age and Aging: A Reader in Social Psychology.* Chicago: University of Chicago Press, 1968.

———. *Racial Oppression in America.* New York: Harper & Row, 1972.

"Blind Father Finally Gets Custody of Sons." *Knoxville News Sentinel,* October 19, 1980, p. B-7.

Blumberg, Paul. *Inequality in an Age of Decline.* New York: Oxford University Press, 1980.

Blumberg, Rae Lesser. *Stratification: Socioeconomic and Sexual Inequality.* Dubuque, Iowa: William C. Brown, 1978.

Blumer, Herbert. "Science Without Concepts." *American Journal of Sociology, 36:*515–533, 1931.

———. "Social Psychology." In Emerson P. Schmidt (ed.), *Man and Society.* New York: Prentice-Hall: 144–198, 1937.

———. "Collective Behavior." Pp. 167–222 in A. M. Lee (ed.), *The Principles of Sociology.* New York: Barnes & Noble, 1951.

———. *Symbolic Interactionism.* Englewood Cliffs, N.J.: Prentice-Hall, 1969.

"Body Language." *Saturday Review* (May):78, 1973.

Bogue, Donald J. *The Structure of Metropolitan Community: A Study of Dominance and Sub-Dominance.* Ann Arbor: University of Michigan Press, 1949.

———. *Principles of Demography.* New York: Wiley, 1969.

Bogue, Donald J., and Calvin Beal. *Economic Areas of the United States.* New York: Free Press, 1961.

Bonacich, Edna, and John Modell. *The Economic Basis of Ethnic Solidarity: General Business in the Japanese American Community.* Berkeley: University of California Press, 1980.

Boorstin, Daniel J. *The Image.* London: Werdenfeld and Nicolson, 1961.

Bouvier, Leon F., and Everett S. Lee. *The Health of Americans. Population Profiles.* Washington, D.C.: Connecticut Center of Information of America, 1976.

Bouvier, Leon F., and Jean van der Tak. *Infant Mortality—Progress and Problems.* Population Bulletin 31. Washington, D.C.: Government Printing Office, 1976.

Bower, Donald W., and Victor A. Christopherson. "University Student Cohabitation." *Journal of Marriage and the Family, 39:*447–452, 1977.

Branscomb, Lewis M. "Taming Technology." *Science, 171:*972–977, 1971.

Brasch, R. *How Did It Begin?* Pp. 71–72. New York: David McKay, 1966.

Braverman, Harry. *Labor and Monopoly Capital.* New York: Monthly Review Press, 1975.

Brickman, William W. *Automation, Education, and Human Values.* New York: School and Society Books, 1966.

Bridenbaugh, Carl. *Cities in Revolt: Urban Life in America 1743–1776.* New York: Capricorn Books, 1955.

Brim, Orville G., Jr., and Jerome Kagan (eds.). *Constancy and*

Change in Human Development. Cambridge, Mass: Harvard University Press, 1980.

Bronfenbrenner, Urie. "The Disturbing Changes in the American Family." *Search* (Fall): 11–14, 1976.

Brooks-Gunn, Jeanne, and Wendy S. Matthews. *He and She: How Children Develop Their Sex-Role Identity.* Englewood Cliffs, N.J.: Spectrum, 1979.

Broom, Leonard. "The Social Differentiation of Jamaica." *American Sociological Review, 19:* 115–125, 1954.

Brown, Lester. *Man, Land and Food: Looking Ahead at World Food Needs.* Foreign Agricultural Report No. 11. Washington, D.C.: Government Printing Office, 1963.

Brown, Lester R. "World Population Trends: Signs of Hope, Signs of Stress." *Population Reports Series J,* Number 13 (January): 237–251, 1977.

Brown, Lester R., Patricia L. McGarth, and Bruce Stokes. "Twenty-Two Dimensions of the Population Problem." *Population Reports Series J,* No. 11 (November):177–202, 1976.

Brown, Turner, Jr. *Black Is.* New York: Grove Press, 1969.

Burch, Thomas K. "The Size and Structure of Families." *American Sociological Review, 32:*347–363, 1967.

Burgess, Ann Wolbert, and Lynda Lytle Holmstrom. *Rape: Victims of Crisis.* Boure, Md.: Brady, 1974.

Cain, Pamela S., and Donald J. Treiman. "The DOT as a Source of Occupational Data." *American Sociological Review, 46:*253–278, 1981.

Cantril, Hadley. *The Invasion from Mars.* Princeton: Princeton University Press, 1940.

Caplow, Theodore. *Two Against One: Coalitions in Triads.* Englewood Cliffs, N.J.: Prentice-Hall, 1968.

Carmichael, S., and C. Hamilton. *Black Power.* New York: Vintage, 1967.

Carns, Donald E. "Religiosity, premarital sexuality and the American college student." Ph.D. dissertation, Indiana University, 1969.

Cartter, Allen M. *An Assessment of Quality in Graduate Education.* Washington, D.C.: American Council on Education, 1966.

Cavan, Sherry. *Liquor License.* Chicago: Aldine, 1966.

Centers, Richard. *The Psychology of Social Classes.* Princeton, N.J.: Princeton University Press, 1949.

Chalfant, H. Paul, Robert E. Beckley, and C. Eddie Palmer. *Religion in Contemporary Society.* Sherman Oaks, Calif.: Alfred Publishing Co., 1981.

Chambliss, William J. "The Saints and the Roughnecks." *Society, 11:*24–31, 1973.

Champagne, Paul J., and Curt Tausky. "When Job Enrichment Doesn't Pay." *Personnel, 55* (Jan./Feb.):30–40, 1978.

Chesney-Lind, Meda. "Juvenile Delinquency: The Sexualization of Female Crime." *Psychology Today* (July):43–46, 1974.

Christ, Carol P., and Judith Plaskow (eds.). *Womanspirit Rising.* New York: Harper & Row, 1979.

Clark, Burton R. "The 'Cooling Out' Function in Higher Education." *American Journal of Sociology, 65:*569–576, 1960.

Clark, Colin. *Conditions of Economic Progress.* London: Macmillan, 1940.

Clark, John P., and Edward Havrek. "Age and Sex Roles of Adolescents and Their Involvement in Misconduct." *Sociology and Social Research, 50:*495–508, 1966.

Coleman, James. *U.S. National Center of Educational Statistics: Equality of Educational Opportunity.* Washington, D.C.: Government Printing Office, 1966.

Collins, Randall. "A Conflict Theory of Sexual Stratification." *Social Problems, 19:*3–21, 1971.

The Commission on Population Growth and the American Future. *Population and the American Future.* Washington, D.C.: Government Printing Office, 1972.

Comte, Auguste. *Positive Philosophy.* Translated by Harriet Martineau. 3 vols. London: George Bell and Sons, 1896.

———. *Positive Polity.* Translated by John Bridges et al. 4 vols. London: Longmans, Green and Co., 1954.

Conroy, Pat. *The Lords of Discipline.* New York: Bantam, 1982.

Cooley, Charles Horton. *Social Organization.* New York: Schocken, 1909.

———. *Human Nature and the Social Order.* New York: Schocken, 1922.

Coontz, Sydney H. *Population Theories and Economic Interpretations.* London: Routledge and Kegan Paul, 1957.

Coser, Lewis A. *The Functions of Social Conflict.* Glencoe, Ill.: Free Press, 1956.

Cottrell, W. F. "Death by Dieselization." *American Sociological Review, 16:*358–365, 1951.

Craig, Eleanor. *One, Two, Three: The Story of Matt, A Feral Child.* New York: McGraw-Hill, 1978.

Cross, Malcomn. "On Conflict, Race, Relations and the Theory of Plural Society." *Race, XII, 4:*477–494, 1971.

Cox, Peter R. *Demography.* Cambridge: Cambridge University Press, 1970.

Curtis, Susan. *Genie: A Psycholinguistic Study of a Modern-Day "Wild Child."* New York: Academic Press, 1977.

Dahrendorf, Ralf. "Toward a Theory of Social Conflict." *The Journal of Conflict Resolution, 11:*170–183, 1958.

———. *Class and Class Conflict in Industrial Society.* Stanford, Calif.: Stanford University Press, 1959.

Daly, Mary. *Beyond God the Father.* Boston: Beacon, 1974.

Davis, A., B. B. Gardner, and M. Gardner. *Deep South: A Social Anthropological Study of Caste and Class.* Chicago: University of Chicago Press, 1941.

Davis, James A. *General Social Surveys, 1972–1980: Cumulative Codebook.* Chicago: National Opinion Research Center, 1980.

Davis, Kingsley. *Human Society.* New York: Macmillan, 1948.

———. "The Role of Urbanization in the Developmental Process." *International Technical Cooperation Centre Review* (Tel Aviv), *1* (July):1–13, 1952.

———. "The Origin and Growth of Urbanization in the World." *American Journal of Sociology, 60:*429–437, 1955.

———. "Population." *Scientific American, 209* (3):62–71, 1963.

Davis, Kingsley, and Wilbert E. Moore. "Some Principles of

Stratification." *American Sociological Review, 10:*242–249, 1945.

Deaux, Kay, and J. Taynor. "Evaluation of Male and Female Ability: Bias Works Two Ways." *Psychological Reports, 32:*261–262, 1973.

DeFleur, M. L. and F. R. Westie. "Verbal Attitudes and Overt Acts: An Experiment on the Salience of Attitudes." *American Sociological Review, 23:*667–673, 1958.

Degler, Carl. *At Odds: Women and the Family in America from the Revolution to the Present.* New York: Oxford University Press, 1980.

De Mause, Lloyd. "Our Forebears Made Childhood a Nightmare." *Psychology Today, 8* (April): 85–88, 1975.

Denzin, Norman K. *The Research Act.* Chicago: Aldine, 1970.

———. *Childhood Socialization.* San Francisco: Jossey-Bass, 1977.

Dobriner, William M. (ed.). *The Surburban Community.* New York: G. P. Putnam's Sons, 1958.

Domhoff, G. William. *The Powers That Be.* New York: Vintage, 1979.

Dominick, Joseph R. "The Portrayal of Women in Prime Time, 1953–1977." *Sex Roles, 5:*405–412, 1979.

Douglas, Ann. *The Feminization of American Culture.* New York: Alfred A. Knopf, 1977.

Douvon, Elizabeth, Helen Weingarten, and Jane L. Scheiber. *American Families.* Dubuque, Iowa: Kendall/Hunt, 1980.

"Down with Human Interference." *The Knoxville News Sentinel,* December 16, 1981.

Drucker, Peter F. *Managing in Turbulent Times.* New York: Harper & Row, 1980.

Duncan, Otis D. "A Socioeconomic Index for all Occupations." Pp. 109–138 in Albert J. Reiss, Jr. (ed.), *Occupations and Social Status.* New York: Free Press, 1961.

Durkheim, Emile. *The Elementary Forms of Religious Life.* Translated by Joseph W. Swain. London: George Allen and Unwin, 1915.

———. *Suicide.* Translated by John A. Spaulding and George Simpson. Glencoe, Ill.: Free Press, 1951 (first published 1897).

———. *The Division of Labor in Society.* Translated by George Simpson. New York: Free Press, 1964 (first published 1893).

Ehrlich, Paul R., and Anne H. Ehrlich. *Population Resources and Environment: Issues in Human Ecology.* San Francisco: Freeman, 1970.

Eichler, Lillian. *Etiquette Problems in Pictures.* New York: Nelson Doubleday, 1922.

Ekeh, P. P. *Social Exchange Theory: The Two Traditions.* Cambridge, Mass.: Harvard University Press, 1974.

Elkin, Frederick, and Gerald Handel. *The Child and Society.* 3rd ed. New York: Random House, 1978.

Engels, Friedrich. *The Origin of the Family, Private Property, and the State.* New York: Pathfinder, 1972.

Erikson, E. H. *Childhood and Society.* New York: Norton, 1963.

Etzioni, Amitai. *A Comparative Analysis of Complex Organizations.* New York: Free Press, 1961.

Farberman, Harvey A. "A Criminogenic Market Structure." *Sociological Quarterly, 16:*438–457, 1975.

Farley, Reynolds. "Surburban Persistence." *American Sociological Review, XXIX:*38–48, 1964.

Faris, Ellsworth. "The Primary Group Essence and Accident." *American Journal of Sociology, XXXVIII,* 1 (July): 241–250, 1932.

Faunce, William A. "Automation and the Employee." *Annals of the American Academy of Political and Social Science, 34:*60–68, 1962.

Featherman, David L. F., Lancaster Jones, and Robert M. Hauser. *"Assumptions of Social Mobility Research in the United States." Social Science Research, 4:*329–360, 1975.

Festinger, Leon. "A Theory of Social Comparison Processes." *Human Relations, 7:* 117–140.

Fidell, L. A. "Empirical Verification of Sex Discrimination in Hiring Practices in Psychology." *American Psychologist, 25:*1094–1098, 1970.

Firey, Walter. "Sentiment and Symbolism as Ecological Variables." *American Sociological Review, 10:*140–148, 1945.

———. "Ecological Considerations in Planning for Ruruban Fringes." *American Sociological Review, XI:*400–421, 1946.

Fishman, Pamela M. "Interaction: The Work Women Do." *Social Problems, 25:*397–406, 1978.

Fleming, Joyce Dudney. "The State of the Apes." *Psychology Today* (Jan.): 31–50, 1974.

Foreit, Karen G., Terna Agor, Johnny Byers, John Parue, Helen Lokey, Michael Palazzini, Michele Patterson, and Lillian Smith. "Sex Bias in the Newspaper Treatment of Male-Centered and Female-Centered News Stories." *Sex Roles, 6:*475–480, 1980.

Franke, Herbert, and James D. Kaul. "The Hawthorne Experiments—First Statistical Interpretation." *American Sociological Review, 43* (October):623–643, 1978.

Freeman, Derek. *Margaret Mead and Samoa—The Making and Unmaking of an Anthropological Myth.* 1983.

Freedman, J. L., and S. C. Fraser. "Compliance Without Pressure: The Foot in the Door Technique." *Journal of Personality and Social Psychology, 4:*195–202, 1966.

Freud, Sigmund. *New Introductory Lectures on Psychoanalysis.* Translated and edited by James Strachey. New York: Norton, n.d.

———. *An Outline of Psychoanalysis.* Translated from *Abriss de Psychoanalyse.* International Zeitschrift fur Psycholoanalyse und Imago, XXV, 1940. New York: Norton, 1940.

Friedl, Ernestine. *Women and Men.* New York: Holt, Rinehart and Winston, 1975.

Fung, Yu-lan. *A Short History of Chinese Philosophy.* Edited by Derk Bodde. New York: Macmillan, 1960.

Gallup, George H. *The Gallup Poll. Public Opinion, 1937–71.* New York: Random House, 1972.

Gans, Herbert J. "Urbanism and Suburbanism as Ways of Life." Pp. 625–648 in Arnold Rose (ed.), *Human Behavior and Social Processes.* Boston: Houghton Mifflin, 1962.

Gans, Herbert J. *The Levittowners.* New York: Pantheon, 1967.

Gans, Herbert J. *Popular Culture and High Culture.* New York: Basic Books, 1974.

Garraty, John A. *The American Nation: A History of the United States to 1877.* 2nd ed. New York: Harper & Row and American Heritage, 1971.

Garwood, S. Gray, Lewis Cox, Valerie Kaplan, Neal Wasserman, and Jefferson L. Sulzer. "Beauty is Only 'Name' Deep." *Journal of Applied Social Psychology, 10:*431–433, 1980.

Gelles, Richard J. "Abused Wives." *Journal of Marriage and the Family, 38:*659–668, 1976.

Gelles, Richard J., and Murray A. Strauss. "Determinants of Violence in the Family." Pp. 550–552 in Wesley R. Burr, et al. (eds.), *Contemporary Theories about the Family.* Vol. 1. New York: Free Press, 1979.

Gendron, Bernard. *Technology and the Human Condition.* New York: St. Martin's Press, 1977.

General Mills. *The General Mills American Family Report 1980–1981: Families Strengths and Strains at Work.* Minneapolis, Minn.: General Mills, 1981.

Georges, Cobert A. (ed.). *Studies in Mythology.* Homewood, Ill.: Dorsey, 1968.

Gerth, Hans, and C. Wright Mills (Translated and edited) *From Max Weber—Essays in Sociology.* New York: Oxford, 1958.

Geschwender, James A. *Racial Stratification in America.* Dubuque, Iowa: William C. Brown, 1978.

Giddens, Anthony. *Sociology: A Brief But Critical Introduction.* New York: Harcourt Brace Jovanovich, 1982.

Gies, Joseph, and Frances Gies. *Life in a Medieval City.* New York; Thomas Y. Crowell, 1969.

Gilchrist, David T. (ed.). *The Growth of the Seaport Cities: 1790–1825.* Charlottesville, Va.: University of Virginia Press, 1967.

Glaser, Barney, and Anselm Strauss. *Awareness of Dying.* Chicago: Aldine, 1965.

Glazer, Nathan, and Daniel Moynihan. *Beyond the Melting Pot.* Cambridge, Mass.: MIT Press, 1963.

Glenn, Norval D., and Charles N. Weaver. "The Marital Happiness of Remarried Divorced Persons." *Journal of Marriage and the Family, 39:*331–337, 1977.

Glick, Paul C., and Graham B. Spanier. "Married and Unmarried Cohabitation in the United States." *Journal of Marriage and the Family, 42:*19–30, 1980.

Glock, Charles Y. *Religion in Sociological Perspective: Essays in the Empirical Study of Religion.* Belmont, Calif.: Wadsworth, 1973.

Glock, C. Y., and R. Stark. *Religion and Society in Tension.* Chicago: Rand McNally, 1965.

Goffman, Erving. *Encounters.* Indianapolis: Bobbs-Merrill, 1958.

———. *Presentation of Self in Everyday Life.* Garden City, New York: Doubleday Anchor, 1959.

———. *Asylums: Essays on the Social Situation of Mental Patients and Other Inmates.* Garden City, N.Y.: Doubleday Anchor, 1961.

———. *Encounters: Two Studies in the Sociology of Interaction.* Indianapolis: Bobbs-Merrill, 1961.

———. *Interaction Ritual.* Garden City, N.Y.: Doubleday Anchor, 1967.

Goldberg, Philip. "Are Women Prejudiced against Women?" *Transaction* 28–30, 1968.

Goldscheider, Calvin. *Population, Modernization and Social Structure.* Boston: Little, Brown, 1971.

Golembeiski, Robert T. *The Small Group: An Analysis of Research Concepts and Operations.* Chicago: University of Chicago Press, 1962.

Goode, William J. *World Revolution and Family Patterns.* New York: Free Press, 1963.

———. *Religion Among the Primitives.* Glencoe, Ill.: Free Press, 1951 and 1964.

Goodwin, Leonard. *A Study of the Work Orientations of Welfare Recipients Participating in the Work Incentive Program.* Washington, D.C.: The Brookings Institution, 1971.

Gordon, Milton M. *Assimilation in American Life.* New York: Oxford University Press, 1964.

———. *Human Nature, Class and Ethnicity.* New York: Oxford University Press, 1978.

Gottman, Jean. *Megalopolis: The Urbanized Northeastern Seaboard of the United States.* Cambridge, Mass.: MIT Press, 1964.

Gouldner, Alvin. "Anti-minotaur: The Myth of Value-free Sociology." *Social Problems, 9:*199–213, 1962.

Granovetter, Mark. "The Strength of Weak Ties." *American Journal of Sociology, 78:*1360–1380, 1973.

Graunt, John. *Natural and Political Observations Mentioned in a Following Index and Made upon the Bills of Mortality* (1692). Baltimore: Johns Hopkins University Press, 1939.

Greeley, Andrew M. *The Denominational Society.* Glenview, Ill.: Scott, Foresman, 1972.

———. *Ethnicity in the United States.* New York: Wiley, 1974.

Green, Arnold W. *Society: An Analysis of Life in Modern Society.* New York: McGraw-Hill, 1972.

Green, Bert F. "Attitude Measurement." Pp. 335–369 in Gardner Lindzey (ed.), *Handbook of Social Psychology.* Reading, Mass.: Addison-Wesley, 1954.

Greenberg, B. S., and B. Reeves. "Children and the Perceived Reality of Television." *Journal of Social Issues, 32:*86–97, 1976.

Greenberg, David F., and Ronnald C. Kessler. "The Effect of Arrests on Crime." *Social Forces, 60:*993–1022, 1982.

Greenberg, David F., Ronald C. Kessler, and Charles H. Logan. "A Panel Model of Crime Rates and Arrest Rates." *American Sociological Review, 44:*843–850, 1979.

Gross, Barry. *Reverse Discrimination.* Buffalo, N.Y.: Prometheus Books, 1977.

Gusfield, Joseph R. *The Culture of Public Problems.* Chicago: University of Chicago Press, 1981.

Gutman, Herbert G. *Work, Culture, and Society in Industrializing America.* New York: Alfred A. Knopf, 1976.

Hadden, Jeffrey K., and Edgar F. Borgatta. *American Cities: Their Social Significance.* Chicago: *Rand McNally,* 1965.

Hagan, John. "The Corporate Advantage." *Social Forces, 60*:993–1022, 1982.

Hage, Jerald, and Michael Aiken. "Relationship of Centralization to Other Structural Properties." *Administrative Science Quarterly, 12,* 1 (June):72–91, 1967.

Hall, Edward T. *The Silent Language.* New York: Doubleday, 1959.

———. *The Hidden Dimensions.* New York: Doubleday, 1966.

———. "How Cultures Collide." *Psychology Today* (July): 97, 1976.

Hall, Edward T., and Mildred R. Hall. "The Sounds of Silence." *Playboy* (June): 139, 1971.

Hall, G. Stanley. *Adolescence.* New York: Appleton-Century-Crofts, 1904.

Hall, Richard H. *Organizations: Structure and Process.* Englewood Cliffs, N.J.: Prentice-Hall, 1982.

Hall, Richard H., J. Eugene Haas, and Norman Johnson. "Organizational Size, Complexity, and Formalization." *American Sociological Review, 32,* 6 (December): 903–912, 1967.

Haney, C., C. Banks, and Philip G. Zimbardo. "Interpersonal Dynamics in a Simulated Prison." *International Journal of Crime and Penology, 1:*69–97, 1973.

Hare, A. Paul, Robert F. Bales, and Edgar Borgatta. *Small Groups: Studies in Social Interaction.* New York: Alfred A. Knopf, 1965.

Harper, Charles L. "Cults and Communities: The Community Inter-Faces of the Three Marginal Religious Movements." *Journal for the Scientific Study of Religion, 21,* 1 (March): 26–38, 1982.

Harrington, Michael. "The New Class and the Left." In B. Bruce-Biggs, *The New Class.* New Brunswick, N.J.: Transaction, 1980.

Harris, C. D., and Edwards L. Ullman. "The Nature of Cities." *The Annals, 242:*8–17, 1945.

Harris, David R. "New Height on Plant Domestication and the Origins of Agriculture: A Review." *Geographical Review, LVII:*90–107, 1967.

Harris, Diana K., and William E. Cole. *Sociology of Aging.* Boston: Houghton Mifflin, 1980.

Harris, Louis, and Associates. *The Myth and Reality of Aging in America.* Washington, D.C.: National Council on Aging, 1975.

Harrison, L. "Cro-Magnon Women in Eclipse." *The Science Teacher, 42:*8–11, 1975.

Harrison, L., and R. N. Passero. "Sexism in the Language of Elementary School Textbooks." *Science and Children, 2:*22–25, 1975.

Harvey, J. H., W. Ickes, and R. F. Kidd (eds.). *New Directions in Attribution Research.* Vol. 1. Hillsdale, N.J.: Erlbaum, 1976.

Hastings, Donald W., Donald A. Clelland, and Robin Danielson. "Gordon's Assimilation Paradigm Revisited: The Issues of Ethnic Communality, Insularity and Return Migration." *Research in Race and Ethnic Relations: An Annual Compilation of Research, 3* JAI:189–206, 1982.

Hauser, Philip M. "Urbanization: An Overview." Pp. 1–47 in Philip M. Hauser and Leo F. Schnore (eds.), *The Study of Urbanization.* New York: Wiley, 1965.

Hauser, Philip M., and Otis Dudley Duncan. "Overview and Conclusions." Pp. 1–22 in Philip M. Hauser and Otis Dudley Duncan (eds.), *The Study of Population: An Inventory and Appraisal.* Chicago: University of Chicago Press, 1959.

Havighurst, Robert J. "Employment, Retirement and Education in the Mature Years." In I. Weber (ed.), *Aging and Retirement.* Gainesville, Fla.: University of Florida Press, 1955.

Havighurst, Robert J., and August de Vries. "Life Styles and Free Time Activities of Retired Men." *Human Development, 12:*34–54, 1969.

Hechter, Michael. *Internal Colonialism.* London: Routledge and Kegan Paul, 1975.

Heer, David M. "What is the Annual Flow of Undocumented Mexican Immigrants to the United States?" *Demography, 16,* 3:417–423, 1979.

Hernandez, Jose. *People, Power and Policy: A New View on Population.* Palo Alto, Calif.: National Press, 1974.

Hessel, Dieter T. *Maggie Kuhn on Aging.* Philadelphia: The Westminster Press, 1977.

Hiller, E. T. *Principles of Sociology.* New York: Harper & Row, 1933.

Hodge, Robert W., Paul M. Siegel, and Peter H. Ross. "Occupational Prestige in the United States, 1925–63." *American Journal of Sociology, 70:*286–302, 1964.

Hodge, Robert W., and Donald J. Treiman. "Class Identification in the United States." *American Journal of Sociology, 73:*535–547, 1968.

Hoffer, Erik. *The True Believer.* New York: Holt, Rinehart and Winston, 1951.

Hollingsworth, T. H. *Historical Demography: The Sources of History-Studies in the Use of Historical Evidence.* London: Camelot, 1969.

Holt, Stall W. *The Bureau of the Census: Its History, Activities and Organization.* Washington, D.C.: The Brookings Institution, 1929.

Homans, George. *The Human Group.* New York: Harcourt, Brace and World, 1950.

Homans, George C. *Social Behavior.* New York: Harcourt, Brace and World, 1961.

———. *Social Behavior: Its Elementary Forms.* Rev. ed. New York: Harcourt Brace Jovanovich, 1974.

Horowitz, David. *Fighting Back! Don't Get Ripped Off.* San Francisco: Harper & Row, 1979.

Horton, Donald, and R. Richard Wohl. "Mass Communication and Para-Social Interaction." *Psychiatry, 19:*3, 1956.

Horton, Paul B., and Gerald R. Leslie. *The Sociology of Social Problems.* New York: Appleton-Century-Crofts, 1970.

Hoyt, Homer. "The Structure of American Cities in the Post-War Era." *American Journal of Sociology, 48:*475–492, 1943.

Howith, Dennis, and Guy Cumberbatch. *Mass Media Violence and Society.* New York: Wiley, 1975.

Hughes, L. W., and W. M. Gordon. *Frontiers of the Law, The Courts and Education.* Chicago: The National Society for the Study of Education, 1978.

Humphreys, Laud. *Tearoom Trade.* Chicago: Aldine, 1970.

"Hungry Asian Refugees Snaring Dogs, Squirrels in Park in California." *The Albuquerque Tribune,* August 18, 1980, p. A–8.

Hunter, Alfred A. "Factorial Ecology: A Critique and Some Suggestions." *Demography, 9,* 1:107–117, 1977.

"Husband Sent to Jail in Rape of His Wife." *Knoxville News Sentinel,* September 3, 1980.

Hyman, Herbert. *Political Socialization: A Study in the Psychology of Political Behavior.* New York: Free Press, 1969.

Inkeles, Alex. *What is Sociology? An Introduction to the Discipline and Profession.* Englewood Cliffs, N.J.: Prentice-Hall, 1964.

International Social Science Association. "Changes in the Family." *International Social Science Journal, 14:*411–580, 1962.

IPPF/WHR. "1981 Outlook for World Food." *Forum* (April), 1981.

Jaffe, Natalie. Attitudes toward Public Welfare Programs and Recipients in the United States.

Janis, I. L. *Victims of Groupthink: A Psychological Study of Foreign Policy Decisions and Fiascoes.* Boston: Houghton Mifflin, 1972.

Jefferson, Mark. "The Law of the Primate City." *Geographical Review, 29* (April):226–232, 1939.

Jeffries, Vicent, and H. Edward Ransford. *Social Stratification: A Multiple Hierarchy Approach.* Boston: Allyn and Bacon, 1980.

Jencks, Christopher. "A Reappraisal of the Most Controversial Educational Document of Time." *The New York Times Magazine* (August 10):10–13, 1969.

———. *Inequality.* New York: Basic Books, 1972.

Johnson, E. A. J., and Herman E. Krooss. *The American Economy: Its Origins, Development and Transformation.* Englewood Cliffs, N.J.: Prentice-Hall, 1960.

Johnson, Harry M. *Sociology: A Systematic Introduction.* New York: Harcourt, Brace and World, 1960.

Kahn, Herman, William Brown, and Leon Martel, with the assistance of the Staff of the Hudson Institute. *The Next 200 Years: A Scenario for America and the World.* New York: William Morrow, 1976.

Kallen, Horace M. "Secularism as a Religion." *Journal for the Scientific Study of Religion, 4,* 2 (Spring):145–151, 1965.

Kammeyer, Kenneth C. W. *An Introduction to Population.* San Francisco: Chandler, 1971.

Kanter, John F., and Melvin Zelnik. "Sexual Experience of Young Unmarried Women in the United States." *Family Planning Perspectives, 4* (October): 9–17, 1972.

Kanter, Rosabeth M. *Commitment and Community.* Cambridge, Mass.: Harvard University Press, 1972.

———. *Men and Women of the Corporation.* New York: Basic Books, 1977.

Kaplan, Charles P., and Thomas Van Valey. *Census '80: Continuing the Factfinder Tradition. U.S. Bureau of the Census.* Washington, D.C.: Government Printing Office, 1980.

Kaplan, H. Roy, and Curt Tausky. "The Meaning of Work among the Hard-Core Unemployed." *Pacific Sociological Review, 17:*185–198, 1974.

Karlins, Marvin, Thomas Coffman, and Jerry Watters. "On the Fading of Social Stereotypes: Studies in Three Generations of College Students." *Journal of Personality and Social Psychology, 13:*1–6, 1969.

Kassel, Victor. "Polygamy After Sixty." Pp. 138–142 in Herbert A. Otto (ed.), *The Family in Search of a Future.* New York: Appleton-Century-Crofts, 1970.

Kastenbaum, Robert. "Death, Dying, and Bereavement in Old Age." *Aged Care and Services Review* (May/June): 1, 3–10, 1978.

Kay, Herma Hill, and Carol Amyx. "Marvin v. Marvin: Preserving the Options." *California Law Review, 65:*937–977, 1977.

Kelley, Harold H. "Two Functions of Reference Groups." In Guy E. Swanson, Theodore M. Newcomb, and Eleanor L. Hartley (eds.), *Readings in Social Psychology.* New York: Holt, Rinehart and Winston, 1952.

Kephart, William M. *Extraordinary Groups.* New York: St. Martin's Press, 1982.

Kepplinger, H. M., and H. Roth. "Creating a Crisis: German Mass Media and Oil Supply in 1973–74." *Public Opinion Quarterly, 43:*285–296, 1979.

Lakoff, Robin. *Language and Woman's Place.* New York: Harper Colophon, 1975.

Lang, Gladys, and Kurt Lang. "Mass Communications and Public Opinion." Pp. 653–682 in Morris Rosenberg and Ralph H. Turner (eds.), *Social Psychology.* New York: Basic Books, 1981.

La Pierre, Richard T. "Attitudes versus Actions." *Social Forces, 14:*230–237, 1934.

Lasch, Christopher. *The Culture of Narcissism.* New York: Norton, 1979.

Latane, Bibb, and John M. Darley. "Group Inhibition of Bystander Intervention in Emergencies." *Journal of Personality and Social Psychology, 10:*215–221, 1968.

———. *The Unresponsive Bystander.* New York: Appleton-Century-Crofts, 1970.

Latane, Bibb, Kipling Williams, and Stephen Harkins. "Social Loafing." *Psychology Today* (October):104 and 110, 1979.

Laudon, Kenneth C. "Privacy and Federal Data Banks." *Society, 17,* 2 (January/February):50–56, 1980.

LeBon, Gustav. *The Crowd.* London: T. Fisher Unwin, 1897.

Lee, Dorothy. *Freedom and Culture.* Englewood Cliffs, N.J.: Prentice-Hall, 1959.

Lemert, Edwin. *Human Deviance, Social Problems and Social Control.* Englewood Cliffs, N.J.: Prentice-Hall, 1967.

Lenski, Gerhard E. *Power and Privilege.* New York: McGraw-Hill, 1966.

Lenski, Gerhard, and Jean Lenski. *Human Societies: An Introduction to Macrosociology.* New York: McGraw-Hill, 1982.

Lerner, Daniel. "The Justice Motive in Social Behavior." *Journal of Social Issues, 31:*1–19, 1975.

Lerner, Melvin J. "Evaluation of Performance as a Function of Performer's Reward and Attractiveness." *Journal of Personality and Social Psychology, 1:*355–360, 1965.

Lerner, Melvin J. *The Belief in a Just World: A Fundamental Delusion.* New York: Plenum, 1980.

Leventhal, Gerald S. "What Should Be Done with Equity Theory?" Pp. 27–55 in Kenneth Gergen, Martin Greenberg, and Richard Willis (eds.), *Social Exchange: Advances in Theory and Research.* New York: Plenum, 1980.

Levy, Marion J. *The Structure of Society.* Princeton, N.J.: Princeton University Press, 1952.

Lewis, Arthur K., Robert Soar, David Harrison, and Carol Blalock. "Social and Economic Forecasts and Their Impact on the Future Organization and Administration of Schools." Research paper prepared for Southeastern Regional Consortium Planning Project. University of Florida, Gainesville, Fla., 1978a.

Lewis, Arthur K., Robert Soar, David Harrison, and Carol Blalock. "Social Trends Influencing Education." Research paper prepared for Department of Education, Florida State University, Gainesville, Fla., 1978b.

Lewis, Michael. "State as an Infant Environment Interaction: An Analysis of Mother-infant Interaction as a Function of Sex." *Merrill-Palmer Quarterly, 18:*97–121.

Liebow, Elliot. *Tally's Corner.* Boston, Mass.: Little, Brown, 1967.

Lifton, Robert. *Thought Reform and the Psychology of Totalism.* New York: Norton, 1961.

Lindgren, Ethel J. "An Example of Culture Contact Without Conflict." *American Anthropologist, 40,* 4 (October-December):605–621, 1938.

Linton, Ralph. *The Study of Man.* New York: D. Appleton-Century, 1936.

———. *The Cultural Background of Personality.* New York: D. Appleton-Century, 1945.

Lippman, Walter. *Public Opinion.* New York: Harcourt, 1922.

Lofland, John. "Collective Behavior." Pp. 411–446 in Morris Rosenberg and Ralph H. T. Turner (eds.), *Social Psychology.* New York: Basic Books, 1981.

Lofland, John, and Rodney Stark. "Becoming a World-saver: A Theory of Conversion to a Deviant Perspective." *American Sociological Review, 30:* 862–874, 1965.

Loftin, Colin, and David McDowall. "The Police, Crime and Economic Theory." *American Sociological Review, 47:*393–401, 1982.

Lombroso, Cesare. *Crime: Its Causes and Remedies.* Boston: Little, Brown, 1911.

Lowie, R. H. *Primitive Religion.* London: Routledge, 1925.

Lueptow, Lloyd B. "Social Change and Sex-role Change in Adolescent Orientations Toward Life, Work, and Achievement: 1964–1975." *Social Psychology Quarterly, 43:*48–59, 1980.

Lyle, Jack, and Heidi R. Hoffman. "Children's Use of Television and Other Media" in Eli A. Rubinstein, George A. Comstock, and John P. Murray (eds.), *Television and Social Behavior, Reports and Papers.* Washington, D.C.: Government Printing Office, 1972.

Lynd, Robert S., and Helen Merrell Lynd. *Middletown in Transition.* New York: Harcourt Brace, 1937.

Maccoby, Eleanor, and Carol Jacklin. *The Psychology of Sex Differences.* Stanford, Calif.: Stanford University Press, 1974.

Madsen, Millard C. "Cooperative and Competitive Motivation of Children in Three Mexican Sub-cultures." *Psychological Reports, 20:*1307–1320, 1967.

Madsen, Millard C., and Ariella Shapira. "Cooperative and Competitive Behavior of Urban Afro-American, Anglo-American, Mexican-American, and Mexican Village Children." *Developmental Psychology, 3:*16–20, 1970.

Malthus, Thomas Robert. *On Population.* Edited and Introduced by Gertrude Himmelfarb. New York: Modern History, 1960.

Marber, Scott, and Robert Shaver. Personality and Social Psychology Bulletin 6, 1981.

March, James, and Herbert Simon. *Organizations.* New York: Wiley, 1958.

Marini, John. "Television Evangelism: Milking the Flock." *Saturday Review, 3:*22–25, 1979.

Marty, Martin E. *The New Shape of American Religion.* New York: Harper & Row, 1959.

Marx, Karl and Friedrich Engels. *The Communist Manifesto.* New York: International, 1848.

Marx, Karl. *Economic and Philosophical Manuscripts of 1844.* New York: International, 1964.

———. *Capital.* Vol. 1. New York: International, 1967.

Maslow, Abraham. *Motivation and Personality.* New York: Harper Brothers, 1954.

Mauldin, W. Parker. "Population Trends and Prospects." *Science, 209,* 4 (July):156, 1980.

Mayo, Elton. *The Human Problems of an Industrial Civilization.* New York: Macmillan, 1933.

———. *The Social Problems of an Industrial Civilization.* Boston: Harvard University Press, 1945.

McArthur, L. Z., and S. V. Eisen. "Achievements of Male and Female Storybook Characters as Determinants of Achievement Behavior by Boys and Girls." *Journal of Personality and Social Psychology, 33:*467–473, 1976.

McCall, George J., and J. L. Simmons. *Organizations: Structure and Process.* Englewood Cliffs, N.J.: Prentice-Hall, 1982.

McCarthy, J. D., and M. N. Zald. "Resource Mobilization and Social Movements." *American Journal of Sociology, 82:*1212–1239, 1977.

McGee, Reece. *Points of Departure.* Hinsdale, Ill.: Dryden, 1975.

McGhee, Paul E., and Terry Fuchs. "Television Viewing and the Learning of Sex-role Stereotypes." *Sex Roles, 6:*179–188, 1980.

McGregor, Douglas. "The Human Side of Enterprise." *The Management Review, 46:*22–28 and 88–92, 1957.

————. *The Human Side of Enterprise.* New York: McGraw-Hill, 1960.

————. *The Professional Manager.* New York: McGraw-Hill, 1967.

McNamara, Robert S. Address to the University of Notre Dame. Washington, D.C.: International Bank, May 1, 1969.

Mead, George Herbert. *Mind, Self and Society.* Chicago: University of Chicago Press, 1934.

Mead, Margaret. *Coming of Age in Samoa.* New York: William Norton and Co., 1923.

————. *Sex and Temperament in Three Primitive Societies.* New York: Morrow, 1935.

Meadows, Donella H., Dennis L. Meadows, Jorgen Randers, and William W. Behrens, III. *Limits to Growth.* New York: Universe, 1972.

Meek, Ronald H. *Marx and Engels on the Population.* Berkeley, Calif.: Ramparts, 1971.

Mellor, Earl F., and George Stamas. "Usual Weekly Earnings." *Monthly Labor Review* (April), 1982.

Melsted, Lillemor. "Swedish Family Policy." Pp. 426–429 in Elizabeth Douvan, Helen Wiengarten, and Jane L. Scheiber (eds.), *American Families.* Dubuque, Iowa: Kendall/Hunt, 1980.

Merton, Robert K. "Bureaucratic Structure and Personality." *Social Forces,* 18:560–568, 1940.

————. *Social Theory and Social Structure.* Glencoe, Ill.: Free Press, 1957.

————. "Notes on Problem-Finding in Sociology." Pp. XV–XVI in Robert K. Merton, Leonard Broom, and Leonard S. Cottrell, Jr. (eds.), *Sociology Today.* New York: Basic Books, 1959.

Michels, Robert. *Political Parties: A Sociological Study of the Oligarchical Tendencies of Modern Democracy.* New York: Free Press, 1911 and 1949.

Mileti, Dennis S., Thomas E. Drabek, and J. Eugene Haas. *Human Systems in Extreme Environments.* Boulder, Colo.: Institute of Behavioral Science. University of Colorado, 1975.

Milgram, Stanley. "Some Conditions of Obedience and Disobedience to Authority." *Human Relations,* 18:57–75, 1965.

Mill, John Stuart. *A System of Logic.* New York: Longmans, 1930.

Miller, H. S., W. F. McDonald, and J. A. Cramer. *Plea Bargaining in the United States (Phase I Report)* Washington, D.C.: Government Printing Office, 1978.

Miller, Stephen. "The Social Dilemma of the Aging Leisure Participant." Pp. 72–92 in Arnold M. Rose and Warren A. Peterson (eds.), *Older People and Their Social World: The Subculture of Aging.* Philadelphia: F. A. Davis, 1965.

Miller, S. M., and Pamela Roby. *The Future of Inequality.* New York: Basic Books, 1970.

Mills, C. Wright. *The Power Elite.* New York: Oxford University Press, 1956.

Mirandé, Alfredo. "The Chicano Family." *Journal of Marriage and the Family, 39* (Nov.) 747–756, 1977.

Mischel, Walter. "Sex-typing and Socialization." In Paul Mussen (ed.), *Carmichael's Manual of Child Psychology.* Vol. 2. New York: Wiley, 1970.

Montague, Ashley. *Man's Most Dangerous Myth.* New York: Harper & Row, 1952.

————. *Statement on Race.* New York: Oxford University Press, 1972.

Moore, Barrington. *Political Power and Social Theory.* Cambridge, Mass.: Harvard University Press, 1958.

Moore, Wilbert E. *Social Change.* Englewood Cliffs, N.J.: Prentice-Hall, 1963.

————. "But Some Are More Equal than Others." Pp. 143–148 in Edward O. Laumann, Paul M. Siegel, and Robert W. Hodge (eds.), *The Logic of Social Hierarchies.* Skokie, Ill.: Markham, 1970.

Moore, Wilbert E., and Arnold Feldman. *Industrialization and Industrialism: Convergence and Differentiation.* Transactions of the Fifth World Congress of Sociology. Louvain: International Sociological Association, 1962.

Moskos, Charles, Jr. *Greek Americans: Struggle and Success.* Englewood Cliffs, N.J.: Prentice-Hall, 1980.

Moskowitz, Milton, Michael Katz, and Robert Levering (eds.). *Everybody's Business: An Almanac The Irreverent Guide to Corporate America.* San Francisco: Harper & Row, 1980.

Muramatsu, Minoru. "Japan." *Country Profiles.* New York: Population Council, 1971.

Murdock, George F. "The Common Denominator of Cultures." Pp. 123–142 in Ralph Linton (ed.), *The Science of Man in the World Crisis.* New York: Columbia University Press, 1945.

Murdock, George P. *Social Structure.* New York: Macmillan, 1949.

Mueller, Carol M., and Charles M. Judd. "Belief Constraint and Belief Consensus." *Social Forces,* 60:182–187, 1981.

Mynatt, C., and S. J. Sherman. "Responsibility Attribution in Groups and Individuals." *Journal of Personality and Social Psychology, 32:*1111–1118, 1975.

Myrdal, Gunnar. *American Dilemma.* New York: Harper, 1944.

National Center for Health Statistics. *Births, Marriages, and Deaths, U.S. 1981.* Monthly Vital Statistics Report 30, 12 (March 18). DHHS Pub. No. (PHS) 82-1120. Hyattsville, Md.: Public Health Service, 1982.

Nelson, Hart M., and H. David Allen. "Ethnicity, Americanization, and Religious Attendance." *American Journal of Sociology,* 79:906–922, 1974.

Neugarten, Bernice L. "Acting One's Age: New Rules for Old." *Psychology Today* (April):66, 1980.

Neugarten, Bernice L., John W. Moore, and John C. Lowe. "Age Norms, Age Constraints and Adult Socialization." *American Journal of Sociology, 70:*710–717, 1965.

Newcomb, Theodore. *Personality and Social Change.* New York: Dryden, 1948.

Nisbet, Robert A. "Sociology as an Art Form." Pp. 148–161 in Maurice Stein and Arthur Vidich (eds.), *Sociology on Trial.* Englewood Cliffs, N.J.: Prentice-Hall, 1963.

Nye, F. Ivan, and Martha B. Lamberts. *School-age Parenthood.* Extension Bulletin 0667 (revised). Pullman, Wash.: Washington State University, 1980.

O'Dea, Thomas. *The Sociology of Religion.* Englewood Cliffs, N.J.: Prentice-Hall, 1966.

Ogburn, William Fielding. "Culture Lag as Theory." *Sociology and Social Research, 41:*167–173, 1957.

———. *On Culture and Social Change. Selected Papers.* Edited by Otis Dudley Duncan. Chicago: University of Chicago Press, 1964.

Omran, Abdel R. "The Epidemiologic Transition: A Theory of the Epidemiology of Population Change." *Milbank Memorial Fund Quarterly, XLIX,* 4 (Part 1):509–538, 1971.

Oppenheimer, Valerie Kincaid. "The Sex-labeling of Jobs." *Industrial Relations, 7:*219–234, 1968.

Orum, Anthony. "On Participation in Political Protest Movement." *Journal of Applied Behavorial Science, 10:*181–207, 1974.

Orwell, George. *1984.* New York: Harcourt Brace Jovanovich, 1982.

Ouchi, William. *Theory Z. How American Business Can Meet the Japanese Challenge.* Reading, Mass.: Addison-Wesley, 1981.

"The Outlook in Detail." *U.S. News and World Report.* December 13, 1982.

Palmore, Erdman. "Ethnophaulism and Ethnocentrism." *American Journal of Sociology, 67:*442–445, 1962.

Park, Robert E., and Ernest W. Burgess. *Introduction to the Science of Sociology.* Chicago: University of Chicago Press, 1921.

Park, Robert E., Ernest W. Burgess, and Roderick D. McKenzie. *The City.* Chicago: University of Chicago Press, 1967.

Parsons, Talcott. "The Social Structure of the Family." Pp. 173–201 in Ruth Anshen (ed.), *The Family.* New York: Harper, 1949.

———. "Suggestions for a Sociological Approach to the Theory of Organizations, I, II." *Administrative Science Quarterly, 1:*63–85 and 225–239, 1956.

Passel, Jeffrey S., Jacob Siegel, and J. Gregory Robinson. *Coverage of the National Population in the 1980 Census by Age, Sex and Race: Preliminary Estimates by Demographic Analysis. Current Population Reports—Special Studies.* P-23 No. 115. U.S. Bureau of the Census. Washington D.C.: Government Printing Office (February), 1982.

Pavlov, I. P. *Conditioned Reflexes.* Translated by G. V. Anrep. London: Oxford University Press, 1927.

Pearson, Willie, Jr., and Lewellyn Hendrix. "Divorce and the Status of Women." *Journal of Marriage and the Family, 41:*375–385, 1979.

Petersen, William. *Population.* New York: Macmillan, 1969.

Phillips, David. "Influence of Suggestion on Suicide." *American Sociological Review, 39:*340–350, 1974.

———. "The Impact of Fictional Television Stories on U.S. Adult Fatalities." *American Journal of Sociology, 87:*1340–1359, 1982.

Pines, Maya. "The Civilizing of Genie." *Psychology Today, 15:*28–34.

Pirenne, Henri. *Medieval Cities: Their Origins and Revival of Trade.* Translated by Frank D. Halsey. Garden City, N.Y.: Doubleday Anchor, 1925.

Playboy Enterprises, Inc. *The Playboy Report on American Men.* Playboy Enterprises, Inc., 1979.

Pleck, Joseph. *The Myth of Masculinity.* Cambridge, Mass.: MIT Press, 1981.

Ploch, Donald R. "Energy and Society: Some Macro Considerations." Paper Presented in Knoxville, Tenn. July 25, 1980.

Population Reference Bureau "Africa Falling Further Behind." "The Potshot That Backfired." *Time,* July 19, 1982.

Quinn, Bernard, Herman Anderson, Martin Bradley, Paul Goething, and Peggy Shriver. *Churches and Church Memberships in the United States, 1980.* Atlanta: Glenmary Research Center, 1982.

Quinney, Richard. *Criminology* 2nd ed. Boston: Little, Brown, 1979.

Reich, Michael, David M. Gordon, and Richard C. Edwards. "A Theory of Labor Market Segmentation." *American Economic Review, 63:*359–365, 1973.

Reiss, Albert J. *Occupations and Social Status.* New York: Free Press, 1961.

Reed, John Shelton. "Getting to Know You: The Contact Hypothesis Applied to the Sectional Beliefs and Attitudes of White Southerners." *Social Forces, 59:*123–135, 1980.

Revelle, Roger. "Energy Dilemmas in Asia: The Needs for Research and Development." *Science, 209:*164–174, 1980.

Rhodes, William, and Catherine Conly. "Federal Sentencing Guidelines. Will They Shift Sentencing Discretion From Judges to Prosecutors?" Pp. 197–224 in James A. Cramer (ed.), *Courts and Judges.* Beverly Hills, Calif.: Sage Publications, 1981.

Richer, Stephen. "Middle-Class Bias of Schools—Fact or Fancy?" *Sociology of Education, 47:*523–534, 1974.

Richmond, Anthony H. "The Sociology of Migration in Industrial and Post-Industrial Societies." Pp. 238–281 in J. A. Jackson (ed.), *Migration.* Cambridge, Mass.: Cambridge University Press, 1969.

———. "Immigrant Adaptation in a Post-Industrial Society." Pp. 298–319 in Mary M. Kritz, Charles B. Keely, Silvano Tomasi, and M. Tomasi (eds.), *Global Trends in Migration: Theory and Research on International Population Movements.* Staten Island, N.Y.: The Center for Migration Studies, 1981.

Riley, Matilda W. *Sociological Research: A Case Approach.* New York: Harcourt, Brace and World, 1963.

Rochberg-Halton, Eugene, and Mihaly Csikszentmihalyi. *The Meaning of Things.* New York: Cambridge University Press, 1981.

Rorig, Fritz. *The Medieval Town.* Berkeley: University of California Press, 1967.

Rose, Arnold M. *The Negro In America.* Boston: Beacon Press, 1948.

———. *Theory and Method in the Social Sciences.* Minneapolis, Minn.: University of Minnesota Press, 1954.

————. *The Power Structure.* New York: Oxford University Press, 1967.

Rosenbaum, James E. "The Stratification of Socialization Processes." *American Sociological Review, 40:*48–54, 1975.

Rosengren, Karl Erik, Peter Arvidson, and Dahn Sturesson. "The Barseback 'Panic'." Pp. 101–116 in Meredith David Pugh (ed.), *Collective Behavior: A Source Book.* St. Paul: West Publishing Co., 1980.

Rosenthal, Robert, and L. Jacobson. *Pygmalion in the Classroom.* New York: Holt, Rinehart and Winston, 1968.

Rosnow, Ralph L., and Gary Alan Fine. *Rumor and Gossip.* New York: Elsevier, 1976.

Rosow, Irving. "The Social Context of the Aging Self." *Gerontologist 3,* 2:83, 1973.

Roth, Julius. *Timetables.* Indianapolis: Bobbs-Merrill, 1963.

Roy, Donald. "Quota Restriction and Goldbricking in a Machine Shop." *American Journal of Sociology, 57:*427–442, 1952.

Rubin, Jeffrey, Frank J. Provenzano, and Zella Luria. "The Eye of the Beholder: Parents' Views on Sex of Newborns." *American Journal of Orthopsychiatry, 44:*512–519, 1974.

Rubin, Lillian. *Worlds of Pain.* New York: Basic Books, 1976.

Rude, George. *The Crowd in History.* New York: Wiley, 1964.

Ruesch, Hans. *Top of the World.* New York: Harper & Row, 1951.

Sandhu, H. S., and L. H. Irving. "Female Offenders and Mental Disorganization." *International Journal of Criminology and Penology, 2:*35–42, 1974.

Sapir, Edward. "The Status of Linguistics as a Science." *Language, 5:*207–214, 1929.

Scanzoni, John. *Sexual Bargaining.* 2nd ed. Chicago: University of Chicago Press, 1982.

Schachter, Stanley. *Psychology of Affiliation.* Stanford, Calif.: Stanford University Press, 1959.

Scharf, Kathleen Rudd. "Teenage Pregnancy." Pp. 136–142 in Jeffrey P. Rosenfeld (ed.), *Relationships.* Glenview, Ill.: Scott, Foresman, 1982.

Scheff, Thomas. *Being Mentally Ill.* Chicago: Aldine, 1966.

Schmeckebier, Lawrence F. *The Statistical Work of the National Government.* Baltimore: Johns Hopkins University Press, 1925.

Schmerhorn, R. A. *Comparative Ethnic Relations.* Chicago: University of Chicago Press, 1978.

Schur, Edwin M. *Crimes Without Victims: Deviant Behavior and Public Policy.* Englewood Cliffs, N.J.: Prentice-Hall, 1965.

Sears, Robert R. "Development of Gender Role." Pp. in F. A. Beach (ed.), *Sex and Behavior.* New York: Wiley, 1965.

Selkin, James. "Rape." *Psychology Today* (Jan.):71–72, 74 and 76, 1975.

Selznick, Philip. "An Approach to a Theory of Bureaucracy." *American Sociological Review, 8:*47–54, 1943.

Sennett, Richard, and Jonathan Cobb. *The Hidden Injuries of Class.* New York: Vintage, 1973.

Service, Elman R. "The Ghost of Our Ancestors." *Primitive Worlds: People Lost in Time.* Washington, D.C.: National Geographic Society, 1973.

Sexton, Patricia C. *The Feminized Male.* New York: Vintage, 1969.

Shapiro, Sam, Edward R. Schlesinger, and Robert E. L. Neslitt, Jr. *Infant, Perinatal Maternal and Childhood Mortality in the United States.* Cambridge, Mass.: Harvard University Press, 1968.

Sherif, M., and C. W. Sherif. *Social Psychology.* New York: Harper & Row, 1969.

Shevky, Eshref, and Wendell Bell. *Social Area Analysis.* Stanford, Calif.: Stanford University Press, 1955.

Shibutani, Tomatsu. "Reference Groups and Social Control." Pp. 128–147 in Arnold M. Rose (ed.), *Human Behavior and Social Processes.* Boston: Houghton-Mifflin, 1962.

————. *Improvised News.* Indianapolis: Bobbs-Merrill, 1966.

Shils, Edward A., and Henry A. Finch (eds.), *The Methodology of the Social Sciences.* New York: Free Press, 1949.

Shupe, Anson, and David G. Bromley. "Reverse Missionizing: Sun Myung Moon's Unificationist Movement in the United States." *Free Inquiry in Creative Sociology, 8:*197–203, 1980.

Shryock, Henry, Jr. "The Natural History of Standard Metropolitan Areas." *American Journal of Sociology, LXIII:*163–170, 1968.

Simmel, Georg. *The Sociology of Georg Simmel.* Translated and edited by Kurt H. Wolff. New York: Free Press, 1950.

————. *Conflict and the Web of Group Affiliations.* New York: Free Press, 1955.

————. "The Metropolis and Modern Mental Life." Pp. 635–646 in P. Hall and A. J. Reiss, *Cities and Societies.* New York: Free Press, 1957.

Simmons, Leo W. *The Role of the Aged in Primitive Society.* New Haven, Conn.: Yale University Press, 1945.

Sirjamaki, John. *The Sociology of Cities.* New York: Random House, 1964.

"Six Years of Neglect. Leave Boy Like Baby." *The Knoxville Journal,* April 24, 1982.

Sjoberg, Gideon. *The Preindustrial City: Past and Present.* New York: Free Press, 1960.

Smelser, Neal. *Theory of Collective Behavior.* New York: Free Press, 1963.

Snow, David A., and Cynthia L. Phillips. "The Lofland-Stark Conversion Model: A Critical Assessment." *Social Problems, 27,* 4 (April): 430–447, 1980.

Snow, David A., Louis A. Zurcher, and S. Ecland-Olson. "Social Networks and Social Movements." *American Sociological Review, 45:*787–801, 1980.

Snow, David A., Louis A. Zurcher, and Robert Peters. "Victory Celebrations as Theater." *Symbolic Interaction, 4:*21–42, 1981.

Sontag, Susan. "The Double Standard of Aging." *Saturday Review* (Sept.):29–39, 1972.

Sorokin, Pitrim. *Social and Cultural Mobility.* New York: Free Press, 1959.

Spencer, Herbert. *The Study of Sociology.* London: Routledge, 1882.

————. *Social Statics.* 1st ed. London: 1855. American ed. New York: D. Appleton and Co., 1896.

Spender, Dale. *Man Made Language.* London: Routledge and Kegan Paul, 1980.

Spengler, Oswald. *The Deadline of the West.* New York: Alfred A. Knopf, 1918.

"Sperm Bank for Gifted Announces Its First Birth." *Chicago Tribune,* May 25, 1982, Section 1, p. 4.

Spitz, Rene A. "Hospitalism." Pp. 399–425 in Rose L. Coser (ed.), *The Family.* New York: St. Martin's Press, 1964.

Stack, Carol B. *All Our Kin.* New York: Harper & Row, 1974.

Stark, Rodney, and Charles Glock. *American Piety: The Nature of Religious Commitment.* Berkeley and Los Angeles: University of California Press, 1968.

Stark, Rodney, and William Sims Bainbridge. "Secularization and Cult Formation in the Jazz Age." *Journal for the Scientific Study of Religion, 20,* 4 (December): 360–373, 1981.

Sterling, Theodor D. "Computer Ombudsman." *Society, 17,* 2 (January/February):50–56, 1980.

Sternlieb, George, James W. Huges, and Connie O. Huges. *Demographic Trends and Economic Reality: Planning and Markets in the 80's.* New Brunswick, N.J.: Center for Urban Policy Research, 1982.

Stoeckel, John, and J. Allan Beegle. "Urban Dominance and the Rural-Farm Status Structure." *Rural Sociology, 34:*56–66, 1969.

Stockwell, Edward G., Jerry W. Wicks, and Donald J. Adamchak. "Research Needed on Socioeconomic Differentials in U.S. Mortality." *Public Health Reports, 93:*666–672, 1978.

Stressin, Laurence. *Pittsburg Business Review.* Pittsburgh: The University of Pittsburgh. November-December. 4 pages. 1971.

Sudnow, David. "Normal Crimes." *Social Problems, 12:*255–275, 1965.

Sullivan, Harry Stack. *The Collected Works of Harry Stack Sullivan.* 2 vols. New York: Norton, 1964.

Sutherland, Edwin H. *White Collar Crime.* New York: Holt, Rinehart and Winston, 1961.

Sutherland, Edwin H., and Donald R. Cressey. *Principles of Criminology.* 10th ed. New York: Lippincott, 1978.

Sumner, William Graham. *Folkways.* Boston: Ginn, 1906.

"Surrogate Mother Tells of Giving Baby Away." *Knoxville Journal,* December 4, 1980.

Sykes, Gresham. *The Society of Captives: A Study of a Maximum Security Prison.* New York: Atheneum, 1966.

Sykes, Gresham, and David Matza. "Techniques of Neutralization." *American Sociological Review, 22:*664–669, 1957.

Tanner, Nancy, and Adrienne Zihlman. "Women in Evolution. Part I: Innovation and Selection in Human Origins." *Signs:* 585–608, 1976.

Tausky, Curt. *Work Organizations: Major Theoretical Perspectives.* Itasca, Ill.: Peacock, 1978.

Thomas, Brinley. "International Migration." Pp. 510–543 in Philip M. Hauser and Otis Dudley Duncan (eds.), *The Study of Population and An Inventory and Appraisal.* Chicago: University of Chicago Press, 1959.

Thomas, W. I. *The Unadjusted Girl.* Boston: Little, Brown, 1923.

Thrasher, Frederic M. *The Gang.* Chicago: University of Chicago Press, 1927.

Thurow, Lester. *Poverty and Discrimination.* Washington, D.C.: The Brookings Institution, 1969.

Toffler, Alvin. *Future Shock.* New York: Bantam, 1970.

Tonnies, Ferdinand. *Fundamental Concepts of Sociology.* Translated by Charles P. Loomis. New York: American Book Co., 1940.

Touhy, John C. "Sex-role Stereotyping and Individual Differences in Liking for the Physically Attractive." *Social Psychology Quarterly, 42:*285–289, 1979.

Travisano, Richard V. "Alternation and Conversion as Qualitatively Different Transformations." Pp. 594–606 in G. P. Stone and H. A. Farberman (eds.), *Social Psychology Through Symbolic Interaction.* Waltham, Mass: Ginn-Blaisdell, 1970.

Treiman, Donald J. *Occupational Prestige in Comparative Perspective.* New York: Academic Press, 1977.

Trice, Harrison M., and Paul M. Roman. "Delabeling, Relabeling and Alcoholics Anonymous." *Social Problems, 17:*538–546, 1970.

Troeltsch, Ernst. *The Social Teaching of the Christian Churches.* Translated by Olive Wyon. Chicago: University of Chicago Press, 1960.

Tsunoda, Ryusaku, William Theodore deBary, and Donald Keene. *Sources of Japanese Tradition.* New York: Columbia University Press, 1958.

Tuchman, Gaye. "Facts of the Moment." *Symbolic Interaction, 3:*9–20, 1980.

Tudor, William, Jeanette Tudor, and Walter R. Gove. "The Effect of Sex Role Differences on the Societal Reaction to Mental Retardation." *Social Forces, 57:*871–885, 1979.

Tumin, Melvin M. "Some Principles of Stratification: A Critical Analysis." *American Sociological Review, 18:* 387–394, 1953.

Turner, Jonathan H., and Charles E. Staines. *Inequality: Privilege and Poverty in America.* Pacific Palisades, Calif.: Goodyear, 1976.

Turner, Ralph H. "Role-taking: Process Versus Conformity." Pp. 20–40 in Arnold M. Rose (ed.), *Human Behavior and Social Processes.* Boston: Houghton-Mifflin, 1962.

Turner, Ralph H., and Lewis M. Killian. *Collective Behavior.* Englewood Cliffs, N.J.: Prentice-Hall, 1972.

Tylor, Edward. *Primitive Culture: Researches into the Development of Mythology, Philosophy, Religion, Language, Art, and Custom.* London: Murray, 1871.

United Nations. *The Determinants and Consequences of Population Trends.* Population Studies, No. 17. New York: United Nations, 1953.

U.S. Bureau of the Census. *U.S. Census of Population: 1960 Detailed Characteristics. United States Summary. Final Report PC (1) 1D.* Washington, D.C.: Government Printing Office, 1963.

U.S. Bureau of the Census. *U.S. Census of the Population:*

1960 Selected Area Reports, Size of Place PC (3) 1B. Washington, D.C.: Government Printing Office, 1964.

U.S. Bureau of the Census. *Trends in Social and Economic Correlations in Metropolitan Areas.* Current Population Reports: Special Studies, Series P. 23 No. 27. Washington, D.C.: Government Printing Office, 1969.

U.S. Bureau of the Census. *U.S. Census of the Population: 1970 Number of Inhabitants, Final Report PC (1) 1A U.S. Summary.* Washington, D.C.: Government Printing Office, 1971.

U.S. Bureau of the Census. *The Methods and Materials of Demography.* By Henry S. Shryock, Jacob S. Siegel, and Associates. Washington, D.C.: Government Printing Office, 1971 and 1973.

U.S. Bureau of the Census. *Census of Population: 1970 General Population Characteristics. Final Report PC (1)—1B United States Survey.* Washington, D.C.: Government Printing Office, 1973.

U.S. Department of Labor, Bureau of Labor Statistics. *Adjustments to the Introduction of Office Automation. Report #137.* Washington, D.C.: Government Printing Office, 1960.

U.S. Merit Systems Protections Board. *Sexual Harrassment in the Federal Workplace: Is it a Problem?* Washington, D.C.: Government Printing Office, March, 1981.

U.S. Water Resources Council. *1972 OBERS Projections. Vol. 1: Concepts, Methodology, and Summary Data.* Washington, D.C.: Government Printing Office, 1974.

Van De Van, Andrew H., and Diane L. Ferry. *Measuring and Assessing Organizations.* New York: Wiley, 1980.

Veitch, Russell. "Radio News Broadcasts." *Sociometry, 40:*383–386, 1977.

Vernon, Glenn M. *The Sociology of Religion.* New York: McGraw-Hill, 1962.

———. *Human Interaction.* 2nd ed. New York: Ronald, 1972.

Vernon, Raymond. *Storm over the Mullinations.* Cambridge, Mass.: Harvard University Press, 1977.

Virginia Slims. *The 1980 Virginia Slims American Women's Opinion Poll.* Virginia Slims, 1980.

Wallace, Samuel E. *The Urban Environment.* Homewood, Ill.: Dorsey, 1980.

Ware, Helen. "Polygyny: Women's Views in a Traditional Society, Nigeria, 1973." *Journal of Marriage and Family, 41* (Feb.):185–195, 1979.

Warner, W. Lloyd, and Paul S. Lunt. *The Social Life of a Modern Community.* New Haven, Conn.: Yale University Press, 1941.

Warner, W. Lloyd, Marchia Meeker, and Kenneth Eells. *Social Class in America.* Chicago: Science Research Associates, 1949.

Washburne, Norman F. *Interpreting Social Change in America.* New York: Random House, 1954.

Wattenberg, Esther, and Hazel Reinhardt. "Female-Headed Households." *Social Work, 24:*460–465, 1979.

Watterlond, Michael. "The Holy Ghost People." *Science, 83,* 4 (May):50–57, 1983.

Weber, Max. *The Protestant Ethic and the Spirit of Capitalism.* Translated by Talcott Parsons. New York: Charles Scribner's Sons, 1930 (first published 1920).

———. *Max Weber: Essays in Sociology.* Translated by H. H. Gerth and C. Wright Mills. New York: Oxford University Press, 1946.

———. *The Religion of China.* Translated by Hans H. Gerth. New York: Free Press, 1951.

———. *Ancient Judaism.* Translated by Hans H. Gerth and Don Martindale. New York: Free Press, 1952.

———. *Max Weber on Law in Economy and Society.* New York: Touchstone, 1954.

———. *The Religion of India.* Translated and edited by Hans H. Gerth and Don Martindale. New York: Free Press, 1958.

———. *The City.* Translated and edited by Don Martindale and Getrud Neuwirth. New York: Collier, 1962.

———. *The Sociology of Religion.* Translated by Ephraim Fischoff. Boston: Beacon, 1963.

———. *Economy and Society.* Edited by Guenther Roth and Claus Wittich. New York: Bedminister, 1968.

Weinberg, Martin S. "Sexual Modesty and the Nudist Camp." *Social Problems, XII,* 3 (Winter):311–318, 1965.

Weinstein, Jay A. *Demographic Transition and Social Change.* Morristown, N.J.: General Learning Press, 1976.

Weitzman, Lenore J., Deborah Eifles, Elizabeth Hokada, and Catherine Ross. "Sex Role Socialization in Picture Books for Preschool Children." *American Journal of Sociology, 72:*1125–1150, 1972.

Wellish, Jean B., Anne H. MacQueen, Ronald A. Carriere, Gary A. Duck. "School Management and Organization in Successful Schools." *Sociology of Education, 51:*211–226, 1978.

White, Theodore. *The Making of the President, 1968.* New York: Atheneum, 1969.

"Who Can Afford College?" *Parade,* April 25, 1982, p. 11.

Whyte, William Foote. *Street Corner Society.* Chicago: University of Chicago Press, 1943.

Wilcox, Preston (ed.). *White Is.* New York: Grove Press, 1970.

Wilkinson, Thomas O. "Functional Classification of Japanese Cities: 1920–1955." *Demography, 1:*177–185, 1964.

Will, Jenie, Felicia Self, and Nancy Datan. "Maternal Behavior and Perceived Sex of Infant." *American Journal of Orthopsychiatry, 46:*135–139, 1976.

William, Thomas Rhys. *Socialization.* Englewood Cliffs, N.J.: Prentice-Hall, 1983.

Williams, Robin M. *American Society.* New York: Alfred A. Knopf, 1970.

Williams, Trevor. "Teacher Prophecies and the Inheritance of Inequality." *Sociology of Education, 49:*223–236, 1976.

Wilson, Kenneth, Louise Zurcher, Diane Claire McAdams, and Russell L. Curtis. "Stepfathers and Stepchildren." *Journal of Marriage and the Family, 37:*526–536, 1975.

Wilson, William J. *The Declining Significance of Race.* Chicago: University of Chicago Press, 1978.

Wimberley, Ronald C., Donald A. Clelland, Thomas C. Hood, and C. M. Lipsey. "The Civil Religious Dimension: Is it There?" *Social Forces, 54,* 4 (June):890–900, 1976.

Wittfogel, Karl A. *Oriental Despotism.* New Haven: Yale University Press, 1955.

Wohlstein, Ronald T., and Clark McPhail. "Judging the Presence and Effect of Collective Behavior from Film Records." *Social Psychology Quarterly, 42:*76–81, 1979.

Wolf, C. P. "The Accident at Three Mile Island: Social Science Perspectives." *Social Science Research Council Items, 33:*56–61, 1979.

Wolff, Wendy C., and Rachel Rosenfeld. "Sex Structure of Occupations and Job Mobility." *Social Forces, 56:*823–844, 1978.

Wood, Robert C. *Suburbia: Its People and Their Politics.* Boston: Houghton-Mifflin, 1958.

Woodring, Paul. "Why 65? The Case against Mandatory Retirement." *Saturday Review* (August 7):18–20, 1976.

Woodward, Joan. *Industrial Organization: Theory and Practice.* London: Oxford University Press, 1965.

The World Almanac and Book of Facts. 1983. New York: Newspaper Enterprise Assoc. Inc., 1981.

Wortman, Sterling. "World Food and Nutrition: The Scientific and Technological Base." *Science, 209,* 4452 (July):157–164, 1980.

Wright, Erik Olin, and Luca Perrone. "Marxist Class Categories and Income Inequality." *American Sociological Review, 42* (February):32–55.

Wrong, Dennis. "Social Inequality without Social Stratification." Pp. 513–520 in Celia S. Heller (ed.), *Structural Social Inequality.* New York: Macmillan, 1969.

Yankelovich, Daniel. *New Rules.* New York: Random House, 1981.

Yinger, M. *Religion, Society, and the Individual.* New York: Macmillan, 1970.

Zajonc, R. B. *Social Psychology.* Belmont, Calif.: Wadsworth, 1966.

Zelnick, Melvin, and John F. Kantner. "Sexual Activity, Contraceptive Use and Pregnancy among Metropolitan-Area Teenagers, 1971–1979." *Family Planning Perspectives, 12:*230–237, 1980.

Zollschan, George K., and Walter Hirsch (eds.). *Explorations in Social Change.* Boston: Houghton Mifflin, 1964.

Zurcher, Louis A., and David A. Snow. "Collective Behavior." Pp. 447–482 in Morris Rosenberg and Ralph H. Turner (eds.), *Social Psychology.* New York: Basic Books, 1981.

Appendix

Sociology and Your Career

The study of sociology is remarkably useful as preparation for a career. One reason is that the concerns of sociology extend to all forms of social behavior and human relationships. Few fields have so broad a scope. This breadth makes sociology relevant to many different career goals. On the one hand, it provides specialized training for a career as a sociologist. But it can provide an excellent background for many other occupations as well.

Another reason why sociology is valuable for career preparation—an increasingly important reason—is that the research methods used and taught in sociology can be used in many fields. The student of sociology learns how to apply the methods of science to problems that are derived from everyday life. Sociology teaches the student to treat all aspects of human behavior rationally and objectively—excellent training for many occupations. Among the specific research skills taught in the field are surveying, interviewing, observational techniques, and statistical analysis. These research methods are in great demand in our science-oriented society. Survey research and statistical analysis, for example, play an increasingly important role in our political processes.

What Sociologists Do

About two-thirds of the professionals in the field of sociology work for colleges or universities, teaching and conducting research. Most of them have Ph.D. degrees, although some, especially in liberal arts schools or community colleges, may have a master's degree only. Professors generally specialize in various subjects within sociology—for example, familial relationships, urban life, education, criminology and penology, sex roles, industrial sociology, health care, social stratification, occupational roles, and gerontology. Sociologists also treat broad topics that cut across these subjects, such as social psychology, social organization and theory, demography (processes of population change), and research methodology (designing and assessing new procedures). In addition to teaching, research, and course planning, sociology professors may also serve as consultants to businesses, governments, and social policy makers.

In the past twenty years, more and more sociologists have taken jobs outside of higher education. Many now work for branches of federal, state or local government. In the federal government, sociologists are found in the departments of Defense, Health and Human Services, Interior, and Agriculture, as well as in various federal agencies. Other sociologists work for international agencies such as the United Nations or the World Health Organization. Still others work for the private sector in corporations, professional and trade associations, consulting firms, and nonprofit corporations or foundations.

Many of the sociologists in business or government are administrators. Typical positions would be as an administrator in a government social service agency, in a community youth organization, or in a corporation's office of personnel development. Being able to understand and supervise social research is a distinct advantage for administrators in many fields.

Research is another typical occupation for sociologists in business or government. Such research might involve gathering and interpreting information for a variety of uses, from sales campaigns or new product development, to occupational or environmental impact studies. Sociologists also conduct research for private research institutes and polling firms. One research position that has become increasingly important is that of program evaluator, a person who assesses the effectiveness of social programs, such as remedial education, job training, and welfare assistance. The requirement for an evaluation study is often included in the legislation setting up a public program, as are the environmental impact studies now required for all large federal projects.

Sociology as Background for Other Career Fields

Persons with a B.A. degree in sociology have many jobs open to them. Depending on your specific major in sociology, you may find work as an interviewer, administrative assistant, research assistant, social worker, counselor, statistician, or survey administrator, to name a few. Each of these jobs could be for a government, corporate, or academic organization. In today's tight job market, a strong undergraduate program in sociology could give you a competitive edge over majors in other academic fields for jobs in a number of highly competitive areas.

The study of sociology is an excellent background for a career in any field concerned with human behavior and human relations. Examples are law, journalism, architecture, business, advertising, politics, social work, recreation, or counseling. For some students planning to enter such fields, either a sociology major or a series of sociology courses would be highly recommended.

A B.A. in sociology can also prepare the student for advanced studies in other academic fields or for the pursuit of an M.B.A. or law degree. If you plan a business career after your sociology B.A., you might take courses in industrial sociology or complex organizations. If you are considering social work, you might concentrate on urban and family sociology or race and ethnic relations.

Future Demand for Sociologists

The strongest demand for sociologists over the next decade will be in applied—or practically oriented—sociology, rather than in teaching. Demand will be strong in such specialties as criminology, deviant behavior, medical sociology, gerontology, and demography. The problem of treating criminals and social deviants shows few signs of disappearing in the near future. In the field of health care, doctors, administrators, and others have become more aware of the social (and familial) aspects of health, as well as of the needs of the growing numbers of elderly in our society. Demography should also be a growing field, as it provides a key tool for long-range planning for developing countries as well as for many government agencies in our own country.

The most marketable skills of sociologists in the near future will be those relating to quantitative research—survey and polling techniques, depth interviews, statistical analysis, and computer-based data handling. Such skills are needed not only for the actual conduct of research and evaluation studies, but also for the administration of research projects and assessment of their results. Research skills can advance a career in the many fields that depend on research methods.

Demand for teachers of sociology—in elementary and high school social studies programs as well as in higher education—will depend on the general level of growth in the educational institutions. At present, little growth is forecast for this area, but such predictions may be subject to change.

The following four occupations are among those for which the U.S. Bureau of Labor Statistics has predicted above average growth over the next decade:

> marketing research
> legal assistant
> health services administrator
> urban and regional planner

Each of these occupations involves the sort of work that benefits from a sound background in the ideas and methods of sociology.

Sociology, with its breadth of subject matter and variety of methods, can provide you not only with an opportunity for personal growth but also with skills and perspectives that will benefit you in many different careers.

Careers in Sociology

Jobs for Which Sociology Is Relevant	Some Typical Employers
market researcher	advertising agency; corporation; market research firm
demographer	government agency; insurance company; pension fund
community planner	urban development agency; urban planning board; community health service
social worker	welfare agency; private charity agency
community financial needs analyst	bank; mortgage agencies
grants administrator	foundation or government agency that sponsors research
writer-editor	publishing firm; government
counselor	welfare agency; rehabilitation program; school or college
environmental analyst	industrial corporation; government
survey researcher	market research firm; political consultant; opinion research institute
equal opportunity specialist	government; large corporation
labor relations specialist	industrial firm; union; consultant firm; government
personnel manager	corporation; department store; manufacturing firm
journalist	newspaper; magazine; freelance
probation officer	court system
ecological impact researcher	architecture firm; government
medical sociologist	schools of medicine, nursing, public health
legal assistant, paralegal	law firm; legal department of corporation
research project director	research institute—private or public; government agency; pollster
social program administrator	welfare agency; community health center; penal institution

Author Index

Subject Index